The Literary Culture of the Reformation

The Literary Culture of the Reformation

Grammar and Grace

BRIAN CUMMINGS

Si enim fallor sum
Augustine

OXFORD

UNIVERSITY PRESS

OXFORD

UNIVERSITY PRESS

Great Clarendon Street, Oxford OX2 6DP

Oxford University Press is a department of the University of Oxford.
It furthers the University's objective of excellence in research, scholarship,
and education by publishing worldwide in

Oxford New York

Auckland Bangkok Buenos Aires Cape Town Chennai
Dar es Salaam Delhi Hong Kong Istanbul Karachi Kolkata
Kuala Lumpur Madrid Melbourne Mexico City Mumbai Nairobi
São Paulo Shanghai Taipei Tokyo Toronto

Oxford is a registered trade mark of Oxford University Press
in the UK and certain other countries

Published in the United States
by Oxford University Press Inc., New York

© Brian Cummings 2002

The moral rights of the author have been asserted
Database right Oxford University Press (maker)

First published 2002

British Library Cataloguing in Publication Data

Data available

Library of Congress Cataloging in Publication Data

Data available

ISBN 0–19–818735–1

1 3 5 7 9 10 8 6 4 2

Typeset by SNP Best-set Typesetter Ltd., Hong Kong
Printed in Great Britain
on acid-free paper by
Biddles Ltd., Guildford and King's Lynn

For MY PARENTS

and MY CHILDREN

Bucer's England—*De Regno Christi*—even then
it was not on, not really.
                    Geoffrey Hill, *Speech! Speech!*

Acknowledgements

ARGUMENT, LEARNING, and the pleasure of books are central to the theme of this study, and it is with gratitude that I record here those who have inspired these things in my own life, among family, friends, and teachers. It was Tony Trott in Birmingham who first made me appreciate the gift of reading, and passed me a copy of a seventeenth-century religious poem with unforeseen consequences. Later at Cambridge, Robin Kirkpatrick and Eric Griffiths pressed on me the virtue of attention to word against word. John Marenbon introduced me to the rigours of medieval philosophy, and Eamon Duffy instructed me in the rough byways of Reformation theology and history with shrewdness and wit. By a stroke of luck I spent four years visiting the rooms of Geoffrey Hill as a doctoral student picking up shards of learning.

All this now seems a long time ago, and my benefactors may have forgotten it, but it was at this stage that this project was conceived. Since then, I have benefited from the careful reading, encouragement, and conversation of many people who had much better things to do, principally Margaret Aston, Anne Barton, Terence Cave, Margreta de Grazia, David Kastan, John Lyons, Margaret McGowan, John Morrill, David Wallace, and Rowan Williams. I owe a special debt to Martin Brooke, who has checked over translations from Latin and Greek.

At Sussex I fell into the lap of the School of European Studies, where it was considered natural to be interested in a wide range of things, and where I was given space next door to people who knew about them. Here my education began over again. I have had the highest good fortune to teach English as a European literature alongside Jeremy Lane, Stephen Medcalf, and Gabriel Josipovici. Stephen has been a source of quotations and aperçus from his bottomless well of learning. Gabriel has been a second father to this book through thick and thin, as well as the most genial of intellectual companions. Successive chairs and colleagues in English have shown a patience in the writing of this book in contradiction of our utilitarian times; Norman Vance, Alan Sinfield, Jenny Taylor, and Tony Inglis are just some of those who have given generous and consistent support. Among friends in other disciplines I single out for many favours Geoff Bennington, Adriana Bontea, Craig Clunas, Rickie Dammann, Paul

Davies, Richard Gaskin, Ben Gibbs, Nigel Llewellyn, Céline Surprenant, Martin van Gelderen, and above all the *genius loci*, Maggie Boden.

Many people who have attended my seminars, undergraduate and post-graduate, have made me think in new and different ways. I thank particularly for their friendship my doctoral students, who have shared the burden of this book while travailing their own paths of scholarship: Penny McCarthy, James Tink, Kate Lyden, Michael Bourke, Anna Martin, David Anderson, and especially (because of the closeness of her work to mine) Andrea Varney. In the Graduate Research Centre for Humanities, Sandy Malcolm and Margaret Reynolds have cheered me up and egged me on, on numberless occasions.

Early research for the book was made possible by a Fellowship at Trinity College, Cambridge, and the first writing was done when the Master and Fellows with customary largesse granted me six months of leave after I had moved to Sussex. Like anyone working in these fields, I have spent more time than I can remember with more enjoyment than proper in research libraries: for which I thank the staff at the Vatican Library; the Bibliothèque Nationale in the rue de Richelieu; the Bodleian Library; the Wren Library at Trinity College; the Libraries of Doctor Williams, of Lambeth Palace, of the Institute for Historical Research, and the Senate House in London; and most of all in homes from home at the British Library, and the Warburg Institute in London; and the University Library in Cambridge.

Part of Chapter 5 first appeared as 'The Theology of Translation: Tyndale's Grammar', in *Word, Church and State: Tyndale Quincentenary Essays*, edited by John T. Day, Eric Lund, and Anne M. O'Donnell (Washington, DC: The Catholic University of America Press, 1998), pp. 36–59, and is reproduced with kind permission. I am especially grateful to the author and to the publishers (Penguin Books and Counterpoint Press) for permission to quote the epigraph from Geoffrey Hill's *Speech! Speech!*

Sophie Goldsworthy and Frances Whistler have been the most encouraging of editors, and nurtured the project when faith was failing. The four OUP readers, one nameless theologian especially, read with such care that I almost couldn't bear to be rid of the manuscript.

The last thanks are easiest to make but hardest to make meaningful. To friends who may have thought this book was my personal Mrs Harris, but who indulged my fiction, who gave us meals, took us on holiday, babysat, lent us their homes, talked about other things, some words of recompense: Mark Archer, Martin Brooke, Christabel and Howard Flight, Gabriel

Josipovici, Claudia Nocentini, Tim and Lynda Thomas; and most of all to Dana English and Tom Whalen for conversation and wine shared in New York, Naples, and elsewhere. Also thanks to members of my family, especially David Cummings, Adrian Butterfield, and Helena Howie. Two people I wished would have seen this book will not: David Howie and Jeremy Maule. Kenneth (while he lived) and Ruth Butterfield supported me and shared in the ideas at every turn. The dedication tells another story. I used to joke with my parents that I hoped the book would come out in time for them, then in time the joke changed to whether my children would live to see it. In the end my parents deserve more than a book, but that is all I can give them. Thomas and Daniel have grown up with two unfinished books for parents. They have made me think everything afresh. To Thomas my thanks for keeping me company, restoring me every day, and reminding me that true inquiry never rests (as well as teaching me new tricks on the computer); to Daniel my apologies that there are no dinosaurs. About Ardis I refrain from saying more, since she already knows.

Putney
Feast of St Scholastica, 2002

Contents

Part Two
The English Language and the English Reformations 1521–1603

Part Three
Literature and the English Reformations 1580–1640

Note for the Reader

SHORT TITLES are used in the footnotes; full references may be found in the bibliographies. For the sake of clarity, signature numbers from early printed editions are cited with arabic numerals throughout. All quotations from contemporary manuscript and printed sources, including quotations in German and French, and a few in Italian and Spanish, retain original punctuation, capitalization and spelling. Quotations in Latin follow the idiosyncrasies of the original citation, except that standard abbreviations and contractions have been expanded, and the use of i and j, u and v, has been regularized. Greek quotations have been supplied with accents and breathings following modern practice. The small number of Hebrew characters has been transliterated. Place-names have been anglicized; names of persons are normally given in the original vernacular, except where common practice uses a Latin name. For ease of reference, translations have been taken from published sources wherever possible; in a few cases where confusion might arise or where the interpretation is crucial, I have indicated corrections. All unattributed translations are my own. Where not indicated, biblical citations are to the Bible Society text (Greek), the Vulgate (Latin), and to the Authorized Version of 1611 (English).

List of Illustrations

Abbreviations

ARCR	Anthony Allison and D. M. Rogers, *The Contemporary Printed Literature of the English Counter-Reformation between 1558 and 1640* (Aldershot: Scolar, 1989–94)
ASD	Erasmus, *Opera Omnia* (Amsterdam: North-Holland, 1969–)
Benzing	Josef Benzing, *Lutherbibliographie: Verzeichnis der gedruckten Schriften Martin Luthers bis zu dessen Tod* (Baden-Baden: Heitz, 1966)
BL	British Library
CC	Corpus Christianorum, series Latina
CHB	*The Cambridge History of the Bible*, ed. P. R. Ackroyd, C. F. Evans, G. W. H. Lampe, and S. L. Greenslade (Cambridge: Cambridge University Press, 1963–70)
CHLMP	*The Cambridge History of Later Medieval Philosophy*, ed. Norman Kretzmann, Anthony Kenny, and Jan Pinborg (Cambridge: Cambridge University Press, 1982)
CHMEL	*The Cambridge History of Medieval English Literature*, ed. David Wallace (Cambridge: Cambridge University Press, 1999)
CHRP	*The Cambridge History of Renaissance Philosophy*, ed. Charles B. Schmitt and Quentin Skinner (Cambridge: Cambridge University Press, 1988)
CR	Corpus Reformatorum
CSEL	Corpus Scriptorum Ecclesiasticorum Latinorum
CSPD	*Calendar of State Papers, Domestic Series, of the Reigns of Edward VI, Mary, Elizabeth and James I*, ed. R. Lemon and M. A. E. Green (London: HMSO, 1856–72)
CSPV	*Calendar of State Papers and Manuscripts, Relating to English Affairs, Existing in the Archives and Collections of Venice*, ed. R. Brown and others (London: Public Record Office, 1865–1947)
CUL	Cambridge University Library
CWE	*Collected Works of Erasmus* (Toronto: University of Toronto Press, 1974–2000)
CWM	*The Complete Works of Thomas More*, ed. L. L. Martz, R. S. Sylvester, and C. H. Miller (New Haven: Yale University Press, 1963–97)

DTC	*Dictionnaire de Théologie Catholique*
EE	*Opus Epistolarum Erasmi*, ed. P. S. Allen (Oxford: Clarendon Press, 1906–58)
EETS	Early English Text Society
ES	*Enchiridion Symbolorum definitionum et declarationum de rebus fidei et morum*, ed. H. Denzinger, 32nd edn. (Freiburg im Briesgau: Herder, 1963)
HMC	Historical Manuscripts Commission
LB	Erasmus, *Opera Omnia*, ed. J. Leclerc (Leiden: Pieter van der Aa, 1703–6)
L & P	*Letters and Papers, Foreign and Domestic, of the Reign of Henry VIII*, ed. J. S. Brewer, J. Gairdner, and R. H. Brodie (London: HMSO, 1862–1932)
LW	*Luther's Works*, ed. J. Pelikan and H. T. Lehmann (Philadelphia: Fortress, 1955–86)
NPNF	*Library of the Nicene and Post-Nicene Fathers*, gen. ed. Philip Schaff, repr. edn. (Grand Rapids: Eerdmans, 1950–89)
PL	*Patrologia Latina*, ed. J.-P. Migne (Paris: Garnier, 1844–62)
Rupp and Watson	*Luther and Erasmus: Free Will and Salvation*, ed. G. Rupp and P. Watson (Philadelphia: Westminster Press, 1969)
SRP	*Stuart Royal Proclamations*, ed. J. Larkin and P. Hughes (Oxford: Clarendon Press, 1973–83)
STC	*A Short-Title Catalogue of Books Printed in England, Scotland and Ireland and of English Books Printed Abroad 1475–1640*, ed. A. W. Pollard and G. R. Redgrave, 2nd edn. (London, 1976–91)
TOT	*Tyndale's Old Testament*, ed. D. Daniell (New Haven: Yale, 1992)
TRP	*Tudor Royal Proclamations*, ed. P. Hughes and J. Larkin (New Haven: Yale University Press, 1964–9)
VD 16	*Verzeichnis der im deutschen Sprachbereich erschienenen Drucke des XVI. Jahrhunderts* (Stuttgart: Anton Hiersemann, 1983–97)
WA	*D. Martin Luthers Werke, kritische Gesamtausgabe* (Weimar: Böhlau, 1883–1999)
WA Br	*D. Martin Luthers Werke, kritische Gesamtausgabe: Briefwechsel* (Weimar: Böhlau, 1930–85)
WA DB	*D. Martin Luthers Werke, kritische Gesamtausgabe: die Deutsche Bibel* (Weimar: Böhlau, 1906–61)
WA TR	*D. Martin Luthers Werke, kritische Gesamtausgabe: Tischreden* (Weimar: Böhlau, 1912–21)

Prologue

I believe we are not getting rid of God because we still believe in grammar.

Friedrich Nietzsche, *Twilight of the Idols*

Prologue

The scholar sits in his study, bent intently over his writing table, pen in hand. From a window to his right sunlight flickers in, illuminating his face. His hat hangs on a peg behind him. A skull lies on the window seat, above a pile of books and cushions. In the foreground, oblivious to the mental labours behind them, a dog and a lion lie sleeping. Albrecht Dürer's engraving of 1514, *St Jerome in his Study* (Figure 1), describes an image of the serenity of learning. Dürer several times presented it to friends and patrons as a gift in company with *Melancholia*, an engraving of the same year: the two prints are regarded, along with *Knight, Death and the Devil* of 1513, as the artist's masterpieces in this medium. Although not designed specifically as a pair, *St Jerome in his Study* and *Melancholia* have come to be known as a diptych devoted to the divergent arts of the sacred and the profane. Melancholia is represented as a brooding angel or woman, surrounded by the scattered objects of philosophical study: geometrical instruments, timepieces, a sphere, a polyhedron, a pair of scales, a magic square of numbers in which each line in every direction has the sum of 34. If Jerome's room is a world in which everything is in order and bathed in light, Melancholia presides over a place of disturbance and crepuscular ambiguity.

Three years later, Dürer's Germany was plunged into confusion by the affair of Martin Luther. Luther became a hero for Dürer, eclipsing even Erasmus of Rotterdam as a new Hercules Germanicus of the intellectual imagination. At Whitsun in 1521 as he travelled through the Low Countries, Dürer condemned Emperor Charles V for the betrayal and arrest of Luther at Eisenach. Fearing for the reformer's life, Dürer called on Erasmus to rise up in God's cause in Luther's place. At the same time, he continued to carry with him copies of the two engravings of *St Jerome in his Study* and *Melancholia*. By now, perhaps, they had acquired new meanings. The aspiration whether to spiritual contemplation or to intellectual creativity had taken on renewed urgency, and with it controversy. Later in the century, Luther was substituted for Jerome in an alternative version of the print. The two engravings represent opposing poles in sixteenth-century thought and learning. The soft light of the saint's cell reflects a yearning for clarity, for a unifying meaning, for a single truth to transcend

Fig. 1. The scholar sits in his study, bent intently over his writing table, pen in hand: Albrecht Dürer, *Saint Jerome in his Study* (1514).

all other truths. The complexities and puzzles of *Melancholia*, on the other hand—the incongruous placing of a dog between geometrical sculptured shapes, a putto sitting disconsolately in the middle-ground, an almost surreal ladder by his neck which leads nowhere—suggest instead a world apparently beyond interpretation. Its strewn objects imply ultimate meaning but never yield their secrets.

The two engravings provide together an emblem of the Reformation, its appeal towards certainty and its conflicts over interpretation. In different guises Erasmus and Luther each epitomize both images: Erasmus, intimate with arcane sources of knowledge yet longing for the simplicity of the philosophy of Christ; Luther, asserting dogmatic faith yet brooding over intense scruples of conscience and spirit, his so-called *Anfechtungen*. This book is a study of the intellectual world of the Reformation, a world poised between the clarity of faith and the melancholy of scepticism. More specifically, this book is a study of the significance of literary culture to the Reformation and of the Reformation to literary culture.

The Reformation promised, it is said, the literal truth. In this it has been judged either a providential success or a historic failure. The literal truth of scripture is commonly regarded as the most sensational doctrine of the Reformation, and the most sensational victim of modern scientific criticism. In such terms it is possible to forget that the phrase 'literal truth' is at best a paradox, perhaps an oxymoron. What is literal is made up of letters, of words. This expression, then, which appears to claim truth by direct revelation, depends on a process inevitably interpretative, properly speaking 'literary'. The Reformation is as much about literary truth as it is about literal truth. The historical events now known as the Reformation are bound up at every level with acts of literature both spoken and written, with the interpretation of language and with the practice of literary culture.

Yet this book is not what would ordinarily be called a study of religious writing. Religious writing appears to be marginal to both religion and writing, a limited activity of pious, sectarian, and personal motivation. Such assumptions misconstrue both religion and writing. Writing was produced in the context of a religious crisis which overwhelmed political and social culture. Only by an odd prejudice of literary history can such matters be regarded as peripheral to literary production. Moreover, a large majority of the writings of the sixteenth and seventeenth centuries was religious. That such writing is not usually described as literature distorts literary history. To define religious writing as non-literary is to beg the question of what 'literature' means, and to call most 'literary' works of the period non-religious completes a circular argument. As an instance, it may be cited that literary history conventionally places at or even outside its margins the single most important literary production of the period in most European countries: the Bible. Without reference to religion, the study of early modern writing is incomprehensible.

By the same token, religion in the sixteenth and seventeenth centuries cannot be separated from writing. The Reformation embodied a massive burgeoning of writing in general. Early modern religion is a religion of books: pre-eminently the Bible, but also a plethora of other books, devotional, doctrinal, controversial. Not only the spread of protestantism, but its identity, is constituted by the exigencies of textual revolution. Catholic reaction, and catholic Reformation, equally consisted in an explosion of literary production. Moreover, a majority of the crucial figures of sixteenth-century religion (protestant and catholic) were writers, usually prolific ones. That they are not regarded primarily as writers distorts religious as well as literary history. Writing is not accidental to the history of religion, since belief and dogma are both mediated by a linguistic and literary process. Without reference to writing, the study of early modern religion is incomprehensible.

A history of such writing encompasses an enormous range of literary genres, some hardly recognized within the discipline of literature, others ordinarily excluded from the discipline of theology: lectures, sermons, and disputations; controversial tracts, catechisms, and primers; vernacular bibles and scholarly bibles in ancient languages; also devotional poems, lives of saints, and meditations. Properly it includes other tangential kinds of writing: theological compendia, biblical glosses, commentaries, marginalia, and annotations. At issue is not only the content of such writing but its material conditions: modes of writing, of production and of dissemination, the medium of print, the conflict between Latin and the vernacular. Such an enquiry involves attention to the politics of writing, the role of propaganda and censorship, the public context of meaning, and its supervision by the state. At issue is the division of interpretation and meaning over the material culture of the book, a division which culminated in sudden epiphanies of conversion and also, frequently, in sudden and brutal death.

What follows claims to be neither a comprehensive survey nor a thematic analysis of such matters. However, it attempts to be compendious in several important ways in order to suggest a large historical narrative. It ranges across a long period rather than concentrates on a single decisive decade; it covers writings from different parts of Europe rather than limits itself to a single nation or language; it negotiates between protestant and catholic writing rather than describes either in isolation; it admits different kinds of writing, poetry as well as theology, controversy as well as commentary, rather than assumes some prior division between these kinds.

Further clarification might be useful of its principles of procedure. First of all, the term 'Reformation' is susceptible of many understandings. It used to be assumed that the term applied exclusively to a protestant historiography, and that it applied to a precise sequence of historical events. This history has come to seem over-determined by its own assumptions, leading to a false and circular narrative based on the perceived corruption of the medieval church and a corresponding need for 'reform'. Such a narrative now seems old-fashioned, and the term 'Reformation' out of date. This book, however, does not use the term to signify a protestant process causally related to a particular political or theological narrative. Rather the term describes what no one denies happened, although historians sometimes forget or refuse to name it. This is a sense in which religion in the sixteenth and the seventeenth centuries, throughout Europe, regardless of a particular polity in force at any one time, protestant or catholic (for these terms, too, are anachronistic and more ambiguous than they seem), was in crisis—divided, extreme, and violent. For this larger crisis, the Reformation is the best available term, although it means something very different from a hundred or even fifty years ago.

A second clarification concerns place. No book could describe in the necessary detail the conditions of writing across so many languages and such a span. On the other hand, no book treating a single region in isolation could do justice to the complexities involved. This book therefore has two different centres, which are neither arbitrary nor causal in relation to each other. One is in the northern European and mostly Latin writing of Erasmus and Luther at the beginning of the sixteenth century: the one perhaps the last true catholic, the other perhaps the first true protestant in Western Europe, although which is which might sometimes be harder to tell. However, their interest here is not as representative of theological factions but of the changing culture of writing in which they each played so large and so different a part. Perhaps no excuse is needed to justify their presence, but this pre-eminence does not mean that they should somehow be seen as originators or authors of the coming catastrophe: their writing and their authorship is symptomatic rather than exemplary.

The second place is England over a whole century. The reason for this is to provide a large body of vernacular writing to balance the Latin which precedes it and competes with it. Here the writers begin with those equally

vexed contemporaries and associates of Erasmus and Luther, Thomas
More and William Tyndale, and continue into later Tudor and Stuart
writing. The presences are both catholic (More, Southwell) and protestant
(Sidney, Greville), as well as somewhere in between or in transit (Wyatt,
Donne) or carefully silent (Andrewes, Herbert). The choice of English
is expedient (it is the writing familiar to me, and presumably to most of
my readers) but has its advantages. England changed religion more
frequently, more equivocally, and with greater political insistence than
perhaps anywhere else. It has been calculated that English religious polity
suffered seven reformations in the space of twenty-five years. A Venetian
ambassador complained it was not possible to tell what religious belief
would prevail from one day to the next. At the same time the English vernacular tells a story different although still contingent to the first centre of
interest. The relationship is fundamental but never exact: English writing
is in no way seen here as the inheritor of some Lutheran or Erasmian code.
As the English story unfolds, two other centres take the stage: the central
European protestantism of Strasbourg and Geneva, eventually subsumed
in Calvinism; and the post-Tridentine counter-Reformation. The wider
argument is that all of this material belongs to a similar literary history of
crisis. This is not to say, in some glib deconstructive gesture, that religious
controversy is really about language, any more than it is to say that literary
controversy is really about theology. It is to acknowledge the interrelation
of these controversies at every level.

The book is in three parts: Part One centres on the Luther controversy
and its relationship to the literary humanism of Erasmus, culminating in
the literary quarrel between the two men at the end of the first decade of
the Reformation. It places this quarrel in the context of debates about literary and linguistic meaning in biblical commentary and translation and
in theories of language and of literature. This part of the book centres on
northern continental Europe. Part Two moves the scene to England, while
still placed in a European context. It considers the campaign against the
Lutheran heresy and the beginnings of vernacular protestantism, before
describing the formation of an independent protestant culture in the
reigns of the later Tudors. Religious argument is discussed alongside
radical changes in vernacular culture and in the status of the English language. Part Three studies the wider life of religion in society in the reigns
of Elizabeth, James, and Charles, through an account of religious poetry
and other literary genres. It considers the ambiguous religious identities of
English culture, the opposing poles of Calvinist and recusant catholic
writing and the struggles in between. The forms of religious quarrel and

linguistic anxiety encountered in Parts One and Two create what is a transformed literary and religious world. In a coda, Milton is described as the inheritor of this long reformation in culture.

The book has no strict chronological boundaries, but tells the story of a literary reformation continuing for well over a century. Although many inaugurations would be possible, it opens with Luther's doctorate in 1512 and Erasmus's New Testament of 1516, rather than the Indulgence crisis of a year later. Although many endings would be possible, and none conclusive, it finishes with *Paradise Lost* in the aftermath of the English Revolution.

*

To apprehend the wider significance of literary culture to early modern religion it is necessary to look no further than Luther. Luther is one of the great writers of the sixteenth century. His literary output is stupendous in its extent as it was staggering in its effect. However, literary culture forms a more pervasive element in Luther's religion than this implies. The story of his religion is a story of reading and writing. Luther began his career as a commentator on the text of scripture. He described his religious conversion—however steeped in mystery and controversy to this day—as a long and complex process of textual interpretation. He was catapulted into fame on a national and European scale by his reputation as a writer. Every point in the subsequent conflict is marked by his literary output and by that of his opponents. Whereas an earlier religious figure might have been celebrated for miracles or for powers of healing, Luther was celebrated even in his own time and by his own acolytes as a bearer of texts. His reliquary came to be the corpus of his Bible and of his voluminous tracts and commentaries. Luther's literary activity is vital to an understanding of his religion and by extension of the Reformation as a whole. At the same time it is symptomatic of the complex literary processes of the sixteenth century, in its tension between vernacular and Latin, popular and learned, scholastic and humanist, oral and literate, manuscript and print.

To examine the Reformation in writing and the writing of the Reformation is to uncover an unfamiliar archaeology of religion: an underground network of text and commentary, of translation and controversy. One view of this textual mass is that it is merely the vehicle for something else, the mechanism by which religion is transferred from one person or group of people to another. According to such a view, religious doctrine is already pre-formed somewhere else before being encoded in texts. Such a view is an illusion: doctrine is textual and exists in texts. Despite the best efforts of theological history, Luther's ideas cannot be understood outside of the context of his methods of writing. Yet this, too, is not enough: for Luther's methods of writing also have to be placed in their own context within a sixteenth-century practice and theory of meaning. Such processes are not an extension of Luther's singular personality, but belong to a linguistic culture as a whole. The first effort of reclaiming the lost textuality of Luther's Reformation must be to abandon the notion that writing is first or last an affect of individual subjectivity. This book attempts to reconstruct a larger context for this historical process of meaning and its analysis.

Equally complex is the theatre of meaning in which texts are received. This is especially true with respect to the religious writing of the Reformation. Religious meaning in the sixteenth century was subject to an appalling apparatus of scrutiny. Writing everywhere faced the prospect of discipline and punishment; not only authors but also printers and readers were burned at the stake or ritually disembowelled. Acts of literature involved summary excommunication or execution. Heretics had been tortured and combusted for centuries, but sixteenth-century religious conflict created an extraordinarily volatile environment of orthodoxy and unorthodoxy, and produced an extraordinarily precise and violent culture of containment. Heresy was hardly discovered before it was proscribed and persecuted. And yet it was not always clear in such a ferment what was heresy and what was not. The identification of heresy involved a hideous process of trial and error, in which writing was exposed as heretical only after the event. At the same time the culture of print introduced forces of dissemination which made heresy theoretically uncontainable. Proclamations of censorship veered towards the arbitrary will of sheer violence, a linguistic and literary paranoia.

Pressure on writing and on meaning in such circumstances was vicious. Linguistic solecism could hardly be distinguished from theological error. The polite forms of modern academic criticism sometimes seem incapable of recognizing such stressful forms. Indeed the extremes of sixteenth-century religious language, its excrudescences in execration, expletive, or scatology, are held up for sanctimonious rebuke, in oblivious disregard for the linguistic ultimatum always at stake. Thomas More did not call Luther *cacangelista* gratuitously or forgetfully. In a similar way, the syntax of Reformation prose is sometimes patronized for its tortuousness, as if in ignorance of the tortures awaiting a small logical scruple or a simple grammatical error. Nowhere is modern writing about the Reformation more at risk of bathos than in its simplistic attention to the Reformation doctrine of the primacy of the Word. The cabbalistic appeal to the sanctity of the word played itself out against a material dispute over material words. Such words were prone to ambiguous interpretation, and every ambiguity concealed a threat as well as a promise. Censorship is widespread but also ambiguous in meaning, and sixteenth-century writers were attuned to the possibilities of self-censorship and of self-concealment. Yet such procedures could have a double-edged effect. As a consequence linguistic usage takes on layers of meaning which require careful unravelling, layers of self-conscious disguise but also of unselfconscious convolution or frank and unredeemed failure. At the same time, religious writing represents an ultimate and self-sacrificial form of aspiration. It is a kind of writing which reaches out beyond itself, perhaps beside itself, to escape the physical laws of gravity which appear to consume all other forms of writing. Perhaps in recompense, it is also capable of miraculous felicities of equilibrium and occasional flashes of extreme grace.

Of all the areas of linguistic usage where this might be latently visible the most promising is that easily forgotten locality of grammar. A revolution in theological vocabulary is a well-known topic of Reformation history. Reformation writing and reading reinvented Christian lexis and often coined new words for its purposes. Yet such words by their very obviousness were in special danger of being construed as *parti pris*. The partisan implications of usage dictated religious fervour but also incited political persecution. Grammar creates a less easily detectable undertow of meaning. If the first aim of this book is to provide a new visibility to the complex cultural processes of writing, the second is to illumine this neglected hinterland of grammar. The inclinations and deviations by which a sentence moves, the countervailing pressures of qualification or concession, the attenuating processes of conjunction or amplification, the rise towards peroration, the threat of sudden cadence, or a quizzical final resistance in defiantly dubious question, each denotes a different significance in the vexed economy of religious writing. Such processes can be as unknown and as baffling to their makers as to their readers. Grammar has the duplicity, and sometimes the advantage, of keeping some of its best secrets to itself. Not by the perilous byways of syntax only: the inflections of single verbs can, and should, give pause for thought.

Alongside the vexatious creativity of Reformation language comes a formidable crisis in the modes of linguistic interpretation. Traditionally, such a crisis has been accorded a different set of causes. Intellectual history has assumed the prime importance of pedagogic method and has concentrated its attention on a recognizable intellectual movement, commonly identified as the rise of literary humanism. This book, too, is conscious of the importance of this academic revolution, and seeks out the arguments of linguistic and literary theory in the schools and universities. However, it also associates these arguments with religious conflict, and finds traces of religious anxiety shot through the texture of humanist debate. By placing academic debate within the context of a theological and political controversy of meaning, this book hopes to produce a new sense of the significance and the signification of the hermeneutic and semantic sciences. Theology and humanism are uncomfortable bedfellows rather than sworn enemies.

*

Amid speculation into the intellectual contexts of Reformation language, a word or two may be said about the intellectual context of this project. It will be evident that such a project places itself within the current of historicism which has overtaken literary study in recent years. Works usually regarded as literature appear in this book but are studied in their historical formation as subject to the structures of power in which they were written and read. No literary product is introduced as the autonomous creation of its self-authorizing creator. And yet this book attempts some modest revision of its own of the historicist endeavour. Religion has come to be seen within literary studies as a transparently ideological construct, an engine of the state. This has become so much an axiom that it might be titled (with an allowable sally at the reverence of its believers) Foucault's Brag. The axiom holds that religion is a fantasy of power which can, by a simple gesture of translation, be demystified back into politics. Yet this in its turn is an exercise in false consciousness. Any sensitive reading of Foucault must confess that no ideology is transparent, and that no construct can simply be translated back into its 'true' original. The inscription of religion in politics, and vice versa, is too deep to be reclaimed by casual inversion.

In this respect, it is the relation of history to language which needs further investigation. Indeed, the first task might be for literary study to reassert its primary burden in the examination of language. To say so is not to return to the celebration of literary language as a transcendent performance of imagination. On the contrary, it is historicism which has sometimes allowed language as a last vestigial carrier of self-consciousness or self-fashioning. Culture is artificial but language, it seems, can still be read for what it means. In contrast, then, this study follows that other brief of Foucault in undertaking what might be called an archaeology of grammar, an excavation of the hidden processes and recesses of discourse. One lesson of the acts of religious language examined in this book is that language is a dense medium, with powers and pressures of its own. These take both writer and reader in unexpected and unacknowledged directions. Language trips up as much as it carries along, since it belongs to no one and lies within no one's power. The user of language is dealing in borrowed currency on borrowed time. Agency in language is a peculiar form of illusion in that the forms of agency are already prescribed in linguistic terms. Before I can call myself my self I have given myself away in language that is not my own even as I make my claim on it.

As evident as the debt in the following pages to literary historicism is an equal debt to the efforts of Reformation scholarship. Having declared this, it is significant that one of the main efforts in such scholarship in recent years has been to argue the 'Reformation' out of existence. Some historians have attempted to avoid historical determinism by emphasizing continuities in a longer sequence. Others have deflected it by distinguishing a plurality of reformations, catholic as much as protestant, in a larger process of religious culture. As in other areas of academic study, an artful use of the plural form has been used to settle the case. Yet whatever revision of historiography is thought necessary, it must respect the fundamental dissentiousness of sixteenth-century religion. The religious culture of this period, catholic as well as protestant, identified itself through division. The Reformation as a historical event has traditionally been seen as a battle between two religious groups, but it might be truer to say that it was a process founded on division: between new and old, protestant and catholic, righteous and sinner, 'faith' and 'works', repentant and reprobate, or elect and damned.

In this respect, the application of literary forms of analysis onto the historical study of the Reformation may also be beneficial. If this book desires a revision of the categories of writing in the name of Reformation history it also desires a revision of Reformation history in the name of writing. For the language of sixteenth- and seventeenth-century religion is also divided against itself. Sometimes it is assumed that differences will easily emerge of fundamental doctrinal significance between catholic and protestant writers. Yet often the protagonists themselves could hardly quantify what the differences were. Indeed, in the effort to locate difference, a writer might deviate all too quickly into his own sense of contradiction. Although Luther is now commonly charged with overmastering certainty, his writing is often overwhelmed with scruples. Perhaps the conclusion will be drawn that after all, little of consequence was at stake, and that the theology of this period was nothing more than a vicious form of shadow boxing. Yet to make such a conclusion is to attempt to withdraw to some place beyond language from which to judge the vanities of controversy. No such utopia exists. The corollary of the turn of history on language is the turn of language on history.

In their entrapment within language, the writers of the Reformation were no different from us. It should come as no surprise in the twenty-first century to find such extremes of abstraction and violence, of scepticism and belief, of desire and anxiety, within the exercise of language. If Luther's religious language seems alien, his sense of alienation from that very language should not. And if one characteristic of sixteenth-century linguistic usage is a lurch into insatiable violence against itself, another is an endless aspiration to escape from itself, to reach out for grace. It may be that in this act of hopeless faith it finds its own redemption.

1 The Reformation and Literary Culture

'Nostre contestation est verbale'.[1] Looking back half a century, Michel de Montaigne described the Reformation as 'a quarrel over words'. This put-down to the Huguenots goes to the heart of the controversies and revolutions that take the name of the sixteenth-century 'reformations'. Montaigne sums up his century, and the religious revolution at its heart, as a world of words, of words at war. The life of the mind is at bay, ravaged by the toil of word set against word, of seemingly endless vituperation and interpretation. Throughout the Seigneur's own lifetime, Gascony and even the small domain of Montaigne itself were devastated by wars of religion. Montaigne had published a translation of a prohibited book and sailed close to persecution while maintaining a careful catholic orthodoxy. He longs for a life set free from language, to escape from 'contestation verbale'.

Montaigne's provocative epithet supplies a commentary to the great narrative of European history. It recalls the clarion cry of the early reformers, beginning with Luther himself, of the word of God alone. With pointed irony, Montaigne reduces *sola scriptura* to words alone or mere verbiage. Luther's words, he says, now raise as many controversies as Luther himself raised about holy scripture. Montaigne combines bathos with a backhanded tribute to the power of the sixteenth-century appeal to *verbum Dei*. Montaigne reconstructs the Reformation as a reformation in and of words, a linguistic, literary, and textual revolution.

Histories of the Reformation, beginning with those of the reformers, have often pictured a revolution of the word. As early as Philipp Melanchthon's *Historia de vita et actis Lutheri* of 1548, the origin of the protestant Reformation was established in a textual event, the publication of Luther's ninety-five theses.[2] This event assumed mythological

---

[1] *Essais*, ed. Villey, p. 1069. The first edn. of 1580 contained only two books; a third was added in 1588. In this and all subsequent edns. 'De l'experience' is placed as the culmination.

[2] *Historia*, B2ʳ. This was an expanded version of Melanchthon's funeral oration of 1546. It was translated into French in 1549, and by Henry Bennet into English in 1561. Foxe incorporated Bennet's text into his *Actes and Monuments* (1563).

significance, and the first centenary was celebrated on 31 October 1617 with a procession culminating at the Schlosskirche in Wittenberg.[3] A Leipzig engraving printed in the Jubeljahr (Figure 2) shows Luther with a gargantuan quill inscribing his theses on the door of the church. The quill skewers the head of a lion (Leo X), going in one ear and out the other, knocking the Pope's tiara off his head. The violently penetrative pen is a witness to the perceived power of the letter; the rest of the engraving swarms with scriptural texts confirming that God wages revolution through writing.[4] The textuality of the Reformation has been taken for granted ever since.

Above all, the status, dissemination, and interpretation of the Bible are central to the historiography of the Reformation. This was not confined to the propaganda of the protesting faction: Johann Eck identified *sola scriptura* as Luther's cardinal sin in 1519, and used it as a means to entrap Luther into explicitly anti-papal statements in a disputation at the university of Leipzig. Not to be outdone, by 1520 Luther was trumpeting the newfound principle in his latter-day blast against Jericho, *An den christlichen Adel deutscher Nation*. After his excommunication in 1521, Luther regarded his most important task as the translation of the Bible into German. He worked on it for the rest of his life. He considered the vernacular to constitute a new religion. It was through textual production that Luther hoped to reform religious life, by reaching beyond the structures of the church to a popular religious movement. The astonishing power of distribution possible with the printed text became evident with the ninety-five theses, said to be known throughout Germany within a fortnight and within a month throughout Europe.[5] The lessons were not lost on the printers: in two years, fifteen imprints of Luther's New Testament appeared in Wittenberg alone, and sixty-six in other towns.[6] Luther understood the textual and technological basis of the Reformation, describing printing as 'God's highest and extremest act of grace, whereby the business of the gospel is driven forward; it is the last flame before the extinction of the world'.[7] Fifty years later, in the primal act of reformed historiography in

---

[3] Schwiebert, 'The Theses and Wittenberg', p. 120.

[4] Conrad Grahle, *Göttlicher Schriftmessiger woldennckwürdiger Traum* (Leipzig: Johann Glück, 1617). By Luther's head in the engraving is a text from Judges 5: 'Out of Zebulun come them that handle the pen of the writer'. Copies were made into the 18th century, and the image became part of an iconography of protestantism, deeply influencing 19th and even 20th-century historiography.

[5] Myconius, *Historia reformationis*, p. 23, writing in the 1530s. Luther's own account in *Wider Hans Worst* (1541), WA 51.540.26, makes the same claim.

[6] M. H. Black, 'Printed Bible', *CHB*, iii. 428.   [7] Black, 'Printed Bible', *CHB*, iii. 432.

Fig. 2. Luther inscribing *vom ablas* ('of indulgence') into the church door at Wittenberg with a giant pen; detail: Conrad Grahle, *Göttlicher Schriftmessiger woldennckwürdiger Traum* (Leipzig: Johann Glück, 1617).

England, John Foxe went further, claiming (in effect) no print, no reformation.[8] Jan Hus had failed while Luther had succeeded because God invented print. At least one modern historian takes Foxe at his word and rewrites the Reformation as an incident in the history of printing rather than the other way round.[9]

It is not difficult, therefore, to justify Montaigne's characterization of the Reformation as a verbal affair. This book explores how a reformation in religion relates to another reformation in language and in texts, placing the Reformation within the early modern culture of writing. At this point it is necessary to enter some caveats. Christianity has always been known as a 'culture of the book'.[10] Cassiodorus referred in the sixth century to an 'apostolate of the pen', praising scribes who 'preach unto men by means of the hand, untie the tongue by means of the fingers . . . and fight the Devil's insidious wiles with pen and ink'.[11] A poem by Alcuin with similar sentiments, written in the eighth century, was inscribed over the entrance to a medieval scriptorium.[12] Before any rush to see the sixteenth century as a textualization of religion, it should be remembered how textual medieval religion is. Its official culture was encoded in decretals, bulls, in the texts of canon law, and in the decrees of church councils. The understanding of these texts was surrounded by a massive culture of commentary. Theology and canon law were the primary disciplines of the medieval university, and operated around textual procedures of immense sophistication: the gloss, the *quaestio*, and the *disputatio*. No book was more glossed than the Bible itself, in the enormous collective effort of the compendious *glossa ordinaria*.

Medieval forms of unorthodoxy were equally founded around the dissemination of texts (just as dissident groups are in modern times) in rural as well as urban areas.[13] Heretical groups have been described as 'textual communities'.[14] From the Cathars of Languedoc, to the Waldensians of the

---

[8] Foxe, *Actes and Monumentes* (1570), i. 837. Foxe derived his argument from Matthaeus Iudex, *De typographica inventione* (1566).

[9] Eisenstein, *Printing Press*, ch. 4. A more moderate account of the relationship of the Reformation and print is found in the comprehensive survey, *Reformation and the Book*, ed. Gilmont.

[10] Perhaps more properly, the Judæo-Christian tradition. The phrase, a 'people of the book', is used in the Koran to describe Judaism; on this and similar terms, see Marrou, *Education in Antiquity*, pp. xiv–xv.

[11] *Institutiones*, 1.xxx.1, quoted in Metzger, *Text of the New Testament*, p. 18. Cassiodorus's ideology of textuality is discussed in Irvine, *Making of Textual Culture*, pp. 195–209.

[12] Leclercq, *Love of Learning*, p. 154.   [13] Aston, *Lollards and Reformers*, pp. 193–4.

[14] Stock, *Implications of Literacy*, pp. 88–92.

fourteenth and fifteenth centuries, to the English Lollards and the Bohemian Hussites, medieval heresy was closely related to a lay culture of literacy in opposition to, although sometimes closely bound up with, clerical literary practice. Usually, this literature had close links also with the vernacular. Heretics guarded their books as a priest might guard his relics; the secret conference of heretical groups would be centred in the reading of outlawed texts. Persecutors of heretics in turn searched houses and property for books as a symptom of heretical activity. The English statute *De heretico comburendo* of 1401 identified book-production as a potentially illicit act.[15] Books were understood to embody heresy, so that books as well as human bodies were the object of official church and state violence.

Both within orthodoxy and unorthodoxy, then, the literary culture of the Lutheran Reformation can be seen not as a break but a continuity. Luther, it is often forgotten, began his reading of the Bible as a medieval glossator, preparing for the degree of *baccalaureus biblicus* at Erfurt university. His concern for the German vernacular is anticipated both by Wyclif's for English and by Hus's for Czech.[16] Translations of parts of the Bible were made in Occitan both by Cathars and later by Waldensians, along with legion other examples of vernacular biblical versions in German, English, French, and Italian.[17] Nor was the idea of *sola scriptura* original in 1520: William of Ockham asserted more than a century earlier that a Christian is required to believe only what can be found in scripture, or can be derived logically from it.[18] Luther cannot even claim precedence in the production of a German Bible in print. Perhaps as many as 10,000 copies in High and Low German were produced between 1466 and Luther's *Septembertestament* of 1522.[19] Print was in no sense the prerogative of protestantism. Even that symbol of monastic manuscript culture, the *glossa ordinaria*, was produced in printed editions which attempted at

---

[15] Wilkins, *Concilia*, iii. 252–4 (*aliquos Libros seu aliquas Scripturas*); see Hudson, 'Laicus litteratus' in *Heresy and Literacy*, p. 232.

[16] Hudson, 'Wyclif and the English Language', pp. 85–103; Aston, 'Wycliffe and the vernacular', reprinted in *Faith and Fire*, pp. 27–72; Frantisek Smahel, 'Literacy and Heresy in Hussite Bohemia', in *Heresy and Literacy*, pp. 245–7.

[17] Bernard Hamilton, 'Wisdom from the East: The reception by the Cathars of Eastern Dualist Texts', *Heresy and Literacy*, pp. 51–2; Anne Brenon, 'The Waldensian books', *Heresy and Literacy*, pp. 140–1.

[18] Roland H. Bainton, 'The Bible in the Reformation', *CHB*, iii. 2.

[19] Black, 'The Printed Bible', *CHB*, iii. 423; Black lists pre-Reformation printed versions in Catalan, Czech, Dutch, and French, as well as in the main centres of vernacular printing in Germany and Italy.

extraordinary typographical cost to reproduce the effect of an island of scripture floating in a vast sea of commentary.[20] Despite Foxe's paean to print and protestantism, pre-Reformation England saw reams of printed papist breviaries and letters of indulgence; well over one hundred editions of Books of Hours survive from English presses, and tens of thousands of copies of Latin primers were published.[21] It was not Foxe, or Luther, who first described print as the work of divine grace, but Cardinal Nicholas of Cusa.[22]

I GRAMMATICAL CULTURE: MEDIEVAL TO RENAISSANCE

To recreate a literary culture of the Reformation it is necessary to pay attention to a longer historical process rather than slip into the charismatic rhetoric of new learning or *Zeitgeist*. A first stage might be to find some alternative and less anachronistic term for a linguistic or literary culture. One source of difficulty lies in the modern distinction between what is called literature and other forms of textual production, another in the distinction between literature and language itself. And although semiotics and other disciplines have worked to break down these barriers, a still more undeclared taboo dislocates the literary as a secular activity visibly independent from the religious or theological.

In this respect one advantage of placing the sixteenth century within a medieval context is to restore the term *grammatica* as the keyword of linguistic culture. Grammar in the middle ages has a far wider resonance than in modern usage.[23] It was the foundation of literacy in general. It was, of course, the first part of the *trivium*, the universal educational practice of the Christian West. But it is a misconception to view it as a merely rudimentary discipline, of however great importance. Grammar was a university as well as a school subject. Medieval curricula show no easy division between the textbooks used for higher and lower levels of learning. Nor is the division between different parts of the *trivium* easy to quantify. There was constant seepage between the boundaries of *grammatica* and its sister arts of *dialectica* and *rhetorica*. Logic and rhetoric were often heavily grammaticalized, just as the study of grammar was often logicalized.

---

[20] Although the first edn. has no colophon, Froelich, 'The Printed Gloss', i. xiii, concludes that it was printed in Strasbourg in about 1480. Later edns. appeared from Venice, Basle, and Lyon.
[21] Duffy, *Stripping of the Altars*, pp. 77 and 212.   [22] Eisenstein, *Printing Press*, p. 317.
[23] In what follows, see Irvine, *Making of Textual Culture*.

Grammar was not, as now, a term reserved either for basic pedagogy or a science within semantics, although it was both of these as well. It was the *ars* before and within every other *ars*. *Grammatica* involved the study of 'literary' authors, classical and modern, Latin, Greek, and sometimes also vernacular. Its syllabus could contain the practice both of speaking and of writing, of producing meaning and of analysing it, of criticism and commentary as well as of what is now called creative writing, of literary theory as well as syntactic analysis. Grammar as a word therefore covered the full range of the linguistic and the literary, the semantic and the semiotic. It contains some of the all-inclusiveness of literary criticism without the well-known exclusiveness of that much abused term. Quite properly the middle ages has been called a 'grammatical culture'.[24]

However, what is not always recognized is how far even the secular theory of *grammatica* was driven by theological needs and aspirations. The subject which ended up in the schoolroom or the university faculty of arts was formulated through a discursive language founded largely by theologians. The *scientia interpretandi* embodied within grammar happily inherited classical models from Cicero or Quintilian but was developed at its most sophisticated level in the exposition of the meanings of the Bible. This fed back in turn into elementary practice in relation to secular authors. Literary theory was motivated powerfully by the need to uncover moral and spiritual levels of meaning within scriptural narrative and poetry.[25] The 'literal' method of interpretation in biblical exegesis on the other hand was often referred to alternatively as the 'grammatical sense'.[26] On a linguistic level, semantic analysis of parts of speech or of the logical behaviour of modal verbs originated in the need to explicate theological questions about God and his relations with the world. By the thirteenth and fourteenth centuries grammatical textbooks covered not only the art *de bene legendi et scribendi* but also an introductory method in understanding *modi significandi* or *proprietates terminorum*. In learning grammar a medieval student was preparing himself to investigate the doctrine of the trinity or the nature of divine providence.

In the sixteenth, and even seventeenth, century a grammatical culture was still in place. Grammar remained the foundation of the *trivium* and the basis of a literate society. Its position in the curriculum of schools and

---

[24] '*Grammatica* thus provided the sole access to the whole library of textual culture', Irvine, *Making of Textual Culture*, p. 15.

[25] Minnis, *Medieval Theory of Authorship*, p. 118.

[26] A survey of descriptions of the *sensus litteralis* is given in de Lubac, *Exégèse médiévale*, ii. 425–87.

universities went unchallenged. Indeed, in states which pursued a reformed religious polity, educational reform entrenched grammar within the syllabus. When Luther interested himself in the school syllabus in 1524 he promoted grammar as the essential scholarly discipline. In England, funds from dissolved chantries and guilds were appropriated to form the 'free Grammer Scholes' of Edward VI. Latin grammar was essential to a career not only in church or law but in any form of administration or government. Grammar continued to encompass not only the acquisition of basic language skills and the engendering of literate 'eloquence', but also the interpretation of linguistic meaning or of literary theory and the study of authoritative Latin texts. These texts included poetry and narrative yet also history, moral or political philosophy, and the natural sciences. Classical authors and sacred books sat alongside each other: Lily's grammar in Edwardian and Elizabethan England used examples from the Psalms to teach the Latin parts of speech. In Germany, Johannes Clajus's *Grammatica Germanicae Linguae* illustrated German usage with citations from Luther's Bible.[27]

At the same time, grammar in the sixteenth century was undergoing a cultural revolution. If anything this further entrenched the position of grammar in the order of things. The humanist programme identified grammar as the first battleground in the conflict over *bonae litterae*. Erasmus lost no opportunity to assert the primacy of grammar over dialectic, and Juan Luis Vives in *De tradendis disciplinis* recommended a reorientation of scholastic pursuits surrounding the reform of grammar.[28] New grammatical texts emerged, beginning with Lorenzo Valla's *De linguae Latinae elegantia* in the mid-fifteenth century, followed by works by (among many others) Niccolò Perotti and Aldus Manutius in Italy, Antonio de Nebrija in Spain, Johannes Despauterius in Flanders and France, Melanchthon in Germany, and Thomas Linacre in England.[29]

Humanist grammars claimed to be motivated first and last by requirements of literary style and to follow the dictates of usage alone. Erasmus's *De recta pronuntiatione* contains numerous righteous pronouncements on the rigours of the new grammar liberally sprinkled with insults against the grammatical (or rather ungrammatical) methods

---

[27] Ed. Meier in *Ältere Deutsche Grammatiken*, ii.
[28] Published as the second volume of *De disciplinis libri xx* in 1531. Vives was born in Spain and trained in scholastic logic at Paris. His attacks on scholasticism date from his arrival in Louvain in 1517, see Jardine, *Erasmus*, pp. 16–20. In 1524 he taught in Oxford (McConica, *English Humanists*, p. 84).
[29] Padley, *Latin Tradition*, pp. 16–29.

of the scholastics.[30] Like much in Erasmus this should not be taken at face value. Scholastic writers were not, as Erasmus claimed, indifferent to grammar, but took it for granted. What was new about grammatical study in the sixteenth century was not that it was newly central (it had never been less than central) but that it was newly controversial. This controversy was not caused, as Erasmus and others frequently insisted, by a simple replacement of old with new methodologies. The newfangled could be determinedly old-fashioned. There were many significant changes in the curriculum, but perhaps the most noticeable feature of the new grammar is its reliance on Priscian, who had appeared on every syllabus of the middle ages. The definition placed at the opening of Perotti's *Rudimenta grammatices* (and plagiarized routinely for a century after) that grammar is the *ars recte loquendi, recteque scribendi*, and an *ars scriptorum et poetarum lectionibus observata*, is, allowing for a few moderately Ciceronian flourishes, virtually repeated from Rabanus Maurus's textbook definition in the ninth century.[31]

Controversy often consisted not in new theory but in a new visibility of tensions that had been present in grammatical theory for upwards of a thousand years. These tensions included the relation between grammar and logic, or between linguistic and literary theory on the one hand and theology and biblical interpretation on the other. One immediate source of new conflict was the new attention in linguistic study to Greek and Hebrew as well as Latin. Erasmus liked to pretend the conflict arose because of the innate antipathy of the medieval barbarians to Sophocles or Pindar, but since these medieval barbarians were lovingly devoted to the study of Virgil or Ovid the explanation is insufficient. The study of Greek became both so widespread and so problematic because, quite simply, the New Testament was written in Greek. On one page of *De recta pronuntiatione* Erasmus complains about the undue influence of theologians on literary studies, while on the next page he recommends urgent scrutiny of Greek grammar because it will assist in the interpretation of St Paul.[32]

What is apparent is how far sixteenth-century study of grammar continues to be bound up with the study of theology and vice versa. Many of the most eminent new grammarians (Colet in England, de Nebrija in Spain, Melanchthon in Germany) were also theologians, and some were actively involved in editing and annotating the original texts of the Bible.

---

[30] LB, i. 919.
[31] *Rudimenta*; Padley, *Latin Tradition*, pp. 30–1; Rabanus Maurus, *De institutione orationis*, i. iv (Paetow, *Arts Course*, p. 13).
[32] LB, i. 922.

De Nebrija made an enormous scholarly contribution to the Hebrew text of the Complutensian polyglot Bible of Alcalá, just as Erasmus himself was most famous or notorious for his edition of the Greek New Testament. Melanchthon earned the epithet *praeceptor Germaniae* precisely because he spanned disciplines which modern academic study prefers to keep apart. He was the most influential interpreter of Luther's theology and also the most serious political ambassador for the Lutheran church. This did not conflict with his reputation as the most learned purveyor in Germany of the humanist arts: his *Grammatica Latina* and *Syntaxis* (like his *Institutiones rhetoricae* and *Dialectices*) became standard texts in German schools.[33] His historical and philosophical pursuits were the widest possible: he wrote a commentary on Thucydides and interpreted the Aristotelian canon on physics, psychology, and metaphysics; his *Liber de anima* went through forty editions and was itself subject to eight separate commentaries.[34] In the university he lectured on everything from astronomy to anatomy. In all these activities he gives the lie to any perception of a fundamental battle between sacred and secular or pagan learning.

The study of Greek and Hebrew raised a conflict in grammatical studies not because of the stylistic beauties or erotic paganism of classical Greek but because of the problem of comparative grammar. The ancient languages exposed an *aporia* in medieval grammatical theory by having a grammatical structure which could not be rationalized fully by the terminology developed in relation to Latin. This was particularly true of Hebrew, which had a radically different system of inflection and syntax. The study of Hebrew therefore forced some immediate revision in grammatical categories. However, it also cast commensurate doubt on how the older Latin categories could be held to be universal or authoritative. And since the issue of the meaning of the Hebrew text was still investigated largely in Latin, it raised a further and profoundly disturbing question of whether texts written in Hebrew and Latin could ever mean exactly the same thing.

If Latin was exposed on the one side to comparison with the other ancient languages, it also faced the threat on the other of the burgeoning influence of the vernacular. The massive growth of writing in the vernacular throughout Europe had an inevitably destabilizing effect on the unity

---

[33] Like the *Syntaxis*, the *Grammatica Latina* was published in 1526 (also in a Cologne edn. as *Elementa Latinae grammatices*). *Institutiones rhetoricae* appeared in 1521, following the *De rhetorica libri tres* of 1519. The *Dialectices* was published in 1528.

[34] *CHRP* (K. Park and E. Kessler on 'Psychology', pp. 479–84, 516–18; C. H. Lohr on 'Metaphysics', pp. 621–6).

of literate culture embodied in the study of *grammatica*. Many of these conflicts of interest seemed initially to be resolved on the side of Latinity: the literariness of Latin was the standard by which the vernacular was found lacking. Even the grammatical structure of Latin was held up as a rebuke to the roughness and uncouthness of its low-class linguistic bastard children. However, such arguments also opened Latin up to counter-attack. Grammar became one more field in the arena of incipient nationalism. In countries riven by arguments for religious reform, the honest plainness of the indigenous national tongue was favourably compared with the devious eloquence of Latin. Here, the ecclesiastical and liturgical function of Latin, which had been a major reason for its enormous power in the Christian West, became a reason for its subversion.

The political and spiritual arguments for vernacular versions of scripture and liturgy thus coincided with a realignment in the order of linguistic culture. The study of grammar was not unaffected. In England, the promulgation of an authorized text of the English Bible and a vernacular Book of Common Prayer is more or less exactly contemporary with the publication of a new English book of grammar. Its authorization is couched in almost precisely the same terms: the reformation government of Edwardian England saw the unification of vernacular culture as encompassing both kinds of text. The English protestant state erected a cultural monopoly in the elementary procedures of education, in which print (and the commercial ambitions of royally sanctioned printers) was a powerful ally.

By whatever means, vernacular grammar posed ambiguities for Latin culture. Vernacular Bibles threatened the visible and legible authority and autonomy of the Latin Vulgate. Vernacular grammar weakened the authority of Latin to explicate and authorize itself. Even in the carefully orthodox form of Lily's *Short Introduction of Grammar*, English is given a peculiar form of subservient ascendancy over its erstwhile master. Latin meaning is verified through the vernacular, and tested in the mind of the schoolboy by reference to vernacular forms. Implicitly, a further problem is created by the fact that these forms are not equivalent: so that unlike is called to explain unlike. This difficulty uncovered a new rupture in the grammatical union, since the emergence eventually of autonomous grammars of vernacular languages could only reveal more starkly the myth of a universal grammar of Latin categories. To endow the vulgar tongue with its own grammatical apparatus was to deliver to it a newfound authority and a potentially divisive power. Just as the difference of Hebrew from

Latin exposed a flaw in Latin grammatical theory, so *a fortiori* did the multiplicity of grammaticalized modern tongues. The Babel of sixteenth-century language is well enough known. But the growth in study of the ancient languages and the rise of the vernacular need to be brought together in an apprehension of the linguistic medium as a whole. The formidable propaganda of humanism has in this respect been a disservice to historical understanding, since humanism has tried so hard to take credit for these developments as a self-conscious intellectual artefact. Instead humanism itself must be located within the larger movement of literate culture. The Reformation can be seen as part of this and as a prime motivator within it. This, too, not in a partisan fashion: catholic writing is as caught up in the conflicts surrounding language as protestant. The issues of control over scripture and theology, and the ideological superstructure of each, are bound up with every question in the linguistic programme, whether of semantic analysis, or literary interpretation, or vernacular textuality. Once again, the master terminology of grammar is evident, as the etymological speculations of grammarians remind us. *Grammatica* is the science of τὰ γράμματα, or *ars literaria vel literatura*, standing for a culture of the written in its entirety.[35]

II WORDS AND THINGS: MONTAIGNE ON LANGUAGE

Montaigne's aphorism about the Reformation is thus not a simple one. Nor is it naïve. Luther, he remarks, who caused such a catastrophic division in the interpretation of the meaning of holy scripture, has himself been subjected to as many divisions in the interpretation of his own meaning.[36] Montaigne thus exposes to scepticism the cardinal doctrine of the reformers, the word alone of *sola scriptura*. Luther aspired to end all doubt by subscription to the one word of God ('l'expresse parolle de la Bible', *Essais*, ed. Villey, p. 1065), but this one word, as all words do, only compounds doubt, and creates difference. Those who aspire to 'appetiser nos debats et les arrester' through scripture only mock themselves. For words, Montaigne says, are constructed in difference, and contain no likeness even to themselves.[37]

---

[35] Brassicanus, *Grammatice institutiones*, A1^r.
[36] 'J'ay veu en Allemagne que Luther a laissé autant de divisions et d'altercations sur le doubte de ses opinions, et plus, qu'il n'en esmeut sur les escritures sainctes' (*Essais*, ed. Villey, p. 1069).
[37] 'La ressemblence ne faict pas tant un comme la différence faict autre' (*Essais*, ed. Villey, p. 1065).

'De l'experience' is an essay in the construction of things in words, but in the encounter between words and things it discovers in the end only bafflement. Self-consciously and self-knowingly it is written after Babel. In ironic imitation it begins with the opening sentence of Aristotle's *Metaphysics*, that nothing is more natural than the desire for knowledge, only to lament that knowledge now is composed entirely of glosses upon Aristotle, and glosses upon those glosses, in an endless division and subdivision of meaning. The effect of these glosses is not to increase knowledge but to augment 'les doubtes et l'ignorance', since 'tant d'interprétations dissipent la verité et la rompent' (1067). What book is there, he asks, 'soit humain, soit divin', whose difficulties have been exhausted by exegesis? Imagine the statement (one can understand Montaigne's excitement at the thought), that such and such a book already has enough glosses, so let no more be said about it. A modern reader feels an irresistible sympathy, perhaps. Such a fantasy proves unattainable, however, since 'Il n'y a point de fin de nos inquisitions; nostre fin est en l'autre monde'.[38]

At the same time this last remark is itself effectively a gloss on *Metaphysics*, I, i. Placing irony upon irony, Montaigne gathers authority for his attack on learning by learnedly quoting Quintilian learnedly attacking learning (*difficultatem facit doctrina*, 'it is learning which creates difficulty'). Montaigne's diatribe against citation and annotation is littered with citations from Crates on Heraclitus, and annotated with references to the ultimate exercise in annotating for its own sake, Erasmus's *Adagia*. Without any obvious humour, a modern editor adds the footnote that it is probably not Crates on Heraclitus after all but Socrates on Delius, a footnote which annotates its own authority via the *Adagia* from Diogenes Laertius on Socrates.[39] Among other things, Montaigne's essay is a commentary on itself:

Il y a plus affaire à interpreter les interpretations qu'à interpreter les choses, et plus de livres sur les livres que sur autre subject: nous ne faisons que nous entregloser (p. 1069)

[There's more adoe to enterprete interpretations, than to interprete things: and more bookes upon bookes, then upon any other subject. We doe but enter-glose our selves (Florio, vi. 327)]

Indeed, he remarks, doing it again, how often his own book has been interrupted and extended in talking about itself.[40] With barely allowable cheek,

---

[38] 'There is no end to our inquiries: our end is in the next world' (tr. Screech, p. 1211).
[39] A footnote seems required here: Screech (tr.) *Essays*, p. 1211, nn.16, 18, 19.
[40] See Cave, *Cornucopian Text*, p. 316.

he adds that he alone is allowed to do so since he is writing in any case about himself.

It is this passage which provides the immediate pretext to the discussion about the Lutheran Reformation and its revolution in language:

> J'ay veu en Allemagne que Luther a laissé autant de divisions et d'altercations sur le doubte de ses opinions, et plus, qu'il n'en esment sur les escritures sainctes. Nostre contestation est verbale. Je demande que c'est que nature, volupté, cercle, et substitution. La question est de parolles, et se paye de mesme. (p. 1069)
>
> [I note that Luther has left behind in Germany as many—indeed more—discords and disagreements because of doubts about his opinions than he himself ever raised about holy scripture. Our controversies are verbal ones. I ask what is nature, pleasure, circle or substitution. The question is about words: it is paid in the same coin. (Screech, p. 1213)]

All that occurs within language is an infinite regression of language within language: 'What is a stone? a stone is a body; but what is a body? a body is substance; but what is substance?'—and so on. No meaning can be said properly to mean itself but must be glossed by another meaning. Yet each gloss is only a substitution, false money paid for good, or rather false for false. Each word can be rendered only and always by more words. Language doubles on itself, and recedes into obscurity and obliquity: 'On eschange un mot pour un autre mot, et souvent plus incogneu'.[41] In resolving one doubt, three more are created: language is the Hydra's head.

In this fabulous parody of the academic metatext, anticipating some of the best jokes in Derrida (and like Derrida including his own text within the frame of the parody) Montaigne encapsulates some of the formidable paradoxes of early modern (and it might be said modern modern) meaning. It is anti-scholastic in the best humanist tradition: the examples of 'nature, volupté, cercle, et substitution' are taken straight out of the dialectic of medieval Paris. But it makes these anti-scholastic gestures in the midst of an attack on Luther, who was as anti-scholastic as anybody.[42] Nor is it at all kindly towards humanist dialectic. For his next parody Montaigne takes to pieces a Socratic paradigm (*homo est animal mortalis et rationalis*) which would be quite at home in humanist dialectic, such as Rudolph Agricola or even Peter Ramus: 'Je sçay mieux que c'est qu'homme que je ne sçay que c'est animal, ou mortel, ou raisonnable' (p. 1069).

---

[41] The intellect, like Apollo, always speaks 'doublement, obscurement et obliquement', p. 1068.

[42] An early instance, using some of the same examples as Montaigne, is Luther's parody of scholastic method in a letter to Georg Spalatin, 22 February 1518, WA Br, 1.149–50.

Something more disturbing is happening here than some polite humanist satire on old-fashioned pedagogy. This is a highly literate piece of language losing faith in the literacy of language. With one of his most winning jokes Montaigne makes a plea for illiteracy: 'I had rather be an expert on me than on Plato', a joke which he made less daring but funnier by substituting in the 1595 edition the humanist darling Cicero for Plato. 'We tell ourselves all that we most need', he says, 'so let us listen to ourselves.' In place of the interminable process of interpretation and the infinite regression of meaning Montaigne turns to what he calls 'experience'. Modern commentators have sometimes called this a replacement of linguistic philosophy by empiricism as if unaware that empiricism, too, is a philosophy of linguistic meaning, whereas Montaigne here risks the much more destructive step of rejecting a philosophy of language altogether. Aware that any such rejection of linguistic meaning can mean logically only a turn to the self, he willingly embraces private meaning. From epistemological high theory and Aristotelian metaphysics Montaigne reconstitutes his text in an ultimate act of self-referential solipsism: he listens to himself by himself and talks about himself to himself. In one of his most memorable phrases he declares that he studies himself more than any other subject: 'C'est ma metaphysique, c'est ma physique' (p. 1072). His solitary exposition of private experience then attempts to recreate with every spasm of physical detail the sensation of being himself: how and when he eats and how and when he shits, what it feels like to sweat or to itch, or to have an orgasm, or to get diarrhoea.

Why at a crucial stage in this extraordinary argument does Montaigne refer to the Reformation controversy about language and to Luther himself (one of only two such references in the whole of the *Essais*)?[43] It seems to be because Luther expressed absolute faith in language, when Luther himself made such faith in language impossible. Luther is denigrated as the apostle of literalism, of the literal interpretation of the sacred text and of the sanctity of literal interpretation. For literal interpretation in Montaigne's analysis is as much a chimera as the non-literal interpretations it is meant to oppose (what, in any case, is a *non*-literal interpretation?). A literal interpretation, like any other, pays words back with words. Luther has promised the ultimate linguistic fiction of a language without fiction, of words which really do render things. In the process he has apparently destroyed all confidence in any language which appears to do less.

[43] The other is in the preamble to the 'Apology for Raymond Sebond', *Essais*, ii. xii.

Montaigne thus places Luther at the centre of what he sees as the sixteenth-century crisis in language. In this he is surely correct, for Luther's Reformation founded itself on a polemic which attempted to reconstruct literate culture at a stroke, on the basis that scripture is a source of authority independent of the church, and the individual Christian an independent authority in the interpretation of scripture. In that sense, Luther's theory of meaning was itself solipsistic—as his catholic detractors were quick to argue—since he made the arbitration of meaning self-referential. Luther, they said, made God subject to private interpretation, and the believer free to believe anything he or she liked. And yet Luther's own place within this crisis is much more ambiguous than Montaigne allows, in ways which reflect back on Montaigne's own deeply ambiguous analysis. He is also closer to Montaigne in this respect than Montaigne, true catholic to the end, had any desire to understand.

III THE TEXTUALITY OF THE NINETY-FIVE THESES

Luther's position within a contemporary linguistic culture is often misunderstood, partly because the available model for such a culture appears to be humanism, and Luther, with whatever ingenuity, will not fit the humanist model. Indeed, he could be said to break it. He uses most of the methods now associated with humanism but evinces none of the principles of *bonae litterae* supposed to motivate those methods. According to some it seems as if the literate culture of the sixteenth century simply passes Luther by, and yet he is powerfully attached to its two great causes: reading in the ancient languages; and writing in the modern vernacular. Arguments are offered in explanation along the lines that he is not interested in 'literature' but in 'scripture' or that his principles are 'theological' rather than 'grammatical', when it is not at all clear that such oppositions make any sense in this period. The insufficiency of humanism as an interpretation of textuality could not be more clearly indicated than by its failure to account for one of the period's most formidable exponents of textuality.[44]

No text is more in need of such a context than the ninety-five theses themselves, which have been more annotated and more explicated than practically any other sixteenth-century text, but with comparatively little

---

[44] Specialist studies of Luther and German textual culture abound: e.g. Gravier, *Luther et l'opinion publique*; Engelsing, *Der Bürger als Leser*; and the survey by John L. Flood in Gilmont (ed.), *Reformation and the Book*.

interest in their own mode of production. Within the historical myth they are not a text but an action: a gesture of defiance; a cry for freedom. The picture of the lonely monk nailing his colours to the church door and waiting for Christendom to collapse around him has obscured the way in which this notorious yet enigmatic document is poised at a peculiar moment in the history of textual culture. In recent years the historicity of the events of 31 October 1517 has been exposed to relentless scrutiny. Doubt has been cast on when, or even whether, the theses were ever posted to any church door. Yet this discussion, too, involves the event more than the text itself.[45] Meanwhile, annotation of the contents of the theses is almost exclusively doctrinal, with the corollary that it is by ideas alone that Luther created such a stir.

The *disputatio* was one of the major textual forms of the medieval university. Some were instructional; some were employed in the examination process for higher degrees (such as the *Disputatio contra scholasticam theologiam*, which Luther composed for his student Franz Günther eight weeks before the ninety-five). Others were written for debate by the faculty at large as a public academic exercise. The ninety-five take the form of this last type. Lecturers drafted theses for this purpose with careful attention to detail and published them in advance. The door of the Schlosskirche in Wittenberg, which lay conveniently between the university library and the law lecture rooms, was the logical site for the university bulletin board, where all official announcements were placed, including the posting of theses and the dates of disputations. Luther's elemental gesture was in this way no more dramatic than pinning up a lecture-list in a modern university.

Publication of the medieval *disputatio* lay somewhere between the literate and the oral, since theses were written and often recorded in official archives but the disputation proper was spoken and even somewhat theatrical, lasting several hours.[46] The ninety-five were never performed, however. On the other hand, if they were posted they were still published in that they would have been on public display just outside the church—a church which a day later on All Saints' Day was full of pilgrims viewing the

---

[45] In a lecture of 1961, Erwin Iserloh caused considerable consternation by describing the posting as a myth. The jury is still out; for contrasting summaries of the arguments see Brecht, *Road to Reformation*, pp. 199–200 and Marius, *Luther*, pp. 137–9.

[46] All promotional disputations at Wittenberg were recorded in the *liber decanorum*; the theses for Luther's own advancement to the doctorate in 1512 survive (Foestermann, *Liber Decanorum*, 11–12). Faculty disputations were not so recorded, however, and there is no mention of the ninety-five in the *liber decanorum*.

Elector's spectacular collection of relics. By being posted on 31 October therefore, the theses received maximum local publicity. The international hullabaloo of the theses none the less surrounds their appearance in print. Since the disputational form of the text fits oddly with its printed dissemination, this too creates an enigma. Many mysteries remain after centuries of bibliographical research. A first imprint in Wittenberg is presumed, perhaps from the house of Luther's earliest known printer, Johann Grunenberg, but if so no copy survives. The three imprints which do survive emanate from three different cities: two take the form of a single folio broadsheet; the third a four-page book in quarto.[47] The title in the earliest printings follows the standard *incipit* format of the university style, with no allowance for a lay audience, not even a reference to indulgences.[48] In two of the imprints, the numbering is not consecutive, and the theses are listed in three groups 1–25 followed by one numbered 1–20. In the third, the numbering is disorderly and the last thesis appears as ¶87. In no copy dated 1517 does the number 95 ever appear.

The subsequent sensation was described by an early chronicler, Friedrich Myconius. Although Luther, he says, did not intend wide dissemination, the propositions spread like wildfire: 'it appeared as if the angels themselves had been their errand-boys, and brought them before the eyes of all the people. One can hardly believe how much they were gossiped about'.[49] Talk of the intervention of angels has concealed the more material process involved. Myconius relies upon Luther's own frequent avowals of indifference to publication, whereas it has been said that 'his surprise at the interest he aroused may have entailed self-deception' and more likely it was a matter of deliberate cultivation.[50] The history of the theses was an elaborate literary fiction from the start, and this has nothing

---

[47] Benzing, 87–9; the printings are described by Honselmann, *Urfassung und Drucke*, pp. 11–17.

[48] *Amore et studio elucidande veritatis: hec subscripta disputabuntur Wittenberge. Presidente R.P. Martino Lutther . . . Quare petit: vt qui non possunt verbis presentes nobiscum disceptare: agant id literis absentes.* At the end of the 2nd column the date is added, M.D.Xvii. There are minor differences in the title in all the extant imprints; text cited here is the BL copy of the Nuremberg imprint, Benzing, 87. The title *Disputatio pro declaratione virtutis indulgentiarum* first appears in the third printing by Adam Petri of Basel (Benzing, 89); see Honselmann, p. 15. Luther always referred to the ninety-five as his *Propositiones*, even in German (e.g. WA 51.540.25, 'meine Propositiones').

[49] *Historia reformationis*, p. 23 (*als wären die Engel selbst Botenläuffer, und trügens für aller Menschen Augen. Es glaubt kein Mensch, wie ein Gered darvon wurd*). Luther, he says, wrote with only *den Gelertender hohen Schulen Wittenberg* in mind (p. 23).

[50] Eisenstein, *Printing Press*, p. 308. More ingenuous interpretations still prevail, e.g., 'it is obvious that nothing was further from his intention than to instigate widespread dissension or theological controversy' (Hillerbrand, *Reformation in its own Words*, p. 32).

to do with the reality or otherwise of their historical circumstances. Like any good fiction it could usefully be interpreted in a number of ways. The piece of paper nailed to the Wittenberg church door, the academic disputation which never happened, the runaway printing success, and the reluctant professor all played their part in this beguiling narrative. As with Erasmus's controversies (for instance, with Maarten van Dorp), Luther's open letters (for instance, to Archbishop Albrecht and the Pope) encircled his other printed works to form a public perception of a world teeming with texts.[51] In the political furore over the scandalous theses an academic setting formed an ideal cover.

Meanwhile the booksellers avidly peddled the printed text. Yet who were the readers? Of all the mysteries of the theses this is the strangest. The text is in Latin in the rebarbative style of the theological faculty. The disputational form was not meant to be read like a book, but consisted of cryptic and allusive notes and dense, unelaborated propositions. The text conforms to the shorthand protocol of disputational theses designed for an expert audience perusing at speed: technical terms are unglossed; academic citations unexplained. A lay reader would have little chance of following the logic, still less of understanding its scholastic context.

A German translation was made by Caspar Nützel, but it has a still more ghostly existence than the Latin edition. Luther acknowledged receiving a copy sent to him by his friend Christoph Scheurl from Nuremberg in January 1518, and Scheurl further refers to this translation in a letter to another friend tracing the dissemination of the theses to Augsburg and Ingolstadt.[52] Myconius used this vernacular version to account for the immediate and overwhelming effect of the theses, but no copy survives.[53] There is no evidence of more than a single print run, and certainly not enough copies to spread like wildfire throughout Germany. Luther did not

---

[51] See Jardine, *Erasmus*, p. 14 and esp. the account of the Erasmus/Dorp 'quarrel', pp. 111–22.

[52] Luther to Scheurl, 5 March 1518 (*positiones meas latinas et vulgares*), WA Br 1.152.1; Scheurl to Kaspar Güttel, 8 January 1518, *Christoph Scheurls Briefbuch*, ed. F. von Soden and J. Knaake (Potsdam: Gropius, 1869–72), ii. 43; see also Scheurl to Ulrich von Dinstedt, 5 January 1518 (*Briefbuch*, ii. 42). Scheurl played a significant role in the spread of the ninety-five, sending copies out as early as 5 November 1517. At this period he was a legal adviser to the city of Nuremberg, but from 1507 to 1512 he was rector of the University of Wittenberg and Dean of the faculty of law.

[53] *wurden bald geteutscht*, Myconius, *Historia reformationis*, p. 23. Modern bibliographies such as Benzing or VD 16 are silent on the German version. A German translation of the ninety-five theses was eventually included after Luther's death in his complete German works, *Der Neunte Teil der Bücher des Ehrwirdigen Herrn D. Martini Lutheri* (Wittenberg: Hans Lufft, 1557), 9B–13A.

authorize this version and his only effort to democratize his arguments through the vernacular was *Ein Sermon von Ablaß und Gnade*, which appeared early in 1518 and was printed widely, beginning with Grunenberg in Wittenberg.[54] This text, too, was propositional in form, but has only twenty 'theses' and is in no sense a condensation of the ninety-five. Luther, in fact, made much of the fact that he never issued the ninety-five theses in the vernacular. He used this to explain his mystification at the popular impact of the theses in the letter to Pope Leo X which prefaced the fully annotated and expanded edition of the theses in 1518 (the *Resolutiones*):

It is a mystery to me how my theses, more so than my other writings, indeed those of other professors, were spread in so many places. They were meant exclusively for an academic circle here. This is shown by the fact that they were written in such a language that the common people could hardly understand them. They are propositions for debate, not dogmatic definitions, and they use academic categories. Had I anticipated their widespread popularity, I would certainly have done my share to make them more understandable.[55]

This is a highly literate account of the shifting rules of vernacular culture, and therefore should not be read too literally. Like the whole letter, it is full of tactical irony, astounded by the *miraculum* of his popularity and shocked by his success in fomenting scandal. Once again, the academic context is used to disguise any political intention, a mask successful enough to have deceived many of Luther's biographers.[56]

For this purpose, Luther acknowledges the popular power of the vulgar tongue even as he denies ever having invoked it. The Latinity of the theses is held up to proclaim his innocence. Had he wanted to provoke his readers, he implies (perhaps threatens), he would have written in German. The corollary is that Luther chose precisely not to do so: he had different cultural work in mind. The academic style of the theses is their point, and obscurity their purpose. This is not to deny the thrilling quality of the Latin. The genius of the ninety-five theses lies in the indirectness of voice which derives from the anonymous manner of the disputational genre. As

---

[54] Benzing, 90–114; Benzing lists 25 imprints in all between 1518 and 1520, from at least 11 printers in 7 cities, including two versions in low German. There were also 18 imprints of Luther's *Defence* of this sermon against Tetzel's reply.

[55] *Beatissimo patri Leoni decimo pontifici maximo*, prefatory epistle to *Resolutiones disputationum de indulgentiarum virtute*, WA 1.528.36, quoted here from Hillerbrand, *Reformation in its own Words*.

[56] Marius, *Luther*, pp. 139–40, is an exception, comparing the use of academic form as a cover by Erasmus and Galileo.

he says in the *Resolutiones*, they are merely 'propositions for debate, not dogmatic definitions', and as such they are unattributable or plausibly deniable. It is not Luther who says with flagrant slander, 'The treasures of indulgence are nets with which one now fishes for the wealth of men' (Thesis 66). Nor is it Luther who presumptuously parodies first the Pope's decrees and then Christ's Beatitudes in order to turn papal policy upside down in Theses 71–2:

71. Let him who who speaks against the truth concerning papal indulgences be accursed. 72. But let him who guards against the lust and license of the indulgence preachers be blessed.

The tone combines formal opacity with stylistic ebullience. Some of the theses are statements of the obvious; others are quotations from scripture or canon law, but these are mixed without any editorial commentary with others which are obvious exaggerations, quaint anecdotes, or wild paradoxes.

In between come invectives against social injustice and Jeremiads of high moral sarcasm which veer close to savage ridicule or even plain jokiness:

48. Christians are to be taught that the pope, in granting indulgences, needs and thus desires their devout prayer more than their money.

In the gap between 'needs' and 'desires' (*magis eget ita magis optat*) a doubt is created which invites a smirk at the Pope's venality competing with his piety, a doubt which becomes aggravated by subsequent hyperbole:

51. Christians are to be taught that the pope would and should wish to give of his own money, even though he had to sell the basilica of St Peter, to those who have been cajoled out of their money by the indulgence hawkers.

Who is supposed to be saying these things, and who is supposed to be listening? With rising volatility and even violence, the theses proceed with a momentum which appears to come from nowhere. Finally, at Thesis 76, a voice in the first person intervenes to give the lie direct ('We say on the contrary that papal indulgences cannot remove the very least of venial sins'). There follow three examples in reported speech, apparently quoted from indulgence sermons by Tetzel and others, which are calmly dismissed as blasphemy.

This is the prelude to the most outlandish section of all, in which Luther adopts the style of the honest citizen protecting the monarch from his worst advisers. Such a trope is a standard mode of satire against a king or other tyrant. It is hard, he says, to rescue the Pope from slander when the uncontrolled preaching of indulgences incites what he calls 'the shrewd questions of the laity'. Theses 82–9 proceed to slander the Pope nine times over with outrageous frankness, protected all the time by the standard formula that these are merely 'the questions of the laity'. How else would it be possible to ask, ' "Why does not the pope empty purgatory for the sake of holy love . . . if he redeems an infinite number of souls for the sake of miserable money?" ' (Thesis 82); or ' "Why does the pope, whose wealth is today greater than the wealth of Crassus, not build this one basilica of St Peter with his own money rather than the money of believers?" ' (Thesis 86).

Before attributing to this style too much radical novelty, it should be recalled that such methods of satire were donnish and even monkish long before Luther. Within the university or the monastery they would have been shocking in the degree of irreverence towards the Pope but even then perhaps not unknown. What is incendiary about the theses is precisely, then, their publication in print. By this means, print yokes together in disturbing alliance clerical burlesque with popular revolution. The theses stand on a knife-edge between private disputation and public propaganda. Latinity is crucial to the effectiveness of the ninety-five theses, but it is a Latinity bordering dangerously on vernacularity. Luther even manages to inveigle popular vernacular culture into his Latin text, and to quote without prejudice the slanderous lyric 'So bald der Gülden im Becken klingt | Im hun die Seel im Himel springt' ('As soon as the coin in the coffer rings, | the soul into heaven springs'). This lyric was a cliché of the broadsheet pamphlets or *Flugschriften* which poured out of the printers' workshops, but in Latin it reads rather differently, almost as if it might be a nominalist quiddity: *statim ut iactus nummus in cistam tinnierit evolare . . . animam* (Thesis 27, WA 1.234.29; see also Thesis 28).[57] Like the theses as a whole, it is ambiguous in its reception. It both incites and resists populism; it is flagrant and obscure at the same time.

In some sense, therefore, the theses did not have readers as such. They were mass marketed for a wide readership, but in different degrees they were unreadable to different parts of that readership. However, this obscurity did not diminish their power, rather it may have enhanced it. The theses were known immediately as a scandalous document. They con-

---

[57] A woodcut caricature of Tetzel with the accompanying verses is reprinted in Hillerbrand, *Reformation in its own Words*, p. 42. It was still going the rounds in 1547 in Lucas Cranach the Younger's woodcut of *Two Kinds of Preaching* (Scribner, *For the Sake of Simple Folk*, pp. 201 and 203).

tained, in Latin, some dark or obscene secret about the papacy. To some, who could not read Latin, this in itself gave the folio sheet ineffable but palpable significance. To others, who could read some Latin, the invective and satire were impressive even if the theology seemed arcane or abstract. But even to those with expert Latin, the theses retained some quality of resistance in their academic coterie allusiveness. No interpretation could quickly explain the theses, and thus exhaust them. They retained some unmentionable, unsatisfiable surplus of force over content. Luther himself comments on this power in the letter to Leo X:

> What shall I do now? I cannot recall my theses and yet their popularity makes me to be hated. Unwillingly I must enter the public limelight and subject myself to the dangerously shifting judgement of men. (WA 1.529.3)

Luther here characterizes himself as a creation of the press and in some degree its creature. He makes a confession of textuality even as he modestly formulates a public *apologia* for his works. Textuality is woven into the ninety-five theses and their effect. They are a sign of the changing rules of cultural formation which come with print. Print enabled a theological controversy to take place even though a formal academic disputation did not: Luther talked over the heads of his faculty to the outside world. The context of heretical discourse metamorphosed, as the papal curia quickly learned. The trial of Luther's opinions before the papal legate Cardinal Cajetan at Augsburg, designed as a platform for recantation and humiliation, became instead a text, cheerfully emitted by Luther's own printers, showing off his verbal triumph against the powers that be.[58] Just as Erasmus shrewdly used (and sometimes authored) opposition to his imprints to increase their fame and their circulation, so Luther seems to have wallowed in controversy. His catholic opponents happily offered themselves as bait and baiters, oblivious to their participation in the Lutheran publicity machine. The campaign was not necessarily orchestrated, but it did not need to be; dissemination was everything. Confutation only amplified Luther's books, and in the process, Reformation controversy became virtually a condition of religion.[59]

Confutation was the staple of the medieval system of censorship: error entailed prohibition which brought persecution. Outlawed books circulated, of course, but did so perforce in secrecy. Printed heresy was open by the nature of the medium. All texts had the status of free distribution,

---

[58] *Acta F.Martini Luther Augustana apud D.Legatum* (Wittenberg: Johann Grunenberg, 1518); Benzing, 234. There were five other imprints.

[59] On opposition to Luther see Bagchi, *Luther's Earliest Opponents*.

however small the actual number of copies. It has never been known, for instance, how many copies of the theses in Latin or German came into existence; but in any case, far more people knew about them and talked about them than can possibly have read them. Censorship laws became all the more strenuous as a result, and state and church hunted down heterodoxy with remorseless violence. Luther's books were burned and he burned some back, and he was at risk of death throughout his life. But the violence is in part a compensation for failure: however many copies are destroyed, within a system of mechanical reproduction complete obliteration is impossible because only theoretical; and there are always reprints, new editions. Argument about the actual circulation of Luther's books, however interesting, is sometimes off the point, since it assumes the only cultural effect worth noticing is that produced by the reading process. Yet books can signify when they are not read, or even seen.

IV LETTER AND SPIRIT: LUTHER'S 1520 PAMPHLETS AND
MORE'S *RESPONSIO*

Textual culture and grammatical culture do not sit in separate worlds. The material texts of the Reformation and their immaterial meanings intersect in formidably complicated ways. Vernacularity is a case in point. The vernacular was not simply for Luther a means of broadening his appeal or of entering into popular culture. It was a new scene of controversy and contestation over words and their meanings. Latin and the vernacular relate in peculiar ways in this period, even in the same writer.[60] Neither medium can be understood in isolation from the other. Montaigne describes in one of the *Essais* how his father brought him up to speak and write Latin, refusing to send him to school in case of contamination. Yet the *essai* which describes this is written, of course, in French. 'De l'experience' commentates with dense illumination on the Latin culture of interpretation, but does so only through a process of translation of the scholastic and humanist discourses which dominate that culture, in ways which only add to the linguistic tension. Erasmus, on the other hand, never published a word in Dutch, and campaigned for Latinity in conscious evasion and repudiation of the vernacular; yet he was adopted as a model for vernacularity by such a virulent anti-Latinist as William Tyndale. Luther himself is now regarded

---

[60] Perhaps the most sensitive modern reading of such issues is Chrisman's study of Strasbourg, *Lay Culture, Learned Culture*.

in Germany as the champion of the vernacular, yet it is often forgotten that Latin was hardly a formal or even a foreign tongue for him to use. Like any university cleric, he regarded Latin as his daily medium and he used it for much of his writing until death. Erasmus considered the style barbaric but it was more of a living language in Luther than in Erasmus (sometimes it is said with justice that humanism killed Latin off rather than revived it).[61] Luther, and Jean Calvin after him, translated his own works from Latin to the vernacular and vice versa as circumstance required.[62]

In 1520, the year of his condemnation in the papal bull *Exsurge Domine*, Luther issued three major pamphlets establishing his position. Of these, one was in German, one was in Latin, and the other was in two versions, one Latin and one German.[63] Luther felt the need to address both cultures, although recognizing the difference between them: *De libertate Christiana* is both longer and more technical than its German counterpart. Whatever his preference between the two media, printers energetically exploited both markets. Learned books represented a large commercial interest: a significant proportion of the literate was made up, after all, of scholars. The Basle publisher Johann Froben acquired some books by Luther in 1518 from a Leipzig printer via the Frankfurt book fair, and quickly reprinted them to reach French and Spanish outlets. He was particularly eager to harvest the rich pickings available in Paris among the doctors of the Sorbonne.[64] By February 1519 he reports only ten copies unsold from an edition of 600; 'I never remember to have sold any more quickly', he tells Luther, although publishers are always saying this kind of thing to hungry authors.[65]

The vernacular market in Germany was less established and therefore more unpredictable, making it all the more attractive to printers seeking new ways of making money. Religious disturbance contributed to this expanding commerce in books: between 1518 and 1524 the output of the German presses grew by a factor of six or more.[66] Luther represented a printing industry in single hands: between 1517 and 1520 he produced

---

[61] 'The decline of Latin was mainly due not to the opponents of classical antiquity but to its supporters, the humanists, whose insistence on classical standards turned it from a living to a "dead" language', Burke, *Art of Conversation*, pp. 35–6, adapting E. Norden, *Die Antike Kunstprosa* (1898).

[62] On Calvin's bilingualism, see Gilmont, *Calvin et le livre imprimé*, pp. 155–65.

[63] *An den christlichen Adel deutscher Nation*; *De captivitate Babylonica*; *Tractatus de libertate Christiana* and *Von der Freiheit eines Christenmenschen*.

[64] Froben to Luther, 14 February 1519; WA Br 1.332–3.

[65] WA Br 1.333.36; by May he says he was sold out (see WA Br 1.335, n.18).

[66] Dickens, *German Nation and Luther*, p. 106.

thirty popular books whether on penance or indulgences, on the Psalms or
the Lord's Prayer, on the sacraments or on preparation for death. One
sermon sold twenty-five editions in eighteen months, and by the end of
1520 over 700 editions of Luther's output had been published.[67] It has been
estimated that 300,000 copies were on the market by this stage.[68] Other
authors complained that their manuscripts lay languishing on publishers'
desks because of the obsession with the Wittenberg daemon.[69]

Editions of Luther's books show the trend towards the vernacular in this
competitive arena. German imprints of *Von der Freiheit eines Christenmenschen* outnumber *De libertate Christiana* by two to one; the Latin *De
captivitate Babylonica* considerably undersold the extraordinarily successful vernacular manifesto *An den christlichen Adel deutscher Nation*.
Melchior Lotter issued 4,000 copies of this latter work in the first printing,
and sold out immediately; Luther was working on a revised edition within
a week. Printers outside Wittenberg quickly sensed an opportunity to
make a similar fortune with a vernacular version of the equally sensational
but learned text of *De captivitate Babylonica*. A Strasbourg Franciscan,
Thomas Murner, filled the gap, believing that a German edition was
necessary to warn the common people of Luther's manifest heresies. This
is a common irony in vernacular culture: Murner's anti-Luther spread
throughout Germany, disseminating Lutheranism as it went.[70] Neither
was the wider European market satisfied entirely with Latin editions:
translations of the three 'Reformation tracts' appeared from 1520 onwards
in Dutch, Italian, Czech, Spanish, and in about 1535 (despite Henry VIII's
ultra-conservative censorship) in English.[71]

Early readers of these books show an emerging sense of a vernacular
religious literacy. Dürer collected Luther's writings from the beginning,
hailing them as icons of German culture.[72] Dürer sent copies of some of his
prints to Luther in January 1518, apparently given in gratitude for a copy of
Luther's theses.[73] A month after Luther's excommunication, in June 1520,
Dürer journeyed to the Netherlands, and his 'Diary' or accounts-ledger
from the period is littered with references to Luther and his texts. In

---

[67] Full list of surviving editions in Benzing, *Lutherbibliographie*.

[68] Holborn, 'Printing and the Protestant Movement', 1. Estimates of this type are speculative since they rely on guesswork about print-runs, but this one is perhaps conservative.

[69] The complaint of Georg Mitzel, a catholic convert from Lutheranism, quoted by
Holborn, 'Printing and the Protestant Movement', p. 11.

[70] It was printed in several editions in Augsburg and Strasbourg before the end of 1520
(Benzing, 712–16; VD 16, L4192–L4196).

[71] Benzing, 697–8, 717, 766–9.   [72] Jardine, *Worldly Goods*, p. 339.

[73] Luther to Scheurl, 5 March 1518, WA Br, 1.152.6.

Antwerp in October he bought the *Condemnatio* of Luther and a Lutheran dialogue.[74] Back in Cologne later the same month he bought 'a tract of Luther's for 5 white pfennig' and another copy of the *Condemnatio* (p. 71). In Antwerp again the following Whitsun he heard the news that Luther had been arrested by the agents of the Emperor Charles V. Fearing Luther's assassination or execution, and panegyrizing him as the great writer of the age (it is explicitly as a writer that he exalts him), he exhorts Erasmus passionately to take up the pen in the same cause (pp. 90–3). A month later, still uncertain of Luther's fate, Dürer received a copy of Luther's *Babylonian Captivity* from Cornelius Grapheus, the Communal Secretary, and gave him in exchange his two 'Large Books' of engravings of the *Apocalypse*, the *Passion*, and the *Life of the Virgin* (p. 98). The version in question was Murner's anti-Lutheran German translation, *Von der Babylonischen Gefengknuss der Kirchen*, only a few months old. Antwerp was a vital centre in the network of vernacular dissemination in a diaspora of tongues: in June 1521 the Portuguese community of Maronite Jews there financed the publication of Luther's works in Spanish.[75]

Two years earlier, Beatus Rhenanus exchanged a number of letters with Huldrych Zwingli in 1519 reporting the progress of Luther's books from printer to bookseller to reader. Rhenanus explicitly commends *ein Teütsche Theologie* 'which will make that clever theology of Scotus appear awkward and dull'.[76] The reference to *Theologia Deutsch* indicates a complex of cultural forces. This was not a new work by Luther but a late fourteenth-century mystical work which Luther sponsored and reprinted. Yet the term stands for more than one work; Rhenanus makes no distinction of authorship between this piece and 'several new tracts of Luther in German' which the Basle printer Adam Petri is about to publish. *Theologia Deutsch* signifies both a reworking of a German religious classic and a new German culture opposed to the Latin culture of Scotus and the universities.

Luther was reaching and perhaps creating a new vernacular readership. Its size, and its unknown nature, encouraged him to proclaim this as a popular movement in religion, a mission to the masses. At the beginning of *An den christlichen Adel*, he declared all Christian believers as members of the spiritual estate, denying any difference between laymen and priests.[77] The laity therefore had equal access to religious truth and independent authority to interpret. This was a truly radical statement, and

---

[74] Dürer, *Diary*, p. 69.   [75] Dürer, *Diary*, Introduction, p. 13. See Benzing, 768.
[76] Beatus Rhenanus to Zwingli, 24 May 1519; *Zwinglis Sämtliche Werke*, vii. 175.
[77] WA 6.407–8.

Luther sensed its democratic ideal as well as its demagogic appeal. Religion, he announced, was not the province of the learned but the common property of the people. Like most such announcements, however, it had ambiguous connotations. Luther addressed it not directly to the people but care of 'the German Nobility'. Similarly, when *De captavitate Babylonica* stated that no Pope or bishop might impose 'a syllable of law' on a Christian without consent, his own syllables assumed interpretation by an already Latinate reader. Dürer, Rhenanus, and Zwingli were all part of this educated readership when they welcomed Luther's new democratic populism. Rhenanus asked Zwingli to use his courier as an entrepreneurial book-agent, peddling Luther's books among the illiterate from village to village and from house to house; but he makes no mention of how the peasants who are to be thus liberated will first learn to read.[78] A rigid distinction between learned and popular is therefore no more viable than one between Latin and vernacular. Nevertheless Zwingli, however unusual, represents a different kind of reader. University trained, but without a degree in theology, he became that new phenomenon, the independent, non-professional theologian, of which Calvin was soon to become the most extraordinary example.[79] Just as Erasmus bypassed the universities through print in becoming an independent scholar, so theology came into a public domain outside clerical authority. German theology may not have been precisely popular but its readership was open and public, radicalizing Luther's writing beyond his control.

For such a theology Luther re-invented the rules as he went along. The priesthood of all believers is immediately linked to an apostolate of readership. The Pope has shored up power by declaring sole entitlement to the interpretation of scripture (*die schrifft niemant ausztzulegenn, den dem Bapst*).[80] Luther turns this on its head: scripture confers no such authority on the Pope. Let the people therefore read, and find authority through their reading. The church's desire to be *meister der schrifft* is not supported by the text it wishes to master (WA 6.411.8). Its claims are thus nonsense, negating the very need for the text which is thereby authorized: why have

---

[78] Beatus Rhenanus to Zwingli, 2 July 1519; *Zwinglis Sämtliche Werke*, vii. 193. Some scholars have taken this letter, unadvisedly, as evidence for the popular dissemination of Lutheran texts (e.g., Eisenstein, *Printing Press*, p. 309; Dickens, *German Nation and Luther*, p. 111).

[79] Zwingli studied at the University of Vienna and then at Basle, receiving the degree of Master of Arts in 1506. He then became a minister at Glarus for ten years before moving to Einsiedeln and finally Zurich. Calvin received his MA from Paris in 1528 and tried out a career as a humanist writer; it is in this light that we may view the first edition of the *Christianae religionis institutio* which he published in 1536 at the age of 26.

[80] 'No one is to interpret scripture, except the Pope', WA 6.406.27.

scripture at all, if the Pope has already decided what it means and no one can challenge him? To this self-authorized monopoly of the reading of scripture, Luther opposes his own scriptural readings:

Doch das wir nit mit wortten widder sie fechten, wollen wir die schrifft her bringen [WA 6.411.21 So as not to fight them with mere words, we will cite scripture]

The text Luther uses to establish his case is 1 Corinthians 14: 30: (to paraphrase Luther's version) 'if the person listening has something better to say, let the person speaking shut up'. Reading conveys authority by the strength of its reading; a bad reading is not made good because a man in authority makes it. Papal power over words is itself composed of mere words, a scandalous linguistic fiction, 'ein frevel ertichte fabel' (WA 6.411.33).

The new theology is thus directly based on an appeal for vernacular culture in its widest sense. The liberation of the German nation from its religious yoke lies in its recovery of power over language. A freedom to interpret is the first freedom of a Christian man, from which (and only from which) all other freedoms derive:

Ausz dieszem allenn und vielen andern spruchen sollen wir mutig und frey werden.

[(WA 6.412.26) Through all these and many other texts we ought to become brave and free.]

The theology of the church is made up only of the *ertichten wortten der Bepst* (WA 6.412.28, 'the fabricated words of the pope') which is reduced to nothing when Christians oppose it with *unserm gleubigen vorstand der schrift* (WA 6.412.30, 'our believing understanding of scripture').

Such a theology is therefore insistently textual. As against papal *wortten* Luther provides *schrifft*. Claims for papal authority are *unvorschampten wortten* ('shameless words'), for which *nit ein buchstaben* ('not a single letter') can be brought in proof; the claim for authority over the explanation (*auszlegung*) of scripture is itself supported by *keinen buchstaben*. If the church refers all to the *character indelebilis* of the priesthood (WA 6.408.22), the indelible mark of consecration granted through Christ, Luther refers all to the *buchstabe* of scripture, the indelible letter or γράμμα given by God. This is an unashamed appeal to literalism. It is as if only the solid ground of *schrifft* can be held stable against the shifting sands of mere *wortten*. Luther uses the word *buchstabe* as an unanswerable rebuke to papal threat, the fact of the letter supplanting the fantasy of canon law, a new radical literate culture striking back against the feudal tyranny of the oral.

However, it is this foundation in the stable text which proves so unstable for Luther. For what is *schrifft* if not *wortten*? He requires every *auszlegung* of scripture to be authorized by a *buchstabe* within scripture, but each *buchstabe* first needs an *auszlegung* to authorize it. Papal *auszlegung* is rejected as brute force: *die schrifft nit macht haben ausztzulegen durch lautter gewalt on kunst* (WA 6.415.1, 'They have no right to explicate scripture through sheer force and without learning'), but the opposition of *gewalt* and *kunst* ('power' and 'culture') begs questions of its own. What does *kunst* consist in, and how is it verified? To this question Luther replies that Christian readers should 'follow the better interpretation and not their own', whereas a methodology for arriving at *dem bessern* as always is ambiguous. The best Luther can manage is *gleubigen vorstand der schrift* ('believing understanding of scripture'), a phrase which seems itself an act of faith.

Catholic controversialists seized on this lacuna in Luther's argument. Thomas More, who entered the debate against Luther in 1523 as part of Henry VIII's campaign to immunize England from heresy, asked: *Et quis erit iudex, quodnam id verbum sit: Lutherus, an ecclesia catholica?*[81] Luther's reliance on the text of scripture, More argued, was self-deconstructing. Quoting Luther's assertion that the word of Christ alone is true, and that *Omnis homo mendax*, More conveniently forgets that this is a citation from the Psalms and treats it as a new and idiotic version of the liar's paradox.[82] All men are liars, and none more so than Luther, who says it himself. More lampoons Luther's literalism, which (he says) thinks that 'scripture is the same thing as Christ, as if a book written about Caesar is the same thing as Caesar' (v. 235). Luther has made scripture his rock and promptly fallen off it (v. 238).

As well as a lampoon, More constructs a theory of interpretation. Luther has rewritten the laws of reading so as to favour the individual against the institution of the church. Rather than the Pope being the arbiter of all meaning, in Luther's account the meaning of scripture is the arbiter of the Pope, so that *Nos non sumus Papae, sed Papa noster est.*[83] Yet the arbiter of that meaning, More reveals, is left undecided; it remains in

---

[81] 'And who will be the judge as to which is that word: Luther, or the catholic church'; *Responsio ad Lutherum*, CWM, v. 240–1.

[82] CWM, v. 236; Luther's text is in *Contra Henricum*, WA 10/2.194.11; see also Psalm 115(6):11.

[83] WA 10/2.194.35; note the play on *pater noster*.

the air, subject to the arbitrary whim of the individual. If one individual, why not another? Luther's only answer to this challenge, More gloats (again ignoring the citation from 1 Corinthians 2:15), is the assertion *Spiritualis enim a nemine iudicatur, et ipse iudicat omnes.*[84] 'Is Luther alone, then, spiritual?', More asks, 'or is the pope alone not spiritual?' (247). Luther's literalism is after all a form of spiritualism. His credulous trust in the text of scripture turns out to hide only the ghost in the machine of his own head. Luther's theory of meaning is a form of false consciousness: look behind the letter and you find that nothing is there.

This turn on the letter recalls a peculiar moment in *An den christlichen Adel*, when Luther the champion of the letter of the text for a moment forgets himself and rejects *buchstabe* as the empty kernel or the useless chaff. The Pope, he jests, is a false money-changer, an alchemist in reverse, who gives *bley umbs golt, fell umbs fleisch, schnur umb den beutel, wachsz umbs honnig, wort umbs gut, buchstaben umb den geyst.*[85] The sudden substitution of *geyst* for *buchstabe*, spirit for letter, throws open the whole controversy of meaning which Luther has attempted to control in his favour. The material culture of the text dissolves instantly into the arbitrariness of meaning. More's identification of this crux is a brilliant moment in the history of interpretation. But it is not as if his own writing does not suffer in due course from this same turn. More is as guilty as anyone of arbitrarily divorcing letter from spirit and he does it in this same work.

The word of God in Luther's terms is entirely a written object. Not so, More replies: John's gospel finishes by saying that Jesus did many things which are not written, which if they were written, the world itself could not contain. The word of God, he counter-argues, is *aliud scriptum . . . aliud non scriptum.* Such, for instance, are the sacraments, supported by evidence which is *partim scripto, partim non scripto* (v. 240/2). Earlier in the *Responsio* it is argued that Luther himself accepts many things not written in scripture, including the assertion that he should believe only what is written in scripture. Repeating a much recited observation of Augustine, More observes that Luther only knows what is in scripture because of the tradition of the church (v. 88). 'If the church did not say that the gospel of John is John's, you would not know that it is John's. For you were not sitting by him as he wrote it' (v. 91). For all the jokes, this argument is riven by paradoxes. The proof that some of the truths of Jesus are unwritten

---

[84] 'The spiritual man is judged by no man and he himself judges no man', WA 10/2.194.36, cited in *CWM*, v. 246–7.

[85] WA 6.450.8, 'lead for gold, hide for meat, the string for the purse, wax for honey, words for goods, the letter for the spirit'.

comes from the written text of scripture, from the same John as Luther's. The conclusion that the church comes before the gospel comes not from hearsay but from Augustine, a writing authorized by the church.[86] At first More is able to keep to his distinction of *partim scriptum, partim non scriptum*, as an each way bet. But his sallies against Luther take him into an ever more volatile form of anti-literalism. Necessary articles of faith are among those teachings which are not written, he asserts; writing is therefore not a necessary condition of doctrine. Indeed, those doctrines which are written could have been left unwritten. If Paul had been able to, he would have spoken everything and written nothing. So much the better, in fact, since:

> Very many of his epistles, as of the other apostles also, are lost, and of those which are extant, some are translated incorrectly, some are translated ambiguously, the copies in the two languages do not agree at all points, and there is incessant controversy about their meaning. Consequently . . . the man who admits nothing but the evident scriptures will never lack pretext for denying what he wishes and asserting what he pleases.   (v. 99–101)

As an example of the baby leaving with the bathwater this could hardly be bettered. In one sentence More does the work of a thousand years of religious scepticism, and tears down the fabric of the church he so earnestly seeks to protect. He employs the most disruptive features of the new grammatical culture (the textual criticism of manuscripts, the comparison of archaic grammars, vernacular translation, humanist hermeneutics) to cast doubt on scripture as a tissue of errors and ambiguities. All the time he litters his text with citations from that same scripture to make his case.[87]

More, just as much as Luther, equivocates between the letter and the spirit. Christ does not promise scripture, he says, but the spirit, and this spirit, he quips, does not say, 'I'll write', but comes directly, in person. Yet this spirit, he says, switching metaphors without pausing for breath, let alone πνεῦμα, is written in our hearts. His metaphor, designed as a cunning riposte to Luther, cancels out his own argument at the same time. The turn of the letter doubles back on More as he seeks to evade it. The teachings of the church, it turns out, are not written down but only prescribed. This is the return of writing with a vengeance. For every instance

---

[86] The most famous of these citations is *Contra epistulam Manichaei*, 5 (CSEL, 25, 197): *ego vero evangelio non crederem, nisi me catholicae ecclesiae conmoveret auctoritas.* See also the episcopal letter, *Epistulae*, 118, 32, CSEL, 34, 696.

[87] Here, for instance, he uses 1 Corinthians 11: 23, 'I myself have received from the Lord what I also delivered to you'.

of the unwritten produced by More is already written: in creeds, in decretals, in bulls, if not in scripture. And there it is in front of the reader's eyes, in More's written text.

More's magnificently deconstructive essay on text and meaning is a symptom as much as an analysis of the crisis in language it reports. This crisis was not a new one. Augustine's *De spiritu et litera* was a medieval classic as well as one of Luther's favourite books. Behind More's argument lies the arch-text from Paul in the first century: τὸ γὰρ γράμμα ἀποκτείνει, τὸ δέ πνεῦμα ζωοποιεῖ, 'The letter killeth, but the spirit giveth life' (2 Cor. 3: 6). Yet this dictum from Paul, eagerly quoted by More, is itself a *gramma*, a dead letter advocating or perhaps inscribing the life of the spirit. *Litera* is grafted onto *spiritus*, *buchstabe* onto *geyst*, whatsoever tries to divide them. Luther, too, was fond of quoting 2 Corinthians 3: 6. Equally, when he alleged that *Spiritualis enim a nemine iudicatur, et ipse iudicat omnes*, he was following Paul to the letter, at least the Latin letter of the Vulgate, from 1 Corinthians 2: 15. More, in deriding Luther's spiritualism, is deriding Paul's, too, and resuscitating the literalism of both Paul and Luther at the same time. Two years later, Luther was chiding Erasmus in *De servo arbitrio* for not following the spirit in his reading. In the same year, he lacerated Thomas Müntzer for the arbitrariness of his appeal to purely spiritual reading: 'he knows as much about the spirit as Dr Karlstadt knows about Hebrew or Greek'.[88] It is a great joke: Karlstadt was a professor in Luther's own university, and a professional windbag much inclined to claim the spirit as the inspiration behind his inflated effusions. Müntzer and Karlstadt, Luther says, echoing More's quips against himself, teach you only how to journey on the clouds and to ride on the wind. Müntzer had denounced Luther as a bibliolater, a textual fetishist, a *buchstäblich* ('literal-minded') indulging in *Buchstabenglaube* ('dogmatism', 'bigotry'). Luther, meanwhile, was prepared to play both *buchstäblich* and *spiritualisch* for all he was worth.

V   THE GIFT OF LANGUAGE

What lies beyond language? The words of 'De l'experience' reflect on themselves, reproduce themselves. At first it seems as if Montaigne proposes experience as an antithesis or even antidote to the interminable

---

[88] Luther's dismissive comments on *Schwärmer* ('enthusiasts') comes in *Wider die himm-lischen Propheten* of 1525 (WA 18).

reflexiveness of language. As interpretation reaches the point of saturation, gloss turned in upon gloss, he seeks relief by returning to himself.
Taking pleasure in the one thing that remains to him, *le souci de soi*, he
retires, sparing no pain in the examination, to introspection. He is tireless
in this attention to himself. And yet there is a paradox here. For what is 'De
l'experience' if not words, words upon words, words exchanged for words?
It is one of the great and moving ironies of the *Essais*, that at the moment
it promises to render the self, it gives back only (mere?) words. 'J'escry de
moi', he writes but, as the *Essai* acknowledges at this very point, it is not he
who is writing; rather he is listening himself to 'mon livre à parler de soy'.
In a pregnant phrase, the *essais* of his life are exactly that: a life of *essais*, in
essais (*Essais*, p. 1079). His life is spent in writing, and the process of writing
becomes his life. Not least of the beauties of this final *essai* is the recognition—*recognoissance*, to use his own term—of himself in his text.[89] It is
with an experience of intense pleasure that he sees his text for who he is.

More than this, he says, he cannot say. To write outside of one's self is to
escape beyond writing into a space which does not exist. Only saints and
madmen aspire to such a rapture, a state of ecstasy which of its nature
eludes other men: 'Ils veulent se mettre hors d'eux, & eschapper à
l'homme. C'est folie: au lieu de transformer en Anges, ils se transforment
en bestes.' This is perhaps another dig at Luther, the maddest of them all,
who really thought his life transformed by grace. Luther has fallen for the
ecstasies of folly to which Erasmus only aspired, at incalculable cost. 'Ces
humeurs transcendentes', Montaigne adds in one of his last revisions,
terrify him. Nothing less becomes Socrates than 'ses ecstases & ses
demoneries'. Montaigne's own writing remains tied firmly to 'la mesure
d'un homme', withdrawing from anything remotely 'outrepasse'.

If 'De l'experience' is stringent in its analysis of the condition of
sixteenth-century writing, it is also defiant in setting itself so utterly against
the ecstasies of theology. For theology is the single, impossible centre of
sixteenth-century writing, and grace is the single, impossible centre of
that theology. Grace is nothing if not 'outrepasse': it is the definitive expression of what is beyond experience, and even beyond language. Grace
inescapably evades writing. And yet the writing of the sixteenth-century
reformations ineluctably exhausts itself in tracking grace down. No other
subject is consumed by so much writing. By taking grace out of the arcana
of high theology and making it the immediate test of vernacular religion,
Luther turned theology into a hazardous undecidable. Calvin's terrifying

---

[89] Cave, *Cornucopian Text*, p. 321.

decisiveness in identifying every practical aspect of divine sanction with inalienable predestination inflamed matters still further. For grace was at once the transcendent, incomprehensible gift of God, and yet also the inevitable locus of all religion. Without grace, there could be no God: God was only in the world through grace, and could only be apprehended by grace. However, grace was at the same time technically unknowable, inaccessible to ordinary investigation. Writing therefore existed in a special place in relation to grace. Grace was at once invisible trace and dangerous supplement, simultaneously grammatological and illegible.

Christian theology of grace developed originally and continually out of controversy: Paul against the Romans, Augustine against the Pelagians, Luther against indulgences, the Council of Trent against Lutherans. Formulation of dogma answered to the necessities of contestation, one word placed in negative relief to counteract another. The meaning of grace was not an object already known and thence defended, but was identified only in opposition to other terms, a *trouvée* of debate and dialectic. Grace thus defined itself within an interpretative discourse, principally of course out of the contestative exegetical metatext and paratext of the Bible. Grace was therefore bound up with grammatical culture. It was produced by literary process by means of literary analysis.

As grammatical culture underwent its tensions in the early sixteenth century two things happened simultaneously. Scholastic categories for explaining the problems of determinism came under suspicion; and the Reformation controversy over the means of grace catapulted such problems into a ferocious public domain. Every syllable and every letter came under relentless scrutiny. Luther complained that Eck undid him in debate on the basis of *uno verbulo*, 'one little word'.[90] The Louvain professor Michael Baius eluded condemnation in 1567 because of an absent comma.[91] The smell of charred vellum or flesh was never far away from these minutiae: Luther scrupled that 'szo solt man die ketzer mit schrifften, nit mit fewr ubirwinden', but More and Calvin, who also wrote voluminously about grace, were not so squeamish in committing heretics to the flame.[92] *Schrifften* and *fewr* were inextricably linked, and the book was burned when the body was not.

---

[90] From the epistle to Leo X prefaced to *De libertate Christiana*, WA 7.45.27; in German, *bey eynem wortle* (*Von der Freiheit eines Christenmenschen*, WA 7.7.16).

[91] The so-called *comma pianum* 'missing' from the papal indictment allowed either of two contrary interpretations; Baius was given the benefit of the doubt. The ambiguity may have been deliberate, although papal documents of the period were very sparing in their use of punctuation. See *DTC*, ii. 48–9; and Brodrick, *Robert Bellarmine*, pp. 27–8.

[92] WA 6.455.21.

The representation of grace collapsed in on itself in the attempt to render it as incontrovertibly free. If late medieval discussion of divine providence was caught up in the intricacies of determinism, sixteenth-century writing struggled incessantly with grace as a radical, eschatological expression of God's free gift. Here it seems that language evanesces entirely. For how is it possible to bring forth the completely gratuitous? This is the final paradox of grace, the impossible paradox of the gift, 'Not impossible but *the* impossible. The very figure of the impossible.'[93] God grants grace *gratis*. If grace is not free, grace is not grace; such has been the self-negating formula since Paul to the Romans (ἐπεὶ ἡ χάρις οὐκέτι γίνεται χάρις (Romans 11: 6)). Yet Paul, too, gives the countervailing refrain, 'Shall we then sin?' and the reflex answer, more in recoil than in reply, μὴ γένοιτο, 'let it not be'. In *De libertate Christiana*, Luther's great cry of freedom, he recognizes this as a contradiction, but urges his readers to live both parts of the contradiction. The Christian is free from the law, free to do as he wishes, unburdened by grace from any obligation to give back what has been given to him. Yet in this freedom, Luther says, the Christian is free finally to give. Work is done only in bondage: but faith 'finds expression in works of the freest service, cheerfully and lovingly done, with which a man willingly serves another without hope of reward' (*LW*, 31, 365).

Yet are such works still free? Luther struggles for some theodical economy which might balance the books. Faith, he says, constitutes an abundance of riches, in relation to which any works are a 'surplus'. This surplus can be rendered back in voluntary contribution. Rather than purchasing grace through works, or else mortgaging grace and surrendering works in repayment, the Christian offers them from an apparently supplementary credit. However, this credit is already in deficit, since it has been granted in advance by God. There is no question of this first and last debt being repaid, even retrospectively, to God, for it has been given free. Only then is giving (in return?) possible, when a man 'most freely and willingly spends himself and all that he has, whether he wastes all on the thankless or whether he gains a reward' (31, 367). Grace given *gratis* is not redeemed, but earns our gratitude, freely given.

Luther knows that he is living on borrowed words here. Extreme paradox is offered in expiation for manifest contradiction. This is not a solely protestant problem. The sixth session of the Council of Trent, which met in the year of Luther's death, agonized for months over some formu-

---

[93] Derrida, *Given Time*, p. 7.

lation that would protect God's unconditional freedom while allowing some residual freedom to man in return.[94] In these proceedings the gratuitousness of grace was exposed to the closest verbal scrutiny. Different theologians adopted different interpretations, following the schools of thought represented by the various religious orders. Some emphasized the free action of God on the passive will of man; others allowed some collateral to the will in part-redemption of grace. One prelate, Sanfelice, went all the way in his definition of the servile will; a cardinal, Grechetto, cursed him for being a fool, whereupon Sanfelice pulled Grechetto by the beard and jostled him to the ground. Sanfelice was barred from the Council and nearly excommunicated.[95] The Council veered away from prejudicially Lutheran assertions.

The effort of doctrine placed unremitting strain on writing of both protestant and catholic persuasion. Indeed controversy as well as dogma emerged only in the writing. It is a grievous historical error to see the partisan approaches as pre-existent, waiting to conflict with each other. Theology is not already there before writing, in some numinous world of ideas. Writing envelopes the articulation of doctrine and dispute as it proceeds. This is, finally, the sense in which Montaigne's dictum might be taken, 'Nostre contestation est verbale'.

Luther self-consciously recognized his own implication in the procedures of language, when in his Table-Talk he commented on the way in which he came to his revolutionary position on the righteousness of God. In a clipped biglot style which itself speaks volumes about the state of contemporary linguistic culture, he recounts to his friend how initially he had interpreted the phrase 'Iustitia Dei' to mean *sein gestreng gericht* ('his severe judgement'). Judged so by God, he could only be damned for ever ('So wer ich ewig verloren!'). Such words therefore seemed hateful to him; but then in front of his eyes they reversed in meaning:

Gott lob, da ich die res verstunde und wiste, das iustitia Dei heiß iustitia, qua nos iustificat per donatum iustitiam in Christo Ihesu, da verstunde ich die grammatica, und schmeckt mir erst der Psalter.[96]

Iustitia is not the justice which judges man, but that by which man is

---

[94] Luther died on 18 February 1546. The sixth session at Trent convened in June, and ended its deliberations with the Canons and Decrees of January 1547.

[95] Jedin, *History of the Council of Trent*, ii. 192.

[96] WA TR 5, No. 5247 (Johannes Mathesius, 1540). 'Thank God, when I understood the matter and learned that the righteousness of God means that righteousness by which he justifies, the righteousness given in Christ, then I understood the grammar, and the Psalter tasted altogether better'.

justified. Luther attributes the new grace to a new *grammatica*. For the active condemnation of God is substituted a passive justification of man. It is in this intervention of passive grammar that he relocates the gift.

This passage is strongly reminiscent of one of the last of all of Luther's writings, the Preface to the first volume of the collected *Opera Omnia* published in 1545. By the time of the second volume, Luther was dead. In his final word to his *pius lector*, Luther offers a *narratio* of his life, of the indulgences affair, what led up to it and what came of it.[97] It is a history full of the ironies of self later to become the idiom of Montaigne in his own final word to the reader. Yet in its way it is also a history of religious *raptus*, of sudden conversion and a life spent *outrepasse*. At the same time it is a life surrounded by interpretation and the gloss. Luther looks back to a life not of action but of books. His path to the indulgence controversy was a decade of reading, which he retraces back through its different stages in the pattern of his lectures in the university halls, from the Psalms via Hebrews, Galatians, Romans, back to Psalms again where he started. He had an overwhelming desire to understand, but one which was obstructed by language, which met resistance in *unum vocabulum*, one word which he found in the text of St Paul. The *unum vocabulum* was, of course, *Iustitia*. Day and night he laboured over its interpretation in a fury of exegesis, until the meaning changed in front of him, from (as he puts it) *active* to *passive*, from one grammar to another.

All at once, he says, he felt transported to the gates of paradise. It is in language that he locates his conversion, in an epiphany of reading, a loving act of interpretation in which he describes the letter of Paul as the transcendent moment of his life. He is narrating this story, he goes on to say, to remind the reader that his was no immediate conversion, but a slow and painstaking process. Above all, it happened *scribendo et docendo*, through writing and teaching. As if to make his point, this too, is a quotation, from Augustine's account of his own conversion in the *Confessions*. Luther rediscovers his own life as a life in reading and in writing. This is not meant only descriptively of his working practice as a scholar and a monk. It is a way of acknowledging the intimate intertexture of life in language, of things in words. Eschewing some false cognitive split of language and experience, he recalls how he was *expertus* and *tentatus* through writing and reading. His experience was in some sense already written, and already read as it was written. Like Montaigne, he rejects finally a division of language and experience, or text and meaning, or literature and inter-

---

[97] Praefatio D. Martini Lutheri pio lectoris, *Opera Omnia* , i. iv^v–v^r.

pretation, or *litera* and *spiritus*, as arbitrary and discontented. In one of his last revisions to the *Essais*, Montaigne held it to be the height of wisdom not to reject the one final given of one's life, the gift of the body.[98] But Luther in apprehending the gift of grace, finds it first in that other primal given of life, the gift of language.

[98] 'J'accepte de bon coeur & recognoissant, ce que nature a faict pour moy: & m'en aggree & m'en loue. On faict tort à ce grand et tout puissant donneur, de refuser son don, l'annuler & desfigurer, tout bon, il a faict tout bon', *Essais* (1595), p. 229.

Part One

Humanism and Theology in Northern Europe 1512–1527

It is evident that grammar, which is the basis and root of scientific knowledge, implants the seed of virtue in nature's furrow, after grace has readied the ground. At the same time, it is grace alone which makes a man good.

John of Salisbury, *Metalogicon*

So how do you imagine a scholar such as Erasmus held such an eminent place in that revolution of the Reformation? The answer is that the smallest change in the relation between man and signifier, in this case in the procedures of exegesis, changes the whole course of history by moving the moorings that anchor his being.

Jacques Lacan, *Écrits*

Part One

Humanism and Theology in Northern Europe
1500–1675?

2 The Reformation of
the Reader

Part One examines the interrelationship between literary methods of reading and writing with the turmoil in theology and religion in the first decade of the Reformation. It studies in detail the literary programme of humanism as it affected the status and practice of theology. It also suggests ways in which humanism itself developed in response to the need to solve certain kinds of theological problem. Its aim is not to establish a causal link between the two kinds of activity, but to demonstrate a larger cultural crisis in which both play a part and which makes them inseparable. The dominant figures, almost inevitably, are Erasmus and Luther. Yet they are not treated as isolated figures of original genius but as readers and writers in a world of books, a literary world which none the less had profound effects on the world outside. What made the reading of books, and the theories of interpretation involved in reading those books, so controversial? How and why was religious belief so intimately bound up with books and their interpretation? Chapter 3 offers an account of the theoretical context surrounding these problems, before Chapter 4 concludes with the sensational literary and theological controversy which broke out between Erasmus and Luther in 1524. Part One opens, as every history of the Reformation does, with Luther. Yet it is, perhaps, an unfamiliar Luther: not Luther the revolutionary, Luther the prophet, or Luther the heretic, but Luther the reader. The argument of this chapter is that without understanding Luther's habits of reading it is impossible to understand the development of his theology.

*

If the political history of the Reformation conventionally begins with the Indulgence crisis of 1517, its intellectual history traditionally begins with Luther's crisis or conversion in the monastery. Luther's *Turmerlebnis* or 'Tower experience' is as much a part of the mythology of the reformer as the nailing of the theses or the stentorian cry in front of the Emperor at Worms, 'Hier stehe ich'. Like them, it has been exposed to some scepticism and satire. Historians prefer now to forget about the tower because of its association with the theory that Luther got his best ideas while *in cloaca*, or in the shithouse.[1] Nevertheless, the search for a 'Reformation breakthrough' has been central to modern study of Luther, even though the search has led to no breakthrough of its own. After nearly a century of research, opinion is divided in relation both to chronology and content. What Luther was thinking before and in the aftermath of October 1517, when he was thinking it, what was original about it, or whether it was original at all, are questions which have attracted a huge bibliography.[2]

It is possible that the argument has become futile and scholastic, and the comment that 'a certain glumness' now hangs over the field is not unjustified.[3] Yet the fault begins with Luther, who himself wrote extensively and with fierce reminiscence about his early theology and its liberating effect on his life, offering intense if sometimes inscrutable detail about ideas and their timing. It is partly the intrinsic fascination of these autobiographical materials, as well as the complex problems involved in interpreting them, which has encouraged the chase. Also the quarry, however elusive, remains powerful. Karl Marx, describing that other great German revolutionary, wrote that Luther 'liberated man from external religiosity by making religiosity the innermost essence of man. He liberated the body from its chains because he fettered the heart with chains.'[4] While history is now wary of sweeping statements of the influence of any single individual, it still appears that modern religion in the West begins with Luther. Luther is the most spectacular symptom both of the processes of religious division and of the religious interiorization which comes to be identified with all religious movements, catholic as much as protestant. As such, he is still frequently cited as one of the authors of modern identity.[5]

Even if final agreement about the 'breakthrough' is implausible, some principles may be observed, as Bernhard Lohse reaffirmed in his systematic survey of *Luther's Theology*.[6] Luther states that his struggle concerned the process of justification, more precisely, the meaning of the phrase 'the righteousness of God'. Here, interpretation of Romans 1: 17 is the key. As Lohse indicates, any reconstruction that does not emerge with a height-

---

[1]   The theory, originated by Erikson in *Young Man Luther*, pp. 204–6, is discussed anew by Oberman, *Luther*, p. 155.
[2]   Bernhard Lohse's two anthologies of essays, *Der Durchbruch* (1968) and *Neuere Untersuchungen*(1988), summarize the field.
[3]   Marius, *Luther*, p. 507.   [4]   'Critique of Hegel's Philosophy of Right', p. 53.
[5]   Taylor, *Sources of the Self*, ch. 1. Taylor's assertion, p. 18, that Luther's quest for identity is not a quest for 'meaning' in the modern sense, is none the less questioned here.
[6]   See particularly pp. 88 and 92.

ened understanding of this phrase in that scriptural context may be considered to have wandered off the point. As for date, there are three main points of interest. The first is Luther's earliest period in Wittenberg, under the influence of his monastic master Johann von Staupitz, up to the point of his first biblical lectures in early 1513. It was to this period that Karl Holl first attributed the 'discovery'.[7] Holl's view has largely been superseded by a further pair of alternatives. The second period at issue is the first series of lectures on Psalms, to which Erich Vogelsang in a breathtaking piece of exegesis assigned the moment of breakthrough, even identifying the precise verse in the lectures, on which Luther commented in the autumn of 1514.[8] Vogelsang long held the field, until Ernst Bizer's study, *Fides ex Auditu* in 1958. Bizer, perhaps surprisingly, was the first scholar to accept authoritatively Luther's own witness to the centrality of, not his first, but his second lectures on Psalms, written after the ninety-five theses. Bizer's book transformed the debate, so that no one since has felt entirely confident in asserting the earlier dates. At the same time, despite Luther's testimony, the later dating of 1518–19 produces its own conflicts.

Perhaps all scholars in this area, as Lohse drily observed, could learn a little from the doctrine of humility which so preoccupied Luther. Perhaps also it is likely that all of the moments identified by Holl, Vogelsang, and Bizer represent breakthroughs of a kind and that, as Heiko Oberman has said, the whole period of 1513–20 is one of fluctuating understanding, rediscovery and reinterpretation.[9] What follows is consistent with Oberman's view. None the less, it has some distinct points of emphasis. Most important of these is a concentration on the act of reading. Although Luther's methods of exegesis have been crucial to the whole tradition surrounding the 'breakthrough', the reading process itself has not been the point of attention. For most scholars Luther's discovery must ultimately be expressed in a point of theology or doctrine, so that, in Lohse's words, 'we should distinguish the exegetical interpretation of Romans 1: 17 from its systematic-theological relevance'.[10] While it is impossible to make such a distinction absolutely, here Lohse's principle if anything is reversed. The primary object is not so much what Luther was thinking as how he thought it. By drawing attention away from theology for a moment it may be easier to escape the thrall of several temptations: the tendency to psychologize Luther's developments; to frame them within a permanently

---

[7] *Gesammelte Aufsätze*, i. 193–7.   [8] *Die Anfänge Luthers Christologie*, pp. 40–61.
[9] ' "Iustitia Christi" and "Iustitia Dei" ', 1–26 (reprinted in *Dawn of the Reformation*); also *Luther*, pp. 165–6.
[10] Lohse, *Luther's Theology*, p. 95.

existential crisis; or to anticipate the great trends of modern, above all Barthian, theology.

Yet this does not diminish the radical nature of Luther's experience. For the early sixteenth century is a radical and volatile moment in the history of reading. The availability of books; the form and construction of those books; the shape and function of the scholar's study; the praxis of silent or private reading; the framework of annotation; the methodology of inter-pretation, are all in flux. Luther provided individual printed texts for his students to gloss from. Yet if Luther is in some ways the prototype of the modern reader, he is also still a medieval reader. Alongside humanist com-mentaries he happily consulted university textbooks. The thousand-year-old daily offices of *lectio divina* preoccupied his life in the monastery. As in so many areas, Luther the reader is poised between two worlds.

The concentration on reading practice has interpretative consequences. The following account involves a detailed study of Luther's exegetical and citational practice. Gloss is related to gloss and annotation to annotation. The resulting account of the 'breakthrough' confirms the complexity of Luther's exploration of the key term *iustitia*. It places renewed emphasis on the grammatical terminology in which Luther couches that explo-ration, and suggests new ways of understanding it. In all of this, with due respect to Bizer's chronology, the earliest lectures on Psalms and Romans are confirmed as powerful locations of exegetical and theological creativ-ity. First of all, though, it is necessary to turn in more detail to Luther's 1545 Preface, already described in brief in the last chapter.

I NARRATIVES OF CONVERSION

Luther's narrative of spiritual autobiography, written in the last year of his life, has become a historiographical fetish. Obstacles in the way of com-mentary are considerable. His memorial reconstruction, full of hindsight after the fact, is written at a distance of thirty years. It covers some of the most difficult ground in the history of Christian doctrine. Yet in the midst of this theological quagmire it is easy to forget that this is also a *narratio*, a story told by Luther, a story of an intellectual conversion that is also a per-sonal conversion. As such, it conforms to the fictional rules of that quin-tessential sixteenth-century genre, the conversion narrative.

Luther's narrative is poised between *apologia* and *retractio*. What pos-terity has described as a Reformation, he refers to off-handedly as a *turba* ('turmoil', 'disturbance') or at best his *causa*. As for his own role, he stumbled into these turmoils, he says, 'by accident', and not 'intentionally': *casu enim, non voluntate nec studio in has turbas incidi.*[11] This remark seems designed to refute the charge that he was an inveterate troublemaker and a deliberate revolutionary.[12] And yet *casu* also has another meaning, revealed a few pages later when he describes himself as *per vim tractus in has turbas necessitate adactus* ('dragged by force into these turmoils, and driven by necessity'). An accident is a proof of God's providence; its contingency is so remote that no other explanation is possible than 'necessity'.

Luther's account veers between doggedly circumstantial record of historical fact and the overriding imprint of God's will. In this, it imitates the structure of the classic conversion narratives of Paul and Augustine: Paul riding his horse to Damascus; Augustine reading a book in his garden.[13] Indeed, Luther tells us that he 'once was a Saul', until one day *prorsus renatum esse sensi* (WA 54.186 'directly I felt myself born again'). And like Augustine, it happened while reading a book: indeed the same book (very properly) Paul's own letter to the Romans. Reading this book was the culmination, for both Augustine and Luther, of months of acute mental anxiety, suddenly resolved in a spasm of mental decision and spiritual conversion. In a moment, as he reached the end of a sentence, Augustine 'felt the light of confidence flooded into my heart'; Luther, 'as though I had entered through the open gates into paradise itself'.[14]

Despite Luther's imitation of the Augustinian pattern, there are significant differences. Augustine's narrative of conversion in the *Confessions* emphasizes its sublime contingency. He is sitting in despair under a fig tree when by chance he hears a child repeating a nursery chant, *Tolle, lege, tolle, lege* (CC, 27, 131). The child is transfigured in his mind into an oracle, ordering him to take up the book lying on his table. In a divine variation of *sortes Virgilianae*, he reads the first words on which his eyes happen to fall (Romans 13: 13–14), and translates them into a personal instruction: to give up sex and drunken parties and to take up Christ instead. The point of this story is the coincidental conjunction of the children's game with words from a codex of the apostle. The sheer gratuitous serendipity of reading is an illustration of divine grace: grace comes when he most needs it but from

---

[11] WA 54.180.3.   [12] See Spitz in *LW*, 34, 325.

[13] Oberman, *Dawn*, p. 111, comments on how these models shape parallel medieval accounts of 'conversion' in Thomas Bradwardine or John Gerson, and also contemporaries of Luther such as Andreas Karlstadt, Gasparo Contarini, or Calvin. See also Donne's conversions below.

[14] *Confessiones*, viii (12, 29), CC, 27, 131.

whence he can least expect it. His own will is absolutely absent. The history of his life in the process confirms the central foundation of his theology: it is the free gift of grace.

However, for Luther the action of grace is discovered not in the happy arrangement of circumstance but through a change in theological understanding about grace. He found grace by better understanding what 'grace' means: 'At last, God being merciful . . . I began to understand that "righteousness of God" as that by which the righteous lives by the gift of God, namely faith'. Luther's narrative redoubles on itself in a series of brilliantly self-reflexive gestures. Conversion was a controversial word in sixteenth-century practice. Luther figures his own conversion around this controversy. He makes it an exemplary illustration of the process known as μετάνοια—the Greek word traditionally translated in Latin as *poenitentia*. *Poenitentia* was the key practice of the monastic discipline Luther is describing: ritual acts of repentance for the life of sin. Protestant exegesis, following Erasmus, rejected this as a misreading of the Greek word, which does not mean 'doing penance' but a 'change of mind'. Luther's μετάνοια therefore surrounds the meaning of μετάνοια. His conversion consists in nothing less than a new understanding of conversion.

Equally powerful in Luther's story, and equally different from Augustine, is the account of the reading process. Luther's act of reading is not gratuitous but laborious, and is provoked not by external surprise but by internal determination. He does not happen to be looking at this book, but has been working at it for months: *miro certe ardore captus fueram cognoscendi Pauli in epistola ad Rom[anos]* ('I had been seized by an extraordinary desire to understand Paul's letter to the Romans'). The passage that catches his attention is not the first one his eyes chance on, but one particular *vocabulum*, over which he has struggled 'day and night':

Furebam ita saeva et perturbata conscientia, pulsabam tamen importunus eo loco Paulum, ardentissime sitiens scire, quid S.Paulus vellet

[I was driving myself mad, with a violent and disturbed conscience, beating away desperately at this phrase of Paul, thirsting most eagerly to know what St Paul meant.]

Augustine's object is to illustrate the pattern of causation in divine action, and his method is that of narrative, a narrative of carefully arranged causes and effects. Every detail in his story plays its part in an elaborate dramatic topography, in which the timing and placing of Augustine's physical and mental movements are intricately recorded. Into this deliberated sequence of causality and temporality the intervention of the child's rhyme is emphatically presented as outside of any pattern, and mysteriously unidentifiable: the disembodied 'voice' may be either a boy or a girl and the chant is from a childhood game which he only half-remembers. It is this clash of narrative structures which creates a sense of God's grace: in this carefully defined story the child's intervention cannot be explained any other way.

In Luther's case, on the other hand, the real story is biblical interpretation. His narrative is bereft of the external props and dramatic characters so crucial to Augustine's history of grace. Whereas Augustine makes gracious acknowledgement of the human instruments used by God in his conversion (the unnamed child, his friend Alypius, his mother Monica), Luther internalizes events, which happened, he stresses, while he was 'all alone' (*me unum*). There is no mention even of his monastic superior Staupitz. The account is full of narrative energy, an energy created not by suspense of events but by argument. If Augustine's encounter in the garden is like a classical recognition scene (ἀναγνώρισις), Luther's dramatic 'recognition' is intellectual. The reader's suspense is concentrated on *peripeteia* of exegesis and theology.

Luther thereby offers to replicate in his readers the reformatory powers he attributes to his own experience of reading. He presents a history of reading which demands of the reader a corresponding energy and patience in interpretation. By reading he was converted, and by reading he hopes to convert his readers. When Oberman calls Luther's reformation breakthrough 'a matter of life, not of thought, study, reflection, or meditation, but of life in the most comprehensive sense of the word', he is guilty perhaps of an academic's scepticism about the academic life.[15] For 'thought, study, reflection' is precisely Luther's subject, and the location of his subjectivity, not at all trivial but a primary part of 'life in the most comprehensive sense of the word'. In the pattern of his conversion his reading becomes his life.

The turning-point is an intricate question of meaning. His problems, he recalls, revolved around the interpretation of his personal *lectio difficilimus*, Romans 1: 17:

Iusticia enim dei in eo revelatur ex fide in fidem sicut scriptum est: Iustus autem ex fide vivit.

On the face of it, Luther's difficulties centre in the lexical signification of the complex word *iustitia*. Romans 1: 17 appears to define the relationship

---

[15] *Luther*, p. 154.

between God and man through this one word. As a result, this one *vocabulum*, he reports, 'stood in the way' of his reading of Paul and of the Bible, to the extent that he hated it, even to the point of hating God. In a remarkable way, Luther equates his religious anxiety with an anxiety over a semantic difficulty. Even more remarkably, he describes his dramatic change of heart as a μετάνοια about what this one word means.

So what was this intransigence in the word *iustitia*? And what is this semantic shift which Luther, thirty years later, perceives as so profound that he can compare it in power with God's redemptive action? It is necessary here to review some of the interpretations proposed in modern Lutheran scholarship. A large part of this effort has involved comparing Luther in detail with his scholastic background.[16] Luther states that originally he interpreted *iustitia* in a 'philosophical' sense, *formali seu activa*, which he glosses as *iustitia . . . qua Deus est iustus, et peccatores iniustosque punit*, the justice by which a just God punishes wrongdoers. This, he says, is how he was taught the word 'according to the usage and practice of all the doctors'. Despite this assurance about his sources, it has not proved easy to identify them.[17]

One possible interpretation of the phrase *formali seu activa* is as follows. The nominalist interpretation of *iustitia* was a juridical concept, derived from Roman law, according to the principle summed up by Cicero as *reddens unicuique quod suum est*.[18] This theory reached its summation in the work of Gabriel Biel, the theological master most frequently quoted in the early Luther's works.[19] God promises to give his grace if man agrees to *facere quod in se est*.[20] The concept is hard to define and easily misunderstood. 'To do what is in one' does not mean to achieve moral perfection, or to satisfy the requirements for salvation. The doctrine follows an orthodox understanding of original sin: man is not capable, after the fall, of satisfying the law.[21] Man cannot ever be, in this sense, *iustus* or 'righteous'. *Facere quod in se est* is rather a moral minimum which is within the power of

[16] Luther's definition of *iustitia* occupies a vast bibliography. Oberman, *Dawn*, and McGrath, *Theology of the Cross*, examine the scholastic context in detail.

[17] It is a polemical issue; Denifle's *Luther und Luthertum*, which inaugurated modern Lutheran scholarship, argued that Luther, in his over-reliance on the nominalist position, had misunderstood the medieval tradition and hence that his 'Reformation breakthrough' was meaningless.

[18] McGrath, *Theology of the Cross*, p. 101.   [19] Oberman, *Harvest*, pp. 131–2.

[20] The doctrine is described in Oberman, *Harvest*, pp. 132–4. *Facere quod in se est* is an integral part of justification in Luther's masters, e.g. Staupitz; see Steinmetz, *Misericordia Dei*, pp. 93–7.

[21] Biel does, however, differentiate various views of original sin; see *Harvest*, p. 122.

every human being ('doing one's bit', perhaps). If this is done, God perfects this little bit with grace. In this process (according to Biel) God, practically, does everything. Grace is not a reward for doing *quod in se est*.[22] None the less, while grace does not correspond to a legal restitution of a debt successfully repaid, it involves a quid pro quo, which makes it conform to the central standard of Roman civil law.[23]

This system of doctrine is evidently both complex and finely balanced. It is crucial to an understanding of Biel's theology to see that he is attempting to rebut Pelagianism, not defend it. The Pelagian assertion is that grace is unjust if it does not involve human moral agency. Biel's system is an attempt to show that grace is divinely operated and yet still just. Nor does Biel in any sense see himself as departing from Augustine; indeed, as Oberman says, 'nominalism was fully involved in the ongoing medieval search for the proper interpretation of Augustine'.[24]

Study of the young Luther, both in his marginal notes on Lombard's Sentences and in his first lectures on the Bible shows how saturated his early thinking is with this nominalist theology. God's 'justice' consists in rendering to each man his due, according to the Ciceronian formula: *Iustitia autem dicitur redditio unicuique quod suum est* (WA 3.91.10). Luther's problem surrounds what this *quod in se* consists in, and a loss of confidence in his, or anyone's, ability to achieve it. One difficulty with Biel's system is that not only is it hard to define what this *quod in se* is, it is impossible to verify whether one has it. Even within Biel's system, it is clear that God does not 'render to each one his due', but rather agrees to make up for a lack. Luther in 1545 records his conclusion that a God who renders justly must condemn. Any principle of *iustitia* relying on *redditio*, therefore, whether derived from Aristotle or Cicero or from canon law, he found to have the most appalling theological ramifications when applied to God.[25]

The phrase *iustitia Dei*, according to the older Luther, became an object of hatred (*oderam enim vocabulum*) because it appeared to add insult to injury. Not only is man born to a life of inevitable crime through original sin, he will inevitably be punished for it throughout eternity, in order to confirm the radical justice of a God who is ineradicably different. And, according to this interpretation, the phrase, 'the just shall live by faith' is a

---

[22] Although in fact sometimes it is called a 'reward' (*pretium*), even by Luther in the *Dictata*.
[23] Justinian, Corpus Iuris Civile; see McGrath, *Theology of the Cross*, p. 105.
[24] *Harvest*, p. 427.
[25] See McGrath, *Theology of the Cross*, p. 112.

malicious taunt, since it is an impossible condition: no one is just ('not one', *quia non est iustus quisquam*, Romans 3: 10), not even a monk (like Luther) who lives an irreproachable life. At this point in Luther's memoir, the narrative action reaches an impasse, seemingly a dead end. The *iustitia Dei* of Romans 1: 17 is synonymous with the *ira Dei* ('the wrath of God') of 1: 18. God is 'just' because he judges rightly between men, and he is angry because human behaviour cannot live up to this standard. In return, Luther 'drove himself mad', with a *saeva et perturbata conscientia*. In a deliberately shocking phrase, Luther reports himself as 'hating God', with sullen blasphemy, *tacita . . . blasphemia*.

Luther now reveals the reinterpretation of the one *vocabulum* through which his whole understanding of God was revised and his life reborn. His readers have been made to cover some dense ground already, and the theological suspense is considerable, but the hard work is not over yet:

as I meditated day and night on the connection of the words . . . then I began to understand the Justice of God as that by which the just lives by the gift of God, namely by faith, and this sentence, 'the Justice of God is revealed in the gospel', to be that passive justice, with which the merciful God justifies us, by faith, as it is written 'The just lives by faith'.

In search for a key to unlock Luther's narrative, commentators have made the most thorough examination of the lexical properties of the one *vocabulum*.

In particular, it has been noted that the word *iustitia* contains a deeply buried interference between three ancient vocabularies, Latin, Greek, and Hebrew.[26] Whereas the Hebrew verb ṣādaq means 'to be acquitted', and is used in scripture in a religious sense, the Greek verb δικαιόω was a technical term from secular law and in the case of the guilty meant 'to condemn'. Septuagint and New Testament Greek struggled with these tensions. The Latin verb *iustifico* did not exist in classical usage and was coined by Christian writers to translate the scriptural sense of δικαιόω. For over a thousand years, these linguistic tensions played a subterranean part in theology of justification, even when no direct knowledge of Hebrew lexicography was involved. The question is how far this ambiguity informs Luther's identification of two separate meanings of *iustitia* in his 1545 memoir. Unlike Augustine, he learned Hebrew (precisely in the years leading up to 1519).[27] Yet, although he refers to Reuchlin's writings on the

---

[26] See McGrath, *Iustitia Dei*, i. §2.
[27] The fullest account of Luther's learning of Hebrew in this decade is Raeder, *Das Hebräische bei Luther*.

Hebrew of the Psalms in his first lectures of 1513–15, he makes no mention of the lexis of the Hebrew root *ṣdq*, or its cognates, until his second Psalms lectures.[28]

Attention to Luther's late scholastic inheritance, and to the linguistic background of the scriptural terminology of 'righteousness', has yielded a profound sense of the significance of Luther's theological struggle. Yet in investigating this theological world it is easy to lose sight of the detail of Luther's own language. It is possible, for instance, that the search for an exclusively lexical explanation of *iustitia* is misplaced. This chapter will take a different approach. It will consider instead the grammatical terms (*activa* and *passiva*) Luther himself uses to explain his enlightenment.[29]

In reading the 1545 memoir, it is significant that Luther constructs his sense of the difference between the two forms of *iustitia* on syntactical grounds. Indeed, it is a syntactic term—*connexio*—which Luther uses to define his problem. This critical word has gone unnoticed by his commentators:

Donec miserente Deo meditantibus dies et noctes connexionem verborum attenderem, nempe: Iustitia Dei revelatur in illo, sicut scriptum est: Iustus ex fide vivit, ibi iustitiam Dei coepi intelligere eam, qua iustus doni Dei vivit, nempe ex fide.

By *connexio verborum*, Luther means the syntax which joins together the two Pauline phrases *iustitia Dei* and *iustus ex fide vivit*. Paul's sentence juxtaposes the cognates *iustitia* and *iustus*, leaving the reader to extrapolate any connection between them. What is it in Paul's syntax to which Luther attaches such significance?

Luther's story, like his theology, has reached a dead end, an impasse. His sentence is given new life, as he himself was *renatus*, by the solution of treating the two clauses *Iustitia Dei revelatur in illo* and *Iustus ex fide vivit* not, after all, as co-ordinate—implying blank conjunction—but as subordinate—implying logical relation (*connexio*). By this syntactic manoeuvre, Luther supplies momentum where before he saw inertia: for it turns out that instead of man being excluded from God's *iustitia*, he is redeemed by it.

All of this is achieved by the little word *qua*.[30] By a delicate use of relative pronouns, Luther crosses the gulf between *iustitia* and man: God's

---

[28] *Theology of the Cross*, p. 101; Raeder, *Grammatica Theologica*, pp. 119–31 on *Operationes in Psalmos* 5: 9, and pp. 209–14 on Ps. 17: 1.

[29] One commentator who did give a grammatical interpretation of *iustitia passiva* is Hirsch, 'Initium theologiae Lutheri', pp. 156–7 (the *genitivus autoris*).

[30] Compare here Barnes, *Aristotle*, p. 25 ('The little word *qua* plays an important role in Aristotle's philosophy').

righteousness is 'that by which' the righteous man lives (*eam, qua iustus
. . . vivit*). Instead of *iustitia* belonging to God, it is something he imparts
to others; exclusive possession is rewritten as inclusive gift. God's *iustitia* is
not something which objectively judges man but something which subjec-
tively enters and redeems him. At the same time, the phrase *Iustus ex fide
vivit* signifies not an impossible condition which human life can never
satisfy, but instead a salutary description of the action of grace, freely given
to man without condition.

Luther's memoir clearly means the reader to experience the same sense
of relief in the reading process as he originally did in St Paul. Yet although
Luther's theological narrative acquires both energy and relief from the
relative pronoun *qua*, it cannot fully explain the idea of a new *connexio* in
his syntax of grace. In fact, another member of the theology faculty at Wittenberg, Andreas Bodenstein von Karlstadt, was using in 1517–18 the same
relative pronoun to describe man's *iustitia*, but without the same consequences as in Luther.[31] Karlstadt, at Luther's instigation, spent the early
part of 1517 testing his ideas of justification against a systematic rereading
of the works of Augustine.[32] Having defended 151 Augustinian theses in
public disputation in April 1517, he expounded Augustine's views at greater
length in a series of lectures commenting on *De spiritu et litera*. Karlstadt's
qua is a direct quotation of Augustine's *qua* in that work: *haec est illa iustitia dei, non qua ipse iustus est, sed qua nos ab eo facti*.[33] Whereas Karlstadt is
attempting faithfully to explicate Augustine, Luther's gloss articulates
something new.[34] Karlstadt was Luther's senior, but now Luther was
leaping ahead. To understand properly Luther's change of mind, we have
to understand more fully his ways of reading.

II LUTHER THE READER

Whether or not Luther was doing so *in cloaca*, he was reading. He describes
himself at the end of his 1545 memoir as one of those who, as Augustine
said of himself, learned *scribendo et docendo* ('by writing and by teaching').

---

[31] Kähler, *Karlstadt und Augustinus*, p. 69 (Non est sensus, quod illa iusticia dei sit per
legem testificata, qua deus in se iustus est, sed illa, qua iustificat impium). Discussed in Sider,
Karlstadt, p. 31.
[32] Reported by Karlstadt in his preface to *De spiritu et litera* printed in 1518 (Kähler, p. 4).
He bought his Augustine at the Leipzig fair in January 1517. See McGrath, *Iustitia Dei*, ii. 21;
also Rupp, *Patterns*, pp. 55–63; McGrath, *Theology of the Cross*, pp. 44–6.
[33] Augustine, *De spiritu et litera*, 18, 31 (PL, 44, 220; CSEL, 60, 185).
[34] McGrath, *Iustitia Dei*, ii. 21.

Although Lutheran scholarship has examined every detail of his early lectures and commentaries, it has done so largely in the interests of doctrinal history. In this enquiry the material processes of a reading practice have often been submerged. Yet Luther the reader is a seminal figure just as much as Luther the theologian; and indeed, without this reading practice the theology would not have taken shape.

The history of reading in Luther's period was in flux in several ways.[35] First of all there was the physical form of the book: print was only thirty years old when Luther was born. Print brought many consequences, including wider availability of a wider range of material. The growing efficiency of the manuscript book-trade had already transformed the conditions of reading which print brought to a head. With more books came more readers, and more individual habits of reading. Readers increasingly owned their own books, and read them on their own. The growth of private reading had unsuspected results. It was a world of incipient heterodoxy, in which a reader could immerse himself in private reflection and foster private opinions.

Luther was a man of books. He bought them, read them, scribbled in them, reread them. In this way he is typical of the new intellectual figure of his day, a man made up by writing. But in this as in so many ways Luther is a man of the old world as well as the new. He stands at the axis of the history of reading, even more than Erasmus, because he was completely a product of the medieval schools. To understand Luther's theology we must understand both Luther the new reader and Luther the old.

In his early years, as for any other theological student of the late middle ages, this meant the routine discipline of examining standard texts and commenting on them for the benefit of students. These everyday habits of method form a fundamental structure in all of Luther's work. Above all, this method was a form of critical practice. Medieval studies were not, as sometimes assumed, a training in a priori logical reasoning, but a set of dialectical procedures founded on a methodical reading and explication of texts. In the midst of Luther's doctrinal sallies and his Reformation controversies, he constantly urges his readers to test his conclusions according to principles of practical exegesis.

The earliest part of Luther's career, with some vicissitudes, followed the prescribed course of academic studies. Up to his sudden translation into

---

[35] The history of reading has been enjoying a renaissance in recent years. See esp. Cavallo and Chartier, *History of Reading in the West*, chs. 3–10; Stock, *Augustine the Reader*; and Jardine and Grafton, 'How Harvey read his Livy'.

the Augustinian monastery in July 1505, he studied the Arts course at the university in Erfurt, then prepared for the law, working on the *Corpus iuris*.[36] But as a novitiate he sold his legal textbooks and was permitted to read only the Bible. Later in life he reported that he had been reading the Bible twice through every year since his youth.[37] After his probation, he was marked out for training for the priesthood, which involved working on Biel's exposition of the mass. At about the same time, in 1507, he renewed academic studies, this time in the faculty of theology, probably under the tuition of the Augustinian professor at Erfurt, Johannes Nathin.

A student of theology began by attending 'readings' (lectiones) and disputations as an *auditor*. There were two types of *lectio*: 'cursory', in which a text was expounded briefly in order to elucidate the sense; and 'ordinary', where a fuller commentary was presented, involving a developed discussion of problems raised in the text. Disputations took the form of a *quaestio* on a local point of difficulty. After a period as an *auditor*, a student became a *baccalaureus biblicus* and himself gave cursory *lectiones* of the Bible while continuing his studies. In due course he became *baccalaureus sententiae* and gave ordinary readings of Lombard's Sentences. After this, as a *baccalaureus formatus* he would take part in disputations, before himself finally becoming a master, usually after at least a decade of study.[38]

Luther's career as a theological student was complicated by the fact that he was moved back and forth by his order between the monasteries of Erfurt and Wittenberg, so that he was schooled at two separate universities. Having begun at Erfurt he became *baccalaureus biblicus* at Wittenberg in March 1509, giving expositions of the Bible as *cursor*. After becoming *sententiarius* in the autumn of 1509 he returned once again to Erfurt.[39] He lectured on the Sentences during the following academic year. However, political troubles within the Augustinian order intervened in his studies; in November 1510 he travelled to Rome as part of a delegation and

---

[36] Brecht, *Road to Reformation*, pp. 44–8.

[37] Ibid., p. 85. Luther later told the story that he first saw a Bible when he was 20 in the university library at Erfurt, when he sat down and read the story of Samuel.

[38] For a summary of medieval practice, mainly based on Paris, see Marenbon, *Later Medieval Philosophy*, pp. 16–24; on Germany, see Overfield, *Humanism and Scholasticism*, pp. 44–6.

[39] Brecht, p. 93, speculates that Luther's progress was unusually quick, but the practice in Germany is rather obscure. Promotions were made more quickly in the later medieval period.

the long journey home occupied him until the following spring. By 1511–12 he was back in Wittenberg.

Luther's reading was dominated by the basic requirements of the syllabus, the Bible, and the Sentences. Some of Luther's marginal notes on the Sentences, which he used for his lectures in 1509–10 at Erfurt, survive.[40] As one would expect of a theologian trained in the *via moderna*, they are littered with references to the interpretations of Ockham.[41] At Erfurt, Luther's theological reading included other standard authors favoured by the *moderni* such as Pierre d'Ailly and Biel. Luther studied Biel thoroughly and not only in his student years: a printed copy of Biel's *Collectorium circa quatuor sententiarum libros*, with Luther's marginal notes, survives in an edition of 1514.[42] The different styles of handwriting prove Luther was consulting it not only while preparing his 1517 *Disputatio contra scholasticam theologiam* but also many years later.[43] Also at Erfurt is found evidence of his early reading of Augustine: both an edition of the *opuscula* and the large late works, *De trinitate* and *De civitate Dei*.

The turning-point of Luther's writing and teaching career came in 1511–12, during his second period at Wittenberg. Staupitz—according to tradition in a conversation under a pear tree in the cloister of the monastery—informed him that he was to take the degree of doctor of theology and succeed Staupitz as professor of Bible. Staupitz seems to have taken the matter personally in hand, and to have persuaded the Elector Frederick to put up the money.[44] The result was that for the next decade— through the controversy over indulgences and its aftermath—Luther was continually employed in lecturing and commenting on the text of the Bible. Whereas his earliest theological work has to be extrapolated from the marginal notes in his copies of textbooks, this period of biblical criticism survives copiously in manuscripts in his own handwriting.

Luther's early lectures on the Bible have dominated twentieth-century Lutheran scholarship. They have been combed for evidence of his early theological positions, whether to show his conformity with late medieval nominalism, or his misunderstanding of earlier high medieval

---

[40] In Zwickau, Ratschulbibliothek; marginalia are ed. in WA 9.42–4; the fullest discussion is still Vignaux, *Luther, commentateur des Sentences*.

[41] Brecht, *Road to Reformation*, p. 94. Luther called himself Ockhamist with pride; see Oberman, *Dawn*, p. 56.

[42] See Oberman, *Dawn*, p. 57. The notes are edited in WA 59.25–53.

[43] On the dating of the glosses, WA 59.27–8. Theses 5–36 of the *Disputatio* are versus Biel. Melanchthon in *Annotationes* commented on Luther's reading of Biel until late in life. See also Oberman, *Dawn* p. 101.

[44] Brecht, *Road to Reformation*, p. 126.

scholasticism, or else his break with all forms of medievalism in the full
thrust of a Reformation 'breakthrough'. However, sometimes in the rush
to identify Luther's theological crises, the occasion and form of these writings have been all but forgotten.[45] Luther in such accounts is treated as the
author and writer of ideas, expressed in such texts; the etymology of the
'lecture' as a *reading* rather than a writing, is elided. Yet even the material
appearance of these lectures is striking and deserves notice.

Luther lectured successively on Psalms (1513–15), Romans (1515–16),
Galatians (1516–17), Hebrews (1517–18), and once again on Psalms
(1518–21).[46] In preparing his first lectures on the Psalms, Luther used a
special edition of the Psalter which he commissioned from the Wittenberg
printer Grunenberg, with wide margins and spaces between the lines for
the reader's annotations.[47] Luther ordered copies of this edition for his students to use in his lectures, and continued this practice with Romans,
Galatians, and Hebrews. The lectures were largely dictated.[48] In form, they
are among the last examples of techniques that, with developments along
the way, had been intact since the late twelfth century, having their origins
in the grammatical and logical schools of Chartres and Laon in the
eleventh century.[49] In medieval lecture rooms, the text was read, individual
words explained, and more difficult clauses paraphrased, with philological
exposition merging seamlessly into brief theological interpretation.
In manuscript, such lectures would be transcribed by placing glosses
between the lines of the biblical text, usually spilling over into the
margins.[50] Hundreds of such commentaries survive from the middle ages,
either as a direct *reportatio* of students' notes or as a polished version dic-

[45] With the magisterial exception of Ebeling (e.g. on the 1st Psalm lectures, *Lutherstudien*,
i); see also Schmidt-Lauber, *Luthers Vorlesung* (on Romans) and Raeder, *Grammatica
Theologica* (on the 2nd Psalms lectures).

[46] No lectures survive from 1512–13. Luther's manuscript copies of the first Psalms lectures
are in Wolfenbüttel, Herzog August Bibliothek (glosses, 'Wolfenbütteler Psalter') and Dresden,
Landesbibliothek (scholia, 'Dresdener Psalter'); of Romans in Berlin, Staatsbibliothek MS
64 theol. quarto 21 (consulted here from a photographic reproduction in the Vatican).
Seventeenth-century copies exist of the MS notes of Romans (Vatican, Palatina Latina
1826) and of Hebrews (Vatican, Palatina Latina 1825). The texts are edited in WA 3 and 4 (first
Psalms; glosses re-edited in WA 55/I); WA 56 (Romans); WA 57 (Galatians and Hebrews); WA
5 (second Psalms).

[47] Ebeling, 'Luthers Psalterdruck', *Lutherstudien*, i, 69–131. Lang also used Grunenberg's
edn.

[48] An early description survives of Luther lecturing by one of his students (dated 1518–22);
quoted in Rupp, *Luther's Progress*, p. 44.

[49] Smalley, *Study of the Bible*, pp. 46–8.

[50] Smalley, *Study of the Bible*, p. 56. There was no formal distinction between interlinear
and marginal glosses, *contra* many Luther scholars.

tated specially by the lecturer to a secretary. In the case of Luther's lectures, the printed text of Grunenberg's edition forms a continuous conversation with handwritten annotations between and alongside. In addition to these *glossae*, in accordance with later medieval practice, Luther provided more extended theological interpretations or *scholia*, again dictated to the students, written by hand onto blank pages bound in after the printed text.[51] In his lectures on Romans, Luther extended the *scholia* still further into vast *corollaria*, and sometimes *corollaria* of *corollaria*, in order to refine, complicate, or qualify his theological exposition of the text. Finally, in the second Psalms series, Luther abandoned the medieval tradition of *glossae* and *scholia* and adopted the new style of a through commentary verse by verse.

However, the early lectures were not intended for publication in this form.[52] Georg Spalatin, the Elector's secretary, wanted him to print the first lectures on Psalms, but Luther refused, regarding them as rough and improvisatory.[53] Although this is partly rhetorical modesty, it also reflects something of the quality of the lectures as they survive. Certainly, Luther would have been astonished at the idea of trying to establish from them a systematic theology. A better description is the one he made himself of his practice, 'ruminating', a complex metaphor of the reading process going back to Augustine himself.[54] The lectures move out from and back into the biblical text in intense and introspective meditation. They survive largely by accident, found among his papers and preserved by acts of piety after his death. Some are conserved in Luther's autograph, others are copied, meticulously reproducing the distinction between printed and manuscript text. In some cases (such as Romans and Galatians) copies survive (see Figure 3) of the students' dictated notes.[55] These can be compared

---

[51] The blank pages have identical watermarks to the printed pages e.g. in Vatican, Pal.Lat.132.

[52] With the exception of Galatians, printed in a somewhat different form as a commentary in 1519, and the second Psalms lectures, painstakingly revised for a reading public and printed in fascicles as *Operationes in psalmos* between 1519 and 1521; Brecht, *Road to Reformation*, pp. 286–90.

[53] He did make preliminary revisions, and published a commentary on the Penitential Psalms (*Die sieben Bußpsalmen* (Wittenberg: Grunenberg, 1517), Benzing, 74–5); see Luther to Spalatin, WA Br 1.56, and to Lang, WA Br 1.72; also Luther's remark quoted in Evans, *Language and Logic*, ii. 95.

[54] WA 3.225.16, 3.261.19, 3.348.1; on the medieval currency of the term, Carruthers, *Book of Memory*, pp. 164–5; and stock, *Augustine the Reader*, p. 219.

[55] Four manuscripts survive of student notes from the lectures on Romans: Dessau, Landesbücherei, MS Georg. 1049a; Gotha, Herzoglichen Bibliothek, Cod. chart. B973; Vatican, MS Palatina Latina 132; Zwickau, Ratschulbibliothek, XIX.VIII.2. These student glosses are edited in WA 57.

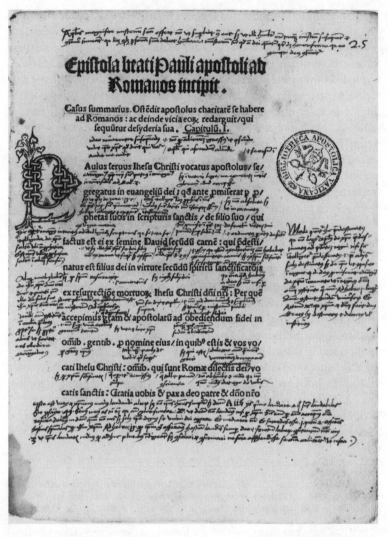

Fig. 3. A student's dictated notes (*glossae*) taken from Luther's lectures on Romans in 1515: Martin Luther, *Divi Pauli apostoli ad Romanos epistola* (1515–16). Vatican, MS Palatina Latina 132, fo. 25.

with Luther's original in order to reveal something of his working practice in the lecture room. While the glosses were given more or less in full, Luther exercised considerable discretion in delivering the *scholia*. In the case of Romans, what the students wrote down is only a small fraction of the original. The interpretations are mostly briefly and tautly argued, with little of the theological energy and bravado Luther shows in his own notes. An example is Romans 1: 17, where the discussion is brief and scholastic, and offending phrases or words are left out as he goes along.[56] Here and elsewhere, controversial points are excised in an effort of self-censorship, with *corollaria* sometimes left out altogether. The students' versions contrast with the almost private nature of the original lecture notes, which have an electric immediacy. In the rushed script of his autograph copies, we can catch Luther in the act of reading and of thinking.

Yet the ideas emerge only through the medium of a reading process. This means that to understand Luther's early lectures, we have to re-educate our own reading methods. Nowadays a commentary is viewed as a secondary activity distinct from a writer's original thinking, which is expected to be propositional in form. In some of Luther's writings—the polemical tracts of 1520, for example—we do find something like propositions, scatological, but still recognizably propositions: the church is a whore; the Pope is a barrel of shit. But Luther's thinking in his lectures is more exigent, even circumstantial. We do not find propositions so much as citations. The Bible is divided into parts, fragments of text, which involve Luther in a linguistic archaeology, recomposing them into theological meaning. These meanings are not always articulated directly, but are discovered in the interstices between words, in the margins of the text, in the friction created by one word or text against another. This is an intensely literary style, but none the less theological for that. Theology, after all, is based historically on acts of interpretation. In this sense it is barely possible to distinguish exegesis and argument, interpretation and doctrine: the two are simultaneous.

Such citational frictions are derived not only from the diverse corpus of biblical texts, Old and New Testament, but also from what might be called the *apparatus criticus* of biblical interpretation. The remarks of previous commentaries commingle with the biblical text in order to provide authority, or to provoke resistance, or to prompt renewed enquiry. Luther used for this purpose a variety of scholarly aids.[57] Primary among them

---

[56] Vatican, MS Pal.Lat. 132, fo.59, 'Ex fide in fidem etc.'. This one page in the student copy covers ground which takes ten pages in the holograph.

[57] The fullest list is in Ficker's Register for Romans, WA 56, pp. l–lv.

was the six-volume edition of the Bible by Johannes Froben, which printed the Vulgate along with two standard medieval commentaries, the voluminous *Glossa ordinaria* and the later *Postillae* of Nicholas of Lyra, along with the corrections and additions to Lyra by Paul of Burgos and Matthias Döring.[58] Froben's work is a typographical tour de force, with the Vulgate appearing as a window in the middle, surrounded by the *Glossa* above and to the left, Lyra to the right, and the corrections to Lyra underneath. It is a printed sixteenth-century embodiment of the characteristic shape of the medieval glossed Bible.

The compendious *Glossa ordinaria* had been compiled mostly in the early twelfth century by a group of scholars surrounding Anselm of Laon, but by Luther's time its origins were uncertain. It forms what has been called a 'divine encyclopaedia', sifting through a huge corpus of sources to form a continuous exposition of scripture.[59] By the end of the twelfth century it had become standard reading, and was itself subject to glosses of 'The Gloss'. Indeed, Lombard's Sentences began as an attempt to clarify and expand the *Glossa* on the Psalter and Paul. Much of this work was incorporated in the eventual text of the Sentences themselves.[60]

Luther's technique of lecturing, elaborating from text to *glossa* to *scholion*, is steeped in this tradition. Like any late medieval glossator, he also made constant reference to Lyra. Nevertheless, the new physical form in which he read these sources is significant. It is as printed artefacts that Luther understood his books, including scholastic classics such as Ockham or d'Ailly. It is alongside a printed text that we find Luther's scribbled notes in the copies of his Biel or his single-volume Vulgate.[61] Here, perhaps, we recover the significance of Luther's tower. The figure of the monk alone in his cell, surrounded by books, is familiar from medieval illuminations. But in the tower at Wittenberg, the monk in his cell meets the modern reader. When the tower was demolished in 1532 during castle refurbishments, Luther recalled nostalgically 'my poor little room', in which 'I stormed against the papacy'.[62] It is a portrait of the reader as individual, making revolutions in his study. The celebrated if cryptic reference

[58] *Biblia cum glosa ordinaria et expositione lyre literali et morali*; the first edn. is 1498; text cited here is Froben's edn. of 1506–8.

[59] Smalley, *Study of the Bible*, p. 63.

[60] Ibid., 64; Lombard's gloss was known as the *Magna glosatura*.

[61] Luther's personal copy of the Vulgate, including notes he made in the Wartburg while translating the New Testament and the Pentateuch, was discovered in 1995 in the Württembergische Landesbibliothek, Stuttgart. It is described in *Eine glossierte Vulgata*, ed. Brecht and Zwink.

[62] WA TR 2, no. 2540.

to the question of heating likens Luther's experience to the familiar context of the humanist *studio*.[63]

The economy of the humanist page also makes its mark on Luther's lectures. The term *scholia* is not Luther's, and was introduced by his nineteenth-century German editors. However, in the manuscript of his first Hebrew lectures he gave the *scholia* the title 'Commentariolus', and elsewhere he used the humanist vogue terms *Enarrationes* and *Lucubrationes* as well as the more common *Commentarius*. His first printed text of the Psalms is described on the title page as 'castigatus', another humanist trademark. Medieval *lectio* (essentially an aural and shared process) merges in Luther's practice into the new literary form of the printed commentary, a handbook for someone else's reading. The public lecture of the schoolroom becomes interwoven with the private reading habits of the study. As late as 1539 Luther recommended 'repeating and comparing oral speech and literal words of the book, reading and rereading them with diligent attention and reflection', in order to understand the meaning of scripture.[64] If it is only by accident of Luther's fame that his lectures survive at all, it is an accident that enables us to see the collision between scholastic and humanist practices at first hand.

Biblical criticism was in a state of flux. This was the high point of humanist critical work on the ancient biblical languages, encouraging a spate of philological and theological reinterpretation. Luther's personal attitude to humanism is debated.[65] None the less, in the period of his early lectures, he took a profound interest in several new productions of philological research. This interest began some years before his earliest lectures on the Bible. He purchased Reuchlin's *De rudimentis hebraicis* in Erfurt in 1508 before his first residence in Wittenberg. Siegfried Raeder, working extensively on Luther's knowledge of Hebrew, shows that he used Reuchlin very thoroughly.[66] By the time of the *Dictata super Psalterium*, Luther was making frequent reference both to this work and to Reuchlin's more recent book on the Penitential Psalms.[67] He continued to refer to Reuchlin when developing his readings of non-Hebrew texts such as Paul. Similarly, in his exegesis both of the Psalms and of Paul, Luther depended

---

[63] The reference to a heated room (*hypercaustum*) is at WA TR 3, no. 3232. Compare refs in Thornton, *The Scholar in his Study*, pp. 43–4.

[64] Preface to German collected works, WA 50.659; *LW*, 34, 286.

[65] The fullest treatment is Junghans, *Luther und die Humanisten*; see also Spitz, *Luther and German Humanism*, chs. 7–9.

[66] *Grammatica Theologica*, esp. pp. 34–46.

[67] *In septem Psalmos poenitentiales hebraicos interpretatio* (Tübingen: Thomas Anshelm, 1512), VD 16, B3406.

a great deal on two works of Lefèvre of Etaples: his textual critical study of the Psalms, *Quincuplex Psalterium* (1509) and his commentary on *S.Pauli Epistolae XIV* (1512, 2nd edn. 1515).[68] In the case of Erasmus, it is possible to observe Luther using the Greek edition of the New Testament and the accompanying *Annotationes* as soon as they appeared in 1516, in the middle of his lectures on Romans. The *Novum Instrumentum* was published in February; in the summer semester, Luther resumed his lectures at Romans 9: 1, and the first named reference to Erasmus's work is at 9: 16.[69] An early example of Luther's use of the *Annotationes* shows him comparing interpretations by Valla, Lefèvre, and Erasmus of a grammatical problem in Greek.[70]

Luther was not unusual among his contemporaries in making eclectic use of medieval and humanist techniques of commenting.[71] Humanist writers often overstated (for polemical reasons) the antipathy of scholastic theologians towards their methods. By availing himself of the Hebrew and Greek scholarship of Reuchlin, Lefèvre, and Erasmus, Luther did no more than fulfil his duties towards his students. He apologized for the amateurism of his efforts in this area, and once Reuchlin's great-nephew, Melanchthon, arrived at Wittenberg in 1518 as professor of Greek, Luther gave over some of his lecturing (including Romans) to someone he considered more expert in biblical philology. Nevertheless, the conflation of divergent sources in Luther's exegesis is significant in the development of his early theology. His working method reflected the instincts of a medieval glossator in its extrapolation of theology from linguistic detail. Luther applied this method not only to the logical cruces that were the staple sources of nominalist theology, but also to the philological cruces of humanist commentary. In this he diverted wilfully from the purpose of humanist exegesis. Reuchlin wished to recover the lost beauties of the Hebrew language; Erasmus wished to revise the biblical text, and reformulate its modes of meaning, in order to revive Christian doctrine on more pietistic foundations. In the process they produced a rich store of semantic observation and speculation. Luther seized on this vast semantic hinterland and subjected it to modes of theological analysis foreign to Reuchlin or Erasmus, neither of whom was a theologian.

---

[68] Luther's annotations in his copy of Lefèvre's work on the Psalms is ed. in WA.4.

[69] Ficker, p. xxix on dating of lectures; ref. at 9: 16 is WA 56.400.

[70] Berlin Staatsbibliothek MS 64 theol. quarto 21, fo.108ᵛ. Pauck, p. 272, assumes Luther refers to the sources independently, but they are all cited in the same note in Erasmus's *Annotationes* (see Reeve and Screech, edn., p. 395).

[71] E.g., among Luther's opponents, John Fisher (see Rex, *Theology of Fisher*, pp. 13–18).

In this merging of old and new, Luther can seem at times an idiosyncratic reader. Yet this is what gives such characteristic energy to his biblical exegesis: for linguistic analysis is directly identified with theological analysis.[72] In the second lectures on the Psalms, the *Operationes in Psalmos*, he found a phrase for his method: *primo grammatica videamus, verum ea theologica*. It is to Luther's *grammatica theologica* that we now turn.

III FROM LUTHER TO AUGUSTINE

The purpose of this section is to move from the material circumstances of Luther's reading to consider the reading practice within which Luther developed the concept of *iustitia passiva*. This is not easy, nor could it be, given the later Luther's obscurity about the origins of this idea. As we have seen, the exigent methods of Luther's biblical commentary require us to seek his theological meaning neither as a clear, deliberative logic, nor as a demonstrable arrangement of identifiable doctrinal sources, but in and between the lines of his glossing and cross-referencing of texts. We thus have to share the commentator's labour of setting one word against another word, building up meaning through a complex compilation of citation and allusion.

The 1545 memoir provides a few scattered clues to retrace Luther's passage through the theological meaning of God's righteousness. He tells us that he was composing his second lectures on Psalms, that he was rereading Romans at the same time, and that afterwards he confirmed his insights by reading (apparently for the first time) Augustine's *De spiritu et litera*. This work of Augustine was one of the classic anti-Pelagian treatises addressed to Marcellinus in 412. Yet at the same time Luther covers over the traces, torturing future historians with his carelessness or deviousness over dates. The beginning of his second lectures on Psalms can be placed in 1518, and yet the lectures on Romans of 1515–16 are already littered with references to *De spiritu et litera*. However, this obscurantism over dates, while it has hampered historians determined to identify a 'breakthrough' with a particular biographical moment, has also hidden an intricate pattern of exegesis between Luther's reading of Psalms, Romans, and Augustine.

The *unicum vocabulum* of Romans 1:17 that was driving him mad had of course already been the object of his own commentary in the lectures on

---

[72] Ebeling, *Lutherstudien*, iii. 32–6.

Romans. Willhelm Pauck calls the relevant *scholion* 'a brief and rather cursory explanation', which he finds astonishing in view of the 'signal importance' of the verse; but this brevity is no sign of a lack of interest.[73] The *scholion* is based on an opposition between *iustitia hominum* and *iustitia Dei*:

Iustitia enim Dei est causa salutis. Et hic iterum 'Iustitia Dei' non ea debet accipi, qua ipse Iustus est in seipso, Sed qua nos ex ipso Iustificamur, quod fit per fidem euangelii　(WA 56.172.3)

[For the righteousness of God is the cause of salvation. Here, too, 'the righteousness of God' must not be understood as the righteousness by which he is righteous in himself, but as that righteousness by which we are made righteous (justified) by him, and this happens through faith in the gospel].[74]

Typically for Luther's style of commentary, this *scholion* is a tissue of diverse citations. The comment on the phrase *iustitia Dei* effectively occupies one single complex sentence, built upon the comparison of two interpretations of *iustitia*, one 'by which [God] is righteous in himself', the other 'by which we are made righteous (justified)'.

This page of Luther's manuscript is very heavily worked. It contains an unusually large number of later additions and interpolations, squeezed onto all four margins. Indeed, it is in the margins of his text that Luther seems to be doing his most urgent thinking. In the abridged version he dictated to his students in the lecture room, he suppressed his gloss of *iustitia Dei*, and elaborated instead a comparison with Aristotle from the Nicomachean Ethics.[75] In Aristotle's view, *iustitia* follows from actions, whereas for God the equation is reversed, and *iustitia* precedes *opera* ('works') which result from it.[76] The rest of Luther's public exposition of 1: 17 is devoted to the crux posed by Paul's obscure phrase rendered in the Vulgate as *ex fide in fidem* ('from faith to faith'). For the benefit of his students he rehearsed the various interpretations of the *Glossa ordinaria*, Nicholas of Lyra, and Paul of Burgos's corrections to Lyra.[77]

These references read like distractions from Luther's argument. His manuscript reflects an intense struggle in which it is easy for later readers to get lost. Indeed, Luther seems to go back over the argument himself, more than once. In the process, he adds several citations from Augustine

---

[73] Pauck (ed.), Luther, *Lectures on Romans*, p. xxxviii.
[74] Tr. from Pauck, p. 18. Further refs in text.　　　[75] WA 57.133.9.
[76] Ficker cites *Nicomachean Ethics*, iii. 7 (1114a). The more common scholastic discussion found e.g. in Luther's masters Arnoldi and Trutfetter, was of ii. 1 (1103a); see WA 56.172.9n.
[77] These are all on the same folio of Froben's 1508 *Biblia*, vi. 5^r.

for further illumination. In the left-hand margin appear two citations from *De spiritu et litera*.[78] A third reference to this work is scribbled into the bottom margin of the same page of the manuscript, once again in reference to Romans 1: 17.

In view of the importance Luther later attached to his reading of this work, these citations are of great significance. They may even help to locate when he read the work. All the early citations in the Romans lectures (including one on the first page of his *scholia*) are afterthoughts in the margins. There is no reference to *De spiritu et litera* in the main body of his text before 2: 12.[79] Did Luther go back over his scholion of Romans 1: 17 and add these citations after reading Augustine a little later in the semester? Or did he already know the work and recalled, either in the course of writing or some time later, the relevance of the citations?[80]

Either way, the citations show how much thinking Luther was doing in his reading. The first of the Augustinian references in the left-hand margin is actually quoted by Luther:

Unde b. Aug[ustinus] c.xi. de spi. et lit.: 'Ideo Iustitia Dei dicitur, quod impertiendo eam Iustos facit. Sicut Domini est salus, qua salvos facit (WA 56.172.5)[81]

[it is called the righteousness of God, because by his bestowal of it he makes us righteous, just as we read that 'salvation' is the Lord's, because he makes us safe (Augustine, *De spiritu et litera*, NPNF, 5, 90)]

The power of this reference for Luther lies in the fact that Augustine here glosses Romans 1: 17, which Augustine has just quoted in order to emphasize how grace excludes all possibility of boasting: 'whatever good life [man] leads he has from the grace of God, and . . . from no other source whatever can he obtain the means of becoming perfect'. Whatever *iustitia* we have, then, is *iustitia Dei*, and is called God's righteousness because God gives it to men. In other words, the phrase uses a genitive of cause and not of possession. The cross-reference to *salus* makes the point clearer. *Salus Dei* could not be a genitive of possession, since God has no need of

---

[78] The references are to *De spiritu et litera*, 11, 18 and 9, 15. Berlin Staatsbibliothek MS 64 theol. quarto 21, fo.33ᵛ.

[79] The first references in the glosses are at 2: 23 and 2: 29.

[80] McGrath, *Theology of the Cross*, p. 114, states that Luther had not read *De spiritu et litera* by the time of the *Dictata* (i.e. before 1515). See Hamel, *Der junge Luther und Augustin*, i. 9–11. There are references to the work in Luther's marginal glosses of Lombard's *Sentences* of 1509, but these may be standard scholastic citations. See WA 9.59.34 and 9.60.26.

[81] *De spiritu et litera*, 11, 18 (PL, 44, 211; CSEL, 60, 171). Pauck (confusingly) presents the Augustinian citation and Luther's comments as seamless, whereas WA records those parts which are marginal interpolations.

salvation himself; therefore the term must refer to the salvation which he bestows on others. Likewise, Augustine says, for *iustitia*.

This definition had become something of a *locus classicus* in medieval thinking, because it was embedded in an important analysis of God's love in Lombard's Sentences (I, dist. 17). The grammar of this passage in the Sentences involves a complex analysis of *De Trinitate*, XV: *amor Dei* means not the love with which he loves, but the love that he gives to us to love him with.[82] To confirm the logic of this signification, Peter directly quotes Augustine's gloss of *iustitia* from *De spiritu et litera*—'not with which he is just, but because with it he makes us just'.[83] Although this passage is not directly concerned with justification, Luther had been familiar with it for a number of years. Indeed in 1509 he had commented on it in his own marginal notes to the Sentences (which he had used for his lectures on that book), while engaged in a discussion of the Trinity. Thus this passage in Augustine had been working indirectly in his mind some time before he himself read *De spiritu et litera*, and it may already have begun to influence his understanding of *iustitia*.[84]

The second reference from Augustine cited by Luther, although not quoted in full, matches the phrasing of his own scholion rather more closely:

iustitia Dei, non qua Deus iustus est, sed qua induit hominem, cum iustificat impium

[not that whereby he himself is righteous, but that with which he endows man when he justifies the ungodly]

We have here the first half of Luther's gloss, in nearly the same words (*non . . . qua ipse Iustus est in seipso*, WA 56.172.4). Furthermore, there is another extract, from the end of *De spiritu et litera*, 18, which Luther does not cite, but which brings us close to the second half of his gloss.[85] Thus Augustine writes *Haec est illa iustitia Dei, non qua ipse iustus est, sed qua nos ab eo [iusti] facti* (18, 31; PL 44, 220; CSEL, 60, 185); whereas Luther writes, *non . . . qua ipse Iustus est in seipso, sed qua nos ex ipso Iustificamur*.

However, to establish the sources of Luther's *scholion* in related citations

---

[82] *Sententiae*, i. dist.17 c.3 (i. 144).

[83] Ibid., c.6 (i. 149), citing *De spiritu et litera*, 32, 56 (PL, 44, 237; CSEL, 60, 215). See Rupp, *Righteousness of God*, p. 124.

[84] Rupp, *Righteousness of God*, p. 97; see also Vignaux, *Luther, commentateur des Sentences*, p. 42.

[85] K. Holl, 'Die iustitia Dei', *Gesammelte Aufsätze*, iii. 175.

from Augustine is not the same as to understand their significance. The citations from Augustine have an evident resonance for Luther beyond the brief quotation in the Sentences.[86] To see how this might have happened we can go back to a point before (in all probability) Luther ever read *De spiritu et litera*—that is, during the composition of his preceding lectures on Psalms, the *Dictata* of 1513–15.

For the significance of Romans 1: 17 was already established in Luther's mind at this earlier date. In his *scholion* of Psalm 31(32): 1, Luther cross-refers his text with Romans 1: 17 and declares: *hec est etiam conclusio totius Epistole b. Pauli Roman.* (WA 3.174.14).[87] This statement led one earlier Lutheran scholar to locate the 'Reformation breakthrough' at exactly this point in the *Dictata*.[88] This was too hasty: again, the search for doctrinal surface has hidden a deeper exegetical logic in the reference. It is a natural step for Luther to adduce Romans in relation to Psalm 31(32): 1, for Paul had himself quoted this verse at Romans 4: 7, and subjected it to his own exegesis. Yet why does Luther bring in 1: 17 in particular? This question takes us into Luther's linguistic analysis of the Psalm, and also the *apparatus criticus* of his exegetical method.

The Vulgate text of verses 1–2 is as follows:

> Beati quorum remissae iniquitates
> et quorum tecta sunt peccata,
> beatus vir cui non inputabit Dominus peccatum[89]

Luther's *scholion* deduces two conclusions from this verse: first, *Nullus est beatus, nisi cui remisse sunt iniquitates* ('no one is blessed, unless his sins have been forgiven', WA 3.174.10); second, as a corollary, *Nullus est sine iniquitate* ('No one is without sin', WA 3.174.11). It is to this logic that he adduces Romans in general and 1: 17 in particular, in support.

Thus Luther derives from this Jewish verse a rigid statement of Christian soteriology. Clearly, the reinterpretation is derived from Paul's use of the Psalmic verse in Romans 4: 7, to be discussed in a later section. However, Luther wants to prove his point not only theologically but exegetically. He therefore has recourse in the middle of his argument to an unexpected piece of Hebraic philology. Hebrew grammar, it seems, happily concurs with Pauline Christology.

---

[86] Or Karlstadt's interpretation in his commentary of 1517.

[87] Pauck mistakes Vulgate and Massoretic numbering here.

[88] Hirsch, 'Initium theologiae Lutheri', pp. 162–6, locating the 'breakthrough' between Ps. 30 (31) and 31 (32).

[89] *Psalmi iuxta LXX*, text as used by Luther.

Est autem in Hebreo haec dictio, que pulchre exprimit hanc remissionem esse sine meritis, dicens, 'Beatus fiens levatus crimine: fiens opertus peccato'. Ecce mere passive ponitur, quia sine penitentia sunt dona et vocatio dei   (WA 3.174.29)

Luther makes a point here which it is easy to miss. In order to do so he contrasts the Vulgate translation, *Beatus quorum remissae iniquitates*, with the original Hebrew formulation. For this purpose he uses newly available scholarship, Reuchlin's literal translation of this Psalm in *Septem psalmi poenitentiales hebraici* of 1512. Reuchlin attempts to express Hebrew grammatical forms in Latin, creating for the purpose his own neo-grammatical translator's pidgin. Luther observes from this extract that whereas the Vulgate uses the Latin participle *remissae*, the Hebrew uses the passive form of the verb nāśā, rendered by Reuchlin literally as *fiens levatus* ('being removed'). The extended gloss in Reuchlin's *Interpretatio* turns into an essay on passive and active forms in Hebrew, and the many ambiguities in their usage. This passage forms a vital index to Luther's use of the terms *activa* and *passiva* in a theological sense.[90]

Theologically, Luther wishes to demonstrate here that righteousness does not come from within, but is given by God. No one is just in himself, but only when his sin is taken from him by God. This is a truth ignored or travestied by heretics, pharisees, and schismatics, who think themselves just in themselves (*confidunt se tanquam iusti*). Paul's whole Epistle, he says, refutes and rebukes this. To achieve this conclusion, he abandons theology in order to say that the idea is already written in the Hebrew language. For the *dictio* of Hebrew *pulchre exprimit* ('beautifully expresses') the theology of forgiveness.

Luther almost makes light of this, the word *pulchre* implying that it is a charming serendipity that connects grammatical *dictio* with theological *distinctio*. But the fact that he feels he is observing something important is shown by the way he makes an identical point in the margin of his copy of Lefèvre's *Quincuplex Psalterium*.[91] These marginalia have been dated as contemporary with the *Dictata*. At Psalm 31(32) alongside the words *Et quorum tecta sunt peccata*, Luther notes: *non dicit, qui texerunt ipsi, sed omnino passive se habent ad remissionem* (WA 4.487.19; 'he does not say, "who covered themselves", but in every way passively they hold themselves in relation to forgiveness'). Here then, he makes the point by substituting

---

[90] *In septem Psalmos poenitentiales hebraicos interpretatio*, C7ʳ–C8ʳ (quia est verbum cuius actio perficitur passive in presenti, seu preterito indeterminato). There are further important remarks on the passive form in Hebrew at D4ʳ and F6ᵛ.

[91] WA 4.465.

the active form of the verb, *texerunt*, in order to show how the Hebrew rejects it, expressing the process of forgiveness instead as being *omnino passive*.

There are important observations to be made here about Luther's working methods. He constructs a theological argument by excavating the semantic structure of the biblical text. At this early stage of his career, this is done largely through the medium of the Latin language, but he collects together evidence from Latin scholarship in Hebrew as well. Reuchlin's literal translation, together with his Hebrew grammar, and Lefèvre's commentary are incorporated into his argument whenever applicable. It is a mistake to say, as one historian has done, that 'for Luther . . . theology governed grammatical considerations'.[92] On the contrary, Luther allows grammar to indicate and articulate his theological directions. In his exposition of this process, he does not line theology against philology, in order to arrive at preordained doctrinal answers; rather, he sees theology and philology as mutually complicit.

What significance might this interest in the Hebrew passive have for the *scholion* on Romans 1: 17 a year or so later?

Et hic iterum 'Iustitia Dei' non ea debet accipi, qua ipse Iustus est in seipso, Sed qua nos ex ipso Iustificamur

The sentence works through an elaborate series of syntactical rhymes, *non qua/sed qua, ipse/in seipso/ex ipso,* and most importantly, *Iustus est/Iustificamur.* The passive form of *Iustificamur* is abutted against the active form of *Iustus est,* in order to imply a gulf of meaning between the two. By means of a beguilingly simple change of grammatical voice Luther attempts to embody a transformation in the system of God's justice. It is not a justice which God enacts but one which is given to man.

In his *Dictata* on the Psalms, Luther emphasizes the passive structure of the Hebrew sentence, but by the time of the lectures on Romans he draws no attention to it. It has become embedded in his thinking as theological shorthand. By means of it he elides all of the Augustinian references from *De spiritu et litera* into one: *Iustitia Dei dicitur, quod . . . eam Iustus facit* is conflated with *non qua . . . Iustus est, sed qua induit . . . cum iustificat,* to produce the simple polarity *non . . . qua . . . Iustus est . . . Sed qua . . . Iustificamur. Iustificamur* is the only word he did not get from Augustine, but it is the most significant. The considerable theological economy must have eluded his students completely: for it contains not only a contrast between

---

[92] McConica, 'Grammar of Consent', p. 94.

God's righteousness as judging versus forgiving, but also man's righteousness as possessed versus received.

By the time Luther wrote his 1545 memoir thirty years had passed since his internal debate over the meaning of *iustitia Dei*. It is not surprising if he showed some confusion over the exact sequence of his ideas. Moreover, he wished to provide his readers with an analysis of the theology which generated his life's experiences, not an autobiography which would explain the origins of his theology. His memories none the less clarify something of the process involved: an intense exegetical labour, developed over a series of years, examining and re-examining the meaning of critical texts in the Psalms, Paul, and Augustine.

In any case, he probably never understood the precise order of his exegetical conclusions, even at the time. Who can review his own reading processes so exactly even a few months, never mind many years, later? Any attempt would be a reconstruction, a form of commentary. The difficulty is exacerbated by the academic methods of the biblical lecturer. Implicit in every text is a layer of other texts adduced in the effort of rendering it intelligible. No text is isolated, or remains stable: as each new source of interpretation is placed alongside it acquires new shades of meaning.

Luther's readings of Psalms, Romans, and Augustine are interfused with each other, and with other sources, so that what emerges is a composite gloss with a structure which has an independent life of its own. By reading across the different texts of his lectures and marginal notes, we are offered glimpses of this structure. At times Luther states it explicitly, only for it then to become hidden again, while still exerting its influence unseen. In his lectures on Psalms, he stated a brief theory of the theological meaning of the grammatical forms of active and passive verbs; in the lectures on Romans, he articulates this theology by means of a play on the grammatical forms themselves, without a restatement of the theory.

This makes his method difficult to retrace, and explains why Lutheran scholarship has missed the grammatical inflection in Luther's use of the words *active* and *passive*. The assumption is made instead that Luther's memoir refers through these words to a metaphysical distinction about divine agency. This assumption appeared natural, since it is in this philosophical sense that the words *active* and *passive* are used, as far as they are used at all, in scholastic discussions of grace. For instance, Aquinas, in his definition of *iustificatio*, refers to *iustificatio passive accepta*.[93] The justification of the unrighteous caused some philosophical difficulty for Aquinas,

---

[93] *Summa theologiae*, 1a2ae, q.113, d.1.

since from an Aristotelian point of view it appears nonsense: the just have no need of justification, since they already possess justice, whereas the unjust can never be justified. Aquinas resolves the contradiction by seeing justification as a transition from one state to another, from injustice to justice. This transformation or movement is what he calls *iustificatio passive accepta*: 'a movement towards justice' which produces a change of state in the individual—*sicut et calefactio motum ad calorem* ('just as heating implies a movement towards heat').

It is also in these philosophical terms of agency that a distinction is made between kinds of grace, in a source Luther certainly knew, Biel's commentary on the Sentences. Drawing on Aquinas's earlier categorical distinction between *gratia gratum faciens* and *gratia gratis data*, Biel distinguishes between senses of grace *accipitur active vel passive* ('understood actively or passively').[94] Grace in the active sense is an action of giving, free and gratuitous, by the divine will: in the passive sense it describes the effect on the person in receipt of this gift.

But the 1545 memoir suggests a much more specific edge in the meaning of *iustitia passiva*. It is an argument at once exactingly local and powerfully generalized. Neither of these things is true of Biel's terminological footnote on the typology of grace. The difference lies in the way that Luther sets up a theological contradiction on the basis of active and passive forms. Biel sees no opposition between the two, making an easy assimilation between God's grace *gratis dans vel gratis datum* ('freely / gratuitously giving or freely / gratuitously given').[95] Active and passive grace are each different aspects of the same God. Luther's manoeuvre is to see the two grammatical forms not as complementary but as adversarial, even dialetical. The one form implies by exclusion its opposite: 'God gives grace to man' so that 'man is given grace of God'. The rules of grammar dictate the composition of the two sentences: if 'man' is the object of God's active grace, 'man' is then the subject of its 'passive' operation.

The idea that 'grace is given by God' is a commonplace so general that no theologian, or even heretic, could have disputed it in fifteen hundred years. But Luther is unusual in drawing attention to the grammar of this sentence as theologically definitive. Biel saw no difficulty in moving from a statement of grace *gratis datum* to a discussion of its relation to how man *facit quod in se est*.[96] Luther, in these comments on Psalms and Romans, declares the active voice of *facit* to be refuted by the grammatical logic of

[94] Ibid., q.111.   [95] I Sent, d.26, q. un art 1, *Collectorium*, ii. 497.
[96] See Oberman, *Harvest*, pp. 135–9.

the grace by which we are *iusti facti*. Blessedness comes not to those who *texerunt*, but *quorum tecta sunt peccata*.

The reasons for this difference are exegetical as well as theological. Indeed it is not clear which comes first. The history of the Reformation has required a theological explanation of its origin: Luther disagreed with Biel because he was repelled by his theology. Luther's reading of Biel is much more complicated than this. First of all, he is schooled in the same theology as Biel—and even at points of disagreement he is trying to find answers to the same kinds of question. He is also schooled in the same logical method: so that he poses both questions and answers in the forms of the *terministi*. Yet in his early lectures on the Bible he was also beginning to be exposed to other kinds of critical practice. His use of terms like active and passive does not come from the Ockhamist categories of *actio* and *passio*.[97] It derives instead from the philological works of Reuchlin and Lefèvre. Reuchlin and Lefèvre's terms have no logical significance: they connote the descriptive enumeration of Hebrew grammatical usage. Luther extracts the grammatical terms and, with terminist zeal, appropriates them to make logical and theological distinctions of vast implication.

IV GRAMMATICA THEOLOGICA: LECTURES ON PSALMS AND ROMANS

Luther's reading becomes his writing. This is true both in the way that the texts of his lectures produce themselves out of citations from other texts, and also in the way that his methods of interpretative analysis reproduce themselves in tropes and habits in his own style, one that could be termed a grammatical theology. In the next few pages I shall illustrate this by examining two extended pieces of Lutheran commentary on short passages of Paul's text (Romans 3: 1–8 and 4: 7). Both texts themselves consist in a form of commentary, since Paul in each quotes tiny gobbets of verse from the Psalms (32: 1 and 51: 4). Both texts are also the subject of analyses by Augustine which are incorporated by Luther into his own discussion. Finally it is significant that at each point, Luther is moved to quote his *locus classicus*, Romans 1: 17.

Luther's lectures amplify gloss and commentary into his own form of textuality. The Pauline text is quoted, extracted, abstracted, and reconsti-

---

[97] A terminology derived from Aristotle; see Ockham, *Summa logicae*, pp. 180–4 and 121–2.

tuted as a new theological narrative. At the same time, the Pauline text (in Vulgate Latin) reverberates within it. Romans 3: 1–8 counterpoises the justice of God and the iniquity of man, God's faith and man's incredulity, God's truth and man's lies. Yet in the characteristic manner of the letter, Paul bewilders the reader by setting up these dichotomies within an effusion of propositions, counter-assertions, and concessions, straining the reader's judgement, faith, and grasp of truth. Interpolated between these vexed oppositions, Paul poses a series of rhetorical and semi-blasphemous questions ('is God unrighteous', 'why yet am I also judged a sinner?'). Not only are these questions not answered (they are rather repulsed, thrown back in the reader's face), it is not even clear who is asking them. Paul protects himself from the charge of blasphemy by apologizing for one of the questions as if it is not his own after all ('I speak after the manner of men'). Another he blames on the gossip of others who have scandalously attributed their own scepticism to Paul. The first problem of Romans 3: 1–8 is to identify who is speaking: is it a man of faith (3: 2), a man of the world (3: 5), a devil's advocate (3: 8), or an advocate of God (3: 4)? The next problem is to discover a simple, indicative proposition: in response to the anguished interrogative of 3: 3—'shall their unbelief make the faith of God without effect?'—the reader finds an expletive, followed by an unfulfilled wish, followed by a quotation, then a conditional, another question, and another expletive.

A less expository manner of proceeding with an argument could hardly be imagined. One obvious task for a commentator of Romans is to transform it into an acceptable paraphrase consisting of a series of logically connected propositions. It could be said (with mild exaggeration) that the effort to perform this task has consumed a large proportion of the history of Christian doctrine, and that difficulties in performing it have resulted in a panoply of heresies and schisms of which the Reformation is only one. Erasmus's own *Paraphrase on Romans*, revised many times, attempted an irenic précis. But Luther's 1515–16 lectures eschew paraphrase. Using the methods of the medieval glossator, he investigates the structures of meaning in the individual words and phrases of Paul's text. Luther's argument emerges not through exposition or proposition but in the gradual accretion of individual acts of glossing. His underlying theological purpose emerges through attention to the grammatical surface of Paul's questions, expletives, concessions, expostulations, and exhortations. The excruciating speech acts of Paul translate themselves into Luther's style, creating a tense debate between nervous qualification and unnerving assertion.

Luther's exposition centres on the verb *iustificare* and its passive form *iustificari*. The Vulgate text of Romans 3: 1–8 uses the verb only once, in a quotation from Psalm 50 (51): 4, *ut iustificeris in sermonibus tuis* (Romans 3: 4). In twenty pages of commentary Luther uses a conspectus of the different inflections of the verb, active and passive, upwards of seventy times. Luther appears to be mesmerized by the connotation and denotation of this verb, and through his puzzlement with it attempts to work through the more general doctrinal conundrum of how a sinner can be held to be righteous.

The puzzlement originates in the curious form in which the verb is used in the Vulgate version of Psalms, *iustificeris*—that is, second person passive subjunctive. Augustine expressed difficulty with the person of the verb, since God seems to be addressed, and yet the verb does not seem to be sayable to God.[98] Why should God need justifying (worse, in what way would he otherwise be unjustified)? Luther shifts his attention to the voice of the verb, since this passive form seems similarly ineffable:

Quia Iustificari Deus in seipso a nullo potest, cum sit ipsa Iustitia, Sic neque Iudicari, cum sit ipse eterna lex et Iudicium ac veritas   (WA 56.212.22)

[For God as he is in himself can be justified by no one, because he is justice himself, nor can he be judged, because he himself is eternal law and judgment and truth (p. 64)]

This is similar to Aquinas's typically Aristotelian problem with the meaning of *iustificatio*, since the just man needs no justification, and the unjust is unjustifiable. Still less does God need justifying, least of all by a sinner.

Luther avails himself here of a pun in the meaning of *iustificatur*. Having rejected as nonsense the sense of God 'becoming just' (*iustificatur*), he approves the alternative sense of God 'appearing just in the eyes of others' (*iustificatur*). Indeed in an important way he makes the two senses identical. Later Lutheran theology, especially in the work of Melanchthon, developed this into the theory of imputation.[99] But here Luther creates an outline of this theology in implicit form by a habit of reading.

The implicit logic is created by means of a barely perceptible grammatical undertow. Collocated with the terms of justification and belief

---

[98] Cui dicat, fratres, cui dicat difficile est advertere (*Enarrationes in Psalmos*, L, 9, CC, 38, 605).

[99] *Loci communes*, H7^{r-v}.

are a concordance of passive verbs: *reputatur, suscipitur, subicitur, petitur,* and of course *iustificatur*. Luther suggests, however indistinctly, a grammatical confirmation of the parallel semantic structure of the verbs *iustificare* and *credere*. Belief, like justification, is structurally passive: it means to receive something, to submit to something.

Typically, Luther compresses the logic of the argument to create a paradox. Why is Luther doing this? Gradually, out of the confusion, a realignment emerges between the meanings of *iustitia* and *iustificatio*. This realignment occurs precisely through the interplay between passive and active senses. The passive reconstruction of the meaning of *iustificatio* begins to imprint itself on his construction of the meaning of *iustitia*. Yet the traces are so faint that at first they can only be seen in the margins of Luther's manuscript, where he seems still to be in the process of identifying them clearly. The earliest indication comes in his *scholion* on 3: 5, where he cites Lefèvre's interpretation that God's *iustitia* is proved by our *iniustitia* in the sense that he punishes it. This Luther rejects, saying Paul means not that man's sin justifies God, but man's acknowledgement and confession of it. In the margin, seemingly in afterthought, Luther adds that Lefèvre has thereby also mistaken the sense of *iustitia*: for Paul does not here speak of 'the righteousness of God, by which he is righteous in himself' (*non loquitur de Iustitia Dei, qua ipse Iustus est*).[100] Later in the same page, he clarifies the point, and draws a line in the left margin to show the connection between the two definitions: *Non hic loquitur de Iustitia, qua ipse Iustus est, sed qua nos Iustificat* (WA 56.215.16). The justice referred to here, therefore, is not that of the just God, but of the justifying God: it is not a justice which is possessed, but one which is given and received. And yet Luther is still not sure: he qualifies himself, adds a lemma, and inserts between *qua* and *nos* the words *Iustus est &*. The full clause finally reads: *Sed qua [Iustus est et] nos Iustificat*.[101] This is the justice of a God who both is *iustus* and who *iustificat*.

A page later, the distinctiveness of the second sense of *iustitia* becomes much more apparent:

Ac Sic in Iustitia, qua ipse me Iustificat, solus ipse glorificatur, Quia solus Iustificatur (i.e. Iustus esse agnoscitur)   (WA 56.216.16)

[And thus in the justice, by which he himself justifies me, he himself alone is glorified, because he alone is justified (that is, acknowledged to be just) (p. 68 corr.)]

---

[100]   MS 64 theol. quarto 21, fo.48^v, WA 56.214.26.
[101]   MS 64 theol. quarto 21, fo.48^v (r.h. margin).

This extraordinary sentence is punctuated by the repeated rhythm of three consecutive passive clauses. The homoeoteleuton of *glorificatur . . . Iustificatur . . . agnoscitur* serves to emphasize that this meaning of God's *iustitia*, like his *iustificatio* and like man's faith, is passive. The *iustitia* by which he himself is *iustus*, on the other hand, and by which he judges others, and punishes them, is active.

Clearly this part of Luther's argument recapitulates his comments on Romans 1: 17 earlier in the lectures. The phrase *Non . . . qua ipse Iustus est, sed qua nos Iustificat* echoes directly the Augustinian locutions which Luther had already been turning over in his manuscript:

Et hic iterum 'Iustitia Dei' non ea debet accipi, qua ipse Iustus est in seipso, Sed qua nos ex ipso Iustificamur   (WA 56.172.3).

In reiterating these words, however, he also gives more explicit shape to the comparison of active and passive forms.

It is in this respect that the *scholia* on 3: 1–8 prove a highly illuminating commentary on the 1545 memoir. For there, we recall, Luther identifies a tension in his mind between two senses of *iustitia Dei*, one *activa* and one *passiva*. These terms are both resonant and yet obscure in derivation. Let us recall the precise wording of Luther's glosses of these terms. *Iustitia activa*, he says, is that *qua Deus est iustus, et peccatores iniustosque punit. Iustitia passiva*, on the other hand, is that *qua nos Deus misericors iustificat per fidem, sicut scriptum est, Iustus ex fide vivit*. Exchanging the active for the passive sense, Luther relates, transported him as if into paradise itself. And it led him to reinterpret a whole set of divine attributes—his 'work', 'power', 'wisdom', 'strength', 'salvation', and 'glory'.

In the midst of his *scholia* of Romans 3: 1–8, Luther summarizes his argument about God's *iustitia* by saying that there are three ways in which we may understand God to be 'justified' (WA 56.220–1). Among these, the first, which he rejects, is *quando Iniustos punit*. This is how he shows himself as just (*se Iustum*). The third way, which he accepts, is *quando Impios Iustificat*, which happens when his word is believed, and for which belief God justifies man. The verbal similarity here to the glosses of 1545 is very close. To make the parallel more striking, twice in the course of the *scholia* on Romans 3: 1–8, he quotes the vital words from Romans 1: 17, *Iustus ex fide vivit* (WA 56.224.23 and 226.26). These are the only two occasions on which he cites this verse in the whole of the lectures on Romans (apart, of course, from the *glossa* and *scholion* on the verse in question). Furthermore, at one point he explicitly states that the same analysis can work by analogy for God's *veritas*, his *virtus*, his *sapientia* and his *innocentia* (WA 56.216.24).[102]

The exact pattern of the analysis of the 1545 memoir is therefore found in the reading in the 1515 lectures of Romans 3: 1–8. He expounds a general account of the meaning of *iustitia Dei*, which centres in an explicit comparison of active and passive verbal forms of the verb *iustificare*, and which follows a syntactic formula pivoting on the relative pronoun *qua*. Even if it is not possible to know whether this is the very passage Luther remembered in 1545, this analysis helps us to interpret the crux he considered instrumental in the vital decade of his career. Over a series of pages of accumulated *corollaria*, the lectures on Romans discover a complementary linguistic economy connecting God and man. God is justified ('understood to be just') by man believing (that is 'justifying') him, which in turn justifies man ('makes him to be just'). By believing in God, man subjects himself to God; simultaneously, God allows himself to be subjected to this belief. God, paradoxically, becomes truly just ('justified') not by acting in a just way (the only sense which Aristotelian ethics would consider meaningful) but by giving justice away, and rendering unjust man just. And man can only be just when thus 'justified' by God.

This makes complicated reading in English, but in Latin these circumlocutions are avoided by the pun in *iustificare* and by the simple converse forms of active and passive verbs (*iustificar[e / i]*, *iustific[at / atur]*, etc.). Man and God co-operate in an elegant symmetry of language: *Deus iustificat, homo iustificatur*. God and man are reciprocally (and homonymously) *iustificantur* by faith. This grammatical parison gratifies Luther, who expresses his gratitude in his own tropes of linguistic pleasure, punning and rhyming with God: *Unde haec dicitur Iustitia fidei et Dei* (WA 56.220.10).

The vicissitudes of memory and polemic render this more crudely in 1545. The delicate weighing of one phrase against another—the necessary business of commentary—is disallowed by the constraints of retrospective narrative, and is replaced by a rigid taxonomy of terms. In 1545 Luther talks of rejecting the active sense of *iustitia* and asserting instead the passive. In 1515, on the other hand, Luther was more interested in the complementarity of the two terms seen in conjunction.

This is revealed in two final *corollaria* of vertiginous virtuosity:

---

[102] The analogy is already in place in the comment on Psalm 71(72) in the *Dictata*, leading Vogelsang to record this as the moment of 'breakthrough'.

Per hoc autem 'Iustificari Deum' Nos Iustificamur. Et Iustificatio illa Dei passiva, qua a nobis Iustificatur, Est ipsa Iustificatio nostri active a Deo. Quia illam fidem, que suos sermones Iustificat, reputat Iustitiam, Ut c.4. dicit et 1.: 'Iustus ex fide vivit' (WA 56.226.23)

[By this [term] 'God [to be] justified' we are justified. And this passive justification of God, by which he is justified by us, is our own active justification by God. For the faith, which justifies his words, he reputes as righteous. As chapter 4 states, and also chapter 1, 'The just shall live by faith']

Passive and active justification mirror each other. God, who is *iustificatur*, thereby *iustificat*. So his passive reception in faith by man initiates his active redemption of man.

The self-referential paronomasia of Luther's commentary is now in free flow. *Iustificare* is used six times in three different senses, in five cognate forms, in four lines of text. This interchangeability of meaning and of verbal form enables Luther to present the act of justification as reciprocal and yet entirely unearned by man. On the contrary, man's 'justification' of God is passive rather than active, for it constitutes a submission to God in a momentary suspense of belief, structurally opposite to the active 'judgement' of God which in turn condemns the unbeliever (WA 56.226.27).

In 1545, Luther construes the *iustitia passiva* of God as the logical opposite of *iustitia activa*. In 1515–16 he describes the relationship of passive and active terms more subtly.[103] Luther finds linguistic confirmation for this in a difference which he notices between the grammar of the Hebrew and Latin texts of Psalm 50(51). For whereas the Vulgate has the reading *iustificeris*—'thou mayest be justified'—Reuchlin's literal translation of the Hebrew (tişdaq) reads *iustificabis*—'thou wilt justify'.[104] Rather than finding this discrepancy a problem, Luther revels in its ambiguity. The asymmetry of Hebrew and Latin grammar makes God doubly graceful:

Ergo dum Iustificatur, Iustificat, et dum Iustificat, Iustificatur. Quare idem per verbum activum Hebreo et per passivum in nostra translatione exprimitur. (WA 56.227.7)

[Therefore, when he is declared righteous, he makes righteous, and when he makes

---

[103] On the complex relationship between grammar and agency, see Jespersen, *Philosophy of Grammar*, p. 165; and Davidson, *Actions and Events*, p. 44 ('philosophers often seem to think that there must be some simple grammatical litmus of agency, but none has been discovered').

[104] Reuchlin, *Septem psalmi poenitentiales hebraici cum grammatica tralacione latina*, p. 6; see Ficker's note on WA 56.227.

righteous, he is declared righteous. The same idea is therefore expressed by an active verb in Hebrew and by a passive verb in our translation (p. 77)][105]

This passage is the culmination of twenty pages of intricate exegesis. God is justified by his word, but he also justifies man through his word. In this sense we 'become' his word. We do this by believing his word—that is, by submitting ourselves to his word, becoming just in the process (justifying ourselves), even as we hold his word to be just.[106]

Justifying God, then, has a powerful double meaning, perhaps a double grammar: our justifying God (our justification of God) is one and the same as our justifying God (God's justification of us):

Iustificatio Dei passiva et activa et fides seu credulitas in ipsum sunt idem. Quia Quod nos eius sermones Iustificamus, donum ipsius eius, ac propter idem donum ipse nos Iustos habet i.e. Iustificat. Et sermones eius non Iustificamus, nisi dum credimus eos Iustos etc.   (WA 56.227.17)

[The passive and active justification of God and faith or trust in him are one and the same. For when we acknowledge his words as righteous, he gives himself to us, and because of this gift, he recognizes us as righteous, i.e. he justifies us. And we do not justify his words, until we believe that they are righteous (p. 78)]

Although Luther's grammar accords with logical rules familiar from the *moderni*, it is not really an example of logical grammar in the style of Ockham or even Trutfetter. Luther in no way attempts to construct a self-supporting or self-explaining logical system of language. His exposition is founded instead on grammatical usage in Latin, and to a lesser extent in Hebrew and Greek. This can be shown in the way he allows the contingencies of usage (such as the different accidence of Hebrew and Latin) to overtake his argument, rather than first conforming them to a single logical rule.

Grammar provides something more than a metaphor for Luther's theological argument. It is no mere analogy that connects his sense of the relationship of God and man with the semasiology of active and passive verbs. At the same time, it does not represent a theory that God is immanent in lexis and accidence. In this sense, Luther is still fully a nominalist. Within the system of language, a coherent understanding of God can be articulated by paying attention to the forms of language.

[105] Note how Pauck invents two different phrasal verbs 'make righteous/declare righteous' to cover the Latin forms iustificat/iustificatur.

[106] Luther may have in mind here the long note in Lefèvre, *Quincuplex*, p. 77 (et veri & iusti sunt sermones tui).

In the *Dictata super Psalterium* Luther once directly quotes Romans 1: 17, commenting *Haec est conclusio totius epistolae Pauli*. The context is his *scholion* of Psalm 31(32): 1–2:

> Beati quorum remissae sunt iniquitates: & quorum tecta sunt peccata. Beatus vir cui non imputavit Dominus peccatum.[107]

One area of theological grammar reverberates into another. Again, we find Luther's theology developing out of a form of complex citationality. This verse is quoted in *De spiritu et litera*, in the same chapter in which Augustine wrote the phrase *Haec est illa iustitia Dei, non qua ipse iustus est, sed qua nos ab eo facti*.[108] The citation reveals an intricate network in Luther's reading: Paul quoting the Psalm, Augustine quoting Paul and the Psalm alongside each other; and Luther himself interpreting both Psalms and Paul through the medium of Augustine in a succession of commentaries and treatises in a variety of enveloping contexts. Each time Luther drives his reading back to Romans 1: 17 in clinching conclusion.

Luther's lecture a year later on Romans 4: 7 takes him back over ground he had already covered in the *Dictata*, and provokes him into several pages of new exposition of the verses of the Psalm, newly interpolated with his discussion of the apostle. As in the *Dictata*, he quotes Reuchlin's literal translation before going on to reiterate his earlier interpretation of the *pulchre dictio* of the Hebrew text:

> Primo dicit: 'Beatus' (i.e. bene illi) 'fiens levatus' i.e. qui per gratiam fit liber ab onere criminis . . . Quod ergo Levatur, immo fiens levatus est, hoc est, Quod non ex Viribus suis, Sed per Deum active et in se passive Liberatur. Quia non dicit: Beautus, qui seipsum Levat, propriis meritis scil., Sed: qui levatur.   (WA 056.277.21)

> [It says first: 'Blessed is he (i.e. well for him) who is being relieved' i.e. who by grace becomes free from the burden of his crime . . . That he is relieved, or rather is being lightened—this means, not by his own powers, but that he is relieved actively by God and passively in himself. For it does not say 'Blessed is he who lightens himself', i.e. by his own merits, but 'who is lightened'   (p. 132) corrected][109]

---

[107] Luther's text of Romans 4: 7–8.

[108] CSEL, 60, 184. Augustine probably wrote his sermon on this Psalm in the same year (collected in *Enarrationes in Psalmos*, also consulted by Luther). Rupp discusses Luther's exegesis in relation to Augustine and Ockham, *Righteousness*, pp. 174–80.

[109] Reuchlin's literal translation (*Septem Psalmi*, p. 2) reads *Beatus fiens levatus crimine fiens opertus peccato*.

The passive construction of the sentence is a sign of the givenness of grace. Justice is not a virtue actively pursued by man *ex viribus suis*, but a gratuitous blessing conferred by a liberal God.

The just man, then, is not the man who has learnt to do just actions, but one to whom God has decided not to attribute sin, and thus to call 'just'. For all men are sinners (*omnes enim peccaverunt*, 3: 23) and are only made just by grace (*iustificati gratis per gratiam ipsius*, 3: 24). The sinner does not 'do' anything, he does not redeem himself but is redeemed, *per Deum active et in se passive*. The difference between the *iusti* and the *iniusti*, then, lies not in the works they do, but in their justification by God. Justification consists in recognising oneself to be a sinner and asking to be justified.

Luther registers these notions through a subtle interplay of grammar. The *iusti*, he says, are those who are *non contenti factis operibus cor etiam querunt Iustificari et Sanari* ('not content with the works they have done and desire the heart to be justified and cleaned', WA 56.268.11). Alongside the passive grammar of justification, then, Luther develops a parallel grammar of subordination and sequence of tenses. Grace is postponed into the future, compared unfavourably with an unjustified past (*factis operibus*). The *iusti* do not know when they are just (WA 56.268.21), but can only 'ask and hope for it'. Their justice is suspended in prayer beyond their present selves.

In the lectures on Romans, this paradox has become startlingly acute. In the *Dictata*, Luther expresses the strangeness of the idea that the sinner can be 'justified' by saying that it is an action continually suspended. The sinner never has 'justice' in the sense that he can stop still and lay hold of it: his justification is rather continually *in motus*. Every goal is only a starting-point (WA 4.364.20), so that the sinner is *semper in via et nondum in termino* (WA 4.328.23). The *iusti* are therefore *semper iustificandi* ('always being made just/justified', WA 4.363.15).[110] There is no end to this journey within life, so that *iustitia* is never a state, but always a process or flux. At every point in this process, man is between sin (from which he started out) and *iustitia* (towards which he is moving).

In the *scholion* to Romans 4: 7, Luther compresses this idea and makes sin and justice simultaneous. This is the final refinement of his paradox of grace: not a process from one condition to another, but two conditions at one and the same time. For the sinner is still a sinner at the point at which he is justified (and thus also just). We are not *iusti* by virtue of what we are

---

[110] It is possible to see this pattern emerging out of the lecture room into the public arena in a sermon on the fear of God, possibly 27 December 1514 (WA 4.665.3).

in nobis nec in potestate nostra (WA 56.269.3). By virtue of our own life and work, we can only ever be sinners. If we were not sinful, after all, God would not need to forgive us. But in the act of forgiveness God also justifies us, that is, holds us to be *iusti*. However, this is not because we have already become (just now) now just, but because we are still sinners. Otherwise we would not need justifying after all. In this sense, in God's eyes justified sinners are just and unjust at the same time: *simul sunt Iusti et Iniusti* (WA 56.269.21). But how can God think such a contradiction: how can he hold us, at one and the same time, to be *peccatores* and *non peccatores* (WA 56.270.10)? After all, this flouts the most fundamental law of Aristotle's logic: it is not possible for something to be both *p* and *not-p*.[111]

Luther gives one kind of answer which is logical, respecting the Aristotelian categories of the *via moderna*. Man as he is in himself (*intrinsice*) is a sinner. But God chooses to see man as different from how he is in himself, and thus *extrinsice* man can also be righteous. From this point of view there is no contradiction, only a change of point of view.[112] Yet Luther also gives another kind of answer, one that asserts and even relishes the lack of logical sense, enthusiastically throwing Aristotle offside. Paradox here becomes Luther's orthodox means of expression:

Ignoranter Iusti et scienter inIusti; peccatores in re, Iusti autem in spe

[unknowingly righteous and knowingly unrighteous, sinners in fact but righteous in hope   (WA 56.269.30), Pauck p. 125 corrected]

Simul manet peccatum et non manet

[Sin remains and simultaneously does not remain   (WA 56.270.10)]

Simul tollitur eorum peccatum et non tollitur

[their sin is taken away and at the same time is not   (WA 56.270.13)]

These phrases are self-consciously counter-logical. Indeed grace, to be grace, according to Luther, needs to run contrary to ordinary logic. The fundamental mistake made by the *stulti* and *Sawtheologen* ('pig-theologians', WA 56.274.14) is to conform grace to everyday ethics. However, while counter-logical, grace is not illogical or arbitrary. Luther's paradoxes are, on the contrary, precisely formulated:

---

[111] *De interpretatione*, 19b19—where he uses as example, 'a man is just' and 'a man is not just'.

[112] Ficker's note (WA 56.269) shows the derivation of this solution from Arnoldi and Trutfetter.

Numquid ergo perfecte Iustus? Non, Sed simul peccator et Iustus; peccator re vera, Sed Iustus ex reputatione et promissione Dei certa, quod liberet ab illo, donec perfecte sanet.   (WA 56.272.16)

[Now, can we say that he is perfectly righteous? No; but he is at the same time both a sinner and righteous, a sinner in fact but righteous by virtue of the reckoning and the certain promise of God that he will redeem him from sin in order, in the end, to make him perfectly whole and sound, p. 127]

This is the first instance in Luther's work of the phrase *simul peccator et iustus*, which was to become one of the mottoes of the Reformation. The sentence is poised on a double subordinate clause, *quod liberet . . . donec sanet*. Man's *iustitia* is predicated only on the qualification that it is contingent on the fulfilment of a providence which is itself contingent on a promise. The sinner cannot be said to be *iustus* either 'perfectly' (as a completed action) or even indicatively, since he is dependent on (subjunctive to) divine justification.

Luther's *grammatica theologica* here comes from a profound rereading of Augustine's reading of the Bible. The *Enarrationes in Psalmos* (cited directly 250 times in Luther's *Dictata*), for example, use over and over again the distinction between *perfectus* and *imperfectus*, even in the particular form *me et imperfectum dico et perfectum* ('I say that I am both imperfect and perfect').[113] After the *Dictata*, and while lecturing on Romans, Luther turned to *De spiritu et litera*. Here we find similar patterns of grammar; grace, Augustine says

ideo datur, non quia bona opera fecimus, sed ut ea facere valeamus   (10,16; CSEL, 60,168)

[is given to us, not because we have done good works, but that we may be able to do them]

The passive form *datur* is merged with a contrast between the perfect form *fecimus* and the subjunctive *valeamus*. It is God who acts, so that *ut velimus et ut credamus* (CSEL, 60, 220). The taking away of sin applies *de futuro*, not in the past or present, a point Augustine makes by explicitly comparing verbal inflections (CSEL, 60, 227).[114] This culminates in an exhortation at the end of the treatise, in which active and passive, subjunctive and indicative, reverberate against each other:

---

[113] *Enarrationes in Psalmos*, 38 (CC, 38, 416); see also CC 38, 407, and 409; other refs in Hamel, *Der Junge Luther*, i. 124–5.

[114] See also *De spiritu et litera*, 29, 50.

omnique homini sit necessarium dare ut detur illi, dimittere ut dimittatur illi et, si quid habet iustitiae, non de suo sibi esse praesumere, sed de gratia iustificantis dei et adhuc tamen ab illo esurire et sitire iustitiam   (36, 65; CSEL, 60, 227)

[it is necessary for every one to give, that it may be given to him, and to forgive, that it may be forgiven him; and whatever righteousness he has, not to presume that he has it of himself, but from the grace of God, who justifies him, and still to go on hungering and thirsting for righteousness   (*NPNF*, 5, 113)]

Luther, like Augustine, developed his theology reactively in the heat of controversy. He, too, works by setting text against text, 'Paul against Paul', creating arguments accretively, adding question to question.[115] It is through the friction of a reading practice that a new theology is developed. In this way, it is Augustine the reader as much as Augustine the theologian who is Luther's acknowledged master.

Rather than providing a key to the mysteries of Luther's theology, Romans 1: 17 radiates outwards throughout his early lectures, setting off patterns of meaning like a pebble in a lake. No one citation holds authority over the others, or represents a singular moment of realization. Nor is the distinction between active and passive forms a systematic discovery, available for formulaic application. Much of the history of Lutheran scholarship can be summarized as a search for a single systematic statement of the theology of *iustitia*, corresponding to the moment described with such ravishment in 1545. There exists no such moment, only a series of insights of reading, which gradually acquire shape in a grounding pattern. Often this pattern is visible only in the citations Luther makes between his master-texts of Psalms, Paul, and Augustine. Sometimes, it is found only outside his text altogether, in the margins and between the lines. This, after all, is where reading takes place.

Over the course of some years these habits of reading became powerful enough for Luther himself to recognize their full significance. By the time of the second lectures on Psalms, the *Operationes in Psalmos*, Luther's sense of the significance of a 'passive' justification had become more explicit. The new text connects it with his famous 'theology of the cross', by means of two different senses of the verb *patior* ('to suffer')—to suffer from an affliction, and to suffer an action to be done to one. Faith is perfected, he says, only 'by suffering' (*patiendo*) 'being passive under an inward divine operation' (WA 5.176.2).[116] Christ's passion and Christian patience come together in the etymology of the beautiful pun *passio*:

---

[115] *Enarrationes in Psalmos*, 31(32) (CC, 38, 229); ipsum Paulum ipso Paulo opponamus.
[116] See Rupp, *Righteousness of God*, p. 229.

vita Christiani magis sit operatio Dei quam nostra i.e *verissima passio nostra* (WA.57.61.10)

[the life of a Christian is much more the operation of God than our own, i.e it is most truly our passion][117]

The old man Luther had a more complete sense of the significance of this theology than his young self ever could. Perhaps this is why he remembers the second rather than the first lectures on Psalms, because by that time the full pattern of what he calls his *via passionis* was in his head.[118] The passive structure of justification as a dynamic transformation given by God and received by man becomes fully articulated as the 'theology of the cross'. The verbal relationship between *iustitia passiva* and the *passio* of the cross, between justification and the 'passions' of the suffering Christian ultimately act as a powerful nexus in protestant thought for centuries to come.[119] Under the pressure of controversy, in the vernacular polemic style which took Luther out of the classroom into international fame, Luther's theology found a startlingly radical voice. Yet the shape of this theology, its intellectual structure, can be found several years earlier in the cryptic glosses and ruminations of his biblical reading. It was the excitement of these private moments of reading that lived with him most strongly in later life.

However, the power of this reading process was not something the young Luther was fully able to understand. This was because, as has been increasingly obvious through this chapter, techniques of reading and theories of interpretation were themselves so much in flux in this period. It is to this crisis of interpretation that we now turn, in order to unravel the complex strands of scholastic philosophy and humanist philology underlying Luther's experience. This requires us to look closely at Luther's alter ego, Erasmus.

---

[117] Lectures on Hebrews (1517–18); quoted by Rupp, *Righteousness of God*, p. 211.

[118] Rupp, *Righteousness of God*, p. 141, citing Hamel, *Der junge Luther und Augustin*.

[119] A 20th-century example is Bonhoeffer, *Ethics*, p. 37.

3 New Grammar and New Theology

In February 1516, the Basle printer Johann Froben published a new edition of the New Testament. It was and is an extraordinary volume. Most famously, it presented the Christian scripture in Greek, audaciously described on the title-page as the original and true text. In addition it provided a new Latin version in parallel with the Greek, apparently superseding the official translation of St Jerome.[1] An enormous apparatus of annotations, which justifies the new readings and explicates their significance to the reader, supports this dual text. Text, translation, and annotation are proclaimed as the work of Erasmus of Rotterdam, whose name is given pride of place, capitalized on the second line of the title-page (Figure 4), and elevated virtually to the place and status of the author.[2] Before anyone had even heard of Luther Erasmus had announced a new religion based on literature.

The year 1516 saw Erasmus at the height of his fame. In May he arrived in Brussels to become councillor to Charles of Burgundy. By October his patron, newly King of Aragon and Castile, and soon to be Emperor Charles V, was trying to make him Bishop of Syracuse.[3] The *Novum Instrumentum* represented the summit of Erasmus's career. In personal terms it was the culmination of twenty years of study, the master project of his learning in Greek, and of his travails in ancient manuscripts. No work could more proclaim his ambition, putting him on the front page, as it were, of Europe. Equally, the publication of the New Testament announced the triumph of his movement: it seemed to show that there were no limits to the power of literary humanism, of textual scholarship, or of liberal philology.

[1] In fact, the translation in the 1st edn. is toned down from the version Erasmus had previously presented to Colet, and is realigned in many places with the Vulgate. The 2nd edn. of 1519 restored these radical readings, including *sermo* for *verbum* in John 1: 1.

[2] *Nouum instrumentum omne, diligenter ab ERASMO ROTERODAMO recognitum & emendatum, non solum ad graecam ueritatem, uerum etiam ad multorum utriusque linguae codicum* (Basle: Io. Froben, 1516), title page.

[3] *EE*, No. 475, Erasmus to Andrea Ammonio, Brussels, 6 October 1516. See also *EE*, Nos. 476, 486, 499.

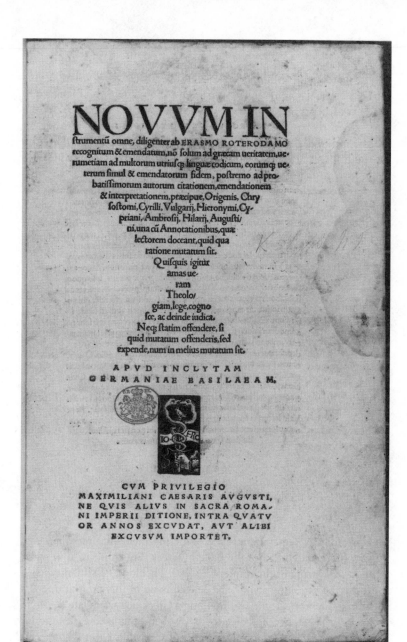

NOVVM IN

strumentũ omne, diligenter ab ERASMO ROTERODAMO
recognitum & emendatum, nõ solum ad græcam ueritatem, ue-
rumetiam ad multorum utriuſqʒ linguæ codicum, eorũmqʒ ue-
terum simul & emendatorum fidem, postremo ad pro-
batiſſimorum autorum citationem, emendationem
& interpretationem, præcipue, Origenis, Chry
soſtomi, Cyrilli, Vulgarij, Hieronymi, Cy-
priani, Ambroſij, Hilarij, Auguſti/
ni, una cũ Annotationibus, quæ
lectorem doceant, quid qua
ratione mutatum sit.
Quiſquis igitur
amas ue-
ram
Theolo/
giam, lege, cogno
ſce, ac deinde iudica.
Neqʒ ſtatim offendere, si
quid mutatum offenderis, sed
expende, num in melius mutatum sit.

APVD INCLYTAM
GERMANIAE BASILAEAM.

CVM PRIVILEGIO
MAXIMILIANI CAESARIS AVGVSTI,
NE QVIS ALIVS IN SACRA ROMA-
NI IMPERII DITIONE, INTRA QVATV
OR ANNOS EXCVDAT, AVT ALIBI
EXCVSVM IMPORTET.

Fig. 4. The first printed New Testament in Greek, with Erasmus's name as 'author'
on the second line: *Nouum instrumentum omne, diligenter ab ERASMO ROTERO-
DAMO recognitum & emendatum, non solum ad graecam ueritatem, uerum etiam
ad multorum utriusque linguae codicum* (Basle: Johan Froben, 1516).

It is perhaps with some envy that the professional critic in the modern university contemplates the example of a man who managed to make the theory and practice of textual studies into one of the most intensely political activities of sixteenth-century Europe. Yet the 1516 New Testament also marks Erasmus's ultimate failure. It created the conditions for the demise of his personal reputation and associated his name with unorthodoxy, sometimes heresy. It involved him in personal quarrels from which he never escaped. In his responses to these controversies he became notorious for an ambiguity, even duplicity, which continues to this day to colour his fame. For his movement, too, far from signalling the triumph of method, it ushers in controversy and acrimony. Erasmus's textual criticism, his skills as a translator, his methods of interpretation, came under intense scrutiny. Humanist studies discovered not a new consensus for religion but became instead a party to a new schism.

In all of this, Erasmus's name became coupled inexorably with Luther's. By 1519, when Froben produced a second, even more daring edition, the question was no longer whether Christian Europe was Erasmian but whether Erasmus was a Lutheran. This story, and the story of their literary quarrel, will be the subject of a later chapter. For the moment, the matter in hand is the context for the Reformation of the conflict over literary method. For the historical coincidence of Erasmus's reform of literary studies with Luther's reform of theology raises important and puzzling questions for each.

I ERASMUS'S *NOVUM INSTRUMENTUM* AND THE NEW GRAMMAR

Froben's folio is remembered chiefly for the incidental reason that it was the first printed text of the Bible in Greek. Erasmus saw it in wider terms, a reordering of the mind of Europe. Theology, Christianity itself, can never be the same again. The central issue in this programme is a revision of literary categories. Providing a Greek text was a late decision, executed in haste, perhaps dictated by Froben's publishing ambitions.[4] Erasmus's first concern was the reform of Christian Latin through his translation and *Annotationes*. By performing a reformation in reading

---

[4] Erasmus described the evolution of his New Testament in his *Catalogus omnium lucubrationum* addressed to Johann von Botzheim in 1523, *EE*, No. 1 (ed. Allen, i. 14); see also Augustijn, *Erasmus: Life*, pp. 90–1.

practices, Erasmus proposed to reform Christian doctrine and moral life. The Greek text here served a subtle purpose, because there was no established praxis for reading Greek ready to be overturned. Reading Latin, on the other hand, was central to medieval culture. A reform in Latinity could be infiltrated by the back door via the less revolutionary medium of Greek.

These claims are set out in *Paraclesis*, the 'summons' or preface to the general reader. *Paraclesis* is one of the most moving and personal of all of Erasmus's works; it was published separately by Froben in 1519. It describes a new Christian reader and a new mode of Christian reading. Erasmus's newly edited text reveals 'the truth itself', *ipsa veritas* (p. 70), shown in its true simplicity and power. Here is scripture in its literal copy, as it is in itself. Christ, our author, is (at last) his own author.[5] In the letters of the Greek his presence is (literally) made known to us. With this volume Erasmus enables Christ the doctor, after centuries of neglect, to supplant the lesser doctors of his church.

A number of profound and complex literary principles underlie these claims. The first is the status of literature itself. Christ is celebrated as the pre-eminent writer of literature, and literature his pre-eminent creation. To be a Christian one must read 'the literature of Christ' (*Christi literas*), no less than to be a Platonist one must read Plato.[6] The second principle concerns the methods of interpretation appropriate to literature. Scriptural literature is self-authorizing, virtually self-interpreting. All other forms of knowledge are *abditum ac retrusum* (p. 70, 'hidden and obscure') in comparison. Christian literature and Christian philosophy are beyond and above interpretation. The New Testament requires 'a pious and open mind' to understand it, informed by a 'pure and simple faith'. Such teaching by definition is universally accessible. And it delivers, without mediation, *ipsa veritas*.

These principles are informed by a powerful and complex system of metaphors. Scripture, truth, presence, authorship, are synonymous. Christ is our author; his authorship is present in his words; his presence guarantees truth; the truth is delivered in these words, written in scripture. Scripture presents a living and breathing Christ, 'almost more effectively', Erasmus breathtakingly declares, than when he dwelt among men. By such tropes, the metaphors of the writing process are turned by Erasmus into literal truths:

---

[5] 'Christ, our Author': *autori nostro principique Christo* (*Préfaces*, p. 70).

[6] *Platonicus non est qui Platonis libros non legerit, et theologus est, non modo Christianus qui Christi literas non legerit?* (*Préfaces*, pp. 78–80).

hae tibi sacrosanctae mentis illius vivam referunt imaginem, ipsumque Christum loquentem, sanantem, morientem, resurgentem, denique totum ita praesentem reddunt, ut minus visurus sis, si coram oculis conspicias   (*Préfaces*, p. 88)

[these writings bring you the living image of his holy mind and the speaking, healing, rising Christ himself, and thus they render him so fully present that you would see less if you gazed upon him with your very eyes   (*Christian Humanism*, ed. Olin, p. 106.)]

The Christian reader, receiving the text of Christ in its true and original form, and trained to understand it according to the canons of classical style, will be transformed into a Christian way of life.

This statement claims the highest possible stakes for literary study. Although scripture has always been described as holy, to make the text the receptacle of Christ 'fully present'—even more than in his human body or implicitly than in the sacrament—is a startling principle. Erasmus presents this claim as if it is self-evident. He is a far too knowing reader of his own culture to believe this. It is, however, his characteristic manner to behave as if his most bitter opponent has already been persuaded of the hopelessness of his own case. Erasmus pursues an intellectual and ideological war, but behaves as if it is barely controversial.

This was not the work of an instant. *Paraclesis* takes its place in a literary campaign that for several years had been preparing the way for the gospel in Greek. Primary in this was a book apparently very different in kind, the *Moriae Encomium* of 1511. The *Praise of Folly*, among other things, is a prototype Preface to the New Testament. Its critique of the old order of learning becomes a manifesto for the new. At one point, in a brilliant pastiche of medieval exegetical style, 'a hasty interpretation of a passage from the gospel' produces a plethora of 'syllogisms, major and minor conclusions, corollaries, idiotic hypotheses and further scholastic rubbish' (*scholasticas nugas*).[7] Earlier, Folly ridicules a monastic sermon, in which the agreement of the parts of speech is made to constitute a proof of the heavenly agreement of the trinity of divine persons, *ut in grammaticorum rudimentis sic expressum ostenderet totius triadis simulacrum.*[8]

Christian literature requires a new grammar to replace old follies. Grammar is the primary discipline for Erasmus, at once elementary and fundamental.[9] In Erasmus's first foray into biblical studies, his 1505 edition of Lorenzo Valla's *Adnotationes*, Erasmus quipped that 'theology, the

---

[7] *Moriae Encomium*, ASD, iv/3, 166.

[8] *Encomium*, ASD, iv/3, 164. The whole passage plays on the metaphysical claims of some of the less philosophically rigorous *modistae* (see below).

[9] Chomarat, *Grammaire et rhétorique*, p. 24.

Queen of all the sciences, will not be offended if some share is claimed in her ... by her humble attendant grammar'.[10] The attack on Queen Theology and her vanities of *amour propre* is systematic. In the Preface to his own *Annotationes* in the 1516 edition, Erasmus disarmingly parodied himself, *Humi reptat inquiunt, in verbulis ac syllabis discruciatur* ('he crawls along the ground, they say, he tortures himself over little words and syllables').[11] The joke is on his opponents. It is they who are covered in mire.

Folly represents the history of Christian doctrine, hitherto. It is typical of Erasmus's complex style to express this as a paradox: to call Christian doctrine 'folly' would be too obviously unorthodox. It is equally typical that he presents his own principles in the form of jokes against himself. But these jokes show that other, blessed folly, the folly of Christ. About this, Erasmus is utterly serious. Questions of grammar, logic, and theology occupied a central place in the controversial reception of the *Encomium*. In particular, the very public 'quarrel' between Erasmus, More, and Dorp in 1514 and 1515 constituted a highly self-conscious discussion of the relationship between the old and the new learning. There is more to this quarrel than meets the eye, as Lisa Jardine has shown.[12] Ostensibly it consisted of a defence of theology against the calumnies of Folly by Maarten van Dorp, a grammarian turned theologian from Louvain; there followed a reply by Erasmus, a new refutation by Dorp, and finally, in October 1515, a defence of the *Encomium* by its addressee, Thomas More.[13] Beyond this simple narrative, ironies and sophistications abound. Dorp was friendly with Erasmus and all three men were part of the same literary circle; the publication of the Dorp and Erasmus letters seems to have involved collaboration, including that of the printing houses. In maintaining this 'quarrel' and so publicly, they participated in what Jardine aptly calls a 'performance' (p. 112). The theme of this elaborate piece of theatre was the justification of two of Erasmus's principal works: the *Encomium*, obviously; but also the New Testament now in preparation. Yet just as important was the subtext: the relationship between secular and sacred learning, and the humanist programme for the arts curriculum.

---

[10] *CWE*, ii. 94. [11] *Préfaces*, p. 160. *Humi serpere* is from *Adagia*, 186ᵛ (II.xmlxxxviii).
[12] *Erasmus*, pp. 111–27 and on the *Encomium* in particular, pp. 180–7.
[13] The *Encomium* was first published in 1511; the early printing history is described in ASD, iv/3, pp. 14–16 and 40 f. Dorp's letters are in *EE*, ii. Nos. 304 and 347; Erasmus's reply is No. 337. The exact dates of the letters are contentious and perhaps factitious; see Jardine, p. 112. In any case, Dorp's first letter was not published until October 1515, included (significantly) in an edition of Erasmus from Dorp's printing house. More's letter is in *Correspondence*, ed. Rogers, No. 15. It, however, was not printed until 1563.

Dorp here possessed crucial qualifications. In representing the theological faculty at Louvain, he placed a debate about Erasmus's work at the heart of sacred studies. He established his conservative credentials while assisting a sympathetic reception to Erasmus's literary aims. The case was made against Erasmus's New Testament before it had even appeared, and at the same time answered. It is a nice example of getting retaliation in first. The debate was held on Erasmus's terms. The question of philology became central to theology, even in the arguments of the opposition. The issue of humanist grammar and logic enters in a more subtle way still. More used his letter to put forward the case for humanist method against scholastic dialectic.[14] Here Dorp, again, contributes in contradictory ways: for in the same year as attacking Erasmus he wrote a commendatory letter for the first edition (published in Louvain) of what was about to be proclaimed the seminal 'new' text of the humanities, Rudolph Agricola's *De inventione dialectica*.[15] What better commendation could there be for the humanist avant-garde than that of the theological orthodoxy?

After 1518, as in so many other instances, Erasmus's arguments in connection with the *Encomium* changed in the wake of the Luther affair, and became more explicitly doctrinal.[16] His New Testament was attacked in 1520 in the *Annotationes in annotationes Erasmi* of Edward Lee, after which Erasmus found himself having to answer suspicions of heresy and blasphemy.[17] Following this lead, the historical reception of the *Encomium* has become bound up with the general concerns of Reformation critique. In this context, the original argument about grammar and theology has become submerged. However, this argument is central to Erasmus's concerns, and in its way, to the history of the Reformation itself.

Erasmus defends himself against Dorp by stating that he has not attacked theology *per se*—true theology is the only branch of learning worthy of the name—but the bad practice of theology.[18] This he characterizes by reference to its understanding of language, in the form of grammar and logic. Erasmus chooses his targets carefully: he lumps together a grammatical text-book (Alexander of Villedieu's *Doctrinale*), the techniques of formal logic, and the *quaestiones* of theological debate—

[14]   Kinney, 'More's Letter to Dorp', p. 179.

[15]   Jardine, *Erasmus*, pp. 116–17, although her interpretation of Dorp's part in this is slightly different from mine. The curious history of Agricola's work, which was not new at all (he had been dead for thirty years) is the subject of a remarkable 'scholarly detective story' in Jardine, chs. 3 and 4.

[16]   Clarence H. Miller, Introduction to ASD, iv/3, pp. 26–7.

[17]   Lee, a former student at Louvain, later became Archbishop of York.

[18]   *EE*, ii. 100 (No. 337).

then ridicules them all by associating them with schoolboy crib-books (the *Catholicon* and *Mammotrectus*). Although he claims to distinguish such methods from theology properly conducted, his caricature of the corner-cutting habits of scholastic dullards tars 'modern theology' with the same brush. It is disfigured by its 'barbarous style', its 'quibbling sophistries', and its dependence on Aristotle.[19] Just as damning, it lacks the hallmarks of the *bonae litterae* now in renewal (*si renascantur bonae litterae*)—'sound learning', and a knowledge of the original tongues. This is the true grammar: far from being unnecessary to an understanding of scripture, as Dorp argued, without philological expertise in Greek and Hebrew it is a monstrous impudence even to claim the title of theologian.

Paraclesis proclaims a transformation in the status of writing and the value of reading. The letters of scripture inscribe the truth within their readers. Erasmus offers to bypass the history of theology (as the interpretation of the divine word) and to render in the words themselves the *imago* of Christ. He proposes a revolution in philosophical method—the elimination of five hundred years of syllogisms, glosses, quiddities—and in the politics of reading. Christ unaccommodated emerges, available indiscriminately and democratically to women, to the poor, to the uneducated, even to the Turks or Saracens, or the Scots or the Irish. In the most famous of his adages, Erasmus longs to hear the farmer singing the words of the gospels at his plough, and the weaver humming them to the movement of his shuttle.

In the appeal of this image it has been easy to forget that very few farmers and weavers knew Greek. Erasmus himself acknowledges that to reach the people holy scripture must be translated into the vulgar tongue. But he makes no explicit assessment of the effect of this process of translation on his central argument about language. The whole premiss of *Paraclesis* is that the letters of the Greek text offer direct access to the original presence of the author. These letters, these γράμματα, do not describe Christ, they *are* Christ. However, in acknowledging the differences between languages, Erasmus admits for the first time that these letters may not, after all, be directly accessible. Translation implies distance, not presence, resistance, not access.

At this focal point of *Paraclesis* are uncovered some of its deepest paradoxes. The publication of the Greek text is also the discovery of its opacity. However much Erasmus proclaims the opposite, Greek is a

---

[19] *quid commercii Christo et Aristoteli, EE,* ii. 101.

secret language. To reveal its secrets, he has to translate it into Latin. Indeed, his very declaration of the openness of the Greek is made in Latin, here in the text of *Paraclesis*. Yet, as he continually reminds his readers, the Latin copy is not the same as the Greek original. The Latin, unlike the Greek, is not the *imago* of Christ. To show forth the truth of the true original, Erasmus not only has to translate it into another language, but has to explicate every difference between the original and the copy in two volumes of annotation. Not the least of the ironies of Erasmus's textual introduction is that having rejected all need for commentary his own text is copiously annotated. By a further irony, Erasmus's *Annotationes* constituted his book's major appeal to originality, and hence his own greatest claim to authorship.

Yet this is by no means the last of the conundrums of the *Novum Instrumentum*. For *Paraclesis* is not even the last word on Prefaces. It is a Preface to further Prefaces (*Methodus* and *Apologia*), followed by a fourth Preface to the *Annotationes* placed after the text of the Greek. At the end of the *Annotationes* a final afterword, by Oecolampadius, Erasmus's assistant, concludes the book. Nor is *Paraclesis* either unprecedented or unprefaced: before introducing himself to the reader, Erasmus introduces his Introduction to Pope Leo X in an open letter; and before this, Froben the printer introduces Erasmus to his own text.

The prefatory apparatus of the humanist text has been well described as one of its essential features.[20] It inscribes the text within an economy of readers and patrons, virtually creating the conditions of its own readership. Each of the Prefaces of Erasmus's volume is a different speech act, addressed to a different question of dissemination. The Letter to Leo X carefully justifies the orthodoxy of the project; the *Methodus* polemically asserts Erasmus's methodological principles of literary analysis; the *Apologia* irenically analyses his attitude to literary and theological polemic. Yet the multiple Prefaces of the *Novum Instrumentum* do something more and less than establish a proper critical reception for his work. They testify to the lets and hindrances in the way of his interpretative project. They manifest a word divided, even as he proclaims its original unity in the γράμμα of the Greek. For the letters of the Greek Christ defer immediately to the lost syllables of an imaginary Hebrew Christ who would have priority and authority even over this unique and originary source of sources. At the same time the traces of the Greek letters are dissipated in the voluminous

---

[20] See the general remarks on the 'physical form' of Renaissance books in Grafton, *Commerce with the Classics*, p. 8; on Erasmus's propagandist uses of epistolary Prefaces, Jardine, *Erasmus*, throughout.

divagations of Latin commentary and interpretation. As Erasmus casts himself adrift in these textual transmissions and translations, he also becomes lost in his own iterability, in the endless need to reiterate himself in Preface after Preface, annotation after annotation, as he seeks to control the meaning of his text and to project his own dissemination.

II ERASMUS AND THE SCHOOLS

If Erasmus promised to reform Europe through reading, first he had to teach Europe to read according to his own principles. This was a life-long task. His earliest important work, *Antibarbari*, is a treatise on reading. With the *Novum Instrumentum* of 1516 his manifesto of the reading process reaches its height. He expounded it in detail in the *Methodus*, a work he reprinted separately in 1518 as the *Ratio verae theologiae*, subsequently revised and expanded on a number of occasions. *Antibarbari* was finally printed in 1520, with revisions that bear evidence of the controversy around the *Novum Instrumentum* in Louvain.[21] On this issue he never gave up, and at the end of his life, in 1535, he summarized his project in the *Ecclesiastes*. While the heart of his manifesto is the knowledge of the three biblical languages, the new grammar goes beyond this to encompass a cultural practice. Grammar consists in the broadest possible rules for good speech and literary style. It includes a loving concern for history, poetry, and the study of antiquity. Literature embodies a living encyclopaedia.[22]

Erasmus conceived his principles as a systematic deconstruction of the old method. His denigration of the medieval schools occurs in its most comprehensive form in two works revised at various points and printed separately in 1528 and 1529, *De recta pronuntiatione* and *De pueris institutiendis*:

as soon as they have learned the declensions and the agreement between nouns and adjectives their study of grammar is finished, and they are introduced to the confusions of logic, where, in effect, they are forced to unlearn whatever skills of correct speech they may previously have acquired. An even more wretched state of affairs prevailed when I was a boy: students were cruelly tormented with modes of meaning (*modi significandi*) and petty enquiries into the 'virtue' of a word, and in the mean time acquired nothing but poor speaking habits. Indeed, the teachers

---

[21] Phillips, *Erasmus and the Northern Renaissance*, p. 23, and Introduction to *Antibarbari*, CWE, xxiii. 11–12.

[22] Chomarat, *Grammaire et rhétorique*, p. 165.

of that time, afraid to teach anything that might seem fit only for boys, would obscure grammar with the complexities of logic and metaphysics[23]

Erasmus presents the argument as straightforwardly pedagogic. The old grammar was subordinated to logic. Believing this (perhaps not surprisingly) to be inappropriate for most schoolboys, he proposed a change in the *ordo studiorum*. A fluent command of languages should precede any training in logic. Grammar must triumph over its rival in the *trivium*.

To understand this we have to consider the implications of the new books of grammar that emerged in the later fifteenth century. These found their inspiration in Valla's *Elegantiae linguae latinae*, written in the early 1440s and published in Venice in 1471. Valla's preference for Donatus and Priscian over later medieval grammatical sources, and his concern for questions of style and usage, was enormously influential.[24] These principles were taken up in a number of new grammars by Sulpitius Verulanus, Antonio Mancinelli, Antonius Illuminatus, and Aldus Manutius. The most widely used was Niccolò Perotti's *Rudimenta Grammatices*.[25] Erasmus, like many others, hailed Perotti as the textbook for a new era.

Perotti defined grammar in a characteristic way as the *ars recte loquendi, recteque scribendi*. As for instruction, he considered the example of poets and authors to be educative, since reading them teaches grammar 'by observation'.[26] Similarly, Aldus Manutius declared that grammatical rules are dictated not by semantic logic but 'by usage, reason and authority'. He cites ancient practice in dividing grammar into two kinds: one *methodice*, a normative study of the rules of speaking; the other *historice*, dealing with the interpretation of passages of authors.[27]

Submerged in the humanist argument is a polemic about language theory. This polemic is coded by means of a subtle redefinition of terms. 'Grammar' is defined within the strict limits of 'skills of correct speech' which are required to avoid 'poor speaking habits'. Erasmus draws a sharp line between this discipline and the 'complexities of logic'. Scholastic practice, he says, has ignored these proper, even natural, limits. The simple art

---

[23] *De pueris instituendis*, quoted here from *CWE*, xxvi. 344–5. Latin text in ASD, i/2, 76–7. As will become apparent, the target of attack in the form of the *modi significandi* is quite specific; for the meaning of *virtus*, see Pinborg, 'Speculative grammar', in *CHLMP*, p. 264 n. 31; also Courtenay, *Schools and Scholars*, p. 260.

[24] See Waswo, *Language and Meaning*, pp. 91–2.

[25] See Padley, *Latin Tradition*, pp. 16–21; on Perotti's German influence see Heath, p. 16. Erasmus approved Perotti as the finest modern gammar in *De ratione studii*, ASD, i/2, 114–15.

[26] *ars scriptorum et poetarum lectionibus observata*; see Padley, *Latin Tradition*, pp. 30–1.

[27] *Rudimenta grammatices Latinae linguae*, pp. 1–2; see Padley, p. 31.

of correct speech is unhappily mingled with the 'confusion' of logical speculation, leading to unnecessary obfuscation.

However, Erasmus's polemic masks several ambiguities. For the *modi significandi* derive not from medieval logical theory but from grammatical theory. Scholastic grammar—as expressed in the *modi significandi*—constituted a philosophical enquiry into semantics. Erasmus denies to grammar any interest in theoretical questions regarding the philosophy of language, and delimits it to practical instruction in the rudiments. All linguistic theory beyond this is hived off into logic. As he makes clear in *De recta pronuntiatione*, even in this form he has little use for such a subject. The student requires only 'enough dialectic to have some acquaintance with it' but should not be 'tortured with all the ridiculous skills of hair-splitting that exist only for the sake of being shown off'.[28]

Grammar is a key word for Erasmus and an iconoclastic one: it represents a new approach to educational practice, and at the same time a reform of the intellectual disciplines. At the heart of Erasmus's critique of old method and of his enthusiasm for the new is the principle of usage. Scholastic Latin, he argues, is an artificial construction. It has been formulated to comply with the demands of an extra-linguistic philosophy. Language is made to follow these rules rather than the other way round. As a result, it has become abstract and recondite, full of barbarisms and neologisms, divorced from ordinary understanding and the common people. The study of language must return to its roots. A reformation of grammar in line with usage will bring about a true philosophy and a restoration of the most eloquent style of expression.

The battle between humanism and scholasticism is a familiar episode in intellectual history. It is not as straightforward as Erasmus would have us believe. Both of Erasmus's central contentions, that scholasticism has no interest in grammar, and that medieval logic has no basis in language, are dubious. The consequences for Erasmus's own method were also complex. His claim to be able to do without a theory of semantics was quickly put to the test. Nowhere was this more clearly at issue than in his forays into scriptural interpretation in his *Annotationes*, and in the vastly influential *Paraphrases* which followed in various editions after 1517. His assertion that the Bible could explain itself—taken up enthusiastically by protestants—was tested severely when those same protestants chose to disagree with Erasmus about these simple meanings. This chapter describes how Erasmus's method, which began by rejecting the heritage of theological

---

[28] *De recta pronuntiatione*, ASD, i/4, 24; CWE, xxvi. 380.

interpretation, was exposed to the return of theology. At the same time it describes how the opposing forces of new and old theories of language were not so easy to unravel after all.

Contrary to Erasmus's caricature, *grammatica* had a broad range of senses in medieval Latin, manifested in this twelfth-century defence of the *trivium* by John of Salisbury:

> it is clear that grammar is not narrowly confined to one subject. Rather, grammar prepares the mind to understand everything that can be taught in words. Consequently, everyone can appreciate how much all other studies depend on grammar.[29]

From John's account of his own education in the school of Bernard of Chartres, this included a study of the rhetorical and moral values of the ancients, training in style as well as the construing of sentences. Grammar is the corner-stone of the educational structure, but also *clavis est omnium scripturarum et totius sermonis mater et arbitra* ('the key to everything written, as well as the mother and arbiter of all speech' (i. 21; p. 61)). It lies at the basis of all forms of knowledge as 'the cradle of all philosophy' (i. 13). Someone unversed in grammar is philosophically 'blind and deaf' (p. 62).

The principal medieval textbooks of grammar were written in late antiquity. Students normally began studying Latin with the *Ars minor* of Donatus (fourth century), a question-and-answer treatment of the eight parts of speech; of the *Ars maior* they used mainly the third part (known as the *Barbarismus*, after its initial word), a list of rhetorical schemes and tropes. More advanced study was found in the *Institutiones grammaticae* by Priscian (sixth century) of which the last two books (*Priscianus minor*) remained for centuries the most comprehensive treatment of syntax.[30]

Medieval language theory projected a complex inheritance. Rather than grammar becoming the prisoner of logic, it would be more accurate to say that logic developed out of the need to explicate ever more fully the depths of language. Priscian's work contained a wealth of material on the fringes of philosophical enquiry, for instance on the relation between language and reality, on the categorical distinctions implicit in proper and common nouns, and on the properties of the verb 'to be'. Glosses of Priscian, such as

---

[29] *omnes aliae disciplinae obnoxiae sint*; *Metalogicon*, i. 21 (CC, 98, 48). Eng. tr. McGarry, p. 60).

[30] The first sixteen books, known as *Priscianus maior*, dealt with the parts of speech, in more detail than in Donatus. Priscian's syntax remained the standard authority for the humanists.

those by John of Salisbury's master at Chartres, William of Conches, in the twelfth century, developed a new and sophisticated tradition.[31] A logician in this early period was likely to be a grammarian as well. Abelard wrote a treatise of *Grammatica*, now lost.

Later, under the influence of newly discovered texts by Aristotle (collectively known as the *logica nova*) logic became formally distinct from grammar. The demands of the university curriculum diverted logic into the formal techniques of syllogisms, consequences, obligations, and the theory of the properties of terms. At the same time, grammar became more formally technical. Peter Helias's commentary on Priscian in the thirteenth century began to supersede the direct study of Priscian in northern universities.[32] An equivalent place in the curriculum was occupied by Robert Kilwardy's commentary on the two syntactical books, *Priscianus minor*.[33]

As significant were new textbooks used in elementary schools, although more difficult questions were left until university. Alexander of Villedieu's *Doctrinale*, composed at the end of the twelfth century, spread rapidly, and by the fourteenth and fifteenth centuries was virtually the universal grammar of most of Europe.[34] Written in verse (to aid memorization), it was usually divided into three parts, one on etymology, one on syntax, and one on quantity, accent, and figures of speech. Many of its concerns were practical—declensions, degrees of comparison, genders, the formation of verbs, irregular verbs, and so on. But the *Doctrinale* is intended to introduce students to more theoretical problems. It shares the complaint of the similarly popular *Graecismus* of Eberhard of Béthune, that Priscian describes constructions without assigning 'causes' to them.[35] In a not especially sophisticated way, these books provoke enquiry into the semantic analysis of language alongside the rote learning of detail. They assume that the incidental features of language are not arbitrary, but explicable.

Medieval grammar insisted that language is an intelligible system. Increasingly such texts were used alongside commentaries with an altogether more systematic approach to grammar, entirely concerned with a theory about language rather than a method of teaching it: this came to be

---

[31] Hunt, *History of Grammar*, p. 18.

[32] Ibid., 12; Thurot, *Notices et extraits*, p. 96. Peter was known simply as 'the commentator'.

[33] See Thurot, p. 97.

[34] See *Doctrinale*, ed. Reichling, p. xxi; on the *Doctrinale*'s use, see Paetow, *Arts Course*, p. 37; on its popularity, see Reichling (ed.), p. xliv. Both Luther and Erasmus were taught from it and later referred to it.

[35] *Graecismus*, ed. Wrobel, Praefatio, p. ix. The complaint goes back to Peter Helias, *Summa*, e.g. i. 180–1.

known as *grammatica speculativa*.[36] Speculative grammar developed out of commentaries on Priscian.[37] In a fateful moment Peter Helias had used the term *modus significandi* to indicate semantic values.[38] The term was then adopted as a mantra to describe an entire theory of meaning. The earliest treatises were by Martin and Boethius of Dacia, and other important exponents include Siger of Courtrai and Radulphus Brito; probably the most widely used work was one of the last, by Thomas of Erfurt (an erroneous attribution to Duns Scotus contributing to its popularity).[39] Although the major thinking on this subject was completed by the early fourteenth century, it was still widely taught in university syllabuses in the late fifteenth century, especially in Northern Europe. As such it was subject to polemical abuse among humanists, often on the basis of late derivative works such as by Michel de Marbais.[40]

Speculative grammar was able to claim its principles as universal by concentrating not on actual words but on *modi significandi* ('ways of signifying'). The particular sounds used to convey meaning are arbitrary, but the rules by which semantic import is conveyed are, it was claimed, unchanging. An individual sound (*vox*) possesses a *significatum speciale* ('lexical meaning') and a *significatum generale* (a term covering the various grammatical categories).[41] By this *ratio significandi* a *vox* becomes a *dictio* (which we might call a 'lexeme'). The *dictio* then becomes a functioning part of speech (*pars orationis*) through the *modi significandi*—a term which is not limited to grammatical categories, but covers categories of meaning as well. The study of *modi significandi* becomes a method of understanding the semantic function of grammatical forms.

The *modi significandi* represent the ultimate medieval attempt to provide a comprehensive explanation for every accident of language. They were even considered to correspond to equivalent *modi intelligendi* ('ways of understanding') and *modi essendi* ('ways of being'). For a time speculative grammar offered what seemed to be a total account of language. However it fell foul of two types of criticism. One, raised by the

---

[36] A bibliography of commentaries on Alexander and Eberhard can be found in Bursill-Hall, *Census*. Several survive in the library at Erfurt; see pp. 62–3.

[37] Pinborg, 'Speculative Grammar', *CHLMP*, p. 254.

[38] *Summa*, i. 182. Reilly comments (i. 34–5) on the history and meaning of the term.

[39] See Bursill-Hall (ed.), pp. 27–8. Most of Thomas's adult life was spent in the schools that became Erfurt university.

[40] Chomarat, *Grammaire et rhétorique*, i. 215. Although commentaries on Thomas survive in the library at Erfurt, there is no mention of him in 15th- or 16th-century syllabuses.

[41] Pinborg, *CHLMP*, pp. 257–61. The link between *vox* and *significatum* is the *impositio*.

nominalist John Aurifaber, was of realism.[42] In the received form of the theory, the criticism was justified, for instance in some commentaries on the *Doctrinale*, where it is assumed that the structure of each sentence imitates a structure in reality.[43] A second criticism concerned the claim to universality. Roger Bacon objected to the notion that the meaning of words is unchanging, arguing, with a prototype theory of complex words, that 'human utterances always belong to a context', which is often tacit and certainly not 'the result of a conscious act on the part of the speaker'.[44] William of Ockham repudiated the view that all grammatical distinctions have semantic relevance, and appealed to the variable *usus* of language against the determinate assumptions of *modi*.

These criticisms concerning the accidentality of language can be compared with the complaint raised by modern commentators that these universal rules are based on the single language of Latin, and follow traditional classifications of Latin grammarians which may be inappropriate to other languages. Yet this criticism is also conversely a source of interest. Medieval logic, unlike modern symbolic logic, was based on the natural forms of Latin. The Latin language provided the virtually exclusive medium for logic; it also provided the principal practical material of philosophical enquiry. This language was both living—its constant use meant that it developed continuously until the antiquarian concerns of the humanists effectively fossilized it in a pristine neo-classical form— and yet also artificial, since the technical requirements of philosophy demanded rigorous forms of terminology not available in nature. It is this fact which makes medieval study of language—even the most 'speculative'—always intensely grammatical no matter how logicalized the study became. But it is also probably responsible for the extremely divergent reputation it has enjoyed: from its championing by modern historians of philosophy and linguistics, to its rubbishing by even the most sympathetic of traditional historians of grammar and philology.[45]

By the time of Erasmus, speculative grammar as an active tradition had run its course. But in a derivative form the *modi significandi* still dominated the theory by which language was understood. In a backhanded way,

---

[42] Pinborg denies the imputation, p. 264.

[43] See the quotations from Gerard of Zütphen's commentary quoted in Heath, 'Logical grammar', p. 48.

[44] Quoted by Pinborg, p. 267. Bacon's criticisms concerned especially the theory of intentionality implicit in the concept of *impositio*. Cf. Derrida's attack on 'la métaphysique de la présence' in *De la grammatologie*, where he refers to the *modistae* (p. 71).

[45] See Marenbon, *Later Medieval Philosophy*, p. 137; contrast Thurot, p. 148 and Chomarat, *Grammaire et rhétorique*, i. 218.

the fierceness of Erasmus's satire is a tribute to the rich legacy of medieval theory of language. Scholastic grammar was not ignorant of, or uninterested in, Latin usage. It attempted to describe a language and at the same time to understand how that language comes to mean. In some cases, it attempted a general theory as to how meaning works altogether. Erasmus's appeal to usage appeared to bypass such concerns by making all linguistic questions a matter of surface. Deep questions of meaning he affected to leave to others. It is best not to take such innocent claims at face value. The application of the methods of humanism to the ideological centre of European culture, the Bible, was an action designed to be as controversial as possible. Grammatical culture was about to become bloody indeed.

III SCHOLASTIC LUTHER OR HUMANIST LUTHER?

No doubt the history of Western Christianity would have been different if it had followed Erasmus's principles to the letter. It was a matter of bitter regret to Erasmus that it did not, an emotion shared, if only half knowingly, by many historians. Erasmus assumed that a reformation in literature would produce a reformation in religion, indeed that a reformed religion was only possible if undertaken according to the new rules of language. Instead, Christian Europe was thrown into convulsion by the Lutheran controversy. To Erasmus, this was an alarming and violent distraction. It was also a cause of bewilderment, because Luther appeared to follow different literary criteria altogether.

Superficially, they had much in common. Luther was a scourge of the 'sophisms' of the late medieval schools, publicly so after the *Disputatio contra scholasticam theologiam* of 1517 (WA 1). Although the main object of this attack was the theological treatment of the doctrine of grace in the work of fifteenth-century schoolmen such as Biel, it also repudiated the way in which such theology was justified by means of arguments borrowed from the Arts faculty. Luther, like Erasmus, took issue with this theology by routinely questioning Aristotelian terminology.[46]

However, what makes Luther's public antipathy to scholasticism different from Erasmus's is that he was himself a scholastic. Luther was schooled in scholasticism and spent almost his whole adult life in universities. Erfurt, where he took his BA and his MA, was a civic university, one

---

[46] For instance, the set of theses against the use of Aristotle in theology in *Disputatio contra scholasticam theologiam*, Th. 41–53 (WA 1.226).

of the oldest foundations in the empire, in a prosperous and populous city.[47] By 1500 it was the third largest in Germany, with a high academic reputation. While theology was well established as a result of the *studia generalia* set up by the three mendicant orders—Dominicans, Franciscans, and Augustinians—each of which provided a separate chair in theology—Erfurt's eminence lay in the teaching of the Arts faculty.[48] Erfurt (along with Heidelberg and Tübingen) was one of the centres of German nominalism, with a special reputation for logic. Although the statutes did not prescribe the *via moderna*, the favoured authors of study were all of this *via*, including William of Ockham, Marsilius of Inghen, Gregory of Rimini, and the derivative works of home-grown masters such as Johan Rucherat of Wesel.[49]

In 1497, logical studies at Erfurt entered an interesting phase. The two most notable professors in the Arts faculty joined together to establish a systematic programme of teaching in logic, following distinctive nominalist criteria. Oberman describes this as a 'real breakthrough' because of the way that it embodied a set of intellectual principles in a change in curriculum.[50] The two professors, Jodokus Trutfetter and Bartholomäus Arnoldi von Usingen, applied these principles over the next few years in textbooks of their own. Trutfetter published commentaries on most of the logical set books, along with two separate handbooks of logic, and a small *summa* of natural philosophy.[51] The works on logic went into many editions. He wrote no theological or devotional works, although late in life he took the degree of doctor of theology. Arnoldi was a few years younger, and did not rise to quite the same eminence in his field, but his writings include introductions to natural philosophy, logic, and grammar.

When Luther entered the university he had no reason to feel he was studying subjects in terminal decline, as Reformation history once implied. Luther's later remarks suggest that he was a proud member of his school. In 1520 he was still prepared to call Ockham the greatest of dialecticians, and the *Table Talk* evinces praise for Ockham for his painstaking methods of analysis.[52] The young Luther often referred to himself as one of the *moderni*, and his colleagues and the university authorities were not in

---

[47] Rashdall, *Universities of Europe*, ii. 345–50.   [48] Oberman, *Dawn*, pp. 115–16.
[49] Brecht, *Road to Reformation*, p. 34; see Kleineidam, *Universitas Studii Erffordensis*, ii. 21–37.
[50] Oberman, *Dawn*, p. 118: see Kleineidam, ii. 147–51.
[51] The logical works were *Breviarium dialecticum* (1500) and *Summula totius logicae* (1501).
[52] WA 6.600.11; Oberman, *Dawn*, p. 120. Brecht, *Road to Reformation*, p. 37.

any doubt of this. There is corroborating evidence from Luther's early appointments. In 1507 it appears that Frederick the Wise decided that his new university in Wittenberg, until now part of the revival of the *via antiqua*, should also have nominalism represented in its curriculum. Trutfetter was persuaded as a result to join the faculty of theology as professor. In 1510 he returned to Erfurt, but in looking for someone to maintain the interests of the *via moderna*, who better than his precocious former student Martin Luther?[53]

Luther retained a warm regard for his former teachers, and the respect was mutual, although it was compromised by the politics of the church. Arnoldi, under his pupil's influence, himself entered the Augustinian monastery in 1512, but later opposed the reformation in Erfurt, publishing defences of the doctrines of merit in good works and of purgatory.[54] Luther in a letter to Trutfetter credited him with being the first to teach him that belief can only be based on the authority of the biblical books, and that critical judgement is to be reserved for all other texts. Yet he also criticized Trutfetter for his failure to live up to such a biblical programme.[55] Trutfetter, he says, will no longer consider his pupil a theologian, since he is no longer a *logicus*.[56]

This remark, directed to his former professor, himself a notable *logicus* and a professional theologian, is crucial to an understanding of Luther's development, and symptomatic of his change of mind on the relationship between philosophy and theology. The polarization of the two concepts in Luther's polemic centred on his virulent attacks on Aristotle, a particular rebuff to Trutfetter since a reappraisal of the texts of Aristotle was one of the chief points of his academic programme. But here too there are considerable ambiguities, as Luther's own works show how thorough Trutfetter's teaching of Aristotle was.[57]

Whereas Luther's outward theology—his public arguments and manifestos of justification and grace—chastized the received intellectual views of Biel and other nominalists, his methods and manners of dispute continued to share the same educational heritage.[58] Long after his theological arguments bypassed his Erfurt teachers Trutfetter and Arnoldi, his ways of expressing these arguments remained under their influence. In this sense,

---

[53] Grossmann, *Humanism in Wittenberg*, pp. 68–9 and 77; Luther did not take Trutfetter's chair directly, being very much his junior.

[54] Brecht, *Road to Reformation*, p. 36.

[55] Luther to Trutfetter, 9 May 1518, WA Br. 1.171.72. See Brecht, p. 35.

[56] Tibi videor non esse logicus, WA Br 1.170.37.

[57] Oberman, *Dawn*, p. 121.   [58] McGrath, p. 36; Brecht, *Road to Reformation*, p. 38.

he may not have been such a good judge of his own mind when he said that he had ceased to be a *logicus*. He may have ceased to believe in logic as the arbiter of all the problems of knowledge, but his mind still followed the methods of the *disputatio* and the hermeneutic practices of the *glossator*.

At the height of his quarrel with Luther in 1526, Erasmus dismissed his opponent as a Sophist.[59] It was the worst insult he could think of. For Erasmus, Luther had gone native. Luther's errant theology was the inevitable result of his retrograde grammar. Erasmus promoted a view that Luther's method and doctrine are out of step. This underestimates the forces at work in the medieval grammar Luther was appropriating to new ends, and it also underestimates the contradictions at work within the crisis of linguistic disciplines that constitutes the 'humanist' programme. Whereas Erasmus sees the battle lines in terms of the choices of polemic, the forces of argument about language emerge as more ambiguous and more persistently and pervasively influential.

Despite Erasmus's polemical caricature of Luther as an unrecon-structed Sophist, Luther's own remarks on the theory and practice of grammar bear out a more complex history. Early in 1524, the same year as Erasmus's attack, Luther reviewed the state of German education in a pamphlet urging the Christian reform of city schools.[60] He also published a Latin version in 1525 with the markedly humanist title *De constituendis scholis*. In this tract he shows a lively concern for the changes taking place in the instruction of Latin and a ready sympathy for humanist arguments. In words Erasmus would approve, he declares that scholarship in the original tongues has brought a new light into the Christian world and has opened the door to the gospel. For this reason, teaching in the ancient languages is vital to the evangelical mission:

we will not long preserve the gospel without the languages. The languages are the sheath in which the sword of the spirit is contained . . . the vessel in which the wine is held.[61]

The Reformation needs scholarship and learning, in order to obtain sound texts and accurate readings. Such knowledge is required not only for the élite but for the whole Christian people, so that a revival of schools is necessary to the renewal of grace. In Bornkamm's gloss of Luther, it is not

---

[59] *Hyperaspistes*, LB, x. 1344C (*Atque hic Lutherus in re sophistica bis Sophistam agit*).
[60] *An die Radherrn aller Stedte deutsches lands: dass sie Christliche schulen auffrichten und halten sollen.*
[61] WA 15.38.7; *LW*, 45, 360. Cf. Ephesians 6: 17.

'enthusiasm' but 'grammar' which does the work of the spirit.[62] Grammar is an instrument of grace, and the grammar schools its nursery.

But the grammar he has in mind is not the scholastic training of his youth. Indeed, he could not sound more Erasmian:

it is not my intention either to have such schools established as we have had heretofore, when a boy slaved away at his Donatus and Alexander for twenty or thirty years and still learned nothing. Today we are living in a different world, and things are done differently   (WA 15.46.23; *LW* 45, 370)

Luther ridicules the 'useless and harmful books' which used to fill the libraries of monasteries, the *Catholicon, Florista, Graecismus, Labyrinthus,* and the *Dormi securi*. His attitude to the old world of grammar has the zeal of Erasmus or the great German humanist Jacob Wimpfeling: 'because of such books the Latin language was ruined' (*LW* 45, 374). He recommends instead the example not only of the scriptures but of the poets and orators, pagan or Christian, Greek or Latin, 'for it is from such books that one must learn grammar' (*LW* 45, 376).

Along such lines, Luther consistently extolled grammar as the most useful of arts, underlying all forms of learning, and above all theology.[63] In his polemical statements, he therefore sounds the model humanist. Yet his own grammatical analysis shows more varied sympathies. This is not surprising, since the Alexander he here vilifies was the companion of his youth. His education was typical in starting with Donatus before progressing to the *Doctrinale*.[64] In private conversation, he acknowledged Donatus as *optimus grammaticus*.[65] As with many humanists, an espousal of anti-scholastic rhetoric does not mean a divorce from scholastic methods, or from the textbook sources so noisily condemned. Until Alexander finally disappeared from schools (that is, at least until after 1525) a denunciation of the *Doctrinale* indicates party interest rather than an abandonment of his principles. Continued attention to Alexander often accompanied a sensitivity to the normative descriptions of (for instance) the widely admired Perotti, and renewed study of the common source of both Alexander *and* Perotti, the ever-reliable Priscian.

Luther's terminology is mobile, showing no consistent affiliation to a

---

[62] *Luther in Mid-Career*, p. 140.

[63] For instance in 1519, during reforms of the Wittenberg syllabus; WA 6.29.7.

[64] Brecht, *Road to Reformation*, pp. 13–14. Luther makes no direct reference to being taught Priscian.

[65] WA TR 3, No. 3490. Luther considers the usefulness of Donatus to depend on the teacher; in TR No.3561A he admits Donatus could be a torture.

particular linguistic doctrine. This is not of itself surprising. Only in the caricature of Erasmus and others do scholastic and humanist methods appear absolutely divorced. Ockham was using the term *usus loquendi* long before the humanist critique in order to attack the semantic reductionism of *modi significandi*. In any case, a penchant for the new grammar is not irreconcilable with a scholastic bias in logic. Among those campaigning for greater latitude in grammatical teaching at Tübingen in the 1490s were Johann von Staupitz, the prior of the Augustinians, later Luther's superior, and Johannes Nathin, Luther's future logical master. While Staupitz followed the *via antiqua*, Nathin was a notable nominalist: which shows how complex the network of linguistic and theological method was.

In Germany, Perotti's humanist grammar was popularized in the form of an adaptation by a Viennese writer, Bernhard Perger. Perger commended his work by tracing it to Priscian and Donatus, distinguishing it from the *ambages variaque dubia* which he attributes to his medieval predecessors.[66] New grammatical work subsequently flourished especially at Tübingen in the efforts of Heinrich Bebel and his pupils, Jacob Heinrichmann, Johannes Altenstaig, and Johannes Brassicanus.[67] Brassicanus's *Grammaticae Institutiones* states that the criterion of good Latin is not *ratio* but *exempla*.[68]

In order to account for the flexible sympathies of Luther's grammar there is no need to search for widely divergent sources, in the manner of those protestant scholars who have been determined to find a humanist Luther in order to make his credentials impeccably anti-scholastic. Late medieval scholasticism is not monolithic; rather it is notably eclectic and flexible in relation to both method and source. Exemplification of this can be found in Arnoldi and Trutfetter. Arnoldi produced a short *interpretatio* of Donatus's *Ars minor* in about 1505, called the *Figure Donati*. His definition of grammar follows the formula characteristic of the humanists: *Grammatica est recte scribendi et loquendi scientia* (A4^r). However, he prefers to call it a 'science' rather than an 'art', and his gloss of this formula shows him attentive to the student's need not only *recte legere* but also *recte intelligere*. Throughout this work, in fact, Arnoldi freely mixes description

---

[66] *Grammatica nova* (Basle, 1506); see Heath, 'Logical grammar', p. 17. Wimpfeling quotes liberally from Perger.

[67] Bebel used Valla's *Elegantiae* as well as Perotti, Sulpitius, Mancinelli, and Manutius. Heinrichmann was a professor of law, Altenstaig of theology; Brassicanus a teacher of Latin outside the university until 1509. See Heath, pp. 24–8.

[68] *Grammaticae institutiones*, A1^r. See Padley, *Latin Tradition*, p. 31.

of usage with short appraisals of principles of signification. He follows the framework of Donatus, and uses many of his definitions *verbatim*, but his analysis is self-consciously more systematic, with elaborate divisions and subdivisions, each explained as following rational principles. As for his sources, he ranges freely, quoting frequently from Alexander of Villedieu, but also from the humanist Antonio Mancinelli.[69] At one moment, he subdivides nouns by means of the logical distinction between *nomen syncathegorematicum* and *cathegorematicum*; at another, he approves Valla's preference for the term *verba participialia* in place of *gerundia* (C6ʳ).[70]

Trutfetter shows similarly varied sources for his textbook on logic, the *Summule totius logice* of 1501. He lists his *authores* as a Preface to the work: they include, as well as standard patristic and scholastic masters, a large number of nominalists: Ockham, Holcot, Gregory of Rimini, Pierre d'Ailly, Biel. But they also include Valla and Perotti; and Trutfetter does not hesitate, even in a treatise of logic, to include literary examples from Horace and Virgil as well as the more obviously relevant Cicero.

Luther is no different from his Erfurt masters, then, in attempting to reconcile nominalism with humanism, and his use of *modi significandi*, however unwitting, may also derive from his mother university, which took pride in the work of the illustrious speculative grammarian, Thomas of Erfurt. In the context of Erfurt nominalism, it is not unusual for him to be concerned with questions of the norms of usage, or for him to mix such concerns with a discussion of signification, however antipathetic this might be to a humanist treatment of usage.

It is not possible in this context to give an answer to the question of whether Luther was a scholastic or a humanist. Put so rigidly, it seems to be the wrong question, for it fails to see what happens when a theory of language is in flux. Different grammars collide, in ways that elude the grammarian's own knowledge. Scholastic methods are applied to humanist problems, and vice versa. One area where the divergence between scholastic and humanist method was at its widest was the grammar of mood. Mood was a key element in medieval language theory. The scholastics were masters of the logic of modality, and had developed centuries of expertise in dealing with it. At the same time, mood was a test case for the humanist concern with usage. Humanist grammars gradually discovered new seas of enquiry by drawing attention to the vast and confusing range of ways in

---

[69] E.g. B3ʳ, C4ʳ, D1ᵛ.
[70] Although here he may be following Priscian ii. 54.5 (see Kretzmann, in *CHLMP*)—but of course, this is a definition abandoned by humanist users of Priscian.

which language uses mood in everyday speech. The late scholastic masters who were exposed to humanism urgently attempted to make sense of this. Yet the gulf between a semantic understanding of mood and a formal one was to prove unbridgable.

Arnoldi, for instance, gives a list of five moods. He also supplies a general theory for their semantic value: to qualify something modally is *significare sub certa inclinatione animi vel indifferenter* ('to signify that something is done by a certain desire of the mind or else indifferently').[71] But he gives no semantic account of the *imperativus*, for example, beyond identifying it as the mood *quod imperatore seu hortatore significat* ('which signifies commanding or urging', D1ᵛ): a definition which is simply a tautology.

There are two ways of classifying moods in medieval discussion, both of which Arnoldi uses, although without reconciling them. Donatus, on the one hand, identifies mood simply by formal inflections. The indicative mood is *lego*, the imperative *lege*, the optative *legerem*, and the subjunctive (or *coniunctivus*) *legam*.[72] On the other hand, Priscian attempts an overall definition of mood itself as a grammatical feature: *modi sunt diversae inclinationes animi, varios eius affectus demonstrantes* ('the moods are the different inclinations of the mind, showing their various dispositions [emotions?]').[73] He therefore attempts to differentiate moods not just by morphology but by signification. For instance, the *indicativus, quo indicamus vel definimus* ('by which we indicate or define'); and the *imperativus, quo imperamus aliis, ut faciant aliquid vel patiantur* ('by which we order other people to do something or to have something done to them').[74]

Even Donatus finds it difficult, none the less, to exclude semantic criteria completely. He recognizes this implicitly by admitting that *legam* is also called (by some) *promissivus* as well as *coniunctivus*: that is, the same inflection seems to have different functions and meanings. In this case, he is consistent with his formal principles, rejecting the category of *promissivus* in order to retain only one mood for each inflection. But in the case of *legerem*, he assigns this to a separate mood (*optativus*), whereas modern grammarians would call it another subjunctive, the changed ending indicating rather the future tense. In any case, Donatus already

---

[71] D1ᵛ. The five moods are *indicativus, imperativus, optativus, coniunctivus, infinitivus*; Arnoldi omits the *promissivus* and *impersonalis* (cf. Donatus, *Ars maior*, ed. Keil, *Grammatici Latini*, iv. 381).

[72] *Ars minor*, ed. Keil, *Grammatici Latini*, iv. 359; cf. also *Ars maior*, ii (*Grammatici Latini*, iv. 381).

[73] *Institutiones*, viii. 63 (*Grammatici Latini*, ii. 421).

[74] *Institutiones*, viii. 63 (*Grammatici Latini*, ii. 421); viii. 67 (*Grammatici Latini*, ii. 423).

uses semantic terms (*imperativus*, etc.), albeit without supplying any semantic explanation.

Priscian, on the other hand, has the opposite problem that his definitions seem to be driven by psychological descriptions, which invade his grammatical categorizations. By importing the terminology of *inclinationes animi*, he begs the question of how these mental categories correspond to grammatical forms in the first place. He himself recognizes this, stating for instance that we use the imperative not only when *imperantes* ('giving orders') but very frequently when *orantes* ('praying, begging').[75] Peter Helias in his commentary identified this problem, and sought to clarify the relation between mental and linguistic categories by redefining grammatical mood as indicating not the relation of the mind to expression in language, but (in strictly linguistic terms) only of the verb to the grammatical subject. This clarification was repeated favourably by the *modistae*.[76] However, for individual moods, their discussion was still almost entirely reliant on Priscian.

The *modistae* give no indication of what the individual moods actually signify. Arnoldi—and many humanists with him—tried to obviate this by means of an apparently unexceptionable tautology (borrowed in any case conveniently from Priscian): the *imperativus* signifies that we *imperamus*. Yet it is only an accident of technical vocabulary that results in the form *lege* being called 'imperative'. For *lege* is used not only to order, but also (as Priscian notes) to beg, or it could be added, to exhort, implore, request or let off steam. Arnoldi hedged his bets by adding only a *hortativus*. There is no end to the terms that might be added. In one direction, Melanchthon shows the discipline of formal description, limiting himself to the indicative, imperative, subjunctive, and infinitive. Yet even he cannot resist adding in the optative by the back door. Brassicanus does the same.[77] Later humanist grammars allowed a Pandora's box of moods to suit every occasion. The history of grammar is littered with unsuccessful attempts to enumerate the moods which language elicits. To take one classic modern example, Otto Jespersen, the eminent philologist, invented what amounts to a thesaurus of moods to correspond to the nuances of inclination. Humanist attention to usage raised the spectre of a grammar without

[75] He gives examples from Virgil, *Aeneid*, i. and viii; *Institutiones*, viii. 63 (*Grammatici Latini*, ii. 424).

[76] E.g. quoted by Thomas of Erfurt, *Grammatica speculativa*, ed. Bursill-Hall, p. 224; Thomas describes the five moods as 'five differences of quality'.

[77] Melanchthon, *Elementa Latinae grammatices*, F2ᵛ–F3ʳ; Brassicanus, *Grammatice institutiones*, M1ʳ. The imperative is *quo imperamus*, the optative *quo aliquid optamus*. The conjunctive is distinguished by syntactic rather than semantic means.

limits. Every usage seemed to require a new grammar to explain it. At times—as in Erasmus's great work *De copia verborum ac rerum* (1512)—it seemed as if the only true grammar would consist in a list of all the possible ways of saying things within the language.

<h2>IV HUMANISM AND THE *MODI SIGNIFICANDI*</h2>

A conflict between the descriptive account of usage championed by humanism and the semantic analysis of meaning practised in the late medieval schools was inevitable. The *modi significandi* were the focus of the humanist critique of scholastic grammar, as shown by Erasmus's description of its 'cruel torments' working to discourage good speaking habits.[78] As with many aspects of Erasmus's humanism, this critique can be traced back to Valla. One of Valla's last works, a sermon 'in praise of Thomas Aquinas' presented in Rome in 1457, demurs the current fashion for *metaphysica et modos significandi*, satirizing the starry-eyed enthusiasm of the theologians for *modi* and calling them instead *impedimenta* to true knowledge.[79]

Erasmus makes many of his comments about scholastic grammar more as clichés confirming party chic than as informed polemic.[80] Erasmus was part of the second generation of critique. At his school in Deventer, many of the causes he later espoused had already been fought when he was a boy. His teacher, Johannes Synthen, and the director of the school, Alexander Hegius, rejected the grammatical works of both Eberhard of Béthune and John of Garland and reformed the elementary study of Latin.[81] Indeed, Hegius was himself the author of a short treatise attacking the *modi significandi*. Hegius rejected the transformation of grammar into rules of signification, or distinctions of *essentiales et accidentales, materiales et formales*.[82] The only proper disqualification for a *grammaticus* is an inability 'to speak and write correctly' (§2). This, he insinuates sarcastically, is the distinction achieved by the *modistae*. To prove his case, he proffers a

---

[78] Overfield, *Humanism and Scholasticism*, p. 76.

[79] The sermon was given to the Dominican order at S. Maria Sopra Minerva three months before his death; *Opera Omnia*, ii. 339–52, this ref. ii. 350. For Valla on the *Doctrinale*, see *Opera Omnia*, ii. 87–96.

[80] Chomarat, *Grammaire et rhétorique*, i. 186.

[81] Chomarat, i. 186. John of Garland's books in fact criticize both the *Doctrinale* and the *Graecismus* of Eberhard (e.g. *Compendium Grammatice*, ed. Haye, p. 63).

[82] 'Invectiva', §2, p. 306; the first part (§§1–10) was published *c*.1480; a revised version was published in 1501 after Hegius's death in 1498.

catalogue of howlers, *orationes ... barbaras et viciosas*, committed by these so-called grammarians (§§5–10).

Concealed within these familiar complaints about incorrect usage is a more sophisticated criticism. Hegius says the *modistae* have introduced alternative grammatical inflections as a way of regularizing grammar into their universal semantic pattern. In Latin, one verb will take an accusative and another a genitive, apparently at random. But the *modistae* are not content to leave language as they find it, and create an artificial semantic orthodoxy at the expense of correct speech. Hegius, on the other hand, with his pedantic insistence on the original locutions, expresses his faith in the arbitrary forms of language.

Synthen, in a commentary on the *Doctrinale* to which Hegius contributed, remarks on the discrepancy between logical rules and grammatical facts. Logicians, he says, articulate four different species of cause (following Aristotle): material, formal, efficient, and final. But grammar does not follow these distinctions. The same grammatical function can be used to imply two different logical relations, with a resulting ambiguity (*amphibologia*) between them. The phrase *epistola Pauli* can mean either that Paul wrote the letter or that it belongs to him—that is, the genitive case can signify either cause or possession. Logic has to create a new expression (*epistola est Pauli*) to establish a distinction which grammar does not dictate.

Similar elements are in evidence in what became a general tirade against the *modi significandi* among those professing the cause of *bonae litterae*. An example is Jacob Wimpfeling's *Isidoneus Germanicus*, an educational manifesto addressed to the German princes which was influential in the reform of German schools and universities. Wimpfeling criticizes *modi significandi* because they lead to 'barbarous' speaking practices, and also because they involve *argumentationes multa dubia & quaestiones de quis & qui*.[83] Its methods involve *perplexa* and *ambages* ('circumlocutions' and 'ambiguities'). Due to its position in the curriculum, boys are too young for it and too much time is spent on it. The result has been that *etiam suos discipulos insanire coegit* ('it has even turned its pupils insane' (cap.xviii).

Wimpfeling does not feel obliged to make more specific criticisms: he does not dispute a philosophical approach to language *per se*.[84] His alter-

---

[83] *Isidoneus Germanicus*, cap. xiii, B3^r. Wimpfeling was also a noted theologian; on the intersection of his work between humanism and theology, see Rummel, *Humanist–Scholastic Debate*, pp. 75–7.

[84] His criticisms of *modi* indiscriminately mix up Alexander, Peter Helias, the *Catholicon*, the *Florista*, and even John of Garland.

native grammar is nevertheless instructive. Teaching methods should abandon 'useless superfluities' and concentrate on what is 'strictly necessary', doing so *clare, distincte et examplariter* ('clearly, distinctly, and using examples', E1ᵛ). This last word *exemplariter* strikes a keynote: grammar works by examples, and thereby sets an example. The true aim of instruction is not a theory of signification, but precepts for elegant composition and *flores poetarum*.

Such criticisms are repeated again and again in the first decades of the sixteenth century. Wimpfeling, like Valla before him and Erasmus after, presented his case as a preference for the authors of classical antiquity. These authors, he suggests, have the best Latin style and the most salutary effect on morals and manners. There has been a tendency in modern criticism to take the humanists at their word on such principles. Such a view has entrenched the humanist prejudice—widely repeated in satiric writings—that scholastic philosophers had either no interest in, or else a violent antipathy to, the teaching of the ancient classics.[85] Primary evidence for this is sketchy and is usually based on the absence of specific prescription of classical authors in university statutes—whereas even textbooks were often omitted from the statutes. Individual cases where evidence does survive suggest a different picture. There is much evidence of sympathy and support for new academic initiatives, both in the promulgation of the ancients, and in the improvement of Latinity. Luther's friendly correspondence with Conrad Mutian is an example.[86]

Controversy over the acceptability of pagan authors is not the true issue in the academic quarrels of the late fifteenth and early sixteenth centuries.[87] The humanist method demolished the link between grammar and logic which lay at the basis of scholastic method. Scholastic disquiet was not due to the effect on grammar but on the two subjects closest to its heart: logic and theology. The established order of studies in the Arts faculties of universities was threatened. The concentration on *exempla* at the expense of *ratio* meant that semantic analysis of language was ignored as outside the proper concerns of *grammatica*. The Arts faculties were at first sympathetic to the pedagogic benefits of a more practical form of language teaching, but gradually it became clear that a lack of foundation in linguistic analysis affected the competence—and the enthusiasm—of

[85] For instance, in *Epistolae Obscurorum Virorum* and Conrad Mutian.
[86] E.g. Luther to Mutian, 29 May 1516, WA Br. 1.40. Mutian in turn was sympathetic to the Reformation. Rummel reassesses the relation of the humanists and the reformers in *Confessionalization of Humanism*, pp. 11–22.
[87] Heath, 'Logical Grammar'.

students for the more developed logical studies of the scholastic programme. The *Doctrinale* and the *modi significandi* had played an important part in the continuous structure of the *trivium*.

The reform of grammar provided an alternative interest in the processes of language by replacing a theory based on the logical proposition with one based on usage and context. This had dramatic effects on the theory and practice of logic. The disturbance in the educational structure explains two long-standing puzzles in the history of sixteenth-century language theory. One is the demise of the *Doctrinale* as a textbook—which saw 150 editions in the early years of printing, and another 100 after 1500, but which disappeared from the presses (at least in Germany) suddenly in 1525.[88] The other is the extraordinary (and equally sudden) vogue for Agricola's *De inventione dialectica*. This became a seminal text in the sixteenth century, but for nearly fifty years had remained largely unknown until an explosion of interest in the 1520s.[89] This new susceptibility to the ideas of Agricola may be traced to the emerging principles of a grammar based on usage. Agricola 'shifts the emphasis from the analysis of term and proposition to organization and construction of argument'.[90] Hence his fascination with *loci* or 'place-logic', a concentration on the topics of argumentation rather than its structure.

However, this transformation in grammatical theory was a gradual process, and more complicated than it appears in retrospect. The disappearance of Alexander's *Doctrinale*, while sudden, was late in coming. Even those who took up the new grammar did not reject it out of hand. Perger used it substantially even in the process of providing a version for German use of Perotti's *Rudimenta*. Synthen and Hegius, while undermining its philosophical basis, none the less collaborated in a commentary on it. Other grammarians created an eclectic mix of old and new grammars without seeing any contradiction.[91] At least at first, the complaint against the *Doctrinale* seems to have been that it was too complicated for elementary use, too prone to 'digressions' to captivate the modern student.

The period in Germany of the most intense debate concerning

---

[88] These figures are from Reichling, pp. xliv–xlviii. The *Doctrinale* continued to appear in northern Italy for some time; Reichling records one from Brescia as late as 1588 (p. xlvi).

[89] The Agricola phenomenon is reinvestigated in Jardine, *Erasmus*. Editions are listed in Ong's *Ramus and Talon Inventory*. On Agricola's significance, see Ong, *Ramus*, ch. 5.

[90] Heath, p. 62.

[91] E.g. in the *Compendium totius grammaticae* (Oxford, 1483) by John Anwykyll, the grammar master of Magdalen College School, Oxford, which combined elements of Valla, Perotti, and Alexander's *Doctrinale*; Weis, *Humanism in England*, p. 169.

grammar, and the most controversial attempts at reform of the curriculum, occurred between 1500 and 1515. Here too, however, the picture is complicated. Erfurt debated the grammatical textbooks for ten years before abandoning the medieval model in 1515. Vienna, too, brought in Perotti and reduced prescribed use of the *Doctrinale*. Leipzig, on the other hand, shows a different pattern. In 1502 reforms were introduced with the support of the duke; but in 1508 there was a move back in favour of the grammar of Donatus and Alexander, and the logic of Peter of Spain. In 1511 the reasons were clarified by the Dean of the Arts faculty (hardly an impartial observer, of course), who declared that the 1502 changes had endangered the university's high reputation in philosophy.[92]

In Tübingen, the proliferation of new grammatical writing was not consistently reflected in the curriculum. In 1496 the Augustinian canons pleaded that their students, who were learning from Perotti's *Grammatica nova*, be admitted to the Arts faculty, and the faculty complied, even admitting that Perotti might be more appropriate to grammatical exercises than 'the long digressions of Alexander'.[93] Bebel's programme of reforms subsequently created a conflict among the masters of Arts, which was formally resolved in 1505. In this, however, Donatus and Alexander were confirmed, and teachers were enjoined 'to retain the grammatical disputations and not pursue novelties'.[94] It may be, as Heath says, that it was as a riposte to this conservative decree that Brassicanus and Heinrichmann decided to publish their own grammatical teaching for a wider audience.[95]

It was only in the 1520s and 1530s that the humanist grammars gained general ascendancy. Wittenberg, as a new university, was in the vanguard of this process; but Leipzig and Tübingen also in turn overhauled the conservative decisions of the previous decade.[96] In 1531 a visitation at Tübingen reported that Alexander and Donatus were no longer taught to new students, being replaced by Brassicanus and Aldus Manutius. For the next generation of students, Melanchthon's grammar and dialectic quickly

---

[92] Altogether, at least seven universities instituted or debated reform in this period. See Overfield, p. 217. Accounts of individual universities in Overfield as follows: Erfurt, p. 221; Vienna, pp. 219–20; Leipzig, pp. 227, 229.

[93] Cited by Heath, p. 29. The Augustinian order was in general sympathetic to curricular innovation, a fact not insignificant for Luther.

[94] Heath, p. 30.

[95] There are dangers in depending too exclusively on either statutes (which reinforce a conservative stasis) or new publications (which give the impression of exciting flux). Padley especially tends towards a latter view. Brassicanus may reflect frustration with a failure to implement favourable reforms.

[96] Overfield, pp. 298–9.

gained ascendency (especially, but not exclusively, in protestant territories).[97] This new pattern of education was repeated all over Germany.

It is evident that the age of Erasmus and Luther represented a crisis of studies in Northern Europe. The approach to grammar that had dominated intellectual training for three hundred years was, in the course of a generation, subverted and ultimately supplanted. The old approach was founded in a sophisticated philosophical theory of signification, which was then applied to the natural forms of language. The new approach resisted abstract analysis of signification and claimed to consist instead in an entirely descriptive account of usage. With the benefit of hindsight we can see that the understanding of language was becoming fundamentally different, with profound consequences for the intellectual history of the seventeenth and eighteenth centuries.

The domino effect which made the new grammar undermine traditional practice in logic was equally significant in its effect on theology. Theology stood at the apex of the medieval system of learning. The most important practitioners of language theory—from Abelard to Aquinas to Ockham—were also theologians. Indeed, much of the most interesting philosophical thinking on language was pursued in the middle ages not in the Arts faculty but in the theological faculty. In a general way, medieval logic and theology are difficult to separate: theology provided a constantly renewed source of problems, for which an ever-more refined logic was required as the only solution to its intricacies. In the life of the medieval schools the two disciplines worked hand in hand, so that it is hard to say whether logic developed according to the dictates of theological requirement, or whether theology chose its targets in order to provide suitable challenges for logic.

One reason for this is simply that every practitioner in theology was required first to study an Arts course, either in a university or, in the case of mendicants, within their religious order. All theologians were thus masters of grammar and logic. However, whereas this might imply that theologians merely transplanted into theology methods learned in the linguistic disciplines, the interrelation of subjects also worked in the other direction. For instance, Aristotle's works on logic provided special problems in relation to Christian metaphysics, which theologians needed to think through; but then in turn these problems in their new context posed the Aristotelian questions in new and complex forms. Medieval writers, there-

---

[97] Only with the *Index librorum prohibitorum* of Paul IV in 1559 did Melanchthon's work in general come to be seen as contaminated by his Lutheranism.

fore, did not separate theological from linguistic questions in the same way that modern writers might. Ockham, for example, developed his theory of universals at far greater length in his theological commentary on Lombard's *Sentences* than he did in his *Summa logicae* and other logical works.[98] For Ockham, the question is an enquiry into the nature of God first and only then of language.

A history of the relation between theology and logic or between theology and grammar is little different from a history of medieval thought. This is especially true of the problem which was about to become, courtesy of Luther, the most controversial problem in Western religion: divine providence. The theory of divine providence was one of the gothic splendours of medieval theology. It also lay at the centre of one of the highest arts in medieval logic. This is because of the way in which theological discussion of divine foreknowledge and human free will was bound up with linguistic theories of modality. On the one hand, it seems as if events in the future are contingent in such a way that it is unknowable in advance how they will turn out. On the other hand, events in the past seem to be describable in terms of causes and effects, such that one event follows another in determinable sequence. Past and future events are therefore described according to different principles, even though of course every future event in the nature of things in time becomes a past one. What was once contingent thus becomes determinate, the same event being described in radically different ways at different points in a temporal sequence.

Aristotle discussed this question in chapter 9 of his *De interpretatione*, with paradoxical and enigmatic results.[99] For, he says, it is axiomatic in every sentence that either *p* is true or *p* is not true (the fundamental principle of logic). It appears to follow also that for every sentence expressed in the future tense, either *p* will be the case or *p* will not be the case. Otherwise future tenses appear to follow different rules (and to possess different truth-values) from present tenses. Augustine and Boethius both recognized early that this problem in the logic of sentences and tense sequences created apparently undecideable difficulties when applied to divine knowledge. For God (presumably) knows the future already; in addition, his knowledge of future events will always be the same (since his knowledge is immutable) as his knowledge of past ones. Within God's knowledge, future events are therefore always determinate. And yet it is only

[98] In fact, twenty times as long as the relevant section in the *Summa logicae*, and forty times as long as the treatment in his commentary on Porphyry's *Isagoge*.

[99] *De interpretatione*, 18ª28–19ª39; see also *Metaphysics*, vi. 3. For analysis of both Greek and medieval versions of the argument, see Gaskin, *The Sea Battle and the Master Argument*.

within a contingent description of future tenses that human freedom appears to make any sense.

God presents acute problems for a theory of future contingents precisely because his knowledge is both infallible and immortal. Thus future tenses uttered by God (for instance, the divine plan ordained at creation, or divine prophecies in the Old Testament) behave like present or past tenses. Such questions entailed, often at the same time, adjustments and improvisations in both the theory of modality and the theology of sin and grace. Not surprisingly, the problem was debated over and over again, from Anselm in the eleventh century, through Peter Abelard, Peter Lombard, Robert Grosseteste, Aquinas, Scotus, to Ockham, Robert Holcot, Thomas Bradwardine, and others in the fourteenth century. In the latter stages, these debates were self-consciously taken up in relation to opposing views of human merit and divine grace in salvation. Bradwardine took up a strongly Augustinian view that God predestines everything, and justified it by means of an intricate theory of how God knows everything at once and yet 'sees' events in sequence as future, present, and past.[100] God thus has an understanding of temporal distinctions, not because he experiences things in sequence but in the act of causing them.[101] These questions were hotly debated in Oxford in the 1330s and in Paris in the 1340s, and they continued to reappear long after, with the same treatments exposed to further scrutiny in Louvain in the late fifteenth century in what came to be called *La Querelle des futurs contingents*.[102] In the sixteenth century, they were given new life in the concept of 'middle knowledge' developed by the Jesuit Luis de Molina.

Fourteenth-century writers such as Ockham concerned themselves with a whole range of problems where God's power tested ideas of modality to their limit. This took many forms. Any definition of 'possibility' had to be tested against a conception of a being for whom nothing was (by definition) impossible. Or again, Ockham tested the theory of consequence (of how a hypothesis relates to an inference) against propositions held to be impossible—such as the apparently valid but contradictory consequence 'God is not three persons; therefore God is not God'.[103] The very contradictoriness of such problems constituted their importance: for the rules of logic turned out to be insufficient and needed further refinement.[104] Medieval logic developed a specialist set of techniques for

---

[100] Normore, 'Future contingents', in *CHLMP*, pp. 374–6; see also Courtenay, *Schools and Scholars*, pp. 276–82.

[101] Bradwardine, *De causa Dei*, Bk iii, ch. 24, p. 699.   [102] Ed. Baudry (1950).

[103] Ockham, *Summa logicae*, iii/3, 42.

[104] 'Obligations', *CHLMP*, p. 332.

questions that seemed to be beyond logic: the *insolubilia*. In time a wild anthology of impossible problems grew up, from the merely difficult—'Can God undo the past?'—to the wilfully shocking—'God commands that none of his commandments, including this one, be obeyed'.[105]

The uncoupling of theology from its established practice in medieval grammatical method left room for something worse than controversy. The medieval arguments, however bitterly contested they might be, were based on a common set of principles as to how the arguments might be resolved. Humanism cast doubt on these principles, and exposed their practitioners to ridicule. Erasmus joined in this ridicule, and applied it especially to the traditions of scriptural exegesis. He offered to read the Bible in a completely new way. In the process, he exposed the new grammar as well as the new theology to enormous pressures.

V SPEECH ACTS: SOLECISMS AND FELICITIES

The revolution in theology, which was about to overtake sixteenth-century Europe, is profoundly connected to the shift in the understanding of language. Religion stands poised, dangerously, between an old culture and a new. Luther is but one, if the most prominent, example of this. The linguistic culture of the middle ages lives in him still, but it is combined with a yearning for the new. As this book will show, the tensions between cultures can be seen far beyond the theology faculty of the late medieval university. Consider the way that the theological discussion of linguistic modality could become a sixteenth-century joke. In Rabelais' *Tiers Livre* Panurge consults the theologian Hippothadée to divine whether or not he should marry. Panurge himself compares his problem to one of the *Insolubilia* of the French nominalist master Pierre d'Ailly (incidentally, one of Luther's own sources, and a favourite of Trutfetter). For he is consumed simultaneously by overwhelming sexual desire and overwhelming sexual anxiety, caught in the horns of a dilemma between marriage and cuckoldry. No matter how powerful his urge he refuses to act on it until he is convinced of the impossibility of his corresponding fears being realized. His problem is therefore an obscene version of a future contingent: he wishes to resolve in advance all the possible counterfactuals of libido and frustration.

In his search for truth, Panurge consults every imaginable form of divination, Virgilian lotteries, the throw of the dice, the interpretation of

---

[105] Courtenay, *Schools and Scholars*, p. 300.

dreams. In a final act of desperation, he places himself at the mercy of the logical and linguistic powers of the theologian in order to unravel the intractable knot of his hypothetical proposition. Hippothadée obliges with a virtuoso display of logical method, following through the dictates of the *quaestio* in a domesticated style: is Panurge's body subject to the demands of the flesh?—Yes; does he have the gift of continence?— No; therefore he must marry, since (in the Pauline cliché so beloved of monkish scholars) 'it is better to marry than to burn'. Panurge concurs, only to ask one last time the question direct, 'un petit scruple' he assures the divine, although in the circumstance it is a *quaestio difficilimus*, 'Seray je poinct coqu?' ('Will I become a cuckold?'). Faced with predicting God's predestined future, Hippothadée hedges his bets: '—Nenny dea, mon amy (respondit Hippothadée), si Dieu plaist' ('Indeed, my friend, if it please God').

Panurge reels from the theologian's equivocating if-clause in consternation:

—O, la vertus de Dieu (s'escria Panurge) nous soit en ayde! Où me renvoyez vous, bonnes gens? Aux conditionales, les quelles en Dialectique reçoivent toutes contradictions et impossibilitez   (*Tiers Livre*, p. 211)

['Oh the Lord help us!' exclaimed Panurge, 'Where are you driving me to, good people? To the conditionals, which in Logic admit of all contradictions and impossibilities', *Gargantua and Pantagruel*, tr. Cohen, p. 371].

Hippothadée's apologetic, hesitating entry into dialectic inspires in Panurge a *tour de force* of pastiche, as he reels off an improvisatory list of his own *obligationes*: 'if a mule could fly, a mule would have wings, if God pleases I shan't be a cuckold, and if God pleases, I shall'. The theologian has transported the unwitting Panurge to the unknown and unknowable mercies of the 'conseil privé de Dieu', to the court of God's secret intentions. Panurge's salvation rests on the interpretation of dizzyingly uninterpretible counterfactuals. God's provisos are unpreventable, leading inevitably to despair in any that dares to predict them. No trap is more dangerous than the linguistic trap of the future subjunctive, in which this passage of the *Tiers Livre* abounds, inveigling the unsuspecting reader as he treads unwarily through the beguilingly democratic prose.

Panurge's horror of subjunctive conditionals becomes all the more understandable in the context of the theologian's reply. This delivers a series of apparently reassuring propositions ('You will find that you will never be a cuckold') only to provide each one with a 'canonical qualification'. The proposition is made to dwindle ever further into unresolved hypothesis ('if you take the daughter of honest parents'). The theologian's discourse is bereft of the safe haven of the indicative mood, and leaves Panurge at sea in conditionals, lost in a contingently undecideable hypothesis which God only knows or can divine. No wonder, then, when Triboulet the fool arrives, that Panurge includes in his encyclopaedic list of suitable epithets the strange locution, 'fol modal' (p. 263), 'modal folly'.[106]

The crisis of sixteenth-century studies is more ambivalent than Erasmus's rough caricature would suggest. Rather than clinging to the wreckage of the old dialectic in defiance of the avant-garde of humanist dedication to usage, Luther is in fact directly concerned with usage. But he is, as Erasmus accuses him, attempting to apply a philosophical method: indeed, his problem is precisely that he is philosophizing about usage without an adequate technical framework. In other words, he suffers not from a superfluity of method but a lack of one.

Erasmus has an opposite problem: he attempts to describe usage without ever having recourse to arguments about meaning. His ideal seems to be grammar without semantics. This is the chimera of sixteenth-century reaction to medieval linguistic theory. Medieval grammarians distorted the natural habits of language, said Melanchthon in a well-worn phrase, because *dialecticen in grammatica trahebant, in dialectica grammaticen* ('they dragged dialectic into grammar, and grammar into dialectic').[107] Meaning for Erasmus is not something requiring long travails in the philosophy of language, but is a simple matter of custom and context. It is a process established in human history and actuated by human intercourse: to find out what we say and mean now we have only to investigate how things have been said and meant in the past. The elucidation of meaning thus requires either a living practice in the art of speaking a given language, or a lifetime of patience and learning in recreating that art. Such an education forms the basis of *bonae litterae*. It is no easy matter, and requires a painful discipline of minutiae, but it does not require a degree in logic or metaphysics.

Erasmus's account of meaning is a theory of speech acts. The *Ratio verae theologiae* summed up his exegetical method in a way suggestive of a general approach to language: the reader should attend 'not only to what is said, but also by whom it is said, to whom, with what words, and on what

---

[106] Among other epithets, Triboulet also receives the scholastic honorifics, 'fol latin', 'metaphysical', 'categorique', 'predicable', 'fol de seconde intention'.

[107] *Dialectices*, cited in Heath, p. 11.

time, on what occasion'.[108] He conceives of meaning in terms of an elementary account of performative utterance, to be judged as a form of illocutionary act.[109] Erasmus makes the claim for his interpretation repeatedly in the *Annotationes*: he approves a reading on the grounds that it is *simplex* or *simplicior*; such readings are said to be in natural accord with the *germanam sententiam*.[110] Having asserted that their respective interpretations are *simplex* and *germana*, what are they to do when the opponent retorts that these senses are not at all evident, but 'distortions' and pernicious nonsense? Erasmus is forced to do exactly what he has denied is either practicable or useful. He has to supply at the very least a theory of how grammatical forms correspond to meanings, if not of how meaning is grammaticalized in forms.

From the time of Valla, humanism sought to find new ways of answering these questions, in ways that corresponded to ordinary Latin usage rather than to the rules of speculative grammar or syllogistic logic. The *Elegantiae* survey the landscape of the Latin language and attempt to understand its formation in terms of natural rules of distinction.[111] In the *Dialecticae disputationes*, Valla extended the grammatical interests of the *Elegantiae* into a more formal treatment of the logic of everyday speech.[112] By the time of Erasmus, with a fuller assimilation of Agricolan method, humanist dialectic was becoming an independent subject. One example admired by Erasmus was *In pseudodialecticos* by Juan Luis Vives, published in early 1520.[113] Vives's work is acutely alive to the philosophical implications of the shift of emphasis in humanist grammar from *ratio* to *exempla*. This is no doubt due in part to the fact that he had himself received a strict education in the *rationes* of language at Paris. None the less, he begins *In pseudodialecticos* with a characteristic humanist swipe at the scholastics, observing that the logic of the university schools is expressed in a language Cicero would scarcely recognize. Far from providing the true path to all disciplines, logic's *via* leads only to solecisms and verbal infelicities.[114] Vives takes the contrary view that it is a defective logic that is based on a language other than that used by most people. For

---

[108] LB, v. 78. See Bentley, p. 180; Barnett, 'Erasmus and Hermeneutics', 558–60.

[109] The term 'illocutionary' is from Austin, *How to Do Things with Words*, p. 99.

[110] Chomarat, 'Les annotations de Valla', p. 220.

[111] Grafton and Jardine, *From Humanism to the Humanities*, pp. 73–5.

[112] Jardine, 'Humanistic logic', in *CHRP*, pp. 178–81; Grafton and Jardine, pp. 76–82. See also Jardine, 'Valla and Humanist Dialectic', pp. 147–9.

[113] The printer was Thierry Martens of Louvain. Erasmus refers to the work in *EE*, iv (No. 1108). The dating of the work is discussed in Fantazzi (ed.), pp. 1–2.

[114] *In pseudodialecticos*, pp. 33–5.

logic no less than grammar or rhetoric is an art of speech (*de sermone*, p. 37). The very word in Greek from which the name of the discipline is derived, διαλεκτική, is a word which means 'speech' (a point derived from Valla).

It is only at this point that the philosophical thrust of Vives's commonplace humanist assertions begins to emerge. For, he says, language came first, and rules followed later. Thus we do not speak Latin in a certain fashion because the rules of grammar so dictate, rather grammar makes its rules to accord with the way that Latin is spoken. Vives now makes his boldest move, by saying that the same is true of the way in which we determine the truth or falsehood of a sentence: 'Logic finds out truth, falsehood, or probability in the common speech that everyone uses, as rhetoric discovers ornament, brilliance, or gracefulness of expression' (p. 36).

Vives thus proposes nothing less than a logic of ordinary language:

Ad eundem modum in dialectica usu venit. Non enim quia praecepit ipsa enuntiationem eam esse veram vel falsam, quae est de indicativo, eam non esse, quae est de aliis modis   (p. 39)

['In the same way, in logic it is usage that ultimately determines whether a certain statement in the indicative mood is true or false, or another statement in another mood is not true or false']

According to Vives, logic does not prescribe good sense, but finds it there already in the language. As good grammar follows common usage, so good logic is derived from the *praecepta* of what *loquentium sive latine sive graece consensus approbat* ('the consensus of speakers, whether of Latin or of Greek, so sanctions' (p. 39)). Thus the rules of logic *ad usum loquendi communem aptanda sunt* ('were adapted to the common usages of speech' (p. 39)).

The 'Sophists', on the other hand, ignorant or unmindful of the resources of common language, have created new languages (indeed *unusquisque*, each having a private language of his own) contrary to 'the custom and use of men', devised exclusively to dispute logic. By way of example, Vives appends a list of 'suppositions, ampliations, restrictions and appellations' in a brilliant satire of scholastic logical method, 'Varro, though a man, is likewise not a man because Cicero is not Varro', or 'two contradictory statements, even in their contradictory sense, are still true'.[115]

---

[115] Varronem cum sit homo, hominem tamen non esse, quia Cicero non ipse sit Varro, p. 41; duas enuntiationes contradictorias, etiam in sensu contradictorio veras esse, p. 45.

This is the logical extension of the humanist credo that *exempla* should replace *ratio* in linguistic study. But Vives goes further by asserting that *exempla* has its own *ratio*. He does this because he sees that otherwise humanist grammar would have no semantics whatsoever: indeed that it would be an empty shell, like Synthen's or Hegius's grammar, recording grammatical forms according to good custom, but unable to explain how they work, or even whether they work at all.

Vives makes a spirited and witty attack on the clumsy alterations scholastic logic made to Latin locutions in order to make them follow its own rules. Elsewhere he makes an effective swipe at the desperate efforts of the *modistae* to invent philosophical rules, which will explain the idiosyncrasies of ordinary grammar. Speculative grammar speculates in inspeculable areas.[116] But herein lies his own problem: which is that grammar does not conform to a strict logic. This, after all, is the reason why logicians debauched the Latin language: not (as he claims) out of sheer ignorance, but in order to maintain the definitions it needed when the language would not supply.

In one of his most interesting and original passages, Vives recognizes that each language has its own ἰδίωμα, its own 'way of putting things' (*sua loquendi proprietas*, p. 57), by which meanings are made. Thus each language has its own logic: in one, a double negative will redouble the negation, while in another, it will cancel it out to form an affirmation (p. 55). But he does not follow through this argument to a natural conclusion: that there is no single essential logic to which all languages conform; or secondly, that no one language contains within it the natural rules of all languages.

Indeed, paradoxically, it is one of the most frequent observations of humanist grammar that Latin forms do not follow logic. Synthen, for instance, objected to the account of the genitive of cause in the *Doctrinale* by saying that grammar uses the same form to express two different versions of causality, and thus equivocates between them in ordinary usage. Vives, however, does not admit to the possibility of such ambiguities and discrepancies, asserting instead that 'accepted usage' corresponds to a 'rational basis of speech' (*rationem loquendi*, p. 49). If someone misconstrues a meaning—interpreting 'you are blonde' to mean 'man is a lion'— then the accepted norms of language can be used against him. When asked to verify this normative account of language, Vives appeals to education or custom. Perhaps seeing the circularity of such an argument, he slips in, in one extraordinary moment, a super-realist gamble: 'its true meaning must

---

[116] *De causis corruptarum artium*, ii, in *Opera*, i. 364.

correspond with what it actually signifies in reality' (*in ipsa re*, p. 49). More characteristic is his bald assertion that the errors of the ignorant may be refuted by the *vero ac germano sermonis sensu*.

Erasmus approved Vives's arguments in a letter to Thomas More in June 1520.[117] He developed no equivalent theory of his own, but in his reply to Luther in the second book of the *Hyperaspistes*, he followed similar principles. Scripture is to be judged not by sophistic logic (as in Luther) but *a more loquendi, sensuque communi* (LB x. 1345A). For instance, common sense concludes that someone has the power to do what he is commanded—at least if the person ordering is not insane (*sed sensus communis colligit esse in illius potestate facere quod imperatur, si modo sanus est qui imperat*, LB, x. 1344F).

Erasmus legislates against Luther's versions of speech acts through a belligerently normative assertion of the 'ordinary' or 'common' usage which he himself defines. Luther, he says, breaks these rules, stating:

Verum iidem pueri sciunt, si quis imperet quod nullo modo fieri possit, aut esse stultum, aut ridiculum, aut tyrannum   (LB, x. 1363F–1364A)

[Indeed the selfsame schoolboys know that if someone commands something which can in no way be done, he is either stupid, or foolish, or a tyrant]

Luther's usages show that *aut insanit, aut est ebrius aut deridet nos* (LB, x. 1364A; 'either he's lost his mind, or he's drunk, or he's having us on'). Whatever, he has entirely abandoned *natura sensusque communis*.

Erasmus's terms of exclusion—the madman, the drunkard, the joker— are reminiscent of J. L. Austin's attempts to shore up an account of speech acts by a doctrine of what he calls the 'felicities', the conditions attaching to a successful performative utterance.[118] Luther, according to Erasmus, has committed his own 'infelicities', and his interpretations can be ruled out of court. Like Vives and Erasmus, Austin expresses a preference for ordinary usage over philosophical usage. Appropriately, Austin describes the process by which speech acts go wrong in theological terms—as kinds of 'sin' against the rules of successful performance.

But, as with Austin, Erasmus's account is open to the criticism raised by Derrida that the legislation of what constitutes an 'infelicity' cannot be guaranteed, that exceptions may turn out to be as possible, and maybe more interesting, than the cases described as 'ordinary'.[119] Erasmus's

---

[117] *EE*, iv. 269.
[118] 'Performative utterances', in *Philosophical Papers*, pp. 237–41; and *How to Do Things with Words*, lecture II.
[119] 'Signature Evénement Contexte', *Marges*, pp. 382–90.

problem, like Austin's, is that language is more ambiguous, and more open to failure, than he allows.

The debate between Erasmus and Luther, which is the subject of the next chapter, shows the paradox of the sixteenth-century crisis in grammar. For we see on the one hand the abandonment of a sophisticated and well-established theory of semantics, which, by putting questions of usage into the background, managed to avoid critical problems of ambiguity. Thus the *modistae* attempted to elucidate *modi significandi* as general semantic laws at a level of abstraction beyond linguistic forms, and then attempted to apply these laws to the forms. Some (like Siger of Courtrai) were interested in formal exceptions to extract further qualifications of the rule. At the same time logicians increasingly ignored natural language in order to provide rules for the behaviour of propositions which could avoid such ambiguity: where a natural form did not exist for the purpose of a particular distinction, then a new form would be adopted. Thus fourteenth-century logicians created a theory of consequences rather than an account of how if-clauses worked in practice.

On the other hand, we see a correspondingly renewed interest among humanist grammarians in the resources of natural language. But whereas they claimed that a return to the examination of utterances treated as performances (according to rules of context and custom) would thereby obviate the need for a semantic account of grammatical questions, in the process they compounded these problems. Speech acts require new and complex theories to explain their behaviour. Thus Erasmus, when forced to explain the meaning of usage, is left prone to the ambivalent exigencies of 'felicities' and 'infelicities'.

The theory of speech acts (as can be seen in modern linguistics) opens up new and radical problems of grammatical explanation—particularly in the area of modality.[120] The description of modality also provides the most complex difficulties of language in a theological theory of grace and justification. Indeed it is in medieval theology of divine foreknowledge and predestination that the most sophisticatedly and articulately designed techniques of discrimination were applied to the logic of modality. Erasmus and Luther dive into this terrifying abyss of modality, but insist on treating it as a grammatical problem rather than a logical one, without any corresponding theory of grammatical modality to apply to it.

The humanist crisis of language in this way merges with the Reformation crisis of theology. For the theological question of grace was the criti-

---

[120] Lyons, *Semantics*, ii. 725.

cal question of the age. Erasmus and Luther attempt to apply an inchoate and unresolved linguistic theory to questions requiring (in a new theological context) a new certainty of distinction. The logical theory of modality was capable at once of making the theological problem so abstract as to be practically incomprehensible to all but a university professor, yet also composed it in such a form that ambiguities could largely be eradicated. The removal of the theological question from the context of scholastic logic to humanist grammar made the arena of interpretation at once more public and more prone to uncertainty and ambiguity. In accordance with Erasmus's historical account of the relation of ambiguity to heresy, this coincided with an exacting demand for ultimate rigour. The problem of grace, for so long one of the arcana of the theological faculty, now became a matter not only of eternal life but also of imminent excommunication and the threat of immediate death. The linguistic activity of grammatical forms, embodying rough distinctions and then equivocating between them, became the acid test of orthodoxy. The political crisis of theological controversy operated in a context of the terrifying ambiguity of everyday grammar.

4   Erasmus *contra* Luther

Luther was one of the first readers of Erasmus's new Bible in 1516. When Froben published *Novum Instrumentum*, Luther had been Professor of Bible at Wittenberg for four years, and was in the middle of his course of lectures on Romans. The long awaited arrival of a Greek text, with textual and critical annotations by Europe's most famous scholar, was of sensational interest, and his lectures show him taking advantage almost immediately.[1] However, from the beginning, Luther expressed reservations with Erasmus's literary criticism. After the summer semester, asked for his opinion by the Elector's secretary Spalatin, he gave voice to some points which 'disturbed' him:

> Deinde de peccato originali (quod utique admittit) non plane velit apostolum loqui cap. V ad Romanos
>
> [Moreover he does not clearly state that in Romans, chapter 5, the Apostle is speaking of original sin (although he admits there is such a thing)][2]

This insight has been called a moment of 'clairvoyance'.[3] Luther picked out from an obscure textual footnote one of Erasmus's most daring philological decisions. Romans 5: 12 describes how 'sin came into the world through one man'—Adam—and 'through sin death'. Death then passed to all men, as the Greek text puts it, ἐφ' ᾧ πάντες ἥμαρτον. For over a thousand years the phrase ἐφ' ᾧ had been translated *in quo omnes peccaverunt*, 'in whom' (or 'in which sin') 'all have sinned'. This has been cited as one of the most notorious mistranslations in history, responsible for the theory of the genetic inheritance of original sin, even for the whole fraught entanglement of beliefs concerning sexuality in the Christian West.[4]

---

[1] The cultural moment of the *Novum Instrumentum* can be observed as it happens in the course of the lectures: there are no references before chapter 9, and frequent ones thereafter. Ficker (WA 56.xxix) surmised that this marked the break between semesters; see also *Lectures on Romans*, ed. Pauck, pp. xlii and 267; and Rabil, *Erasmus and the New Testament*, p. 160.

[2] Luther to Spalatin, 19 October 1516, WA Br 1.70.7; *LW*, 48, 24.

[3] Kohls, 'La position théologique d'Érasme', p. 73.

[4] For instance Pagels, *Adam, Eve and the Serpent*, p. 109. In his most elaborate treatment in *De civitate Dei*, 13, 14, Augustine argued that the mechanism for the dissemination of sin was male semen; Christ was exempt because conceived without semen.

Augustine used it profusely as a proof-text in his controversy with the Pelagians.[5]

This was the reading accepted in the Vulgate.[6] But Erasmus's *Annotationes* queried the reading, preferring *quatenus* to *in quo*, and glossing the new sense as *proinde ad omnes pervenisse mortem quatenus omnes peccatum habuerunt* ('in the same way death came to all in so far as all had sin').[7] Luther was quick to see a change of doctrine in Erasmus's usage. Whereas *in quo* establishes the connection between the sin of Adam and the sin of all other human beings, *quatenus* makes it a matter of analogy: just as Adam's sin brought his death, so the sins of all others bring theirs in turn. Luther's lecture on this text during the winter semester of 1515–16 categorically opposed such an interpretation ('The Apostle speaks here of original and not of actual sin') using liberal supporting quotations from Augustine.[8] In his letter to Spalatin he sarcastically supplied a bibliography of Augustine's works to aid Erasmus's future studies.[9]

Luther was among the first but he was not the only theologian to raise such objections. Edward Lee in 1520 and Frans Titelmans in 1529 both published refutations of the reading of Romans 5: 12 as part of a general attack on Erasmus's methodology.[10] Erasmus published counter-rebuttals to each author (*Responsiones*), and in subsequent editions of the *Annotationes* defended his reading at length. By 1535 (the fifth and final edition of his lifetime) he had turned a small lexicographical footnote into an extended theological essay.

I THE POLITICS OF INTERPRETATION

The controversy over Romans 5 is a portent of a greater quarrel between literature and theology, which found dramatic expression in the debate between Erasmus and Luther over free will a decade later. The most illustrious of humanists challenged the most controversial of theologians at the

---

[5] *De peccatorum meritis et remissione*, i. 10, 11 (CSEL, 60, 12); compare *De spiritu et litera*, 27, 47 (CSEL, 60, 201), and *De natura et gratia*, 41, 48 (CSEL, 60, 268).

[6] Erasmus's first translation in 1516 was careful to avoid contradicting the Vulgate head on, on this as on many points. The 1516 reading *in eo quod omnes peccaverunt* was replaced in the 1519 2nd edn. and all subsequent versions with *quatenus omnes peccaverunt*.

[7] *Annotationes in Epistolam ad Rhomanos*, in *Novum Instrumentum* (1516), p. 432.

[8] WA 56.309.21.

[9] Especially the anti-Pelagian works; Luther even supplies the volume number in Johan Amerbach's Basle edition of 1506 (WA Br 1.70.12). Spalatin passed on the advice, but Erasmus strangely enough failed to reply.

[10] See Rummel, *Catholic Critics*, i. 95–110 and ii. 14–22.

heart of his theology on the basis of literary interpretation. Erasmus's *Diatribe de libero arbitrio* provoked Luther into a trenchant literary and theological *tour de force*, *De servo arbitrio*, excoriating Erasmus as both grammarian and theologian. The wounded Erasmus produced two further works, the two parts of *Hyperaspistes*.[11] The debate marked a schism in the virgin world of protestant doctrine. It also represents a crisis in literary method, the subject of Part One of this book. What follows is an examination of Erasmus's and Luther's principles of literary criticism in action.

The use of literary interpretation in theology had been part of humanist polemic for many years. In 1504 Erasmus discovered in a monastery library near Louvain a manuscript of Valla's *Adnotationes* on the New Testament, which he published in Paris the following year with a Preface which self-consciously promoted literary categories above theology in the interpretation of scripture. Valla had claimed to be motivated only by philology and correct Latin and Greek usage. Erasmus praised Valla in such terms, and has been praised in turn for his assertion of 'literary categories' against the 'demands of medieval theology' which dominated in the commentaries of Nicholas of Lyra.[12]

For others, the Vulgate text of Jerome was sacrosanct: one glossator of a late medieval grammatical text refuted one of Valla's rules of usage simply by citing a line of the Psalms in disagreement. Titelmans' work undertook a full-frontal attack on the new philology of Valla, Erasmus, and Lefèvre, vindicating the Vulgate at every turn. However, the relationship between the 'literary' and the 'theological' is not simple. Despite Valla's assertions, he could not avoid theology by foreswearing it.[13] Valla was more conservative in his treatment of the New Testament than of classical texts.[14]

By contrast, the young Luther's swipe at Erasmus over Romans 5 appears to involve a preference for theology against usage. Yet Luther, too, characterizes his dispute not as doctrinal but as exegetical: he not only admires Augustine's theology, he considers him to be a better reader than

---

[11] Erasmus's *Diatribe* was published in Basle, Antwerp, and Cologne in September 1524; four other printings followed quickly. *De servo arbitrio* was published in Wittenberg in December 1525. The first part of *Hyperaspistes* (attacking Luther's Preface and Introduction) was produced at speed for the Frankfurt spring book fair in 1526, and was published by Froben in Basle in February, with a reprint in July. Book II of *Hyperaspistes* (dealing with the scriptural arguments) followed in Froben's edition of September 1527.

[12] Bentley, *Humanists and Holy Writ*, p. 183; see also Chomarat, 'Les *Annotations* de Valla', p. 222. On Erasmus and Lyra, Chomarat, pp. 218–19.

[13] Chomarat, 'Les *Annotations* de Valla', p. 216.   [14] Tracy, *Erasmus of the Low Countries*, p. 62.

Erasmus (and Erasmus's master Jerome).[15] Erasmus, in turn, accepts in his 1516 edition that the *sensus* of the passage is changed. Just how profound a change is reflected in the contrast in later editions between the simplicity of his lexical assertions and the prevarication of his interpretative explications.

By 1524 any difference between the two was no longer a private matter. Indeed, Erasmus's *De libero arbitrio* constituted a very public statement. In the first years following Luther's denunciation of indulgences, Erasmus's reaction to the Lutheran affair had been guarded, consisting of enigmatic refusals either to endorse or to condemn. Sometimes (disingenuously, one assumes) he declared that he had not read Luther, so that he could plausibly deny having an opinion regarding him.[16] If this was unlikely in 1519, by 1521, when he was still repeating it, it must have seemed blatantly untrue.[17] Yet it was not simply political cover: Erasmus was conscious of the power of his silence, which gave encouragement to reform without attracting a counter-charge of heresy. His indecision was a form of political action, 'not vacillating but firmly ambivalent'.[18]

However, the Lutheran controversy had a way of making political sides unavoidable. Erasmus found himself coerced into abandoning his careful equipoise, since catholic bishops took his silence as tacit support for Luther, while Lutherans saw it as a form of betrayal.[19] In 1521 (without yet implying a critique of Luther) he was saying in letters printed publicly that the malady was *immedicabile*, and that Luther's remedy was worse than the disease.[20] In 1522 he admitted ruefully to the German humanist Willibald Pirckheimer that he was now a heretic on both sides.[21]

Dissension now threatened Erasmus's ideals of *bonae litterae* and reformed evangelicalism. Luther's supporters began to attack Erasmus as

---

[15] In the letter to Spalatin, 19 October 1516, he made the much-quoted remark 'I esteem Jerome in comparison to Augustine as little as Erasmus himself in all things prefers Jerome to Augustine' (*LW*, 48, 24).

[16] To Elector Frederick of Saxony, 14 April 1519, *EE*, iii. 530 (No. 939). This letter was never published by Erasmus, unlike others more critical. None the less Spalatin distributed it to enhance Luther's position; Luther greeted it with pleasure on 22 May (WA Br 1.404.4).

[17] To Justus Jonas, 10 May 1521, *EE*, iv. 487 (No. 1202). He also made the same remark (sensibly, in view of the addressee) to Leo X, 13 September 1520, *EE*, iv. 345 (No. 1143): *nec libros illius unquam legi, nisi forte decem aut duodecim pagellas, easque carptim.*

[18] Gerrish in *Essays on Erasmus*, ed. DeMolen, p. 191.

[19] *EE*, v. No. 1352. There is a clear exposition of Erasmus's complex involvement in the 'Luther question' in Augustijn, *Erasmus*, pp. 119–33.

[20] *EE*, iv. 494 (No. 1203); *EE*, iv. No. 1202. Both these letters were published in *Epistolae ad diversos* (Basle: Johann Froben, August 1521), a volume designed to set out Erasmus's impeccable position.

[21] *utrique parti sum haereticus, EE*, v. 16 (No. 1259).

mercilessly as they did the cardinals and monks who had been the butt of Erasmus's satires. Luther himself wrote to Oecolampadius in June 1523, dismissing Erasmus's usefulness to reform (WA Br 3.626). Oecolampadius, who had assisted Erasmus in the preparation of the _Annotationes_ but whose involvement in the Basle Reformation was now an embarrassment to his old friend, was told that Erasmus should abandon his work on the New Testament. Like Moses, Erasmus was destined to die in the fields of Moab, short of the promised land.

Erasmus's natural allies were leaving him. Ulrich von Hutten, in his last illness, published an _Expostulatio_ in Strasbourg in the summer of 1523, complaining of Erasmus as a fair-weather friend. Erasmus's treatment of Reuchlin and the papal inquisitor Jakob von Hoogstraten, and now of Luther and the papal nuncio Girolamo Aleandro, followed the pattern of his career: in the end Erasmus sided with the victors. Everything else was politics and dissembling. By sleeping with the enemy, he had become a traitor to the truth. Power, not knowledge, was Erasmus's master.[22] Stung into reply, Erasmus published _Spongia_, which, when Hutten's death intervened in the meantime, blackened his reputation further. _Spongia_ also confirmed his distance from the Lutheran cause. A year later, in September 1524, Erasmus explicitly repudiated Luther in _De libero arbitrio_, announcing melodramatically 'the die is cast'.[23]

The controversy between Erasmus and Luther of 1524–7 is famous largely on account of the celebrity of its participants. The significance of its topic—free will and divine grace—is also acknowledged as a premonition of the primacy of predestination in later Reformation theology. Otherwise, the debate is something of an embarrassment on both sides. Scholars of either sympathy wish their protagonist had chosen another enemy. Half-heartedly, the quarrel is revisited to see who won. Meanwhile, the manner of the debate—remorseless exegesis of textual minutiae—is taken by everyone to be regrettable. The controversy emerges as a dialogue of the deaf. For Erasmians, Luther is not enough of a humanist, and for Lutherans, Erasmus not enough of a theologian, for either to be seriously engaged by the other.

By this analysis the true nature of the debate is missed. For literature and theology cannot, after all, escape each other. The New Testament is central to Erasmus's conception of _bonae litterae_. The explication of scripture is not at the periphery of Erasmian humanism; it is its test case. _De libero_

[22] _Schriften_, ii. 192–214; on the quarrel between Erasmus and Hutten, see Augustijn, _Der Humanist als Theologe_, pp. 168–89.

[23] _EE_, v. No. 1493; see Gerrish in _Essays on Erasmus_, ed. DeMolen, p. 192.

arbitrio is in a direct line from the *Novum Instrumentum*, just as that work was the culmination of Erasmus's career up to 1516. Equally, the Bible is central to Luther's conception of theology. The interpretation of literature is not an irrelevance to Lutheran protestantism, it is its proof-test. The incapacity of Erasmus and Luther to agree about almost any matter of literary interpretation shows not how the debate was meaningless but that it was, fundamentally, about meaning. Erasmus and Luther could not agree about how words come to have meanings. They met head to head at a moment of crisis not only in religious doctrine but also in the philosophy of language. It is this, rather than the epic personalities of the contestants, which makes the quarrel so important in sixteenth-century cultural history. What makes it so typical of its century is that the argument was also so public and so violent.

It is not a pretty argument to read. The debate is not to modern taste either in philosophical or in literary method. The lack of a propositional framework has been a source of disappointment to commentators, even one as sympathetic as Gordon Rupp:

It was the tedious manner of the age to deal with one's opponents line by line or at least paragraph by paragraph. That is how Luther began, and it was fatal.[24]

Criticism line by line seems alien to Rupp because he stands on the other side of a shift in critical method. Foucault characterized this shift in *Les mots et les choses* as a movement from *commentaire* to *critique*.[25] Modern critical method, 'faced with existing and already written language . . . sets out to define its *relation* with what it represents'.[26] Language in such a context is simply a medium, 'neutral and undifferentiating', for the expression of ideas. For Foucault this forms a break with the pre-modern human sciences, where, far from being a transparent medium, language has a 'massive and intriguing existence', which 'preceded, as if by a mute stubbornness, what one could read in it' (p. 79). *Commentaire*, as opposed to *critique*, makes no distinction between the thing represented and the words representing it, but is called into being by 'the brute fact that language existed' (p. 79) as a way of stirring 'the enigma of the mark'.

As often, Foucault places his epistemological break too late and too rigidly. Sixteenth-century method is caught in a tension between *commentaire* and *critique*. Erasmus and Luther, for all their differences, are

---

[24] Rupp and Watson, p. 10. [25] *Les mots et les choses*, p. 92.
[26] *The Order of Things*, pp. 80–1.

alike in apprehending language as 'le fait brut', and interpretation as 'l'énigme de la marque'. Line by line commentary is therefore not a tedious redundancy but a methodological necessity. The argument about the theory of predestination or about the philosophy of free will cannot be separated from an argument about hermeneutic theory, the modes of linguistic analysis, and the practice of literary criticism. Rather than one man representing grammar and the other theology, grammar and theology are in tension throughout the debate.

Luther and Erasmus are not only arguing about texts, they are also arguing about how to argue about texts. *De libero arbitrio* is prefaced by an elaborate discussion of Erasmus's interpretative principles, which he admits might seem too lengthy 'if it were not almost more relevant to the main issue than the disputation itself'. His central concern in this Preface is not ascertaining a doctrine of free will but assessing the means by which a doctrine may be formulated. For he and Luther agree that the text of scripture is the only arbiter of doctrine:

> the authority of scripture is not here in dispute. The same scriptures are acknowledged and venerated by either side. Our battle is about the meaning of scripture (*de sensu scripturae pugna est*).[27]

The question of free will has produced centuries of conflict. Indeed, Erasmus says in his opening sentence, 'there is scarcely a more tangled labyrinth' (*vix ullus labyrinthus inexplicabilior*, LB ix. col. 1215A; p. 35) in all of holy scripture. Free will provides a test for scriptural interpretation as much as the other way around.

The solution to this *labyrinthus* must lie in scripture. Whereas the ruminations of philosophers on free will have produced only *negotium* ('labour', col. 1215), attention to scripture may bear 'fruit'. This makes his method circular: for it is the obscurity of scripture that has created the 'mist' (*caligo*, col. 1219) that scripture will elucidate. And if scripture cannot be its own interpreter, he is left with the question of who can arbitrate the meaning of the arbiter. How do we know who has been given the spirit to interpret?

If, as some believe, this spirit has been given to all, then every interpretation must be listened to, and meaning becomes literally 'arbitrary': *incerta erit omnis interpretatio* (col. 1219C). If on the other hand we conclude from the *obscuritates* which 'torment' the learned that no one has this

---

[27] LB ix. col. 1219B; tr. from Rupp and Watson, p. 43. Further refs in text citing page nos. in both edns.

spirit, then equally, *nulla erit interpretatio certa*. The church asserts that the apostolic spirit has been certified to the officers of the church, giving unique sanction to its interpretations. To this, Erasmus acerbically replies that evidence for apostolic behaviour within the church does not lend much optimism for a corresponding certainty in its powers of reading. Yet if we demand a character reference for each interpreter, we have total confusion. There are scholars on both sides and sinners on both sides, so that neither learning nor holiness can properly test the spirit (*probari spiritus*) (col. 1219E; p. 44).

As a result of these enquiries Erasmus establishes two broadly opposing theories for determining meaning: inspiration and consensus. He has to allow some credit to the possibility of inspiration, since Christ thanked God for revealing to 'the simple and foolish' what he hid from pharisees and philosophers. St Paul, and even St Francis and St Dominic, Erasmus says, were 'inspired' in this sense. But he is mainly hostile to the claim of inspiration, using the charge that was to become a standard form of catholic critique of protestant hermeneutics, that inspiration is equivalent to subjectivity, even solipsism. Spiritual interpretation appears to imply a private theory of meaning: 'if we grant that he who has the Spirit is sure of the meaning of the scriptures, how can *I* be certain of what he finds to be true?' (col. 1220; p. 46). Furthermore, two people may disagree who both claim the inspiration of the Spirit, so that their arguments still require some external test. In this way *circulus ad caput redierit* ('the argument returns full circle', col. 1220C; p. 46).

Erasmus is therefore more attached to a second form of theory based on consensus, since it appears to have greater chance of objective status— indeed it seems of itself to form a verifying principle. Certainly, he wishes Luther to heed the weight of opinion massed against him. From centuries of argument over free will, Erasmus musters the testimony of Greek and Latin Fathers, and of later medieval doctors, to his opinion; and on Luther's side finds only two writers, Manichaeus and John Wyclif (hardly reassuring company, since both are condemned heretics). After loading the dice to his advantage in this way, Erasmus asks the reader rhetorically whether 'my own argument meets the other with equal weapons'? Does more weight apply to 'so many saints, so many martyrs, so many theologians', or to 'the private judgement (*privato iudicio*) of this or that individual?' (col. 1219A; p. 43).

Erasmus admits the old adage that the truth is not revealed by counting opinions, since 'those are not always the best things that are approved by a majority' (p. 43). Yet he tries cleverly to reverse this argument by saying that if a majority does not disprove a falsehood, a minority does not prove a truth:

> I hear you say, 'what has a multitude to do with the meaning of the Spirit?' I reply 'What have a handful?' . . . You say, 'What has the knowledge of philosophy to do with the knowledge of sacred letters?' I reply, 'What has ignorance?'   (col. 1219; p. 45)

Erasmus appears to have found a common-sense solution, since agreement seems itself to be a proof that a 'meaning' has been understood, even 'correctly' understood. Yet he struggles to clinch his case, as he has to go outside the language to test his inference of meaning. He has offered nothing like a proof of meaning; the proof of this is that his own case of disagreement (over free will) entirely baffles his theory.

Consensus will only work in cases where consensus already exists—and by definition consensus does not exist wherever meaning has been found to be a problem. If a consensus could be found on the question of free will, then the *sensus Scripturae* would no longer be obscure, and so would not need the clarification that consensus might provide. So by way of conclusion, Erasmus provides as proof of his credentials not a theory of meaning, but a quietly defiant modesty topos:

> I claim for myself neither learning nor holiness, nor do I trust in my own spirit. I shall merely put forward with simple diligence (*simplici . . . sedulitate*) those considerations which move my mind   (col. 1220D; p. 46)

To close the circle, Erasmus offers his open mind: 'if anybody shall try to teach me better, I will not knowingly withstand the truth', thus begging the question still further. With a knowing dig at Luther, he asks for similar forbearance in his opponents.

Erasmus was fond of such scholarly disclaimers. But there is something uncharacteristically winsome about his insouciance in this case, when only a few paragraphs before he was promising a comprehensive theory of textual explication. The insouciance is indicative of a tension underlying his whole treatise, over the production and establishment of meaning, a tension surrounding the opposing terms *assertio* and *ambiguitas*.

Erasmus's discussion in *De libero arbitrio* was the culmination of first-hand experience of five years of the Lutheran affair, the violence of which he reacted to with revulsion bordering on panic. Yet although he described his personal antipathy to conflict in pathological terms, he also saw it as the clear moral teaching of Christ.[28] In addition, the deep fissures brought

---

[28] E.g. *EE*, v. 159 (No. 1331) and esp. *EE*, v. 220.705 (No. 1342); repeated in *De libero arbitrio*, p. 36, and in *Hyperaspistes*.

about by the 'Luther business'[29] delayed or even destroyed his own hopes for evangelical reform, and in any case constituted in themselves the worst form of political evil. The world has been caught up in a 'tempest' that has reached into private relationships and friendships: human affairs are 'seething with public and private hate, so that there is scarcely a vestige of true friendship anywhere'.[30] For Erasmus, this is the destruction of the most basic principle of the ethical life.

Conflict in Erasmus's view is directly caused by *assertio*. In 1523 Erasmus published a careful analysis of the processes of theological controversy as a Preface to his edition of the works of Hilary, the fourth-century Bishop of Poitiers, a principal campaigner against the Arian heresy. Erasmus clearly intended his remarks to apply equally to the Lutheran furore.[31] He states his own view that *summa nostrae religionis pax est et unanimitas*.[32] However, such peace can scarcely exist 'unless we define as few matters as possible, and leave each individual judgement free on many matters'.[33] This is because although many matters are shrouded in *obscuritas*, the mind of man appears to suffer from 'a morbid instinct' never to give in once controversy has begun. Consequently, once the debate has 'warmed up', each side defends its tenuous position as if it were absolute truth (*verissimum*) and social pressures conspire to constrain every person to join in and take sides (*EE*, v. 177–8).

Erasmus adopts the contrary opinion that nothing should be defined beyond what is proclaimed (*proditum*) in holy scripture; *problemata* and *quaestiones* should be left alone, since only God's revelation can take away their 'enigma'. Hilary is held up as an example of interpretative restraint and doctrinal reticence. Erasmus continues with an analysis of the historical processes of heresy. In the early church, Erasmus says, faith was a way of life, not a 'profession of articles'. It was the existence of heretics which brought about a need for more precise scrutinizing of the divine books, and heretical intransigence then required definitions prescribed by authority.[34] This process acquired an inner momentum: new articles produced new sources of contention, which required new forms of power to suppress that contention.

In this complex account of the processes of ideology Erasmus argues that heresy created both the need for the arguments which were used to

---

[29] *EE*, v. 204 (*negocio Lutherano*): an Erasmian joke (*negocium* = 'business' and 'trouble').

[30] *EE*, v. No. 1342, quoted here from *CWE*, ix. 390; see also *EE*, v. No. 1268.

[31] Olin, *Six Essays*, p. 93, comments movingly on the personal resonance in Erasmus's life. The Preface is written as a letter to Jean de Carondelet, an official in the Habsburg court in the Low Countries.

[32] *EE*, v. 177 (No. 1334).   [33] *CWE*, ix. 252.   [34] *EE*, v. 180–1; *CWE*, ix. 257.

refute it, and also the conditions for its own suppression. This worked to increase the wealth and the power of the church, and to encourage the intervention of secular authority in ecclesiastical affairs. Yet these forms of power in turn created new forms of heresy. Articles of faith can only be maintained by *terrores ac minae* ('terrors and threats'), so that, in a hideous irony, 'by terrorization we drive men to believe what they do not believe, to love what they do not love, to know what they do not know'.[35]

Erasmus aims to show how the violence of controversy operates at the level of the finest minutiae, yet more than this he argues a strong connection between violence and precision. It is the exactness of definition, applied to the subtlest areas of belief, which creates the optimum conditions for heresy, and the severest sanctions in eliminating it. The Preface to Hilary is a tract for Erasmus's own times. The analysis of the workings of controversy is prophetic: this Preface was itself exposed to inquisitional scrutiny at Paris in 1526 and at Valladolid in 1527.[36] With belligerent irony, the theologians at Paris censured the very opinion that 'the sum of our religion is peace and unanimity'. On the contrary, *pax & unanimitas* are only a proper pursuit of the church if they are *pia & recta*, and the only verification of rectitude is, of course, orthodox doctrine. Peace should not dictate dogma, but on the contrary, derives from it; anything *a catholica veritate aliena* is merely a 'consensus of the wicked'.[37] In discussing heresy, Erasmus came within a hair's breadth of being declared a heretic himself.[38]

It is in reaction to such forms of theological precision that Erasmus formulated his notion of interpretation and doctrine in *De libero arbitrio*. Free will has caused a philosophical labyrinth because it allows no fast distinctions. In this sense, it is not just a matter of dispute, but a disputable matter. Different opinions have developed about it and differences of opinion are allowable. In effect, he has free choice over free choice. This is both a careful rhetorical pose (he is 'the debater, not the judge', p. 38), and a statement of hermeneutic method: interpretation itself is 'free'.

Openness to the variability of meaning is the distinguishing feature of his practice as literary critic. His opponent, on the other hand, is the great maker of 'assertions'. Erasmus had used the title of Luther's reply (*Assertio*

---

[35] *EE*, No. 1334.378f, as translated by Bainton, *Erasmus of Christendom*, p. 225.

[36] For details, Olin, *Six Essays*, pp. 93–4. The Paris *censurae*, with Erasmus's replies, are reprinted in LB ix. 920–1, 925–8. The passages considered incriminatory at Valladolid (which concerned Arianism) are described by Bataillon, *Érasme et l'Espagne*, i. 276–8.

[37] Quoted from LB, ix. col. 926C.

[38] The smell of heresy remained with Erasmus throughout the century, and his works were famously added to the Indexes of prohibited books of Paul IV (1559) and Pius IV (1564). See Menchi, *Erasmus als Ketzer*; on Italian perceptions of Erasmus's 'Lutheranism', see pp. 33–66.

omnium articulorum) to the papal bull of excommunication as a catch-word for Luther's flaws since 1521.[39] ΔΙΑΤΡΙΒΗ makes this the occasion for a series of jokes lampooning Luther's brash certainties. *Assertio* is the mark of someone 'uncontrollably attached' to his opinion, who 'twists' (*detorqueat*) meaning into 'conviction'. As for himself, Erasmus sums up his position, in words which were to cause him trouble in turn, not least from Luther himself:

so far am I from delighting in 'assertions' that I would readily take refuge in the opinion of the Sceptics.   (col. 1215; p. 37)

Despite Luther's interpretation, this is not a position of unlimited scepticism: in the same breath Erasmus submits himself to 'the inviolable authority of the holy scriptures' and 'the decrees of the Church'; adding even 'whether I grasp what it prescribes or not' (p. 37). His statement can be taken rather as an appeal to the traditional distinction between *fundamenta* and *adiaphora*: the essential dogmas of the church versus those areas of thought where the church makes no prescription. Bainton believes 'Erasmus was the first to use this distinction extensively in the interests of religious liberty'.[40] Yet in limiting religious conflict, Erasmus also rewrites the distinction. Despite his references to decrees and councils, Erasmus replaces doctrinal judgement with exegetical judgement. Passages in scripture that fail to produce consensus among commentators can be considered areas about which God prefers to maintain 'mystic silence'.[41] The evidence for a doctrine being one of the *adiaphora* comes not from the church but from the history of interpretation.

This may explain how Erasmus comes to form such an unlikely view of the *fundamenta*. Among those doctrines he considers inessential are the trinity, the divine-human nature of Christ, and predestination.[42] The essentials are the *bene vivendi praecepta*, the 'precepts for a good life'.[43] The doctrines Erasmus rejects inspired the major schisms of the Christian West. It is not surprising Bainton hails Erasmus as the prophet of modern ecumenism, when his approach to controversy is to deny the validity of

[39] *EE*, iv. 494 (No. 1203).   [40] Bainton, *Erasmus of Christendom*, p. 225.
[41] LB, ix. col. 1217. 'Le silence mystique' is identified as a key element in Erasmus's theology by Margolin, 'Érasme et le silence', pp. 173–7; see also Screech, *Ecstasy*, pp. 48–61.
[42] Erasmus uses the metaphor *conglutinatio* to express the physical inexpressibility of the trinity. Erasmus had been under suspicion on the trinity ever since his omission of the *comma Johanneum* in the text of 1 John 5: 7. Lee had identified this issue in his critique of the *Annotationes* in 1520. It was on the Arian heresy that Erasmus was charged, although not formally condemned, at Valladolid in 1527; see Bataillon, *Érasme et l'Éspagne*, i. 267–78.
[43] See O'Malley, 'Erasmus and Luther', p. 49.

any controvertible proposition. It is equally unsurprising that Erasmus's cavalier treatment of these doctrines brought him the attention of the inquisition.[44] But such questions hide what is a central lacuna in Erasmus's hermeneutic theory, one none the less of great interest.

Erasmus appears to construe a divide—perhaps a total divide—between areas of obscurity and areas of clarity in the scriptural texts. Some areas are opaque to interpretation; others transparent. Erasmus gives no criteria as to how discrimination between the two areas is to be maintained, or how his eminently practical criticism may be learned. This manifests itself in the way that it is the same Erasmus who apparently embraces flexibility of interpretation, championing the cause of *multa varia*, yet who shuns the fruits of such variety as *contentio* and *turba*. Ambiguity in the exegete is the proper attribute of scepticism, yet ambiguity in the text is to be hidden away as a mystery of God. Similarly, his rejection of *assertio* in controversy and antipathy to the quibbling distinctions of philosophers in difficult points of doctrine is matched by an earnest assertion of scriptural truths (*notissimae* or even *inviolabiles*), and an admiration for the punctilious literary exegesis of (for example) Hilary of Poitiers in expounding them.[45]

There is a conflict in Erasmus's approach between a belief in ambiguity as an escape from violence, and a horror of ambiguity as a cause of violence; and between assertion as a suppression of tolerance, and assertion as an expression of peace. This conflict is then translated into his detailed examination of scriptural texts, which he begins with a sentence that is both dogmatic and equivocal: 'it cannot be denied that there are many places in holy scriptures which seem to set forth free choice. On the other hand, others seem to take it wholly away'. His promise is to 'review' (*recensere*) the former and to 'dissolve' (*diluere*) the latter. It is unclear whether he means to let the contrary texts stand side by side, or to play one off against the other: to enforce the contradiction, or to resolve it away altogether. To understand his critical theory, it is time now to look at his critical practice.

II THE PROOF-TEXT: ERASMUS AND LUTHER ON ECCLESIASTICUS 15

Among the texts that 'support' (*statuunt*) free choice, he gives priority to Ecclesiasticus 15: 14–18:

---

[44] For instance, at Paris, see LB, ix. 920–1.   [45] *EE*, v. 190–2.

Deus ab initio constituit hominem, & reliquit illum in manu consilii sui. Adiecit mandata & praecepta sua: Si volueris mandata conservare, conservabunt te, & in perpetuum fidem placitam servare. Apposuit tibi aquam et ignem, ad quod volueris, porrige manum tuam. Ante hominem vita & mors, bonum & malum, quod placuerit ei, dabitur illi.

[God made man from the beginning, and left him in the hand of his own counsel. He added his commandments and precepts. If thou wilt observe the command-ments, and keep acceptable fidelity forever, they shall preserve thee. He hath set water and fire before thee; stretch forth thine hand for which thou wilt. Before man is life and death, good and evil; that which he shall choose shall be given him.][46]

Erasmus's treatment of this passage encapsulates the process by which interpretation turns into doctrine. At the end of his Preface, a paragraph before, he preached the virtue of *suspendentem sententiam* ('suspended judgement', col. 1220E) in elucidating commentary. Now, he considers the lines from Ecclesiasticus to constitute something like an article of faith: 'to paint most clearly (*planissime videatur depingere*) the origin and power of free choice' (col. 1224E; p. 54).

The exigencies of commentary, however, involve Erasmus in a series of qualifications, diverting his doctrinal thrust. *Planissime* is an odd word to use for a discussion requiring more than two thousand words of com-pressed argument, and Erasmus has to apologize that it is for the sake of the 'inexpert' reader. In the path of his assertion he encounters numerous obstructions. First of all, the authority of this text, on which he wishes to base his authoritative conclusions, was in doubt. It was included in the Vulgate, but as Jerome had noted, it was not part of the Hebrew scrip-tures.[47] Canonicity was not established within the catholic church until after Erasmus's death, at the Council of Trent in 1546.[48] Protestant traditions later either consigned it to the Apocrypha or else rejected it altogether. Erasmus sidesteps these difficulties by averring on his own authority that there is nothing 'to disturb the reader' in the book, and quipping that the Hebrews had less reason for excluding it than for the canonical but otherwise dubious Song of Songs.

[46] The Latin text is that given by Erasmus, col. 1221A. As will be seen, he makes a number of emendations from the Vulgate text by cross-referring to the Septuagint. As should be obvious from what follows, any translation of this passage is itself an act of interpretation; the version given here is from *Free Will and Salvation*, p. 47. The passage had been discussed by Origen and Augustine.

[47] Erasmus discusses the question in *De libero arbitrio*, LB, ix. col. 1221.

[48] Session IV, 8 April 1546; *ES* 1502; in the same session the Vulgate was declared the authoritative edition ahead of texts in the original languages (*ES* 1506). The canonicity of Ecclesiasticus was discussed in 1439 at the Council of Florence (Mansi, *Collectio*, xxxi. 1736).

He has problems establishing a text at all: his Latin version differs from the Vulgate but also involves emendations of the Greek text, restoring the reading *conservabant te* in verse 15.[49] Neither the text, nor the authority, of this authoritative text could be taken for granted. From here Erasmus's queries proliferate. His attempt to find a unitary explanation of the passage fragments as one doctrinal question leads to another. He apologizes for the need to qualify himself: to divide the law into three kinds; grace into two; or to elucidate three views of how grace might relate to free choice. He is not able (as he promises) to limit his discussion to exegetical matters: his arguments require the support of the Fathers as an alternative proof of orthodoxy. He continually wards off association with the arguments of heretics, and distinguishes his own view from a variety of 'Pelagian' ideas. In the section on grace, he is forced to provide a hasty synopsis of opinions from Augustine to Duns Scotus.

It is nearly impossible, indeed, to provide a paraphrase of Erasmus's argument at this point: not only because it is so condensed, but also because every phrase is so calculated in its wording and in its context, in order (successfully or not) to maintain a line of orthodoxy. If Erasmus's avowed aim is to forge a middle path between opposing heresies, it involves him in a tortuous route.

Notwithstanding these complex prevarications, Erasmus opens with a definition of free choice outstanding in its boldness:

Porro *Liberum Arbitrium* hoc loco sentimus vim humanae voluntatis, qua se possit homo applicare ad ea quae perducunt ad aeternam salutem, aut ab iisdem avertere (col. 1220F–1221A).

[By free choice in this place we mean a power of the human will by which a man can apply himself to the things which lead to eternal salvation, or turn away from them, p. 47]

Luther reacted to this definition with scarcely rhetorical astonishment: 'Erasmus far outdoes the Pelagians (WA 18.664.18; p. 173), he 'leaves Pelagians, Sophists [i.e. Scholastics], and every one else far behind' (WA 18.664.30; p. 174). For once Luther meant more than a 'calumny' by such remarks.[50] In attributing to free choice a power of applying itself to salvation, Erasmus has produced a definition quite foreign to medieval theology. Medieval theologians commonly tried to find a number of ways of preserving the sovereignty of God's will in relation to salvation without

[49] See col. 1224E. There was no Hebrew text in the 16th century, and Ecclesiasticus was only available in the Septuagint.
[50] *Calumnia* is Erasmus's word in *Hyperaspistes*, i. (LB, x. col. 1321).

disposing of the human capacity to will contingently; it is hard to think of anyone who baldly asserted the human capacity to will salvation. Luther provides a standard reference to Peter Lombard's *Sentences* to this effect. He might just as easily have appealed to Gabriel Biel.[51]

Modern apologists for Erasmus have been embarrassed by this passage, and have tried hard to protect him from a charge of Pelagianism.[52] This misses the point, partly because it is hard to decide what a 'Pelagian' point of view is: Pelagius himself may not have been a Pelagian in the sense Augustine took him to be, never mind in the terms of medieval cliché. Even if Erasmus is called 'Pelagian' here, this definition of free will is not representative of his views in general. As Luther noted, on the next page Erasmus states that 'apart from the help of grace, [man] could not attain the happiness of eternal life' (p. 48). In this sense, Luther says, Erasmus is as much at cross-purposes (*dissidet*; WA 18.664.32) with himself as with others.

The text from Ecclesiasticus, Luther says, is *obscura et ambigua*, and 'proves nothing for certain' (WA 18.666.25). What is required of Erasmus is a text that will show his case in *claris verbis*: but he cannot find one. At the same time, Luther objects that Erasmus's exegesis is far from showing his doctrine *planissime*. In order to say anything like this, his argument has been tortured by qualifications, so that Erasmus writes as if walking on eggs,[53] and quotes so many opinions on free choice that 'you almost turn Pelagius into an Evangelical'.

III IMPERATIVE VERSUS INDICATIVE

So what is it that leads Erasmus to base a general doctrine of free will on this single text, and what justification does he provide? This question dominates the middle part of his treatise. The arguments work more implicitly than explicitly, eluding many commentators as a result.[54] At first, Erasmus presents his case as an ethical argument: sin depends on a supposition of voluntarism, no criminality is attached to the victim of rape, for instance. This is the only way in which the system of rewards and

[51] *Sententiae*, ii. dist. 25, 5. For the scholastic context, Oberman, *Harvest*, pp. 131–45.

[52] Beginning with Erasmus himself, e.g. *Hyperaspistes*, ii. LB, x. 1339. There is a subtle discussion by Chantraine, *Érasme et Luther*, pp. 236–40.

[53] WA 18.666.29, literally 'on ears of corn' (*super aristas incaedis*). The phrase is also used at WA 18.624.1. Tr. from Rupp and Watson, *Free Will and Salvation*, p. 176; further refs in text citing page nos. in both edns.

[54] With the exception e.g. of Gerrish in *Essays on Erasmus*, ed. DeMolen, pp. 193–4.

punishments envisaged in the Old Testament Law is comprehensible.[55] God otherwise seems unjust and even arbitrarily powerful. But as the next section of the *Diatribe* turns to other Old Testament texts for corroboration, it emerges that Erasmus does not consider the ethical case to be merely prudential. He cites God's words to Moses in Exodus, 'I have set before your face the way of life and the way of death. Choose what is good and walk in it', and comments 'It would be ridiculous to say, "Choose", if the power (*potestas*) of turning one way or the other were not present' (col. 1224–5; p. 54). Similar examples are produced from Deuteronomy 30: 15–19.

Erasmus implies that these biblical phrases make no sense except on a premiss of free will: 'If there really is no power in man of free choice toward good or, as some say, no freedom either for good or for ill, what do these words mean?' (*quid sibi volunt haec verba?*, col. 1225C; p. 55). From these tentative beginnings Erasmus eventually formulates a general linguistic law in relation to Isaiah 21:12 'If you will inquire, inquire; turn and come':

Quorsum attinet hortari, ut convertantur & veniant, qui nulla ex parte suae potestatis sunt?   (col. 1225D)

[What would be the point of such an exhortation, to turn and come, if those who are in question have no such power in themselves? (p. 55)]

Erasmus provides about twenty Old Testament references in corroboration. He goes so far as to say that there is very little left in the Bible besides promises, threats, expostulations, reproaches, exhortations, blessings, and curses, and that these expressions would all be in vain if Luther's understanding of free choice were to prevail (col. 1226A). In this sense, he says (quoting from his own *Adagia*), looking for proofs of free choice in the Bible is like looking for water in the sea: citation is superfluous, since illimitable.[56]

This goes some way towards explaining the extraordinary divergence between the confidence of Erasmus's initial definition of free will and the prevarication of his explanation of this definition. In place of interminable philosophical distinctions requiring a scholarly apparatus of scholastic authorities and dogmatic history, his exegetical argument rests on what appears to be a simple linguistic rule. He derives a theological principle from the seemingly incontrovertible speech acts of the Bible.

---

[55] For a modern version of this argument see Küng, *Justification*, p. 182.
[56] *Adagia*, I.ix.75, LB, ii. 359.

This rule, it has been pointed out, has a modern counterpoint in the principle known as 'ought implies can', associated in post-war ethics with the Oxford philosopher R. M. Hare.[57] Hare even uses the same joke to clinch his case. Erasmus compares making an exhortation of someone powerless to fulfil it with saying to a man in chains, 'Get up and follow me'. In the same way, Hare comments 'it would not do to tell a soldier to pick up his rifle if it were fixed to the ground'.[58] Hare, like Erasmus, follows the Aristotelian principle that 'it is only voluntary actions for which praise and blame are given'.[59] Like Erasmus, he gives this a linguistic logic. In a case where I cannot but do something, the question 'what shall I do?' makes no sense as a practical question, and operates only as a 'request for a prediction' (p. 60). Like Erasmus, Hare sees this as an argument against naïve determinism.[60]

So far Erasmus has only provided examples from the Old Testament, and agrees that it may be objected that the juridical framework of the Law makes the Hebrew scriptures especially prone to this form of exegesis. However, he argues that the gospels and epistles are also full of exhortations, and repeats his theory that *ipso facto* they are 'intended to incite us to striving, to endeavouring, to industry, lest we perish by neglecting the grace of God' (p. 60).[61] The same theory applies to threats and reproaches—'You serpents, you brood of vipers, how are you to escape the damnation of Hell' (Matthew 23: 33), which will 'lose their meaning' (will become *supervacanea*, col. 1227F) if interpreted according to Luther's interpretation. Furthermore, in relation to New Testament texts, Erasmus extends his case into new areas by asserting a law of speech acts for conditionals as well as for commands. Not only does 'ought' imply 'can', but 'if' does too, at least when attached to an 'ought'. In this way he comments on John 14: 15 'If ye love me, keep my commandments'

Quam male coniunctio *si* congruit merae necessitati   (col. 1227C)

[How inapposite the conjunction 'if' when all was necessity! (p. 59)]

---

[57] Pigden, 'Ought-Implies-Can', referring to Hare, *Freedom and Reason*, ch. 4. A convenient statement of the doctrine can be found in Lyons, *Semantics*, ii. 746: 'One cannot appropriately command, request, entreat, advise, or exhort someone to perform an action, or demand that he perform an action, which one knows or believes he is incapable of performing'.

[58] *Freedom and Reason*, p. 54.   [59] *Nicomachean Ethics*, 1109b.

[60] Although he is careful, unlike Erasmus, to say that he is not trying to 'solve' any of the tangle of problems that go by the name of 'the problem of free will' (p. 61).

[61] That negative conditional or counterfactual sentences of this type themselves raise extraordinary problems for a theory of speech acts hardly needs emphasizing; Dummett, *Philosophy of Language*, pp. 465–6.

If the protasis of the conditional is impossible, then the 'if' appears redundant: 'With what effrontery would it be said "If you will" to one whose will is not free?' (p. 59).

The argument from speech acts has exciting implications for Erasmus since it seems to solve immediately the problem of interpretation in his Preface. It bypasses the difficulty of consensus by seeming to eliminate *ambiguitas* and *obscuritas*: whereas the meaning of theological terminology is open to disagreement, the inferences of exhortations and conditionals appear to be unarguable: they are transparent issues of usage. As such his practical exegesis has produced an equally transparent sense. If 'ought' implies 'can', then since the Bible is manifestly full of 'oughts', the Bible must, and repeatedly, imply 'the power of free choice'.

Erasmus's attempt to derive a theory of signification from bare speech acts is a bold move. He does not attempt to provide a logical analysis: by contrast, in scholastic logic, a conditional sentence is meaningless only if its protasis and apodosis are contradictory.[62] Rather, he appeals over the head of logic to conversational implication: a sentence in which the condition is impossible is nonsense in anything other than a logical sense.[63] Similarly, he does not argue that an impracticable exhortation is incoherent, but that there is no point to it, so that a God who made one would be sadistic or mad—like someone saying to a crippled man 'Walk!' The appeal is the stronger because it combines a semantic argument with an ethical one, so that it is not quite clear whether he is discussing what it is possible to say or what it is reasonable or even right to say. Yet to call this an argument from common sense would be to underestimate its power and subtlety: it is more an argument from common meaning.

Despite its attractions, of course Luther rejects it. He does so, interestingly, not by repudiating Erasmus's theology, but by offering an alternative analysis of the signification of speech acts. His theory is equally prescriptive, and he offers it as a comprehensive disproof of Erasmus's argument.

He begins by noting how the question of free choice first arises in the text from Ecclesiasticus at the words *Si volueris* ('If thou wilt', 15: 15). But contrary to Erasmus, he takes this passage as evidence against, not for, *liberum arbitrium*:

---

[62] For instance Ockham, *Summa logicae*, ii. 31.

[63] This might be compared in a modern context with the attempt to bypass formal logic through an appeal to the logic of ordinary sentences in Grice's theory of implication and 'implicature'; see esp. 'Logic and conversation'.

non video, quomodo istis verbis liberum arbitrium probetur. Est enim verbum coniunctivi modi (Si volueris) quod nihil asserit, sicut Dialectici dicunt, conditionalem indicative nihil asserere (WA 18.672.31)

[I do not see how free choice is proved by these words. For the verb is in the subjunctive mood ('If thou wilt'), which asserts nothing. As the logicians say, a conditional asserts nothing indicatively (pp. 183–4)]

This is a nice retort to Erasmus's supposition that the sentence 'If you are willing and obedient, you shall eat the good of the land' (Isaiah 1: 19–20) implies that man has a power to will and obey. As counter-examples Luther wittily suggests, 'If the devil is God, it is right to worship him' and 'if an ass flies, an ass has wings'. Neither of these sentences proves that the devil is God or that asses can fly. To clinch his point, he compares, 'If free will exists, grace is nothing': a proposition which Luther takes as true and Erasmus as false, but which Erasmus's *ad hoc* logic of conditionals appears to prove irrefutably.

However, Luther recognizes that Erasmus is not making a strictly logical argument, but one based on the 'inferences' (*sequelae*) of conversation. When God says 'If you will keep the commandments', it is not that logic dictates the performability of the condition, but that *ratio humana* finds it unreasonable for God to say this (or at least to say it seriously) if he knows the condition to be practically impossible. Luther in response to this formulates a lucid and concise summary of Erasmus's theory:

if I ask how it is proved that the presence of free will in man is signified or implied (*significari vel sequi*) every time it is said 'If thou wilt, if thou shalt do, if thou shalt hear', Reason will say 'Because the nature of the words and the use of language among men (*natura verborum et usus loquendi . . . inter homines*) seem to require it. (WA 18.673.13; Rupp and Watson, p. 184)

Luther queries whether the ordinary rules of human speech apply to God, but since in practice he cannot speculate on the unusual conversational habits of the divine person, he proposes instead to offer his refutation in accord with 'the usage and concerns of men'.

Both writers base their appeal on an understanding of speech acts. Erasmus follows his habitual principles of literary practice. Luther does so in the more specialized context of his nominalist masters. Indeed this passage can be seen as a direct tribute to his Erfurt teacher Trutfetter. His reference *Dialectici dicunt* implies as much; in addition, the rule that *conditionalem indicative nihil asserere* is a close quotation from Trutfetter's textbook on logic: *Condictionalis proprie dicta non asserit alicquam.*[64] Trutfetter argues that conditionals only tell you about true and false consequences, they do not tell you whether the initial proposition is itself true. This whole passage shows how Luther was still using the techniques and vocabulary of the *moderni* some years after his break from Rome. The key word *sequelae*, used repeatedly by Luther as a term for semantic analysis, also comes from Trutfetter (as in this same passage, where a conditional is said 'to denote only consequence' (*sed denotat solam sequelam*)). The phrase *usus loquendi*, too, is a staple of Ockham's theory of language.

What gives the edge to Luther's argument here is that he applies the scholastic framework on consequences to show himself a better humanist than Erasmus in paying respect to the limits of ordinary language. Of all the cases offered by Erasmus, Luther recognizes the primacy of scriptural commands and exhortations, because of their sheer frequency, because of the ingenuity of Erasmus's treatment of them, and because of the theological and historical importance of the ten commandments. Yet he claims Erasmus has failed to observe elementary distinctions. Erasmus takes no account of natural obstacles which may prevent a command being obeyed, or a condition being fulfilled—for instance imprisonment, physical inability, or even fear or contrary desires. Erasmus also makes no distinction between endeavour and fulfilment. He assumes that whatever is desired can always be attempted, and that whatever is attempted can be achieved. In this way, Luther says, Erasmus begins by meaning to prove human desire and striving for good, and ends by proving 'a complete act, everything fully carried out by free choice' (p. 197). Yet the vicissitudes of life show 'how often there are slips between the cup and the lip, so that what you have commanded and indeed was possible enough, nevertheless does not happen' (p. 190).

Luther attacks what he sees as a facile understanding of what it means to 'will' something, as if it were enough simply to 'decide' to do the good, unhampered by the complex constraints hemming in on all sides. Such a criticism could fairly be levelled also at the bland complacency of Hare's rule that 'ought implies can'. Luther also has a more general argument against Erasmus's linguistic inferences, which he expresses with stinging contempt. Moses in the Pentateuch does not say 'thou hast the strength or power to choose' but 'Choose, keep, do!' Erasmus, far from developing a new linguistic theory, has ignored the most basic linguistic forms. Moses 'issues commandments about doing' he does not 'describe man's ability to

---

[64] Trutfetter, *Summule totius logice*, ii. MM3ᵛ.

do'. Erasmus can only make his inferences (*sequelae*) through bad reasoning and even worse, through 'blindness and carelessness' (p. 191).

Erasmus, therefore, can collect as many exhortations as he pleases—he can spend the rest of his life hunting the major concordances—but his case will not be proved in this way. For in juxtaposition to Erasmus's theory of commands, Luther places his own:

Atque id etiam grammatici et pueri in triviis sciunt, verbis imperativi modi nihil amplius significari, quam id quod debeat fieri. Quid autem fiat vel possit fieri, verbis indicativis oportet disseri. Qui fit igitur, ut vos theologi sic ineptiatis velut bis pueri, ut mox apprehenso uno verbo imperativo inferatis indicativum, quasi statim, ut imperatum sit, etiam necessario factum aut factu possibile sit   (WA 18.677.24)

[This is something that even schoolteachers and schoolboys in their grammar lessons know, that by verbs of the imperative mood nothing else is signified but what ought to be done. What is done, or can be done, must be expressed by indicative verbs. How is it, then, that you theologians drivel like people in their second childhood, so that as soon as you get hold of an imperative verb you take it as implying the indicative, as if once a thing is commanded, it must forthwith necessarily be done or be possible to do? p. 190, corrected]

There are several distinctions Luther is making in this passage. The simplest is that commands and statements are grammaticalized by means of different forms, at least in Latin. But Luther recognizes that such a strictly formalist distinction will easily break down: in this same argument he notes that Hebrew often uses a future indicative to express an imperative (similar to the English translation 'thou shalt not kill'). Alternatively, he may be intending a broader semantic distinction between types of sentence: a sentence can never be both imperative and indicative (whereas it can be both interrogative and indicative).[65] On this matter, modern grammarians concur with Luther's analysis, sometimes using the term 'mand' in place of Luther's 'imperative': 'whereas a statement tells the addressee that something is so, a mand tells the addressee that something is to be made so'.[66] Yet in this case, it is interesting that Luther uses this distinction to disprove what is equally an axiom of modern linguistics: that an imperative implies performability.

Certainly, Luther seems to be right in arguing that Erasmus is too easily inclined to imply that 'once a thing is commanded it must forthwith necessarily be done', but he is in greater difficulties showing that it is not necessarily 'possible to do'. He sees that he is required to provide some

---

[65] See Lyons, *Semantics*, ii. 748.   [66] Ibid. 751.

examples of alternative speech acts from everyday discourse. Parents, he says, frequently tell their children to do this or that, 'simply for the sake of showing them how unable they are, and compelling them to call for the help of the parent's hand' (p. 184). Although Luther's psychological explanation may have dubious moral value, it is certainly the case that parents often tell their children to do things when they are fully aware that they will not or cannot carry them out. All Luther needs to show is not that man cannot follow divine commands, but that in practice he will not succeed; this is Augustine's argument at the start of *De spiritu et litera*. More plausible is Luther's next example. When a doctor tells a patient 'to stop doing things that are either impossible or painful to him, so as to bring him through his own experience to an awareness of his illness or weakness, to which he could not lead him by any other means'. Here even the moral seems more secure: its logic is familiar from the treatment of alcoholism or addiction.[67]

Luther's objection is that the world of 'ought implies can' is one in which men and women are always in control of their circumstances, a situation familiar enough in the sentences of moral philosophers, but remote from the world in which human beings actually live. In life, other powers, other people, not to say appetite, emotion, physiology, and pathology interfere, so that what we ought to do turns out to be precisely what we cannot do.[68] It needs to be said, however, that he also creates a problem for himself by trying to argue that commands never assume that they can be fulfilled— that such an inference can only be derived from an indicative, not an imperative. This would make nonsense of many everyday commands ('put down this book, now'), and also of much of the New Testament. It would not, for instance, be a very convincing explanation of Jesus's behaviour in Matthew 4: 19–20: 'And he saith unto them, follow me, and I will make you fishers of men. And they straightaway left their nets, and followed him'.

This example from Matthew appears to follow Erasmus's rule and not Luther's. Indeed at certain points in his argument Luther admits that, despite his attempt to provide a definitive law, there are sets of conditions under which the speech acts of an imperative sentence will behave differ-

---

[67] Pigden considers the example of a doctor ordering a patient to give up smoking; 'What the patient *really* ought to do is what he can't do' (p. 12). Even so, Pigden perhaps underestimates the difficulties of the smoker, and the banality of Hare's rule in such a context.

[68] The fullest recent articulation is Nussbaum's attack on Kant and Hume in *The Fragility of Goodness*. See especially the account of practical conflicts (pp. 31–2), and ch. 1 ('Luck and Ethics') in general. See also Williams, 'Moral Luck'.

ently. For this purpose he invokes one of the central antinomies of his theology, between 'divine' and 'human' spheres of action.[69] From time to time he concurs with Erasmus that 'within his own province, so far as observation goes' (WA 18.674.7) man makes orders which can be performed (presumably like that in Matthew). This concurs with his general principle that in everyday affairs man has freedom of choice 'to milk cattle, build houses, etc.' On the other hand, Luther is unequivocal that man does not have the freedom to do anything in 'divine and spiritual matters were they never so small'. That is, man does not have the ability to choose salvation, follow the law, or in this sense to be righteous, without grace. This is why Luther finds Erasmus's definition of free choice (*qua se possit homo applicare ad ea quae perducunt ad aeternam salutem*, col. 1220F–1221A) so extraordinary.

IV THE THEOLOGIAN AND THE GRAMMARIAN

This brings Luther into an area fraught with difficulty. A distinction between a natural and an eschatological sense of freedom (ἐλευθέρια) appears in the New Testament, but even the disciples appear to have found it hard to understand. As Hans Küng remarks, 'when Jesus Christ proclaimed to his countrymen that the truth would make them free, they replied in anger that they were already free'.[70] The disciples understand the word in a political sense—they are 'in bondage to no man' (John 8: 33); but Jesus retorts that they are in bondage to sin. Only if the Son frees them will they be 'free' in this religious sense (8: 36).

A distinction between a man being *liber* and him having religious *libertas* is found, if obscurely, in Augustine. Anselm in *De libero arbitrio* clarified the concept, defining *libertas* as the capacity not to sin.[71] But the relation between senses of *liber* continued to provoke argument, for which a number of complex solutions were proposed. The classic scholastic solution—developed by Aquinas (out of Boethius and Augustine) but subject to discussion until the generation before Erasmus and Luther—made a distinction between different kinds of necessity. A full discussion is impossible here, but put briefly, *necessitas consequentiae* ('of the consequence') is a statement of logical relation—the necessity by which the inference of a conditional proposition follows from its premiss. Aquinas calls this kind

---

[69] Ebeling, *Luther*, pp. 119–24.
[70] Küng, *Justification*, p. 180, referring to John 8: 32–3.
[71] See the discussion of *libertas* in Gilson, *L'étude de Saint Augustin*, p. 213: 'La terminologie augustinienne s'est clarifiée et fixée chez Anselme'.

of 'necessity' *conditionalis*.[72] Everything that God wills has 'conditional' necessity, but this does not eliminate free will in man: God can will that things happen contingently, through our free will. *Necessitas consequentis* ('necessity of the thing consequent'), on the other hand, could be called a statement of ontological necessity: something that is necessary from the nature of the thing or event in question.

Aquinas's argument was important because it showed that the assertion of God's providential will was not incompatible with the assertion of man's natural free choice. Nevertheless, Luther expressed discontent with the distinction between necessities as early as 1515–16 in his Lectures on Romans.[73] By the time of his reply to the papal bull *Exsurge Domine* (threatening excommunication) in 1520, he was wilfully abandoning it, making a leap between saying that when the will 'does what it can it commits sin', and continuing that 'all things happen by absolute necessity'.[74] According to Aquinas, such a leap is simply illogical. But there are several indications that Luther is less interested in the question of 'necessity' than the related question of what the will does when 'it does what it can' (*facere quod in se est*). By the fifteenth century this had become the dominant issue of grace in relation to freedom. In practice, no one accepted the Pelagian position that the will can (though with difficulty and only after careful moral education) achieve the good on its own. But there were a number of other positions available.

Erasmus himself borrowed two possible formulae for resolving this question. First, the will after original sin is incapable of achieving righteousness, but can strive towards it, such striving being rewarded with the grace that subsequently fulfils righteousness. Second, the will has severely impaired freedom but still has some scintilla of original perfection which, when aided by grace, can recover its full righteousness. Luther, however, rejected both solutions as a misunderstanding of original sin, and dismissed them as intellectual evasions of a radical truth. If original sin meant

---

[72] *Summa contra gentiles*, i. 67, 10. See McSorley, p. 151, who collects a variety of citations.

[73] From the student copies edited by Ficker in WA 57, it appears that Luther left these controversial thoughts in his private notes. By 1517 in the *Disputatio contra scholasticam theologiam* (Thesis 32, WA 1.225.33) he is saying that the distinction *nihil quoque efficitur* (i.e. that it is irrelevant, see below).

[74] *Assertio omnium articulorum*, xxxvi: *sed omnia . . . de necessitate absoluta eveniunt* (WA 7.146.7), citing the articles of Wyclif condemned at Constance in support. In the German version (*Grund und Ursach*) there is no such reference. McSorley (p. 265) speculates that the word 'absoluta' is contrary to Luther's meaning, citing the German text; but it is clearly too controversial to be a slip exactly. In *De servo arbitrio* he never uses the term *absoluta* in relation to *necessitas*.

anything it meant precisely that for a human being *facere quod in se est* means to sin. In other words, human beings have all kinds of natural freedom, but none of these freedoms affects the one central necessity of sinning. Since salvation has nothing to do with contingent freedoms, he professes himself uninterested in them: the only freedom which concerns him is the eschatological freedom of salvation, the freedom described by Jesus in John 8. He can see no other interpretation of the words, 'If the Son shall make you free, you shall be free indeed', or of Paul's theological explanation of freedom in Romans, or of Augustine's expositions of Paul in his controversial works against Pelagius.

This is the reason why he finds the question of speech acts so significant. Erasmus has tried hard to avoid making a Pelagian argument, or anything that could be construed as such. He has tried to reconcile his defence of free will with a reaffirmation of grace, and to maintain a position which makes allowance to both sides of the argument. But the *sequela* of 'ought implies can' appears to go beyond this. If the logic of biblical exhortations is as Erasmus suggests, then the moral imperatives of the Bible must be performable. This implies that the will is capable even of keeping and fulfilling commands.[75]

According to Erasmus's principles, it would be 'ridiculous' if an imperative only implied 'can try but won't succeed'. In this sense, Luther says, Erasmus is constructing an argument only Pelagius can win (WA 18.675.7): from the point of view of his anti-Pelagian intentions, he has proved too much for his own good:

I have the idea that you are mightily pleased with these similes of yours, but you fail to see that if they hold good, they prove a good deal more than you set out to prove; in fact, they prove what you deny and want condemned, namely that free choice can do everything   (WA 18.678.20; p. 191)

As stated earlier, Erasmus's alleged 'Pelagianism' is an academic question. What is more interesting here is Luther's claim that although Erasmus professes a theology that is explicitly not Pelagian, he uses in effect a Pelagian grammar. His logic of speech acts is out of step with his asserted principles: 'you have said that free choice can do nothing without grace, and yet you prove instead that free choice can do everything without grace' (p. 191; WA 18.678.24). This is because, according to Erasmus's understanding of exhortations, they either imply that free choice *can* do the things commanded, or else these things 'are commanded to no purpose, ridiculously and irrelevantly'.

[75] WA 18.674–5.

On the contrary, Luther says, original sin dictates that there are certain things man cannot do (of his own natural powers). These are, of course, exactly the things which man *ought* to do—in some final religious sense of 'ought'. In this special sense, original sin actually means 'ought implies cannot'. The purpose of the imperatives (their pragmatics) is not to prove man's ability, but precisely to demonstrate his inability: divine commands are given not to elicit human ethical action, but to alert humanity to its final ethical failure. This is Luther's understanding of Romans 3: 20 'for by the law is the knowledge of sin'. By the words of the law man is warned and instructed as to what he ought to do, not what he is able to do; 'their purpose is that he may know his sin, not that he may believe himself to have any power' (p. 190; WA 18.677.17).

This is why Luther wishes to preserve a total divide between the 'imperative' and the 'indicative' as modes of speech. In another sense, however, he implies that original sin places special demands on the logic of sentences: that ordinary grammar breaks down under this pressure. According to *ratio carnalis*, it would be insane to say to a man at a crossroad 'Take either route' if only one road is open. But original sin envisages just such a situation: the only road open is the 'broad and easy' one that leads to Hell. 'It would not be ridiculous, therefore, but a matter of due seriousness, to say to a man standing at such a crossroad "Take which way you like", if he was inclined to imagine himself strong when he was weak, or was contending that neither road was closed' (p. 190; WA 18.677.4).

This is the only understanding of grammar, Luther says, which preserves some room for grace. For again, according to Erasmus's examples, it is unreasonable to say to a crippled man 'Walk!' Indeed, only a sadist would ever make such a command. And yet, of course, in the New Testament, Christ does say to a crippled man 'Walk!' at which point the cripple indeed walks. Not that the cripple walks of his own will (and thus finds that he 'can' do what is commanded, as Erasmus might have it); rather, he is ordered to do something which he cannot do, but which (miraculously) it turns out he does. Grace thus fills out what the will cannot perform, even when 'ought' implies 'cannot'. The commands are made, then, not only in order to show the impotence of free choice, but also 'to intimate that some day all such things will be done, though by a power not our own but God's' (*verum aliena virtute, nempe divina*) (p. 209; WA 18.691.24).

Here Luther offers a provisional solution to the problem of necessity, which has dogged his argument all along. He agrees that these expressions (*sermones*) would 'rightly' be called pointless or ridiculous if they were used in cases which were 'absolutely impossible', that is if even God could not make them happen. The scriptural examples, however, command things, which, though impossible by human powers, are possible by divine power. Grace transcends ordinary possibilities: this is what makes grace grace. In this sense grace supplants or transgresses ordinary grammar: not by creating a new language, but by rewriting its speech acts.[76]

Luther increasingly dismisses Erasmus's interpretations. *Diatribe*, he says, holds 'it is all the same, whether a thing is said imperatively or indicatively' (p. 222). As a grammarian, never mind as a theologian, Erasmus should have seen through such a solecism. In this Luther underestimates Erasmus's argument, for Erasmus has not bungled his way into this grammar, he has articulated a careful theory of his own. Yet Luther has successfully identified a problem that Erasmus has in relating this grammar to his theology, and particularly in Erasmus's failure to provide any linguistic account of the action of grace.

Erasmus's motive in his argument is piety: piety is enhanced by a repentant moral striving, and also by attributing all goodness to God.[77] Erasmus sees no contradiction between these pieties—and any difference between scriptural passages in this respect can be explained by a difference of rhetorical purpose. Sometimes the Bible urges us to higher moral effort; sometimes it rebukes our moral pride and humbles our presumption. Rather than contradiction Erasmus finds rhetorical and moral coherence. He discovers what has been called, in the context of Valla, a *theologia rhetorica*.[78] For the Bible is the ultimate *ars rhetorica*, at once an instruction and inspiration to the good life.

However, for Luther the two forms of piety are incompatible. Erasmus's attempt to make both assertions—that we have free choice, but that we can 'ascribe' it to God as the ultimate source—is for Luther proof of the duplicity at the basis of Erasmus's treatise. In his opening remarks he complains that Erasmus is everywhere *lubricus et flexiloquus* (WA 18.601.34; 'evasive and equivocal', p. 103). Luther even charges Erasmus with a general scepticism, scornfully dismissing Erasmus's stated preference for the 'opinion of the sceptics' over *assertio*. In answer to this, Luther insists that Christianity is based on 'assertions', indeed that if assertions are taken away, there is scarcely anything left (WA 18.603.28). He turns Erasmus's sentence back on him, quipping his own epigram, *Spiritus sanctus non est scepticus* (WA 18.605.32).

---

[76] This is a characteristic example of Luther contradicting himself to suit his argument; here he is reaffirming a version of 'ought implies can'.

[77] See Gerrish, in *Essays on Erasmus*, ed. DeMolen, p. 194.

[78] Trinkaus, *In Our Image*, i. 126–7.

Too much has been made of this phrase on both sides of the argument, either in proving Erasmus's (supposed) fastidious dilletantism or Luther's (supposed) boorish dogmatism.[79] Erasmus's lengthy and bitter reply to this charge in *Hyperaspistes* is justified to the extent that *De libero arbitrio* is clearly not the work of a religious sceptic. Yet in any case this is not Luther's main argument: he wishes to show that Erasmus's treatise is full of assertions, but false ones. Luther, too, is quite prepared to admit a distinction between the *adiaphora* and the *fundamenta* of doctrine, but the question is which is which.

Far from being a theological puzzle for Luther, demanding discreet handling, and censorship before the uncomprehending masses, the argument of this controversy is the foundation of faith. Indeed, it is one half of the Christian *summa*, since on it depend both knowledge of oneself and knowledge of God (WA 18.614.17). The other half of this *summa* is 'whether God foreknows anything contingently, and whether we do everything of necessity'. The choice of the word *summa* is an explicit statement of Luther's new theology.

It is in this light that we can approach Luther's reply to the problem in hermeneutic theory posed by Erasmus as the central part of his Preface. Erasmus, as we saw earlier, is vexed by the conflicting interpretations to which scripture has been subject. The mere existence of controversy over some issues (such as free will) leads him to conclude that scripture leaves these matters finally obscure. The problems of interpretation thus define for him the limits of what is sayable about any doctrine. Free will is among the most obscure of scriptural questions, and is best left in such obscurity, beyond some basic moral maxims necessary to underpin the pious practice of religion.

. At the end of his treatise, Erasmus addresses this question once again and offers an even more radical account. There are conflicts of opinion concerning scripture, and yet scripture, having one author (the Holy Spirit) cannot be in conflict with itself. Only one explanation is possible: 'since different men have assumed different opinions from the same scripture, each must have looked at it from his own point of view, and in the light of the end he is pursuing' (p. 86). Some base their interpretation on a desire to stamp out moral apathy, and so approve free choice; others, more concerned with the dangers of the arrogance of good works, increase the emphasis on grace, or bring in a doctrine of absolute necessity. Erasmus is

[79] Jedin, *History of the Council of Trent*, i; Huizinga, *Erasmus and the Reformation*, p. 164. It is a kind of boisterous joke, similar to Luther's joke about his own aggressive manner on p. 105.

even-handed between these interpretations, indeed he has to be, for his hermeneutic circle has completed its revolution: interpretation is dependent not on the text but the interpreter. The text itself is irresolute, even opaque: difference can only be resolved by reference to the mind of the critic.

Erasmus does not seem to notice the radical nature of this new theory, and it does not affect the conviction with which he expounds his own exegeses as inviolable truths. Luther none the less feels it incumbent on him to tackle the question of whether scripture is obscure or ambiguous. His first argument is that the texts which are obscure are so not because (as Erasmus claims) of the majesty of the subject-matter, but because of our ignorance of their vocabulary and grammar (*ob ignorantiam vocabulorum et grammaticae*, WA 18.606.23). God is unknowable, but scripture is not: even the most sublime ideas of the Bible—the incarnation, the resurrection—are comprehensible to the human mind.[80] None the less scripture makes considerable linguistic demands on the understanding, requiring constant care and attention. Far from enjoining a pious refusal to inquire further, the Bible forces us into ever more exact investigation of its complex words and grammar. Luther speaks here from practical experience: his main preoccupation in the preceding years was his biblical translations.[81]

None the less, he admits that for many people the Bible remains unclear. This is not the result of the opacity of the text, but the blindness of the reader. It is not the abstruseness of the word of God which deceives these readers, but their own 'blasphemous perversity' (*blasphema perversitate*, WA 18.607.17; p. 111). Luther concludes that scripture itself is clear, although there are two kinds of clarity and two kinds of obscurity. One—*externa*—requires the painstaking efforts of critical exegesis; the other—*interna*—is closed except to grace itself: 'For the Spirit is required for the understanding of scripture, both as a whole and in any part of it' (p. 112).

On the face of it, this falls straight into the trap of subjectivity anticipated by Erasmus: for who can prove the presence of the Spirit in his own interpretation? By 1525, it was no longer possible for Luther, either, to make a straightforward appeal to the Spirit, since he had his own religious enthusiasts (*Schwärmer*) to deal with, 'boasting of the Spirit' (p. 158). It is easy to forget that *De servo arbitrio* came out in the same year as the

---

[80] Referring to Romans 11: 33, quoted by Erasmus.
[81] Luther's remarks on the demands of translation are instructive; in *On Translating: An Open Letter* (1530) he commented on how single words would take him weeks.

Peasants' War, and that the darker side of its apocalyptic theology may be connected with this.[82] As on the question of free choice, where he found himself eventually arguing with radical predestinarians in the Antinomian controversy, Luther was fighting battles on two sides. So although he claims final recourse to the Holy Spirit he argues that this 'internal' clarity is not useful for the purposes of proof in exegetical controversy, since an internal judgement only works internally. A person cannot be persuaded by another person's inner conviction (WA 18.653.20).

Luther therefore falls back on 'external' judgement—and thus on the semantic criteria of *vocabulorum et grammaticae*. His proof of the clarity of scripture comes from the testimony of scripture itself, from its claims to be a 'witness', a 'light', and a 'pathway' to understanding. However, in practice he can only argue for it through his own exegesis. In this way his argument hangs on a knife-edge, with the minutiae of lexical and grammatical explication bearing the weight of overwhelming doctrine which only the Holy Spirit can persuade us to, since carnal reason will always regard it as folly and deny its existence.[83] Hence his extraordinary emphasis on grammar—since here at least there seems to be the possibility of an external criterion which can carry internal conviction. If sin has made the intellect perverse and intractable to the truth, grammar makes the intractable truth of grace tractable.

But his problem is that grammar, too, is ambiguous. Erasmus has attempted to bridge the divide between the texts and his assertion by a grammatically prescriptive interpretation of the speech acts of conditionals and imperatives. A rule of implication, one might say of pragmatics, provides an authority for dogma. Luther refutes him by interpreting a different rule, and by a new prescription. Between the two forms of prescription, grammar ambiguates. Each claims grammar to be transparent to his interpretation, but finds it opaque. God's commands seem resistant to a single semantic explanation. And yet far from being a distraction from theology, the linguistic cruces have brought Erasmus and Luther to the substance of their philosophical disagreement. The perplexity of theology is profoundly related to the perplexity of language.

In his reply to Luther in 1526 in the first part of *Hyperaspistes*, Erasmus articulated this impasse with brutal frankness. Luther keeps appealing to *Verbum Dei, Verbum Dei* ('the word of God, the word of God'); but the

---

[82] Bornkamm, *Luther in Mid-Career*; compare Luther's *Wider die himmlischen Propheten* (1525).

[83] As often, the supporting quotation is Psalm 14: 1, 'the fool has said in his heart, there is no God'.

problem lies not in the words but in the interpretation of those words.[84] Erasmus and Luther in turn marshall as many texts as they like to prove the case once and for all, but still their interpretations contradict each other. Neither argument exists as a stable unity. Instead refutation and defence follow on from each other in a vortex of mutual recrimination.

V THE POTTER AND THE CLAY

The culminating case is the interpretation of Romans 9. In this chapter Paul wrestles with some of the most problematic texts in the Old Testament. God chooses some and not others. He even chooses one twin above another. Of the two children of Isaac and Rebecca, 'Though they were not yet born and had done nothing either good or bad, in order that God's purpose of election might continue, not because of works but because of his call, she was told "The elder will serve the younger". As it is written "Jacob I loved but Esau I hated" ' (Romans 9: 10–13).[85]

God's seemingly arbitrary preference for Jacob over Esau, and his consequent division of Israel into two peoples, provokes Paul's torturing refrain: 'what shall we say then? Is there unrighteousness with God? God forbid'. Paul provides no analysis justifying God's justice, only a further series of Old Testament proof texts. 'I will have mercy on whom I have mercy, and I will have compassion on whom I will have compassion' (Exodus 33: 19); 'I have raised you up for the very purpose of showing my power in you' (Exodus 9: 16); 'Will what is moulded say to its moulder, "Why have you made me thus?" Has the potter no right over the clay, to make out of the same lump one vessel for beauty and another for menial use?' (Isaiah 29: 16; Jeremiah 18: 6).

To these texts, Paul interpolates his own glosses: 'So it depends not upon man's will or exertion, but upon God's mercy' (Romans 9: 16); 'So then he has mercy upon whomever he wills, and he hardens the heart of whomever he wills' (Romans 9: 18). But he makes no further comment on the relation of his texts to their glosses. Paul's argument is constructed more as a series of reflexes than of propositions: he raises the spectre of God's injustice, and then does not refute it so much as redefines it as God's justice. It is a self-confessingly paradoxical piece of writing, and Erasmus laboured over

---

[84] LB, x. 1283–4. See the discussion in Augustijn, 'La «Claritas Scripturae»', esp. pp. 742–4.
[85] Quoting Genesis 25: 21–3 and Deuteronomy 21: 15; see also Malachi 1 (mentioned by Erasmus). The text used here is Erasmus's version, not the Vulgate.

it for at least twenty years in a succession of public wrangles of which the dispute with Luther formed only a part. Erasmus had been engaged in controversy since the publication of his *Paraphrases* on the Epistle in 1517. Here he took the view, supporting himself with citations from Origen and Jerome, that Paul is able to justify the righteousness of God because 'some part of it depends on our own will and effort, although this part is so minor that it seems like nothing at all in comparison with the free kindness of God'.[86] In 1522, Pirckheimer warned Erasmus that the Lutherans were quoting this passage against him, accusing him of 'turning upside down . . . Paul's words and intentions'.[87]

Erasmus defended his orthodoxy against such a charge, and publicly vindicated himself in a letter to Martinus Laurinus. This was a major exercise in apologetics in relation to the Luther crisis; Erasmus's sense of its importance is shown from the fact that he published it as an appendix to the catalogue of his complete works, the *Catalogus lucubrationum* printed by Froben in April 1523.[88] The letter includes a trial run for the *Diatribe*. He describes the extraordinary control of language necessary to establish a position between this Scylla and Charybdis: between giving in to fatalistic despair, and arrogating all ethical power to human motivation.[89] But he confesses himself ill inclined to devote more time to this dispute, 'since this is an abyss no man can get to the bottom of' (*quando abyssus est impervestigabilis*; *EE*, v. 226; *CWE* iv. 400). In what were by now familiar words, he urged people to leave these areas of obscurity, to desist from the precision which leads to uproar and violence, and to trust to the concord of the gospel.

When Erasmus turned to these verses in his *Diatribe*, then, he had a quite specific sense of the factionalism of interpretation. Erasmus privately wished that scholarship could be incubated from the grubby domain of partisan politics, but his own *Paraphrases* demonstrated that the act of exegesis in 1517 was inescapably political: however wittingly, he had placed himself among party views, and for the moment uncomfort-

---

[86] *CWE*, xlii. 153.

[87] Pirckheimer to Erasmus, March 1522, *EE*, v. 29 (No. 1265). In his reply to Pirckheimer, 30 March 1522, Erasmus insisted that he had checked it out beforehand with the theologians; *EE*, v. 35 (No. 1268).

[88] The catalogue was written as a letter to Johann von Botzheim; Allen prints it as a Preface to *EE*, i. The letter to Laurinus was omitted from the 2nd, expanded edn. of the *Catalogus* in 1524, but was reprinted in the 1529 *Opus epistolarum*. It is given the date 1 February 1523, but Allen comments justly (*EE*, v. 203), that it 'has the air of a composition', and was probably extensively worked over.

[89] *EE*, v. 226 (No. 1342). The Homeric allusion was repeated in *De libero arbitrio*.

ably between parties.[90] And yet his account in *De libero arbitrio* still attempts to remain above the battle, appealing to a consensus beyond contention. Erasmus tries to show that this problem is within the grasp of scholarship.

Romans 9 occupies a classic position in Erasmus's hermeneutic programme. In some respects it represents part of the beginnings of modern historical criticism.[91] For he implicitly chastises Paul (as Jerome had done) for quoting Old Testament texts out of context, and for applying them with a 'polemical force' foreign to their historical meaning.[92] In removing the doctrinal and philosophical gloss which Paul has applied, he is restoring the original speech act which must finally be viewed as the arbiter of intended meaning. His readings take their cue from who is speaking, to whom, in what circumstances.[93]

In Exodus, Pharaoh is repeatedly appealed to by Moses to 'let my people go', but despite a series of prognostications that it may be an offer he would be unwise to refuse, and despite his own devious promises to comply, Pharaoh remains obstinate. Yet there are signs that this obstinacy is in any case part of God's providential scheme, particularly at 9: 12: 'And the LORD hardened the heart of Pharaoh, and he hearkened not unto them, as the LORD had spoken to Moses'. This is even given a purposive explanation (9: 16) that it is to show God's power, so that his name should be declared through all the earth. Paul, in turn, translated the verse into a general theory of predestination: 'Therefore hath he mercy on whom he will have mercy, and whom he will he hardeneth' (Romans 9: 18).

Erasmus was not the first to feel that it was absurd and appalling that God 'who is not only just but good also' should not only permit but even initiate evil actions, simply as a means of enhancing his own power. Origen, who was noted for the doctrine that it was God's intention to save all men, had special reason to confute such an implication; the effort called forth considerable powers of critical ingenuity, imitated and emulated in turn by Erasmus. In Περὶ Ἀρχῶν, Origen used a simile of the action of the rain and the sun: the same rain brings forth crops and fruit in one place, thorns and thistles in another; and the same sun melts wax and 'hardens' mud. In the same way, he says, God's forbearance makes some people obstinate in their wrong doing, but brings others to repentance. God's will

---

[90] In the 1532 edition of the *Paraphrases*, in order to attempt a new *rapprochement* with the Lutherans, he changed his interpretation; see Payne, 'Lutheranizing changes', pp. 323–4.

[91] See Bentley, *Humanists and Holy Writ*, esp. ch. 1 and pp. 183–4.

[92] Jerome, cited in Rupp and Watson, p. 70n.

[93] See Bentley, p. 31 and Chomarat, 'Les *Annotations* de Valla', p. 223.

accords not with rules of behavioural intentionality, but with laws of physics: it is no more proper to blame God than to blame the rain. Jerome went further: the hardening of Pharaoh's heart was even (seen from God's perspective) an occasion for repentance, and thus properly speaking an act of mercy.

Erasmus found in these interpretations a solution to his problem, and perceived God's agency in this passage ('the LORD hardened the heart') as a rhetorical trope. This trope is found all the time in common speech, he says, as when a father is said to 'spoil' his son by failing to punish him. It is a subtle piece of linguistic analysis, attentive to the way in which a grammatical subject is not equivalent to a philosophical agent—and it is acknowledged as such by Luther (WA 18.702.10). But Luther is less impressed by it as a piece of literary criticism. The question, Luther says, is not whether the trope is used in common speech, or whether it is possible linguistically to interpret the passage in this way, but 'the use the writer makes of it', and 'whether Paul intended it to be so used' (p. 223). On this point Luther demurs, accusing Erasmus of *licentia interpretandi* (WA 18.703.29).

According to Luther, Erasmus has not only read the passage rhetorically, he has emended it grammatically:

cum Deus dicit: Ego indurabo cor Pharaonis, mutatis personis suis accipias: Pharao indurat sese mea lenitate   (WA 18.703.30)

[When God says, 'I will harden Pharaoh's heart', you change the person and take it to mean 'Pharaoh hardens himself through my forbearance', p. 225]

First Erasmus has expounded the passage in Exodus by means of the explanation 'he is described as the agent who merely provides an opportunity'. Without further comment he has also replaced 'And God hardened the heart of Pharaoh' with the gloss 'Pharaoh was created with a will that could turn either way, but of his own wish he turned to evil'. As Luther comments, the passive 'his heart was hardened' is thus changed to the active 'he turned to evil'.

Luther calls this a *nova at inaudita grammatica* ('new and unheard of grammar'). The change of person has enormous effects on theology. For the direction of grace is effectively reversed. And the problem with Erasmus's method of interpretation is that these reversals cannot be halted, but may be recapitulated indefinitely, as Luther proceeds to show with satiric gusto:

In this way, his sending of Christ as saviour into the world will not be said to be an act of mercy on God's part, but an act of hardening, because by this mercy he has given men occasion to harden themselves ... When he takes the saints up to heaven on the Day of Judgement, this will not be an act of mercy, but of hardening, in as much as it will provide an opportunity for them to abuse his goodness. But when he thrusts the ungodly down into hell, he will be having mercy on them, because he is punishing sinners. I ask you, whoever heard of such acts of divine mercy and wrath as these?   (p. 225).

If we follow Erasmus's analysis, Luther argues, 'anything might be made of anything' (p. 224). Yet Erasmus has not intended such a deconstruction of the semantics, rather he has presented his own version as the proper sense of the passage. But if Erasmus's analysis collapses from emendatory conviction into uncontrollable instability, there is something equally problematic about Luther's assertion of his own interpretation in turn as following the *naturalis significatio* (WA 18.702.21). His insistence that

tropum hic nullum esse posse, simpliciter vero, ut sonant verba, sermonem Dei esse accipiendum   (WA 18.702.33)

[there can be no trope here, and what God says must be taken quite simply at its face value, p. 223]

implies that an easy distinction can be made between 'trope' and 'face value'—that Erasmus has embellished the sense, whereas Luther sticks to the 'natural meaning'. Luther asks us to take the words *ut sonant* ('as they sound', repeated at WA 18.703.9), and to respect the exact verbal forms of the passage, in terms of their grammatical person and voice. But this is to assume a natural correspondence between grammar and ontology, which Luther even in this same passage argues against. It is hard to know what a rigidly ontological interpretation of grammatical voice would make, for instance, of Latin deponent verbs, where a passive form is used in place of an active.

As this confrontation between Erasmus and Luther shows, interpretation is more difficult than either writer, for the sake of polemic, will admit. The reason is not that they have suddenly forgotten their rudiments—both treatises are full of subtle and intricate linguistic analysis—but because so much is at stake in these minute modulations of language.

As his final instance of exegesis, Erasmus takes Paul's citation of Jeremiah:

And when the vessel that he made of the clay was marred in the hands of the potter, he made again another vessel, as seemed good to the potter to make it. Then the word of the LORD came to me, saying, O house of Israel, cannot I do with you as with this potter? saith the LORD. Behold, as clay in the potter's hand, so are you in mine hand, O house of Israel   (Jeremiah 18: 4–6)[94]

Erasmus searches for some rhetorical explanation of the passage.[95] He reacts with repulsion to 'the polemic force' Paul attributes to it. For if man is simply clay in God's hands, the marred shape of the pot is no one's fault but the potter's, who created the clay and moulded it. 'Yet here a vessel which has been guilty of nothing because it is not its own master is thrown into eternal fire' (p. 71). It must be some fault in the pot which makes the potter reject it; just as it must be some fault in Esau which makes God prefer Jacob to him: 'those whom God hates or loves, he hates or loves for just reasons' (p. 70). So Erasmus interprets the potter and the clay metaphorically: the clay is an instrument, but not an ignorant or inert one; this is why the clay can be exhorted and incited (as occurs soon afterwards) to improve itself. Such exhortations, as we have seen, are for Erasmus proof enough of free choice.

Erasmus admits his interpretation is contrary to 'the literal meaning' (p. 74, also p. 72). His reasoning is that this is the only way to avoid making God unrighteous: 'anyone would deem a master cruel and unjust who flogged his slave to death because his body was too short or his nose too long or some other inelegance in his form' (p. 88); and even worse if he himself was understood to be responsible for those deformities. In a similar way, a master who gave incessant commands to a slave bound by his feet to a treadmill, 'Go there, do that, run, come back', with 'frightful threats if he disobeyed', would be mad and cruel, 'beating a man to death for not doing what he was unable to do' (p. 89).

Erasmus's *De libero arbitrio* is a passionate defence of a God of reason and justice. In this his linguistic analysis and his interpretative methodology are of a piece. Where scripture is obscure, where the literal meaning is 'absurd', 'we are forced whether we like it or not to forsake the literal sense of the words and seek their meaning modified by interpretation' (col. 1248; p. 97).[96] This rationalization of the literal sense by means of figures of speech is required, Erasmus says, 'in order to have something to impute justly to the wicked, who have voluntarily come short of the grace of God, in order that the calumny of cruelty and injustice may be excluded from

---

[94] Compare also Isaiah 45: 9.

[95] On this complex passage, see the illuminating arguments of Davies, 'Potter, Prophet and People', esp. pp. 27–30.

[96] On the tensions and reconciliations in Erasmus between the literal and the allegorical sense, see Payne, 'Hermeneutics of Erasmus', although Payne is heavily reliant on the late *Ecclesiastes* (1535).

God' (p. 97). Erasmus comes as close as blasphemy permits to saying that, in the literal sense, God is unjust.

Erasmus's theology is founded on legal grounds, by which God's actions must be fulfilled according to natural justice. Erasmus also has moral grounds, for free choice seems to him to keep human beings from despair, and to incite them to endeavour (p. 96). For Erasmus, the concepts of the justice of God and human responsibility are inseparable. The notion of a man created to be incapable of good, and entirely dependent on grace for salvation, is not just foreign to him, it contradicts every religious value.

By contrast, Luther's doctrines seem to him a hideous form of exaggeration, of 'hyperbole' and 'paradox'. Luther even appears to delight in such statements: *Id genus hyperbolis delectatus videtur Lutherus* (col. 1246F). Luther has abandoned ἀξίωματα and espoused παράδ οξωτερα ('more than paradoxes'). The sarcasm is heightened by this word being a paradox in itself. Luther's paradoxes are directly related to the confusion and hatred that have overwhelmed Christian Europe. As early as the letter to Justus Jonas in 1521, Erasmus bemoaned Luther's incorrigible preference for *paradoxa*, which will always lead to trouble.[97] The letter to Laurinus in 1523 expresses his convinced belief that doctrinal quiddities lead only to discord. But even these remarks of conciliation had fractious results. Ulrich von Hutten found in them a confirmation of the increasing sense among the embattled religious dissenters that Erasmus was deserting the cause in favour of a quiet life. And whereas Erasmus finds concord a proof of the *pax Christi*, Hutten sees in it a proof of apostasy. 'Anyone who proclaims the gospel sows the apple of discord', he wrote in his formal attack on Erasmus.[98] Rejecting moderation, he constructs a rapturous apocalyptic of violence: 'Did not Christ say there would be hate and dissension, wars and bloodshed on account of his teaching?' In the same year, the first Lutherans were burned at the stake in Brussels. In such a context, Erasmus's reply hovers between horrified equity and pusillanimous aloofness: 'I am of no mind to die for the paradoxes of Luther'.[99]

Luther, like Hutten, sees in dissension the trial of orthodoxy. Erasmus asks at the end of *De libero arbitrio* whether it is reasonable to accept, in place of 'the consensus of many centuries', *paradoxa quaedam, ob quae nunc tumultuatur orbis Christianus* (col. 1248C). Luther halts for a moment to acknowledge Erasmus's arduous and well-intentioned efforts

---

[97] *EE*, iv. 487 (No. 1202).   [98] *Expostulatio, Schriften*, ii. 226–7.
[99] *Spongia*, ASD, ix.1; see also pp. 208–9.

for peace, then reflects: 'to wish to stop these tumults . . . is nothing else but to wish to suppress and prohibit the word of God. For the word of God comes, whenever it comes, to change and renew the world' (p. 129).

Luther's argument is that 'tumult' exists as much within the word of God as it does outside in the world. Doctrine works in contradictions, so that when God 'justifies he does so by making men guilty' (p. 138). Erasmus's very effort to free scripture from contradiction in this respect is an act of suppression and prohibition. For the argument of absurdity could apply to virtually any article of faith. After all, according to Paul, Christ crucified 'is a stumbling block to Jews, and folly to Gentiles' (I Corinthians 1: 23). In this sense, 'tropes are no use, and there is no avoiding the absurdity' (p. 230). Outdoing even the author of *Encomium Moriae, De servo arbitrio* offers to play the fool for Christ. Far more than Erasmus's own exercise in folly, Luther took risks with the grounds of rational humanism itself. It is a measure of his success that Erasmus failed to see the joke.

Luther's triumphant embrace of paradox is a rational defence of irrationalism rather than an irrational attack on rationalism. It involves a sharp attack on what he sees as the lack of ethical density in Erasmus's interpretations. Erasmus describes a world in which choices can always be made, and justice can always be done, because he believes that otherwise the world is irredeemably unjust, and God with it. But the Old Testament texts of the potter and the clay, or of Jacob and Esau, represent for Luther more vexed contingencies:

But as for the idea that freedom of choice is not lost if we are as clay in God's hands when he afflicts us, I do not see the point of it or why Diatribe contends for it, since there is no doubt but afflictions come upon us from God against our will, and put us under the necessity of bearing them, nor is it in our power to avert them, although we are exhorted to bear them willingly   (p. 255).

If Erasmus argues that this risks making God seem unjust, then Luther replies that this is exactly the difficulty that the Old Testament texts force us to consider: Jeremiah 18: 6 is shot through with the terrifying possibility that God is unjust, a suggestion which it struggles to repress. Why else should Paul so tortuously ask, 'Is there then unrighteousness with God?' before abjuring the very question, 'God forbid'? Paul confronts the possibility, then vigorously denies it; but the whole point of his argument would be lost if the fault were seen to lie so self-evidently 'with the vessel and not with the potter' (p. 257).

With similarly racked paradoxicality, Luther writes that 'this is the highest degree of faith, to believe him merciful when he saves so few and damns so many, and to believe him righteous when by his own will he makes us damnable' (p. 138). Such paradoxes involve not only public discord, but a violent dissension of the self with the self:

Ego ipse non semel offensus sum usque ad profundum et abyssum desperationis, ut optarem nunquam esse me creatum hominem, antequam scirem, quam salutaris illa esset desperatio et quam gratiae propinqua   (WA 18.719.9)

[I myself was offended more than once, and brought to the very depth and abyss of despair, so that I wished I had never been created a man, before I realized how salutary that despair was, and how near to grace, p. 244]

With these words, Luther willingly threw Christianity into crisis. Erasmus challenged Luther to back his theology with literary principles. Luther responded by taking Erasmus's axiom of interpretative freedom at its word. Humanist theory—however distorted Luther's version of it was— had never seemed so powerful. The Lutheran speech acts, confident and paradoxical at the same time, appeared to give the reader—any Christian reader—limitless power to construct doctrine. Far from settling the matter of free will and predestination, the literary quarrel of Erasmus and Luther gave it new urgency and uncertainty. In these violent controversies of meaning, the anxieties of ambiguity are suppressed in prescriptions of terrifying exactitude. Erasmus abandons *varia* in the hope of a *sensus simplex*; Luther asserts scriptural *claritas*, then occludes it with *paradoxa*. The burden placed on language redoubles both in the relentless efforts at precision, and in the way precision suddenly evades their grasp. In a manner that provides a premonition for the coming century, theology seems at once insoluble and in need of immediate solution. As if the terrain of grammar and grace were not already muddied enough, it was now about to enter the open field of the vernacular.

Part Two

The English Language and the English Reformations 1521–1603

Bot lat vs haif the bukis necessare
To commoun weill and our Saluatioun
Iustlye translatit, in our toung Vulgare
    David Lindsay, *Ane Dialog betwix*
        Experience and ane Courteour

Whereto our language giveth us great occasion, being indeed capable of any excellent exercising of it. I knowe some will say it is a mingled language: And why not, so much the better, taking the best of both the other? Another will say, it wanteth Grammer. Nay truly it hath that praise that it wants not Grammer; for Grammer it might have, but it needs it not, being so easie in it selfe, and so voyd of those combersome differences of *Cases, Genders, Moods,* & *Tenses,* which I think was a peece of the Tower of *Babilons* curse, that a man should be put to schoole to learn his mother tongue.

                    Philip Sidney, *Defence of Poesie*

Part Two

The English Language and the English Reformations 1521–1662

5   Vernacular Theology

Part Two now moves the scene to England. This is a move of more than location. From a European perspective the religious changes in England are a messy offshore affair. They lend themselves much less obviously than Luther's Reformation to intellectual or cultural analysis. Partly this is a matter of politics, since the religious world of sixteenth-century England is dominated by the murky factional milieu of the Tudor regime and its court. The shadow of political violence falls over most of the figures in the pages that follow. However, the centre of attention is not on religious politics narrowly defined but on the emergence of a vernacular religion, which comes to occupy a central place in English culture as a whole. Part Three studies that wider culture in the form of religious literature. Part Two focuses on the extraordinary history of the English language as a medium for a new theology and national church. This is a history which combines ideological brutality with intellectual creativity. The English language became the carrier of a national religious culture and as such was invested with a peculiarly heavy charge. Yet it was not a neutral medium. For the vernacular itself was in flux. As a linguistic entity it was barely understood or studied. Part Two is therefore a study of the translation of religious authority from Latin into the vernacular, and also of an emerging discourse for understanding these processes of translation. In this way, Part Two brings together two stories which are well enough known in their own fields, but which together represent a complex network of language and belief.

*

The papal bull *Exsurge Domine*, promulgated on 15 June 1520, condemned forty-one statements extracted from Luther's works, and assigned him sixty days in which to recant. On 3 January 1521, this 'wild boar, at loose among the vineyards of the Lord' was formally excommunicated. In England, the importation and sale of books by Luther was banned by Cardinal Wolsey early in 1521. On 12 May, in Ascension week, Wolsey publicly declaimed *Exsurge Domine* in the churchyard of St Paul's Cathedral, and ceremonially incinerated a selection of Luther's works.[1] This exemplary piece of ecclesiastical theatre concluded with a sermon preached by the Bishop of Rochester, John Fisher.

Wolsey's action inaugurated the English campaign against the Lutheran heresy. Fisher's sermon inaugurated a literary campaign of orthodoxy against the forces of unorthodoxy. Against the background of the temporal turmoil of the king's divorce, in which parties and sects enjoyed favour and disfavour with alarming regularity, this literary struggle for the soul of England continued throughout the reign of Henry VIII. In this struggle, writers on both sides proved themselves, if sometimes reluctantly, children of the world of Erasmus and Luther. For the battle between prominent catholic humanists and Luther's English supporters was as much about the English language as it was about the new theology. The effort to win this battle, on both sides, involved a controversy about translation and meaning, about modernity and the ancient classics. It also involved the reception of the new humanism into the vernacular field, as English was given an independent analytic tradition in grammar, logic, and rhetoric. The story of the English Reformation is the story of the politics of the vernacular, and at the same time of what we may call vernacular theology.

Fisher's sermon has a prime place in the history of religious controversy in England, identifying immediately Luther's three principal arguments: denying papal supremacy; affirming the sole authority of scripture in determining doctrine; and asserting justification by faith alone.[2] However, Fisher's theological essay is also notable for being written in English. To dispute with Luther, Fisher had to translate him, and develop a theological language in a tongue unaccustomed for the purpose. For a hundred years, theological writing in English had been associated with dissidence. Arundel's Constitutions of 1408 condemned vernacular theology, unless approved by the ordinary, as heresy, and threatened it with censure or even death. Lollards, not bishops, spoke religion in English.[3]

Fisher was writing a sermon, not a treatise, and he was doing so at the behest of the archbishop. Yet the oddity of writing theology in the vernacular can be seen from the fact that after its initial publication in English, the sermon was reprinted in a Latin version in 1522.[4] Fisher's

---

[1] BL, MS Cotton Vitellius B.IV, fo. 115 (formerly fo. 111); see also *CSPV*, 3, 210, and 213.

[2] See Clebsch, *England's Earliest Protestants*, p. 31; and Rex, *Theology of Fisher*, p. 80 and esp. pp. 116–17.

[3] The Constitutions are printed in Wilkins, *Concilia*, iii. 314–19; see Strohm, 'Lancastrian Court', in *CHMEL*, 645–6.

[4] The English version was reprinted three times in the 1520s (*STC* 10894 and 10895–7). Latin version (by Richard Pace): *STC* 10898.

further offensives against Luther were also, naturally, in Latin.[5] Latin was the language of the church and of scholarship. This made Fisher's first essay in English difficult, for several reasons. One was a lack of technical terms of established usage, leaving no stable ground for discussion and interpretation, and a necessity for coinages. A second difficulty lay in the sense (often expressed in the sixteenth century) of indecorum in the vernacular, and discomfort for the writer in addressing abstract ideas in an inappropriate medium.[6] But the third was the most problematic for Fisher. His argument concerned the authority of doctrinal tradition, a tradition inscribed exclusively in Latin. On what authority could Fisher claim tradition in English, in which that tradition was as yet unwritten?

Fisher's difficulties are most apparent in areas where he perceives Luther to be most novel (that is, precisely those points where Luther is accused of heresy), since Fisher has to find novel words to rebut him. The area of his greatest difficulty, occupying the second part of the sermon, concerns justification by faith:

But now to what purpose serueth this instruccyon. To this. It subuerteth one grete grounde of Martyn Luther whiche is this y^t faythe alone withouten workes doth Iustifye a synner. Vpon ye whiche ground he byldeth many other erroneous artycles & specyallye y^t the sacramentes of christes chirche dothe not Iustyfye but only faythe. A perylous artycle able to subuerte all ye order [of?] the chirche. (B5^v)

The verb 'to Iustyfye', in its theological sense, was untried ground in English.[7] Early sixteenth-century examples cited in the *OED* are from biblical translations—all of them protestant—mainly in relation to Romans. Fisher was trying to define a particular theological meaning with a word not yet coined for the purpose. In the same decade his opponents were appropriating the word for a different meaning.

Other senses of 'to justify' were current. The word was commonly used in a legal context, to mean 'to administer justice to, to treat justly' and hence also 'to execute justice upon, to punish'—exactly the senses explicit in the Greek δικαιόω, and implicit in the Latin *iustificare*, against which Luther grappled in the previous decade. A third meaning, less common, was 'to show a person to be just or in the right'. This had been used in the Wyclifite translation of the verse in Psalms quoted in Romans 3, in turn so problematic for Luther, 'That thou be iustefied in thi woordis' (Psalm 50

---

[5] Principally the *Confutatio* (1523).
[6] See Jones, *Triumph of the English Language*, chs. 3–4.
[7] See Cummings, 'Justifying God', esp. 152–7.

(51): 4). But even as Fisher was writing, the word was acquiring further nuances.

Justification by faith, as Fisher perceptively foresaw, was to become the great battleground between English Christians. This was due to the prominence of this doctrine in the Lutheran affair. But the battle was vexatious for other reasons. Perhaps more than any other word, 'justification' involves all the latent forces and tensions of humanism. The word incorporates three different linguistic traditions in the ancient languages in collision with each other. Formidable expertise in Hebrew, Greek, and Latin was required to understand it, yet this expertise was likely to increase tensions rather than resolve them. The difficulties were only exacerbated in that other humanist arena, the vernacular.

In the theory of justification, the great paymasters of humanism—political, theological, and legal—came to a head. 'To justify' was a volatile word, with a specific and sometimes violently applied legal resonance. The *OED* records five new meanings during the course of the sixteenth century.[8] Fisher attempts to restore the natural justice of the legal meaning, so that a man is 'iustifyed by his deedes' in the sense that he is 'shown to be right, vindicated'. But he can only do so by showing that Luther has misconceived the meaning applied to the word in scripture. To demonstrate in English Luther's misconstruction Fisher has to dispute the meanings of scripture in English. Translation of scripture into English had been illegal since Arundel's Constitutions; in a technical sense, Fisher was in breach of these regulations by Englishing a single verse.[9] Fisher's problem is not just that there are no agreed meanings for the Bible in English, but that there is not even an agreed text of the English Bible.

I DIFFERENT TONGUES: MORE VERSUS TYNDALE

One of the New Testament texts Fisher cites against Luther's assertion of justification by faith alone is Galatians 5: 6. He quotes it in Latin and in his own English rendition: '*fides que per dilectionem operatur*, that is to saye, Faythe which is wrought by loue' (C3ʳ). Love, Fisher says, therefore constitutes a separate, and prior, duty for the Christian than faith.

In 1528, William Tyndale chided the cardinal for an elementary grammatical blunder:

---

[8] *OED* 5b,5c,6a,7a,9a. The dating in *OED* should be taken only as a rough guide.
[9] Wilkins, *Concilia*, iii. 317; see Justice, 'Lollardy', in *CHMEL*, 676 and 678.

Rochester . . . intendinge to prove y^t we are iustified thorow holy workes/allegeth halfe a texte of Paul of the fyfte to the Galathiens (as his maner is to iugle and convaye craftily) *fides per dilectionem operans*. Which texte he this wise englisheth: faith which is wrought by love/and maketh a verbe passive of a verbe deponente. Rochester will have love to goo before and fayth to springe out of love. Thus Antichrist turneth the rotes of ye tree upwarde.[10]

If the linguistic point is complicated, the doctrinal point is anything but trivial.[11] For Tyndale, the verse is a proof-text that 'fayth . . . iustifi-eth a man' (J2^v). True faith will result in love, and indeed in works, but only as the 'fruit' of faith, not as its predisposition. For Fisher, the text shows the opposite: faith, works, and love are part of a mutually suppor-tive spiritual economy, all of which 'be requyred to the iustyfyenge of our soules'.

The problem for both Fisher and Tyndale is that to settle their contro-versy over interpretation, they need to settle on a text to interpret; and arriving at such a text in English requires a theological controversy. Construing Galatians in English takes them back into the semantics of both Latin and Greek texts. But retranslated into English the text does not stay the same. For the signification of English is different from the signifi-cation of Greek and Latin. For instance, English, unlike Greek and Latin, has no deponent form. English grammar, as well as Lutheran theology, divides Tyndale from Fisher.

By 1528, Tyndale had secretly published his translation of the New Testament in Germany. He worked from the Greek text of Erasmus's edition, in consultation with Erasmus's Latin translation, the Vulgate (more occasionally), and Luther's German translation of 1522.[12] The authorities moved quickly to suppress Tyndale's version. The Bishop of London, Cuthbert Tunstal, ordered the investigation of London book-sellers and merchants, and the confiscation of any copies found. In March 1528, Tunstal wrote to Thomas More, urging him to employ his literary

---

[10] *Obedience*, J1^r; *Doctrinal Treatises*, ed. Walter, pp. 221–2. In his 1526 NT Tyndale trans-lated the verse 'faith which by love is mighty in operacion'.

[11] *Operatur* is clearly deponent, and 'is wrought' is a mistranslation. Surtz, *Works and Days*, p. 204, comments: 'What induced Fisher to this particular English translation is not clear'. In his *Sermon* on Barnes's abjuration (1526), he translated 'faith whiche worketh by loue'. Fisher's Latin text is not the Vulgate but Erasmus's translation, yet Fisher for some reason ignored Erasmus's Annotation: ἐνεργουμένη, *quod agens rectius verti poterat* (LB vi. 822).

[12] Tyndale worked from Erasmus's 3rd edn. of 1522. He may also have used the Wyclifite version (which was banned, but circulated in a large number of MSS); Cummings, 'Justifying God', 147–9. The first print at Cologne was intercepted and stopped, and work moved to Worms.

talents against heretical books and translations. More had already written in Latin the polemical *Responsio ad Lutherum,* and had been employed by Wolsey in searching German merchants in the Steelyard in 1526. Tunstal, however, had something different in mind: he wished More to write in *lingua nostra vernacula,* in order 'to reveal to simple and uneducated men the deceitful malice of the heretics'.[13] Tunstal perceived a necessity to refute English Lutherans not only in kind but also in their own language. The battle could not be won in Latin alone.

More's contribution to the controversial campaign was staggering. From 1529 to 1532 he was Henry's lord chancellor; and yet between Tunstal's commission and his own imprisonment by Henry in April 1534 he contributed one million words of polemic, all in the vernacular (some of it very much so).[14] It quickly became an argument also about the vernacular. More attacked Tyndale's translation for being heretical but also faulty. Indeed, errors of language and of theology are for More virtually synonymous. Tyndale, he says in the *Dialogue Concerning Heresies,* has 'many textys vntrewely translated for the mayntenaunce of heresye'.[15] It would be easier to retranslate the whole book than to correct its errors (p. 293). He expresses himself astonished that anyone should 'complayne of the burnynge of that booke' (p. 285).

The brunt of More's argument about Tyndale's version concerns its rendering of words such as 'church', 'priest', and 'charity' by the words 'congregation', 'senior', and 'love'. Worst of all, perhaps, Tyndale replaces 'grace' with 'favour'. It is obvious why More should object: these are some of the key concepts of catholic ecclesiology. Yet he grounds his objection not on dogma but linguistic usage: 'Nowe do these names in our englyshe tonge neyther expresse the thynges that bi ment by them' (p. 286). Tyndale has removed 'yᵉ comon knowen worde' and replaced it with a coinage ('senior') which is foreign to the ear and practically incomprehensible: 'in our englysshe tonge this worde senyor sygnyfyeth no thynge at all but is a frenche worde vsed in englysshe more than halfe in mockage' (p. 286).

The effect of these new-fangled words, More says, is 'mischeyuous'. For by 'the turnynge of these names' the reader is made to feel as if they were never used or intended in the New Testament but were fabricated by the church:

[13] *Correspondence,* ed. Rogers, No. 160, p. 387. The novelty of the request is shown by the fact that Tunstal's own letter is in Latin.
[14] List of works in Fox, *More,* p. 145; discussion, pp. 144–6.
[15] *Dialogue, CWM,* vi. 290.

And then wolde he with his false translacyon make the people wene further that suche articles of our faythe as he laboreth to destroy and whyche be well proued by holy scrypture were in holy scrypture nothynge spoken of but that the prechers haue all thys .xv. C. yere mysse reported yᵉ gospell and englyshed the scrypture wronge to lede the people purposely out of the righte way   (p. 290)

Some profound problems of translation are raised here. Tyndale replied that he made coinages to render the original Greek more accurately. Mockingly, he quoted More's 'derelynge Erasmus' in his own support.[16] None the less, he can hardly find English equivalents that will do. For English usage has developed in line not with the connotation of first-century Greek but with the usage and signification of fifteen hundred intervening years of church Latin. As a social meaning, the Greek ἐκκλησία has been occluded by the Latin *ecclesia*, and is not recoverable in English. More's problem, on the other hand, is that while he can easily support his doctrinal arguments by reference to the Vulgate, in English he is groundless.[17]

Hence it is that More argues that 'it is dangerous to translate yᵉ texte of scrypture out of one tongue into another as saynt Hyerome testyfyeth for as moche as in translacyon it is harde alwaye to kepe the same sentence hole' (p. 315). Arundel's Constitutions, too, had used Jerome's admonition to justify censorship. The obvious irony is that it was Jerome who translated the Greek text into Latin, the very translation which More uses as his authoritative 'text'. His argument thus opens out from the question of interpretation of scripture into a question about the interpretability of language and, more vexingly still, from language to language.

This is what lends interest to his strictures against the professed reliance of Tyndale and Luther on 'scripture alone', a doctrine More calls 'a playne pestylent heresye' (p. 290). Within the dialogue form, More dramatizes his heterodoxical interlocutor as spouting forth gobbets of scripture, and interpreting them to mean what he likes. The most extended example is where More represents his opponent (in a direct pastiche of Tyndale) as expounding the idea of justification by faith alone. This chapter in Book IV of the *Dialogue Concerning Heresies* amounts to a practical and dramatic analysis both of Lutheran doctrine and of Lutheran exegesis, and the relation between the two. At the same time it indicates the difficulties of inventing a new exegetical practice in the vernacular.

---

[16] *Answere*, p. 14.
[17] On More's use of Greek in the controversy, see Marius in *Confutation*, CWM, viii. 1350–51.

More's imaginary heretic is examined by some 'ryght honorable vertu-ous and very cunning persons'.[18] Asked to explain justification by faith, he refers to four texts from Romans, two from Galatians, and one from Mark. However, he does not quote them accurately: he paraphrases, leaves words out, and elides two different texts together. Then he pronounces squarely 'By all these textys . . . yt playnely appered that all of our salvacyon came of fayth' (p. 391). His examiners dispute his exegesis at length. They accuse him of interpreting words too narrowly and without respect to context. Paul denied only that we are saved by good works before baptism: 'there ys neuer a texte of them nor eny other in scrypture' which implies that after baptism we may be saved by faith without good works. More's heretic has simplistically extracted a phrase for his own purpose without respect to its fuller signification and context.[19]

Earlier in the *Dialogue*, More satirically ventriloquizes the methodol-ogical principles of his opponents. It is no crude parody, for More presents him as neither stupid nor unlearned: instead, he is made to undo his own principles even as he explains them. The heretic says that he has 'gyuen dylygence to the latyn tonge', but is doubtful of other academic disciplines such as logic ('but bablynge') and philosophy ('the most vanyte of all'), which have together 'lost all good dyuynyte with the subteltye of theyr questyons'.[20] Instead he concentrates only on scripture, from which he endeavours to elicit 'the sentence and vnderstandynge therof'. He has no time for 'interpretours' and 'gloses', but finds the text itself illumination enough; difficulties, he claims, are solved by simple cross-reference within scripture; if all else fails, he is aided by the help of God 'which neuer fayleth them that faythfully trust in his promise'.

However, More is a careful enough reader of Tyndale to know that his opponent has an answer to the examiners' assertion that faith is not suffi-cient without good works. The heretic is represented as saying that 'fayth hath alway good hope and charite wyth it and can not but worke well no more than the fyre can be without hete and lyght' (pp. 382–3). As proof-text, interestingly enough, the heretic uses the verse Galatians 5: 6, '*Fides quae per dilectionem operatur* fayth worketh by cheryte', but his proof is the

---

[18] *Dialogue*, Bk. IV, ch. 11, *CWM*, vi. 379. Tyndale, in his *Answere*, p. 194, identifies the heretic as Dr Forman; but More has more than one target, including Tyndale himself, whom he quotes and tendentiously misquotes throughout.

[19] 'And that thys ys thus we maye well knowe by the textys of holy scrypture yf we sette theym together and take not one texte for our parte and set a nother at nought' (*CWM*, vi. 392).

[20] *Dialogue*, i. 1, *CWM* vi. 33. Perhaps unwittingly, More thus ascribes to the heretic a reasonable summary of Erasmus's views in e.g. *De pueris institutiendis*.

opposite of that proposed by Fisher a few years before: 'it can not but be that thys charyte is alway ioyned vnto fayth' (p. 383).[21]

A true faith, the heretic is made to argue, 'hath alway good hope and charite wyth it', and a trust in God's promises, otherwise it is not faith at all, but only a dead faith. This argument the examiners dismiss as an 'equyvocacyon of the word fayth' (p. 387). The heretic has failed to use 'the word in hys ryghte sygnyfycation'. But 'equyuocacyon' (a word More repeats several times) is the very opposite of the fault otherwise charged by More, that the heretic uses words simplistically and without contextual understanding. And what else but 'equyuocacyon' is More's own argument that 'justification by faith' applies only to those before baptism, or his argument that this constitutes only the 'first iustyfycacyon', followed by a second in which good works are necessary and performable?

More attempts to satirize his opponent as simplistically bound to a rigid and incoherent exegetical rule, but even within his own drama he shows protestant exegesis as more complicated than he admits. Indeed in some respects it is not so unlike his own. In the event, Tyndale simply returned More's charges back upon him:

Master More declareth the meaninge of no sentence he describeth the propir significacion of no worde ner the difference of the significacions of any terme/but runneth forth confusedly in vnknowen wordes and general termes. And where one worde hath many significacions he maketh a man some time beleue that manye thinges are but one thynge/and some time he leadeth from one significacion vnto another and mocketh a mans wittes.[22]

Tyndale's interpretative principles, as this passage shows, are not so easily paraphrased or parodied as More claims. On the one hand (as More disapprovingly noted) Tyndale distrusted the medieval glossatory tradition.[23] The right method of reading Jonah, the *Prologe* to his translation says, is 'interpretinge it spiritually with out glose', so that 'thou fele in thyne herte'.[24] In the *Obedience of a Christen Man* he made the by now commonplace attack on the fourfold interpretation of scripture, and the equally habitual assertion of the literal sense as the true spiritual sense.[25] His

[21] More, like Fisher, here uses Erasmus in preference to the Vulgate.

[22] *Answere*, p. 195.

[23] An account of Tyndale's putative university training at Oxford is given by Daniell, *Tyndale*, ch. 2.

[24] *The prophete Jonas*, C1r; *TOT*, p. 638. Nevertheless, Tyndale's Prologue is four times the length of the prophet's book.

[25] *Doctrinal Treatises*, p. 309 ('His literal sense is spiritual, and all his words are spiritual'). See also p. 304. Tyndale is close to Lefèvre here.

Prologue to the Pentateuch also commends only 'the playne texte and literall sense'.[26] But as with Luther's theoretical claim of *claritas scripturae*,
the relationship of these party cries to exegetical method is tenuous. In
practice, interpretation involved Luther in complex logical and philological arguments. Similarly, Tyndale's wish to lay scripture 'plainly' before
the eyes of the lay people is not a slogan for abandoning learning and
discrimination. He commends, in humanist style, 'ye processe/order and
meaninge of the texte'.[27]

The Messenger in the *Dialogue Concerning Heresies* says that scripture
takes precedence over the church, and that 'the texte is good ynough and
playne ynoughe' by itself. More replies that it is hard 'to fynde any thynge
so playne that it shold nede no glose at all' (Book. 1, ch. 28; *CWM*, vi.
168). On this account More rests his appeal to the authoritative status
of church and tradition. Scripture cannot provide authority, but only
argument. However, in the vernacular, More's own claim to authority is
vitiated by the lack of a canonical tradition of interpretation in that
language. Here, what has been termed his case for 'semantic pluralism'
actually works against him.[28] Exactly because the interpretation of scripture is arguable, and the meaning of the English Bible an open field, More
is reduced to arguing over and over again. Tyndale ridicules his contest for
'ryghte sygnyfycation' as 'the propir significacion of no worde ner the
difference of the significacions of any term'. More needs to be able to take
his 'sygnyfycation' for granted, but this he cannot do, so that he too is
reduced to 'equyuocacyon'. More's own glosses, and his glosses of
Tyndale's glosses, are reduplicated in Tyndale's *Answer unto Sir Thomas
More's Dialogue*, and then again, at ever-greater length, in More's *Confutation of Tyndale's Answer*. Not even a million words can give More the last
word on English meaning. Only death (his execution for treason in 1535
followed by Tyndale for heresy a year later, both on the order of Henry
VIII) could interrupt the endless glossing.

II THE FALL OF LANGUAGE

In one respect, Tyndale happily accepts More's dispraise: he has neglected
other sciences of learning 'saue grammar'.[29] On the prime status of

---

[26] 'A prologe shewinge the vse of the scripture', *The fyrst boke of Moses called Genesis*, A5^r.
[27] 'W. T. To the Reader', *Fyrst boke of Moses*, A2^v; *TOT*, p. 4.
[28] Marc'hadour and Lawler, 'Scripture in the *Dialogue*', *CWM*, vi. 498.
[29] *CWM*, vi. 122.

grammar Tyndale concurs with his master Erasmus: understanding the words of the ancient languages is the only way to understand the word of God.[30] After devoting (and risking) his life over some years in the study of Hebrew and Greek accidence, Tyndale presumably took less kindly to being told that his motive in preferring grammar to other sciences was 'partely in slouth refusynge the labour and payne to be susteyned in that lernynge'.[31] How to render the grammar of one language in the grammar of another was a question that caused Tyndale much labour. In 1534 he brought out a revised edition of his New Testament. Introducing his painstaking revision, in which he has 'weded oute of it many fautes', he considers the complex relation between the two languages:

> If ought seme chaunged, or not all to gether agreynge with the Greke, let the fynder of the faute consider the Hebrue Phrase or maner of speche lefte in the Greke wordes. Whose preterperfectence and presenttence is ofte both one, and the futuretence is the optative mode also, and the futuretence is ofte the imperatyve mode in the actyve voyce, and in the passive ever. Lykewyse person for person, nombre for nombre, and an interrogacion for a condicionall, and soche lyke is with the Hebrues a comen vsage.[32]

Tyndale raises profound questions about the translatability of grammar. Translatability was taken for granted in medieval speculative grammar, which conceived all languages to be governed by the same fundamental principles. Tyndale follows humanist principles in assuming instead that grammatical structures are peculiar to each language. None the less, one grammar may be compared with, and even influence, another. First-century Greek, as written by Palestinian Jews, takes on some of the characteristics of classical Hebrew.

The consequences of such an argument are more complicated for Tyndale's translation. He has to transfer the locutions of Greek (including its residual Hebraisms) into sixteenth-century vernacular. Moreover (as we see from his controversy with More) he does so against the grain of an intervening tradition in Latin, which he believes in some ways has traduced the original meanings. Yet he is still unavoidably under a Latin influence. Latin was his primary academic tongue, in which he received all his theological training. In addition, the Bible in which he was educated and from which he practised as a priest was

---

[30] Erasmus, Preface to *Annotationes, Préfaces*, pp. 160–2. Tyndale refers to Erasmus more than any other writer (including Luther).

[31] *CWM*, vi. 122.

[32] 'W. T. vnto the Reader', *Newe Testamente*, p. 3.

the Vulgate.[33] Furthermore, the terminology in which he learned English grammar was derived from Latin grammatical theory. The evidence of this appears in this same passage, where the terms 'preterperfect', 'optative', and 'condicionall' are from the Latin grammatical tradition of Priscian and Donatus.

Tyndale insisted, however, that English possessed advantages over Latin in the rendition of scripture:

> They will saye it can not be translated in to oure tonge it is so rude. It is not so rude as they are false lyers. For the greke tonge agreeth moare with the english then with the latyne. And the propirties of the hebrue tonge agreth a thousande tymes moare with the english then with the latyne. The maner of speakynge is both one so y^t in a thousande places thou neadest not but to translate it into ye english worde for worde.[34]

Effusions of linguistic patriotism were common in the first half of the sixteenth century and often used in polemic about the English Bible. Tyndale's remarks combine populist chauvinism with original linguistic theory. In saying Hebrew can be translated 'worde for worde' into English he means the structure of the Hebrew sentence can be mirrored word by word, rather than (as with Latin) laboriously negotiated by circumlocutory rephrasing. The point is purely syntactic, and whatever its accuracy (Tyndale gives no examples to justify his case) it shows how far questions of syntactic structure guided his ideas about meaning.

More took Tyndale's commendation of the sufficiency of scripture as a prescription for total subjectivity of interpretation.[35] Tyndale replied that he prescribed no such thing: he rejected the interpretative methods of the doctors ('their predicamentes/vniversales/seconde intencions/quidities hecceities & relatives') in order to replace them with his own.[36] These amount to principles of literary criticism. In the Preface to *The Obedience of a Christen Man* he warns the reader that scripture is not understood suddenly, but requires patience and diligence, like an apprentice learning from his master. This discipline consists in 'the propirties and maner of speakinges of the scripture'.

It is commonly assumed that as More was a humanist, Tyndale must be anti-humanist. The strikingly humanist vocabulary of 'the manner of

[33] Latin usage in the Vulgate, of course, is itself under the influence of both Hebrew and the Greek of the Septuagint and of the New Testament.

[34] *Obedience*, B7^v; *Doctrinal Treatises*, pp. 148–9. Further references in text, citing page numbers from both edns.

[35] See especially *Dialogue* Bk I ch. 22 and Bk III ch. 16.

[36] *Obedience*, C2^v; *Doctrinal Treatises*, pp. 157–8.

speaking' and 'the circumstances of the text' (p. 156) belies this. In his controversial works as in his translations, Tyndale labours to justify English theological usage through an emerging philology of the English language. The central argument of the *Obedience* is that 'ye scripture ought to be in ye mother tonge' (B4^r; p. 144). The law of Moses, and the prophets and the Psalms were written for the children of Israel 'in their mother tonge'. Moses himself said: 'Heare Israel let these wordes which I commaunde the this daye steke fast in thine herte/and whette them on thy childerne'.[37] Socially embedded acts of language are only possible, Tyndale argues, in the common vernacular.

The bishops have forbidden the vernacular supposedly in order to protect God's meaning from random opinion, in which 'the laye people understonde it every man after his owne wayes' (B5^v; p. 146). Yet this, Tyndale argues at the end of the Preface, is precisely the effect of leaving scripture in Latin, where every university doctor, even every priest and friar, renders the text according to his own glosing. It is through Latin that 'mans wisdome scatereth/divideth and maketh sectes' (C3^r; p. 160). By a radical twist of argument, Tyndale turns the tables and makes English the protector, not the destroyer, of God's singular wisdom:

God is not mans imaginacion/but that only which he saith of hym selfe. God is no thinge but his law and his promyses/that is to saye/that which he biddeth the doo and that which he biddeth the beleve and hope. God is but his worde: as Christ saith John. viii. I am that I saye unto you/that is to saye/that which I preach am I (C3^v; p. 160).

This is the argument of Erasmus's *Paraclesis*. God exists in language, he is incarnated in the word. But here Tyndale encounters a typically Erasmian problem: is Christ the same in every language, can he be the same 'word' in a different tongue? Is he a Hebrew word (in the original), or an Aramaic (in his own vernacular), or a Greek (into which his words were translated in the New Testament), or perhaps a Latin or an English?

Tyndale creates a problem for himself. It appears the word is received by an infinity of possible auditors, as if by simultaneous translation, each in his vernacular. The consequence of this argument is that scripture should always be written in the mother tongue. But Tyndale also wishes to argue that English reproduces God's original words more authentically, both

---

[37] Deuteronomy 6: 6–7, cited in *Obedience*, B4^v. As if to prove his point, Tyndale translated the verb 'whette' literally, using the Hebrew metaphor against the paraphrased version preferred both in the Septuagint and the Vulgate (and also later in the AV, 'teach them diligently').

from the Hebrew and from the Greek. However, Latin, too, was once a
mother tongue (it was, for instance, Jerome's), and in that sense is just
as good as (though by the same token no better than) English. Tyndale is
caught between asserting the equality of all languages, and proclaiming
the superior virtues of English. In the tension between these arguments, he
encounters a more fundamental problem of how the word can be translated at all. For in the proliferation of tongues, how can we know that God
says the same thing in each?

In the *Obedience*, Tyndale is able to claim that 'the greke tonge agreeth
moare with the english then with the latyne', but by the time of the 1534
revision of the New Testament, after several more years grappling with the
ancient languages, his view is tempered with doubts. His English version is
now 'not all to gether agreynge with the Greke' as he is caught in the complexity of the linguistic exchange. What vexes him especially is the lack of
interchangeability between grammatical forms. He notes in particular
that in Hebrew 'the futuretence is the optative mode also, and the futuretence is ofte the imperatyve mode in the actyve voyce, and in the passive
ever'.[38]

What had happened in the mean time was that Tyndale had been spend-
ing years of labour translating the Pentateuch from the original Hebrew.
He was the first Englishman to do so, for the study of Hebrew in England
was only a generation old.[39] The genesis of Tyndale's Old Testament is
therefore a primal event in the English language. Its significance can be
seen in the language of original sin in the Hebrew story of the Fall.
Tyndale's Fall shows him negotiating ambiguously between alternative
forms of language, carefully modulating English grammatical categories
in substitution for Hebrew originals.[40]

Here must be remarked some idiosyncracies of Hebrew grammar. In a
strict sense, Hebrew has no system of tenses, but uses instead what in
modern grammatical theory is called two 'aspects'. The imperfect aspect
denotes an uncompleted action, while the perfect aspect denotes a completed one. By this means, Hebrew articulates a number of distinctions,
which in another language would be covered by distinctions between
tenses.[41] The radical problems involved in describing a Semitic language

---

[38] Tyndale's judgement, interestingly, is confirmed by Butler, *Moods and Tenses*, p. 35, who
identifies an 'imperative future' in the second person as a frequent NT usage (§67), an
idiom which 'shows clearly the influence of the Septuagint', i.e. a Greek translation from
Hebrew.

[39] See Lloyd Jones, *Discovery of Hebrew*, chs. 4–5.

[40] On Tyndale's knowledge and use of Hebrew, see Hammond, 'Tyndale's Pentateuch'; and
Daniell, *Tyndale*, pp. 291–308.

[41] Weingreen, *Classical Hebrew*, pp. 56–7.

within the terminology of Latin grammar indeed led sixteenth-century grammarians to describe some uses in Hebrew as examples of 'tense'. For instance, the Hebrew imperfect can be interpreted in many cases as working analogously like a future tense, to signify an action which has not yet happened. Reuchlin, in the Hebrew grammar most widely used in the early sixteenth century, happily described such a usage as a 'future indicative' in order to aid his European readers.[42]

This process is complicated by the fact that the imperative in Hebrew is formed like an imperfect, only without the prefix. However, the imperative is never used with a negative. A negative command is expressed in exactly the same way as a negative imperfect. There is thus no way of distinguishing, formally, between the two.[43] This is of critical importance for God's prohibitions in Genesis 2 and 3, where a series of sentences involving the contrast of imperfect and perfect aspects is combined with a parallel pattern of positive and negative commands. Within this brief narrative the entire future of the human race is contained, and the economy of human sin, punishment, and redemption predicted. The rendering of this complex Hebrew grammar into another language is therefore paramount. And yet the grammar of another language inevitably encodes a different set of differences, with potential confusions and ambiguities abounding. To express this in Saussure's terms, 'The distinctions of tense which are so familiar to us are unknown in certain languages'.[44] Saussure comments specifically on the absence of a tense system in Hebrew, and uses it to argue that far from different languages embodying the same innate ideas, each language system creates a different set of values.

Tyndale renders the initial prohibition in Genesis 2: 15–17 as follows:

And the LORde God toke Adam and put him in the garden of Eden/to dresse it and to kepe it: and the LORde God commaunded Adam saynge: of all the trees of the garden se thou eate. But of the tre of knowlege of good and badd se that thou eate not: for even yᵉ same daye thou eatest of it/thou shalt surely dye.[45]

God makes two types of 'command' here, the second expressed in the negative. Because of the difference in the way an imperative is formed

---

[42] *De rudimentis Hebraicis*, Book III, p. 585. Reuchlin divided Hebrew verbs between the *imperfectus* and the *perfectus*, but also delineated three tenses (present, preterite, and future) and three moods (indicative, imperative, and infinitive), thus accommodating Hebrew within a recognizable Latinate paradigm. His conjugations of individual verbs as a result follow a familiar pattern, present indicative, preterite indicative, future indicative, present imperative, etc.

[43] Weingreen, *Classical Hebrew*, pp. 76–7.

[44] *Cours de linguistique générale*, Part II, ch. 4; quoted here from *Course*, p. 115.

[45] *The fyrst boke of Moses called Genesis* (Antwerp, 1530), B3ʳ; *TOT*, 17.

in Hebrew, there is a subtle distinction. The first clause ('āḵōl tōḵēl), concerning 'all the trees', is interpreted in rabbinic commentary in a number of different ways. Some take it as merely permission to eat any of the trees; Ibn Ezra emphasizes that this verse does not in fact contain a command at all, which is restricted to the prohibition alone. The verb is after all in the imperfect form. Others, however, take this imperfect verb as implying a command that man must partake of the food of the garden.[46] This is the sense Tyndale adopts: 'of all the trees of the garden se thou eate'. Possibly, Tyndale was influenced here by the Vulgate, which uses an imperative verb (*ex omni ligno paradisi comede*); if so, he preferred it to the more literal Latin translation of Pagninus, who made extensive use of rabbinic commentary and here employs the Latin future (*Ex omni ligno orti, comedendo comedes*).[47] Later, the Authorized Version endorsed a more emphatically permissive interpretation, 'Of every tree of the garden thou mayest freely eat.'

In the second, negative, command (lô tōḵal), Tyndale continues with the English imperative form, 'se that thou eate not', whereas in the Authorized Version this is given as 'thou shalt not eat'. Tyndale was familiar with the latter usage, and in Exodus 20 chose the form, 'Thou shalt not kyll'.[48] He was also familiar with Luther's German version. Luther with great simplicity uses the modal auxiliary 'sollen' in both clauses: 'du sollt essen von allerlen bewme ym gartten, Aber von dem bawm des erkentnis guttis und bosis soltu nicht essen', identical with the form he prefers in Exodus, 'Du solt nicht'.[49] Luther's German auxiliaries in Genesis 2: 16–17 could be interpreted either prescriptively or permissively. But Tyndale prefers to emphasize an imperative meaning by choosing an English imperative verb in place of any possible auxiliary, 'se that thou eate not'.

On the face of it, this is unfortunate, since 'Thou shalt not eat' appears to correspond exactly to the ambiguity in the Hebrew, where a negative command is identical with a negative future tense.[50] Tyndale's reason, however, seems to be that in the very next clause God repeats his grammar but with a slightly different inflection, backing up his command with the statement, 'for even yᵉ same day thou eatest of it, thou shalt surely dye'.

---

[46] Zlotowitz, *Bereishis*, pp. 100–1.

[47] Pagninus, *Biblia*, 1ᵛ. Tyndale's direct knowledge of rabbinic exegesis has not yet been quantified (for a summary, see Daniell, *Tyndale*, p. 296), but his knowledge of Pagninus has been established by Lloyd Jones, *Discovery of Hebrew*, pp. 118–20. On the use of rabbinic sources (including Ibn Ezra as well as Rashi and the brothers Kimchi) by Christian Hebraists such as Pagninus, see Lloyd Jones, *Discovery of Hebrew*, pp. 40–52.

[48] *The seconde boke of Moses called Exodus*, 35ʳ; *TOT*, 116.

[49] *Das Alte Testament* (1523), 1Moses, 2 and 2Moses, 20; WA DB, 8.42.1 and 8.262.11.

[50] On modality and negation in general, see Palmer, *Mood and Modality*, pp. 98–100.

God's grammar here, when put into English, is less clear. He might be using 'thou shalt' as a command again, stating his irrevocable Law; alternatively, he might mean it as completing a conditional, 'if you eat it . . . you will'; or else he might just be making a prediction about the future ('surely you will die').

It is exactly this ambiguity which the Serpent exploits in the next chapter:

But the serpent was sotyller than all the beastes of the felde which ye LORde God had made/and sayd vnto the woman. Ah syr/that God hath sayd/ye shall not eate of all manner trees in the garden. And the woman sayd vnto the serpent/of the frute of the trees in the garden we may eate/but of the frute of the tree y^t is in the myddes of the garden (sayd God) se that ye eate not/and se that ye touch it not: lest ye dye. (B3^v; *TOT*, 17)

Tyndale's God has made two unequivocal commands, both addressed to Adam: of trees in general, 'se thou eate', but of one particular tree, 'se that thou eate not'. The serpent plays on this, trying to create confusion in Eve's mind, who had, after all, never heard the interdiction directly from God. Tyndale's serpent does so by introducing an English grammatical ambiguity, true to the Hebrew forms, asking Eve whether God has said 'ye shall not eate of all manner trees in the garden'. This could be either a statement about the future or a direct imperative not to do so. Despite the verbal tricks, at first the woman remembers scrupulously (presumably as reported by Adam), 'of the frute of the tree y^t is in the myddes of the garden (sayd God) se that ye eate not and se that ye touch it not: lest ye dye'.

But the serpent treats God's words as if he had been making an idle and inaccurate prediction. In a wonderfully dismissive phrase, using the mild expletive 'tush', he retorts:

Then sayd the serpent vnto the woman: tush ye shall not dye: But God doth knowe/that whensoever ye shulde eate of it/youre eyes shuld be opened and ye shulde be as God and knowe both good and evell.   (B4^r; *TOT*, 17)

What the woman has understood as a command, the serpent has turned into a wish or perhaps a suggestion, to be bargained over or reasoned with. Luther captures this perfectly: Eve insists that God has said, 'Esset nicht davon . . . das yhr nicht sterbet', while the serpent replies with calculated looseness, 'yhr werdet mit nicht des tods sterben'. God's knowledge of the future is not unequivocable, but open to interpretation, even contingent, a characteristic caught by Tyndale in translating a further set of future tenses by the conditional modal auxiliary 'shuld': 'whensoever ye shulde eate of it youre eyes shuld be opened and ye shulde be as God'.

The Hebrew text uses a mixture of imperfects and imperatives for different purposes in this passage—to signify a range of semantic functions variously described by Tyndale as 'the imperatyve mode' and 'the optative mode' as well as the simple future indicative. The Authorized Version uses 'shall' in every case, but Tyndale attempts to preserve a linguistic difference by using 'shuld', 'shall', and the imperative 'se' in carefully delineated distinction. Theologically, it is easy to see why he should want to respect these distinctions. A God who makes commands and a God who merely makes predictions are two different Gods, as the serpent brilliantly realizes. One God predetermines whereas the other God only foresees. The serpent's equivocal tongue seizes on the indeterminacy of Hebrew in order to confuse Eve as to which God has been speaking. The original serpent in the garden could therefore be said to be the possibilities of misinterpretation implicit in human language.

Many of the most important passages in the New Testament play on similar areas of language, often quoting the Old Testament in the process. When Tyndale returned to the New Testament after 1530, he encountered further complications, since Greek has a different set of modal locutions from either Hebrew or English. In addition to a distinct future tense, Greek possesses separate modal forms for the subjunctive, optative, and imperative. English has only the much looser set of differences implied by the modal auxiliaries, 'shall', 'should', and so on. Although often described as a future tense, 'shall' is no such thing, as the example 'thou shalt not kill' neatly shows. Consequently, modal distinctions embodied in Greek inflections cannot be rendered by precise correspondences in English.[51]

Tyndale usually reserves 'shall' for the Greek future, and uses 'might' to distinguish the subjunctive. Thus at Romans 3: 3, he translates μὴ ἡ ἀπιστία αὐτῶν τὴν πίστιν τοῦ θεοῦ καταργήσει; 'shall their vnbeleve make the promes of god with out effecte?'; while at 3: 4 he renders Ὅπως ἄν δικαιωθῇς ἐν τοῖς λόγοις σου as 'That thou myghtest be iustifyed in thy sayinge'.[52] The third person imperative he distinguishes by using 'let', as at 3: 4, γινέσθω δὲ ὁ θεὸς ἀληθής, which he gives as 'Let god be true'. Similarly, he uses 'let' to translate the first person subjunctive as a notional imperative, as at 3: 8, ποιήσωμεν τὰ κακὰ, 'let vs do evyll'. The optative,

---

[51] See Butler, *Moods and Tenses*, p. 34, on the distinction between 'assertive' and 'promissory' uses of the predictive future in NT Greek, which requires 'delicate discrimination, but is often important for purposes of interpretation'. He comments further: 'its representation in English is complicated by the varied uses of the auxiliary verbs *shall* and *will*'. The general significance of these remarks will (shall?) be seen below.

[52] Greek text quoted from Erasmus's 3rd edn. (1522), as used by Tyndale.

μὴ γένοιτο, repeated several times throughout Romans, which he might literally have rendered 'let it not be', he chooses instead (following the revised Wyclifite Bible) to express figuratively with the impersonal command 'God forbyd'.

However, sometimes he also uses 'shall' to translate a subjunctive. He is especially prone to do this in cases where the Greek uses a first person subjunctive in a question, to express a putative wish or obligation. Conversely, occasionally he uses 'shuld' to translate a simple future (for example, νικήσεις at 3: 4). Part of his problem is the sheer diversity of means by which Greek can express contingent purposes, results, intentions, expectations, and so on. He is also hampered by the fact that English has no rigorous rules in this area but uses modal auxiliaries interchangeably to do different jobs. The result is that Greek and English use complex, but complexly different, sets of grammatical forms to signify similar sets of semantic relationships.

A good instance of the syntactic friction between New Testament Greek and Tyndale's English can be seen in his version of the beginning of Romans 6:

What shall we saye then? Shall we continue in synne, that there maye be aboundaunce of grace? God forbyd. How shall we that are deed as touchynge synne, live eny lenger therin? (6: 1–2)

Here Paul uses a future tense (τί οὖν ἐροῦμεν;) almost in place of an imperative ('What shall we saye?'), followed by a present subjunctive (ἐπιμένωμεν), as a kind of negative imperative in question form ('Shall we continue?'); then a further future indicative (ζήσομεν) implying a doubtful possibility ('How shall we that are deed . . . live eny lenger'). Tyndale, on the other hand, simply repeats 'shall' three times.

The succeeding sentences force Tyndale into further improvisations of modal auxiliaries in order to cover a variety of different constructions in the Greek:

This we must remember, that oure olde man is crucified with him also, that the body of synne myght vtterly be destroyed, that hence forth we shuld not be servauntes of synne. For he that is deed, ys iustified from synne. Wherfore yf we be deed with Christ, we beleve that we shall live with him. (6: 6–8).

In the space of a paragraph, Tyndale uses a whole lexicon of auxiliaries—'shall', 'shall', 'maye', 'shall', 'shuld', 'must', 'must', 'myght', 'shuld', 'shall'—in a scrupulous attempt to match the exacting syntax and elusive theology of Paul's intricate prose. Paul's theology modulates between a statement

of how things are, an assertion of how things can be, a description of the
conditions prescribed by God if this might happen, a prediction of how
he will reward us, and finally an exhortation as to what we should do
about it. Each clause is superimposed on the last with exacting discrimination. The concatenation of questions, Τί οὖν ἐροῦμεν; ἐπιμένωμεν τῇ
ἁμαρτίᾳ; 'What shall we saye then? Shall we continue in synne?' encapsulates this equivocation by catching the reader between God's intentions
and man's intentions, and questioning whether language can bear the
weight of either. Paul exerts unremitting pressure on Greek grammar in
order to test the concentration, linguistic and philosophical, of his
readers. In the process he places an intolerable burden on his later
translators.

III ENGLISHING GRAMMAR

In making his comments on the translatability of grammatical forms from
Hebrew to Greek to English Tyndale could not avail himself of any
grammar of the English language, since none existed until William
Bullokar's *Bref Grammar for English* of 1586, followed by P.G.'s *Grammatica Anglicana* of 1594 (written in Latin).[53] In Tyndale's time 'grammar'
meant the rules not of English usage but of Latin. Latin grammar stood as
a paradigm for all languages. Indeed, even early grammarians of English
such as Bullokar assumed the norms of Latin applied equally in English,
and advertised their works as much as aids towards the acquisition of
the learned languages as primers in the better use of the vernacular.[54]
Tyndale's own terms, used indiscriminately of Hebrew, Greek, and
English, bear this imprint of Latin indoctrination. The effect is paradoxical, as Tyndale's efforts to rid himself of the stain of Latin theology are
themselves impregnated with Latin linguistic concepts.

In vindicating English usage as distinctive from Latin, Tyndale goes
against the grain of early sixteenth-century linguistic theory. For contemporary with his writings there arose the first systematic attempts to
assimilate English within Latin regulatory categories. This occurred not in

---

[53] Bullokar was printed in London. Although the attribution has sometimes been
questioned, P. G. is identified as Paul Greaves in a copy in the CUL unknown to Padley. Each
survives in only two copies. The 17th century saw a burgeoning of interest, with fourteen
new grammars of English. For bibliographical details of all these early grammars, see Alston,
Bibliography of the English Language, i.

[54] Bullokar, *Bref Grammar*, title page. See Padley, *Vernacular Grammar II*, p. 230.

independent treatments of the grammar of English but in pedagogic schoolbooks of Latin grammar written in English. Up to the end of the fifteenth century the main school texts continued to be Donatus and Alexander of Villedieu, supplemented by early humanist grammars such as Valla and Perotti and some English derivatives (all in Latin).[55] Further developments surrounded the foundation by John Colet, the Dean of St Paul's, of his school in 1509, and his attempts to provide it with new textbooks. At his suggestion, Thomas Linacre, the most original scholar of the Latin language in the country, whose pupils at various dates included More, Colet himself, and Prince Arthur and Princess Mary, wrote in English a *Progymnasmata grammatices vulgaria*, but Colet rejected it, perhaps as too erudite.[56] Instead Colet worked himself on an accidence (later called *Aeditio*), and commissioned the High Master of St Paul's School, William Lily, to compose a syntax, known as the *Rudimenta Grammatices*.[57] Both of these seminal works were incorporated into what became the standard grammar in English schools for three hundred years, first authorized under King Edward with the combined titles *A Shorte Introduction of Grammar* and *Brevissima Institutio* in 1548.[58]

Colet's and Lily's work had no pretensions to linguistic theory and followed Colet's original precept that 'al lytel babys al lytel chyldren' should be encouraged to 'procede and growe to parfyt lyterature and come at the last to be grete clarkes'.[59] For the pupils of St Paul's School to command Latin semantics, they are given scraps of English usage by way of comparison, even though they have not been provided with any equivalent science in vernacular grammar. Nevertheless, by being constructed in English at all, the *Aeditio* and *Rudimenta* encountered profound questions of translatability. This process periodically compelled the authors to abandon the inculcation of rules and indulge in improvisatory theorizing. At times Colet and Lily fell back on modistic concepts.[60] Elsewhere they made extemporary semantic analyses of English forms arising out of the

---

[55] For a list of grammars printed in England before 1500, see Watson, *English Grammar Schools*, pp. 232–3. Weis, *Humanism in England*, pp. 168–72, cites the case of John Anwykyll's *Compendium totius grammaticae* (Oxford, 1483), which freely blended medieval and humanist sources. See also Nelson, 'Teaching of English'.

[56] It was later re-issued as *Rudimenta Grammatices* (1523?).

[57] Published together in 1527 after Colet's death in 1519 and Lily's in 1523.

[58] On the complex origins of these works and their equally complex publishing history see V. J. Flynn, Introduction to *A Shorte Introduction* (New York, 1957), pp. iv–ix; and Padley, *Latin Tradition*, pp. 24–7.

[59] 'A lytell proheme to the boke', *Aeditio*, A6ʳ.

[60] For instance in the differentiation of substantives and adjectives, A6ᵛ; see Padley, *Vernacular Grammar II*, p. 236.

need to provide parallels between the two languages as an aid to Latin prose composition.

The most significant examples of this occur in Lily's section of rules 'To make latyn' at the beginning of the *Rudimenta*. Lily attempted to provide English phrases to correspond to Latin parts of speech. Of course, in many cases the vernacular did not possess identical categories. To make up for this, Lily developed a theory of 'sygnes'. Wherever English grammar failed to have an exact equivalence to Latin, a vernacular linguistic feature is said to be a 'sign' or 'token' of some corresponding aspect of Latin accidence. In other words, whenever English morphology differed in function from Latin grammar, it could be seen after all to be identical in fundamental semantic structure.

This theory was not original to Lily. Italian grammars commonly treated vernacular prepositions and articles as *segni* of Latin cases, and Linacre characterized French prepositions in a similar way.[61] Padley's history of grammatical theory describes Lily's terminology of 'signs' as a 'mere pedagogical device' (p. 234). None the less, *pace* Padley, it does force Lily into some structural analysis of English. This takes the form of listing English morphemes and attributing to them Latin semantic values. This is a crude example of the widespread practice of submitting vernacular grammar to a foreign paradigm. Yet by virtue of recognizing their morphological distinctness and calling them 'signs', Lily dislocates English from Latin usage. The most striking example is Lily's treatment of verbal auxiliaries. For, according to Padley, Lily was original in extending the theory of 'signs' to cover these forms as well as the simpler case of prepositions:

I may knowe the verbe by any of these wordes/do/dyd/haue/had/wyl/wold/sholde/ mai/myght/am/arte/is/be/was/were/can/cowde/let it/or/must, whiche stande eyther as sygnes before the verbe/or elles they be verbes them selfe. I cal them verbes comynly whan a nowne or pronowne foloweth after them.[62]

Lily here identifies the verbal auxiliaries as forms unknown in Latin, but struggles to assimilate them to the Latin model. This results in uncertainty whether to define them as 'sygnes before the verbe' or as verbs in their own right.

In rudimentary fashion, Lily stumbles into the virgin field of vernacular signification. The step proves more audacious than he realizes, and too problematic for his grammatical methodology to cope with. For the

---

[61] Padley, *Vernacular Grammar II*, p. 234.
[62] 'To make latyn', *Guillelmi Lilii Angli Rudimenta*, in Lily and Colet, *Aeditio*, D7^v.

English auxiliaries cover a minefield. Their usage is so diverse they defy immediate categorization.[63] Lily does not even conceptualize them as a category. Instead, he uses the auxiliaries to codify Latin semantic properties in English usage. To every Latin conjugation, he attempts to marry a partner chosen from among the myriad auxiliary forms.

In the *Aeditio*, this process is restricted to translating the Latin tenses, for example defining 'shall' as a 'sygne' of future time, and a brief treatment of 'Modes'. By the time of the *Shorte Introduction of Grammar*, this project had been expanded. To the five 'modes' of the *Aeditio* ('indicatyue', 'imperatyue', 'optatyue', 'coniunctyue', and 'infinitiue') was added a sixth, the 'potencial'.[64] The terminology shows the influence of Linacre.[65] For this mood, indeed, his criterion seems to be strictly grammatical, defining it by means of morphological characteristics:

The Potenciall mode is knowen by these signes, *maie, can, might, would, shoulde*, or *ought*: as Amem, *I can or maie loue*, without an aduerbe ioyned with hym.   (B2ᵛ)

Lily comes close at this point to identifying auxiliaries as a grammatical category with a modal function. However, once again he stumbles because of his determination to assimilate the two languages. Linacre's *modus potentialis* leads him astray, as it is not a grammatical distinction in Latin at all: *amem* is an ordinary subjunctive. Possibly English usage influences him here, since 'can' and 'may' might be thought to have a distinctive modal function which could be characterized as 'potential'. In that case, Lily is further confounded by the profusion of auxiliary types; failing to choose between them, he adduces six in a wild gesture of theoretical optimism: '*maie, can, might, would, shoulde*, or *ought*'.

The indeterminacy of 'signes' implicit in English modals defeats Lily, but he makes a last desperate effort to master them. His brief definitions of the 'modes', 'tenses', and 'persons' give way to an exhaustive catalogue of verbal inflection, with every permutation of six moods, five tenses, and four conjugations. In Latin this requires repetition, since the forms of his 'optatiue', 'subiunctiue', and 'potencial' are identical. However, Lily attempts to register differences even between identical forms by attaching to each a separate English verbal phrase. This extraordinary attempt to keep up linguistic appearances thus labours to regularize Latin categories

---

[63] The term 'auxiliary' was not invented until 1653 by John Wallis; see Padley, *Vernacular Grammar I*, p. 204, and ch. 10 below.

[64] *Shorte Introduction*, B2ᵛ.

[65] The *modus potentialis* appears to be Linacre's invention, *Progymnasmata*, C3, *De emendata structura*, 13ᵛ; see Michael, *English Grammatical Categories*, p. 115; and Padley, *Latin Tradition*, pp. 48–9.

by appealing to the uncategorized irregularities of English. These become more and more complicated, culminating in the optative, where he is forced to conjure up an entirely arbitrary order of English phrases which he treats as if he were parsing the inflections of a Latin verb (B4^r):

Optatiue present tens	*Amem*	God graunt I loue
Preterimperfect tens	*Amarem*	Would god I loued
Preterperfecte tens	*Amaverim*	I praie god I haue loued
Preterpluperfecttens	*Amavissem*	Would god I had loued
Future tense	*Amavero*	God graunt I loue hereafter

The same Latin forms declined as a 'potencial' produce a new range of auxiliaries, respectively 'I maie or can loue', 'I myght or coulde loue', 'I myght, shoulde or ought to haue loued', 'I myght, should or ought to had loued', 'I maie or can loue hereafter' (B4^v).

With tongue-twisting ingenuity, Lily's grammar finds twenty-eight different phrasal forms of 'to love' in order to satisfy the conjugal demands of his Latin exemplar, and another twenty-eight for the passive equivalents. The result is a grammatical monstrosity, born of Lily's desire to marry two languages. However, through this effort of misalliance, Lily coincidentally exposes some of the idiosyncracies of English that will not fit his Latinate paradigm, features which cry out for independent analysis. Paradoxically, the transliteration of Latin grammar into vernacular forms leads, indirectly but inevitably, to the grammatical invention of English.

Questions of translatability generated analysis of vernacular linguistics just as problems of biblical translation motivated investigation of vernacular meanings. In the 1520s both activities were covert at a time when the political implications of vernacular usage remained volatile and prone to arbitrary suppression. However, Henry's reversal of ecclesiastical policy endowed the English language with political and theological signification of immense and as yet uncalculated power. By the 1540s, the apparatus of state power was being wielded in order to subject all kinds of linguistic process to systematic supervision. Tyndale's English Bible, a work so heterodox that it forced its author into fugitive exile, by a savage ideological irony was incorporated within two years of his death into the semi-official Matthew Bible, and in 1539 his revolutionary words were placed in every pulpit in the country. By the end of the decade the language of English liturgy had been similarly encoded in the Edwardian Prayer Book.

The English Grammar of 1548 was part of this same imposition of vernacular authority. It prescribed not only the elements of Latin signification but the methods of vernacular instruction and the processes of vernacular translation. By this means, according to a royal proclamation addressed 'to all schoolemaisters and teachers of grammar' which was annexed to the treatise, 'Ye shal herein not onely shewe your selues obedient to the powers, but also profitable to the realme, and easy to the learners.' Henceforth this was the universal grammar to be referred to both 'openly and priuately', in all circumstances 'the same and none other to bee vsed'. The printer was Reynold Wolfe, his majesty's printer of the three ancient and biblical languages. The motive of linguistic control was explicit: to establish 'one lyke and agreable faschion of grammar, to be vsed of euery mayster in instructyng al youth committed to the gouernaunce of his teachyng', thereby to eradicate 'the endless diuersitee of sundry schoolemaisters', and more specifically 'diuersitee of grammars'.

In this proclamation, 'gouernaunce' and 'powers' go hand in glove with the disciplinary categorization of the procedures of linguistic meaning. Politically and grammatically, its methodology is prescriptive and unitary. The state legislates the submission of linguistic 'diuersitee' to 'one kynd of grammar', and its interests are repeated in the grammarian's own letter 'To the Reader' which follows in the text:

As for the diuersitees of grammars, it is well and profitably taken awaie, by the Kynges Maiestees wysedome, who . . . caused one kynde of grammar by sundry learned men, to be diligently drawen, and so to be set out.   (A2^r)

The *Shorte Introduction* stipulates one kind of language as well as one kind of teaching. Its singular explanations aim to extirpate ambiguity, and to establish a uniform practice of grammatical interpretation. Translating Latin forms by means of one-to-one correspondences with English forms, it attempts to transpose this uniformity onto vernacular modes of meaning, too. In grammar, 'there is but one bestnesse' (A2^r).

Yet Lily's work manifests some difficulty in dictating the 'bestnesse' of English. Its features evade definition and provoke uncertainties in interpretation, causing him, like his recalcitrant pupils, to 'stumble in trifles'. In 1586, writing the first independent grammar of English, William Bullokar commented on the character of his language in similar ways. Largely copied from Lily, Bullokar's grammatical rules also try to fit English into a Latin system.[66] Like Lily, Bullokar is hampered in his methods by the proneness of English to 'equiuocy'. Remarkably, Bullokar sees this as a characteristic of English grammar as well as lexis:

---

[66] Michael, *English Grammatical Categories*, p. 214.

Not that som on word hath Diuers significations or mæninges, yet al of on part of spech . . . such word is caled an Equiuoc: but if such word of Diuers Mæninges may be vsed in diuers partes of spech, or in particular partes of any-on part of spech, it may be caled An Equiuocal   (pp. 16–7)[67]

Bullokar constructs a miniature treatise on ambiguity. A synonym he defines as a 'Co-significatiue', a homonym as an 'Equiuoc'; but the most interesting term is the one he invents for a specifically grammatical form of ambiguity, the 'Equiuocal', when the same morpheme may be construed as having more than one part of speech. This kind of ambiguity is particularly hazardous to the user of English, who is liable to mistake the meaning, especially since it might be 'som tym perceiued only by other wordes in the sentenc^e'.

Whereas other languages make distinctions by adding extra syllables to form inflections, English relies on 'diuisions or partes in the voic^e'. Quick to defend his native tongue as being 'as sencibl^e as theirs', and praising it for its economy and density of meaning, Bullokar none the less warns his fellow English-speakers that its short words are especially prone to 'equiuocy' unless protected by Bullokar's own reformed orthographical system. Nowhere is the equivocation of English more evident in Bullokar's grammar than in his elucidation of those notorious monosyllables, the modal auxiliaries.

Bullokar consigns the modal auxiliaries to a separate class of verb, which he treats as 'the third Coniugation'. He calls them 'Verbes-Neuters-Vn-perfect', 'Neuters' meaning 'intransitive' and 'Vn-perfect' that 'they reqyr the Infinitiu^e-mood of an other verb too expres their signification or mæning perfectly' (pp. 22–3). There is a dim realization in this classification that the auxiliaries behave according to their own pattern of rules, independent of Latin. Bullokar is confused, and includes within his ordinary conjugation 'I shal or wil lou^e' as a 'futur tenc^e' and forms of 'I would' among his special cases of 'doutful' tenses (p. 27). None the less, he identifies unusual features of the auxiliaries such as their being indeclinable except in the second person and also their combination with infinitive verbs without the intermediate 'to' (with the exception of 'ought to'). There are the beginnings here of an understanding of the special grammatical status of auxiliaries. Fleetingly, Bullokar also recognizes their peculiar semantic fluidity:

[67] *Pamphlet for Grammar 1586*, pp. 16–17. This text prints facsimiles of both surviving copies of Bullokar's work (referred to here as *Bref Grammar*) in the Bodleian and in the library of Christ Church, Oxford. Bullokar used his own unique system of orthography. Padley discusses Bullokar in *Vernacular Grammar II*, pp. 234–43.

Mor is sayed in my Grammar at-larg͏͏ᵉ tuching the equiuocy in Wil, Wilt, and Would, som tym shewing wilingnes, som tym a commaundment, som tym a wishing mæntt by them.   (p. 33)

The 'equiuocy' of the modals perplexes Lily's grammar without producing a theoretical model. Bullokar ascribes to them a category without properly defining its function. In both grammars the modals carry an indeterminate signifying charge that acts as a surplus which cannot be accommodated within the available linguistic system. English modality remains an open field of meaning without a clear semantic explanation. Latin structural analogies only complicate their analysis still further. Lily crudely forces the auxiliaries into a contorted inflectional typology. Bullokar at one moment ascribes to them the mood, number, and tense of their accompanying infinitives, and in the next breath realizes an independent but unquantifiable semantic register of 'wilingnes', 'commaundment', or 'a wishing'. These troublesome English forms play havoc with the grammarians' Latin modes of signification even as they attempt to utilize the same Latin modes to explain English usage.

IV THEOLOGY WARS: THE REIGN OF HENRY VIII

Encouraging his young scholars to learn through plentiful examples that they might 'soonest conceaue the reason of the rules, and beste bee acquaynted with the faschion of the tunge' (A3ʳ), Lily recommends a peculiarly self-reflexive schoolroom exercise:

A great helpe to further this readynesse of makynge and speakynge shall be, yf the mayster geue hym an Englyshe booke, as the Psalter, or Solomons Prouerbes, or Ecclesiasticus, and to cause hym ordynaryly to tourne euery daye a chapiter into Latin.   (A3ᵛ)

It is a measure of the political gulf traversed between 1521 and 1548 that *The Shorte Introduction* can refer so lightly to the Bible as 'an Englyshe booke'. Equally striking is the blithe pedagogic incitement to re-render in Latin (no doubt in a form more vulgar than Vulgate) a text of which the de-rendering from Latin had been so contentious. There is some historical comedy in the picture of Edwardian schoolboys routinely travestying Tyndale's or Coverdale's English back into broken Latin syntax. The exercise is anyway circular: pupils struggle to reconstruct in Latin grammar English sentences which they have already been taught to misconstrue according to Latin rules, sentences which are in any case translations (via the Latin Vulgate) from Hebrew and Greek grammatical locutions.

The translations of Tyndale and Coverdale were themselves forged out of the friction between the rough edges of biblical and vernacular grammar. Unacquainted with any grammatical theory of English usage, Tyndale struggled to articulate biblical language in English. This was an incredible undertaking, not the least of his difficulties being to reconstruct a theology in English grammar. He laboured under the necessity of combining faith to the original linguistically with faith to the original doctrinally, two faiths not always commensurate with each other. Since doctrine did not yet exist in English, he had in effect to invent a new language to accommodate it. Although More accused Tyndale's English of newfangledness, neologism was for Tyndale a necessity poised on the edge of solecism even as his neo-theological statements constantly risked heresy; the instinct to avoid linguistic blunder might easily lead him into committing doctrinal error, or else vice versa.

Tyndale's writing is fraught with an awareness of the possiblility of mistakes of either kind. In 1526, his text of Romans 6: 14 read:

Synne shall not have power over you. For ye are not vnder the lawe, but vnder grace.[68]

But in 1534, he changed his version of Paul's Greek:

ἁμαρτία γὰρ ὑμῶν οὐ κυριεύσει, οὐ γάρ ἐστε ὑπὸ νόμον ἀλλ᾽ ὑπό χάριν

Let not synne have power over you. For ye are not vnder the lawe, but vnder grace.

The 1526 reading interprets Paul's statement as a prediction that for those 'vnder grace' sin's power will be destroyed. It appears to understand οὐ κυριεύσει as a straight future tense, in line with the Vulgate reading *non dominabitur* but also with Luther's *wird nicht herrschen können.*[69] The 1534 rendering represents a radical change of mind. It no longer predicts but commands, possibly making the fulfilment of the command a condition by which (and perhaps only by which) grace is able to operate.

Grammatically, Tyndale now reads οὐ κυριεύσει as an imperative, making it parallel in meaning to the phrase in 6: 12, 'Μὴ οὖν βασιλευέτω ἡ ἁμαρτία ἐν τῷ θνητῷ ὦ ὑμῶν σώματι', which he translates (in both ver-

---

[68] Ed. Hardy Willis, p. 327.

[69] Clajus's discussion of mood in *Grammatica Germanicae linguae* used examples from Luther's German Bible (ed. Meier, *Ältere Deutsche Grammatiken*, ii. 73–6). On Clajus's treatment of the German modal verbs (possibly derived from Melanchthon), see Padley, *Vernacular Grammar II*, pp. 287–8.

sions) 'Let not synne raygne therfore in youre mortall bodyes'. However, in Greek the form of κυριεύσει (future indicative) is different from βασιλευέτω, which is a third person present imperative. The reason for Tyndale's change may be traced to his observation in the 1534 Preface concerning 'the Hebrue Phrase or maner of speche lefte in the Greke wordes'. Romans 6: 14 shows him acting out his interpretation of New Testament grammar that 'the futuretence is ofte the imperatyve mode'.

In English, though, Tyndale uses neither a 'future' nor an 'imperative', but rather the modal auxiliaries 'shall' and 'let'.[70] The grammar of 'shall' works differently from either the Greek future or the imperative. Although 'shall' is used to signify action taking place in the future, in practice it is often difficult to distinguish this from an obligation or an undertaking.[71] Thus 'he shall come tomorrow' sometimes predicts a future action but sometimes orders the action to take place, and often it will do both. In this sense, 'Synne shall not have power over you' acts less as a statement about the future than as the guarantee of a promise.

Modern linguistics differentiates these senses of 'shall', in common with other English modals, by using the terms 'epistemic' and 'deontic'. 'Epistemic modality' is defined as concerned with questions of knowledge or belief about the truth of a proposition, 'deontic modality' with 'the necessity or possibility of acts performed by morally responsible agents'.[72] The nomenclature is not entirely satisfactory, relying as it does on a cumbersome metaphysical explanation which hardly corresponds to the delicate modulations of grammatical inflections. Yet some such dual system, often with the same forms used for both kinds of modality, can be found not only in English and many other European grammars but in languages from all over the world—Dravidian, Arabic, Australasian, Uto-Aztecan.[73] In English, for example, 'he may come tomorrow' means either (epistemically) 'perhaps he will' or (deontically) 'he is permitted to do so'; and 'this book should be finished soon' means either 'probably it will be' or 'there is a serious deadline'.[74]

---

[70] Bullokar recognizes the oddly impersonal grammar of 'let' ('vsed imparatiuᵉly or permissiuᵉly', p. 36), seemingly a command without a commander, but his analysis will not suffice for all cases: who exactly is the 'persᵒn vnderstanded' in Romans 3: 4, 'Let god be true, and all men lyars'?

[71] See Palmer, *English Modals*, pp. 74–5. Barber, *Early Modern English*, p. 260, comments '*shall* could be used all through our period to signal obligation or necessity'.

[72] Lyons, *Semantics*, ii. 823.

[73] For examples of the very different forms used in different languages, and the different degree to which the same form is used for both types of modality, see Palmer, *Mood and Modality*, pp. 121–3.

[74] See Palmer, *Mood and Modality*, p. 19.

Tyndale in his 1534 revision effectively substitutes a deontic meaning (which he calls 'imperatyve') for an epistemic, only with a further complication. For Tyndale seems to be negotiating three competing modal interpretations of οὐ κυριεύσει. One epistemically describes the sinlessness of grace, a second guarantees a promise of sinlessness to those under grace, a third sees it as an exhortation to those under grace not to sin. The third of these meanings is possible in his first translation, 'Synne shall not have power over you', but it is much the weakest of the three.[75] In 1534 he opted decisively for this third meaning, possibly under the influence of the 'theology of contract' which he had carried over from his translation of the Pentateuch.[76] Certainly, the new version 'Let not synne have power over you' works to exclude the other two meanings, and to imply that grace involves a moral imperative. Yet his new version also is not free from modal ambiguity. This is because of the indeterminacy of 'Let' as to grammatical person. The primary sense seems to be 'you should not let it happen', but 'let' often works impersonally, in which case the meaning is 'let it not happen that'. In the context of the Bible, on the other hand, the meaning of 'let' is frequently ascribed as if in the third person to God, producing a third possibility, 'let God not allow it to happen'.

These ambiguities are characteristic of modal sentences. A modern grammarian, F. R. Palmer, comments, 'there is no obvious reason why the same forms should be used for expressing the speaker's degree of commitment to truth and for getting other people to do things'.[77] Yet theologically, the connection is both intuitive and disturbing, so that the 1526 and 1534 versions of Romans 6: 14 hesitate between grace seen as a logical precondition, or a promise to be fulfilled, or an obligation to be satisfied. Such theological friction is created by many kinds of modal uncertainty. John Lyons convincingly argues that 'reference to the future, unlike reference to the past, is as much a matter of modality as it is of purely temporal reference'.[78] Many languages do not have a future tense at all, and those Indo-European languages that do often derive their future tense forms

---

[75] Although in modern English the meaning is strained, it seems to be present in a phrase such as 'money shall have no power over you', perhaps uttered by a prison chaplain to a former cabinet minister.

[76] That is, God's grace only operates if man fulfils his part of the contract to 'Let not synne have power over you'. On Tyndale's increasing affiliation with 'the theology of contract' or 'covenant theology', see Clebsch, *England's Earliest Protestants*, pp. 185–95. Clebsch believes such influence in the 1534 NT is confined to the marginal notes, and that 'textual changes' were not much affected by 'theological considerations'. He discusses some examples of such change on p. 192, however, and the distinction is perhaps hard to maintain.

[77] Palmer, *Mood and Modality*, p. 123.

[78] *Semantics*, ii. 816.

from the subjunctive mood.[79] The English form 'shall' derives from a Teutonic root meaning 'debt' or 'guilt', and 'will' is still used as a verb to mean to 'desire' or 'intend'. Statements about the future usually prove nearly impossible to make, and languages hedge them around with various modalities of supposition, inference, wish, fear, stipulation, threat, hope, or resignation.

Such tensions run deep in the history of Christian doctrine. One of the classic accounts of the modality of futurity is in Book XI of Augustine's *Confessions*. What status does prophecy have, he asks, if statements about the future are impossible? God's time, Augustine says, bends language.[80] The modality of tense is made more complex still by divine providence. When God makes his covenant with Noah and says 'I will make myne apoyntement with the', he could be (epistemically) foreseeing a future that he already knows, or (deontically) expressing his intention so to do, or (more strongly deontic) predetermining Noah's salvation.[81] The slippage between modal interpretations is simultaneously a slippage between theological interpretations of divine predestination (deontic) and fore-knowledge (epistemic). Paradoxically, however, the modal implications are reversed when seen from man's point of view. For when the rich man asks Jesus, 'what good thinge shall I do, that I may have eternall lyfe?' his question implies a deontic interpretation, and at the same time assumes theologically that he has free will to determine his own salvation.[82] Yet if he asked the question 'shall I be saved?' epistemically, the answer would seem to lie within God's mind alone.

These logical involutions repeat themselves when we turn to another area of grammatical modality. For the same modal forms (at least in European languages) again ambiguate between categories of necessity and obligation, and possibility and permission. 'You must be reading this' means either 'it is necessarily true' (epistemic) or 'you are required to' (deontic); 'you may enjoy it' either 'it is possibly the case' or 'you have been given permission'. Further confusion is created in English by the fact that the negatives of 'must' and 'may' work differently: 'must not' must be deontic, while 'may not' may be either; at the same time there is an inter-esting correlation between 'possible not'/'not necessary' and 'necessary

---

[79] Including some Latin forms: see Handford, *Latin Subjunctive*, p. 15. Greek often uses a subjunctive as a future.

[80] *Confessiones*, xi (18, 23–20, 26).

[81] Genesis 6: 18 [Tyndale], *Fyrst boke of Moses*, Cı^r.

[82] Matthew 19: 16 [Tyndale], also Mark 10: 17 and Luke 18: 18. Interestingly, Tyndale trans-lates the same verb (τί ποιήσω, i.e. future tense) as 'what shall I do' in Mark and 'what ought I to do' in Luke, whereas the AV twice uses 'must' and once 'shall'.

not'/'not possible'.[83] Theologically, once again, an uncertainty over grace is perfectly expressed in such an uncertainty over modality. When Paul says 'even so must we be in the resurreccion' (Romans 6: 5), he could mean either 'it is certain that we are' (epistemic) or 'we are obliged to be' (deontic). Yet here there is contradiction as well as ambiguity. For if the phrase is epistemic, any obligation is made redundant, or otherwise we 'must' do what we 'may not' (or rather 'might not', since 'may not' might mean that 'we are not permitted to' although not, of course, that we 'cannot').

Much of medieval theology and logic is bound up in such problems, as we saw in Chapter 3. In the theological politics of the late 1520s the ambiguity could hardly be more tendentious. Fisher and More attempted to maintain social and ecclesiological order by establishing a theology of justification that produced ethical imperatives. Grace included the freedom to follow these imperatives since the only alternative was political and religious anarchy. More's position is especially complex because this freedom forms the only barrier between the burden of original sin and an apprehension that physical compulsion ultimately constitutes the only means of reforming it. The *Dialogue Concerning Heresies* struggles constantly to validate a theory of free will within the inevitable truth of the church even while its author was confirming that inevitability by more strenuous methods outside the confines of the text. As a result, More is at pains to show that grace works both to guarantee the church's ability to interpret truly and to enable the Christian truly to follow the church's teaching. Grace necessitates the freedom to act with grace:

Well sayd quod I /then yf we must /we may. For yf we may not /we must not. For our lorde byndeth no man to an impossybylyte.   (*CWM*, vi. 117)

This sentence forms part of an argument that 'as far as ye necessyte of our saluacyon requyreth /god gyueth the chyrch the ryght vnderstandynge therof' (vi. 116). More thereby creates a powerful nexus of literary theory, theology of justification, and linguistic theory, all of which he sums up in the neat modal formula 'yf we must /we may'. This logical *coup de grace*, slipped into the text with characteristic inscrutability, works by means of a pun between epistemic and deontic modalities. 'We must' is deontic ('it is our duty to construe scripture correctly') but is used to corroborate an epistemic 'we may' (not 'we are permitted to' but 'we are able to do so'). The logic is confirmed by a similar turn on the negative forms—if (epistemic)

---

[83]   Palmer, *English Modals*, p. 9.

'we may not' (that is, 'cannot') then (deontic) 'we must not'. All of this is confirmed by the doctrinal cliché 'God cannot command an impossibility'—itself a complex conflation of modalities between God's demands and the demands of logic.

The notion that God only makes possible demands, and that if we must (deontic) do something, we must (epistemic) therefore be able to do it, was one of the cardinal principles of Erasmus's *Diatribe* against Luther, written five years previously. Tyndale, who may have been in Wittenberg at the time of Luther's reply in 1525, used a standard Lutheran argument on the topic when he made his first essay in protestant polemic in 1528: God makes commands, not that they might be done, but to show that they cannot be done.[84] This statement was in turn extracted as one of Tyndale's 'heresies and errors' by the king's commissioners and satirically glossed as saying 'The commandments be given us, not to do them'. Later, Foxe's defence was that Tyndale did not 'say that we should not do the commandments, but that we cannot do them'. Yet the point is not altogether easy to maintain. Tyndale implies that some forms of 'must' translate as 'may not'. *The Parable of the Wicked Mammon* reverberates with such complexities of interpretation. Written as a justification of Luther on justification, it also needs to protect Luther from the charge of immoralism and the antinomian belief that the Christian need do nothing towards salvation.[85] This structure of controversy sees Tyndale looking both ways, arguing both that 'faith only justifieth' and that faith after all enables a man to do good works, in such a way that God's commands once more become possible.

The result is mobility between different kinds of statement on grace. On the one hand, good works necessarily come of grace, and cannot be performed by man. Yet once the believer is possessed of saving faith, this epistemic 'must' elides easily into moral recommendation, expressed in a deontic 'must':

Even so we with all oure workes maye not seke oure awne profit/nether in this world nor in heven/but must and ought frely to worke/to honour God wyth all/and without all maner respecte/ seke oure neyghbours profit and do hym service.[86]

One modality modulates into the other. *The Parable* juxtaposes contrary impulses. In one sentence he states: 'The law when it comaundeth that

---

[84] *Parable of the Wicked Mammon*, in *Doctrinal Treatises*, p. 81. See Ch. 4 above.

[85] The *Parable* consists partly of a translation of a *Sermon von dem unrechten Mammon* by Luther (17 August 1522, WA 10/3.273–92), and also incorporates other direct quotations from Luther's works. See Rupp, *English Protestant Tradition*, p. 51.

[86] *Parable*, C3ʳ–C4ʳ; *Doctrinal Treatises*, p. 62.

thou shalt not lust/geveth the not power so to do/but damneth the/because thou canst not so doo' (A7ᵛ; pp. 47–8), a view subsequently extracted as Article IV of Tyndale's 'heresies' ('The law requireth impossible things of us'). Yet the very next sentence, over the gulf of a paragraph break, exhorts the reader to follow a command: 'Iff thou wylt therfore be at peace with God and love him/thou muste turne to the promyses of God and to the Gospel' (A7ᵛ; p. 48).

A moralist strain has been identified in Tyndale's writing later in life, and has been associated with a preoccupation with the Hebrew Law after his translation of the Pentateuch in 1530.[87] Yet rather than see this as a radical change of mind, or a specific renunciation of Luther's doctrine of justification, it is more a realization of a modality which is already there in his earliest tracts. There is a tension from the beginning in Tyndale's theology between the constraints of faith, and of works as the fruit of faith: in that sense his Lutheranism was moralist *avant la lettre*. The Pentateuch gave him a Hebraic grammatical and theological idiom in which to allow this aspect of his doctrine full expression, but it is doubtful that Tyndale ever saw this as a departure from Luther. It is more the authentic signature of faith, a faith which even in the 1526 Prologue to Romans (itself a paraphrase directly from Luther) is defined as:

evyr doynge/evyr frutefull/so that it is vnpossible/that he which is endued therewith/shulde not worke all wayes good workes with oute ceasing.[88]

This reflex in Tyndale's theology, by which an assertion of faith redoubles as an exhortation to do good works, occurs throughout early English evangelical writing. Robert Barnes, prior of the Augustinian friary in Cambridge, was made to recant during a service at St Paul's in February 1526 at which Fisher gave the second of his vernacular rebuttals of Luther. Placed under house arrest, late in 1528 he escaped first to Antwerp and then to Wittenberg. There he attempted in late 1531 to mediate between the Lutheran theologians and Henry VIII on the matter of the dissolution of the king's marriage to Catherine of Aragon. His *Supplicatyon . . . vnto the most excellent and redoubted prince* also took the opportunity to justify his own past actions and to promote the principles of Reformation theology. Having failed comprehensively in this self-appointed mission, he continued in similar ingenuous but hopeless embassies, vainly negotiating between the dictates of regal policy and the ambivalences of regal theology, until he was burned at Smithfield in 1540.[89]

---

[87] Clebsch, p. 155.   [88] *Prologe to Romayns*, A6ᵛ; *Doctrinal Treatises*, p. 493.
[89] A full account of Barnes's career is given in Rupp, *English Protestant Tradition*, ch. 2; and Clebsch, ch. 4.

The 1531 *Supplicatyon* appended a theological essay aimed to prove that 'Only faythe Iustifyeth by fore god'. Like Tyndale, he is careful to distinguish faith from mere belief, 'imagination', or 'opinion', which even 'deuils and infidels' have.[90] In order to show that saving faith is more than this, Barnes has to improvise some modal logic: 'but the faith that shall iustifye vs/must be of a nother maner strength/for yt must come from heuen' (xlviii^v). This sentence clearly works epistemically, 'the faith that justifies necessarily comes from heaven'. Barnes next moves in another direction:

My lordes this is the faythe that dothe Iustifie/and be cause it is geuen from heuen in to oure hartis by the sprete off god/therfore it can be no ydille thynge/But it must nedis do all maner of thingis/that be too the honour off god/and also to the profite of oure neyboure/in so muche that at all tymis necessary yt must nedis worke well/and also brynge forthe all good workes/that may be to the profitte and helpynge off any man.   (xlix^r)

In this complicated sequence of dependent clauses, Barnes begins as if continuing his description of the necessary condition of faith that, being heavenly, it must (epistemic) 'do all maner of thingis' that are godly. But once these actions are defined not only generically as 'too the honour off god' but also purposively, as needing to be 'to the profite of oure neyboure', Barnes seems to switch modalities and to create obligations for faith to fulfil. Thus the second instance of 'must nedis' appears to be deontic: 'at all tymis necessary yt must nedis worke well/and also brynge forthe all good workes'.

Barnes thereby implicates himself in a double logic, the full consequences of which he does not appear to be in control. As if realizing this, he tries to assert that these works still do not work salvation: 'these workys be not done/too Iustifye the man/but a iuste man must nedes do them'. Barnes here uses a familiar Lutheran epistemology, reversing the Aristotelian view that a good man is defined by his actions and redefining 'good' as an ontological status conferred by God which then (necessarily) produces good actions. For this logic to apply epistemically, however, it must mean that *in all cases* a just man does good actions, whereas the countervailing possibility remains that the just man does not necessarily do so, and so must endeavour to do the best that he can. Barnes's theology is poised between these two interpretations. When he says that 'the Iuste man must nedys do good workys' (xlix^v), his grammar divides between 'he is certain to do them' (as in 'a large man must needs fall heavily') and 'he ought to do them' (as in 'a large man must needs go on a diet').

---

[90] E.g. the belief that there is one god, that he is eternal, that the gospel is true, *Supplicatyon*, xlviii^v [STC 1470]; see also Tyndale, *Doctrinal Treatises*, p. 492.

The vicissitudes of Tudor policy encouraged Barnes to revise the *Supplicatyon* in 1534. He moderated his attitude to episcopacy and advocated royal sovereignty over spiritual as well as temporal affairs, urging the king to throw off all vestiges of papal authority over doctrine and to submit himself under God to the truth of vernacular scripture.[91] Apart from the last clause this made happy reading for Henry, for whom perhaps were also designed some curious alterations to the section on justification, which abandoned Luther's radical stance on the canonicity of the Epistle of James and argued its compatability with Paul. Works, Barnes says, are 'an outwarde declaration and a testimonie of the inwarde iustification'.[92]

Clebsch argues that Barnes through his 1534 revisions marks his 'withdrawal from a strict Lutheran stand on justification', and it is true that this last remark of Barnes is an extraordinary travesty of the protestant trademark 'only faith justifies', re-rendering it as 'only that faith justifies, which does good works'.[93] It is not so clear that this represents either the emergence of a new theory or a clear break with Barnes's previous view. The 1531 *Supplicatyon* was already caught in a tension between the assertion of *sola fides* and the reaffirmation of the moral obligation to perform good works, a tension between theological logic and deontic grammar. In this respect, he followed Melanchthon in revising the early Luther, a supposition made more likely by his stay in Wittenberg.[94] Barnes in 1534 still tried to assert unequivocally the primacy of faith, but his grammar continued to equivocate, creating new conditions for the operation of grace.[95] This habit of conditional grammar is also found in the work of another early English evangelical, John Frith: 'If we be deliuered from sinne through Christ, then must we walke in a new conuersation of our life, or els we are still in darknes.'[96] Clebsch astutely observes in Barnes and Tyndale the seeds of Calvinism and more especially English puritanism.[97] No doubt this

---

[91]   On the differences between the two editions, and the mistakes made by some interpreters of Barnes because of their reliance on Foxe's 1573 edition of Barnes's *Workes* (which conflated the two early texts), see Clebsch, pp. 58–60.

[92]   The 1534 edn. [*STC* 1471] is quoted here from a reprint (1550?) [*STC* 1472], N4ʳ.

[93]   Clebsch, p. 60. The view is challenged in Trueman, *Luther's Legacy*, pp. 190–4.

[94]   The fruit of Melanchthon's revision of the Lutheran account of works, specifically using the word *necesse*, is found in his 1535 revision of the *Loci communes* (e.g. CR, 21, 429).

[95]   'For it is no worke that receyueth the promise made in Christes bloude, but fayth onely' (N5ʳ).

[96]   'An other booke agaynst Rastell, named the subsedye or bulwarke to his first booke, made by Iohn Frithe prysoner in the Tower', probably written in 1532 and published in Antwerp perhaps sometime after 1537; see Clebsch, pp. 109–10 and n. 9. Quoted here from Foxe's edited text of *Whole Workes of Tyndall, Frith, and Barnes*, p. 71.

[97]   See pp. 68, 138, 167–8, 199.

encouraged the Elizabethan puritan John Foxe still further in his decision to collect together the work of the three martyrs Tyndale, Frith, and Barnes in a folio edition designed for the theological establishment of 1573. Yet it may be wrong to see in the Henrician theologians too articulate a doctrinal revision. They are engaged in an effort to formulate a theological language, which continues to elude them, and which traps them in a nexus of linguistic modalities which they cannot unravel. Calvinism, too, was to have its struggles with these double meanings as an official protestant doctrine developed in the England of Elizabeth.

V WYATT'S WRITING LESSON: THE *PENITENTIALL PSALMS*

Robert Barnes was burned for heresy on 30 July 1540 in perhaps the grimmest ritual of the Henrician Reformation. With gruesome evenhandedness, Henry put to death three evangelicals and three papists on the same day. For all its calculated intimidation, however, this was just a sideshow; the main event had preceded it by two days, when Cromwell was executed for treason.

It was not the best time for a show of faith, on justification or any other article. After Cromwell was executed, his papers were exhaustively scrutinized by the authorities. Among those implicated was his protegé Sir Thomas Wyatt, former Marshal of Calais and ambassador to the courts of Spain and France. Wyatt was arrested at Hampton Court in January 1541, accused of treason and immorality by his old enemy, Edmund Bonner, the Bishop of London. Wyatt prepared a meticulous and witty Defence, exacting in its analysis of the chillingly subtle regulation of the processes 'by worde, message or wrytinge' embodied in the examination of treason.[98] These processes he summed up in the lapidary phrase 'the lawe of wordes': 'Reherse here the lawe of wordes. Declare, my lords, I beseke you, the meaninge therof' (p. 196). This 'lawe', he says, is subject to manifold 'mysreportinge and mysvnderstandinge':

For in some lyttell thynge may apere the truthe which I dare saye you seke for your consciens sake. And besydys that, yt is a smale thynge in alteringe of one syllable ether with penne or worde that may mayk in the conceavinge of the truthe myche matter or error (p. 197).

Writing is a matter of difference, of 'greate dyfferaunce' discovered in small differences.

[98] *Life and Letters*, ed. Muir, p. 190.

Wyatt composed his *Penitentiall Psalms* (it is believed) while waiting for his indictment.[99] It is hardly likely, then, that Wyatt would allow the law of words in this work to be casually misplaced. And yet his Psalms alternate between scandalous outspokenness and guarded prohibition. It is a strange fashion of forgetfulness which makes Wyatt so sensitive in the Defence to 'the hygheste kynde of naughtines and maliciousnes' in the interpreting of his everyday conversation, and yet which gives him leave to allude (in the Prologue to the Psalms) to a king who does not scruple 'By murder for to clok Adulterye.'[100] This from a man who was himself according to hearsay the former lover of Anne Boleyn.

At the same time the *Penitentiall Psalms* provide themselves with multiple prophylactics against suspicion. They are, of course, a translation, in this case a double translation, since Wyatt's work paraphrases (often verbatim) Pietro Aretino's *Sette Salmi de la Penitentia di David*. The Psalms were the traditional vehicle for biographical immolation, intrinsically sanctioned by scriptural authority. Adulterous murder is here the prerogative not of Henry and Anne but of David and Bathsheba, who in Aretino's and in Wyatt's versions are the protagonists of a framing narrative into which the seven Psalms are lyric interpolations. The Penitential Psalms had become in the early sixteenth century the most widespread of devotional modes, eminently respectable for any side of the religious and political divides (Luther, Fisher, and Reuchlin, for instance, brought out versions within a few years of each other). Stephen Greenblatt has written of the way in which the Psalms provide a form of textual self-fashioning for Wyatt, in which conventionality is not opposed to identity but precisely constitutes it: translation works as a form of appropriation, a 'representation of his own voice and culture'.[101]

The opportunity provided by religious writing in the dire political context of the Henrician court is that it can keep secrets without telling lies. The laments of the Psalms become a covert means of expressing the laments of these latter days. However, it is characteristic of Wyatt's Psalms that they are as much self-concealing as self-revealing. Indeed the poems work by a contradictory logic in which redemptive discovery is achieved only through obliquity and displacement. Wyatt's David is caught

---

[99] *Life and Letters*, p. 174, although Mason has argued that they were written during a previous period of imprisonment in 1536.

[100] *Penitentiall Psalms*, line 37, from *Collected Poems*, ed. Muir and Thomson. Further refs in text.

[101] Greenblatt, *Renaissance Self-Fashioning*, pp. 119–20.

between the 'secrete wound' (241) of sin and the salvatory grace by which he would become 'open in thi syght' (251), and yet is oppressed by the very thought of exposure to this desired openness. He is therefore caught in a very Tudor bind. The Henrician proclamations project with unrelenting tension both a pitiless privacy and a transparent openness to interrogation. They desire that every secret should remain hidden and that it should be ruthlessly searched out from its hiding place. In this respect, it is ironic yet symptomatic that Wyatt's indictment was based on an accusation of obscene frankness. It was said that he had 'maliciously, falcely and traytoursly' sworn that he feared 'the kinge shulde be caste owte of a Cartes arse and that by goddis bloude yf he were so, he were well served'. Equally characteristic is that when faced with his own quoted outspokenness he should prepare several careful paragraphs of analysis interpreting the unspeakable phrase into uninterpretable obscurity.[102]

Wyatt's Psalms (like his Defence) are prolix and roundabout, but they are circumlocutory to a purpose. If they hedge their bets they cannot afford to do otherwise. This applies not only to the more or less overt narrative of David and Bathsheba's royal adultery but also to the less openly covert processes of the poem's theology. Grace is not a freely available subject: it is controversial and political. By 1540 the Psalms were swarming with Lutheran connotations. Of all doctrines, the action of penitence was least suited to unguarded treatment. Psalm 32, second of the penitential seven, was virtually the battle-hymn of the Lutheran republic of the spirit. It was the site of Luther's shattering insights in his early lectures on Psalms and Romans. Its verses had become a code for justification by faith and for the imputation of God's righteousness.

Wyatt's version is contorted by this doctrinal burden:

> Oh happy ar they that have forgiffnes gott
> Off their offence (not by their penitence
> As by meryt wych recompensyth not
> Altho that yet pardone hath non offence
> Withowte the same) but by the goodnes
> Off hym that hath perfect intelligens
> Off hert contrite
>
> (217–23)

This is not out of the Hebrew or the Latin but Aretino's Italian. Even so, the careful syntactical logic of Aretino ('non per le opere de la contritione, ne

---

[102] 'Let ther declarations be rehersed, yf thei have bene in that examyned, wherby it may appere what I mene by the proverbe . . .', *Life and Letters*, p. 198; see also p. 189.

de la penitentia . . . ma per beneficio de la gratia sua'[103]) has given way to a dizzying counterfactual complexity in which the opening clause is bedevilled by four self-qualifying qualifying clauses. The disjunctive causal logic is unravelled and re-ravelled: 'not by . . . As by . . . Altho that yet . . . Withowte . . . but by'). H. A. Mason has noted with scholarly care the Lutheran strain in this translation, but he modestly fails to note the pains he has taken to discover it.[104] This is a poetry that represses its own radicalism. The countervailing rhythm of the Lutheran passive verbs is heard, but only as a faint echo amid the self-censoring burden of Henrician prohibition.

In the last years of the reign of Henry's father, Fisher had made a famous series of sermons on the Penitential Psalms which became one of the religious best-sellers of the age, reprinted in seven editions.[105] Fisher's account of Psalm 32 makes the late medieval division between contrition, confession, and satisfaction, leaving no doubt of the efficacy of penance as sacrament. God 'imputes not sin' because of 'the hole & perfyte doynge away of synne by satysfaccion'.[106] The sinner does 'satysfaccion' (makes up for sin, makes perfect his penitence) by 'doynge good werkes' (CC2^v). Sin is done away with by what Fisher construes as a law of erasure:

Whan we be aboute to rase & do awaye ony maner wrytynge, we fyrst scrape the paper, & by that rasure or scrapynge somwhat is taken awaye of the lettres, & as a deformyte of the very perfyte knowlege, that the lettres may not be perceyued & dyscerned but derkly, yf we rase it agayne the lettres shal than be vtterly done away and put out of knowlege, and yf we do so the thyrde tyme than shal no thynge of the leest lettre be sene but as clene as euer it was.   (CC1^v–CC2^r)

By the time of Wyatt's Psalms thirty years later the rules of writing had changed. The enforcement of the Reformation, which accompanied the Act of Supremacy, interpreted erasure literally. In 1535 Fisher was executed for treason. In the same year, a circular from Cromwell to the bishops and later to the secular authorities ordered the word *papa* to be erased from prayers, mass-books, canons, rubrics, and other books in church. Any mention of the power of the Bishop of Rome was 'utterly to be abolished, eradicate, and rased out' and his name to be 'perpetually suppressed, and obscured'.[107] In the long run, in the treatment of evangelical as well as

---

[103] Aretino, *Sette Salmi*, C3^v.   [104] *Humanism and Poetry*.

[105] Rex, *Theology of Fisher*, p. 48.

[106] *Penytencyall psalmes*, CC2^r; *English Works*, ed. Mayor, p. 25.

[107] Wilkins, *Concilia*, iii. 773, also printed in *TRP*, i. No.158; discussed by Elton, *Policy and Police*, pp. 231–2.

catholic writing Henry proved more even-handed. By 1540 he had turned his censorship towards scripture. The 1543 Act of Reformation ordered all 'annotations or preambles' to the Bible to be banned. These are subject to a rigid act of cancellation, cut out or blotted so utterly that 'they can not be perseyued nor red'.[108]

Fisher's sermons, with their vision of letters that 'may not be perceyued & dyscerned but derkly' provide an awful premonition of things to come. Wyatt's religious writing is altogether more circumscribed, and can no longer indulge in quaint metaphors. This is writing under pressure. With a palpable reference to the physical torture exercised by the Henrician regime in the examination of religious belief on all sides of the spectrum, Wyatt's translation of Psalm 32 (for once abandoning his Italian model entirely) describes 'my hert in presse' (246). Wyatt's writing veered on the edge of heresy as well as treason trials. The first of his poems to be printed appeared in *The Court of Venus*, which barely saw the light of day, surviving only in fragmentary copies. The first poem in this anthology was *The Pilgrim's Tale*, a late Lollard verse tract which, according to hearsay, was placed by William Thynne, clerk to the king's kitchen, in one of his editions of Chaucer until it was censored out at the last moment. Another heterodox work included in Thynne's Chaucer, *The Plowman's Tale*, was sometimes attributed apocryphally to Wyatt himself. With staunchly anti-clerical references to episcopal oppression, these works were easy targets for conservative bishops such as Bonner and Stephen Gardiner. As for Wyatt's Psalms, they were highly suspicious. Vernacular scripture after the first vent of enthusiasm was regarded as a subversive genre. Wyatt refers darkly in his Defence to Bonner's desire to suppress it (p. 204), and within a year of Wyatt's death Gardiner drafted the infamous 1543 Act which made all but the most official versions illegal. Latin scripture was another matter: the modern Hebrew scholar Campensis's *Enchiridion Psalmorum*, another of the direct verbal sources for Wyatt's English, was owned by the monarch himself, with his monogram on the title-page. Wyatt wisely did not (could not?) print his English Psalms at all, but kept them safe in his personal manuscript (the Egerton MS), revising them from time to time. They were copied into one contemporary manuscript collection of verse, the Arundel Harington MS. In 1549 they were finally printed as *Certayne Psalmes*, with Henry safely dead: their publication indicates a new phase in Tudor religious polity, in which the Lord Protector Seymour

---

[108]   34 & 35 Henry VIII, *Actes*, A2ᵛ.

attempted to entrench the Edwardian evangelical faith with reams of printed evangelical piety.

Wyatt's *Penitentiall Psalms* therefore represent a new kind of literature. Writing and religion relate in this in complex ways. Biographers have searched Wyatt's work for signs of religious affiliation, as if assuming that belief is always antecedent to language. Yet in Wyatt this can hardly be the case, since language carries with it such an insistent purchase, and is the text on which belief is founded. Religion for Wyatt is a discourse without limits:

> In slepe, in wach, in fretyng styll within,
>   That neuer soffer rest vnto the mynd;
>   Filld with offence, that new and new begyn
> With thowsand feris the hert to strayne and bynd.
>
>   (283–6)

At the same time his Psalms are a search for limits, an attempt to take the measure of the emergent forms of sixteenth-century religion. In the coda to Psalm 32 which follows these lines, Wyatt strains beyond his confinement for evangelical liberation:

> But for all this he that in god doth trust
> With mercy shall hym sellff defendid fynd.
> Joy and rejoyse, I say, ye that be just
>
>   (287–9)

Of course, the question of who are 'ye that be just', and how they become so, is the most difficult of all sixteenth-century questions. Tyndale had given a distinctively Lutheran response to such questions in English ten years before in the *Answere to More* (1531):

How then/to loue the law of god and to consent therto and to haue it written in thine hert and to professe it/so that thou art ready of thyne awne accorde to doo it and wyth out compultion/is to be righteous: that I graunt and that loue maye be called rightwysnesse before God passiue and the life and quickenesse of the soul passiue.[109]

Here is Luther's *iustitia passiva*, ready Englished. Indeed it has arrived in England before he wrote in his memoir of 1545 how it had opened for him the gates of paradise. Following Luther, Tyndale cites in support the classic Pauline texts of Romans 1: 17 and 4: 7–8, the latter citation in turn borrowed from Psalm 32: 1–2.

---

[109] *Answere*, p. 205.

Having quoted the Psalm ('blessed is the man whose transgression is forgeuen & his synnes hid/and vnto whom the lorde rekeneth not vnrightwysnesse'), Tyndale sums up:

So that the only rightwysnesse of him that can but synne and hath nought of hym selfe to make amendes/is the forgeuenesse of sinne/which faith only bringeth. And as ferforth as we be vnryghtwese/faith only iustifieth vs actiuely and else nothinge on our parte. And as ferforth as we have synned/be in sinne or do synne or shall synne/so ferforth must fayth in christes bloud iustifie vs only and else nothynge (p. 207)

This has the authentic Lutheran signature, and as if in confirmation Tyndale cites his author by name in another connection a paragraph below. It is an interpretation of Psalm 32: 1–2 far removed from Fisher's affirmation of satisfaction. The sinner here makes up for nothing, for he 'can but synne and hath nought of hym selfe to make amendes'; he is justified passively, or 'else nothynge'. By a Lutheran turn on grammar, Tyndale then states that this passive justification by faith also 'iustifieth vs actiuely'. It is active to the extent that it is passive.

None the less, Tyndale admits that these 'termes be darke to them that be not experte and excercysed' (p. 207). In Wyatt the terms of justice are all the more darkened. A standard trope is the double negative:

> Nor in his sprite is owght vndiscoverd
> (236)
> And not to hide from the my gret vnryght.
> (253)

It is as if a direct statement is a form of rhetoric closed to the elucidation of these vexed areas of personal theology. Rather than risk solecism or heresy, Wyatt qualifies himself twice over, perhaps in the hope that one error will cancel another out. Wyatt deliberately placed himself beyond the imputation of heresy.

To some degree he can be said to have succeeded, in the way that the sonnet by Surrey, 'Praise of certain psalmes of Dauid, translated by sir T. W. the elder', portrays Wyatt's David as a devout catholic penitent in the image of Fisher:

> Where he doth paint the liuely faith, and pure,
> The stedfast hope, the swete returne to grace
> Of iust Dauid, by perfite penitence.[110]

---

[110] *Tottel's Miscellany*, 16ᵛ.

However unlikely a reading this is, it is a misreading useful to a man who might be in peril of his life for being read more closely. Surrey, too, as his own biblical paraphrases show, saw the advantage of inscrutability in the presentation of his more catholic sensibilities.

In the same vein, another of Wyatt's favoured tropes is repetition, sometimes to the point of tautology:

> And pray and seke in tyme for tyme of grace
> (260)

> But thou thy sellff the selff remaynist well
> That thou wast erst
> (625–6)

This is repetition not as renewed emphasis but as diminishing returns, a process of abrasion by which the word subjects its own meaning to erasure. This is the symptomatic cadence of these most deeply self-conscious of poems, a figure involving not so much self-reference as self-cancellation.

The *Penitentiall Psalms* approach their own justification with wary carefulness. This, then, is Wyatt's version of the other locus classicus of Luther's *sola fides*, Psalm 51: 4 (again recited in Romans 3: 4):

> This know I and repent; pardon thow than,
> Wherby thow shalt kepe still thi word stable,
> Thy justice pure and clene; by cawse that whan
> I pardond ame, then forthwith justly able,
> Just I ame jugd by justice off thy grace.
> Ffor I my sellff, lo thing most vnstable,
> Fformed in offence, conceyvid in like case,
> Ame nowght but synn from my natyvite
> (451–8)[111]

This dense essay in theological vocabulary takes verbal repetition into new territory: five cognates of 'justice' are used in three lines, including three in one: 'Just I ame jugd by justice off thy grace.'

The tautology is in delayed reaction to Luther's fetish of *ut iustificeris in sermonibus tuis*, with its unspeakable counter-logic of a God who is not only unjustified but even unjustifiable. Wyatt wards off these unconscionable suggestions by turning God's justice into a triple tautology: God

---

[111] As Muir and Thomson note (p. 376), this is mostly an independent paraphrase from the Bible; but there are hints from Campensis, *Enchiridion Psalmorum*, N2ʳ: *& in servandis promissis constantissimus, & in damnandis illis qui resipiscere nolunt iustissimus.*

is justified because he is justified because he is justified. In the process Wyatt comes up with virtually unsayable verse. It gave trouble to his sixteenth-century editors: in *Certayne Psalmes*, 'justly able' was emended to 'justiciable', hardly a solution since the word was unknown in English except as a term in French law meaning 'subject to another's jurisdiction'.[112] Neologism that it is, 'justiciable' nicely expresses the taboo of justification in Henrician England. The *King's Book*, the official dogma of the church in England in the latter years of the reign, praised God that such subjects as predestination, free will, and justification were things hidden by God, and instructed English subjects to leave well alone. Wyatt's poem shows the necessity of dealing with them all the same, as the sinner attempts to work out his salvation in the face of political repression. As a result he trips over his own tongue, the words of prohibition sticking in his throat:

> Off deipe secretes that David here did sing,
>   Off mercy, off fayth, off frailte, off grace,
> Off goddes goodnes and off Justyfying,
>   The grettnes dyd so astonne hymselff a space,
> As who myght say who hath exprest this thing?
> I synner, I, what have I sayd alas?
>
> (509–14)[113]

Wyatt works between revelation and concealment, between freedom and bondage, between epiphany and damnation. He hardly knows what he himself is saying. His *Penitentiall Psalms* are a masterpiece of suppressed scandal and of scandalous suppression, a triumph of obliquity in which, as he puts it, 'His sylence semid to argew and replye' (296). As such, the work is a formidable model for the state of writing in the wake of the English Reformation.

[112] A reading unique to the printed *Certayne psalmes*. See also *OED*.

[113] These lines build on Aretino but are largely independent, especially in their use of technical theological terminology.

6   Protestant Culture

Acts of literature under Henry VIII were a dangerous business. The Reformation of 1534 engulfed the nation in literary radicalism, as evangelical printers rushed into publication not only new evangelical texts and new imprints of old Lollard tracts but also newly radicalized editions of Langland, Gower, and even Chaucer, dressed in reformed royalist national colours.[1] Cromwell and Cranmer joined in promulgating a royal national vernacular Bible. But in the wake of conservative reaction and regional rebellion this cultural propaganda gave way to a second phase of censorship and literary suppression. The same texts that had been promoted were now indexed as seditious scandal. In the statutes of 1543, Henry proscribed the reading of the Bible for all but the most official purposes. Even reading the *Canterbury Tales*, although allowed for the moment, was threatened with future sanctions. The Henrician regime created a literature of suspicion, on its guard against the imputation of treason or heresy.

The later Tudor reigns, which form the subject of this chapter, tell a different story. Under Edward and Elizabeth, there was a more consistent and thoroughgoing attempt to justify protestantism through literature. The Marian interregnum saw creativity as well as conflict, sowing the seeds of a catholic literary revival (to be discussed later in the book) and of a nascent protestant identity. Although fitful and often contradictory, the last Tudor years see the creation of a protestant literary culture. There was also a movement to create a protestant humanist method for understanding and interpreting literary categories. Indeed, at its highest point this culture held ambitions for reformed protestant hegemony, a unified literary method that would make the triumph of the Reformation complete and permanent. Yet, like its counterpart in the Elizabethan puritan political movement, this protestant literary culture was prone to division and, perhaps inevitably, final failure. For if the Tudor state aspired to a literature without limits, in practice it created a literature with formidable limits on the sayable, the writable, and the readable.

[1] Cummings, 'Reformed Literature and Literature Reformed', pp. 845–9.

I CULTURAL REFORMATION: BUCER IN ENGLAND

At first sight, the accession of Edward VI brought a cultural revolution. This is the high water mark of English protestantism. Contemporaries acclaimed the entry of a new boy-king Josiah to sweep away the tyrannical ambiguities of Henrician religion.[2] The new reign ushered in royal injunctions, which reversed the anti-evangelical laws of the Six Articles and stamped out the vestiges of catholic practice. Within two years, England at last had a proper vernacular Prayer Book.

This triumphant picture no longer characterizes histories of the English Reformation. It could have turned out differently.[3] The struggle to control the succession continued up to the day of Henry's death. Had he died four months earlier, the opposite party would have been in the ascendant, and a catholic reaction led by Bishop Gardiner could have prevailed. As it was, a coup d'état in December put the Duke of Norfolk and his son, the poet Henry Howard, Earl of Surrey, in the Tower. Gardiner was denied access to the king. On 19 January 1547, Surrey, 'the foolish proud boy' was executed for treason, just nine days before the king died in his bed. A new will was written but as yet unsigned; with the collusion of Sir William Paget, secretary of state, Edward Seymour daringly sidled himself into power. Even so it took two months of plotting before Seymour established himself as 'the first protestant to enjoy independent control of the state'.[4]

If the terminology of revolution is rejected in terms of an inevitable, popular demonstration of protestant sentiment, it can be understood in a different way as part of Seymour's exercise of power. Seymour was a ready purveyor and user of culture. He oversaw an 'explosion of radical Reformist publication during Edward's reign'.[5] This included the appearance in print of matter too dark for Henrician proclamations, such as Wyatt's *Certayne Psalmes*. That this rush to print was orchestrated by Seymour is shown by his personal patronage of writers and printers.[6] Thomas Becon and John Hooper resided in his household as chaplains; William Turner was his physician. William Cecil and Thomas Smith—his secretaries—acted as conduits for the patronage of humanistic writing. The two came under Latimer's influence at St John's College, Cambridge,

---

[2] Cranmer applied the epithet in his coronation address, 20 February 1547. On the contemporary (and iconoclastic) meanings of Josiah, see Aston, *England's Iconoclasts*, i. 247–50, esp. 249 n.

[3] The definitive revisionist restatement is Haigh, *English Reformations*, esp. pp. 166–7.

[4] Dickens, *English Reformation*, p. 280.

[5] King, *English Reformation Literature*, p. 20.

[6] Ibid., 107–9.

in the 1530s; both had a reputation for Greek learning. Other aristocratic patrons of evangelical writers close to Seymour included the Duchess of Richmond, who housed John Bale and John Foxe together. Catherine Brandon, Duchess of Suffolk, supported John Day, the printer, later to produce Foxe's *Actes and Monuments* and his collected folio of Tyndale, Frith, and Barnes. Turner (who ranged from catholic-baiting to herbalism), Bale (bibliographer, bibliophile, and bibliolater supreme), and Becon (who published seventy odd works between 1541 and 1567) were prolific writers. Many of them provide a continuity between the late repressive years of Henry, through exile or persecution under Mary, to eventual restoration under Elizabeth; their literary heyday is the six-year reign of Edward.

John King has asserted that Seymour's regime showed 'an unprecedented degree of religious toleration and freedom of speech, reading and publication' (p. 26). It is certainly the case that Royal Injunctions repealed some draconian aspects of Henrician censorship, and also Arundel's infamous Constitutions, which had remained on the statutes for nearly a hundred and fifty years. Seymour also enjoys the accolade of being the only Tudor ruler not to execute anybody for heresy. The statute for religious burnings, *De heretico comburendo*, was among those repealed. However, catholic writing was effectively suppressed. Richard Smith, a noted controversialist in favour of the mass, was sacked from the Regius chair in divinity at Oxford, going into exile at Louvain.[7] New forms of radicalism were identified as dissent. Perhaps Seymour did not last quite long enough to become a persecutor. There were tribunals against heretics in 1548 and 1549; on 2 May 1550, six months after his fall, burnings resumed, when Joan Bocher went to the stake for her views on the divine and human natures of Christ.[8] It seems better to interpret Seymour's enthusiasm for literature in other ways. The most significant statistic is that three out of every four books printed under Seymour were religious. Seymour seems to have conceived religious writing as a form of cultural capital. Religious ideology encouraged conspicuous displays of solidarity designed to bolster the new polity. Henry VIII had shown a similar liking for religious radicalism during the great matter of the divorce, but quickly became murderously suspicious of its volatile force. The Seymour years mark the next phase in this enforced visibility of religion, followed by the 1580s under Elizabeth. In each case a political crisis is ridden out on a wave of

---

[7] On the suppression of catholic writing in 1548, Haigh, *English Reformations*, p. 173.
[8] MacCulloch, *Cranmer*, p. 474.

enthusiasm. In each case the status of religious writing rises to national significance.

It does not much matter what Seymour believed in all this. Perhaps he was as radical a protestant as some historians have accorded him. His contemporaries were not so convinced. Evangelicals hoping for true theocracy quickly became disillusioned; the independence of the bishops was rigorously suborned to royal power. Radicals and evangelicals, even moderates, frequently expressed disappointment at religious policy. Edwardian political religion is marked less by theological purity than by a campaign of ideology. On the one hand, it promoted the breaking up of the rite of the mass, the cult of saints, and the veneration of images; on the other, the vigorous promulgation of alternative media, most especially printed books.[9] This began as early as August 1547, when Seymour rode north for his Scottish campaign, bombarding the natives not only with weapons but also with loads of Bibles.[10]

Theologically, this material could be contradictory. In the summer of 1547 every parish was ordered to purchase two books for regular dissemination during divine service. One was Cranmer's *Book of Homilies*; the other was Nicholas Udall's translation of Erasmus's *Paraphrases* of the New Testament. This is like promoting *De servo arbitrio* and *De libero arbitrio* at one and the same time. The books had in common, however, a reverence for moral sobriety, quietist piety, and political conformism. Service to Christ is peaceably compatible with obedience to Caesar.

Some controversial matter was deliberately promulgated. Thirty-one printed tracts against the mass survive from one single year, 1548, including two by Seymour's tirelessly angry chaplain Turner.[11] Other texts presented themselves as unexceptionably edifying, such as the sixty editions of the Bible produced in Edward's reign. Yet it is the nature of all Reformation literature that controversy is just round the corner. The leading literary principle of Edwardian and Marian evangelism is of the translucent plainness of the literal meaning, as in Cranmer's definition of the Bible as self-explicating (in his Preface to the second edition of the Great Bible in 1549). It is a claim not borne out by the need for a thousand folio pages of Erasmian paraphrase alongside it. The truth is that the gospelling of Bale, or Becon, or Hooper was altogether too hot for some. The catholic exile

---

[9] The two sides of this ideological war are best described respectively by Duffy, *Stripping of the Altars*, pp. 448–77; and Aston, *England's Iconoclasts*, i. 246–77; also Simon, *Education and Society*, pp. 268–87; and King, *English Reformation Literature*, pp. 87–109.

[10] Dickens, *English Reformation*, p. 281.

[11] King, *English Reformation Literature*, pp. 89 and 287.

Richard Smith sniped that Hooper was treated as a 'prophet, nay they looked upon him as some deity'.[12] Such objections came not just from reactionaries like Smith or Gardiner (largely silenced) but from the heart of the evangelical establishment. Thomas Smith, one of Seymour's secretaries of state, wrote to Seymour's wife, the Duchess of Somerset (herself a patron of evangelical writing). He complained of those that 'kneel upon your grace's carpets and devise commonwealths as they like, and are angry that other men be not so hasty to run straight as their brains crow'.[13] Yet Smith was happy to ally himself with notable gospellers such as Latimer and Robert Crowley in pursuit of the religio-political aims of the group known as the 'commonwealth men'.[14] Crowley as writer, editor, and printer was a principal author of Edwardian culture: he published the first printed editions of the Wyclifite *General Prologue* and Langland's *Piers Plowman*, as well as a host of biblical works.[15]

Biblical literature was itself not uncontroversial. Even the Psalms—of all biblical books the easiest to present as conventional piety, and the most widely printed—could take on the tincture of faction. *Goostly psalmes and spirituall songes*, edited by Coverdale in about 1539, contained unharmonized metrical settings of thirteen psalms, the Magnificat, Nunc dimittis, the Lord's Prayer, Creed, and Commandments, intended for pious, domestic use. The presence of some German hymns gives away its 'unmistakably Lutheran flavour', based on Luther's own *geistliche Lieder*.[16] The Act of Six Articles that year was unpropitious for any act of literature, and according to Foxe the book was suppressed immediately after the fall of Cromwell, Coverdale's patron. One copy only survives. For the last years of Henry's reign singing Psalms seems to have been too subversive to be permissible; Crowley's *Psalter of David newely translated into Englysh metre*, of 1549, was the first for a decade. It is the first complete English metrical psalter and the first to contain harmonized music.[17]

Harmony, too, was controversial: Turner (in *The huntyng and fyndyng out of the Romysh foxe*), Bale (in *The Image of both Churches*), and Becon (in *Jewel of Joy*) all objected to anything beyond the simplest, plainest settings.[18] Thomas Sternhold, a minor royal householder, appealed to the king's personal patronage to circulate his abbreviated metrical Psalter of

[12] Quoted in Brigden, *London and the Reformation*, p. 459.
[13] BL Harleian MS 6989, 146ʳ, quoted in Brigden, *London and the Reformation*, p. 458.
[14] Dickens, *English Reformation*, p. 310.
[15] On Crowley, see King, *English Reformation Literature*.
[16] Le Huray, *Music and the Reformation*, pp. 370–1.
[17] Ibid., 371.   [18] Ibid., 12.

1549, promising 'more delyght in the holy songes of veritie than in any fayned rymes of vanitie'.[19] Although a second edition and several reprints appeared in Edward's reign, none had music: this had to await the more fertile ground of Geneva, where a musical edition of Sternhold and Hopkins, with an order of prayer by Calvin, was produced in 1556. This work was forbidden in England during the reign of Mary; but even the Genevan version contains a defensive Preface rejecting complicated music 'to tickle the ears and flatter the fantasies': the music is not harmonized and the underlay is syllabic.[20] Such carefulness is striking in a book that became possibly the most widely used work of literature in English before the end of the seventeenth century, with over five hundred editions. Less public versions of the Psalms were all the more illicit. Just as Wyatt had justified himself in prison by Englishing the Psalms in secret, so Thomas Smith, arrested after the fall of his patron Seymour late in 1549, paraphrased the Psalms while imprisoned in the Tower.[21]

The cultural polity of the early Edwardian regime was energetic and ambitious, incorporating the pious with the theological, the private with the public, the popular with the aristocratic, in ways which the preceding government would have found insanely heterodox. In one further respect, Edwardian culture adopted a distinctly un-Henrician tenet: the cultivation of European protestant literature. A xenophobic trait is found in two proclamations against books written in 1530 by Chancellor More. This banned not only heresy but any book 'being in the English tongue and printed beyond the sea, of what matter soever it be . . . or the same books in the French or Dutch tongue'.[22] Other government pronouncements throughout the reign endeavoured to protect England from infection from 'beyonde the see'.[23] Through political coincidence, within a few months of Henry's death an opportunity arose to reverse this policy of theological isolation. This was instigated through the personal influence of Cranmer, who had perhaps felt most keenly the separation of English from European reform.

In April 1547, Charles V's victory at Mühlberg put continental reformers at risk throughout the empire. More than four hundred clergy may have left southern Germany at this time. Pietro Martire Vermigli (known in England as Peter Martyr) and Bernardino Ochino, already exiled from their native Italy, accepted in October an invitation to leave their

[19] Quoted in King, *English Reformation Literature*, p. 217.
[20] Le Huray, *Music and the Reformation*, pp. 372–3.
[21] King, *English Reformation Literature*, pp. 233–4.
[22] *TRP*, i. 194–5 (No. 129).   [23] Wilkins, *Concilia*, iii. 735.

temporary refuge in Strasbourg for England. Peter Martyr was given the golden handshake of Richard Smith's Regius professorship of divinity at Oxford, where the Students of Christ Church were horrified to find him bringing his wife into residence.

The Italians brought letters of commendation from the doyen of Strasbourg reform, Martin Bucer. In the same letter, Bucer encouraged Cranmer to invite another Italian from Strasbourg, the Hebrew scholar Emmanuel Tremellio.[24] If the first arrivals were from Strasbourg (like Pierre Alexandre, who became Cranmer's secretary), the influx soon came from all parts of the protestant diaspora, taking in most of the nationalities of Europe. In 1548, Cranmer received Francisco de Encinas (known as Dryander), a Spanish Lutheran and pupil of Melanchthon. The distinguished Polish exile, Jan Laski, former archdeacon of Warsaw and friend of Erasmus, came from the Frisian church of Emden, followed by the Fleming, Jan Utenhove. Between them, the refugees represented the different wings of evangelical thought: from Zurich came Bullinger's assistant, Johan ab Ulmis; emergent Calvinism had a voice in Vallerand Poullain, who had succeeded Calvin as minister to the French congregation in Strasbourg.

The star in this firmament, however, was Bucer himself. Bucer had been interested in English affairs since 1531. His long and fruitful correspondence with Cranmer shows a friendship of complex mutual deference and influence which reflected the odd relationship of England and the continent at this time.[25] The lure of English power and wealth made it the most attractive potential protestant ally for the league of the Schmalkalden; at the same time the English looked up to the intellectual sophistication of a city such as Strasbourg at the heart of Europe. In a similar way Bucer offered elaborate flattery to Cranmer as a potentate even while Cranmer paid tribute to his mastery of theology. The relationship is summed up by the dedication to Cranmer in 1536 of Bucer's commentary on Romans, the first volume in a projected commentary on all the Epistles.

Bucer was given his own promise of preferment in the form of the Regius chair at Cambridge, along with his colleague Paul Fagius, who was to become university Reader in Hebrew. Yet if Cranmer, and Seymour, saw Bucer as the final key to the cultural reform of England, Bucer arrived to find a rather different situation from the optimistic portents of October

---

[24] MacCulloch, *Cranmer*, p. 381. Tremellio, a Jew originally from Lucca, had first been converted by Reginald Pole.
[25] On Bucer's first engagement in English affairs, see MacCulloch, *Cranmer*, pp. 61–7, who is the best authority on Cranmer's contact with Bucer.

1547. Leaving Strasbourg only at the last minute, in April 1549, and escorted by Alexandre from Calais to Lambeth Palace, he finally met Cranmer in person after eighteen years of fulsome letters. It was only in December that Bucer officially took up his professorship, by which time Fagius had died, falling victim to his first Cambridge summer.[26] The embarrassing delay in Bucer's advancement was due to the political cataclysm overtaking Seymour's protectorate. It could be said that these events justified, after all, the Henrician prophecy about the dangers of too much theological culture.

Rebellions were endemic in Tudor England, and had complex causes. In 1549, unrest seems to have been started by protest against the enclosure of common land. None the less, this most serious outbreak of public violence since the Pilgrimage of Grace in 1536 followed directly from the most visible cultural project of all: the English Prayer Book. Even more than the English Bible, the English Prayer Book was a definitive act of ideology. English services were introduced at St Paul's and other London churches as early as the spring of 1548. After long debate, compromise, and revision between Cranmer, the bishops, and the lords, an official Order of Service was finally passed in January 1549. While some parishes introduced the new forms straightaway, final abolition of the Latin services was set for Whit Sunday, 9 June 1549.[27] Some Devon parishioners ordered a priest to say mass on 10 June; on the next day, Seymour worried that priests were using economic concerns to incite wholesale rejection of the English liturgy. The Western Rebellion led to a siege of the city of Exeter against 'heretics and two-penny book men'. While this was the only armed resistance to the new religious measures, and London stayed loyal, there were riots in Hampshire, Oxfordshire, Buckinghamshire, Yorkshire, and East Anglia.[28] Peter Martyr fled from Oxford to London, and Bucer spent just one night in Cambridge before retiring to the safety of Ely. Although Seymour blamed reactionary clergy and agrarian unrest, the council blamed him, and in October he was sent to the Tower. In Oxford college chapels, as is often the case on such occasions, Latin mass was celebrated in anticipation of a return to the old ways.

However, the response to the commotion was not retreat but cultural

---

[26] Ibid., 422.

[27] Duffy, *Stripping of the Altars*, p. 464.

[28] Haigh, *English Reformations*, pp. 174–5. Haigh's tendency to argue for effect suppresses evidence about London, where most parishes complied with the new orders; see Brigden, *London and the Reformation*, pp. 444–6. MacCulloch, p. 432, remarks that evidence of unrest being anti-evangelical can only be found in the West; in Eastern counties, rebels concerned about rural poverty asserted their loyalty to the new religion.

expansion. On Sunday 21 July, Cranmer personally supervised a service at St Paul's, preaching a sermon, celebrating English communion, and leading the singing of his new Litany. Outside, his chaplain preached a vigorous sermon at Paul's Cross. For his own sermon, Cranmer was assisted by Peter Martyr, who produced two drafts in Latin on the text of rebellion, which Cranmer modified into English.[29] Meanwhile, Bucer and Ochino were commissioned to research the political theology of sedition and resistance.[30]

Bucer was involved in controversy about the Prayer Book throughout his sojourn in England. He did not like the book: not for being too radical, but too moderate, an opinion shared by evangelical opinion in England. Cranmer did not altogether like it either, and Bucer accepted Cranmer's need for political compromise. He was requested to write a detailed critique, now known as the *Censura*, which he completed in January 1551, virtually the last theological act of his life (he died on 28 February). Cranmer assimilated much of this criticism in his revised Prayer Book of the following year.

Bucer found the religious temper of England during his emigration vitiated by uncertainties, worrying that his theological reputation had been compromised. Calvin wrote from Geneva suggesting his old mentor had gone soft. Nevertheless, Bucer was consulted with deep respect on the issues of the day, particularly on ordination, on vestments, and on the eucharist. His summary of the practical concerns of the church in society, *De regno Christi*, was received with acclaim in 1550. During these years, England found itself briefly at the centre of a European theological tradition. For this reason, history has accorded the refugees of the Edwardian reign a crucial status in the progress of an English Reformation. At this time English religion became marked by a central-south German and Swiss character rather than by the Lutheran north.[31] This might have been different if Melanchthon had accepted Cranmer's solicitations to succeed Bucer in the Cambridge professorship; but Melanchthon warily anticipated the accession of Mary and declined.[32] The subsequent exile of many English evangelicals to Zurich and especially Geneva confirmed the theological trend.

As a result of the public debates in England between the two editions of the Edwardian Prayer Book, study of the influence of Bucer has tended to concentrate on the eucharist and on outward ceremonies. However, the

---

[29] MacCulloch, *Cranmer*, pp. 435–6.   [30] McNair, 'Ochino on Sedition', pp. 36–49.
[31] MacCulloch dates the realignment back to the mid-1530s (*Cranmer*, p. 173 ff.).
[32] MacCulloch, *Cranmer*, p. 539.

cultural impact of Bucer can be traced in less visible ways. In little more than a year in Cambridge he made a lasting impression. Among his acolytes was John Bradford, who had passed from law at the Inner Temple to divinity at Pembroke Hall, Cambridge, 'where he heard D. Martin Bucer diligently, and was right familyar and deare vnto hym'.[33] A contemporary biography of Bucer describes Bradford as nursing him on his deathbed.[34] One of Bradford's pupils at Pembroke was John Whitgift, future Archbishop of Canterbury; Whitgift cited Bucer regularly throughout his career.[35]

Bradford played a leading role in a serious quarrel among evangelicals that began in 1552 when Bishop Ridley went to Kent to investigate a group dubbed 'the Freewillers'. It is a premonition of the dissension now emerging in protestant culture, and at the same time of the preoccupation with predestination, which developed later in the century. The Kent conventicle was also suspected of being Anabaptist; Cranmer threatened it with imprisonment. In a remarkable prophecy, one of the leaders warned Cranmer that soon the tables might be reversed and the archbishop himself could face death for heresy.[36] Within two years, the argument broke out again, this time in prison, where representatives of both factions faced persecution together under Mary.

Bradford was arrested in Fleet Street on 13 August 1553, less than a month into the new reign, oddly enough after protecting a catholic priest from an evangelical mob. He was sent to the Tower and thence to the King's Bench prison in Southwark. Here in 1554 he renewed debate with the Freewillers, writing various letters of admonition and rebuke, and composing a 'Defence of Election' or 'Treatise of Predestination' which confuted six 'enormities' perpetrated in the confessional articles of the leading Freewiller Henry Hart.[37] Bradford's treatise was enclosed in a general letter of 18 January 1555 to the three great bishops now imprisoned in Oxford: Cranmer, Ridley, and Latimer.[38] Bradford complained of his opponents

[33] Thomas Sampson, Preface to Bradford, *Two notable Sermons*, A3ᵛ.

[34] 'De obitu M. Buceri', in Bucer, *Scripta Anglicana*, p. 875.

[35] Pauck ascribes this to Bradford's influence, *Melanchthon and Bucer*, p. 172, n. 24; see also Collinson, *Godly people*, p. 31.

[36] Foxe recorded the story in his notes and in the Latin *Commentarii* (1559), but censored it from his English text; it is transcribed in the 19th-century edn., v. 860.

[37] 'A treatise of predestination with an answer to certain enormities calumniously gathered of one to slander God's truth' is the MS title, Bodleian Library MS Bodl.53. The text of Part 1 was printed by John Hall in 1562.

[38] The letter was signed by Bradford, Robert Ferrar, Rowland Taylor, and John Philpot. An early copy survives in an Emmanuel College, Cambridge, MS; it was printed by John Day in Coverdale's edition of the *Letters of the Martyrs* (1564).

that 'In freewyl they are playn papists, yea Pelagians'.[39] It is an extraordinary episode at such a point of duress: Bradford was arraigned at the end of the month and burned at Smithfield on 1 July. Ridley found the controversy regrettable but also acknowledged its gravity: it struck a blow at the heart of the new gospel.[40] Ridley distributed a treatise of his own, now lost.

Bradford's views on predestination have been attributed to his reading of Calvin.[41] It is Calvin's destiny to have become the proleptic source of every argument about predestination since the foundation of the earth. Yet there is no need to hunt for Calvin in 1554, when he was still a middle-ranking intellectual figure. Predestination is only briefly mentioned in the 1536 *Institutio*, and the long chapters devoted to it in the 1559 edition were not yet written.[42] In any case, justification by faith, including a predestinarian outlook, was fashionable already in Catherine Parr's circle in the 1540s.[43] Melanchthon's Latin treatise on justification was translated into English in 1548.[44] Predestination was entrenched in the Forty-Two Articles of Religion of 1553, in a wording hardly changed to the present day.[45] Moreover, Bradford's sources can be identified specifically. One book he certainly had with him in prison is Bucer's *Metaphrases et enarrationes*, the commentary on Romans dedicated to Cranmer in 1536. Probably after his condemnation, awaiting death, Bradford wrote a consolatory tract entitled 'The Restoration of all Things' addressed to Joyce Hales, consisting largely of translations from annotations on Romans 8 in *Metaphrases et enarrationes*.[46]

Because of Bucer's mediatory role in so many contentions, his theology is often misrepresented as moderating in every respect. In his public theology, Bucer was forever the diplomat, searching a form of words to satisfy both parties. This quality earned him a prominent place in debates between Zwinglians and Lutherans on the eucharist and on justification; and also in the famous efforts to bring a rapprochement between catholicism and protestantism at Regensburg and Ratisbon. The exigencies of biblical commentary are different, however. Theology does not work in

---

[39] Coverdale, *Letters of the Martyrs*, p. 359.

[40] Ridley to Bernhere, Oxford, probably 19 January 1555, in *Writings of Bradford*, ii. 172–3.

[41] Dickens, *English Reformation*, p. 278.   [42] Wendel, *Calvin*, p. 265.

[43] Davis, *Heresy and Reformation*, p. 35.

[44] *The Justification of Man* was a translation by Nicholas Lesse of *De iustificatione* of 1531.

[45] None the less, this wording, too, is commonly wrongly ascribed to Calvin's influence.

[46] See e.g. *Writings*, i. 355, where Townsend provides a passage from Bucer for comparison. There is a copy of Bucer's text in Bradford's College Library, Pembroke. Thomas Freeman has demonstrated that books were smuggled into prison for Bradford by bribing jailers.

the same way in all places, despite the best hopes of doctrinal and intellectual historians. The pressure of reading Paul took Bucer in other directions from those of public meetings, just as it had done also for Augustine or Luther, or, for that matter, Aquinas. In turn, Bucer's way of reading Paul had considerable influence on Calvin.[47]

Bradford's short treatise is based almost exclusively on citations of two biblical books, Romans and Ephesians, the two Pauline books on which Bucer had published commentaries.[48] Against Hart's claim that predestination leads to licentiousness and despair, Bradford replied, following Bucer, that the doctrine is both necessary and sufficiently explained in scripture: 'of all things which God requireth of us, not only the most principal, but also the whole sum'.[49] Bucer argues that predestination is of special comfort to martyrs (p. 363), a consideration that did not escape Bradford at the King's Bench. Far from leading to the 'dungeon of despair' the defence of the doctrine of election is an aid to piety and love at the expense of pride and self. The doctrine was directly relevant to men awaiting death in prison, because it promised God's salvation for his faithful. The Freewillers denied this promise. 'The effectes of saluation they so mingle and confounde with yᵉ cause' that they put the cart before the horse.[50] Bucer's proper order of salvation—*praedestinatum . . . vocatum . . . iustificatum . . . glorificandum*—is therefore for Bradford a matter of eternal life and death, far outweighing his earthly fate.[51]

In his reading of Paul, Bradford reaches back via Bucer to the Luther of *De servo arbitrio*, in one place closely enough to suggest the possibility of direct quotation:

As for the testimonies of the scriptures, which he bringeth for free-will, a child of two years reading in the scriptures may see them to be legal sentences, and prove not that man can do as they require, but telleth man as the law doth, what he ought to do.[52]

[47] Bucer's commentary is summarized usefully by Parker, *Commentaries on Romans*, pp. 34–62; Calvin's use of Bucer is discussed on pp. 71–4.

[48] Bucer also lectured on Ephesians at Cambridge in 1550; Pauck, *Melanchthon and Bucer*, p. 158.

[49] *Writings*, i. 308; see *Metaphrases et enarrationes*, p. 399. Hall, without evidence, states there is no evidence of Bradford using Bucer except in 'The Restoration' ('Bucer in England', p. 157). It seems improbable that Bradford eschewed the use of a commentary on Romans by his master when he had one available.

[50] To Cranmer, Ridley, and Latimer, January 1555, in Coverdale, *Letters of the Martyrs*, p. 358; and also 'Treatise of Predestination', *Writings*, i. 318.

[51] *Metaphrases et enarrationes*, p. 359. See also McGrath, *Iustitia Dei*, ii. 35.

[52] *Writings*, i. 321; compare WA 18.677.24, and Ch. 4 above, esp. p. 165.

It appears here that Hart has been reading Erasmus, in assuming that biblical injunctions can be taken as a proof of free will.[53] Bradford answers him not with doctrine but by means of an interpretative reflex concerning the grammar of verbs, a staple of commentary tradition. To confirm Bradford's adoption of a Lutheran style of biblical reading (perhaps derived from Melanchthon, perhaps directly), there is a striking reference in another of Bradford's treatises:

> One man therefore which is regenerate may well be called always just, and always sinful: just in respect of God's seed and his regeneration; sinful in respect of Satan's seed and his first birth.[54]

Whereas Hart made free will the opposite of justification, so that acts of virtue are an operation of deliberate choice, Bradford's reading of Paul follows Bucer's in drawing any good will back to the will of God. In his own actions, man can only be righteous by the grace of God, which produces the choice to will good.[55]

Bradford's deeply inward meditations on predestinatory scripture show how he learned from Bucer not so much a set of doctrinal assertions as a method of reading embedded in protestant culture. This is perhaps not surprising in one of Bucer's pupils in divinity. Yet Bucer's influence can also be seen in less expected quarters. Ralph Lever's *The Arte of Reason, rightly termed, Witcraft* appeared in print in 1573. It was the second logic produced in England, following Thomas Wilson's *Rule of Reason*, and the last before Ramism took over.[56] It was clearly composed many years earlier, perhaps before Wilson. In the dedicatory letter to the Earl of Essex, Lever remarks that 'Martine Bucer read ouer this arte, in his old days, and renewed in his age, the rules that he learned thereof in his youth'.[57] It is a passing reference to the breadth of Bucer's interest in emergent English culture.[58] Bucer also occupies a place in Wilson's career. They shared the patronage of Catherine Brandon, Duchess of Suffolk, perhaps the most evangelical of Edwardian aristocrats. She asked Bucer to oversee the education of her sons in Cambridge; Wilson was their tutor, until the boys

[53] Hart's bill is lost; however, Penny, *Freewill or Predestination*, pp. 89–96, suggests Erasmus (perhaps the *Paraphrases*) is a source for Hart.

[54] 'A Comparison between the Old Man and the New', *Writings*, i. 298. The treatise was printed by Wiliam Seres in *Godly Meditations* (1567). Trueman, *Luther's Legacy*, p. 282, notes the Lutheran vocabulary.

[55] *Writings*, i. 321; see *Metaphrases et enarrationes*, p. 360.

[56] Howell, *Logic & Rhetoric*, p. 57.

[57] *Witcraft*, *3ʳ.

[58] On Bucer's influence at Cambridge, see also Simon, *Education and Society*, pp. 261–3.

died of plague in 1551, shortly after Bucer himself. In his *Arte of Rhetorique*, Wilson made a glancing elegy of the reformer, citing as his example of synecdoche, 'All Cambridge sorowed for the death of Bucer' adding, somewhat bathetically, 'meanyng the moste parte'.[59] It was a bathos justified by the posthumous history of poor Bucer's bones: in 1557, Bucer and Fagius were disinterred, condemned as heretics, and their remains put to the flames, along with their books, in Cambridge market-place.

Bucer's place in a general European humanism is shown by his long association with Johannes Sturm, dating from 1533. Sturm became the leading humanist and grammarian in Strasbourg and had earlier introduced Agricolan logic to the university in Paris, where he probably taught Peter Ramus. In April 1550, Roger Ascham wrote to Sturm praising Bucer as a new Cicero, and proclaiming him as the ornament of English humanities. Bucer's presence in England, he said, promised a new golden age, combining Christian piety, humanist learning, and public eloquence.[60]

These three Cambridge *literati*, Ascham, Wilson, and Lever, together show logic as the handmaiden of protestant theology in Edwardian England. Indeed, after Wilson was arrested by the inquisition in Rome in 1558, he claimed that his works of logic and rhetoric had been cited against him as evidence of heresy.[61] The dedicatory letter in the *Rule of Reason* to Edward, 'Kyng Iosias', advances its cause as the first vernacular English logic and puts itself at the service of the 'Gospell'. Whereas its structure is conventionally Aristotelian and Agricolan, and self-consciously old-fashioned, the examples are professedly protestant and provocatively novel. Syllogism is used to prove that 'none trusting to his workes, is iust before God'.[62] Wilson uses the treatment of Invention to make the doctrinal point more emphatic:

And therfore I maie saie, man is not iustified by his workes, because he is iustified by his fayth onely. For if mercie come by grace, and that frelie, then workes cannot saue us. Paul proueth the first, therfore the seconde is for euer true'. (16ᵛ)

It seems as if Wilson could have been listening to Bradford. The compliment is repaid when Bradford finishes his 'Treatise of Predestination' by

---

[59] *Arte of Rhetorique* (1560), M1ʳ. The 1st edn. was 1553. Wilson contributed an epigram to Bucer (along with Henry and Charles Brandon, Walter Haddon, Nicholas Udall, and many others) to the funeral oration of Sir John Cheke, *De obitu doctissimi et sanctissimi theologi doctoris Martini Buceri* (London: Reginald Wolff, 1551).

[60] Ascham to Sturm, *Works* (ed. Giles) i. 183 and 189.

[61] *Arte of Rhetorique*, A4ᵛ ('for the which I was coumpted an heretike').

[62] *Rule of Reason*, H1ʳ.

averring that 'Truth is plain and simple, but untruth must be obscured with ambiguous phrases'.[63] Wilson gave to his *Rule* the task of eliminating 'Ambiguitee' from the realm of truth: 'Consideryng ambiguite bredeth error, moste wareness ought to be vsed, that the doubleness of no one worde deceaue the hearer' (C4ᵛ).

In his position as presiding master of the arts of theology and logic, Bucer cast a shadow from Edwardian and Marian evangelism into the reign of Elizabeth. Ascham was already tutor to the princess, and exercised considerable influence in the new regime. Whitgift, Bradford's pupil, rose to be primate of England and privy councillor. Even Wilson, in his minor way, occupied a position as a secretary on the edges of power, in a manner all the more telling of the operation of Tudor political culture. Command of the arts of humanist literacy and of theology was the key to its ideological system and to preferment. The two went hand in hand, so that it is hardly possible to write a history of one without a history of the other. In this respect, too, the controversies that are the particular legacy of Bucer's influence, over freedom and predestination, and over the status of vernacular writing, are characteristic of the new age.

II CALVIN'S COMMENTARIES

In the control of the literary arts, as in other matters, the stakes were raised by the greatest of Bucer's inheritors, Calvin. While Bradford, Ridley, and Cranmer suffered under the Marian persecution, others escaped to the continent, above all to Geneva, where Calvin had finally settled, on Bucer's advice, in the 1540s. English evangelicals found in Geneva a heavenly city, seemingly immune from the political vicissitudes that hampered religion under the Tudors. Above all, they found a city with a seemingly unified religious culture. Ruled from above by the ecclesiastical *Ordonnances* of 1541, Geneva lived under Calvin's mastery in other ways. Remembered by history as the narrowest of theocrats, Calvin was known in his own time as a prince of learning and of humanist literature. Whatever his theological differences from them, Calvin modelled his scholarship on the pillars of French humanism, Erasmus, Lefèvre, and Guillaume Budé. He was deeply schooled in the methods of Latin oratory. The title of his theological lifework, the *Institutio*, with its reference to Quintilian's *Institutio oratoria*, showed this humanist stamp.

[63] *Writings*, i. 326.

Calvin's role as absolute ruler was always as much fiction as fact. The Geneva seen by Englishmen in the 1550s was riven by faction. What made Geneva attractive was not so much theocracy in practice as a vision of a godly culture. Calvin was a supreme maker of ideology, a massively productive man of letters. He delivered sermons on the New Testament on Sunday mornings, Psalms in the afternoons, and the Old Testament on weekdays. Just as important was his textual production: from 1551 his principal labour was in literary efforts, above all the many editions of the *Institutio* and a comprehensive series of biblical commentaries.[64] Calvin was also committed to control of the educational system. Eventually this resulted in the foundation of the Collège in 1559 (projected as early as the *Ordonnances* of 1541).[65] The Genevan academy followed Calvin's humanist principles to the letter. It was an Erasmian trilingual institution, with a curriculum based on Virgil and Quintilian in grammar, Livy and Xenephon in history, Cicero in dialectic.[66]

Calvin's theology was worked out under the bewildering linguistic pressures of sixteenth-century religion. The publication of Erasmus's New Testament provoked a fundamental problem: it created a bilingual Bible. In time this turned into a polyglot Bible, with parallel texts of Hebrew, Greek, and Latin. Simultaneously and interdependently the vernacular movement created Bibles in German, English, French *ad finitum*. Theology claimed to be unitary, to make one explanation of one God. At the same time theology is pre-eminently a textual activity because it arises out of commentary on a text. In medieval theology a semblance of unity could be maintained because the Bible appeared to be one text in one language. But the sixteenth-century Bible was transparently two texts in two languages, or even a multiplicity of texts in a panglossia of languages. How could it possibly yield one single theology?

This problem vexed catholic theology, evident at either end of the century in the work of Thomas Cajetan and Robert Bellarmine, threatening the autonomy of doctrinal authority. The Council of Trent provided a kind of solution by restoring the fiction of the one Vulgate to which the original languages were subordinate. Calvin adopted a different method to restore the disintegrated unity of the text. His theology attempted to reunite the single *parole* of God, but it could only do so by reinventing linguistic and hermeneutic theory in the process. This he did by working with the grain of humanist grammar, logic, and rhetoric even as he rejected

---

[64] These editions are surveyed in Gilmont, *Calvin et le livre imprimé*, pp. 63–92.
[65] Parker, *Calvin*, pp. 126–9.   [66] Bouwsma, *Calvin*, pp. 14–15.

absolutely its theology. From his early edition of an essay by Seneca, Calvin remained a good humanist.[67]

Calvin's theological writing divided itself around a clear demarcation of the processes of meaning. The *Institutio Christianae religionis*, first published in Latin in 1536, was formulated as a catechistical work, in octavo size, beginning with an *apologia* addressed to François Ier. Compelled to leave Geneva for Strasbourg, in 1539 he produced a revised version in folio, three times the length, of greater theological ambition. This was followed by his beautiful translation into French, the *Institution de la religion chrestienne* of 1541. The 1539 text provided full chapters on penitence and justification and a first essay on the question of predestination and divine providence.[68] In his Preface to the new edition, however, he explained that he intended the *Institutio* merely as a prolegomenon of doctrinal discussion in advance of the true labour of biblical commentary.[69] The 1541 French text announced itself as 'comme une clef et ouverture' to give access to the understanding of the scriptures.[70] The doctrine of the *Institutio* and the hermeneutics of the *commentarius* formed a holy triangle with the text of the Bible, in the Greek and Latin editions of Robert Estienne and the new French version of Calvin's mentor Pierre Robert Olivétan.[71] The new theology was a triumph for new learning.

Calvin lectured on the Bible (beginning with the gospel of John and the letters to the Corinthians) in Strasbourg in 1539 under the aegis of Sturm.[72] In 1540, he published his first commentary on the deliberately chosen text of Romans. The division of meaning between *Institutio* and *Commentarius* now became clear. The *Institutio* ordered scripture into theological *loci*, following the practice of Melanchthon's famous *Loci communes*, in turn based on the logical principles of *loci* developed in Agricola's *De inventione dialecticae*.[73] *Loci communes* is a classic of the age, enormously influential

---

[67] Calvin's humanism is well documented by Breen, *Calvin: A Study in French Humanism* and 'Calvin and the Rhetorical Tradition', Wendel, *Calvin et l'humanisme* and others; the summary here is from Bouwsma, *Calvin*, pp. 9–14.

[68] *Institutio* (1539), cap.viii, pp. 244–71. The successive Latin and French editions of the *Institutio* are described in detail by Wendel, *Calvin*, pp. 112–22.

[69] 'Epistola ad lectorem', verso of title-page (dated August 1539). Here he announces his forthcoming commentary on Romans.

[70] *Institution*, i. 25.

[71] Calvin wrote a Latin Preface to Olivétan's *La Bible qui est toute la Saincte escripture* (Neuchâtel: Pierre de Wingle, 1535).

[72] Wendel, *Calvin*, p. 61. Sturm had recently returned from Paris; he wrote a eulogy of Calvin for the 1543 edition of the *Institutio*.

[73] *Loci* or 'place logic' was of course largely derived from Aristotle's τόποι. On its Agricolan development, see Jardine, 'Humanistic Logic', *CHRP*, p. 182; and Ong, *Ramus*, pp. 104–12.

in protestant culture for its summatory brevity and lucidity on the prime theological issues.[74] Protestant commentary now developed a new humanist form, distinct from Luther's early lectures. Melanchthon used the new method in his *Commentarii* on Romans, tying Paul's text to leading concepts.[75] Heinrich Bullinger's commentary of 1533 espoused the humanist principles of brevity, faithfulness to the original, and attention to context. It was to these ideals that Calvin devoted himself in the first sentence of his introductory letter to Simon Grynaeus prefacing the commentary on Romans. The proper aim of the interpreter is *perspicua brevitas* (in the French version, 'une brièveté sans obscurité'), a rhetorical virtue allied to his sole task of elucidating the meaning of the text, what Calvin terms *verborum proprietas*, 'the exact sense of the words'.[76]

Because of the multiple texts of the Bible this could mean many things. Calvin showed care both in his choice of a Greek text and in his use of modern Greek grammars. But he wrote the commentary in Latin alongside a Latin text of scripture, a translation he made himself in consultation with Erasmus's version and Estienne's revision of the Vulgate. Rather than work purely from the Greek his method conflated Greek and Latin readings with a bilingualism typical of the age.[77] He also noted many cases where Paul's Greek is influenced by Hebraic usage. As if three languages were not enough, in 1550 he produced a French translation of his whole commentary.

Potentially this Babel of Bibles provided him with an insuperable problem of signification. One solution he consistently rejected: although Calvin habitually referred to scripture as dictated by the Holy Spirit, he denied the faith of linguistic cabbalism in the individual signifiers of the original text.[78] The text of the Bible is a human production in human words, through which God 'communicates' with man.[79] It is through this theory of divine communication ('accommodation' in French) that he finds a solution to the proliferation of tongues. For although there are many Bibles in many languages there is only one word of God. According

---

[74] The *Loci communes* were first published in 1521 and frequently expanded in revised editions.

[75] Published in 1532. Melanchthon's first lectures on Romans had been printed as the *Annotationes* in 1522 at Luther's behest. Bizer argues that Melanchthon referred to Luther's lectures on Romans in MS. Calvin did not know them, however.

[76] *Commentarius*, e.g. pp. 1 and 42. See Ganoczy and Scheld, *Die Hermeneutik Calvins*, pp. 111–20.

[77] Girardin, *Rhétorique et théologique*, p. 167.

[78] For references, see Vincent, *Exigence éthique*, p. 65.

[79] See Parker, *New Testament Commentaries*, pp. 56–8.

to Calvin, this word must always be the same in whatever language. It is therefore innately translatable. Tyndale wanted to say this but stuck stubbornly to the linguistic differences between the tongues he had so lovingly mastered. Calvin insisted that there is only one *sensus* even though there may be various linguistic forms of this *sensus*. In this way he goes behind *mots* to find a world of divine *parole* which always inhabits our parochial verbal media of *mots*.

Calvin's Bible is one of *signifiés* not *signifiants*. This is the basis of the key term of his hermeneutics, the *genuinus sensus*, a term that engenders multifarious synonyms, *germanus sensus*, *simplex sensus*, *literalis sensus*, all subject to the primary *signifié* of the *verus Scripturae sensus*.[80] Some historians of Calvin's thought take this *simplex sensus* as unproblematic and to herald the beginnings of modern 'scientific' exegesis. But Calvin's own acts of interpretation are complex and the variety of terms he uses to describe the scriptural *signifié* suggests that his insistence on *genuinus* is special pleading. He justifies it, however, by appealing to *sensus* as only an adjunct to a logically prior *mens scriptoris* ('mind of the author'). Derrida's ultimate 'metaphysic of presence' is found in Calvin, in the ascription of *parole* to a single intentionality lying behind biblical meaning in the *scriptor* of the *textus*.[81] The letter to Grynaeus declares the task of the interpreter to be to 'unfold' the *mentem scriptoris*, and his stock phrase in rejecting readings of other critics is *alienum a mente Pauli*. In a crucial statement on the relationship between language and mind, the commentary on I Corinthians describes language as the *character mentis* by which others perceive the *affectus* of the writer.[82]

In the fashion predicted by Derrida, it is this *character mentis* that guarantees the singularity of meaning. In practice, Calvin arrives at meaning by examining the context and connotations of the words before him rather than by appeal to an extratextual 'author'. But his linguistic theory still makes him look for one meaning alone. It is a technique of 'désambiguïsation'.[83] In this way, whatever his view of Erasmus's theology, he confirmed Erasmian method.[84] A resonant example is Calvin's exposition of the classic Lutheran verse, Romans 1: 17. Fully conscious of the weight of exegetical prehistory attaching to the phrase *iustitia Dei*, Calvin refers obliquely to Luther's interpretation of *iustitia passiva*

---

[80]   For examples, ibid., 64.   [81]   *De la grammatologie*, p. 103.

[82]   *Opera Calvini*, xlix. 341. The Latin term *character* is used in the connotation of the Greek χαρακτήρ, 'an image on wax of a seal' (Liddell and Scott). This is an Erasmian trait.

[83]   Girardin, *Rhétorique et théologique*, p. 154 (also 'délimité et stable').

[84]   For instance, Erasmus's treatment of *loci theologici* in *Ratio verae theologiae*, LB, v. 130–1.

(glossed by Calvin *quae a Deo nobis donatur*) only to reverse Luther's theology of the *actus imperfectus*. Calvin rewrites *Sed Iustus per fidem vivet* according to his own theological grammar: 'The verb in the future tense designates that the life of which he is speaking is not only for the moment but for eternity.' To make the future all the more secure, he revised his gloss on two occasions, eventually endowing salvation with all too solid certainty.[85]

Like Melanchthon, who praised Romans because *iusto ordine rem exponit planeque methodice*, Calvin called its style 'methodical'.[86] *Methodus* emerged from the rhetorical dialectic of Agricola to become one of the key words of the sixteenth century. Melanchthon used it to appropriate the logic of Aristotle (whom he dubbed *qui unus ac solus est methodi artifex*) for protestant purposes.[87] His definition of μέθοδος in his logical textbook, *Erotematum dialectices*, shows how he applies the terms of logic to theological and scriptural explication: 'a science or art to make a path through impassable and overgrown places.'[88] Logic provides the *inventio* ('the way through') the hard places (*loci*) of scripture. The illumination of *loci* provided the leading method for the masters of biblical commentary acknowledged by Calvin in his 1540 Preface to Grynaeus.[89] Next in order after Melanchthon he praises Bullinger. Bullinger's commentary on Romans is not written chapter by chapter, but is instead divided into a series of arguments surrounding theological topics—*de peccato, de iustitia*, and so on.[90] Surpassing both, Calvin singles out Bucer. Bucer, as the principal theologian of Strasbourg, was a looming presence in Calvin's crucial years in that city, during which he composed new Latin and French editions of the *Institutes* as well as his first biblical commentary. Calvin's theology was influenced strongly by Bucer before he met him, and even more afterwards.[91] Bucer was at this date regarded as the prince of protestant biblical commentators. Calvin in the Romans Preface of 1540 praises his 'profound learning' and 'perspicacity'; in 1555 he went further, stating in

---

[85] *Commentarius*, p. 27: 1st edn. (1540) *futurum verbum designat eius vitae de qua loquitur, non fore momentaneam, sed perpetuo*; in 1551 he added *constaturam* and in the final edn. of his lifetime (1556) *solidam perpetuitatem*.

[86] Melanchthon, *Commentarii in Romanos* (1532), *Werke*, v. 33; Calvin, *Commentarius*, p. 1.

[87] *Oratio de vita Aristotelis*; *Opera*, xi. 349.

[88] *per loca invia et obsita sentibus, per rerum confusionem, viam invenit et aperit*; *Opera*, xiii. 573.

[89] Preface to *Commentarius in epistolam Pauli ad Romanos*, p. 2. Parker, *Calvin's New Testament Commentaries*, ch. 2, describes Calvin's methods and sources.

[90] *Commentarii*, pp. 9–54.

[91] On Calvin and Bucer, see Bouwsma, *Calvin*, pp. 21–4; on Bucer as a source for the *Institutes*, Wendel, *Calvin*, pp. 137–44.

the Preface to his commentary on the synoptic gospels that he has copied Bucer more than any one else.[92]

Peter Martyr's writings were also turned into *Loci communes* by his acolyte Massonius. Bucer's little treatise on practical exegetical method, the *Instructio*, explicitly espouses Agricolan principles and recommends its readers to learn *dialectica Rudolphi*. Nevertheless, his commentaries, while widely owned and consulted in England, proved too compendious to be culturally lasting. Luther notoriously called Bucer 'the chatterbox', and even Calvin allowed himself a few jokes at the expense of his master's prolixity.[93] Just as Calvinist theological method superseded Bucer's influence after Elizabeth's accession, so Ramus supplanted Agricola. Indeed Ramist theory proved precisely amenable to Calvinist theology. Its *unica methodus* seemed to unite all the arts, in a way that could cover all languages, vernacular and biblical. It could therefore authorize the single *sensus Scripturae* and place it within a comprehensive order of discourse. In addition, it granted autonomy to the linguistic system of the vernacular with its own independent *dialectique*.

III THE LOGIC OF CALVINISM

The pages that follow examine this legacy in the development of an English puritan tradition in the humanist arts and especially in the treatment of language. Lily's grammar, protected by law as the *Regia grammatica* and granted exclusive use in English schools, held dominion over grammatical studies in England throughout the sixteenth century and well beyond. New grammars of Latin avoided the royal prohibition only by couching their proceedings as translations or annotations of Lily into the vernacular, justifying their work as an aid to 'the weaker sort' of pupil.[94] Vernacular grammar of English in fact developed as a way round the injunction.

One exception that slipped through the royal monopoly was a translation into English of Ramus's *Grammatica Latina*. Ramus's work on

---

[92] Romans, *Opera Calvini*, x/1, 404; *Bucerum praesertim sanctae memoriae virum & eximium Ecclesiae Dei doctorem sum imitatus* (*Harmonia ex tribus Euangelistis composita*, A4ᵛ).

[93] *Commentarius*, p. 2; it was perhaps a fair comment in view of Bucer's 4,000 words on the first verse alone.

[94] Examples are John Stockwood's *Rules of Construction* (London, 1590); Thomas Granger, *Syntagma Grammaticum* (London, 1616); John Danes, *A Light to Lilie* (London, 1637); and indeed Milton's *Accedence Commenc't Grammar* (London, 1669).

grammar followed his *Dialectique* of 1555 (and its Latin version, the *Dialectica* of 1556) in a series of books published in 1559. These consisted of two textbooks, the *Grammatica* and *Rudimenta*, along with a much longer theoretical justification of his pedagogic approach in twenty books of lectures known as *Scholae grammaticae*. Ramus's dialectic, accompanied by the rhetoric of his junior collaborator Omer Talon (Talaeus), enjoyed a vogue in Elizabethan England which reached its height about the time that *The Latine Grammar of P. Ramus, translated into English* was published in separate editions in London and Cambridge in 1585. Presumably the perceived importance of Ramist studies allowed this relaxation of the law, but Ramism acquired no further currency in Latin grammar. Instead it was in the field of vernacular accidence that Ramist grammar gained ground.[95]

Ramus had himself produced a *Grammaire* of the French language in 1562.[96] His so-called 'single method' was applied to English in what was the second ever vernacular textbook, the *Grammatica Anglicana* of 1594 by Paul Greaves.[97] A strictly Ramist approach, more complex than Greaves, was also adopted by Ben Jonson in his *English Grammar*, written before 1623 but not published until the folio of 1640.[98] Other writers combined Ramist theory with traditional approaches taken from Lily, Linacre, or from the Latin framework that went back to Priscian. Alexander Hume, an Edinburgh schoolmaster, in what nearly became the standard Latin grammar in Scottish schools, named Linacre as his master but cited prominently among his sources Ramus, *cuius methodus in multas apud nos penetraverat*.[99] In 1617 he dedicated a much briefer and less systematic 'British' grammar to James I, once again eclectically mixing Ramus and Linacre.[100] Far more ambitious was the 1619 *Logonomia*

---

[95] Ong's statement on the significance of the vernacular in *Ramus*, p. 11, is in this respect quite mistaken.

[96] Published anonymously in Paris as *Gramere*; a second edition under his name (*Grammaire de P. de la Ramée*) followed in Paris, 1572. Padley, *Vernacular Grammar I*, pp. 28–44, analyses Ramus's vernacular theory in detail.

[97] An appendix to the grammar contained a lexicon of words used by Chaucer.

[98] Printed at the end of ii. 31–84 (paginated separately with Horace's *Art of Poetrie* and *Timber; or, Discoveries*). Jonson probably used Ramus's *Scholae grammaticae* as well as his *Grammatica*. Herford and Simpson note that Jonson owned copies of Lily's *De octo orationis partium constructione* and Linacre's *De emendata structura*, and Padley (*Vernacular Grammar I*, p. 58) comments that he must also have known Scaliger's *De causis linguae Latinae*.

[99] *Grammatica noua* (1612), Preface, dated 1608. This work, an expanded version of Hume's *Prima elementa grammaticae* (also Edinburgh, 1612), was accepted by the Scottish parliament as a replacement for the grammar of Johannes Despauterius, but then rejected by the bishops; see Padley, *Latin Tradition*, p. 112.

[100] *Orthographie and Congruitie of the Britan Tongue*, preserved only in a BL MS and not published until 1865.

Anglica of Alexander Gil, like Lily and Mulcaster before him High Master of St Paul's School (where his pupils included Milton). Padley describes this as 'the most comprehensive early grammar of English' (*Vernacular Grammar I*, p. 69). This work combined Cambridge Ramism with an interest in historical philology (Old English and modern vernaculars as well as Greek and Hebrew): many of his examples come from Spenser's *Faerie Queene*.

Just as Melanchthon's grammar, logic, and rhetoric became standard texts in German protestant schools partly on his authority as the twin pillar of Luther's Reformation, so Ramism acquired respectability in Britain because of its association with Calvinism. Conversely, Calvinism stopped Ramism from developing further in Germany. Ramist studies were banned in some universities and found root more easily in the form of a doctrine conflated with Melanchthonian Aristotelianism known as Philippo-Ramism.[101] In Britain, on the other hand, the smack of Calvinism was a positive advantage. Enthusiasm for Ramus emphasized his status as a protestant martyr (he was killed in Paris in 1572 in the St Bartholomew's Day Massacre) and the suitability of his doctrines for promulgating the true word of God. Ascham, the first Englishman to refer to Ramus, commented on the congeniality of his logical theories to true religion, and aligned him with the influence of Bucer.[102] Later, in *The Scholemaster*, however, Ascham worried that Ramus's logical 'singularitie' might lead to religious dissent or political faction.[103]

Cambridge was a centre for Ramist studies and a centre for radical puritanism: facts not unconnected. The first lectures on Ramist logic at Cambridge were given by Laurence Chaderton, a fellow of Christ's College, between 1571 and 1577.[104] Historians of logic have largely neglected Chaderton's role as a leading exponent of presbyterianism, arguing in the same decade for a presbyterian eldership to reform the public government of the church.[105] Christ's College was the leading home of puritanism in

[101] An excitable survey of German Ramism is given by Ong, pp. 298–300; and a more tempered analysis of its influence in grammar by Padley, *Vernacular Grammar I*, pp. 46–53.

[102] Ascham to Sturm, 29 January 1552 (*Works* (ed. Giles); i. 319). See Howell, *Logic and Rhetoric*, pp. 173–4.

[103] *English Works*, pp. 243–4.

[104] Although the lectures have not survived, they are mentioned by Abraham Fraunce as one of the sources for his *Sheapheardes Logike* (see below). On Chaderton's lectures, see Howell, pp. 179 and 206; and on Fraunce, p. 222.

[105] E.g. Howell, p. 206; Padley, p. 54. Church historians, on the other hand, have often missed his importance to logic. On Chaderton and puritan politics see Collinson, *Elizabethan Puritan Movement*, pp. 125–7, 235–7, and 401–2; and especially Lake, *Moderate Puritans*, ch. 3.

Cambridge until the foundation of Emmanuel in 1584 (of which Chaderton was first master). Edward Dering was a fellow there, as was later William Perkins. Christ's was also the mother of Cambridge Ramism. Gabriel Harvey was Sophister there when he first read Ramus, before lecturing on Ramist rhetoric in the 1570s and later controverting against Thomas Nashe on Ramus's behalf. The list of Ramist students and teachers at Christ's includes George Downham, William Ames, and ultimately Milton, who wrote an *Ars Logicae* on Ramist principles.[106]

This is no coincidence. Chaderton believed Ramist logic to be an essential tool both in public preaching and in religious controversy. In some notes on the qualifications needed in a minister of God, he listed (after knowledge of the biblical tongues) the arts of rhetoric and logic. Ramist theory is necessary for 'the true interpretation of the word and to confute contrary errors by unanswerable arguments and reasons'. Combined with the presbyterian practice of regular and intensive 'conferences' of ministers and other godly people, it will establish a consensus of interpretative understanding of scripture and doctrine.

English versions of Ramist method in all three elementary arts were frequently aimed at preachers. The first British edition of Ramus's *Dialectica* and its first translation into English were both undertaken by Roland MacIlmaine of St Andrew's University, also friendly to puritanism. MacIlmaine addressed his translation to a general educated public but stressed its utility to 'Pastors of the Churche' who will apply 'this our rule of veritie' (that is, Ramus's second law, the so-called *lex veritatis*) in order to dispute 'the trickes of poysonable sophistrie' of their Romanist opponents.[107] He sets out a guide to structure a sermon, both in dividing the text and in the 'invention' of the discourse. Dudley Fenner's *The Artes of Logike and Rethorike* (1584), which combined an unattributed translation of parts of Ramus's *Dialectica* with the first English reworking of Talaeus's *Rhetorica*, also aimed itself towards a puritan ministry.[108] Some years later, Thomas Granger followed his *Syntagma Grammaticum* with a *Syntagma Logicum*, advertising its summary of 'Ramus *Christianus*' as 'especially for the vse of Diuines in the practise of preaching' and using the sub-title *The*

---

[106] On the Ramist connection at Christ's, see Howell, *Logic and Rhetoric*, ch. 4 generally; on Harvey, pp. 178–9 and 196–9. Harvey moved to Pembroke in 1570. See Jardine, 'Dialectic teaching'.

[107] *Logike*, p. 11. The *Dialecticae libri duo* edited by MacIlmaine were also published under his name by the Huguenot Vautrollier in 1574. A 2nd edn. of the English version appeared in 1581.

[108] This was the first combined Ramist logic and rhetoric. Fenner was expelled from Peterhouse because of his puritan tendencies. See Howell, p. 220.

Diuine Logike.[109] Although less rigidly Ramist in construction, the most famous of all Elizabethan treatises on preaching, William Perkins's *The Arte of Prophecying*, can also be seen as an application of Ramist logical procedures to the method of the sermon.[110]

Ramist logic was seen as instrumental in serving two fundamental purposes of puritanism: propagating the gospel through preaching and confounding Roman doctrine through religious controversy. Ramist method promised, on the one hand, a transparent system of discourse and, on the other, an infallible method of refutation. At the same time its discursive basis (Ramism is above all a theory of the text) meant that both purposes could be achieved through apparently rigorous attention to the signification of holy scripture. Above all, it could be used with equal facility in relation to Latin (the primary mode of controversy and of education) and the vernacular, the polemical medium of the protestant Bible as well as the practical language for the conversion of all classes. The puritan networks of logical theory, religious controversy, and political faction thus easily interrelated. William Temple defended Ramus's *vnica methodus* in Cambridge against Everard Digby and then dedicated an edition of the *Dialecticae libri duo* to Sir Philip Sidney in an attempt to ally himself not only to humanist learning but also to the political patronage of Leicester's party.[111] Sidney was a prime mover in the dissemination of Ramism. He was the dedicatee of another Ramist work, Abraham Fraunce's *The Sheapheardes Logike* (with examples taken from Spenser's *The Shepheardes Calendar*).[112] In his Ramist guide to legal logic, *The Lawiers Logike*, Fraunce claims Sidney as a fellow admirer of Ramus and his own inspiration. In addition, Sidney was an enthusiastic supporter of protestant interventionism in foreign policy. Temple accompanied Sidney as his secretary on his fatal expedition to the Netherlands in the war against Spain. Later, in Dublin, Temple established a chair in religious controversy while promoting a colonial version of Irish Ramism.[113] Meanwhile, in Cambridge in

---

[109] See Howell, pp. 229–32.

[110] First published in Latin, *Prophetica* (1592); posthumously translated into English and printed in 1606. Perkins's Ramism is discussed by Howell, *Logic and Rhetoric*, pp. 206–7 and by Miller, *New England Mind*, pp. 338–9.

[111] On Temple's argument with Digby, see Howell, *Logic and Rhetoric*, pp. 194–6; *contra* Howell, however, Francis Mildapet is Temple's pseudonym. On the dedication to Sidney, see Howell, pp. 204–5, where Sidney's reply is quoted. Temple also wrote a Ramist commentary on Sidney's *Defence of Poesie*: see below.

[112] Never published but preserved in MS at the BL. The importance of Sidney as a patron of Ramism and his connections with Hubert Languet (a friend of Ramus) and the Frankfurt printers' firm of Wéchel, which published 172 editions of Ramus's works, are discussed by Ong, p. 302.

[113] On Temple as provost of Trinity College, Dublin, see Morgan, *Godly Learning*, p. 257.

1587, the new master of St John's, William Whitaker, a prominent puritan controversialist, started proceedings against Digby the anti-Ramist as an alleged Roman sympathizer.[114]

Even handbooks of logic purporting to be translations of Ramus's theory moved in a theological direction. In place of Ramus's illustrations of logical invention through quotations from Virgil, Horace, Cicero, or Ovid, MacIlmaine substituted texts taken from the Bible, particularly from Matthew and Genesis. The effect was not so much pietistic as doctrinal: for instance, in discussing arguments transferred 'from the speciall to the generall', he cited '*Abraham was iustified by faythe, therfore man maye be iustified by faythe*' (*Logike of Ramus*, p. 59), thus radically compressing the reading of Genesis 15: 6 in Romans 4. This principle was carried farther by Fenner, whose title page openly boasted the relevance of 'Methode' for 'the resolution or opening of certayne parts of Scripture'. Fenner liberally interspersed both *Logike* and *Rethorike* with selections from the Calvinized Geneva Bible, and concluded the volume with a 'resolution' of the Lord's Prayer.

In the First Book of the *Logike*, the treatment of causes becomes a typology of different kinds of divine cause in the Bible. In the Second Book, the analysis of syllogisms returns again and again to examples taken from Romans on the theology of justification.[115] In the sixth chapter, the last and most complex form of syllogism is justified as follows:

> As thus
> *Faithfull men must eyther be saued or condemned*:
> *But they shalbe saued*:
> *Therefore not condemned* (C4^r).

Ramist syllogistic results in a piece of pure Calvinism. Luther asserted all men are sinners, including the righteous, so that his theology resolved itself only in the paradoxical formula *simul iustus et peccator*. Calvinist logic dictated that it is a necessary truth about a person that *either* he is saved *or* he is condemned. A man must be one or the other, and if one then not the other.

It has been argued that Fenner's 'logic was in no way affected' by his use of scriptural texts, but this is to misunderstand the dynamics of his text.[116]

---

[114] For an account of this dispute see Lake, *Moderate Puritans*, pp. 171–80. St John's before Whitaker's time as master was on the conservative side in logical studies; Nashe, for instance, was a student there.

[115] *Artes of Logike and Rethorike*, C3^r. An almost identical example is given as a 'disiunctiue Sillogisme' on C4^r.

[116] Morgan, *Godly Learning*, p. 109.

In the treatment of justification in the chapters on syllogism, the doctrinally incontrovertible examples appear to buttress the authority of his logical method as much as the categorical procedures of inference appear to make absolute his theological propositions. The true Christian already knows implicitly that '*No man is iustified by his workes*' but is gratified to find that his techniques of logic must be in good order because they (naturally) concur with divine truth. The *Artes of Logike* therefore emerges as an art of theological dialectic.

Theology and logical theory coexist and even coalesce in Fenner, in such a way that it is hard to see whether his logic explains divine providence or the other way round. The predetermination of method confirms proleptically the doctrine of predetermination. Ramus himself wrote a *Commentarius de religione christiana*, published posthumously and dedicated to Sidney by its printer. Fenner's *Sacra theologia* came out the year after his *Artes*. Yet it would be a mistake to see Ramism as an explanation for the shape of English Calvinist theology, or Calvinism as an explanation of the forms of English Ramism. Rather the two make a marriage, perhaps a marriage made in heaven (hell in the minds of opponents). Ramism attracted English theologians because it provided a theoretical groundwork for explaining the linguistic and logical assumptions of their true *doctor*, Calvin himself.

Elizabethan methodical theology reached its apogee in Perkins. A pupil of Chaderton and a protégé of Whitaker, his astonishing popularity as preacher and writer in the 1590s eclipsed both mentors and acquired for him an international reputation as a Calvinist divine. Younger than Chaderton, his political ideology was not presbyterian and his logic not purely Ramist. He made voluminously eclectic lists of his sources and nowhere mentions Ramus. But a marginal note written by hand into a Cambridge University Library copy of his *Workes* attaches him to Bernard Keckermann and Johann Alsted, two German authors of Ramist systematic theologies, showing where contemporaries thought Perkins's intellectual affiliations lay.[117] The dichotomous principle of Ramus's method, whereby every proposition is divided into two more, is found everywhere in Perkins's systematic works. In reverse form this affects his theology: every dichotomous logic leads back eventually to a single origin, and this origin for a theologian must be God. Ramus's 'three rules' of 'du tout', 'par soy', and 'vniuersel premierement' determine Perkins's view of God.[118]

[117] MS note in *Workes*, ii. 762 (CUL copy Syn 2.61.5).
[118] Known among Latin writers following Ramus, rather clumsily and pretentiously, as the *lex veritatis, lex iustitiae*, and *lex sapientiae*.

God is the premiss of all Perkins's arguments, responsible for every concatenation in the world or in language.

Prophetica, Perkins's treatise on preaching, included discussion of interpretation, of logic and rhetoric, and matters of style and doctrine, all
organized dichotomously with frequent employment of syllogisms. Interpretation, he says, is 'the *Opening* of the wordes and sentences of the
Scripture, that one entire and naturall sense may appeare'.[119] Perkins
conflates the Calvinist *genuinus sensus* with a conventional attack on the
medieval *quadriga*, 'There is onely one sense, and the same is the literall'
(ii. 737).[120] In alliance to this hermeneutic Perkins recommends a logical
order of theological 'common-places' (in other words, *loci*): 'Haue in
readinesse common-place heads of euery point of diuinitie' (ii. 736).

In spite of his theory of the *sensus simplex*, Perkins finds many parts of
scripture which are 'difficult and darke'. Here it turns out (against his own
methodology) that the natural signification 'disagrees' with the 'Analogie
of faith' (ii. 740). This problem he tries to 'resolue' through rhetoric. Like
Fenner and Whitaker, he describes 'This is my body, which is broken for
you' as a 'Metonymie'; other difficulties are 'opened' by terms such as
'Synecdoche' or 'Anthropo-pathie'.[121] But there remain places where
'Grammatical and Rhetoricall proprieties of words signifie diuersly with
those words' (ii. 744). Perkins finds himself embroiled in the contingent
speech acts of the Bible taking him ever further into 'diuersitie' and away
from the 'one entire and naturall sense'. Even common uses of the verb
involve diverse interpretation:

An Interrogation signifieth, 1. an earnest affirmation, or asseueration . . . Secondly, it signifieth a denial . . . 3. It signifieth a forbidding . . . 4. It argueth sundrie
affections, as admiration, compassion, complaining, and finding of fault.   (ii. 746)

How else but by such complex critical readings of signification are we to
understand Christ's anguished interrogative on the cross, 'My God, My
God, why hast thou forsaken me?' Minutiae of tense, aspect, and mood pre-
occupy Perkins's analysis.[122]

These problems, scrupulously recorded in the *Prophetica*, prey on
Perkins's theology in his systematic works of dogma. *Armilla Aurea* came

---

[119] *Workes*, ii. 737. All quotations from Perkins (unless otherwise noted) from the
Cambridge edition of 1608–9 (3 vols.).
[120] Cummings, 'Literally Speaking', pp. 208–17.
[121] *Workes*, ii. 741; see Fenner, *Artes*, D2ʳ; and Whitaker, *Ad rationes decem*, p. 45. 'Analogie'
was a key puritan term (e.g. in Whitaker).
[122] E.g. ii. 746 (on concessives), 747 (on 'compleat' and 'vncompleat' time), 752 ('continually' = *indefinenter*).

out two years before *Prophetica*, and was translated in 1591 as *A Golden Chaine; or, The Description of Theologie, containing the order of the causes of Saluation and Damnation*. A work of no little ambition, it posits a comprehensive theory of divine cause and effect. Perkins's method characteristically dividuates the totality of theological discourse back to a single point of origin, God. This originary point (by definition) cannot be further divided, or logically derived from any other point, leading Perkins to define God as lying outside the otherwise all-embracing system of logic and language: 'The Simplenesse, of his nature, is that by which he is void of all Logicall relation in arguments. He hath not in him subiect or adiunct' (i. 11). God is defined as without relation, without syntax even. If Perkins had taken this proposition literally, his *Armilla Aurea* would have been short. Yet the rest of Perkins's treatise attempts contradictorily to apply a relational syntax between God and every contingency in every conceivable ramification within the world and its history. For 'the Lord, according to his good pleasure, hath most certainely decreed euery thing and action, whether past, present, or to come, together with their circumstances of place, time, meanes, and end' (i. 15).

Perkins appears to be on the point of hermetically sealing God off in a world outside language, before instead engaging him inextricably in its every jot and tittle. The resulting strain on Perkins's linguistic theology is intense. God becomes coterminous with the interminable plenitude of language. Everything that has been, or will be, or even could have been or might be, must be from God. One immediate inference is that 'Yea, he hath most iustly decreed the wicked workes of the wicked. For if he had nilled them, they should neuer haue bene at all' (i. 15). This is part and parcel of a doctrine inferred by Calvin and elaborated by Beza that God wills the reprobation of the wicked as certainly as he does the election of the blessed. Yet the final consequences of Perkins's logic are more extraordinary, for he collapses entirely the distinction that might be held to exist between what is contingently possible and what God wills, something Calvin at least is careful not to do. The effect is that the epistemic is merged completely into the deontic:

For that, which beeing hereafter to be, is foreknowne of God, that assuredly will come to passe, and shall be, and that either by the will of God, or without his will: if with his will, then no doubt, he both decreed and preordained the same: if without or against his will, how is GOD then omnipotent?   (i. 98)

All modal meanings are constrained in Perkins's linguistic system by this overpowering deontic 'shall' of God. Every epistemic prediction of what 'will come' is expressible only as a deontic 'shall be' attributed to the direct agency of 'the will of God', so that what will be shall be his will. This results both in some neat arguments and in ultimate linguistic chaos. Perkins adroitly counters his opponents by suggesting that if the divine order of salvation is based on foreknowledge of sin, then God must constantly be changing his mind, as he surveys every nuance of human motivation. The result is one of two impossibilities, one that 'he might have taken better aduise', the second that 'he seeth that he could not bring his former purpose about as he would' (i. 98–9). But Perkins's alternative is one in which (in a macabre game of consequences) God foreordains every last vicissitude of human psychology in order to confirm retrospectively his own predestination. It could be called God getting his retaliation in first, and it results in many similar Irish bulls of theological grammar. Nowhere is the logic more convoluted than in the discussion of the reprobate who falls away through 'vneffectual calling'. Perkins tries to blame this on the reprobate—for the reprobate is always to blame even though condemned by God's own decree—as if the calling is 'vneffectual' because of a failure properly to listen. But this would imply conversely that the elect are saved because they are not so hard of hearing, which Perkins cannot allow because it makes election dependent on a merit of human will. His own explanation appears to conjure up a God who decides to damn some whom he calls only half-heartedly, as if *pour encourager les autres*; except that it can neither encourage or discourage the others since they are already either elect or damned in any event. God calls them now knowing that in the future they will not after all have heard, thus proving that they were never going to be called in the first place. Effectively, God calls their bluff.

The idea of the 'temporarie professour' of the gospel troubles Perkins's whole enterprise. It creates for him an irremediable loop of temporal and modal logic, in which the 'simplenesse' of God's linguistic integrity is exposed to the arbitrary processes of human mood. God's true purposes are revealed only through the minutest examination of human motivation. As a result, Perkins's theological *corpus* abandoned logical *summa* in favour of psychological encyclopaedia in the form of his *Cases of Conscience*, for God ordains even the smallest scruple and grace depends on the tiniest inflections of mind and soul. After *Armilla Aurea*, Perkins turned his attention to works such as *A Treatise tending vnto a declaration, whether a man be in the estate of damnation or in the estate of grace: and if he be in the first, how he may in time come out of it: if in the second, how he may discerne it, and perseuere in the same to the end*.[123] This title is itself an Irish bull: for how can someone 'come out of' what is already past?

Except that Perkins, too, realizes he cannot: 'the Reprobate may haue a loue of God: but this loue can be no sincere loue' (i. 358). If it were sincere, he would turn out not to be reprobate at all, but one of the elect who had not yet shown his true colours. Similarly, when a seemingly sincere love turns out to be insincere it was never sincere in the first place. Perkins thus commits himself to an endlessly circular logic: 'We say that the Elect alone may be, and indeede are made sure of their election: that so we may exclude the reprobate hypocrites: for considering they are not elected, they can neuer be truly perswaded that they are elected'.[124] The circle is fully compassed in the 'practicall syllogisme' defined in *How to liue, and that well* as follows:

> He that beleeues the Gospell, shall haue all the benefits and blessings of God promised therein.
> But I beleeue the Gospell, and I beleeue in Christ;
> Therefore the benefits promised therein are mine.

(i. 475)

Here Perkins's Ramism and Calvinism unite as sheer discourse replaces dialectic and becomes doctrine. Self-assertion assumes the status of logical proof, called by Perkins 'experimentall certentie'.[125]

In this purely rhetorical theology, axiom blurs into exhortation: 'For we must haue a faith, whereby we must be assured that our callings are good, and lawfull in themselues' (i. 478). Perkins over and over again tries to treat epistemic and deontic meanings as tautological, so that we must do what we must: 'Againe, faith is required, whereby euery man must beleeue, that the calling in which he is, is the particular calling in which God will be serued of him' (i. 478).[126] Yet if the epistemic certainty of these sentences is truly axiomatic, it begs the question of whether deontic obligation is really necessary. Hence the peculiar modality of Perkins's urging us 'to make examination whether we be in conscience conuicted of the certaintie of the word or no. If we be not, we must labour to be conuinced' (i. 480). For according to 'experimentall certentie' such a statement is either self-fulfilling or redundant. Perkins labours to convince his readers and so

---

[123] See Breward, *Perkins*, p. 355 on the progeny of this work. Dated 1595 in the *Workes*.

[124] *A Case of Conscience, the greatest that euer was: how a man may know whether he be the childe of God, or no*, *Workes*, i. 429.

[125] On the 'practical syllogism', see Kendall, *English Calvinism*, pp. 69–74.

[126] Further examples in *How to live, and that well*: i. 480, 482, 483, 484; in *A Reformed Catholike*, i. 558; in *A Graine of Musterd-Seede*, i. 632, 634.

exposes his own conviction to disbelief. For what he assures us is 'the certaintie of the word' is only the uncertainty of words, a 'we must' which
needs to be self-authorizing but which might as easily be other things: an
expression of opinion slightly contrary to the facts; a wish on our part
unlikely to be fulfilled; a statement of moral obligation in half-rebuke of
our lack of responsibility; or an order uttered with semi-expletive contempt, acknowledging its own failure.

Marlowe's Doctor Faustus had studied Ramism, too. Marlowe was a
student in Cambridge at the time of Ramus's first popularity, and included
the scene of his assassination in *The Massacre at Paris*. Ramus is allowed
to die nobly, defending himself and his method against the murderous
sarcasms of the Duke of Anjou (the future Henri III) and the Duke of
Guise, who cites

> this quidditie,
> *Argumentum testimonii est inartificiale.*
> To contradict which, I say *Ramus* shall dye[127]
> (ll. 399–401)

before stabbing the logician in cold blood. It is the classic university
student's sick joke, turning the professor's doctrine into a reason for killing
him. In *The tragicall History of Doctor Faustus*, Marlowe's hero shows a
similarly keen eye for theological semantics:

> When all is done, Diuinitie is best.
> *Ieromes* Bible, *Faustus*, view it well.
> *Stipendium peccati mors est*: Ha, *Stipendium, &c.*
> The reward of sinne is death: that's hard.
> *Si pecasse negamus, fallimur, & nulla est in nobis veritas.*
> If we say that we haue no sinne,
> We deceiue our selues, and theres no truth in vs.
> Why then belike
> We must sinne, and so consequently die.
> I, we must die an euerlasting death:
> What doctrine call you this, *Che serà, serà,*
> What wil be, shall be? Diuinitie, adieu.
>
> (ll. 65–76)

Like Dudley Fenner in *The Artes of Logike*, Faustus puts two biblical citations together and formulates them as a syllogism, leading to an incontrovertible conclusion, 'we must die an euerlasting death'. He may be rejecting

---

[127] All citations are from *Works*.

Calvinism but he has mastered its logic as well as its theology: his syllogism is the logical obverse of Perkins's 'practical syllogism', and could be called the epitome of 'experimentall' uncertainty, or the impractical syllogism. He ends with a polyglot doctrinal pun, '*Che serà, serà*, What wil be, shall be', where the English shows more felicity than the Italian original. For in the shift from 'wil' to 'shall', Faustus effects the transference from epistemic to deontic, and thus renders future contingency as divine predestination. Whereas the Italian cliché is merely resigned to the future, Faustus's English paronomasia encapsulates a terrifying theology of determinism. It is a good example of how sensitivity to linguistic detail encompasses a fierce and deadly struggle over doctrine. The Englishing of theology left its traces on English as well as on theology.

IV ORIGINAL DEFECTION: SIDNEY'S *DEFENCE OF POESIE*

Elizabethan England is known as the age of religious settlement. In literature it is credited as an age of renewal and invention. What does religious settlement have to do with literary invention, or literary invention with religious settlement? Modern literary history sometimes ignores such questions, forgetting that Elizabethan politics involved an argument about the status of writing conducted along theological lines. Protestant culture—encompassing both Whitgift and Perkins—was in the ascendant, and accorded to literary culture an enormous power of persuasion. The Elizabethan period saw a burgeoning analysis of the conditions of writing, the properties of fiction, and the theory of interpretation.

Although this has been studied usually as a corollary of strictly literary practice, its writers were inclined to justify themselves in religious and political terms. William Temple, Sidney's secretary, writing a Ramist commentary on the *Defence of Poesie* within a few years of its composition, observed that the *tota controversia* of that work lies in its theory of imitation.[128] The theological resonance of Temple's word *controversia* is not misplaced. Sidney's *Defence*, although formally derived from the Aristotelianism of Minturno and Scaliger, makes its claims in a protestant humanist framework.[129] In the same years, Sidney with his sister Mary, Countess of Pembroke, reformed the art of divine poetry in their version

---

[128] *Haec est illa definitio . . . quae totam controversiam continet*; from 'Analysis tractationis de Poesi contextae a nobilissimo viro Philippe Sidneio equite aurato', *Temple's Analysis*, p. 80.

[129] On Sidney's protestantism, see Worden, *The Sound of Virtue*, pp. 34–7.

of the Psalms.[130] Wyatt's clandestine forms are replaced by a literature of spectacular confidence and transparency. The following pages examine how Sidney makes perhaps the ultimate claims for a protestant aesthetic of writing. However, the claims cause him difficulty: indeed the sense of poetic creation as analagous to divine creativity, and the attempt to fix the didactic purpose of poetry to an account of original sin, prove more problematic than any other part of the *Defence*. Although within the scope of the courteous and witty temper of his apologetic he somehow carries it off, Sidney does not resolve his theology.[131]

Sidney attempts to graft onto a conventional account of aesthetic persuasion an identification of the poetic ideal with an 'erected wit' from before the Fall. This is in answer to what Spingarn has called the central problem of Renaissance literary criticism, the ethical justification of poetry: 'Action being the test of all studies, poetry must stand or fall in proportion as it conduces to righteous action'.[132] According to Sidney, the creations of poetry, since they are not subject to nature, are not subject to the consequences of the Fall. As well as new beings, they are also new creatures in the moral sense. Such is the confidence of Sidney's aesthetic scheme that he claims a moral independence in works of art, making them morally efficacious. The poet, by creating one Cyrus through fiction, creates many more by example. Although Sidney is unclear as to means, he is assertive of the end: fictions act as persuasions to virtue.

Sidney's argument is largely limited to the natural sphere. None the less his claim to make new Cyruses endows poetic creativity with a power that is 'erected' above the natural so that it can transform the 'infected wil'. On this basis, Sidney's *Defence* has been seen as a 'poetics of protestantism'.[133] Yet no sooner does Sidney initiate this theory than he is forced onto the defensive. At one point he consciously has to ward off blasphemy, as he justifies his sources concerning the poet's 'divinity'. Sidney here draws on a tradition making the poet's capacity equivalent to the power of divine ordinance. His argument adapts Scaliger's *Poetices* of 1561, that 'the poet produces another nature altogether', and 'in this process makes himself

---

[130] Philip translated Pss.1–43; Mary completed the version in the 1590s after his death. See Prescott, 'King David as a "Right Poet" '; Hannay, *Philip's Phoenix*.

[131] *Prose Works*, iii. 9. Further refs in text. On the problems of the *Defence*, see Ferguson, *Trials of Desire*, pp. 138–62; and Sinfield, *Faultlines*, pp. 197–205.

[132] Spingarn, *Literary Criticism*, p. 12.

[133] Weiner, *Poetics of Protestantism*; see also Shepherd (ed.), *Apology*, p. 27; and Hamilton, *Sidney*, p. 114. Waller, ' "This matching of contraries" ', 23–4, presents a more modulated view.

almost into another god'.[134] Calvinism cannot contain Scaliger's Italian urbanity so easily. To avoid the controversial suggestion that the poet has divine powers, Sidney omits the phrase 'another god'.

Sidney's zealous care in his use of the word 'divine' paradoxically has the effect of concealing the theological force of his subsequent argument concerning the moral freedom of poetry. Attention to the question of divinity has obscured this more vital question in Sidney's work. For the feature which led others to call poetry 'divine' is its ability to create 'an other nature', and about this Sidney has no doubts and is even explicitly radical. A comparison with George Puttenham's *The Arte of English Poesie*, which also bears the stamp of puritan humanism, shows how radical Sidney is being:

> It is therefore of Poets thus to be conceiued, that if they be able to deuise and make all these things of them selues, without any subiect of veritie, that they be (by maner of speech) as creating gods.[135]

'All these things' that Puttenham says poets make, are the 'Princely persons' of Homeric Greece. Sidney's 'new formes' are similarly '*Heroes, Demigods*' (p. 8), and so on. Puttenham's poets 'make all these things of them selues' and 'without any subiect of veritie', in other words, without copying them from a model in nature. Sidney's poet, too, is 'lifted up with the vigor of his own invention', and, unlike the *Historian* and even the *Metaphysicke*, is not 'tied' to the 'subjection' of 'what nature will have set forth'.

Sidney omits from this argument the conclusion that the poet, being a creator *ex nihilo*, is like a God. Yet Puttenham himself only says it 'by maner of speech'; and he goes on to reduce the force of his idea by adding qualifications:

> If they do it by instinct diuine or naturall, then surely much favoured from aboue. If by their experience, then no doubt very wise men. If by any president or paterne layd before them, then truly the most excellent imitators & counterfaitors of all others.   (p. 4)

Puttenham, in his artless way, is prepared to use the idea of 'creating gods' (but only 'by maner of speech'), if it helps his argument that poetry is a respectable art. Yet he has no confidence that poets do in fact 'make all these things of them selues, without any subject of veritie'. One of the ways

---

[134]   *Poetices*, i/1, p. 3 (at poeta & naturam alteram . . . ac demum sese isthoc ipso perinde ac Deum alterum efficit).
[135]   *Arte of English Poesie*, p. 4.

he envisages that they 'make . . . these things' is 'by . . . experience', or in other words, from nature, and another 'by . . . president or paterne', or in other words, by using someone else's invention.

Although Sidney does not use the term 'creating gods', and although superficially this makes him 'more discreet', in fact his claims are less modest. Puttenham makes a claim that is ultimately shallow, because he does not take the creativity of the poet seriously; for Puttenham the poet is like a conjuror or a counterfeiter. On the other hand, Sidney assigns a fully creative power to the poet, only to omit the word 'divine' (at least in this context) in order to make his argument less obtrusively controversial.

The crux of Sidney's argument concerns the grounds of the poet's creativity, and not his alleged 'divinity'. On this question his reasoning is complex, and depends upon an ambiguous conflation of Platonic and Christian ideas. But his conclusion is so bold that it is worth considering the full course of his thinking. He pursues his argument with such a slack rein, and passes from one point to another so fluidly, that it is necessary to quote at length to follow the idea through:

> Neither let it be deemed too sawcy a comparison, to ballance the highest point of mans wit with the efficacie of nature: but rather give right honor to the heavenly maker of that maker, who having made man to his owne likenes, set him beyond and over all the workes of that second nature, which in nothing he sheweth so much as in Poetry; when with the force of a divine breath, he bringeth things foorth surpassing her doings.   (pp. 8–9)

The first problem is the meaning of 'nature', which alters as Sidney proceeds, making it difficult to understand what he means by the 'other nature' produced by the poet. Poetry ('the highest point of mans wit') is envisaged at first as being on a level with 'nature', but subsequently as above it. In one sense it has the same 'efficacie' to create, but in the other, it 'bringeth things foorth surpassing her doings'.

Up to this point, Sidney's argument is not a simple one. But as a last sweeping gesture, as if casually, he slips in the doctrine of the Fall:

> with no small arguments to the incredulous of that first accursed fall of *Adam*, since our erected wit maketh us know what perfection is, and yet our infected wil keepeth us from reaching unto it. But these arguments will by few be understood, and by fewer graunted: thus much I hope wil be given me, that the Grekes with some probability of reason, gave him the name above all names of learning.   (p. 9)

Before we know it, Sidney passes on to other matters. But he leaves us with the theological puzzle of what we are to understand by the 'erected wit' and its relation to the 'infected wil'.

This argument is an entirely new, and contentious, concern. English protestant culture was formulated around very different terms. Whatever their differences in other respects, Cranmer and Bradford, Whitgift and Cartwright were agreed in their radical position on free will. Tyndale expressed the orthodox English position early:

Because y^t the will of man foloweth the witte & is subiecte vnto the witte and as the witte erreth so doth the will /and as the witte is in captivitie /so is the will /nether is it possible that ye will shuld be fre where the witte is in bondage.[136]

Sidney reverses the argument used by Tyndale; for Tyndale the will is 'infected' exactly because the 'witte' (or rational understanding) is itself in 'bondage'. The first result of original sin is the bondage of the wit.

None the less, several attempts have been made to identify Sidney's idea of an uncorrupted natural intelligence as the position of an orthodox Calvinist. A citation from the *Institutio* is used to prove the point:

Quum ergo ratio qua discernit homo inter bonum et malum, qua intelligit et iudicat, naturale donum sit, non potuit in totum deleri   (2, 2, 12, *Opera selecta*)

[Since reason, therefore, by which man distinguishes between good and evil, and by which he understands and judges, is a natural gift, it could not be completely wiped out   (Battles, p. 270)]

The arts and sciences have been given to man by God in order to make him conscious of the existence of the gift of grace. It is this consciousness which distinguishes man from the beasts. Through the arts, man is deprived of all excuses, since he cannot claim ignorance of God. In this sense, the arts are a considerable gift, and deserve man's gratitude:

discamus quot naturae humanae bona Dominus reliquerit, postquam vero bono spoliata est.   (2, 2, 15)

[Let us learn . . . how many gifts the Lord left to human nature even after it was despoiled of its true good   (Battles, p. 275)]

It has been concluded that Calvin's description of the rational faculty corresponds to Sidney's. But there is a difference between saying 'not entirely corrupted' and 'not at all corrupted'. Calvin makes this point in his next paragraph:

Verissime enim Augustinus . . . ut gratuita homini dona post lapsum detracta esse, ita naturalia haec quae restabant, corrupta fuisse docet   (2, 2, 16)

---

[136] *Obedience*, 34^v.

[For with the greatest truth Augustine teaches that as the free gifts were withdrawn from man after the Fall, so the natural ones remaining were corrupted . . . (p. 275)]

Calvin limits very precisely the claims which the 'erected wit' may make. It is not 'completely wiped out', but it survives only in a condition which is *debilitata* and *vitiata* (2, 2, 12).

Calvin carefully distinguishes the perfection of the object known from the perfection of the means of perceiving it:

non quod per se inquinari possint, quatenus a Deo proficiscuntur: sed quia polluto homini pura esse desierunt, nequam inde laudam consequatur. (2, 2, 16)

[Not that the gifts could become defiled by themslves, seeing that they came from God. But to defiled men these gifts were no longer pure, and from them he could derive no praise at all. (p. 275)]

The arts and sciences in themselves are perfect, but the understanding which apprehends them is not. In this sense human knowledge, too, is imperfect. Sidney, by contrast, sees reason as uncorrupted. He certainly does not derive this idea from Calvin, although he might have inferred it incorrectly from the *Institutes*.

In Calvin's account, art cannot be 'pure' in a world that is fallen. Sidney indeed seems to realize that he may have overstepped the mark in making so extravagant a claim:

with no small arguments to the incredulous of that first accursed fall of *Adam*, since our erected wit maketh us know what perfection is, and yet our infected wil keepeth us from reaching unto it.

The 'first accursed fall of Adam' is used more as an analogy than as an explication of his ideas, and this makes it difficult to evaluate the precise nature of the effect of the 'wil' on the creations of the 'wit'. The most important question to be asked about Sidney's argument concerns the force of 'and yet'. However, the logical syntax is slippery here, and fails to make the exact connections that it claims: 'with . . . since . . . and yet . . . But . . . '. The result is that the two parts of the sentence—the 'no small arguments'—pass each other by.

The full sentence ('Neither let it be deemed . . .') has so many subordinate clauses that the final disjunctive locution 'and yet' loses its grammatical function of qualification, and serves as an afterthought. The literal sense of Sidney's argument is that the perversity of the flesh undoes the effect of (since it 'keepeth us from reaching unto') the 'erected' knowledge retained by the intelligence. Perfection, after all, is impossible, since the 'infected wil' makes it unrealizable in nature. Sidney in this way provides the counter-argument to his own theory even as he evolves it. At this point Sidney seems to abandon theology for more favourable territory. In one uncomfortable sentence, Sidney takes extraordinary theological risks, before taking similar pains to cover over his traces. It is a sign of the pressures puritanism places on literary culture.

V LITERATURE ANTI-LITERATURE

Fulke Greville, Sidney's schoolfriend and biographer, left remarks about the *Arcadia* which pay attention to its moral and religious purposes but in a language far removed from the *Defence*. His career allowed no absoluteness of choice: he ran into opportunity and suffered from occasion through fifty vitiating years in court life during the reigns of three monarchs.[137] This recalcitrant server of the interests of monarchs ended up murdered by his own servant in a mundane quarrel over his will. He wrote no comparable treatise on poetry, but what can be gleaned from his *œuvre* as a whole emerges as a very different statement.[138] It is precisely on the power of the poet's images to move the will that Greville demurs. Greville attends to the same theology informing Sidney's discussion, and his arguments provide an insight into the protestant aesthetic at the turn of the century. By the end of the Tudor period, protestant culture appears to occupy two contradictory positions in relation to the literary act: it is literature's most enthusiastic friend and its most articulate enemy.

At various points in his *Life of Sidney*, Greville makes an oblique commentary on the critical vocabulary of Sidney's work. Greville writes a brief autobiography of his poetic career, the tone of which is at variance with Sidney's extravagant conceits:

For my own part, I found my creeping Genius more fixed upon the Images of Life, than the Images of Wit, and therefore chose not to write to them on whose foot the black Oxe had not already trod, as the Proverbe is, but to those only, that are weather-beaten in the Sea of this World, as having lost sight of their Gardens, and groves, study to saile on a right course among Rocks and quick-sands.[139]

---

[137] Greville's moribund career under Elizabeth, which was ruined by his association with the Earl of Essex, was revived under James I. He became Chancellor of the Exchequer in October 1614, was created Baron Brooke in 1621, and was a prime councillor of Charles I after James's death in 1625. For all details of his life, see Rebholz, *Greville*.

[138] Maclean, 'Greville's "Poetic" ', p. 170.

[139] *Life of Sidney*, p. 224. Further refs in text. The original title of the work is a 'Dedication to Sir Philip Sidney'. The date of this, as of all Greville's works, is debatable, but is usually given as 1610–12.

In his laconic account of the aims of his poetry, Greville sets himself against the phrasing of the *Defence of Poesie*. His 'creeping Genius' contrasts ironically with the 'high flying libertie of conceit' (iii. 6), claimed by Sidney as proper to the poet. The 'Images of Wit', expressly preferred by Sidney to the 'Images of Life', are resisted by Greville. His weather-beaten readers are deprived of the poetic world described with rapture in the *Defence*:

Nature never set foorth the earth in so rich Tapistry as diverse Poets have done, neither with so pleasaunt rivers, fruitfull trees, sweete smelling flowers, nor whatsoever els may make the too much loved earth more lovely: her world is brasen, the Poets only deliver a golden (iii. 8).

Greville's friendship with Sidney is so well known, it can go unnoticed that this passage in the *Dedication* is diametrically opposed to the *Defence*.[140] Greville doubts Sidney's very principles of writing, though there is a guarded politeness about the work as a whole. He grumbles about the *Arcadia*, without perhaps being sure of his reasons: 'Greville's feelings about his old friend seem impenetrable even to himself'.[141] He casts his reservations about *Arcadia* ('not onely the imperfection, but vanitie of those shadowes') in the form of Sidney's dying thoughts about the work. The realization that beauty is 'more apt to allure men to evill' (p. 16) is so natural to him, his imagination cannot conceive of Sidney thinking in any other way. But, as has been noted, these feelings do not fit with those of the work they supposedly describe.[142] Greville attributes to Sidney a moral position antipathetic to him.

Greville confides that Sidney wished him to burn the work (p. 17), but he has not finished with the matter: after all, he helped to get the *Arcadia* published.[143] Even here, though, Greville's role is ambiguous. In promulgating the *New Arcadia* he simultaneously suppressed the *Old*, a work he described in a letter to Sir Francis Walsingham, Sidney's father-in-law as 'so common'.[144] In the same letter he lobbied to prevent the publication of Sidney's translation of Philippe du Plessis Mornay's *De la verité de la religion Chrestienne*, now completed by Arthur Golding. If he promised to

[140] E.g. Rees, *Greville*, p. 197, although she contradicts herself within three pages (see p. 194).

[141] Woudhuysen, 'Enigmatic Relations', p. 895.

[142] Connell, *Sidney: The Maker's Mind*, p. 12.

[143] The revised version of *The Countess of Pembroke's Arcadia* was published, incomplete, in 1590. See Woudhuysen, *Circulation*, p. 226.

[144] The letter of November 1586 is ed. by Woudhuysen, *Circulation*, pp. 417–18, and the full context described pp. 225–6.

make good this last work in a complete edition of Sidney's religious works, it was a promise he failed to fulfil.[145] As always, Greville's intentions are double-edged.

Greville refers to *Arcadia* again when discussing his own writings at the end of the *Dedication*. Once more, he remarks on Sidney's 'dexterity', and how he made 'the dashes of his pen . . . beautifie the Margents of his works'; once more, he alludes to Sidney's higher purpose:

> his end in them was not vanishing pleasure alone, but morall Images, and Examples (as directing threds) to guide every man through the confused *Labyrinth* of his own desires, and life. (p. 223)

What is notable here is the gravity of Greville's understanding of 'the confused *Labyrinth* of his own desires, and life'. The 'morall Examples' are reduced to tenuous 'directing threds', a far cry from the metaphysical exuberance of Sidney's 'scope to know, & by knowledge to lifte the minde . . . to the enjoying his owne divine essence'.

Equally extraordinary is Greville's final eulogy of the *Arcadia*, hedged with qualification:

> So that howsoever I liked them too well (even in that unperfected shape they were) to condescend that such delicate (though inferior) Pictures of himselfe, should be suppressed; yet I do wish that work may be the last in this kind, presuming no man that followes can ever reach, much lesse go beyond that excellent intended patterne of his. (p. 223–4)

This is muted praise. It is hard language, to ask, even rhetorically, whether the work 'should be suppressed'. The poise of his last sentence is enigmatic. It is true that his reason for hoping this work 'may be the last in this kind' is that no one could better it, but the reason is given only after the statement, and is therefore vitiated. The graver point, scarcely concealed, is that just as no poet can emulate the writing, so no man, in the corrupted state of the world, can hope to 'reach . . . that excellent intended patterne of his'.

If one half of Greville's difference with Sidney concerns the 'infected wil', the other is a formal attack on the notion of the 'erected wit'. His views on this subject appear in *A Treatie of Humane Learning*, a work of different character from the *Dedication*. The logical starting-point for Greville's re-estimation of the mental faculties in this work is not a subjective distrust, or a homespun world-weariness, but a deduction from the Fall, or 'originall defection' (st. 4).[146] The imperfection of the senses is axiomatic: only

---

[145] Duncan-Jones, *Sidney*, p. 251–2.
[146] *Poems and Dramas*, ed. Bullough, i (cf. st. 5, 15, 19, 33). Further refs in text.

the 'God-head' is infinite, stable, and uncorrupted. Any kind of relative perfection is, in this light, imperfection. This is in direct contradiction of Sidney's assertion of an 'erected wit', which 'maketh us know what perfection is'. Perfect knowledge for Greville is impossible outside the innate perfection of God. The imperfect mind cannot 'containe' perfection, just as a finite space cannot 'containe' an infinite (st. 23). All it can reach is a knowledge of how far it falls short; this, Greville concludes, is what distinguishes man's mind, for man has the unique mental power of understanding his mental limitations.

Greville extends this argument about the rational faculty to the imagination and thence to poetry. In this respect he explicitly rejects Francis Bacon as well as Sidney.[147] The imagination, Bacon says in *The Advancement of Learning*, is 'not tyed to the Lawes of Matter'.[148] Poetry, being a work of the imagination, brings 'satisfaction' in those places 'wherein the Nature of things doth denie it'. It represents 'a more ample Greatnesse, a more exact Goodnesse, and a more absolute varietie, then can bee found in the Nature of things' (ii. 17ᵛ). In this respect Bacon is close to Sidney's idea of the poet 'disdeining to be tied to any such subjection' of nature. Bacon continues in a vein directly reminiscent of Sidney's valuation of Poesy:

And therefore it was euer thought to haue some participation of diuinesse, because it doth raise and erect the Minde, by submitting the shewes of things to the desires of the Mind; whereas reason doth buckle and bowe the Mind vnto the Nature of things. (ii. 18ʳ)

For Greville, poetry and the imagination cannot be divided from the rational faculty in this way. Poetry is subject to the limitations of nature, and must 'buckle and bowe' as it can.[149]

When Greville turns to the arts, his language involves a radical rewriting of the terms of Sidney's *Defence*:

> But these vaine Idols of humanity,
> As they infect our wits, so doe they staine,
> Or binde our inclinations borne more free
> (st. 38)

Sidney's words are seen in reverse: the wit is infected.[150] This in turn works to 'binde our inclinations', a witty reinterpretation of Bacon's quality of

---

[147] Bullough (i. 54) and Wilkes ('Sequence of the Writings of Greville') disagree on how direct the relation between the two works is.
[148] *Advancement of Learning*, ii. 16ᵛ.   [149] See Rebholz, *Greville*, p. 85.
[150] Sidney's terms have become embedded in Greville's rhyme of 'erects/*infect*' in st. 54.

'submitting the shewes of things to the desires of the Mind.' The inclinations are bound, and do no binding.

If Bacon appeals to an ultimate poetic justice, Greville subjects poetry to
an ultimate reduction:

> *These Arts, moulds, workes can but expresse the sinne,*
> *Whence by mans follie, his fall did beginne*
>
> (st. 47)

Greville's statement is extraordinary when we consider he is constructing
an aesthetic theory on the basis of this view. Sidney made his *Defence*
against the 'idle tongues' of the detractors of fiction; those who say that
poetry is a form of lying, and that lying corrupts. Greville is not saying that
poetry is sinful, but rather that it 'expresses' sin, as every mental product
does. It therefore acts as a means of recognizing and understanding the
state of sin:

> In this Mortalitie, this strange priuation,
> What knowledge stands but sense of declination?
>
> (st. 48)

Greville makes the poet closer to Sidney's historian, bound to 'what is, hath
bin, and shall be', than to Sidney's poet, attentive to 'what may be and
should be'(p. 10). Greville wishes to bring poetry back into line with 'the
Lawes of Matter' from which Bacon claimed it to be free:

> Since, if the matter be in Nature vile,
> *How can it be made pretious by a stile?*
>
> (st. 112)

This is a principle of Christian rhetoric familiar from Augustine's *De doctrina Christiana*, that truth is its own eloquence, and that a superabun-
dance of eloquence is merely a distortion of the truth.[151] There can be no
divorce between 'matter' and 'stile' because the 'matter' remains doggedly
what it was.

Greville's attack on the moving power of rhetoric reveals a profound
tension in puritanism about the status of poetry. Even Calvin adopts a
softer line on the power of eloquence. In 1543 he wrote a prefatory epistle
on the devotional effect of listening to the Psalms which was later
attached to an edition of the metrical versions of the Psalms made by
Clément Marot and Theodore Beza. The experience of devotion inspired
in the listener is not, says Calvin 'vne chose morte ne brutiue', but 'vn

---

[151] *De doctrina christiana*, iv. 25–6 (CC, 32, 160–3).

mouuement vif, procedant du sainct Esprit, quand le coeur est droite-
ment touché. . . .'[152]

Calvin expands this idea of 'mouuement' a little later into a miniature
poetic:

Et à la verité, nous cognoissons par experience, que le chant ha grand force &
vigueur d'emouuoir et enflammer le cueur des hommes, pour inuoquer & louer
Dieu d'vn zèle plus vehement & ardent   (A5^v)

The power 'd'emouuoir et enflammer le cueur' recalls the 'scope' which
Sidney attributes to the poet to 'delight to move men to take that goodnesse in hand'. According to Calvin, the experience of poetry inculcates in
the listener 'vn zèle plus vehement et ardent'. The moral implications of
this are clear: poetry has the capacity 'pour nous inciter'; this brings the
listener vital benefits, for it enables him 'à prier & louer Dieu, à mediter
ses oeuvres, à fin de l'aimer, craindre, honorer et glorifier' (A7^r).

Calvin makes these comments in the context of holy scripture, and is
careful to make the Holy Spirit the author of these effects. In fact, as we
sing the Psalms, Calvin says, we have a certainty that God puts the words
in our mouths, and that 'luy mesme chantoit en nous' (A7^v). But Calvin
borrows for this scriptural purpose a rhetorical language unchanged
from secular sources, where moral rather than spiritual virtues are incited.
In Fenner's *Artes of Logike and Rethorike* a union is declared between
Calvinist theology and humanist literary theory, to the mutual discursive
advantage of each. Yet in a different context the same rhetorical ideas could
have dangerous consequences for theology. Abraham Fraunce's *Arcadian
Rhetorike* was produced in the same year as a second edition of Fenner's
treatise, 1588. Like Fenner, Fraunce without acknowledgement translated
large parts of Talaeus's *Rhetorica*, the standard Ramist rhetoric.[153] Yet
unlike Fenner, as its title indicates, the literary examples are taken from
Sidney's *Arcadia*, along with Homer and Virgil, Tasso and du Bartas. There
are also some from Spenser's *Faerie Queene*, Book II.[154] Fraunce thus abandons the safe haven of Fenner's biblical precepts for the riskier field of contemporary vernacular authors.

Similar tensions can be found in Henry Peacham's *The Garden of
Eloquence*, first produced in 1577. The second edition of 1593 shows the

---

[152] *Pseaumes Octantetrois de Dauid*, A1^v.

[153] Howell, *Logic and Rhetoric*, pp. 255–8; see also Jones, *Triumph of the English Language*,
p. 187.

[154] Fraunce gained access to Sidney's MSS from the Countess of Pembroke, who may also
have provided him with an MS copy of *The Faerie Queene* (which was not printed until 1590);
see Woudhuysen, *Circulation*, pp. 338–40.

ubiquitous influence of Ramus.[155] Peacham calls wisdom, and her sister eloquence, 'the gifts of God'.[156] The terms he uses are a secular parody of salvation and the Fall: 'by her the true felicitie of man is found out and held up, without her it falleth by a sudden, and wofull ruine' (AB2ᵛ). The gift of wisdom, here a 'felicitie', is likened to 'a blessed state of life', whilst the lack of it is to be 'utterlie confounded', and characterized, in line with Pauline eschatology, as 'miserie and death'.

The Orator, as the purveyor of wisdom, therefore has great powers. Orpheus, says Peacham, continuing his parody of the terms of sin and grace, converted man 'from that brutish condition of life, to the loue of humanitie'. Peacham conceives the utterances of the Orator as inherently performative: 'what he perswadeth is obeied, & what he disswadeth is auoided' (AB3ᵛ). Peacham's conclusion is dramatic:

he is in a maner the emperour of mens minds & affections, and next to the omnipotent God in the power of perswasion, by grace, & diuine assistance (AB3ᵛ)

This is enticing praise, reminding us of the heady excitement of Sidney's desire 'to lifte up the minde . . . to the enjoying his owne divine essence'. Peacham, however, is more daring in his vocabulary even than Sidney is. To call rhetoric 'next to the omnipotent God in the power of perswasion' is to elevate it to a state of supernatural efficacy, as in Peacham's phrase 'by grace, & diuine assistance'. The agency of the terms appears to be transferred from God to the poet, who has his own techniques of 'grace', and his own 'diuine' creativity. A little further on, the poet's 'figures and formes of speech' are even called the 'instruments' of grace, which have veritable 'vtilitie, power, and vertue'. (AB4ʳ)

Peacham's phrasing, although unusually explicit, is no more than a metaphorical extension of the commonplace sixteenth-century idea of the power of poetry to move. There is an absolute divide between this point of view, and Greville's insistence that knowledge consists solely in the 'sense of declination'. Rhetoric, according to Peacham, is the most effective means of changing people's minds, and can persuade even where reason fails. To Greville, on the other hand, nothing can change a man's mind except the grace of conversion. A rhetoric of persuasion, he believes, is only appropriate within a moral philosophy which accepts the rational virtues; he, on the contrary, derives his rhetoric as well as his theology from St Paul, as in these stanzas from *A Treatise of Religion*:

[155] Howell, *Logic and Rhetoric*, p. 137. The more traditional concerns of the 1st edn. are described pp. 132–7.
[156] *Garden of Eloquence* (1593), AB2ᵛ.

Yea, these impressions are so firmlie fixt
In understandinge, and the conscience too,
That if our nature were not strangelie mixt,
But what it knewe, it could as easilie doe;
    Men should (even by this spirit) in fleshe and blood,
    Growe happilie adorers of the good.

But there remains such naturall corruption
In all these powers, even from our parents seed,
As to the good gives native interruption;
Sense staines affection; that, will; and will, deed:
    So as what's good in us, and others too
    We praise; but what is evill, that we doe.[157]

Greville's attack on rhetoric appears to be a reduction to nothing; the writer has no effect at all. This aspect of the work has made it unattractive to modern commentators, who find in it a negation of every achievement of Elizabethan and Jacobean literature. Yet Greville's arguments, negative as they are, contain a literary force much more powerful than the simplistic puritan attacks on theatre and poetry against which Sidney constructed his *Defence*. Greville creates a literature and an anti-literature at the same time. For Greville's resistance to poetry does not erase Greville's own poetic remains. For someone who has closed his mind to the value of letters, Greville is remarkably persistent in his literary efforts: there is good reason to believe that he continued to write (and constantly to revise) verse over fifty years of his life.

Greville provides a grave commentary on the state of English writing in the century spanning from Wyatt's to Mary Sidney's Psalms. His theological arguments concerning the power of literature are evolved with a precise attention to language and the way language works. They provoke a new interest in religious language, which far from being stultifying and puritanical, is creatively provocative. This helps to resolve some of the difficulties raised by the argument between Sidney and Greville. In addition it offers insights into the practice of writing in the period. Puritan humanism hardly understands its own contradictions. It stakes its faith in a literary power apparently without limits, and then places the severest constraints on the powers it has invoked. As we see in the final part of this book, this gives birth to a literature with a creative ambition only matched by its own doubts about that ambition and that creativity.

[157] St. 12–13. All citations from *Remains*, ed. by Wilkes.

Part Three

Literature and the English Reformations
1580–1640

Predestination: one can only write this under a most fearful suffering: and then it means something quite different. And so no one can utter this as a truth, unless he is in torment. Rather than a theory, it is a sigh, or a cry.

Ludwig Wittgenstein, Culture and Value

All the *natural* movements of the soul are controlled by laws analogous to those of physical gravity. Grace is the only exception.

Grace is the law of the descending movement.

Simone Weil, Gravity and Grace

Part Three

Literature and the English Reformations
1530–1630

7   Calvinist and Anti-Calvinist

The last part of this book concerns a wider culture of religious identity in sixteenth- and seventeenth-century England. The story so far has been of parallel revolutions in theology and in literary method, different in origins but inextricably entangled. The remaining chapters describe writers and modes of writing from worlds beyond those of humanist linguistic philosophy or of Reformation theological controversy. In Chapter 7, the focus will be on how writers responded to the demands of Calvinist theology. In Chapter 8, attention will shift to the dissensions and exclusions felt outside the Elizabethan orthodoxy among recusant and exiled catholic writers. In Chapter 9, the religious writing of John Donne will be examined, as a figure caught in the crossfire between opposing theologies. In all of these chapters, it will be clear how far a struggle over theological meaning permeated English cultural life. However, Part Three also proposes a connection between literature and religion in the opposite direction. Most accounts of religious writing are founded on an unacknowledged conceptual separation of the surface of discourse from the beliefs that motivate them.[1] Religion comes first, writing follows after. This goes hand in hand with the attempted identification of a writer's beliefs in terms of a doctrinal position or party. Yet the first two Parts of this book have questioned any such division. It is at the surface of discourse that the nexus of grammar and grace is found. It is here that the anxieties and tensions of early modern religion are revealed. These chapters will attempt to follow the lines of writing without reducing them to a doctrinal statement. The surface of discourse will be observed at the level of the smallest detail. For God (or the devil) is indeed, if anywhere, in the detail.[2] The language of early modern writing is perhaps a better representation of culture than the apparently more neutral terminology preferred by many historians.[3] Disentangling the literary forms of writers such as Greville and Herbert, Southwell and Donne, teaches us about the discursive pressures exerted in theology and belief throughout English culture in its extended reformations.

[1] Foucault, *Archaeology of Knowledge*, pp. 121–2.
[2] Ibid., pp. 131 and 139–40; and especially the epic turn on his own method in 'Conclusion', pp. 199–211, which could be taken as a refutation of many of his followers.
[3] For a similar argument, see Lake, 'Religious Identities', pp. 58–9.

*

Calvinism, it hardly needs saying, was the dominant feature in the landscape of English political and intellectual life from the accession of Elizabeth to the English revolution.[4] Predestination, equally, has been seen as the central motif of Calvinism.[5] How far a Calvinist ideology held sway has none the less proved debatable. Indeed predestination could be said to be as controversial among historians today as it was in the seventeenth-century conflicts they study. In a previous generation the issue concerned Anglican piety and its bitter relations with an increasingly strident puritan radicalism, a conflict regarded as responsible for the outbreak of civil war. More recently, the terms 'Anglican' and 'puritan' have appeared anachronistic. Since Nicholas Tyacke's seminal work of revisionism, Calvinism has been seen as the established rather than dissident voice of the Elizabethan church, and the quarrels of the 1630s as a reaction to the threat to that consensus provided by a new anti-Calvinism centred on William Laud.[6]

This chapter offers no new revision of the history of Calvinist doctrine. It is concerned more with the question of how doctrine works within culture than with the question of which doctrine was dominant. In particular, it rejects a residual dualism that has divided religion into two parties in clear opposition, and then attempted to define the doctrines around which the parties divide. English religion was a deeply divisive world in the late sixteenth and early seventeenth centuries, but its lines of division were not clear.[7] To make a position clear was indeed dangerous. Theologians and divines often went to considerable lengths to avoid public clarity, sometimes to avoid clarity in the first place. Public assertion on predestination was a rarity. The official position was articulated in the Articles of Religion, originally drafted by Cranmer and printed in 1553, then revised by Matthew Parker and reduced to the canonical Thirty-Nine of 1563. The version of predestination expressed in Article 17, although strongly formulated, was scrupulously limited to scriptural citation. An attempt to

---

[4] Like its sister term 'puritan', 'Calvinist' began life as an insult and only gradually acquired positive valuation as a term of self-identification. See Collinson, *English Puritanism*, p. 7: 'For many decades, it was principally a term of more or less vulgar abuse'. Collinson dates the use of 'puritan' as a substantive to polemics of catholic exiles in the 1560s. On more positive overtones, see Lake, 'Puritan Identities', pp. 112–23.

[5] This has been established dogma since the pioneering studies of puritanism by Haller, *Rise of Puritanism*, p. 83; and Knappen, *Tudor Puritanism*, p. 368. Among the most important recent restatements are Lake, *Moderate Puritans*, p. 279, and Tyacke, *Anti-Calvinists*, p. 1.

[6] A counter-view, itself much disputed, continues to make a claim for an Elizabethan and Jacobean *via media*; see White, *Predestination, Policy and Polemic*.

[7] See the arguments in Milton, *Catholic and Reformed*, e.g. p. 542.

codify doctrine further in the Lambeth Articles of 1595 was never promulgated as church policy. In 1604, the Hampton Court conference assembled by King James finally gave up on the matter unresolved. A clearer definition in the 1615 Irish Articles was never adopted on the English mainland. The conclusions of the Synod of Dort in 1619, in which English Calvinists enthusiastically joined with their Dutch brethren in outlawing the Arminian positions, never achieved official endorsement in the Church of England.

I ENGLISH CALVINIST CULTURE

Calvin has some claim to be the most widely cited of all sixteenth-century authors. He wrote voluminously and, despite a reputation for the strictest consistency, very variously. The *Institutes* exist in several radically different editions and in two different languages. Modern scholars who are used to the Latin can be surprised by what is in the French, and vice versa. Calvinism, even within the bounds of Calvin's own corpus, is multifaceted. It has numberless afterlives and counter-lives in the writings of his followers and, for that matter, their opponents, who were forever attributing views to 'Calvinism' which may be found in no known 'Calvinist' author. Followers themselves disagreed constantly, but maintained a conviction that theirs was the true source of incorrigible correctness. Jacobus Arminius, identified in the seventeenth century as the arch-enemy of Calvinism, remained a follower of Calvin in his way. Theodore Beza (who was Arminius's tutor, but with wildly different views), is probably more responsible than Calvin himself for the ideas which have posthumously come to be known as Calvinism. Beza first articulated a full theology of predestination in the *Tabula praedestinationis* of 1555, written in defence of Calvin. This contained a diagram (Figure 5) showing the absolute division of humanity into mutually exclusive groups: one elect and one reprobate. In 1582 he published a more elaborate theoretical treatment, *De praedestinationis doctrina*, derived from his lectures on Romans 9.[8] The pupil here outdid his master. It has been said with some justice that Calvin himself was not a Calvinist.[9]

Recently there has been a move away from the chimera of precise party

---

[8] On the obscure origins of the *Tabula*, Geisendorf, *Théodore de Bèze*, pp. 74–5. Both works were reprinted, with revisions, in *Tractationes theologicae*. See Bray, *Beza's Doctrine*, pp. 70–81.

[9] Hall, 'Calvin against the Calvinists'; also Kendall, 'The Puritan Modification of Calvin's Theology'.

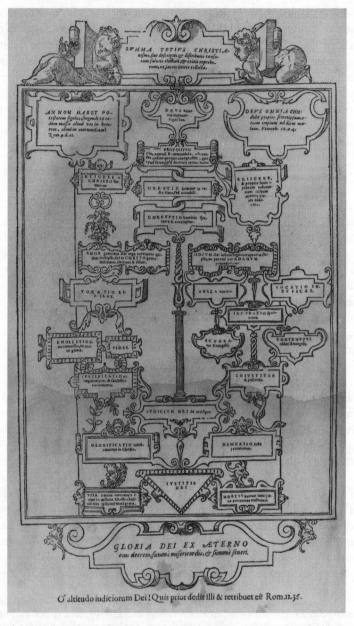

Fig. 5. The table of predestination: a diagram dividing the saved from the damned: Theodore Beza, *Tabula praedestinationis*, originally published in 1555, reprinted here from *Tractationes theologicae*, 3 vols. (Geneva: Eustace Vignon, 1576–82), i. 170.

lines towards the apprehension of a more general 'puritan culture'. Foremost in this historical effort has been the work of Patrick Collinson.[10] This chapter sees itself as part of this effort. Yet this is not a movement away from doctrinal history. Rather, it is to see doctrine as part of a continuous writing and rewriting of the self and of society, and indeed to see these processes of writing and rewriting as part of the practice and experience of doctrine. To understand doctrine culturally is to expand the horizons of religious history in a number of ways. Doctrine exists as a single stratum of dogmatic propositions only in the artificial world of intellectual history; within its historical formation it is a complex series of intersecting speech acts. At different times, Calvin discussed predestination in sermons and in biblical commentaries; in a more extended form in theological treatises and controversial tracts; and in precise, truncated, assertions in official religious Articles and formularies. In each literary context, predestination is articulated differently, for different purposes and with different meanings. It is a travesty of history to reduce this to a generalized reconstruction of underlying 'Calvinist' theory.[11]

However, the history of predestination is a history not only of complex acts of language: it is a history of silence, of totem and taboo. Calvin himself wrote of predestination as an unbridgable abyss in which language could not but lose itself. The *lex abominabilis*, the unpronounceable word of theology, was prone to material forms of prohibition. Government proclamations throughout the Tudor and Stuart reigns made periodic efforts to curb the tongues of theologians. Any utterance of the unutterable doom of divine sanction was considered in such circumstances a danger to civil peace.

Yet any account of censorship also encounters the strange compulsion to speak out on this most dangerous of subjects. An Italian visitor to England at the turn of the sixteenth century wrote sarcastically to a friend that the common people of England should be considered wiser than the most learned of Italians:

here the very *Women* and *Shopkeepers*, were able to judge of Predestination, and to determine what Laws were fit to be made concerning Church-government.[12]

[10] The term 'protestant culture' is used as a chapter title in *Birthpangs of Protestant England*. See also collections such as *Culture of English Puritanism*, ed. by Durston and Eales; and *Religion and Culture in Renaissance England*, ed. by McEachern and Shuger.

[11] Walsham, *Providence in Early Modern England*, gives a full account of the popular culture of providentialism which may be read in parallel with what follows; on the question of Calvinist theory, see pp. 15–20.

[12] Walton, *Life of Hooker*, pp. 186–7.

Like the citizens of fourth-century Alexandria who could discriminate between the divine and human natures of Christ, every Elizabethan Londoner, its seems, was a theologian. This picture of ubiquitous discourse has been questioned, and one analysis of religious writing in the period has attempted to show predestination lower on the list of priorities than the staple of faith, charitable works, and repentance.[13] Yet such an analysis fails to comprehend the way in which predestination invades these areas as well, and exerts a power when unspoken as well as when spoken. Thomas Wilson wrote approvingly in 1560 that in theology silence is sometimes the better part of valour:

But shall I saie of soche wilfull men, as a Spaniarde spake of an earnest Gospeller, that for woordes spoken against an Ecclesiasticall lawe, suffered death in Smithfield? *Ah miser, non potuit tacere & viuere?* Ah wretche that he was, could he not liue and hold his peace.[14]

Presumably many Elizabethans took Wilson's advice and lived. The significance of predestination in Calvinist England lies not in its precise formulation, nor in its pseudo-psychological effects, but in the way that it saturates the discourse of culture beyond the understanding of its speakers.

The purpose of this chapter is to uncover what might be called a literature of predestination. This entails studying the kinds of writing used in giving voice to predestination, and also (with more difficulty) the kinds of literary style and trope associated with predestination. Some points need to be made in advance. The 'literature' of predestination includes, but is not restricted to, forms of writing which now go by that name. 'Literature' in its modern sense (as a reading of Sidney's *Defence* shows) is not a useful term in the Elizabethan and Jacobean period. This chapter includes genres of writing now peripheral to or even excluded from literary study, such as sermons and theological treatises. Yet it treats these writings in what would now be called a 'literary' way, in the close reading of rhetorical style, grammar, use of figures. At the same time it pays attention to forms of writing usually regarded as irrelevant to histories of religious doctrine or politics, including poetry. Poetry is interesting to a study of religion because it mediates between public and private expressions of belief. Also, even when written by someone in religious or political employment, it has the character of a lay voice. Religious poetry, whether or not it expresses an identifiable doctrine, is distinguishable from official assertion of that doctrine.

---

[13] Green, *The Christian's ABC*, p. 356.　　　[14] Wilson, *Arte of Rhetorique*, 17ʳ.

This chapter will consider the relationship between a general culture and the peculiar milieu of the theological schools, and the conditions of writing which attach to each. To do so, it is divided into four parts: the first examines Calvinist theologians; the second a writer of poetry associated with Calvinism, the third anti-Calvinist theologians; and the last a writer of poetry associated with anti-Calvinist theology. The division between Calvinist and anti-Calvinist will not be clear cut, and will sometimes break down. More than this, the power of predestination will appear above mere faction as a source of complex anxieties and desires. Two poets from succeeding generations will be compared, who, in different ways, straddle the worlds of politics and religion. Each was a minor aristocrat and an aspiring but often unsuccessful courtier; each was educated at Cambridge and caught up in the bitter brand of theological politics peculiar to that university. Interlocking with their lives and writings and caught in the same web of patronage and clientage are a variety of academics, clerics, and bishops who similarly trod their paths between Cambridge, Oxford, London, and the court. Traversing the years from the rise of the Earl of Leicester to the eve of the civil wars, the careers of Fulke Greville, civil servant and theologian manqué, and George Herbert, country parson and flâneur manqué, are together symptomatic of the religious crisis which haunted a century.

II PREDESTINATION AND CERTAINTY: THE LAMBETH ARTICLES

In 1595, the Church of England nearly acquired a fully articulated doctrine of predestination. Yet it happened more by accident than by manifest destiny, and after a few months, just as arbitrarily, the matter was dropped. The Lambeth Articles represented a near triumph for a Calvinist mainstream, yet became its worst missed opportunity. However, their status was not properly established even in defeat. Although never officially adopted, they were never officially denied. Not printed until 1613, they cannot none the less be said to have been of no effect. From time to time, most importantly at the Hampton Court Conference in 1604, they were appealed to as having liminal authority; but it was an authority which, while powerful when implicit, had a habit of disappearing when brought into the open. When King James asked innocently what they were, Richard Bancroft, shortly to become Archbishop of Canterbury, behaved as if they did not exist.[15]

[15] See Tyacke, *Anti-Calvinists*, pp. 23–5.

The origin of the Articles was also obscure. The story has been described elsewhere and does not need to be repeated in detail.[16] On 29 April, William Barrett, a chaplain of Gonville and Caius College, preached a sermon in Latin in the University church. He was immediately accused of teaching 'the papiste doctrine of doubtfullnes of our salvation' and examined in a series of interviews by the Vice-Chancellor and the Consistory Court of the University.[17] Although Barrett recanted in Great St Mary's a fortnight after the offending sermon, the affair would not go away and was referred both to Archbishop Whitgift at Lambeth, and to the University's Chancellor, Lord Burghley. The intricacies of predestination were now in the hands of the highest ecclesiastical and secular powers in the land. As a result of the complex proceedings that ensued, Barrett first revoked his recantation in July, and then, in January of the following year, was required to make another.

In the meantime, in November 1595, William Whitaker, Regius Professor of Divinity, drew up nine Latin propositions setting out true orthodoxy. He hoped to use the occasion of the Barrett controversy to produce a clear settlement on the issue. After some conference at Lambeth, Whitgift and the ecclesiastical commissioners on 20 November approved a revised set of nine Articles. There the matter might have rested. However, to shore up his position Whitgift sent a copy of the Lambeth Articles to Burghley. Burghley in a letter expressed grave doubts about the propositions. More ominously, the queen was now reported to dislike the whole procedure. Years later, Thomas Fuller reported Elizabeth as joking that Whitgift, by calling an ecclesiastical council without her permission, had forfeited all his goods to her. While the joke may be apocryphal, it has the right smack of Tudor grimness about it. Whitgift certainly reacted as if stung by the experience. Feeling caught between a rock and several hard places, he turned on the theologians for having exposed him to such risk, and the Articles dropped from sight.

The affair of the Articles is a defining moment in English theology, and the divisions they entailed an important interpretative register in an understanding of available theological positions. Yet it is possible to overestimate their status as a doctrinal imprimatur. The Articles represent not a statement but a moment of controversy. Even the points of assertion are

[16] Porter, *Reformation and Reaction*, pp. 344–75; and, with a different interpretation, Lake, *Moderate Puritans*, pp. 201–42.

[17] The proceedings against Barrett, and a large body of other material relating to the Lambeth Articles, are preserved in Whitgift's copybook, Trinity College, Cambridge MS B.14.9, this citation fo. 23.

products of controversy. Whitaker's bracing certainty in the Lambeth Articles is only skin deep: every phrase is won at a huge cost of theological effort, with heavy awareness of possible positions on the other side. Clause is built stringently on every last sub-clause. Although battle-lines came to be drawn up, they were not known in advance, but emerged as one side fell away in recoil from the other. And even as new doctrinal authority emerged, it dissipated in a counteraction of censorship.

Historical interest in this episode has concentrated on the question of which side in the debate represented the consensus, and which side achieved dominance afterwards. Yet it is not clear that the language of consensus or dominant ideology is appropriate here. The speech acts of controversy are more fraught. Dogmatic articulation meets half way with recantation. Although Calvinism is famous for its assertiveness, a pattern of rebuttal and suppression is more redolent of Calvinist culture than the partisan history of opposing factions with iron-fast certainties.

Equally interesting are moments of self-censorship or surprised self-doubt. Take the case of Whitgift—first aligning himself with the Cambridge masters, and then persuading himself he had not done so after all; then attempting to rebuke the culprits who had made him think he had. Whose side was Whitgift on? It may be mistaken to think even Whitgift knew what he thought, certainly that he knew all along. Which is not at all to say that he was theologically either ignorant or indifferent. Whitgift, however powerful he became, was always the diligent pupil of his martyred mentor, Bradford. Yet Bradford, hard-liner in opposition to the Freewillers, could not have prepared Whitgift for arguments yet unknown. As Peter Lake has commented, Whitgift's response to the post-Calvinist inheritance was 'complex and contradictory'.[18] At times he tried to be a 'better Calvinist' than anyone (p. 220). However, Whitgift was more interested finally in authority than theology. He was always searching for the limits of orthodoxy: and his greatest principle was the force of silence beyond those limits. His final response to the Lambeth Articles, that they were correct in principle but nevertheless unutterable in practice, is characteristic of his zeal for inhibition.

The cause of offence in Barrett's sermon was his assertion that no one 'by certainty of faith' (*certitudine fidei*) can be sure of his own salvation (*de salute sua debet esse securus*).[19] To this he added a number of other propositions: that justifying faith can be lost, that the gift of perseverance is not

---

[18] Lake, *Moderate Puritans*, p. 220.
[19] Quoted here from the summary by the Heads of the Cambridge colleges (7 July 1595), Trinity College MS B.14.9, fo. 53.

certain, and that sin, not the divine will, is the cause of reprobation.[20] These theological arguments were spiced with gratuitous insults against the protestant canon, Calvin, Peter Martyr, Beza, Zanchius, and others. Such effrontery added to the scandal, but the issue of certainty in any case placed the sermon in an emotive framework. It cut a link between high abstract philosophy and the everyday pastoral concerns of moral theology. It also brought predestination face to face with the concerns of the individual. This made for a lively reaction among the Cambridge congregation, but the response of Calvinist traditionalists shows that they, too, were concerned with practical humanity as with logical purity.

Certainty of salvation played a powerful role in disputes throughout the sixteenth century. At the sixth session of the Council of Trent in January 1547, it was asserted (following Augustine) that no one should have *fiduciam et certitudinem remissionis peccatorum suorum* ('confidence and certainty of the forgiveness of . . . sins'), since this would be *vana . . . et ab omni pietate remota fiducia* ('vain confidence, remote from all piety'), found only among *haereticos et schismaticos*.[21] The church offered a passage to salvation through the sacraments, but it could not guarantee their effectiveness without reference to individual conscience. Nor could it promise the Christian's faithful perseverance to the end. Grace was acquired by a Christian over a lifetime, and was subject to the collective fears, hindrances, and persuasions of a lifetime. Grace was envisaged as a process and, like any process, it was prone to intermission and open to doubt.

However, protestants objected that grace was sovereign, without respect to personal will or conscience, and offered freely through the death of Christ. Confident assurance of salvation was made essential to the doctrine of predestination, which Calvin set out to prove in the *Institutio*. Taking to a logical conclusion the principle that grace is entirely the gift of God, and that man is by nature irrevocably sinful and incapable of returning himself to God, Calvin eradicated all sense of conditionality in the action of grace. Grace was a manifestation of God's will. He, too, quoted Augustine: the will of God is certain and eternal, and thus the number of the faithful or elect is also certain.[22] It followed that the elect were certain of their election. Anything less than certainty implied grace was condi-

---

[20] Barrett's sermon may be reconstructed from his recantation, Trinity College MS B.14.9, fos. 39–41 (10 May 1595). The recantation is also printed in Strype, *Whitgift*, iii. 317.

[21] *ES*, 372. Eng. tr. *Sources of Catholic Dogma*, pp. 252–3.

[22] Calvin, *Institutio*, 3, 24; Augustine, *De correptione et gratia*, 13; CSEL, 92, 233. Of all the anti-Pelagian works, this is the one most cited by Calvin; see Smits, *Augustin dans l'oeuvre de Calvin*, i. 239.

tional on good behaviour, conscience, or proper observance of the sacraments. To apply such conditions was, Calvin said, to 'bargain' with God: *hac conditione pacisci*.[23] The alternative to certainty of salvation was not humble doubtfulness, but certainty of damnation. Assurance was a refuge in the face of horror. Calvin, in a gesture of defiance, called predestination a voyage *tuta et pacata, addo et iucunda* ('safe and calm, I even add pleasant,' *Institutio*, 3, 24, 4). Beza developed the doctrine of certainty even further. The person who is elect is as certain of his salvation as if he had heard the eternal decree from God's own mouth.[24] In England, Beza's imitators took certainty of faith in the believer as a signifier of salvation, fundamental to predestination. The relation of assurance and salvation was not so much logical as syllogistic: the elect are certain of their election; this man is not certain: therefore he is not saved.[25]

Against this background Whitaker devised the Lambeth Articles, which asserted from the first clause the sheer gravity of Calvinist predestination:

Deus ab aeterno praedestinavit quosdam ad vitam, & quosdam ad mortem reprobavit

[God from all Eternity predestinated some to Life, and reprobated some to Death].[26]

The cause of election is defined in Article II as *sola, absoluta & simplex voluntas Dei*, and from this it follows that the number of the elect is fixed and certain (Article III). Since faith is the gift of God, and his decision eternal and irrevocable, it is inferred in Article V that grace in the elect cannot be lost *aut totaliter aut finaliter*. A further step makes the elect certain of their election:

Homo vere fidelis, id est, fide iustificante praeditus, certus est certitudine fidei, de remissione peccatorum suorum & salute sempiterna sua per Christum.

[A truly faithful Man, that is, one that is indued with justifying Faith, is certain with a certainty of Faith, of the Forgiveness of his sins, and of his eternal salvation by Christ.]

Whitaker was in the forefront of English anti-catholic writing, and thought the issue of certainty a cardinal point of difference between the

---

[23] *Institutio*, 3, 24, 5. All quotations from the Latin text are from *Opera selecta*, ed. by Barth and Niesel; Eng. tr. by Battles, *Institutes*. Further references in text citing page numbers from relevant edn.

[24] ex ipso Dei ore arcanum illud decretum intellexisses (*Tractationes theologicae*, i. 200).

[25] See Kendall, *Calvin and English Calvinism*, chs. 1–3.

[26] *Articuli Lambethani*, p. 9; Eng. tr. Ellis, *Thirty-Nine Articles*, p. 127.

faiths. This was how the heads of colleges saw Barrett's sermon: in their reply to his appeal to Whitgift, they observed that Barrett had used arguments from 'the Tridentine Council and popish writers' in order 'to prove popish doubtfulness and that we cannot assure ourselves of our salvation'.[27] Barrett's conversion to catholicism after the case subsided naturally occasioned some puritan smugness.

Notwithstanding, the stark clarity of Whitaker's sixth Article cannot conceal a deep sense of trouble over the question of certainty of faith within the protestant camp. Whitgift's first reaction to Barrett's sermon is instructive: 'to affirme *Neminem debere esse securum de salute*, to what Article of Religion established in this churche yt ys contrarye I see not'.[28] The point led Whitgift to some carefulness, it might be said anxiety, in relation to words. At this early point he allowed that a man who was *certus* should none the less not be *securus*. Later, when perusing the detail of the Lambeth Articles, he changed Whitaker's draft, *certus est certitudine fidei*, to *certus est plerophoriâ fidei*. Having first said that the elect could be 'certain' but not 'secure', he now thought they should be 'assured' but not 'certain'. Whitgift's misgivings on Christian assurance have divided historians. Porter made much of them, aligning Whitgift with an incipient Anglican *via media*. Lake has argued that they are to be taken as details of difference in what is otherwise substantive agreement with the Calvinist cause. Both judgements are concerned with Whitgift's alliances, while we might wish instead to pause for a moment over a deeper question of motivation. Whitgift is troubled because of the enormity of personal consequence. This is where predestination becomes a matter of eternal life and death. What does it mean for the Christian to have assurance about his or her condition?

Both Calvinist and anti-Calvinist writing is capable of being misunderstood on this point. The Calvinist impulse towards an ever more certain process of election and damnation is not meant to be either sadistic or depressing: on the contrary, it is supposed to give the Christian overwhelming comfort. It does, however, place enormous strain on the concept of assurance. For the dark side of certainty of election is certainty of damnation. Yet the opponents of Calvinism did not prefer the alternative route out of incipient liberalism: rather they did so to preserve the notion of common human sinfulness, and of a universal requirement for humility and patience in relation to God's forgiveness. Calvinism, strictly speaking, seemed to leave them with nothing to be

---

[27] Quoted in Lake, *Moderate Puritans*, p. 207.   [28] MS B.14.9, fo. 3.

forgiven for, since the elect were always already redeemed before the beginnings of time.

After Barrett had submitted and resubmitted, the cause was taken up by Peter Baro, Lady Margaret Professor of Divinity. Like Barrett, Baro went out of his way to make trouble in what must have seemed hopeless circumstances. Unlike the irascible Barrett, however, for Baro this was out of character. A protestant refugee from the St Bartholomew's Day Massacre, he had been quietly lecturing in Cambridge for more than twenty years. Although suspected of heterodoxy by the Calvinist establishment at least since 1583, it took the Lambeth Articles to fish him out.[29] Examined by Whitgift in December 1595 he complied with the Articles but maintained reservations on two points: he insisted the reprobate are damned on account of their sins; and that no man can be secure of his salvation. Now Baro behaved like a man at the end of his theological tether. Risking his place in the university and even his safety as a resident alien, he flouted the queen's ban on further public disputation of the doctrine of election in another sermon *ad clerum* at Great St Mary's on 12 January 1596. The vice-chancellor complained immediately to the archbishop of 'the great offence and grief' caused by the sermon to the godly, but even he noticed the emotion of Baro, who spoke 'with more earnestness and vehemency, than is remembered that ever he showed before'.[30]

Baro had been working on these questions for the last year. Before the storm over Barrett, who was one of his disciples, he wrote *Summa trium de praedestinatione sententiarum*, which directly attacked Calvin's version of predestination. Baro argued that the rigid interpretation of election by the *absoluto . . . voluntas Dei* made God 'the Author of . . . men's destruction as well as of their salvation'.[31] Baro associated this 'first opinion' with Calvin, as well as the late works of Augustine and Luther; it was an opinion also endorsed by Whitaker in the first Lambeth Article. Yet in the fourth Article, Whitaker made a crucial addition to the cause of reprobation, which places this Article more in line with the second of Baro's 'Three opinions concerning predestination'. Article IV was as follows:

Qui non sunt predestinati ad salutem, necessario propter peccata condemnatur

[Those who are not predestinated to salvation, shall of necessity be condemned for their sins]

---

[29] On Baro in 1583, see Collinson, *Elizabethan Puritan Movement*, p. 236.

[30] Goad to Whitgift, 13 January 1596, MS B.14.9, fo. 131. See also MS B.14.9, fos. 184–5 (Heads of Colleges to Burghley, 18 March 1596).

[31] *tamque hominum exitii quam salutis author habendum*; Baro, *Summa trium*, p. 2 (tr. in Nichols, *Works of Arminius*, p. 93). Further refs in text, citing page nos. in both edns.

There is a dislocation in the argument caused by the juxtaposition of *necessario* and *propter peccata*: for if reprobation is 'of necessity', how is it also conditional on sin? The reason for the addition, reinforced by the bishops in commenting on and emending the Articles, was that otherwise God was made *peccati autorem*—'the author of sin'. However, Baro argued that this was the effect in any case:

Cur enim Deus . . . hos potius quam illos in ea deserit? Peccatum huius discriminis causa esse non poterit, cum in illis qui liberantur, non minis sit, quam in illis, qui deseruntur. Illis ergo consistendum est ab absoluta Dei voluntate hoc pendere (p. 5)

[Why does God desert in that mass some of them rather than others? Sin cannot possibly be the cause of this difference, because it is no less in those that are delivered than in those who are deserted. They are forced therefore to confess, that this difference depends on the absolute will of God   (Nichols, p. 95)]

It is a subtle piece of reasoning, the inference being that the phrase *propter peccata* in the Lambeth Articles is no more than a reflex of mitigation, and fails to alleviate the rigid determinism of its premisses. Baro's alternative, set out as the 'third opinion' (p. 98), recalls Aquinas's distinction between the 'antecedent' and 'consequent' will[32] of God, and makes reprobation the result of God's foreseeing of sin (a point of view denied in Article II at Lambeth). In replacing sin at the centre of reprobation, Baro simultaneously replaced repentance at the heart of salvation. Neither reprobation nor, crucially, election was therefore in Baro's eyes a matter of necessity. They were therefore not matters of certainty either. Baro's impulse to absolve God of blame for reprobation caused him to reject the notion of the certainty of the elect in their own salvation.

Baro was now under threat. But Whitgift was also receiving advice from individuals in a stronger position. Lancelot Andrewes was Master of Pembroke, Whitgift's old college, and was also Whitgift's personal chaplain at this time. To Andrewes, argument over the origin in God's will of reprobation was of mystical nicety; what mattered was that Christianity should be morally educative. He affected ignorance on the doctrinal issue, saying he preferred 'to listen to these things, than speak of them'; this modest gainsaying protected a different aim, 'relating to a holy and well-governed life'.[33]

His case was that certainty of grace leads to moral negligence, and cer-

---

[32]   *Summa theologiae*, 1a.q.23.d.4. See Ch. 4 above.
[33]   Ellis, *Thirty-Nine Articles*, p. 140.

tainty of reprobation to apathetic despair. The view goes back to Aquinas, who attributed certainty only to a few, by special revelation.[34] Aquinas used the word *securitas* to describe a state akin to *neglegentia*, and does not seem to have distinguished it from *certitudo*. To English theologians of the 1590s, 'certainty' was a sensitive word. Andrewes, along with Whitgift and another of the archbishop's chaplains, Hadrian Saravia—and even Barrett (when forced to recant)—preferred to make his stand against *securitas* than *certitudo* itself.[35] The implications of the distinction seems to lie in *securitas* being the attitude of a person once he has taken account of his own *certitudo*. *Securitas* represents a degeneration of moral effort; fear and insecurity are required to keep the will in check.

Andrewes recommends a life of 'insecurity' in order to guard against moral nervelessness. He cites a quotation from Augustine's *Confessions* in his comments on the censure of Dr Barrett:

Et nemo securus esse debet in ista vita, quae tota tentatio nominatur, ut qui fieri potuerit ex deteriore melior, non fiat etiam ex meliore deterior

[No body ought to be secure in this Life, which is a state of Temptation, inasmuch as he that can rise from worse to better, may also fall from better to worse.][36]

John Overall's *Sententia de Praedestinatione* was printed alongside Andrewes's opinions on the Lambeth Articles (and the Articles themselves) in 1651, although it may have been written after 1595. He also emphasized the place of repentance in salvation, and exhorted believers 'to be rooted and confirmed in Charity' (*in charitate radicati & confirmati fuerint*), in order that they should have 'a stedfast Faith of obtaining salvation through Christ' (*fidemque de salute per Christum consequenda stabilem habere*).[37]

As such, the arguments of Baro, Andrewes, and Overall appear in mere contradiction of Calvin. They endorse a view of the co-operation of the will that is Calvin's first principle to deny. The language of 'repentance' and 'charity' is appropriated from exactly the kind of catholic anthropology

---

[34] *Summa theologiae*, 1a.q.23.d.1: *quia sic illi non sunt praedestinati desperarent, et securitas in praedestinatis neglegentiam pareret.*

[35] MS B.14.9, fo. 33 (Barrett to Whitgift, 16 May 1595): *certi sunt de salute fideles, securi esse non debent.*

[36] Quotation from Augustine, *Confessions*, 10, 32, cited here from Andrewes, *Censura censurae D.Barreti de certitudine salutis*, in *Articuli Lambethani*, p. 38 (Ellis, *Thirty-Nine Articles*, p. 159).

[37] John Overall, *Sententia ecclesiae Anglicanis de praedestinatione*, in *Articuli Lambethani*, p. 55 (Ellis, *Thirty-Nine Articles*, pp. 176–7).

which Calvin repudiated (*Institutio*, 3, 24, 3). In this way, it seemed the only alternative to the adoption of 'certainty of faith' lay in a retreat into a position incorporating the cooperation of the will in grace. Certainty of salvation is seen as the necessary consequence of Calvin's radical interpretation of predestination by God's will; objection to it as a covert reassertion of the freedom of human will.

However, there was a different objection to certainty that is compatible with Calvinism. Among a series of citations from Augustine, Andrewes drew attention to the work *De dono perseverantiae*. Calvin argued that not only is grace the gift of God, but also faith; there are no claims that man can make on salvation. Yet Augustine in *De dono perseverantiae* went further than this; even perseverance in faith is in the gift of God, and thus also is assurance. And because this is in God's gift we cannot know we have it for sure. Augustine argues that we cannot claim certainty for ourselves, because we eradicate the sense that it is given. It is possible for something to be certain about us, without our being sure of it. Knowledge of salvation is possible only for those who have died, not because they have had to prove themselves during life, but because God's gift is outside knowledge:

Ad quam vocationem pertinere nullus est homo ab hominibus certa asseveratione dicendus, nisi cum de hoc saeculo exierit.

[To which calling there is no man that can be said to be with any certainty of affirmation to belong, until he has departed from this world][38]

Baro, when examined by Whitgift, insisted his arguments did not disagree with the Lambeth Articles.[39] He was adamant that his views remained within a central protestant tradition. After all, he had been ordained by Calvin, and had suffered exile for his beliefs.[40] It was to no avail. In April 1596, he wrote to the Danish Lutheran Niels Hemingsen, enclosing a copy of the *Summa trium*. In this letter he complained:

In this country we have hitherto been permitted to hold the same sentiments as yours on grace, but we are now scarcely allowed to teach our own opinions on that subject much less to publish them.[41]

By the end of the year Baro's prediction came true. He failed to gain re-election to his professorship. Attempts by friends to provide him even a stipendiary lectureship in Hebrew came to nothing. He left Cambridge a broken man, and died three years later in London.

---

[38] *De dono perseverantiae*, 13, 33; PL 45, 1012. Cited by Andrewes, *Articuli Lambethani*, p. 40.
[39] MS B.14.9, fo. 85 (14 January 1595/6).
[40] Porter, *Reformation and Reaction*, p. 376.   [41] Arminius, *Works*, i. 91.

III FULKE GREVILLE'S BELIEFS: THE CONFIDENCE
OF THE FLESH

In March 1595, a month before Barrett's sermon, Baro sent a copy of his treatise on predestination to Greville. Baro's letter praised Greville as a patron (*fautor*) of learning and literature, and offered his efforts on election and reprobation to Greville's *acri solidoque . . . judicio* ('penetrating and substantial . . . understanding').[42] This letter from Cambridge to the court indicates a wider life to the controversy surrounding the Lambeth Articles. Baro's influence is found elsewhere among literary humanists, such as Harvey and possibly Spenser.[43] Greville's circle of patronage includes other players in this episode. In 1601 he helped Overall, now Master of St Catharine's College, Cambridge, to become Dean of St Paul's. In the same year he wrote to Robert Cecil commending Andrewes for the vacant deanery at Westminster.[44]

Conventional wisdom might place Greville, on the basis of this evidence, on the side of the anti-Calvinists. And yet Greville, on the contrary, is commonly identified as among the most Calvinist of contemporary writers.[45] In many places he follows an expressly Calvinist position on predestination. In *A Treatise of Religion*, he describes 'God's elect, which cannot from him fall'.[46] The proposition that the elect cannot fall from grace was one of the cardinal principles of Calvinism discussed at the Synod of Dort. In fact, he also patronized Cambridge puritans: in 1615 he was promoting the career of John Preston, fellow of Queens' College, later giving him a pension of £50 a year.[47] Preston, one of the apostles of puritanism, was chosen in 1626 to defend the ground of orthodox Calvinism at York House.[48] Ronald Rebholz has explained the discrepancy between Greville's patronage of different parties in 1601 and 1615 by concluding that Greville changed his mind, or even experienced a conversion, to embrace Calvinist predestination in his old age (*Greville*, pp. 24–5).

Patronage does not suggest such an easy story, however. After all,

---

[42] Dr P. Baro to Foulke Grevil, 7 March, 1594/5, Earl Cowper MSS, HMC, 12th report, Appendix, Part 1 (London, 1888), p. 16.

[43] Stern, *Gabriel Harvey*, p. 109; Norbrook, *Poetry and Politics*, p. 123.

[44] Rebholz, *Greville*, p. 142.

[45] Bullough (ed.), Greville *Poems and Dramas*, i. 9.

[46] *Religion*, st. 95 in *Remains*, p. 226. The date of the treatise is not known, but must be later than 1612 (Wilkes (ed.), *Remains*, p. 16).

[47] Rebholz, *Greville*, p. 310. In 1622 Preston was elected master of Emmanuel after Chaderton retired at the age of 86; see Porter, *Reformation and Reaction*, p. 414.

[48] Tyacke, *Anti-Calvinists*, pp. 166–7 and 171.

Burghley was one of Whitaker's most consistent supporters at court, yet in 1596 was ready to take the side of Baro, Whitaker's bogey man. Rather optimistically, some at the time took this as a sign that Burghley, on the issue of predestination, 'coincided in his opinions' with Baro, Overall, Andrewes, and others such as Richard Clayton and Samuel Harsnett.[49] This was to take too simple a view of the meaning of theology. Burghley was used to playing both sides. When Whitaker died suddenly in his prime, a month after composing the Lambeth Articles, Burghley presided with princely equivocation over the succession to the mastership at St John's. Clayton slipped into the vacancy between the claims of two other men: one favoured by the puritans; the other by Whitaker's widow.[50] In a similar way, Whitgift balanced the factions by letting Overall into Whitaker's Regius Chair, then scarcely a year later watched Baro succumb to the witch-hunt, before making known his preference for Thomas Playfere, a staunch Calvinist, to take the Lady Margaret professorship in Baro's place.[51]

Yet we should not conclude that politics was a bigger or different game from theology. Under Elizabeth, Greville was attached to the cause of international protestantism, which found its leader in the Earl of Leicester. Leicester was described in 1568 by the French ambassador as 'totally of the Calvinist religion'. Like Sir Francis Walsingham, and like his fellow-poets Sidney and Edward Dyer, Greville energetically promoted the alliance of English foreign policy with the religion of continental protestants in France and the Low Countries.[52] Yet this did not make them all Calvinists. Hubert Languet, Sidney's mentor, although he worked in the service of a Calvinist, was a Melanchthonian Lutheran.[53] Religious politics and religious belief interrelate in complex ways. Overall was tutor at Cambridge to the Earl of Essex, who throughout the 1590s was Greville's overlord. This made Overall a natural client of Greville. Clients and patrons do not always concur, although it may be convenient for clients to pretend they do.

Many interpretations of the pattern of Greville's religious patronage are possible. Greville may have regarded Overall and Preston, anti-Calvinist and Calvinist or no, as having much in common. He may have seen them both as representatives of the high learning of his old univer-

---

[49] Cooper, *Athenae Cantabrigiensis*, ii. 276.
[50] The puritans favoured Henry Alvey; Whitaker's wife, and his closest Cambridge friends, campaigned for Lawrence Stanton. See Porter, pp. 201–5.
[51] Lake, *Moderate Puritans*, p. 236.
[52] Rebholz, *Greville*, pp. 19–20; Worden, *Sound of Virtue*, pp. 50–1.
[53] Worden, *Sound of Virtue*, p. 52.

sity. He may also have seen them both as guardians of the godly within the conformity of the English church and its royal patron. Andrewes, Overall, and Preston, after all, were alike in seeking the favour of the king.[54] They all stood robustly against catholicism, and resolutely opposed to any move towards presbyterianism. If Greville's religious affiliation sometimes seems ambiguous, this can be said of the national church as a whole.

Greville's Calvinism needs to be seen in a broader context than the narrow confessional labelling of Rebholz's account.[55] Naturally, it differs from the purer strains of university discourse. Academic Calvinism is specialized in its vocabulary, and in its doctrinal contexts. Controversy flares up at precise moments, and entails specific conclusions. Nevertheless, Greville's lay Calvinism has considerable interest in showing how the arcana of predestination relate to a larger moral theology. It also shows how issues such as assurance of faith are equally critical in academic and in lay circles. Greville's religious reading may have been wider than often assumed, like other so-called Calvinists with broadly protestant interests.[56] This interrelates with other intellectual contexts, ingrained in Greville but alien to Cambridge theology, such as his stoicism and moral pessimism, drawn particularly from Roman history and philosophy, especially Tacitus and Seneca. Greville's Senecan phase is best represented by his claustrophobic closet dramas, two based on complex Islamic story-lines (*Mustapha*—which survives in two recensions—and *Alaham*); the third, *Antonie and Cleopatra*, Greville burned in 1601 in order to save his skin in the wake of Essex's execution.[57] *Alaham* is a savage exercise in theological pessimism; while *Mustapha*, in the *Chorus Sacerdotum* at the end of Act I, has been called 'the most penetrating attack on the conventional Christian concept of the good God before *King Lear*'.[58] Its first line is Greville's most famous—'Oh wearisome Condition of Humanity', while its last can be taken as an epitaph for his complete works:

[54] Preston was made chaplain to Prince Charles in 1621; Hill, *Puritanism and Revolution*, p. 235.

[55] See the often subtle account of Waller, 'Greville's Calvinism', e.g. 301–5.

[56] Bush and Rasmussen, *Library of Emmanuel College*, p. 19, show how even a noted Calvinist institution had substantial collections of Luther and his followers. For evidence of private ownership in Cambridge of Luther, see Leedham-Green, *Cambridge Inventories*, ii. 509–13. To take two very different cases, Donne and Preston both refer frequently to Luther in their works.

[57] *Life of Sidney*, pp. 156–7.

[58] Rebholz, *Greville*, p. 107. As Bullough (ii. 34) notes, however, the priests in the chorus are not Christian.

> Yet when each of vs, in his owne heart lookes,
> He findes the God there, farre vnlike his Bookes.[59]

The irony of these lines cuts hard both ways.

Greville's lifelong interest in Tacitus was confirmed by his endowment of a lectureship at Cambridge in 1627. Having attempted to lure the Dutch grammarian and theologian Gerhard Voss from Leiden in 1624 and 1625, he persuaded Isaac Dorislaus to speak to puritan Cambridge on his favourite Roman historian.[60] Like most of Greville's initiatives, it ended in disaster. Yet the incident also shows Greville's persistent intellectual adventurousness. Lurking in the shadows of his mind is Giordano Bruno, who wrote of metaphysical speculations at an Ash Wednesday supper at Greville's lodgings in Whitehall in 1584.[61] These sources complicate Greville's Calvinism by grafting theological assertion onto instinctive philosophical scepticism. If Calvinist scepticism sounds a contradiction in terms, it is a contradiction Greville lives to the full. The term is appropriate for the verse treatises that, composed in a style of terse gravity unique to him, preoccupied Greville for a large part of his life: the *Treatise of Monarchy, Of Warres, An Inquisition upon Fame and Honour, A Treatie of Humane Learning,* and *Of Religion.* In Greville is found what is commonly supposed not to exist: the ambiguity of Calvinism.

These questions are here examined in relation to a series of twenty-three religious poems, which forms the culmination of Greville's sonnet sequence *Caelica.* These poems are frequently anthologized, and are commonly regarded as the crown of Greville's literary career. *Caelica* as a whole was written over a long period. Greville composed the earliest poems in companionable competition, or 'social textuality', with Sidney and their mutual friend Dyer.[62] The early love poems follow Elizabethan court fashion, addressed to a series of heavenly ladies with names (Caelica, Myra) reminiscent of Sidney's Stella. In the mid part of the sequence love sonnets begin to merge with longer, stanzaic, philosophical poems, some of which may be off-cuts from Greville's dramas or his verse treatises. *Caelica* LXXXIV is a 'farewell to love', and LXXXV is a sonnet on divine love. The pair together marks an introduction to the final sequence on religion.

---

[59] *Poems and Dramas*, ii. 137. In the later version in the Warwick MS the chorus is placed at the end of the play.

[60] Rebholz, *Greville*, p. 293; on Voss, Padley, *Latin Tradition*, pp. 118–19.

[61] Bruno, *La Cena de le Ceneri*, A2ᵛ–A3; the circumstances are discussed in detail by Bossy, *Bruno and the Embassy Affair*, pp. 42–9.

[62] Marotti, *Manuscript, Print*, pp. 161–2. The three poets are described as 'Mates in Song' in Davison's *A Poetical Rapsody* (1602).

There is no outward evidence of the dates of any of the poems in *Caelica*. The manuscript copy is heavily revised, in different hands including Greville's own. Traditionally it is thought the poems are placed in chronological order, although the overriding logic of this is clearer to a modern editor than to the poet himself, perhaps. Nevertheless, the fashion for love sonnets in the reign of Elizabeth, which gives way to religious and philosophical meditations under James, suggests poems late in the cycle were written later.[63] At the same time, there is a formal, rather than strictly autobiographical, passage from the world of love to the life of religion.

Greville's Calvinism is often taken for granted, then applied to his poems. In a circular process, the poems are adduced as evidence of his doctrinal beliefs. In either event, the poetry is seen as a passive recipient of doctrine that has already been formulated. However, poetry is an active participant in belief and doctrine. Greville's starkly intellectual verse makes minute adjustments of ideology, from stanza to stanza and from line to line. Rather than theology happening elsewhere, before the poem is made, the poem shows theology in the making. This tells a different story about Calvinism than that found in doctrinal formularies. It is a story in which every detail, every scruple counts. The theology that emerges is full of movement rather than static, articulating subtle counter-balances of thought and feeling. It is a theology with a living syntax rather than a fixed order of ideas.

Caelica LXXXIX, 'The *Manicheans* did no Idols make', compares different experiences of faith, at first appearing to contrast 'our' faith favourably with that of the Manicheans:

> We seeme more inwardly to know the Sonne,
> And see our owne saluation in his blood;[64]
>
> (ll. 7–8)

Yet the 'seem' is an expression of reservation; and scepticism of this 'inward' belief is increased by the wary lines:

> As if true life within these words were laid,
> For him that in life, neuer words obey'd.
>
> (ll. 11–12)

The final stanza completes this mistrust, darkly dismissing the merely 'said' as 'a pleasant way'. With terse gravity, Greville suggests a more purgative 'way':

---

[63] On changes in literary taste from sexual to theological, see Marotti, *Coterie Poet*, pp. 179–81.

[64] All refs to *Caelica* from *Poems and Dramas*, i.

> If this be safe, it is a pleasant way,
> The Crosse of Christ is very easily borne:
> But *sixe dayes labour makes the sabboth day,*
> *The flesh is dead before grace can be borne.*
> *The heart must first beare witnesse with the booke,*
> *The earth must burne, ere we for Christ can looke.*
>
> (ll. 13–18)

These lines are crucial to the interpretation of the poem. They give voice to a divorce between 'flesh' and 'grace', rather than to a sanctifying transformation of one into the other. The 'Manicheans' poem suggests how faith fails to be 'inward'.

Greville follows Calvin's view of the unregenerability of man, and of the unconditional grace of God. Such a view was made more rigid in the Calvinism of Greville's day, when English theologians were under the influence of Beza and the 'practical syllogism' of faith and salvation. At the same time, however, Greville seems to share doubts with Andrewes and Baro, which strike at the root of Calvin's doctrinal solution of personal certainty of election. Greville's poems show a consciousness of sin, even 'such as contumaciously continue in sin' (which Baro identified as the cause of reprobation) and also the 'insecurity' recommended by Andrewes.[65] Yet Greville goes beyond Baro and Andrewes in not finding satisfaction through repentance. For whereas they propose repentance as part of a scheme of salvation, Greville, following Calvin, finds such an effort incapable of regeneration. By sharing a lack of confidence in the virtue of man, and a lack of confidence (also found in Augustine) in the certainty of divine intervention, Greville creates an impasse.

Greville locates a contradiction between 'flesh' and 'faith'. Greville agrees with Andrewes in finding life as likely 'to fall from better to worse' as the other way round. Yet paradoxically, the grounds for his lack of confidence are found not in Baro's universalist theology, whereby God desires to save all provided they repent, but from a version of predestination akin to Calvin's. The lack of confidence is more serious in that there is no possibility of remedy: Greville deserves Hell, and God has no need to save him. Greville's diffidence is derived from the combination of a violent consciousness of sin and temptation and of the absolute power of the Lord to save or to perish. Calvin does not acknowledge the contradiction, but he provides the reasons for it. Greville's doctrinal Hell could perhaps be said

---

[65] *rebelles vero & in peccato contumaces*; Baro, *Summa trium*, p. 7. (Eng. tr. *Arminius*, ed. by Nichols, i. 96).

to be Baro's *insecuritas* grafted onto Calvin, a Hell that is Augustinian as much as Calvinist or Arminian.

In such a perspective it is possible to understand the late lyrics of *Caelica*. In the crucial sequence of XCVII–XCIX, we see an imagination of sin under the threat of damnation.

> Eternall Truth, almighty, infinite,
> Onely exiled from mans fleshly heart,
> Where ignorance and disobedience fight,
> In hell and sinne, which shall haue greatest part:
>
> (XCVII, 1–4)

'Eternall Truth' stands inviolate to the 'fleshly heart'. In this poem the promises of grace constantly run into the obduracy of flesh. The two vocabularies, material and abstract, are out of sorts with one another, and this results in an awkward inconclusiveness of metaphor:

> When thy sweet mercy opens forth the light,
> Of Grace which giueth eyes vnto the blind,
> And with the Law euen plowest vp our sprite
> To faith, wherein flesh may saluation finde
>
> (ll. 5–8)

There is no figurative continuity between 'opens forth', 'giueth eyes', and 'plowest vp'; this might be taken to be maladroit if it did not point to a literalness in the metaphors which relates uncomfortably to the abstract nature of the process described. How does abstract spirit, come to be 'plowed vp'? 'Flesh', indeed, could be 'plowed'; but this only reinforces its distance from metaphysical 'faith' and 'saluation'. To borrow a phrase from *A Treatise of Religion*, 'fleshe cannot beleeue'; a discrepancy between 'flesh' and 'faith' emerges from Greville's persistent manner of making the conceptual and physical puzzle each other. 'Flesh' is made impervious to 'faith' in that there is not even metaphorical correspondence between the two.

The aspiration implied by 'When' in line 5, of a temporal end to 'exile', in fact leads nowhere; there is no progress of time in the poem during which flesh is recalled to God. The enjambements 'the light / Of grace' and 'plowest vp our sprite / To faith' induce uncomfortable pauses which provide a momentary stutter of disbelief. The poem removes the benefit of the doubt from a belief in grace. This is especially revealing in two moments of qualification, in lines 9–10, and line 17:

> Thou bidst vs pray, and wee doe pray to thee,
> But as to power and God without vs plac'd
>
> (ll. 9–10)

By repeating the word 'pray', the poet casts doubt on the validity of prayer. Reiteration puts pressure on the word, compromising its sincerity and even its meaning. Another prayer is put in mind by the repeated word:

> But wherefore could not I pronounce Amen? I had most need of
> Blessing, and Amen stuck in my throat.[66]

Greville's prayer also has 'stuck in the throat', and on re-examination, the prayer seems only an act of wishful thinking.

The confessions of the poem are placed as if between oblique inverted commas.[67] The words seem uttered by someone else, not so much in reservation as retraction. This leads to disappointment and self-disgust:

> For while wee say *Believe*, and feele it not
> Promise amends, and yet despaire in it,
> Heare *Sodom* iudg'd, and goe not out with *Lot*,
> Make Law and Gospell riddles of the wit
> We with the *Iewes* euen *Christ* still crucifie,
> As not yet come to our impiety.
>
> (ll. 17–22)

Greville's poem remains emphatically unredeemed, apparently irredeemable. Its prevailing tone is an incapacity to believe its own statements.

Calvin thought of *diffidentia* in different terms:

Quin potius dicimus perpetuum esse fidelibus certamen cum sua ipsorum diffidentia　(*Institutio*, 3, 2, 17)

[On the other hand, we say that believers are in perpetual conflict with their own unbelief　(p. 562)]

The idea of *certamen* signifies the believer's difficulties as lying outside him, to be fought off. This is a consistent habit of Calvin's imagination:

fidem scilicet variis dubitationibus impelli . . . sed, quibuscunque machinis quatiantur, vel ex ipso tentationum gurgite emergunt, vel in statione sua permanent. (*Institutio* 3, 2, 37; p. 47)

[faith is tossed about by various doubts . . . but whatever siege engines may shake them, they either rise up out of the very gulf of temptations, or stand fast upon their watch　(p. 584)]

Calvin's conception of doubt is different from Greville's. Greville's doubts assail from within, seemingly inherent in his experience. Striving against the self is the opposite of striving against external *machinae*. Rather than

---

[66]　Shakespeare, *Macbeth*, II. ii. F 687–8.
[67]　See Hill, 'Our Word is Our Bond', in *Lords of Limit*, p. 143.

seeing the believer as struggling against his own worst nature, Calvin instead imagines him as returning to the rock of essential faith. Greville sees him as having to strive first of all against his own inability to strive.

Greville struggles in this poem to find a confidence akin to certainty of salvation, judging confidence out of key with his estimate of his own condition. The condition of sin seems unable to aspire to salvation. A conventional Calvinist analysis might argue that in the process of avoiding *securitas*, he has found the 'despaire' of the reprobate. Yet Greville reaches this insecurity through emphasizing one part of Calvinism at the expense of another, failing to find sanctification because of the gravity of sin. The poems work themselves out around a narrow circle of negative abstract nouns—'degeneration', 'desolation', 'transgression', and 'desperation'— which 'deprive' the capacity to believe in salvation.

Greville's poems show this resistance to confidence especially in their scrupulous rigour over grammar. They contain no inflection that can secure future grace in some imagined anticipated past. *Caelica* XCVII is caught in the present: apart from the past participle 'exiled' in line 2, and the 'shall' of sin in line 4, the present is the only tense in the poem. A redeeming future is looked for in vain. The phrase:

> Thou bidst vs pray,
> (l. 10)

strains for fulfilment, but is answered only by the unsatisfactory present:

> . . . and wee doe pray to thee,
> But as to power and God without vs plac'd.
> (ll. 10–11)

In the same way,

> We with the *Iewes* euen *Christ* still crucifie,
> As not yet come to our impiety.
> (ll. 21–2)

Like Augustine in his famous confession, salvation comes 'not yet'. The poem does not look forward.

The two poems which follow 'Eternall Truth', present the same knowledge of sin:

> Wrapt vp, O Lord, in mans degeneration;
> The glories of thy truth, thy ioyes eternall,
> Reflect vpon my soule darke desolation,
> And vgly prospects o're the sprites infernall.
> (XCVIII, 1–4)

The metaphor 'Wrapt vp . . . in mans degeneration' is old in the Christian imagination. Augustine described the sinner as *curvatus* ('bent down to earth'). Luther rewrote this as *incurvatus in se* ('bent upon itself').[68] It is possible Luther was influenced by Reuchlin's literal version of Psalm 31 (32): 4, *Incurvatus sum*.[69] Greville's 'Wrapt vp' is close to the Lutheran figure, glossed by Anders Nygren as 'it means that man is egocentric, that his will is determined always by his own interest' (p. 486). Greville makes a new penitential Psalm in which 'even the soul that is turned towards Heaven can be bent upon itself' (p. 486). The 'glories' of God 'reflect' only 'desolation'. This is an inverse, or perverse, reflection.

The turn at the end of the stanza is therefore a surprise, as nothing in the previous lines has anticipated it:

> yet Lord deliuer me.
>
> (l. 6)

However, the prayer has not been earned by the verse, but forced out of it. 'Yet' implies a tension between 'knowledge of sin' and 'prayer for mercy'. The sin in fact stands in need of prayer. This prevents a movement from hope for righteousness to assurance of righteousness. Greville does not rationalize the prayer into an act of penitence, as Baro suggests he should, in anticipation of grace. In fact the positive offer of 'deliuer me' is retracted in the second stanza, as doubts overtake the poem once more:

> Thy power and mercy neuer comprehended,
> Rest lively imag'd in my Conscience wounded;
> Mercy to grace, and power to feare extended,
> Both infinite, and I in both confounded
>
> (ll. 7–10)

Line 9 appears to bring in the absolute power of grace to transform (expressed by 'infinite'); but once again this movement is balked by 'confounded'.

If the poem makes a prayer, it is uncertain. The rhymes of the first stanza are all feminine, with the exception of the last line, where 'deliuer me' should be masculine but is dragged into dying cadence by the weight of the rhymes preceding. In the second stanza, the rhyme almost disappears in a funereal sequence of four past participles, whilst the refrains work deflatingly, the prayer diminishing in force, losing confidence as it continues to be unanswered.

---

[68] *Agape and Eros*, p. 486; also cited in Hill, *Lords of Limit*, pp. 152–3.

[69] *Septem psalmi poenitentiales*, p. 4. Luther makes the verb reflexive (contrast *versatus sum in miseria mea* in Jerome's *Psalmi iuxta Hebraicum*).

The poem concludes with an extended conditional clause:

> If from this depth of sinne, this hellish graue,
> And fatall absence from my Sauiours glory,
> I could implore his mercy, who can saue,
> And for my sinnes, not paines of sinne, be sorry:
> Lord, from this horror of iniquity,
> And hellish graue, thou wouldst deliuer me.
>
> (ll. 13–18)

The poem shapes itself towards resolution, the pressure of reading giving an apparent power to 'thou wouldst deliuer me'; but this is potential, it is not yet completed. 'Thou wouldst' is governed retrospectively by 'If'. The meaning of the stanza in fact is strangely neutral, a statement of doctrinal position: 'If . . . I could implore his mercy, who can saue . . . thou wouldst deliuer me'. All the same, perhaps, the downward momentum of the conditional clause lends to the poem a momentary illusion of grace.

Caelica XCIX ('Downe in the depth of mine iniquity') again enumerates the condition of sin:

> And in this fatall mirrour of transgression,
> Shewes man as fruit of his degeneration,
> The errours ugly infinite impression,
> Which beares the faithlesse downe to desperation;
>
> (ll. 7–10)

'Transgression', 'degeneration', 'desperation': these feminine rhymes are culled from the centre of Greville's vocabulary. Again, too, the last stanzas make an approach towards 'assurance':

> In power and truth, Almighty and eternall,
> Which on the sinne reflects strange desolation,
> With glory scourging all the Sprites infernall,
> And vncreated hell with vnpriuation;
>   Depriu'd of humane graces, not diuine,
>   Euen there appeares this *sauing God* of mine.
>
> For on this sp'rituall Crosse condemned lying,
> To paines infernall by eternall doome,
> I see my Sauiour for the same sinnes dying,
> And from that hell I fear'd, to free me, come;
>   Depriu'd of humane graces, not diuine,
>   Thus hath his death rais'd vp this soule of mine,
>
> (ll. 13–24)

The crucial changes are contained in the refrain. In the penultimate stanza, 'not' already makes an alteration. In the first two stanzas, Greville is described as 'depriu'd' of divine and human graces; the new reading appears to offer divine grace in the absence of human 'graces'. The reason is contained in the start of the new stanza: Christ on the cross offers to redeem 'priuation'.

Yet the poem has not yet reached the other side. There is no surge to confidence, no sense of achievement, least of all in the grammar of the poem, which resists the rise of the idea. Christ is still to come. In Greville, Calvinism comes up short, colliding with the certainty of its own conclusions. The resistance to confidence, to a show of salvation, is instinctive to Greville. As Norbrook puts it, his writing is 'fissured by ellipsis, abrupt transitions, by sudden curtailments of dangerous lines of thought'.[70] Yet perhaps this should not be seen as a reluctance to show his meaning, so much as a meaning which contains a measure of reluctance. Greville's resistance is embodied in the scruple of not claiming salvation to be possessed since it is 'not his own' but God's. This scruple too is Calvinist: it is an insistence on not taking grace for granted.

IV PURLOINED LETTERS: ANDREWES, HOOKER, HERBERT, AND ANTI-CALVINISM

Sometime after 1619, Izaak Walton tells us, Andrewes, now Bishop of Winchester, sought out the friendship of George Herbert, fellow of Trinity College, Cambridge and recently elected Orator of the University.[71] He dedicated some translations of the Psalms to Herbert, the future author of *The Temple*, whom he declared to be 'the best Judge of *Divine Poetry*' (*Lives*, p. 273). As well as a shared taste in verse, the two men talked theology:

And for the learned Bishop, it is observable, that at that time, there fell to be a modest debate betwixt them two about *Predestination*, and *Sanctity of life*; of both which, the *Orator* did not long after send the Bishop some safe and useful *Aphorisms*, in a long Letter written in Greek; which Letter was so remarkable for the language, and reason of it, that after the reading it, the Bishop put it into his bosom, and did often shew it to many Scholars, both of this, and forreign Nations; but did alwaies return it back to the place where he first lodg'd it, and continu'd it so near his heart, till the last day of his life. (p. 273)

---

[70] *Poetry and Politics*, p. 171.   [71] Walton, *Life of Herbert*, p. 273.

What the contents of the letter were, we will never know, for Walton remains as secret as Andrewes's bosom. It is an anecdote as pregnant as any in the *Lives*, garrulous and guarded at the same moment, yet it yields almost nothing. Herbert's views on predestination—a secret worth knowing for any scholar—are shrouded in a series of enigmas. They are encrusted in aphorisms, rendered in Greek, sealed in a letter, hidden in a close pocket, buried no doubt in the bishop's grave. Even the bishop's opinion of them is concealed, save that the 'language, and reason' is said to be 'remarkable': we are never told whether Andrewes agreed, only that he showed the paper to selected scholars, English and continental. Naturally, the names of these scholars are withheld.

Andrewes's clandestine carefulness in the keeping of this letter may seem somewhat Trappist, but it was habitual to him. His experience gave him good reason, particularly where scholars of 'forreign Nations' were concerned. In October 1617, the Dutch Arminians had claimed to have in their hands copies of letters by Andrewes 'in countenance of their cause'.[72] At the same time, Hugo Grotius, doyen of Dutch scholarship, reported to King James on his farewell from a visit to England, that Andrewes was of the opinion that '*a Man who is truly justifyed and sanctifyed, may excidere à gratia*, although not *finaliter* yet *totaliter*'. This was dangerous stuff: the *Remonstrance to the States* by the Arminian party of January 1610 had denied three crucial Calvinist doctrines, that Christ died for the elect alone, that divine grace is irresistible, and that the elect are incapable of falling from grace. Grotius evidently regarded Andrewes as a considerable feather in his cap; the ancient Bishop of Ely was a legendary presence in the Church of England, described by a contemporary as 'an interpreter general at the confusion of tongues'.[73] The king was reported to be visibly displeased, and Andrewes deeply embarrassed. For one thing, the king was known for his anti-Arminian views, but in addition this was a highly sensitive moment in European theological politics. An impolitic word at this point, even on a scintilla of dogma, might spark a war. Andrewes denied the story and offered to controvert Grotius; Archbishop Abbott, despite being a noted Calvinist, persuaded him not to, warning that silence on this subject was the best policy.

What did Andrewes really say to Grotius, and what was in his letters? Andrewes had been introduced to Grotius by Isaac Casaubon in Spring 1613, hardly foreseeing the trauma it would cause him. Grotius had supper

---

[72] *CSPF* Holland, 84/79/182.
[73] Fuller, *Church History*, vi. 39. The whole episode is described in Welsby, *Andrewes*, pp. 165–71.

with him at Ely House, and Andrewes thought little of it, save that Grotius
was so talkative, wondering 'what a Man he had there, who never being in
the Place or Company before could *overwhelm them so with talk for so long
a time*'. Indeed he only recalled the occasion at all when asked to give a total
account of his dealings with Grotius by the ambassador to The Hague, Sir
Dudley Carleton, in the wake of the 1617 episode. Interviewed in London
by John Chamberlain, Andrewes was at pains to exculpate himself from
any imprudently Dutch association. He had eaten with Grotius twice,
hardly getting a word in edgeways, and had had no other communication,
'though he understands since that [Grotius] gave out and fathered many
things upon him that were neither so nor so'. Andrewes remarks felinely
once again on Grotius's prodigious powers: this time, his exact memory
for whole conversations several years earlier lasting nearly two hours.

So much for hearsay: but the question of letters caused Andrewes more
vexation. Chamberlain expressed astonishment to Carleton at the lengths
Andrewes went to in order to deny the existence of written memoranda of
any kind; but one piece of paper Andrewes did acknowledge, a memory
still sore over twenty years after its inscription:

> wherupon he fell into long speach, of a writing that the archbishop Whitgift got
> from him in some parts of that argument, and that he knowes not what became of
> yt, for he never gave copie of yt but one onely to Master Hooker, who promised to
> return yt but never did. But he expressed not all the while which opinion he
> inclined to, but still insisted that yf they had any writing of his they shold shew yt,
> concluding that I shold assure you they have no letter of his, and with that
> vehemencie that he wold geve me leave to send you his head in a platter yf they
> could shew any letter of his.   (Chamberlain, *Letters*, ii. 111)

This takes us back into the murky world of the Lambeth Articles, when
Andrewes was among those consulted by Whitgift. Andrewes has usually
been taken as the author of the *Censura Censurae Dr. Barreti*, later
published during the Commonwealth with other papers relevant to the
Lambeth affair. Possibly it was a copy of part of this (which survives
in manuscript among Whitgift's papers in Trinity College, Cambridge)
which he remembered later having given to Richard Hooker; perhaps
it was some other memorandum now lost. As ever, the direct trail
of Andrewes's authorized opinion trails into oblivion. The survival of
Hooker's own papers is a detective mystery in itself: his friends collected
what they could; Andrewes himself came into possession of some.[74]

---

[74] Andrewes later passed his own copies to Bishop Usher, who had them published;
Shuger, *Habits of Thought*, p. 18.

Whitgift's agents scrubbed around in Hooker's study at Borne, near Canterbury, for everything they could find, especially the lost books of the precious *Ecclesiastical Polity*. However, Hooker's son-in-law, one Ezekiel Charke, got there first with another local minister, prevailing upon the lamentable Mrs Hooker, 'to look upon some of his Writings: and . . . there they two burnt and tore many of them, assuring her, that they were Writings not fit to be seen'.[75]

Perhaps, even so, the elusive paper found its way into the hands of Grotius. One or two of Hooker's close friends, such as Hadrian Saravia, who as Whitgift's chaplain had himself been involved in the affairs of 1595, had connections which could have led such a manuscript into the hands of Dutch Arminians. There are other possibilities. It is not impossible that Walton got his dates wrong, and that Andrewes had his debate with Herbert before 1617. Possibly Grotius was one of those scholars of 'forreign Nations' given access to Herbert's Greek epistle, which he mistook for Andrewes's own. We are embroiled in conjecture and counter-suggestion here, in a kind of furtive espionage of predestinarian controversy. Perhaps the wily elusive Andrewes, like Edgar Allen Poe's Dupin, purloined his own letter and substituted Herbert's in its place in an elaborate joke against Grotius, only to be put back in trouble by the meddlesome Dutchman.

It is no longer of any significance which letter was which. Both letters are lost, even if they ever existed. Searching for the contents of the letters, for a message that was delivered, is misguided, since what is so striking is the failure to deliver any message, even the deliberate erasure of its contents. Carleton was more than content with such erasure, thanking Chamberlain for his cross-questioning of Andrewes, sharply noting 'with what fictions and fancies some busy brains and one in particular you name do delude the people', a clear reference to Grotius.[76] In his zeal to secure the passage of the upcoming Synod of Dort of the following year, he deliberately omitted Andrewes's name from other references to the affair in his letters at the time.[77] Archbishop Abbott suspected Andrewes inclined to the Arminian view, but noted that Andrewes had always been mindful enough not to broach it.

It is a measure of the care Andrewes needed to show that his silence has indeed subsequently been taken as tacit Arminianism, so much so that it is taken for granted by modern scholarship. Yet Andrewes's silence deserves

---

[75] Walton, Appendix to *Life of Hooker*, p. 231.
[76] Carleton to Chamberlain, The Hague, 8 November 1617, *Carleton to Chamberlain*, p. 247.
[77] Carleton to Sir Ralph Winwood, 29 September 1617, *Letters in Holland*, p. 183.

greater respect. Its rigour was lasting and resolute, laconically opaque. Even when pressed by Whitgift (that most persuasive of enforcers) to render up an opinion, he replied that he had refrained from preaching on such points from the time of his ordination. During his 'long conference' with Chamberlain, 'he expressed not all the while which opinion he inclined to' (ii. 111). Even the persistent Dutch eventually gave up. In 1618, the year of the synod, the Arminians published extracts from English theologians supporting their cause. There is not a single citation from Andrewes. Andrewes was anyway a notorious non-publisher. He printed nothing except two controversial writings against Cardinal Bellarmine in his long life: his celebrated Ninety-six Sermons are posthumous. Old Possum kept mum to the last. Whenever poor Grotius wrote to him, even from prison, Andrewes always found some excuse not to reply.[78]

Thirty years earlier a colleague and intimate of Andrewes at Pembroke Hall, Cambridge, had not been so wise. On 27 October 1584, Samuel Harsnett, a green 23-year-old, preached a sermon at Paul's Cross on the text of Ezekiel 33: 11, *As I live (saith the Lord) I delight not in the death of the wicked.*[79] It was a text capable of uncontroversial treatment, but Harsnett chose the most controversial reading possible. He turned it into a jeremiad worthy of the prophet himself against the wickedness of predestinarianism. Only a mad God, Harsnett says, would create a race of people in order to destroy it. To make the point, he recalls the neo-Homeric story of Odysseus and Palamedes, where the hero feigns madness to avoid going to the war at Troy. Palamedes tricks Odysseus by placing his baby son Telemachus under the plough in front of him: 'so they discovered that he was but counterfeitly mad; but, if he had ploughed up his Son, they would have accounted him perfectly mad indeed'.[80]

It is perhaps an unfortunate comparison. Was Abraham only pretending when he took the knife to slay his son Isaac as 'a lamb for a burnt offering' (Genesis 22: 7–10)? Or was he mad? Or was God only bluffing when he offered his own son to die in place of mankind? Yet Harsnett risks such blasphemies in order to suppress the greatest blasphemy of all: 'that *God*

---

[78] In a typical episode, in 1617 Grotius asked Overall to show a copy of *De Imperio* to Andrewes, who first managed to be away, and then could not read it until he sought His Majesty's permission. See H.-J. van Dam, '*De Imperio*', in Nellen and Rabbie, *Hugo Grotius Theologian*, p. 30.

[79] Maclure, *Register of Sermons*, pp. 63–4.

[80] Steward, *Three Sermons*, p. 133. The story of Palamedes and the plough is from Hyginus, *Fabulae*, 95, printed in Basle in 1535. Harsnett's copy of the *Odyssey* contains a collection of ancillary Homeric fables from Heraclides Ponticus; Goodwin, *Catalogue of the Harsnett Library*, p. 87.

should designe many thousands of soules to Hell before they were, not in eye to their faults, but to his own absolute will and power, and to get him glory in their damnation' (pp. 133–4). The horror of the idea produces increasingly unrestrained rhetorical violence in recoil:

this opinion saith, that not one or two, but millions of men should fry in *Hell*; and that he made them for no other purpose, then to be the children of *death* and *Hell*, and that for no other cause, but his meer pleasure's sake' (p. 134)

God predestinating the reprobate to damnation is like Saturn eating his children, or Herod massacring the innocents (p. 139). This is not the God of grace but the god of fate, the god of the Greeks, 'that gave their God a glorious *Title* for killing of *Flies*' (p. 141). Harsnett rails against this God like blind Gloucester to his mad son:

> As Flies to wanton Boyes, are we to th' Gods,
> They kill vs for their sport.[81]

The whole sermon is written with a tone of high sarcasm, with a target that is not hidden. He calls the tropes of predestination the '*Genevian* conceit', and it is Calvin's God Harsnett rears from as from an angel out of Hell. Yet within weeks he found that his Church had decreed an attack on this hell as out of countenance. Forty years later, he reports he was 'checked by the Lord Archbishop Whitgift, and commanded to preach no more of it, and never did'.[82] His profit from silence was a gradual rise to the ultimate preferment of an archbishopric: he succeeded Andrewes into the mastership of Pembroke in 1605, and in 1609, when Andrewes was translated to Ely, into the bishopric of Chichester. Eventually, in the reign of Charles I, he moved via Norwich to the see of York. Yet the smell of controversy and censorship, of heresy and even treason, never left him for long. He came out on Baro's side during the Lambeth Articles controversy, and in 1599 was nearly imprisoned for failing to censor a book found to be favourable to the disgraced Earl of Essex.[83] In 1616 the Fellows of Pembroke alleged fifty-seven Articles against him, headed by those cardinal Cambridge crimes, popery, embezzlement, and absence from college. His parishioners in Norwich were no happier: in 1624, perhaps at the instigation of

---

[81] *King Lear*, IV. i. F2221–2. Shakespeare was reading a later work by Harsnett (*A Declaration of Egregious Popish Impostures*, on Jesuit exorcisms), while writing *King Lear*; see esp. Greenblatt, 'Shakespeare and the Exorcists', in *Shakespearean Negotiations*, pp. 94–128.

[82] *Lords' Journals*, 19 May 1624, iii, 389.

[83] Harsnett's part in the publication of Sir John Hayward's *Henry IV*, which he claimed (disingenuously?) to have passed without reading, is reassessed by Clegg, *Press Censorship*, pp. 63–4.

Sir Edward Coke, he was accused of setting up images in churches, and of extortion.[84] He died in 1631, perhaps the luckiest septuagenarian of his time.

What provoked the will to silence on predestination, the periodic outbursts of violence and menace from official quarters, and the techniques of evasion in response to this menace? One explanation is doctrinal: silence proves one way or other the characteristic stamp of church policy. Yet arguments from silence are always difficult: and here silence is thick and scarcely fathomable. The silence of predestination has the power of a shibboleth, drawing all within the magic of its awesome decree and yet rendering all speechless in apprehension of such power. Lurking within protestant culture is an overwhelming desire to explain and expound the depth of silence; yet any effort to broach silence is prone to immediate suppression. Such suppression may involve either sympathy or else disillusion with the ethic of predestination, or it may involve a refusal to acknowledge anything so temeritous as an opinion on the subject. It is a silence between scruple and censorship, between awe and evasion.

Government injunctions and episcopal warnings from time to time took active efforts to ban public discussion, but often they did not need to. Self-censorship was an ingrained habit and did the work of government for it. Foremost among such willing self-censors was Hooker. It has been remarked how in all the bulk of the eight books *Of the Lawes of Ecclesiasticall Politie* his interventions on the subjects of predestination or election are extraordinarily rare.[85] Yet they created a spectre throughout his career from which he struggled to escape. His first public appearance away from the womb of Oxford was to deliver a Paul's Cross sermon in 1581, for which he chose the subject of the two wills of God, antecedent and consequent. Walton spends much of his narrative at this point (for which he is the only source) on Hooker's severe bout of hypochondria, which drove him into the clutches of Mrs Churchman and her daughter, out of his solitary Eden into marriage and the world of men.[86] Yet Walton also notes in passing that the sermon 'seemed to cross a late Opinion of Mr *Calvins*, and then taken for granted by many that had not a capacity to examine it' (p. 177).

This ominous footnote carried over into Hooker's subsequent career. The dubious sermon (unfortunately now lost) was recalled in an acrimonious row in 1585 between Hooker, now Master of the Temple, and the man passed over in his favour, Walter Travers. Travers was a presbyterian, at

---

[84] Goodwin, *Catalogue*, pp. xv–xvii.   [85] Lake, *Anglicans and Puritans?*, p. 184.
[86] *Life of Hooker*, pp. 176–8. The sermon is described in Maclure, *Register of Sermons*, p. 61.

least covertly, but enjoyed some patronage at court for his strict Calvinist views. Indeed both men jostled for the favour of the new Archbishop Whitgift (appointed in 1583) even as they battled with each other over points of theology. For a few months, as Thomas Fuller later waggishly put it, 'the Pulpit spake pure *Canterbury* in the *Morning*, and *Geneva* in the *Afternoon*, until Travers was silenced'.[87] Travers made a *Supplication* to the privy council to have Hooker removed, citing the Paul's Cross sermon as well as a series of four sermons at the Temple Church. In a reply addressed personally to the archbishop, Hooker answered the charges.[88] They read like a lexicon of sixteenth-century controversy: justification and works, the status of the church of Rome, certainty of election, assurance of faith, predestination. Hooker stressed that this last 'matter was not broached in a blind alley' or 'huddled in amongst other matters, in such sort that it could pass without noting'.[89] By preaching at Paul's Cross he had opened himself beyond the audit of 'private interpretation' or book learning into the arena of public doctrine. He insists his remarks had passed the scrutiny of the Bishop of London 'without rebuke or controlment afterwards' (iii. 577). Nevertheless, on points of detail he is now scrupulously silent. Of the original words of his sermons he repeats not a syllable, making silence speak for him. He still has the texts, he declares, and has allowed many to look over them; the tacit approval of his readers is sufficient testimony. Yet on no point does he risk seeking Whitgift's seal of approval. The sermons were not published until long after his death; they were reprinted, around the time of Andrewes's trouble with Grotius, in the wake of the Synod of Dort. By 1618 these words of the dead provided a protection behind which the living could hide.[90]

Hooker survived his brush with Travers but was chastened by the experience. From now on, in Lake's usefully Freudian phrasing, the matter of predestination became subject to 'displacement'.[91] Hooker attempts to deflect predestination from the centre of Christian doctrine. Yet he does not quite succeed. Instead it is a site of anxiety, present even or especially because of its unutterable absence. In the meantime, he was regarded with suspicion by the presbyterian party, for whom even the mention of the antecedent and consequent wills of God meant guilt by association.

---

[87] *Worthies*, p. 264.
[88] Travers's *Supplication*, Hooker's *Answer to Travers*, and several of his sermons (compiled into two works, *A learned and comfortable sermon of the certaintie and perpetuitie of faith in the Elect*, and *A learned discourse of iustification*) were published in 1612 by Joseph Barnes, *STC* 24187 and 13706–8.
[89] *Works of Hooker*, ed. Keble, iii. 576.   [90] *Certayne Divine Tractates*.
[91] *Anglicans and Puritans?*, p. 186.

In Lake's careful analysis, Hooker managed to stay quiet about predestination by implying it was a matter of obsession only for those tainted with non-conformism on church discipline. Finally, just once, a presbyterian tract called his bluff by countering that Hooker was only anti-presbyterian because he was first and foremost anti-predestinarian.

The anonymous *Christian Letter of certaine English Protestants* appeared in 1599, the first printed response to the *Ecclesiastical Polity*. By this time Hooker was already in his final illness. Before he died, he made marginal notes in his copy of *A Christian Letter*, and drafted fragments of a manuscript reply. It was never published, not even posthumously. Even his indefatigable literary executors were understandably wary of this subject. Yet this obscure notebook is the location of Hooker's only substantial surviving treatment of the *decretum terribile*.

Even so, whatever the insinuations of his opponents, Hooker is by no means a denier of predestination, any more than other conformist theologians of his time. His statement is full of logical resistances rather than dogmatic assertions. This very lack of assertiveness would have indicated to the 'purified crew' (as in an unguarded moment he calls the authors of *A Christian Letter*) theological impurity. However, logical qualification is fundamental not only to Hooker's methods of epistemology but even to his principles of piety or godliness. Only God can afford to make dogmatic assertions about predestination, because God only knows. What God knows for certain he alone knows for certain. For mere mortals, the number and the identity of the predestinated is 'a Gulfe of bottomles depth, Gods unsearchable purpos'.[92]

This criticism was made repeatedly against the Calvinists. In 1621, in a sermon preached at Whitehall in the presence of James I, Andrewes compared the decrees of God with the decrees of the king: they are '*magna & mirabilia super se*, and so *super nos*: points too high, too wonderfull for us to deale with'.[93] Cunningly accusing his opponents of *lèse-majesté* rather than false doctrine, Andrewes wondered aloud whether God enjoyed the way that his interpreters were telling him what his own decrees were. Paul and the Psalmist themselves, the doctors of the doctors, had lowered their eyes before the great depth of divine judgement:

---

[92] *Works of Hooker*, Folger edn., iv. 123. The so-called 'Dublin Fragments' are in Trinity College, Dublin, MS 121 and 364. Hooker's marginal notes to *A Christian Letter* are in Corpus Christi College, Oxford, MS 215 b.

[93] Andrewes, Easter Sermon, No. 15 (Whitehall, 1 April 1621) printed in *XCVI Sermons* (1629), p. 548.

Yet are there in the world, that make but a *shallow* of this great deepe: they have sounded it to the bottome. GOD's secret *Decrees*, they have them at their fingers ends, can tell you the number and order of them just, with 1.2.3.4.5. Men, that (sure) must have beene in GOD's *cabbinet*, above the *third heaven*, where *Saint Paul* never came. (p. 548)

Andrewes sardonically imagines the Calvinists in God's private apartments, counting off the number of the elect. There appears to be a covert allusion to the Lambeth Articles, ticking off God's innermost thoughts '1.2.3.4.5'. Yet Andrewes's unusually outspoken satire offers no alternative theological position. He does not refute the Calvinist system. It is a position of resistance, a reactionary refusal to say more than is necessary. The difference between Calvinism and anti-Calvinism is not the difference between one doctrine and another but between assertiveness and uncertainty, articulation and inarticulateness.

If Hooker's drafted reply to *A Christian Letter* seems equivocal, this does not reflect theological scepticism but rather Hooker's more reticent faith. True faith never claims more than it can. It does not take bets with providence. Nevertheless, there is a tension in Hooker's epistemology between the desire to explain the rationality of God's will as fully as possible, and the inhibition created by the sense that reason can only go so far. To this effect, Hooker in the *Ecclesiastical Polity* was as critical of puritan philosophical method—particularly Ramism—as he was of its theology.[94] Similarly, reason is Hooker's weapon against the conclusions of *A Christian Letter*, for his main objection to the *Letter* is that it allows no limits to what reason can say.

What can be known, ultimately, about God's first intentions? In Hooker's epistemology, to the extent such a question is rational at all, it can only be answered by means of the finest possible philosophical distinctions between necessity and contingency. 'Sensible experience' shows that 'all things come not necessarily to passe' (iv. 124). On the one hand, 'those effects are necessarie which can be noe other then they are'. The sequence of their causes has 'but one only way of working'. On the other hand, the causes of contingent effects 'may divers wayes varie in their operation' (iv. 124). Hereon distinctions become harder to maintain. Hooker, now into his stride, begins to extemporize the permutations and probabilities. The crucial feature in Hooker's method is the counterfactual, or in the Aristotelian terminology used by Hooker, δύναμις ἀντιφάσεως ('the

[94] *Ecclesiastical Polity*, i. pp. vi, 4; *Works of Hooker*, Folger edn., i. 76. See also Morgan, *Godly Learning*, p. 111 and Miller, *New England Mind*, pp. 148–9.

possibility of contradiction'). In the case of some things, it is possible for them not to have been the case. It is this which truly distinguishes the contingent from the necessary. For a thing to be necessary it can be said that it is not possible for it not to be; whereas for a thing to be contingent, it is able to be one thing or the other, it 'may as well be, as not be' (iv. 126).

So far, so good. This discussion requires of Hooker a dense commentary on passages in Aristotle concerned with this fundamental area of logic, most especially the notorious ninth chapter of *De interpretatione*, with its discussion of the logical imbalance between sentences expressed in the future and sentences expressed in the past. How does the radical uncertainty of the future translate into the radical certainty of the past? How is it that the same event offers itself to opposite interpretations merely according to the time at which the interpretation is made? It is in solution to such questions that Aristotle constructs his most complex and extensive model of the concepts of necessity and contingency. This model in turn provided the source for any number of Christian treatments of the relationship between providence and foreknowledge, in Boethius, in Augustine, in Aquinas. The margins of Hooker's manuscript are riddled with references to these sources.

Yet Hooker's treatment is different, because between him and them lies the brooding presence of Calvin. It is Calvin who has made the peculiar speech act of predestination all the more difficult to say. It is only with the most extraordinary effort of will that Hooker brings himself to say anything at all. In the context of his time, the sheer reticence of the million words of *Ecclesiastical Polity* on this subject is incredible. The logical prolegomenon on necessity and contingency in the fragmentary reply to *A Christian Letter* is one more way of putting off the inevitable; even here, Hooker almost gets away with not asking the questions he knows his reader knows he should be asking. Is his sin a matter of necessity or contingency? Is his salvation? Is his knowledge of either, either necessarily or even contingently possible? Calvin made such questions both more terrible and more awkward because he has seemingly left less and less room for divine contingency.[95] He has changed the rules so that all God's future sentences behave like past ones anyway. If all God's sentences, past or future, necessary or contingent, break ordinary rules of logic, then can logic be any use in constructing some medium between them?

Hooker retains his faith in such a possibility, but only just, and only by means of the barest logical equilibrium and grammatical finesse. Even in

---

[95] See esp. *Institutio*, 1, 16, 9, and 3, 23, 6.

the peerless company of Aristotle, Hooker's manuscript is a staggering essay in the use of the double negative, sometimes the double double negative:

for during the tyme, whyle as yet they are not, it is butt possible that they shall be; when once they are, their not being is then impossible

being once made actuall, they are then soe necessarie, that God himself cannot possibly cause them not to have beene   (iv. 126)

Perhaps we might call this a double negative theology. Hooker makes a classical defence of the distinction between divine prescience and causal necessity, but in a Calvinist context it is more of a balancing act than ever. Unlike Boethius or Augustine, Hooker has to dance on the wire while under public examination, with sudden penalties for the merest failure. He summons up his resources, logical and syntactic, to find some room, however small, to assert at one and the same time that man is responsible for his sins but cannot do otherwise than do them; that such sins are nevertheless contingent and not necessary; that God knows them for certain in advance but does not make them happen; that he chooses by grace to forgive some men for their sins but not others; that such grace is finally certain but not immediately irrevocable; that the cause of this grace lies not in the person given it but in the God who gives. In an act of supreme theological courage, at the end of the essay he subjoins a revised version of the Lambeth Articles, concluded with such painful political struggle only four years before. Yet at the heart of his essay is not a doctrinal statement but the pious reflex contained in a sentence such as this: 'Though grace therefore bee lost by desert, yet it is not by desert given' (iv. 165). It is a sentence which barefacedly admits to the possibility of its own illogic, or the self-contradiction of false correspondence. How can one half of the sentence be true if the other is? This is Hooker's final chance with providence: it is the risk he takes in believing the goodness of God, in surrendering to the givenness of grace.

V HERBERT'S *THE TEMPLE*: GRACE AND THE GIFT

For a century and more, protestant theology struggled with the paradox of the gift inaugurated by Luther. Luther pushed back the boundaries of givenness to their limits and even beyond. There is no work, no merit in man that can earn the grace of God. Even faith is not an action required by God, but a response of gratitude in the face of a divine generosity that is uncalled for, unexpected, uninvited. Yet for Calvin, even this was not enough, or else too much. Did not the Lutheran demand of faith imply that it was a reciprocal exchange for a benefit received? Grace could not even ask for this. It must ask for nothing. Predestination, in its extended Calvinist form, was a device to guarantee the absolute givenness of grace.

Calvin's theology, as Natalie Zemon Davis has written, can be seen as a fundamental attack on the systems of reciprocity to be found at the core of the catholic faith.[96] The elaborate bonds of mutuality by which priest is joined to laity, church to Christ, body to soul—the implicit contracts of exchange embodied in the offices of charity, in the oblations of the dead, in indulgences, in the mass itself—came to seem anathema. To Calvin they were an attempt to buy God off, to commit him to a contract, which he is under an obligation to fulfil. Calvin, Davis asserts, undertook to dismantle this theological system, 'recasting reciprocal relations in terms of gratuitousness wherever he could' (p. 191). God is characterized (he says in a comment on Deuteronomy 32) by 'pure gratuité'.[97] Calvin reconfigures theology so that at every point the vocabulary of the gift is pellucid: 'bonté gratuite', 'bénignité gratuite', 'don gratuit', 'élection gratuite'.[98] Calvin delights in rhetorical figures of graceful dependence: 'A celuy qui aura, il luy sera donné'. In Latin, the connection between grace and the gift is tautological: *gratuita Dei gratia*.[99]

The history of theology defines predestination in doctrinal terms but it is just as important to understand the techniques of writing needed to define it. For the concept of the gift places special pressures on language. Indeed at times it seems impossible to find a language that will bear the weight. It may be helpful here to consider the classic account of the gift in the work of Marcel Mauss. In his anthropological analysis of the culture of gift-making in archaic societies, he observed that gifts are not given in isolation. Gifts are returned: every good favour deserves another. Gift systems are in effect exchange systems. The gift is offered with the understanding that it will in turn be given back in the form of a new gift (a 'counter-gift'), which requires one more in turn.[100] Social harmony relies on this mutual, unspoken rule of reciprocity. Emile Benveniste suggested that language itself (in its Indo-European forms) has developed so that this mutuality is

[96] *The Gift*, p. 191.
[97] *Commentaires sur les cinq livres de Moyse*, p. 693. A more extended treatment is given in the *Sermons sur Deuteronomie*; they were translated into English by Arthur Golding in 1583 (*STC* 4443.5). See the vocabulary of 'gratious giftes' and 'Gods owne freegoodnesse' (p. 1117).
[98] *Institution*, ed. by Benoît, ii. 70 (2.3.10–11).
[99] Ibid., ii. 71; *Opera selecta*, iii. 287 (2, 3, 11).
[100] Mauss, *The Gift*, pp. 65–70 (originally published in 1923–4 as 'Essai sur le don').

confirmed. 'Giving' and 'taking' are bound in a mutual linguistic system, whereby one vocabulary can be exchanged for the other.[101]

This may explain how Derrida, in his commentary on Mauss's work, found that the gift, in its pure form, appears to be philosophically impossible:

> On the one hand, Mauss reminds us that there is no gift without bond, without bind, without obligation or ligature; but on the other hand, there is no gift that does not have to untie itself from obligation, from debt, contract, exchange, and thus from the bind.[102]

This is a good account of the complexity of the gift in sixteenth-century thought. For the gift to be a gift, it must oblige no one, and be obliged to no one. It must be free, gratis. And yet the ties that bind seem to return without asking; the gift calls forth, without even knowing it, something in return. Between these poles the arguments crossed back and forth. To allow mankind even a gesture of reciprocity in matching the gift of grace with some motion of answering merit—even if only desired, or foreseen, or preveniently called into being by the act of giving itself—seemed to Calvin to make it untrue. It is this which perhaps motivates the more extreme Calvinist solutions to the problem of grace, such as supralapsarian election. Supralapsarianism—the doctrine that election and reprobation were determined even before the Fall of man, in a sovereign act of divine will—is an attempt to place election one step further back from any association with human merit or volition. And yet in response, the anti-Calvinist argued that to insist that the gift of election could be apprehended by the elect—and possessed by the individual as a certainty—was precisely to rid God of his power of giving, to reduce him to an onlooker of his own providence. It made the elect feel, paradoxically, that grace was his own.

Certainty and uncertainty, then, rather than originating from opposing theological positions, both endeavour to preserve the sanctity of the gift. Calvinism and anti-Calvinism are in this sense not so unlike. Yet each side is driven to ever more paradoxical formulations in order to achieve its aim. Indeed, according to Derrida's analysis, it would not be possible to expect them to do otherwise. The gift is already a paradox. The nearer a gift reaches to the proper structure of the gift, the more impossible it becomes to find a language adequate to it. The gift, in its pure form, subverts language itself. The rules of language—of subject and object, of copula and complement,

---

[101] *Le Vocabulaire des institutions indo-européennes*, i. chs. 5–7.
[102] *Given Time*, p. 27.

of active and passive—have to be ignored or overturned. The unrequited, unneeded gift is not so much against nature as against language.

Protestant thought would hardly accept Derrida's more extreme formulations ('the truth of the gift is equivalent to the non-gift' (p. 27)). Yet they are not so far from Paul's famous dictum that if grace is not free, then grace is not grace. Sixteenth-century protestant theology seems constantly to risk the impossibility of grace. It attempts to place grace somewhere almost beyond language, to wrest some sense from those places where syntax apparently breaks beneath its unbearable lightness.[103] If Calvinism, at one extreme, searches for a logical system which will bear the weight, a super-logic which will articulate everything, and demonstrate the relationship of every joint and ligature to the next, anti-Calvinism seems to be just as interested in those moments where language breaks down.

One such author is Herbert. Yet to call him anti-Calvinist is a complete misnomer. Herbert shows the difficulty of precise theological labels when no explicitly doctrinal literature survives. His affiliation with Andrewes makes it tempting to place him in a similar party, except that, as we have seen, Andrewes took great lengths to avoid identification with any party. Herbert, like Andrewes, no doubt saw himself in the tradition adumbrated by the Thirty-Nine Articles of the Elizabethan and Jacobean mainstream. Yet this category also included Whitgift, Whitaker, and even Perkins. For this reason, one or two lone voices have placed Herbert happily within the Calvinist consensus.[104] Debora Shuger, in an aside, speculates instead that what interested Andrewes in that elusive stolen letter was precisely that 'it said something different from the stock arguments of either Calvinist or anti-Calvinist dogma'.[105]

If Herbert remains elusive, however, this is not because Herbert's poetry is un- or anti-theological. There was once a tradition that found considerable comfort, not to say satisfaction, in the idea that what makes Herbert so quintessentially Anglican was his rejection of dogma, perhaps of any kind of intellectual process whatsoever. Rather, *The Temple* is difficult to interpret according to rigid categories because he has absorbed so much theology. Take the typically beguiling opening of the poem 'Grace':

> My stock lies dead, and no increase
> Doth my dull husbandrie improve:
> O let thy graces without cease
> Drop from above![106]

---

[103] On 'breaks' in French syntax in relation to the gift, see *Given Time*, p. 53.
[104] Veith, *Reformation Spirituality*, pp. 35 and 84; also Nuttall, *Overheard by God*.
[105] *Habits of Thought*, p. 91, n. 1.
[106] All quotations from Herbert are from *Works*, ed. by Hutchinson.

Despite the simplicity of the metaphors, and the studiedly mundane meter, this is a poem very exact in its theology. It is carefully aware of the complex economics of the gift. No 'husbandrie' of human will or effort can 'improve' his stock. He cannot 'increase' his own state, but must submit to grace. Grace comes always from outside.

This one-way motion is confirmed by the repeated refrain 'Drop from above!' Cut off from the ordinary visual form of the poem by a dramatic caesura, it seems, too, to have no syntactic relation to what precedes it in each stanza. The implication is that the sinner finds grace as the passive object of a free gift. He no more causes grace to come than he causes an apple to fall on his head. Grace indeed seems to be an act of gravity. And yet, with an additional scruple, Herbert notices that the turn of the gift still rebounds on him. He has made the call, 'Drop from above!' Is the desire implied by the call a form of propitiation which has produced grace? As if in acknowledgement, the final stanza places grace a step yet further off:

> O come! for thou dost know the way:
> Or if to me thou wilt not move,
> Remove me, where I need not say,
> *Drop from above.*
> (ll. 21–4)

Not even the imperative is spoken by the sinner: everything, even the first motion, comes from above.

The endings of the poems in *The Temple* are instructive because they so often resist any sense that grace has been willed or desired into being. They absolve themselves of the least claim on grace:

> Ah my deare God! though I am clean forgot,
> Let me not love thee, if I love thee not.
> ('Affliction (I)', ll. 65–6)

This odd grammatical form, virtually a solecism, performs a ritual of unsaying itself: of unwilling the will, or giving back its own gift. At the end of 'The Pearl', once again, he takes away any credit from himself:

> Yet through these labyrinths, not my grovelling wit,
> But thy silk twist let down from heav'n to me,
> Did both conduct and teach me, how by it
> To climbe to thee.
> (ll. 37–40)

The complex syntax here, with its network of subordinate clauses, sub-tends the action of grace ever further from the 'I' of the poem. His own 'wit' is not an actor in his salvation; it is a bystander. He waits for the delicate cord of grace to come his way.

Just as in the religious poems at the end of *Caelica*, there is a concentration of energy in the final stanza. This is where grace takes place, where sin is redeemed. Yet the endings are a location of anxiety as well as power. It is an anxiety which can only be described as theological. Herbert, like Greville, takes great pains to establish the grounds of this salvation. Modern criticism often takes less care, and assumes a satisfaction or bland self-assurance that simply is not there in the poem. Modern criticism also often assumes a sense of closure, which is alien to the strangely open-ended and tentative conclusions of these religious lyrics. If studied closely, Herbert's endings contain a series of checks and balances in order to figure forth a particular theology of the gift.

This is equivalent to an art of regulated syntax. It takes a number of forms. One is a persistent use of the passive voice, as at the end of 'The Pearl', also of 'Life', and 'Obedience'. Word order is arranged so that the passive reception of grace as a gift is articulated clearly. Another is the use of complex conditional clauses, as in the counterfactual quoted above which concludes 'Affliction (I)'. Grace is drawn back to source (see also 'Affliction (IV)', 'Artillerie', 'The Pilgrimage'). A third is the use of a modal grammar of imperatives, asking God to fulfil a need that cannot be fulfilled any other way: examples of this are 'Sighs and Grones'(which consists of importunate imperatives throughout), 'Submission', 'Affliction (V)', 'Mortification', and 'The Method'. Related to this are optative auxiliaries, most typically that odd English verb, 'let', which (as has been observed several times in this book) has a grammar all of its own, poised between a reflexive exhortation ('let me') and a second-person order ('let me not'). 'Complaining', 'The Forerunners', and 'Judgement', all finish using as a main verb 'let'.

These habits of syntax form a complex theology but it is not one that is articulated directly. Instead it consists in a subtle and pertinacious resistance to the theology of the gift-exchange, of gift and counter-gift. Herbert scrupulously avoids the temptation to ascribe grace to any authorship of his own making. The poems are full of the expression of subjective fears, desires, hopes, but these signs of the will are cut off from the final action of the drama, a redemption which comes (if it comes) without asking or waiting. Even the smallest slips of volition are checked back, in a series of habitual gestures of self-rebuke, as in the peculiar end to 'Miserie', with its dangling qualification, 'My God, I mean my self'. In this way the poems evade any easy categorization as either Calvinist or anti-Calvinist. In their

rejection of voluntarism it is not surprising that commentators have occasionally found them radically protestant or even Calvinist; but in their
erasure of any ethic of the certainty of salvation they are classically anti-
Calvinist.[107] The notion of grace as possessed, as already taken for granted
by a certified member of the elect, is anathema to them.

Herbert is a virtuoso of what might be called a self-corrective syntax of
qualification. Take the first stanza of 'Peace':

> Sweet Peace, where dost thou dwell? I humbly crave,
>   Let me once know.
> I sought thee in a secret cave,
>   And ask'd, if Peace were there.
> A hollow winde did seem to answer, No:
>   Go seek elsewhere.

The quiet music of reflection here is created by an effect so subtle as to
be barely noticeable. In six short lines seven different kinds of verbal
grammar are used, not one the same as any other. Vocative address merges
into direct question; a simple indicative appeal prefaces the optative use of
'let'; the main clause 'I sought thee' translates into a question, which is
none the less posed in the form of a conditional 'if'. A miniature narrative
('A hollow winde') finishes abruptly with a negative exclamation, after
which the stanza ends with an imperative, 'Go seek', itself ambiguous, as it
delays resolution to some point in the unknown future. What is the variety
of grammar, punctuation, and phrase-length doing if not imitating a
process of thought? The reader is made to imitate the same faltering
rhythm of ratiocination: sudden questions and doubtful pauses, uncertain orders and meditative afterthought, assertive proposition and
self-reflexive counter-argument.

In this way theology comes to life as a way of feeling and as a language of
the self. Yet what marks out this language is the exact limits it places on the
sphere of the self. The relationship between self and God is always subject
to the peculiar economics of the gift. This is the message of 'Gratefulnesse':

> Thou hast giv'n so much to me,
>   Give one thing more, a gratefull heart.

Reciprocation of the gift of grace is pre-empted; even gratitude is denied as
a voluntary motion of the spirit. The gift cannot be bought back, it can
never be cashed in. Herbert plays with the terminology of quantity and of

---

[107] See Strier, *Love Known*, p. 84. Clarke, *Theory and Theology*, p. 185, comments 'it would
have been extraordinary if Herbert did not believe in double predestination'.

value, breaking the laws of supply and demand. Strictly, the gift is without limit:

> Gift upon gift, much would have more
> ('Gratefulnesse', l. 15)

Sin is a debit without end, a system incapable of being in credit. Perhaps the best example of this is 'The Holdfast':

> I threatned to observe the strict decree
> Of my deare God with all my power & might.
> But I was told by one, it could not be;
> Yet I might trust in God to be my light.
> Then will I trust, said I, in him alone.
> Nay, ev'n to trust in him, was also his:
> We must confesse that nothing is our own.
> (ll. 1–7)

Herbert's interlocutor presses him back on every point; whatever instinct of power or trust he has, he has been given. Then in an extraordinary moment of self-reflexiveness, even the acknowledgement of the givenness of the given is taken away from him. The idea is so odd that it is expressed in a tortuous double negative reminiscent of Hooker:

> Then I confesse that he my succour is:
> But to have nought is ours, not to confesse
> That we have nought.

For a moment Herbert admits himself baffled by his own movement of thought ('I stood amaz'd at this'). Even the confession of confession is a gift. This is a reflex with a whole century of theological thought behind it. Not only grace but the desire for grace, not only faith and repentance, but even the very instinct towards faith and repentance, in fact even the retrospective acknowledgement of the apprehension of faith or repentance, even this comes from elsewhere. In an equally characteristic seventeenth-century reflex, Herbert then states that it is only in this givenness that it can become his own: 'all things were more ours by being his'.

Protestant theology was searching for a language or logic that could encapsulate this central paradox. This can be seen, as the early chapters of this book showed, in the early Luther. The sinner is never made righteous, he is always being made righteous. Or, alternatively, the sinner is always righteous, but still always sinful. In one peculiar passage in the lectures on Romans, Luther states in a paradox that can almost be called a contradiction, that the sinner is just precisely at the moment when he knows that he is not just. These paradoxes are thrown out by Luther without resolution. The phrases are experimental, desperate measures to express the immeasurability of grace. It was left to Calvin and his followers to attempt to codify these reflections in a full theory of the gift. Yet in giving a rigorous logic to the idea, Calvinism also took terrible risks, making fully explicit the contradictions and aporia which Luther left as paradox. In reaction, those theologians and writers who have come to be known as anti-Calvinists rejected the full articulation of predestinatory theory.

Yet this did not resolve the tensions in protestant theology, or end the search for a language which could express the authenticity of grace. In occasional reflexes of syntax, Herbert attempted to capture what could hardly be captured. In a way which was never quite possible in academic theology, he subverted the ordinary rules of language to express the strangeness of the gift. In 'Deniall', he does it by the extra-linguistic means of rhyme: five stanzas of discord are ended with a last, unexpected parison. It is a moment of grace which happens outside language, almost outside the poem itself. In the sonnet 'Prayer (I)', he extends clause upon clause in order to suggest some effect of redemption, as if, in Simone Weil's words, to defy gravity. The casual reader may not notice, but the poem is a single sentence. It is a poem which never stops to take breath, which apparently exhausts the resources of its own language. It is also, strictly speaking, without closure: twenty-eight clauses are piled on one another, but there is no main verb. It is a poem without proper syntax, and a poem which stops without ending. In that sense it is a trope for the gift of grace.

8   Recusant Poetry

In June 1595, in the midst of the furore surrounding Barrett's sermon, the heads of the Cambridge Colleges wrote to Whitgift about a literary revival in catholicism:

> In these times instead of godly and sound writers, and among our stationers . . . there are not books more ordinarily bought and sold than popish writers; Jesuits, friars, postill writers, Stapleton, and such like . . . upon the search that was made by your Grace's appointment many divines' studies being searched there were found in diverse studies many friars', schoolmen's, Jesuits' writings and of protestants either few or none.[1]

It is a characteristic piece of puritan scare-mongering designed to persuade the archbishop that his cause and theirs was equivalent. However, Whitgift hardly needed reminding of the power of catholic literature. A literary campaign had been at the centre of efforts to keep alive the old faith for more than twenty years. The Elizabethan settlement originated with 'the great controversy', when John Jewel's Paul's Cross sermon of November 1559 challenged the catholics on twenty-six points extracted from scripture and the Fathers.[2] Jewel's 'Challenge Sermon' was answered initially by Thomas Harding, the former Regius professor of Hebrew and warden-elect of New College, Oxford.[3] Claim and counter-claim followed as both sides realized the power and significance of literary controversy. Another refugee from New College, Thomas Stapleton, entered the fray in 1562 with a translation of the work of one of the first converts back from Lutheranism to catholicism, to which Stapleton appended his own remarks on the 'fathers' of the protestants, Luther, Melanchthon, and Calvin. The titles of such works set the scene: Stapleton's *Fortresse of the Faith* brought forth Fulke's *Overthrow . . . to the feeble Fortresse*; a followup work elicited Stapleton's *Counterblast to M.Horne's Vayne Blaste*.[4]

It is hardly surprising the Cambridge heads singled out Stapleton by

---

[1] Heads to Whitgift, 12 June 1595, Trinity College, Cambridge, MS B.14.9, pp. 17–20.

[2] Southern, *Elizabethan Recusant Prose*, p. 59. Jewel's sermon was repeated at court in March and again at Paul's Cross shortly before Easter in 1560, in which year it was also printed.

[3] *Answere to Iuelles Chalenge*, STC 12758, ARCR 371.

[4] Milward, *Religious Controversies of the Elizabethan Age*, Nos. 30, 33, 36, 39.

name. When William Allen founded the English seminary at Douai, Stapleton was almost immediately made professor of religious controversy. Whitaker's name was particularly bound up with Stapleton's. In 1588, Whitaker published what was perhaps his major work, the *Disputatio de sacra scriptura*, a systematic refutation of catholic theology which had as prime targets Stapleton and Robert Bellarmine, Jesuit professor of the Gregorian university and later cardinal and Archbishop of Capua. Stapleton and Whitaker replied to each other in voluminous tomes at two-year intervals for the rest of Whitaker's life.[5] If from an English vantage point Whitaker has come to be seen as the senior contender, it should be remembered that by 1590 Stapleton had risen to the eminence of professor of scripture at Louvain. As such, he could be viewed as the most internationally prominent English theologian of his day. It was he who referred patronizingly to his adversary in 1592 as one 'not to be disregarded or despised', as he invited the countrymen of his small island to rejoin the mass of catholic Europe.[6]

As the remnants of catholic England settled themselves in for a long war, the literary field became perhaps the most important battle to win. While history has concentrated on the bloody story of missionary priests in hiding or on the scaffold, or else on the fate of those recusant families (high and low, although mostly high) whom they served, the leaders of the catholic exile movement clearly saw the printed word as a most potent weapon. This fourth estate of catholic England took three main forms. Controversy came first. As tales of martyrdom grew up, controversy gained a persuasive ally in a new literature of persecution. Beginning in 1581 with a work by the Jesuit leader Robert Persons, *De persecutione Anglicana*, this literature served a double function of moving the faithful to endurance and inspiring the apostate to conversion. It also had a controversial register in countering the claims of Foxe's famous *Actes and Monuments* to a true apostolic succession from the early Christian martyrs. A third form of literature was devotional, supplying breviaries, catechisms, and postills for liturgical use by recusants and, for missionary purposes, new genres of pious material.

Historians of both religion and of literature have been muted in their response to this material. Controversy and persecution play their part in debates about the dissemination of the English reformations. They have contributed to the understanding of recusancy and of that larger and more

---

[5] See ibid., Nos. 543–52.
[6] *Authoritatis ecclesiasticae*, ARCR 1142, p. 17 (*neutiquam etiam a nobis negligendus aut despectui habendus*).

ambiguous body of 'church papists'.[7] Literary history has been content to consider some devotional poems at the margins of protestant production. Much of this work has been left to the pietistic efforts of the Catholic Record Society and of historians of the Jesuits and other movements.[8] It has been less easy to formulate a different kind of understanding, one that encompasses all kinds of literary production as part of the same movement, and that pays attention to the interaction of diverse confessions and opposing beliefs.

I ROBERT SOUTHWELL'S TEARS

In 1595, perhaps in March, a slim volume appeared from the press, which still baffles conventional literary categories.[9] It consists outwardly of a prose letter of dedication and of fourteen poems. Of these poems, one is a further dedication 'To the Reader', the second is the title poem of the collection—the long narrative *Saint Peters Complaint*—and the rest are short lyrics. The subject-matter of the poems is apparently uncontentious and edifying. And yet there is something immediately uncanny about the book. The title page bears the name of the printer but not of the author. Bibliographers know the reason for the absence, but have been reluctant to treat that absence as itself a sign. The author is hidden but revealed obliquely as a clandestine presence.

It cannot now be known how many of the original readers of *Saint Peters Complaint* knew it as the work of Robert Southwell. Yet his erased signature is the most noteworthy feature of a book that is in any case far more significant than it seems.[10] Southwell was hanged, quartered, and disembowelled for treason as a Jesuit priest at Tyburn on 21 February 1595. It was a sensational event. From the admittedly hagiographical account that survives in an Italian manuscript letter by Henry Garnet, we can take it that the execution moved its protestant audience, as well as Southwell's fugitive coreligionists, to excited sympathy and admiration.[11] The small volume of poems makes a subtler memorial of the dead poet, which also marks something of a rewriting of the rules of martyrdom. This literary

---

[7] See Walsham, *Church Papists*; and Questier, *Conversion in England*.

[8] A recent exception is Shell's *Catholicism and the English Literary Imagination*.

[9] *Saint Peters Complaint, With Other Poemes*, STC 22955.7.

[10] Shell, *English Literary Imagination*, p. 63, speculates that the semi-anonymity of the book may be 'a collusion between officialdom, publisher and public'.

[11] Southwell's execution is recorded in Stow, *Chronicles*, p. 443. Garnet's letter is cited at length in Janelle, *Robert Southwell the Writer*, pp. 86–91.

survival brings with it a life beyond death to match the deathless tale of heroism embodied in the more traditional narrative of martyrological history. The body of the saint is memorialized in the saint's own book. Southwell's book is prepared for more than one readership, and it appeals to its readers in more than one way. Straightforwardly devotional in content, the poems none the less suggest beyond themselves, without directly uttering it, the persecutory context of the poet's death. The title poem, and the two poems that first follow, 'Mary Magdalens Blush' and 'Marie Magdalens complaint at Christs death', concern Christ's passion. This is not the order found in any of the surviving manuscripts of Southwell's poems.[12] It is part of the effort of his posthumous editors to present him to the world in the light of his martyrdom. The sequence of poems in the printed edition alludes to the central act of martyrdom in the Christian tradition. Yet rather than meditate directly on the moment of heroic death, they refer obliquely to its prelude and aftermath, in the experience not of Christ himself but of his bystanders and disciples. In this way, they speak also to the bystanders and potential disciples of the poet's passion at Tyburn.

In a similar way, the Petrine context of the volume also brings the reader into the metaphorical context of the church of Peter without making the connection too obvious. Indeed in several ways the volume deliberately eschews any direct association with catholicism. All of the poems in the manuscripts that make flagrant reference to catholic liturgy or sacraments are excluded. This shows the way in which catholic literature had learned to display the subtle arts as well as the strong-arm tactics of Persons and other early practitioners. Southwell's poems aim to convert by not protesting too much. This enabled them to evade the censor and be printed in London.[13] They also quickly found an avid London market. A second edition by Wolfe followed shortly after the first, making textual revisions and adding eight new poems. In April, Gabriel Cawood obtained the copyright and entered what was now the third edition of *Saint Peters Complaint* in the Stationer's Register.[14] In an act which appears ironic in the light of the complaints in puritan Cambridge two months later, ecclesiastical licence for this book by a sectarian traitor was granted by Abraham

---

[12] The MSS are described in McDonald and Brown's Textual Introduction to Southwell's *Poems*, pp. xxxvi–lv, and the order of the lyrics on pp. xcii–ix. The long narrative title-poem is found in only two, imperfect MSS, in each case as a separate item. Wolfe's decision to place it so prominently is original to him (p. liii).

[13] Clegg, *Press Censorship in Elizabethan England*, p. 80, nevertheless fails to note that the author's name is omitted and the contents of the book tailored for a protestant readership.

[14] *Saint Peters complaynt. With other Poems*, STC 22956.

Hartwell, Whitgift's secretary. In October, another volume was entered in the Stationer's Register by John Busby. *Maeoniae*, whose classical title makes its poet a new Lydian lyric genius, contains a fresh collection culled from Southwell's manuscripts not covered by Cawood's licence.[15] Once again, overtly Roman subjects are excluded. Three early editions of this collection survive, all bearing the date 1595. The date in the latter two editions probably does not reflect the truth, but shows the way in which all these collections are strongly connected in the public imagination with the calendar year of Southwell's martyrdom.

Cawood made three further editions of *Saint Peters Complaint*, in 1597, 1599, and 1602. There was also a Scottish edition by Robert Waldegrave of Edinburgh, probably in 1599.[16] The fact that this volume bears the insignia Cum Privilegio Regio, and Waldegrave's position as printer to James VI, shows how successfully this clandestine material found patronage in orthodox protestant circles. Whereas Southwell's literary achievement was once discussed in an exclusively counter-Reformation context, the assimilation of Southwell's devotional verse into protestant culture deserves some comment. There are different aspects to this. Southwell was a missionary, and his entire life was dedicated to his mission. He did not write poems for his own or for others' recreation: he aimed to convert. Southwell therefore consciously used modes of writing that would be likely to appeal to an as yet unconverted audience. Devotional verse was not a common genre when Southwell was writing. His poems therefore answered a need. Yet he made them, and his editors shaped them within a structure, that was acceptable to protestant taste, and even designed with their concerns in mind.

This may explain how *Saint Peters Complaint*, and also his prose meditation *Marie Magdalens Funerall Teares*, passed the censors so comfortably. The *Funerall Teares* were published in Southwell's lifetime, and entered in the Stationer's Register on 8 November 1591.[17] The title page bears the initials S.W., which, while hardly open, are openly coded. It has been described as somewhat surprising that the approval of the Archbishop of Canterbury was granted at the same time as Topcliffe and the pursuivants were hunting down the author with a view to torturing him to find out his beliefs.[18] Yet there was no reason why Whitgift or his secretaries would not find these works spiritually edifying. Elizabeth herself,

---

[15] *Maeoniae; or, Certaine excellent Poems and spirituall Hymnes*, STC 22955.
[16] *Saint Peters Complaint. With other Poems*, STC 22960.
[17] Under the name of 'master Cawood'; Arber, *Stationers' Register*, ii. 598 (STC 22950).
[18] Janelle, *Robert Southwell the Writer*, p. 146.

at least anecdotally, is said to have read and admired one or other of these books.[19]

The common theme of Southwell's two longest devotional works was repentance. Repentance, of course, was a persistent point of difference in controversies between confessional groups in the sixteenth century. However, the two sides of the argument led to mutual influence as well as public antipathy. The weight given to the anthropology of inwardness in post-Tridentine catholicism was a tribute in its way to the arch-enemy Luther. Southwell's long narratives of contrition, with their soliloquies of personal crisis, are strongly part of this tradition. Both are modelled on continental and particularly Italian precedents. Luigi Tansillo's *Le Lagrime di San Piero* was published in Venice in 1560. It was widely imitated throughout the century: one of the last works of Orlando Lassus is a cycle of seven-voice spiritual madrigals taken from Tansillo.[20] In 1587 an edition of Tansillo was produced in Genoa which also included Erasmo da Valvasone's *Le Lagrime di S. Maria Maddalena*. Valvasone's work formed the basis for Southwell's *Funerall Teares*. There were many other works in this 'literature of tears'. Having originated in a need to counter Reformation forms of spirituality, this catholic literature in turn filled a gap among protestants: Southwell's books of tears were widely imitated by English protestant poets.[21] Indeed, it has been pointed out that Calvinism had produced hardly any narratives of Christ's passion.[22] Calvinist England, while always alert to any whiff of popery, proved a receptive home for a literature of sentiment which it could not produce for itself.

In this way, the literary relationship between Calvinism and catholicism is much more complex than meets the eye. This in turn shows how the religious culture of post-Reformation Europe, and particularly of England, has been divided too rigidly according to sectarian principles. The tradition of literary complaint—in which St Peter is represented as expressing contrition for his past—was in some ways part of a counter-Reformation movement to express atonement for the sins of the catholic past. Southwell as a careful missionary was aware of this conciliatory message to his protestant flock. While he excoriated his countrymen for any conformity with the divine services or liturgy of the schismatic Church of

---

[19] She is reported in a text of 1599 (Yepes, *La persecucion de Inglaterra*, p. 647), *de auer visto vn libro que auia compuesto el mismo Padre de diuersos pios y deuotos argumentos en lengua Inglesa.*

[20] Lassus dedicated the music to Pope Clement VIII shortly before he died; published posthumously in Munich in 1595.

[21] Shell, *Catholicism and the English Literary Imagination*, p. 80.

[22] Shuger, *Renaissance Bible*, p. 89.

England, he also wanted to convert them back.[23] To do so, he had to understand their language. This chapter will describe the literature of repentance created by Southwell, and will place it in the context of the Tridentine arguments about justification in the wake of the Lutheran heresy. In the process, it will try to show how controversy and piety meet half way, and how a vexed language of the psychology of the will permeates both sides of the theological debate. Whereas it would be foolish—especially in the light of Southwell's own excruciating death—to underestimate the differences between the polemical positions of catholic and protestant, this does not mean that the intellectual and linguistic problems were not a shared inheritance in the path of controversy.

The structure of inwardness in the literature of repentance practised by Southwell had a number of different sources. Here, it is necessary to examine the special circumstances of his education. His family background shows mixed signals of religious affiliation. His grandfather, Sir Richard Southwell, a typical Henrician courtier, made money out of the dissolution of the monasteries. Under Elizabeth, on the other hand, his father, uncle, and two of his brothers were suspected of recusancy. Yet they did not appear on the rolls of recusants in 1592–3, and his father conformed enough to enjoy some favour at court. It is not known, therefore, exactly what propelled Robert at the age of 14 into a life of exile and an education in catholic seminaries overseas. By this time catholics were barred from taking degrees at Oxford and Cambridge. Southwell arrived at Douai in June 1576, and enrolled in university studies at the English College. He did not complete his education there, however, and went on to Paris and later to Rome, where he had arrived by December 1581. In Paris, Southwell became a novitiate in the Jesuit order; in Rome, he studied at the Jesuit university (called the Roman College), soon renamed the Pontifical Gregorian university. He was ordained priest around June 1584. In 1586 he set out with Henry Garnet on his fatal mission back to his native country, arriving in London on 18 July.

The Society of Jesus provided a complex pedagogic context for the literary identity Southwell developed in his maturity. It taught a distinct moral theology and philosophy of religion, as will be discussed later in the chapter. It also promoted a peculiar form of interior piety. This amounted to an education in the passions. The *Spiritual Exercises* of the order's founder, Ignatius Loyola, is one of the most influential books in the history of Christian practice. Ignatius's work embodied a holistic

---

[23] For Southwell's views on conformity, see Walsham, *Church Papists*, pp. 33 and 44.

approach to the life of religion, a discipline for the body, for the emotions, and for the mind. It utilized a complex theory of somatics and of psychology, and made that somatics and that psychology, in the practice of the experienced religious, a matter of performative instinct. There is no doubt of Southwell's personal investment in this method: a manuscript survives in Brussels of Southwell's own adapted version of spiritual exercises.[24]

The literary life of Ignatian method was made the object of a full study by Louis Martz in *The Poetry of Meditation*. Martz created a picture in which literary form and religious practice were united. Southwell performed a crucial role in his book as a founder of this art and as a model for Donne and Herbert, whose work is claimed as the pinnacle of the meditative method. Ignatian psychological theory—with its trinity of memory, understanding, and will—is made into a template for a comprehensive literary praxis. Martz's approach, although somewhat narrow in its application, explains well the odd combination of argument and passion that runs through Southwell, Donne, and Herbert.[25] More generally, Ignatian method provides Southwell with a whole range of techniques for constructing inwardness, which appear again and again in his short lyrics and his longer meditations.

Indeed, the Jesuit example also provided Southwell with a more direct motivation for the expression of inwardness in poetry and other literary forms. Unlike many religious movements, the Jesuits actively encouraged acts of literature. As the first of the post-humanist orders, the Society introduced a reformed syllabus more easily than the Dominicans or Franciscans, with their long-standing structures based on scholastic principles. The *Ratio studiorum*, which organized the levels of study for Jesuit schools and universities, and was also used in the preparation of the novitiate, encompassed a full flowering of Renaissance humanism.[26] The study of the classics was regarded as an aid in the propagation of the faith.[27] Although now famous for its ascetic forms of piety, the early Jesuits were just as noted in their day for the cultivation of style and culture. This is one of the features they had in common with Calvinism: for Ignatius, like Calvin, saw no contradiction between rigorous humanism and rigorous

---

[24] *Exercitia et deuotiones R.P. Roberti Sotwelli*, Brussels, Bibliothèque Royale MS 5618.

[25] For a revised view of Martz, taking into account protestant meditative traditions, see Lewalski, *Protestant Poetics*, pp. 147–8.

[26] The *Ratio studiorum* was formally introduced in 1581, late in Southwell's education, but its principles were developed from the beginnings of the order in the 1550s.

[27] Examples from Jesuit syllabuses in Germany in the 1560s may be found in *Ratio studiorum*, ed. by Pachtler, in *Monumenta Germaniae Paedagogica*, ii. 163, 195, 209–10, 213–14.

theology. The *Ratio* reserved its most profound distaste for any manifestation of 'barbarity'.

Humanism was taught both at the Collège de Clermont, where Southwell studied in Paris, and at the Roman College. In Rome, Franciscus Bencius, who lectured on eloquence, rhetoric, and classical literature, may have taught him poetry. Bencius wrote on poetic theory as well as rhetoric.[28] It is quite possible, in fact, that Southwell was encouraged to think of poetry as part of his training and mission. Poetry was not only legitimate in Jesuit eyes, it was one of the foremost arts of instruction and persuasion. A number of Jesuit treatises at this time, such as Jacobus Pontanus's *Poeticae Institutiones*, published in 1594, extolled poetry as an aid in moral development and even religious conversion. Janelle suggests that Pontanus's literary theory was too constrained for Southwell, and that its rigid didacticism allowed too little for the expression of the self, but he perhaps expects the wrong kind of argument in a poetic treatise. The literary models encouraged by the Jesuit theorists—which included Catullus and Lucretius as well as the more obvious Virgil—allowed Southwell surprising latitude in the cultivation of emotional expressiveness.[29] Jesuit neo-classicism also provided Southwell with a ready method for applying the registers of erotic poetry to a religious purpose.

In this regard, Southwell followed the tenets of Italian poets such as Tansillo. Southwell's grasp of the Italian language was fluent and idiomatic, and he was an avid reader of Italian vernacular poetry. Petrarch was his main model here. As the master of the conceited style, and of a complex language of the self, Petrarch showed how the Jesuit ideal of emotional inwardness could be realized in poetic form. This also gave Southwell a clue as to how to apply his art in the English vernacular, since Petrarchism was the dominant mode of mid-century English verse. In some cases— such as his versions of two poems by Dyer—Southwell can be seen applying his method in deliberate exercises of sacred parody. Dyer's love lyrics are transliterated phrase by phrase into litanies of the religious self.

As an example, let us consider the techniques of inwardness in one of Southwell's short lyrics, 'Sinnes heavie loade':

> O prostrate Christ, erect my crooked minde,
> Lord let thy fall my flight from earth obtaine;
> Or if I still in earth must needes be shrinde,

---

[28] *Orationes et carmina* contains two orations on poetry (Nos. 7 and 8); the book also contains a treatise *De stylo* (pp. 404–24).

[29] *Orationes et carmina*, pp. 117–19.

> Then Lord on earth come fall yet once againe:
> And eyther yeeld with me in earth to lie,
> Or else with thee to take me to the skie.
> (ll. 37–42)[30]

The poem's self-reproach issues not in self-pity but in submission. This movement is apparent in the first couplet of the poem:

> O Lord my sinne doth over-charge thy brest,
> The poyse thereof doth force thy knees to bow;
> (ll. 1–2)

There is a subtle realignment of pronouns here. 'My sinne' we expect to 'over-charge' *my* 'brest'; but instead it is 'thy brest' (Christ's) that is overloaded: what might be self-dramatizing soliloquy is redeemed as confession. Confession, however, may not be sufficient, for the poem ends with an unsatisfied exclamation of anxiety. We are thus faced with the question of what change of devotional feeling there is between the first and last stanzas.

Martz sees the poem as a three-fold structure, consisting of 'acts of composition and memory' (stanzas 1–2), followed by 'formal, theological analysis of the scene' (stanzas 3–6), resulting, in the last stanza, in a 'colloquy (petition)'. Martz thus views the poem as 'under the influence of methods of meditation'.[31] One might take issue, none the less, with his 'impression of a "predetermined plan"'. This fails to take account of the gap between the undemonstrative excogitation of the penultimate stanza, and the cry of distress which opens the last.

The phrase ' "predetermined plan" ' underestimates the emotive threat to meditation involved in the 'cry'

> O prostrate Christ, erect my crooked minde,

The cry, 'O' runs against the grain of the analysis that has gone before, or strains to confirm it, rather than enthusiastically halloos it. A similar reservation could be attached to Martz's characterization of the last stanza of the companion poem 'Christs sleeping friends', as 'simultaneously . . . colloquy . . . and . . . exhortation':

> Alas the glorie of your arbor dies,
> Arise and guarde the comforte of your lives.
> (ll. 39–40)

---

[30] All quotations from Southwell's verse are from *Poems*, ed. by McDonald and Brown.
[31] *Poetry of Meditation*, pp. 41–3.

'O Lord' and 'Alas' are supplications that cry for mercy. These cries are acts of submission and expressions of weakness. The poems make a 'formal, theological analysis' of the grounds for remorse; but remorse itself is expressed not in reasoned 'colloquy', but in a loud and inarticulate utterance of grief or pain. A cry is not meant, but barely voiced: at best it registers a consciousness of sin, rather than a 'theological analysis' of sinfulness.

This question of the grounds for remorse, both in a theological and a devotional sense, occupies a central place in Southwell's work, and especially in the successive versions of *Saint Peters Complaint* and the prose *Marie Magdalens Funerall Teares*. There is a clear connection between these two longest of Southwell's non-controversial works, and Nancy Pollard Brown argues that they may have been prepared for distribution at the same time, although *Saint Peters Complaint* was probably written over a number of years.[32] Brown sees *Saint Peters Complaint* as 'embodying the Catholic doctrine of penance as defined at the Council of Trent, which explicitly stated that when no priest was available reconciliation with God might be obtained through perfect contrition'.[33] Brown comments that this doctrine was of special significance to the recusant community of English catholics.

Brown is referring to Session XIV of the Council of Trent, concerning the Sacraments of Penance and Extreme Unction, the decree of which was delivered on 25 November 1551. Contrition is defined in Cap. 4 as *animi dolor ac detestatio . . . de peccato commisso, cum proposito non peccandi de cetero* ('a sorrow of mind and a detestation for sin committed, with the purpose of not sinning in the future').[34] The impulse to 'sorrow of mind' is clearly in evidence at the beginning of *Saint Peters Complaint*, where St Peter urges his soul:

> Divorc'd from grace thy soule to pennance wed.
>
> (l. 10)

However, interest in penitence in the poem goes beyond the practical difficulties 'when no priest was available'. The doctrine of penance, set out in Session XIV at Trent, has to be understood in the broader context of the whole process of justification, as set out in the famous Session VI of 13 January 1547. In effect, Session XIV is an extended footnote to the pro-

---

[32] *Poems*, Introduction, p. xc.

[33] Introduction, pp. lxxviii–ix. Her argument is expanded in 'Structure of "Saint Peter's Complaint"'.

[34] *ES*, §1672; Eng.tr. Schroeder, *Council of Trent*, p. 91. Further references in text.

ceedings of 1546–7, which were recognized at the time to be the most important theological debate of the whole council.[35] The wording of the chapter on contrition clearly originates in Cap. 6 of Session VI, which discusses the *odium aliquod et detestationem* (*ES* §1526) of the sinner towards his sin, and in Cap. 14, which presents in outline the sacrament of penance itself.

II REPENTANCE AND JUSTIFICATION AT THE COUNCIL OF TRENT

The question raised in *Saint Peters Complaint* is not limited to the sacramental value of penance. The poem treats of the whole nature of the 'disposition' of the sinner, and his 'preparation' for grace, a subject central to Session VI at Trent. These questions were among those first proposed for discussion by the General Congregation in June 1546.[36] The theologians were asked to consider, among other problems, how much of the cause of justification was to be attributed to God's part, and how much to man's. In addition, how the process of justification was envisaged to take place— what was felt to precede, accompany, and follow the act of justification in the sinner. Repentance is a part of this process, but how large a part, and whether the feeling was initiated by the sinner or inculcated in him by God, was open to question.

The question at issue can be seen in the sentence following the definition of contrition in Cap. 4 of Session XIV:

Fuit autem quovis tempore ad impetrandam veniam peccatorum hic contritionis motus necessarius

[This feeling of contrition was at all times necessary for obtaining the forgiveness of sins (*ES* § 1676. Schroeder, p. 91)]

The decree goes on to declare that contrition *praeparat ad remissionem peccatorum* ('prepares . . . for the remission of sins'). Such statements, magisterially made, none the less rely on controversial assumptions. Significant among these are the idea that the sinner has the power himself to 'prepare' for the remission of his sins; that some *motus* of his own is even

---

[35] See the report of the leaders of the Council to Rome, 21 June 1546: 'The significance of this Council in the theological sphere lies chiefly in the article on justification'; quoted in Jedin, *History of the Council of Trent*, ii. 171.

[36] See Jedin, ii. 175–6. Jedin's analysis of justification at Trent is modified by Fenlon, *Heresy and Obedience*, pp. 127–30.

'necessary' for forgiveness; and that his own action is capable of 'obtaining' grace at all. The controversy surrounding these ideas is described succinctly by Hubert Jedin at the beginning of his account of the Decree of Justification. For it is a premiss of Luther's account of the process of justification that the sinner, enslaved as he is to sin, is 'incapable of any kind of active co-operation' in his salvation, and that he cannot 'actively concur with grace' (p. 170).

In this way Luther envisages the sinner to be 'passive' to the action of grace. In its strict sense this involves psychological difficulties which the prelates at Trent were quick to notice. But it is worth attending first to Luther's reasons for going so far as to deny 'any kind of active co-operation', for they included principles just as important to the catholic theologians as to the protestants. As Jedin puts it, 'The absolute gratuitousness of justification was and always remained the basic concern of Luther's religion' (p. 170). But 'gratuitousness' was a notion also precious to the catholic tradition of Augustine. Jedin expresses the problem at Trent in this way: 'In order to counter this notion, catholic theologians were bound to own that, according to their teaching, the sinner is incapable of crossing, by his own strength, the chasm created by sin between himself and God' (p. 170). The difficulty arises in the force attached to the phrase 'incapable of crossing'. Does this incapacity, the blindness of sin, mean merely an inability by natural powers alone to obtain salvation, or does it mean an absolute powerlessness, which negates even the possibility of the sinner's disposing himself for salvation, or co-operating, once given the aid of grace, in that salvation?

Essentially there are three ways in which the preparation of the sinner for justification might be conceived. First, the process might be invited, initiated, or else operated by the sinner himself. Secondly, at the other extreme, justification might be thought to be a process that simply happens to him, in which the sinner is 'merely passive', like the clay of a potter. Thirdly, seemingly as a medium between the extremes, justification could be a process to which the sinner actively consents, and in which he co-operates, even though he does not initiate the process, still less can be said to be its 'agent'.

In practice the first of these positions is adopted only by heretics, and most obviously by Pelagius. However, co-operation is also often confused with operation, partly because in neither case is the will conceived to be 'merely passive'. But another reason why these two positions might be confused is because of the attribution of merit. If co-operation or consent is necessary to salvation, then it seems to be deserving of merit, since it clearly distinguishes the justified from the reprobate. In this case it appears to be co-operation that is the operative agent, since grace is offered to both saved and damned, but only accepted by the saved.

The problem comes to a head in the phrase eventually used at Trent, that repentance is 'necessary for obtaining the forgiveness of sins'. If repentance is 'necessary', then it appears that grace can only operate on condition of some response of the human will. This conditional is of great importance.

Vitam enim in Deo quaerit, quae non in mandatis, aut poenarum edictis, sed misericordiae promissione reperitur, eaque nonnisi gratuita: quoniam conditionalis, qua ad opera nostra remittimur, non aliter vitam promittit, quam si perspiciamus esse in nobis sitam.   (Calvin, *Institutio*, 3, 2, 29)

[For in God faith seeks life: a life that is not found in commandments or declarations of penalties, but in the promise of mercy, and only in a freely given promise. For a conditional promise that sends us back to our own works does not promise us life unless we discern its presence in ourselves.   (p. 575)]

According to Calvin's account, the two terms *gratuita* and *conditionalis* are mutually exclusive: what is freely given can have no condition attached to its being given. The commandment that contrition is 'necessary' appears to apply just such a condition, one that is antecedent to grace, since contrition *praeparat ad remissionem peccatorum*. The reference to *opera nostra* conforms to the commonplace of Reformation controversy that catholic dogma did 'send us back' to our works, and that this was contrary to the sense of a promise 'freely given'. However, the Council of Trent also confirmed the idea of the 'gratuitous' gift of God:

Si quis hoc Adae peccatum . . . vel per humanae naturae vires, vel per aliud remedium asserit tolli, quam per meritum unius mediatoris Domini nostri Iesu Christi . . . anathema sit.   (*ES* 1513)

[If anyone asserts that this sin of Adam . . . is taken away either by the forces of human nature, or by any other remedy than the merit of the one mediator, our Lord Jesus Christ . . . let him be anathema   (p. 22)]

This decree is from Session V of June 1546, concerning original sin. The language has changed from Calvin's expression of 1539, which signifies an eschatological promise (*misericordiae promissione*), to the more catholic description of the atonement implicit in the phrase *per meritum unius mediatoris*. Nevertheless, the two statements are in agreement over the question of an unconditional promise, without respect to what we 'discern in ourselves' as the 'forces of human nature'.

The following discussion considers closely the first four canons of justification from Session VI in the context of the lengthy and complex discussions which preceded the decree, and which are recounted in Hubert Jedin's history. Firstly, we note the clear opposition between Calvin's statement above, and the new Canon 4 of January 1547:

Si quis dixerit, liberum arbitrium a Deo motum et excitatum nihil cooperari assentiendo Deo excitanti atque vocanti, quo ad obtinendam iustificationis gratiam se disponat ac praeparet . . . anathema sit.   (*ES* 1554).

[If anyone says that man's free will moved and aroused by God, by assenting to God's call and action, in no way cooperates towards disposing and preparing itself to obtain the grace of justification . . . let him be anathema   (p. 42)]

Calvin's argument would seem to imply that Canon 4 is itself in contradiction of the decree on original sin quoted above. To argue the 'cooperation of the will' in assenting to grace is to introduce a condition into the action of grace, since without this prior assent grace is understood not to operate.

Need the two statements be seen in simple contradiction, however? 'Not by force of human nature' does not necessarily infer 'without any cooperating effort of human nature'. This is the reasoning implied in Canon 1 of the same session: the co-operating will is not operative of grace, but only concomitant with it. Human nature has no power on its own, the argument runs, but its assent assists a process already begun.

The extent and nature of the co-operation of man's free will in his justification was, in any case, a source of some difficulty at Trent. Four theologians in the original discussions held the will to be purely passive to grace. Although suspected of Lutheran influence, at least one of them—Gregory of Siena—was a strict Thomist.[37] A more representative opinion in the early congregations, on the other hand, was that of the Scotist Musso on 9 July 1546, who declared (in direct opposition to Luther) that 'the faith spoken of by St. Paul resulted from the cooperation of grace and freedom'.[38] However, when the legate Cardinal Cervini drew up a draft of the decree at the end of August, with the assistance of Cardinal Seripando (general of the Augustinians), the substance of man's role was changed considerably from the decisions of July.[39] Good works done without faith were said 'not in any way' to 'contribute to justification'. The exposition of man's freedom is reduced to a terse statement of 'the concurrence of grace and the human will'. Whereas the July draft 'clearly declared life eternal to

---

[37] The four theologians comprised two Augustinians, a Dominican, and a Servite; Jedin, *History of the Council of Trent*, ii. 177.

[38] Ibid., 186.

[39] The new draft is referred to by Jedin as preliminary draft B, ii. 241.

be the reward of merit', Cervini's new draft 'describes it as a favour promised and a reward due to us'.

In the opinion of Jedin, this new draft 'breathed the spirit of the bible and Augustine and was formulated in their words' (p. 241). But the revisions made to this draft in the early days of September, in consultation with other theologians, resulting in the so-called September draft, once again shifted the emphasis. The major alteration, according to Jedin, is that 'the contribution of the human factor in the preparation for justification is more positively assessed' (p. 243). One reason for this is the effort to differentiate the catholic from the Lutheran conception of justification. Nevertheless, the new draft was clearer than its predecessors and was generally approved; Jedin praises its 'high quality' (p. 246). The November draft made only stylistic changes in this respect and in turn was adopted in substantially the same form in the final decree of 13 January 1547.

Some of these shifts of emphasis are reflected in the eventual wording of the decree itself. The decree on original sin in Session V, quoted above, is restated in the first canon of the new session, but with an important difference:

Si quis dixerit, hominem suis operibus, quae vel per humanae naturae vires, vel per Legis doctrinam fiant, absque divina per Christum Iesum gratia posse iustificari coram Deo: anathema sit (ES 1551).

[If anyone says that man can be justified before God by his own works, whether by his own natural powers or through the teaching of the law, without divine grace through Jesus Christ, let him be anathema (p. 42)]

The difference between the new canon and the decree of Session V is less explicit than implicit. There are clear repetitions of phrasing, for instance in *humanae naturae vires*. None the less, the new wording is written from the point of view of the limits of the power of man, rather than from the point of view of the saving power of God to remit sin. The earlier decree insists that the *humanae naturae vires* are useless, and that sin cannot be removed *per aliud remedium . . . quam* ('by a remedy other than') the merit of Christ. However, the new phrasing *absque divina . . . gratia* ('without divine grace') only stipulates that *humanae . . . vires* are ineffectual on their own, and thus require the aid of divine grace. It is this distinction between 'powerless in any event' and 'ineffectual on their own', which allows the idea of co-operation embodied in Canon 4 of Session VI.

The operation of grace is still necessary under these terms to effect justification, but is it thereby unconditional? Trent asserts that grace is gratuitous 'because none of the things which precede justification, whether faith or works, merit the grace itself of justification', going on to quote, brazenly it seems, the Pauline text which stood as the emblem of protestant opposition, 'else grace is no more grace' (Romans 11: 6). However, as we saw earlier, Calvin argues that *gratuita* is equivalent to *non conditionalis*. The question posed is whether the sentence structure of the Tridentine statement amounts grammatically to a conditional proposition. Clearly, in the decree on original sin it does not: 'by any other remedy than the merit of . . . Christ' implies 'without respect to human action'. But the phrase in the first canon of justification, 'without the aid of divine grace', implies in reverse some part may be played by man. Canon 4 goes further than this: since it is possible to refuse grace, assent (in the minimal sense of the absence of refusal) is a necessary part of the preparation of grace. The will in this case is not 'merely passive' to God's will but is a participatory agent of grace.

There is an obvious danger implicit in this logic, one foreseen and prepared for in Canon 2. This denies that grace acts only 'that man may be able more easily to live justly . . . as if by free will without grace he is able to do both, though with hardship and difficulty'. The qualification does not quite cover the case however. The Pelagian formula denied in Canon 1, 'by free will without grace', is not the only possible inference from 'able more easily to live justly'. Calvin argued that putting assent alongside grace in the process of justification makes assent a second necessary term. In this sense, grace does make the will 'able more easily to live justly', albeit in the stronger sense of 'not without the aid of'. For equally, grace acts 'not without the aid of' the assent of the will. Co-operation, according to Calvin's logic, entails that there are two necessary conditions of justification. Free will cannot act on its own, but neither can grace; therefore grace is 'conditional' and not 'gratuitous'.

The canons and decrees do not involve a logical contradiction. The assertion that the human will cannot justify itself by its own powers alone does not imply that no impulse of the human will is involved. Yet although there is no logical contradiction there are contrary impulses at work within the same Chapter. Cap. 5 first asserts that the beginning of justification 'must proceed from the predisposing grace of God . . .' (p. 31). Cap. 5 further explains that justification proceeds *ab eius vocatione, qua nullis eorum existentibus meritis vocantur* ('from this vocation, whereby, without any merits on their part, they are called' (*ES* 1525; p. 31). Yet in the space of the same sentence, the passive construction (*ab eius vocatione . . . vocantur*) is abandoned for the active description of the sinners converting themselves 'to their own justification by freely assenting to and cooperating with that grace' (pp. 31–2). No sooner has the assertion of grace been uttered, than the anticipated imbalance is corrected by a restatement of the function of the will. The Augustinian strain is tempered by the Scotist modulation. But if there is an ambiguity here, between 'being called' and 'convert themselves', it is deliberate. Jedin concurs with Loofs in finding the decree ' "clear and precise" ' in points of essence, but ' "ambiguous and obscure from sheer caution" ' when dealing with the divergent opinions of the Schools (p. 309).

Inevitably this caution could not satisfy all parties, although all parties declared themselves satisfied. There thus remains a tension within the decree itself, a tension which matches the perennial difficulty in the doctrine of grace of reconciling the freedom of God with the freedom of man. Such tensions do not exist only on an intellectual level, however, but involve the whole structure of religious devotion. As Jedin says of Seripando, when he argued the case for 'two-fold justice': 'For Seripando these questions were no mere problems of technical theology; his discourse, perfect as to its literary form, quivered with all the subdued passion of a man fighting for the life of his spirit' (p. 248). Seripando to some extent moderated his public opinions; he confided only to his diary that he felt the treatment of merit in the final November draft to be ' "lavish and generous in extolling good works" ' and yet ' "niggardly and sparing in proclaiming God's grace" '.[40]

When he came to deliver his own discourse to the congregation on 26–7 November, his words, as Jedin describes, had the tone of a lost cause, but Jedin sees him as fighting for 'toleration of his own piety' (p. 287). For Seripando's conception of the power of grace was for him a matter of private piety as well as intellectual conviction. Significantly, his misgivings about the language of merit originate in an appeal to the prayers of the liturgy as well as in his reading of Augustine, Bernard of Clairvaux, and Aquinas:

'Does not the Church', he asked, 'pray thus at the obsequies of the dead: "Enter not into judgment with thy servant, O Lord, for no man is justified before thee, unless thou grant him remission of his sins"?' (Jedin, *History of the Council Trent*, ii. 287).

The accent of this cry 'Enter not into judgement with thy servant, O Lord', is a long way from the positive assertion of the co-operating assent of man's will. When Seripando came to suggest amendments to the November draft, he had in mind those who could not find in themselves that

---

[40] Quoted ibid., 285. Seripando's understanding of justification is reassessed by Marranzini, 'Il problema della giustificazione'.

inherent charity which Trent went on to describe as the sanctifying effect of grace. Such people were conscious of 'not having acted with such fervour or charity as to have complied with the commandments of God and thereby merited eternal life'. Seripando wished it to be written into the decree that such a person 'repent and call upon God's mercy'.[41] The wording of the Augustinian General puts us in mind of the cries of distress at the felt recognition of sin which interrupt Southwell's penitential poems. The personal admission of powerlessness seems a far cry from the theological explanation of co-operation.

These activities at Trent have been dealt with at length because they show both how difficult this subject was felt to be, and how much latitude of opinion was given even among the arbiters of orthodoxy. Indeed, in 1541, Seripando's associate Cardinal Contarini had agreed a formula on justification with protestant theologians including Melanchthon and Bucer at Regensburg.[42] This rapprochement came to an end after the death of Juán de Valdes at Naples in 1541, followed by Contarini himself a year later. The *spirituali* then declined in influence.[43] Trent reflects a new entrenchment of division, but it also shows continuing tension. The personal dilemma of Seripando shows the depth of feeling at stake in decisions about justification. The theological explanation of justification adumbrated the sinner's own conception of himself. Each stage of the process described by the decree at Trent (the detestation of sin (contrition), the appeal to God for mercy, the forgiveness for sin supplied by grace, the subsequent infusion of sanctifying charity, and the gradual accretion of personal justice in the reborn sinner) involves a complex psychological as well as theological problem.

III CONFESSIONAL POETRY

Saint Peters Complaint held pride of place in Southwell's corpus in his own time, but it has become resistant to modern readers, especially in comparison to the short lyrics. Formally and emotionally it can seem an alien work. Yet there is one feature which is so modern that it is possible to fail to register the originality which it once possessed. This is that the poem from the start is expressed in the first person. What is noticeable in this early stanza is the repeated use of the personal pronoun 'I':

---

[41] Quoted ibid., 288.
[42] Matheson, *Contarini at Regensburg*; Fenlon, *Heresy and Obedience*, pp. 45–8.
[43] Fenlon, *Heresy and Obedience*, pp. 143–4.

> I fear'd with life, to die; by death, to live:
> I felt my guide, now left, and leaving God.
> To breath in blisse, I fear'd my breath to geve:
> I fear'd for heavenly raigne, an earthly rod.
> These feares I fear'd, feares feeling no mishaps:
> O fond, O faint, O false, O faultie lapse.
>
> (ll. 49–54)

The manner is in complete contrast to the model Southwell found in Tansillo's *Lagrime di San Pietro*. Tansillo's work is a third person narrative, with occasional direct addresses 'al suo caro Signor', Christ.[44] *Saint Peters Complaint* is a dramatic monologue. Like any dramatic monologue, it feels like a confession to the reader. Here the presence of confession is not merely an analogy. This is St Peter's confession to Father Southwell, or in some sense Southwell's own confession to himself.

Confession is a central religious practice in the history of Christianity yet it is also as Foucault observed a discursive form with laws all to itself.[45] Confession is a way of speaking. If it is a ritual means of uncovering the truth, it is also a ritual way of constructing the language of truth. In this space, and in this space only, the final truth about a person appears knowable, beyond even the forensic processes of law. This is the truth as God knows it, or as far as such knowledge is permissible. In its formal structure confession is always a shared process, between the maker of the confession and the confessor; between speaker and listener. Yet it also provides a discursive space for self-examination, for internalization. In this way, it provided a ready model for a literature of self-examination, beginning with Augustine. This is a literature which has not yet ended: among its legacies are the confessional novel (via Rousseau) or, in another direction, Freud or Lacan.

Because of the Reformation, confession had a specially charged place in sixteenth-century literatures of the self. Of all the catholic sacraments, it had perhaps the most broadly controversial status, since confession not only performed a central function in catholic doctrines of sin and justification, it also in part defined the exclusivity of the Roman mass. Although Luther at first allowed auricular confession, by the later sixteenth century the rite of confession had been transformed within protestant traditions. The General Confession of Cranmer's liturgy was a communal and public act. It removed confession from the closed formal space of speaker and

---

[44] Tansillo, *Lagrime*, p. 43; for an example of direct address, p. 49.
[45] *La Volonté de savoir*, Eng.tr. *History of Sexuality*, p. 58. The standard historical treatment is Tentler, *Sin and Confession*.

listener, subject and object. Nevertheless, even in protestant England, the confessional form retained a residual power. The cultural memory of individual confession was strong. At the same time, it was rendered clandestine and scandalous. When the missionary priests returned to England, the ritual of confession, just like the mass, became the source of a mysterious semi-magical force. In hiding, confession was more private than ever: not only its content, but its very performance was a shibboleth. To protestant persecutors, confession created a powerful signifier of the recusant and missionary community as a secret society.

This outer history places further pressure on the confessional structure of *Saint Peters Complaint* and of its companion *Marie Magdalens Funerall Teares*. Both works expose their subject to an ever-more exacting scrutiny of conscience. It seems there is no area of consciousness too private for confession to uncover. As each layer of truth about the self is unveiled, another is exposed to examination. In this way, the two works conform to Foucault's description of the peculiar literary forms produced by confession:

a literature ordered according to the infinite task of extracting from the depths of oneself, in between the words, a truth which the very form of the confession holds out like a shimmering mirage   (p. 59)

Southwell drags the truth out of his interlocutors with relentless pertinacity. Here, no doubt, a part is played by that other instrument of confession, the apparatus of examination used by Topcliffe and the other pursuivants in seeking out the priests from their hiding-places. Yet whereas Southwell allowed any legal or justifiable practice of equivocation or dissimulation in the defence of the priests against their torturers, in his literary works he redeems the processes of confession by letting his subjects tell the truth.

Whatever the fate of his own works, this left an important inheritance for future literatures. By providing a discourse of truth, which can survive the fiercest of self-examination, Southwell created a language of authentication for the self. Not only the dramatic monologue, but the theatrical soliloquy is a product of this literature of confession. Yet, as with any literature of inwardness, the risks are high. Authenticity has to be continually reinvented in each layer of examination. At every stage it is prone to the criticism of fabrication and falsehood. Every truth may be a lie. Southwell's repentant sinners suffer agonies in the effort to deliver their souls. In addition, they face the constant danger that the very effort of self-examination may expose them to further sin, in the possibility that this very process of scrutiny is itself a form of self-centredness or self-vaunting.

The accents of shame and self-reproach are unwearied and wearisome. They wear both speaker and reader down. But in these shouts of self-contempt there seems to be an effort to enhance or exaggerate the 'sinne' itself as well as the 'shame':

> O sinne, of sinnes; of evils, the very woorst:
> O matchlesse wretch: O caitife most accurst.
>
> (ll. 59–60)

Janelle calls this 'the unallayed bitterness and darkness of remorse' (p. 211). Yet the lines which he quotes as being strong 'in their suggestion of self-contempt' also have the sound of being self-obsessed, especially if we recall the last line of the previous stanza:

> Most teares I wish that have most cause to weepe.
>
> All weeping eies resigne your teares to me:
> A sea will scantly rince my ordurde soule:
> Huge horrours in high tides must drowned bee:
> Of every teare my crime exacteth tole.
>
> (ll. 42–6)

These lines make a strident effect, and use exaggerated gestures and expressions. Even superlatives are not enough for Peter: 'most, is not too much' (l. 48). His demands are emotionally imperialist, as he claims for himself 'All weeping eyes'; and the phrase 'ordurde soule' reiterates the shrieking tone of

> An excrement of earth, to heaven hatefull
>
> (l. 29)

several lines earlier.

The very fact St Peter feels so strongly that he has let Christ down is evidence that he still relies on himself, and the strain for self-dependence reveals itself in the strain to make himself heard. The mortification is shouted, and in the shouting it is possible to find a false note. In his asseverations of shame, no less than in his boasts of love for Christ, we feel Peter to be a 'Gyant, in talke' (l. 63); the shame, in its stridency, is a kind of inverted 'pride' (l. 64).

Janelle writes 'from beginning to end Peter voices Southwell's own feelings, and his words sound utterly sincere' (p. 227). But in accepting a simple correspondence between Peter's words and Southwell's feelings, does this suggest falseness in the poet's understanding of remorse? Such a judgement is peremptory. Geoffrey Hill warns: 'for Southwell to have "lost himself" merely in a poem would have required more self-centredness than he was capable of'.[46] However, Peter, if not Southwell, does seem to have ' "lost himself" ' in the passion of remorse.

When Martz talks of 'excessive parallelism and antithesis' (p. 193), and charges Southwell that he 'indulges in all the worst extravagancies of Petrarchan poetry' (p. 186), we should bear in mind Hill's comments on Southwell's use of the word 'excess'. Southwell can mean by it, both the mystical practice of 'ecstasy', and the more common sense of immoderate behaviour: ' "Excessus" signifies "ecstasy" . . . But deeply versed though Southwell may have been in the methodology of "excessus", he was alert to the dangerous implications of excessive behaviour' (p. 36). Hill quotes Southwell in *Short Rules of a Good Life* to the effect that 'excess in voice and immoderate loudness are always certain signs of passion'.[47] 'Passion' is a word to make alert in Southwell; Peter may be ' "beside himself," either with a frenzy of egoistic inclinations or with a disciplined indifference to them'.[48]

It is possible Southwell means us to find Peter's violence of feeling dangerous. Hill writes with absolute accuracy of Southwell as 'this man of discipline', and it is part of the effort of this poem to bring discipline to repentance, to control this 'excess' or 'mannerism' of remorse. To make this judgement we have to have confidence in Southwell's control of the dramatic monologue. Martz, who finds 'the poem does not display impressive powers of construction', does not share such confidence (p. 193); and doubt is increased by Janelle's finding it so easy to say that 'from beginning to end Peter voices Southwell's own feelings'. But this difficulty always exists with a dramatic monologue, where there is often an important change of heart or feeling, which can only be gauged by the tone of the first-person voice, since there is no third-person narrator to adjudicate.

Both Janelle and Martz none the less recognize a change in quality in the poem as it progresses. Janelle writes that there is 'a steady progress in the successive parts of the poem, and it seems as if, when Southwell moved on from Peter's denunciation of himself to the hope of forgiveness obtained from Christ's love, his powers had risen with his feelings' (p. 226). Martz believes this rise to take place 'under the impulse of . . . meditative methods' (p. 195). This is a strange judgement. The passage Martz berates for showing 'all the worst extravagancies of Petrarchan poetry'—that is, the address to Christ's eyes—is one of the clearest examples of

---

[46] 'The Absolute Reasonableness of Robert Southwell', *Lords of Limit*, p. 36.
[47] Southwell, *Short Rules of a Good Life*, ed. by Brown, p. 36; quoted by Hill, p. 36.
[48] Hill, p. 37, commenting on the 'radical pun' in the word 'ecstasy'.

meditative method in the poem. It is perhaps the fault of Martz's book that meditation is offered as a kind of poetic elixir. Meditational practice is important in this poem (as in others by Southwell) as Martz shows. But it is not clear that Southwell only acquires control of feeling when he makes use of Ignatian method. Helen Gardner, after all, makes the opposite judgement of the effect of meditative practice in Donne's 'Holy Sonnets'. 'The almost histrionic note of the "Holy Sonnets" may be attributed partly to the meditation's deliberate stimulation of emotion; it is the special danger of this exercise that, in stimulating feeling, it may falsify it, and overdramatize the spiritual life.'[49] Peter's early laments give exactly this impression that by 'stimulating feeling' he falsifies it; but the 'deliberate stimulation of emotion' is foreign to the effort of the latter part of Southwell's poem.

A change of heart first seems to take place in the poem with the memory of the cock crowing (l. 259 ff.), the event recounted in Matthew 26: 75: 'And Peter remembred the word of IESVS which he had said, Before the cocke crow, thou shalt deny me thrise. And going forth, he wept bitterly' (Rhemes NT; cf. also Mark 14: 72 and John 18: 27). Peter's memory of the cock's crow at this point in the poem seems to repeat the process which had originally occurred; previously, the cock-crow led him to recognize the crime of his denial; now, the thought of the cock-crow in turn recalls him from the depth of his misery:

> O wakefull bird, proclaymer of the day,
> Whose piersing note doth daunt the Lyons rage:
> Thy crowing did my selfe to me bewray,
> My frightes, and brutish heates it did asswage.
> (ll. 259–62)

The very thought of the cock-crow seems once again 'my selfe to me bewray'; to take Peter out of himself, and out of his self-accusation. But it does not yet 'asswage' his feelings, but rather brings him to a just recognition of his sin:

> O bird, the just rebuker of my crime,
> The faithfull waker of my sleeping feares:
> Be now the dayly clocke to strike the time,
> When stinted eyes shall pay their taske of teares.
> (ll. 265–8)

This is one of the essential problems with which the poem deals. The consciousness of sin must be a passionate affair, it must amount to a

---

[49] *Divine Poems of John Donne*, Introduction, p. xxxi.

'detestation'; but how is the passion of self-rebuke to be kept distinct from the selfish passions of the sin itself? The soul of man is 'selfe-loaden', Southwell says in line 403, but hatred of the self is equally burdened with self. So no sooner has Peter met the 'just rebuker' of the cock than he returns to mauling himself, comparing himself unfavourably with great sinners of the Old Testament past:

> O no their fault had show of some pretence.
> No vayle can hide the shame of my offence.
> (ll. 305–6)

Southwell in *Saint Peters Complaint* imagines repentance in a very different way. It comes by turning to Christ; or rather, Christ turns to Peter:

> In time, O Lord, thine eyes with mine did meet,
> In them I read the ruines of my fall:
> Their cheering raies that made misfortune sweet,
> Into my guilty thoughts powrde flouds of gall.
> (ll. 325–8)

Peter is unprepared for this meeting of eyes, and is undisposed to feel he merits it. In the apprehension of Christ, Peter learns to forget his 'selfe':

> Much more my image in those eyes was grac'd,
> Then in my selfe whom sinne and shame defac'd
> (ll. 371–2)

Peter's 'image' of himself is thus made graceful, and also made full of grace. There is a conscious strain in the use of the theological noun as a verb ('grac'd') tantamount to the strain involved in conceiving the active power of God to be infused into and inherent in the individual. We also note the passive construction: this new 'image' is a gift from outside, which replaces the effort of the 'selfe' which had only 'defac'd' its own image with 'sinne', and also the effect of sin in 'shame'.

At the same time, the poem is 'grac'd' by Christ's eyes. The self-abuse of Peter's lament is redeemed by the encounter with Christ's forgiveness. Whereas before Peter seemed to be straining to rely on himself, he now resigns himself:

> I worthles am, direct your beames on me,
> With quickning vertue cure my killing vice.
> By seeing things, you make things worth the sight,
> You seeing, salve, and being seene, delight.
> (ll. 375–8)

The simplicity of the syntax is sacrificial: Peter's cry 'I worthless am', which at the start of the poem was part of the noise of remorse ('O caitife most accurst') is now made subject to Christ, as Peter makes his supplication, 'direct your beames on me'. There is a discipline about the theological accuracy, and the syntactic plainness, of

> You seeing, salve, and being seene, delight.

By simple parison this declares the relation of Christ to man.

What takes place in the poem is an emptying of the self from the self. This exercise of discipline in religious feeling is mirrored closely in Southwell's prose work, *Marie Magdalens Funerall Teares*. But in neither work is the process a simple transfiguration of passion into devotion. Each work deals in tears, although those of Mary Magdalen are shed in sorrow rather than remorse. Each is concerned with central episodes in Christ's passion and resurrection, and each is imbued with the vocabulary of the gospel accounts and patristic commentary on them. Janelle believes *Saint Peters Complaint* to be an early work, and is inclined to discuss the work in terms of Southwell's lyric development; Nancy Pollard Brown, however, sees close connections between the poem and the prose-poem, in date as well as subject-matter. It is thus the more surprising that she sees the poem in the simple terms of the doctrine of contrition.

Southwell's knowledge of the complexity of religious feeling is clear from the finely weighed words near the start of the 'Epistle Dedicatory', 'Passions I allow, and Loves I approve'. His treatment of such feeling is distinguished at once by its rigour and its amplitude. The religious apprehension of the passion needs to be passionate, and Southwell delicately seals his approval of passions often disapproved:

Hatred and Anger are the necessary Officers of Prowesse and Iustice . . . Sorrow is the Sister of Mercy, and a waker of Compassion, weeping others teares, & grieued with their harmes . . .[50]

Having given account to the root meaning of 'Compassion' (suffering with and for another), however, Southwell goes on to quantify and qualify his approval. He applies 'Vertues Correction': 'But as too much of the best is euill, and excesse in Vertue is vice: so Passions let loose without limmits are imperfections, nothing being good that wanteth measure' (p. 48).

Mary is depicted outside the tomb, 'complaining' of Christ's death. We

[50] *S. Peters Complaint and Saint Mary Magdalens Funerall Teares* (1616), pp. 46–7. Further references in text.

are struck by Southwell's sense of the paradoxical nature of her feelings, and the strictness of his distinctions:

But *Mary* hoping in despaire, and persevering in hope, stood without feare, because shee now thought nothing left that ought to be feared. (p. 60)

'Hoping in despaire' is a paradox of the Petrarchan type. Here Southwell seems to be indebted to the Italian verse *Lagrime della Maddalena*.[51] But there is logic in the paradox in this case, since 'shee now thought nothing left that ought to be feared'. If she feared for the worst, the worst has already happened: Christ has died. Mary is at the bottom of her feelings, and therefore fearless. The style is Euphuistic but philosophical, as Southwell rings the changes on the words 'life' and 'death' (another 'Petrarchan' paradox):

But now she thought it better to die then to liue, because she might happily dying find, whome not dying she looked not to enioy, and not enioying she had little will to liue. (p. 61)

In the early stages of the work, Southwell carefully builds up sympathy for Magdalen's tears: 'The time hath been that fewer teares would have wrought greater effect, shorter seeking have sooner found, and lesse payne have procured more pitty' (p. 67). Even Christ is gently chided for not being moved to compassion by the sight: 'O good Jesu what hath thus estranged thee from her?' (p. 68). Lack of compassion is against Christ's nature, the poet affects to argue; Mary's tears seem testimonies to her faith, in comparison with the two Apostles who have left the scene. Southwell attempts to elucidate (in the terms of the 'Epistle Dedicatory') the 'limmits' of approvable feeling, by interceding with Christ on her behalf:

if this import not any offence but a true affection, and be rather a good desire than an euill desert, why art thou so hard a Judge to so soft a creature . . . ? (p. 69)

But it is the very strangeness of Christ's obduracy, that proves the point: 'it seemeth too strange that he . . . should give thee over, to these paynfull fits, if in thee he did not see a cause for which he will not be seene of thee' (p. 73). Having made allowance for her passion, Southwell returns upon himself, showing his verdict not to be closed: 'I doubt there is some trespasse in thy teares, and some sinne in thy sorrow' (p. 73). This is the same doubt that comes over *Saint Peters Complaint*. The movement of qualification is the essence of Southwell's method: to take Mary over the brink of excess, and to encourage us in following her, only to

---

[51] *Lagrime di San Pietro con le Lagrime della Maddalena*, 169^{r-v}.

pull us, with Mary, back. For Christ has forbidden tears and weeping is a lack of trust in his promise, even though the fault is a fault of love. Southwell continues:

The fault must be mended, ere the pennance be released, and therefore eyther cease to weepe, or never hope to finde. But I know this logicke little pleaseth thee, and I might as soone win thee to forbeare living, as to leave weeping.   (p. 73)

Southwell's gentle humour has the tone of an affectionate confessor. He shows her love to be excessive, but he means it to be moving as well. Yet this emotion of sympathy, too, is tempered, for 'it well appeareth, that excesse of grief, hath bred in thee a defect of due prouidence' (p. 83).

As in *Saint Peters Complaint*, 'Vertues Correction' comes in the form of an appeal to Christ: 'And to thee I appeale, O most loving Lord, whether my afflicted hart do not truly defray the tribute of an undeuided Love' (p. 77). So begins what constitutes a long lyric by Magdalen, addressing Christ directly. Once more, Southwell is concerned with fine distinctions of feeling, as Magdalen's appeal is hedged with qualifications: 'O too fortunate a lot, for so unfortunate a woman to crave: no no, I do not crave it. For alas I dare not, yet if . . . And though . . . yea, & . . . for my part . . . but even . . . But alas I dare not . . .' (pp. 79–80).

IV CONDITIONS OF GRACE: *SAINT PETERS COMPLAINT*

However, the encounter with Christ is slow in coming. Southwell follows the gospel account in John 20 closely, using his quotation of the gospel with a fine sense of climactic tension. The appearance of Christ to Mary after the resurrection is one of the great recognition scenes in literature, like a classical ἀναγνώρισις in one of Euripides' tragicomedies. Its twists and turns of emotion supply Southwell with his material, as Jesus appears to Mary, but is not recognized as such by her. She takes him for the gardener until he calls her by name. In expanding the account, Southwell maintains suspense. The sense of relief, which overcomes the work when Christ finally makes himself known, itself imitates an act of grace. The mercy of Christ is unlooked for, unhoped for; delay only increases its happiness (in both senses of the word). The moment is both blissful and providential:

And as all this while she hath sought without finding, wept without comfort, & called without answere: so now thou satisfiest her seeking with thy comming, her teares with thy triumph, and all her cries with this one word *Mary* (p. 140)

Mary has 'sought without finding, wept without comfort, & called without answere'; her own 'seeking' does not instigate Christ's coming, so that she does not herself 'obtain' this grace. On the contrary, Christ comes to her freely, to 'satisfy' (make whole) her loss. Yet on reflection this does not quite fit the case. Just before Mary's recognition of Christ, the poet makes this promise to Mary:

Yea this only water hath quenched Gods anger, qualified his iustice, recovered his mercy, merited his love, purchased his pardon, and brought forth the spring of all thy favour   (p. 138)

Such a vocabulary has a different ring. The rub of the matter comes in the word 'purchased', which clearly implies a 'faculty' in Mary to procure Christ's forgiveness through repentance. Indeed Southwell goes so far as to reassure Mary that 'thy teares will obtain'; although the primary meaning here is 'succeed' there is also the oblique sense of 'acquire'.

There is a suggestion of contract, in the legal and financial sense, in the word 'purchased', which was also present in Mary's question earlier posed to Christ, 'whether my afflicted hart do not truly defray the tribute of an undeuided love' (p. 77). By 'tribute' we understand an obligation or necessity of payment, which Mary believes she may 'defray' through her affliction. The same word 'defray' comes up in a crucial context in *Saint Peters Complaint*:

> Come sorrowing teares, the ofspring of my griefe,
> Scant not your parent of a needfull aide:
> In you I rest, the hope of wishde relief,
> By you my sinfull debts must be defraide.
> Your power prevailes, your sacrifice is gratefull,
> By love obtayning life, to men most hatefull.
>
> (ll. 463–8)

There is a complex of important ideas present in this stanza. Here again there is a sense of obligation, of a 'needfull aide'. Such an obligation is confirmed in line 466,

> By you my sinfull debts must be defraide

in which penance is made to be the instrument of justification. The legal 'defraying' of debt is a clear indication of the doctrine of a meritorious disposition, as we see also in *Marie Magdalens Funerall Teares*, where 'this only water hath . . . merited his love'. Nancy Pollard Brown comments that the stanza states 'the sacramental value of contrition' (*Poems*, p. 164);

such a view is certainly suggested by the use of the word 'sacrifice'. And the 'sacrifice', in addition, is efficacious, as is shown by the residual pun in 'gratefull' of 'grace-bearing'. Once again the key-word 'obtayning' occurs when the contractual language of 'purchase' is used in association with the theology of justification.

Yet this language seems strange in view of a later use of 'defray' in the poem:

> O forfeyture of heaven: eternall debt,
> A moments joy: ending in endles fires:
> Our natures skumme: the worlds entangling Net:
> Night of our thoughts: death of all good desires.
> Worse then all this: worse then all tongues can say,
> Which man could owe, but onely God defray.
>
> (ll. 655–60)

Whereas in the earlier example the 'debt' of sin is presented as being 'defraide' only by the tears of penance, here all is made dependent on God's mercy. The 'tribute' requires reimbursement by a grace of pardon, rather than by the 'purchase' of human 'sacrifice'. Once again we are left with a sense of conflict between a 'free' and a 'purchased' act of God. Southwell gestures at one moment to Seripando's sense of the permanent need to subject to God's pardon, and at another to the Tridentine notion of 'obtayning' justice.

To understand the poem, and indeed Southwell's whole treatment of repentance and justification, in terms of what Janelle calls the post-Tridentine literature of remorse (p. 205), is possible only with a sense of the difficulty of these issues in his work. But it is a mistake to assume, as Brown does, that there is one simple post-Tridentine doctrine. The council itself, in its preliminary stages, gave voice to a range of opinions, and to some extent these differences of opinion are maintained in equilibrium in the decree itself. It is therefore worth considering the efforts of theologians in the latter half of the sixteenth century to interpret this difficulty.

As a Jesuit seminarist at Douai and at Rome, Southwell received an orthodox training in theological doctrine. Southwell trained as a priest, and so spent a total of four years in the superior school of theology, although he probably took longer because of his responsibilities as a tutor at the English College.[52] Although he lived from 1581 in the English College at Campo dei Fiori, he pursued his theological studies at the Roman

---

[52] Devlin, *Life of Southwell*, p. 47.

College, at the foot of the Capitoline Hill.[53] Bellarmine, Suarez, and Clavius were among the professors at this time. Suarez was developing the Jesuit theory of middle knowledge in countering protestant explanations of predestination. Bellarmine, who became Professor of Controversial Theology at the Gregorian University in 1576, was a formidable controversialist on justification and other matters. Southwell later wrote admiringly of Bellarmine to the detriment of his English opponent, Whitaker.[54]

The teaching of theology in the Jesuit College was divided into several parts: the study of Thomas Aquinas's *Summa Theologiae*, of scripture, of moral theology, of cases of conscience, and of religious controversies.[55] Aquinas was studied at Rome morning and evening, under two separate tutors; the Lutheran controversies were given a thrashing once a week.[56] Among other authors, Lombard's Sentences, a traditional favourite, was clearly important; but on difficult questions the *Ratio Studiorum* also makes special mention of later scholastics such as Biel, whose work was so important in Luther's education, and Cajetan, the leading catholic reformer who tried Luther at Augsburg.[57]

So much can be gleaned of the specific nature of Southwell's theological studies. But much can be learned from the example of his English contemporary Stapleton, Southwell's tutor for two years at Douai before Southwell moved to Paris and thence to Rome.[58] Stapleton, the most intellectual of the English exiles, wrote important treatises on the church, on scripture, and on justification in his controversies with Whitaker.[59] Whitaker's death in 1595 (followed shortly by Stapleton's in 1598) prevented him from completing his reply to the treatise on justification: he was able only to complete a few hundred pages on original sin.[60]

This is not the place for an examination of the 350,000 words Stapleton wrote on justification, but to show the kind of problem which occupied a catholic intellectual (and an Englishman) in the post-Tridentine period. In fact, the sticking points remained the same as at Trent: whether man was 'merely passive' to the action of justification; whether justice in man was to be confined to the righteousness of Christ; whether justification consisted

---

[53] Devlin, 46.
[54] Ibid., 156–7. Bellarmine's knowledge of protestant sources at this period is discussed in Biersack, 'La conoscenza delle fonti protestanti'.
[55] *Monumenta Paedagogica Societatis Iesu*, ii. 45.   [56] Ibid., 180.
[57] Ibid., 268–9.   [58] Devlin, *Life of Southwell*, p. 23.
[59] See O'Connell, *Stapleton and the Counter Reformation*, p. 23.
[60] Stapleton, *De universa iustificationis doctrina hodie controversa*; Whitaker, *Tractatus . . . de peccato originali*. See Milward, *Religious Controversies of the Elizabethan Age*, Nos. 551–2, pp. 150–1.

only in remission of sin, or was also a process of infusion or sanctification as well; and in what sense man could be understood to have merit.

Stapleton, following the conclusions of Session VI, Canons 4 and 5, denied that the will was only passive to grace, as argued by protestants. He went so far as to argue against the moderate protestant Martin Chemnitz, who allowed freedom of choice after conversion, but not before. In this way, Stapleton reaffirmed the participation of the will even in the first conversion of the sinner, participation he calls *spontanea, non coacta* ('free, not constrained').[61] His conclusion is that *conversio enim est actio* ('conversion is an action', p. 93), an action which, moreover, *voluntas agit* ('the will performs', p. 93). To make his point clear, he quotes Luther in opposition, that justification is *solius Dei opus, actio & agitatio* ('the work, action, and operation of God alone', p. 93).

Stapleton insists his view is not Pelagian, arguing instead that it is scriptural and Augustinian. He uses four arguments for the co-operation of the will, all of them well known. Three recall the controversy between Luther and Erasmus. Free will is obvious from the use in scripture of the form of command (*forma iubendi*); it is necessary for the understanding of reward and punishment; and it is mentioned in scripture (with the passage from Ecclesiasticus 15, discussed in Chapter 4, well to the fore). His fourth argument, that without the notion of the co-operation of the will, men would be like cattle, is clearly spurious, since it fails to acknowledge the distinction between natural and religious freedom.

Such is Stapleton's doctrinal basis for the idea of co-operation: but he still needs to give it psychological life. The will does not achieve justification on its own, Stapleton says, as such an idea would be Pelagian. The process is instead a meeting of two minds. Stapleton uses a series of words to explain his idea: man has a *vis consentiendi* ('a power of consent'); God gives him *adiutorium* ('assistance'); the will of God and the will of man *concurrere* ('concur'). Stapleton makes frequent recourse to the Tridentine phrase that the will is *a Deo excitata* ('roused by God'). But herein lies the problem: is the will 'moved by' God, or simply 'helped along'? It is at this point that Stapleton's psychology becomes blurred, hiding behind technical terminology. The agency of the action is crucially vague.

To make sense of the problem Stapleton distinguishes three kinds of grace. Trent was content with two—remission of sins and sanctification— but Stapleton acknowledges a third, which he calls *gratia cooperans*.[62]

---

[61] Stapleton, *Opera omnia*, ii. 93.
[62] The term was originated by Peter Lombard, *Sentences*, ii. q.26 d.1 (*PL*, 192, 710); Calvin discusses it in *Institutio*, 2, 2, 6.

What is immediately odd, however, is the way he describes the first two. The first justification he calls *electio* or *vocatio*; it is 'extrinsic' to us, and antecedent to our will. Then Stapleton drops his bombshell: we are 'passive' to this grace: *in his omnibus mere passive nos habemus* ('to all these actions we hold ourselves merely passive', p. 107). The definition which he goes on to make is one of which Luther himself would be proud: *est motio illa divina, in qua mens nostra movetur tantum, & non movet* ('it is a divine motion, by which our mind is only moved, and does not move itself' p. 107).

The second justification 'the infusion of supernatural qualities in us', Stapleton also describes as the 'gift' (*donum*) of God; and in this also we are passive to the *gratia operans* of God. However, Stapleton argues that there is yet a third kind of justification, which God does move in us without our consent. This seems to be a conflation of Thomist theory with the idea developed from the Sentences by Biel of *gratis dans vel gratis datum*.[63] As part of this, Stapleton lists *omnia opera & actiones, illae, quae ad nostram iustificationem concurrunt* ('all those works and actions, which concur in our justification', p. 107). They include *credere* ('to believe'), *diligere* ('to love'), *poenitere* ('to make penance'), and they enable us to *avertere a peccato* ('to turn ourselves from sin'). Such *opera* are, properly speaking, *actiones nostrae*: they amount to *gratia cooperans*.

This term gives him great difficulty. The two words seem to run in opposition to each other: if it is the operation of *gratia*, something given to us *gratis*, what is our part in it? And if we operate it, if it is *actio nostra*, then how is it grace? It is odd, too, for 'assent' to be termed a 'cooperation'. Once again, Stapleton's argument makes clear the extreme difficulty of reconciling dependence on God's power for forgiveness with the free assent of the will. Yet this tension is implicit in the concept of grace. The word has traditionally been understood in two quite different senses, firstly as 'the free and unmerited favour of God as manifested in the salvation of sinners' and secondly as 'the condition of one who is under such divine influence'.[64] Grace goes between God and man. Catholic theology always understood grace to make commands about human action whilst reaffirming that grace in fact obviates the need for a law of commandments.

Equally, as we have seen in the present chapter, the notion of the preparation or disposition of the sinner for grace, and the idea of the sinner's consent to grace, raises questions in catholic theology. Trent affirms this consent to amount to a co-operation of the will in grace, a co-operation

---

[63] Biel, I Sent., d.26, q. un art 1.   [64] *OED*: GRACE 11a and 11d.

which merits some reward. Stapleton clearly has difficulties with these ideas. He wishes to argue that the gift of grace is gratuitous, and that man is passive to it, and at the same time that the will actively co-operates in this gift; and yet he hesitates to say that the will achieves something. Affirming both the supernatural operation of grace, and the natural co-operation of the will, leads him to use the term *gratia cooperans* as if it encapsulated both.

A rather different implication is found in the prayer for the dead which Seripando found of such significance in his understanding of the remission of sins: 'Enter not into judgment with thy servant, O Lord, for no man is justified before thee, unless thou grant him remission of thy sins'. The prayer is an appeal that grace be implemented from outside; 'no man is justified' unless God justifies him. The imperative mood of the cry signifies a need to be fulfilled. Yet at the same time the making of the prayer is a kind of passive disposition for grace.

It is this sense of prayer going against the grain of doctrine that is found in *Saint Peters Complaint*. The confessional parts of the poem are differentiated from the railing against sin with which the poem opens. The 'denunciation' of self is first arrested by Peter's appeal to Christ following line 325. This movement is itself displaced by a further access of self-blaming, reaching its acme in the comparison with Cain in line 523. But self-hatred is distinguished from acknowledgement of sin. Peter's confession has a Pauline ring (from Romans 7):

> A thing most done, yet more than God can doe,
> Dayly new done, yet ever done amisse:
> (ll. 643–4)

Janelle admits to finding the last part of the poem the most successful; one reason is that he shares the sense of relief which Southwell induces in Peter. It is in this part of the poem that Peter finds his true voice, the humble (and passive) voice of prayer:

> Prone looks, crost armes, bent knee, and contrite hart,
> Deepe sighes, thicke sobs, dewd eyes and prostrate prayers,
> Most humbly beg reliefe of earned smart
> (ll. 769–71)

The marks of penance and contrition 'humbly beg reliefe', they do not exhort, demand, or buy it. Brown has it that contrition is efficacious in the poem; but Southwell in fact leaves us with a prayer for remission of sins, a prayer which in the very utterance is 'prone' to God. Southwell uses the word 'contrite' with the same accent as he does the significant words 'prone', 'crost', and 'bent': Peter does not offer to make restitution, but places himself in the way of grace. The adjectives themselves are genuflections to Christ.

The effect of relief can be seen most clearly in miniature in the early draft version of 'Saint Peters Complaynte', on which, in terms of its careful depiction of the action of grace, Southwell did not improve but only elaborated in the longer version. In its initial stage, the poem is one of unbridled, abasive self-reproach. This culminates in bitter self-involved calumny:

> What Jewish rage, yea what infernall sprite,
> Could have disgorg'd against him greater spite.
>
> (ll. 65–6)[65]

However, from this pitch of abasement, there is a sudden reversal of feeling into the last stanza, as reproach is transformed into remorse:

> With mercye, Jesu, measure my offence:
> Lett deepe remorse thy due revenge abate:
> Lett teares appease when trespas doth incense:
> Lett myldnes temper thy deserved hate.
> Lett grace forgive, lett love forgett my fall:
> With feare I crave, with hope I humbly call.
>
> (ll. 67–72)

The discipline and 'measure' of the verse here is itself a kind of penance for the passion of reprobation that has preceded. The poet is relieved from his haranguing of himself by turning to Christ in straightforward appeal: he supplicates, he petitions Christ. But he finds special relief in the optative 'Lett'. After the extravagance of the vocabulary in the previous stanza: 'Jewish rage', 'disgorg'd', 'spite', the extreme plainness of beginning four consecutive lines with the word 'Lett' is ravishing. Each line ends with a colon or a full stop, so that the punctuation itself provides checks to pride, by limiting self-expression to the bounds of single lines. The very regularity of the beat makes its own contrition, and the poem ends on consecutive downbeats, the rhyme resigned rather than resolute.

It is Southwell's grammar which calibrates this tone of humility. The successive use of 'Lett' places the sinner in the way of grace, without congratulating itself on the achievement. The gracefulness of this reaction is prepared for in the longer poem:

---

[65] Compare the tempered anger of the later version, ll. 137–8.

> A poore desire I have to mend my ill:
> I should, I would, I dare not say, I will.
>
> I dare not say, I will; but wish, I may:
> (*Saint Peters Complaint*, ll. 761–3)

The auxiliaries 'should . . . would' are preferred to the future 'will'. Peter 'dare not say, I will' in the sense that he cannot promise his own sanctification. His 'poore desire' is itself a kind of co-operation in grace, but is restrained from becoming an operation, by being expressed by an unfulfilled verb: 'wish, I may'. These lines provide an exegesis of Southwell's use of 'Lett' in the above stanza: the intention to act 'I will' is qualified by the optative desire 'I wish'. In the process, Southwell says, 'My pride is checkt' (l. 764), for the human will is subsumed into the divine will:

> My good, O Lord, thy gift; thy strength my stay:
> Give what thou bidst, and then bid what thou wilt.
> (ll. 765–6)

The sinner's will, in fact, is subsumed grammatically, for the speaker's imperative forms a tautology with the divine bidding, 'Give what thou bidst', 'bid what thou wilt'. It is a reflex taken from Dante's *Paradiso*, part of Southwell's Italian education.[66] The bidding in the later stanza takes a different form:

> Lett grace forgive, lett love forgett my fall:
> (71; *Saint Peters Complaint*, l. 785)

The manner of forming the optative mood in English with the modal verb 'let' allows a crucial ambiguity, between the use of 'let' as a form of inflexion, consignifying a wish, and of 'let' as an imperative addressed to an unnamed third party, to 'let' the action occur. Southwell creates a grammatical place for grace within 'Lett' as the instigator of the action implicit in the order. The future is conditional ('I dare not say, I will'), but the action of grace is unconditional; the optative 'Lett' is Southwell's way of making a future tense that is unconditionally God's.

The short version of the poem ends with self-reproach redeemed as resigned appeal:

> With feare I crave, with hope I humbly call.
> (72; *Saint Peters Complaint*, l. 786)

---

[66] 'E'n la sua voluntade è nostra pace', *Paradiso*, iii. 85.

The 'call' itself is a humble act, a 'cry for mercy'. The later version attempts to go further, making Christ 'say' Southwell's words for him:

> Cancell my debtes, sweete *Jesu*, say Amen.
>
> (l. 792)

The 'say' is both imperative and imprecatory. 'Amen', as an end-rhyme, seems to be spoken by someone else, in affirmation of the rhyme. If this appears to be a syntactical accident, this in itself is providential, in that it is provided from outside. It is a poetic trope to provide a resolution which in dogmatic theology appeared impossible to achieve. As with the 'Lett grace' of the penultimate stanza, we are faced with the felicities of syntax, sudden falls from grace, and unexpected redemption. Southwell fashions from the ambiguous legacy of the post-Tridentine practice of confession a model for interiority to rival the Lutheran tradition. In turn, through the influence of his anonymous poems, this devotional inwardness and sensitive self-analysis passed back into English protestantism.

9   God's Grammar

The conversion of John Donne, which led eventually to his becoming Dean of St Paul's, has never quite shared the reputation of the Damascene experience of the patron of his cathedral church, the revolutionary Saul:

And as he journeyed, he came near Damascus: and suddenly there shined around about him a light from heaven: And he fell to the earth, and heard a voice saying unto him, Saul, Saul, why persecutest thou me? And he said, Who art thou, Lord? And the Lord said, I am Jesus whom thou persecutest: it is hard for thee to kick against the pricks. And he trembling and astonished said, Lord, what wilt thou have me to do? And the Lord said unto him, Arise, and go into the city, and it shall be told thee what thou must do.   (Acts, 9: 3–6, AV)

Donne's conversion has appeared more like Paul becoming Saul, more pricks than kicks. After all, young Donne was a recusant, educated by Jesuits in the old faith. His conscience was marked by the Elizabethan witnesses of that faith, such as Southwell, whom he may have met in prison shortly before Southwell's savage execution in 1595, when Donne was in his early twenties.[1] Donne's conversion has seemed, like the unreformed Saul, a betrayal of conscience. Rather than a road to Damascus, Donne's route led to preferment, its end not in martyrdom at Rome but worldly gain at Westminster. Instead of submitting to blinding light, Donne went 'into the city' (Acts 9: 6) with his eyes wide open knowing exactly what he wanted.

Conversion is a defining experience in religious culture, appearing to guarantee the authenticity of religion itself. As such, it has been exposed to all kinds of test. The initiate must establish both sincerity and conformity, since without one the other is invalid. As a result, conversion is a deeply significant process within the operation of culture, monitoring the boundaries between interior and exterior, private and public, or orthodox and heterodox.

The narrative of conversion was a controversial form in Reformation Europe. Paul, zealot turned apostle, and in a different way Augustine, Manichee turned missionary, passed from conspicuously religious anti-Christianity to conspicuously Christian anti-paganism. The case of

---

[1] Bald, *Donne*, pp. 64–5 and 68.

Luther disarranged these examples, since he was considered by protestants to have passed to apostolic Christianity but by catholics to heretical apostasy. His conversion posed a direct question about the true meaning of the 'Christian', since in each phase of his life he had adopted the name unambiguously. Donne's conversion seems a comparatively mundane affair, hardly one to endanger nations and empires in the manner of Luther. But in the convoluted history of the English Reformations it is more symptomatic than might appear. A catholic by birth and education, at times recusant and at times conformist, perhaps reluctant in both, he came eventually not only to embrace the reformed faith but to minister it. For the last ten years of his life he occupied one of the most important positions in the English church, one which—if not in the first rank of ecclesiastical and political influence—was peculiarly visible and public. He was the public face of the church in its most public cathedral, much in demand as a preacher both at Whitehall and at Paul's Cross. These two venues, respectively the highest court and the most general crowd in the country, were the most important audiences in English culture. Paul's Cross was an open theatre of the streets in a way which makes the Globe Theatre seem like a private club in comparison.[2] It is a strange arena in which to encounter the intricate, inward, reflexive, verbal ingenuities of Donne's prose. Yet in this obtuse juxtaposition of catholic and protestant, devotional and opportunistic, sincere and insincere, Donne's writing from the death of Elizabeth to the eve of the English revolution forms a summary and archetype of English religion in its most difficult century.

I DONNE'S CONVERSIONS

A representation by Caravaggio of the *Conversion of St Paul* (Figure 6), painted in the same decade as Donne's *Holy Sonnets*, shows some of the newly ambiguous meanings of conversion.[3] Commissioned for a chapel in a prominent church in Rome (as chance would have it next door to the convent where Luther the monk stayed a century earlier) Caravaggio's painting none the less shows muffled marks of being influenced by a protestant economy of conversion. The composition is dominated on the left-hand side by the fleshy mass of the back end of a horse, the torso of which stands astride the whole frame of the image and takes up almost half

---

[2] MacLure, *Paul's Cross Sermons*, p. 167.
[3] Rome, Chiesa di Santa Maria del Popolo, commissioned by Cardinal Tiberio Cerasi (1600–1).

Fig. 6. 'And he fell to earth, and heard a voice saying unto him, Saul, Saul, why persecutest thou me?' Caravaggio, *The Conversion of St Paul* (1600–1), commissioned by Cardinal Tiberio Cerasi.

of the total visual space. By contrast, the prostrate figure of the saint underneath the horse is lumped into a foreshortened periphery. His outstretched hands catch the light while his face, upside down and expressionless, dwindles into shadow in the bottom right corner. Unlike another version of the same subject by Caravaggio (almost certainly earlier) this painting has virtually no narrative and no sense of epic style. There is no Christ and no angel beckoning to the saint, no military gesture in the horse or the standing groom, who in the other version guards his master with a spear but who here looks down with glum inattention.[4] The painting is static and momentary, frozen in a single inarticulate event.

From early on the picture has been criticized for its ungainliness and its low style. Howard Hibbard recalls that 'one wag has likened it to an accident in a barber's shop'.[5] The painting describes one of the charismatic events of the Bible but seems studied in its lack of visual charisma. This vision of grace is resolutely graceless. Yet by representing the obliviousness of horse and groom Caravaggio shows his scene to be precisely 'accidental' and in that sense uncalled-for. Paul does not call for grace but is called by it against his will. In this respect the lighting of the picture is peculiar and even extraordinary. At most times of day the chapel is shrouded in gloom and details can only painfully be observed. At such times the light figured as landing on Paul's face appears to disobey the laws of physics: nothing else is illumined. Only in afternoon sunlight does this effect have a naturalistic explanation, when the eye is directed back to an apparent source in a sunbeam refracted through a window in the vault. This window is decorated with the dove of the Holy Spirit.[6]

By means of its radical and discomforting composition, the *Conversion of St Paul* represents grace as 'action without meaning, mere happening'.[7] It has been noted how close such a theology is to ideas developed among members of the Augustinian order to which this church belongs, under the unattributed influence of the heretic Luther. If so, and if Caravaggio was aware of such a theology, it must be recognized as deeply implicit. Luther was to a Roman public a figure of anathema. Yet in the internal quarrels of the counter-Reformation, as was evident at Trent, catholic reaction could take contradictory forms. One of these was to recognize a version of grace, which virtually eliminated any voluntary co-operation from the sinner. And yet in the pressure of controversy, under the gaze of the papal curia, such a version could be allowed to exist only in a repressed form. In this

---

[4] Rome, Collezione Odescalchi Balbi di Piovera.   [5] *Caravaggio*, p. 123.
[6] Ibid., 128.
[7] Giulio Argan's gloss of Bellori; see Hibbard, p. 300.

way, Caravaggio's image appears too incongruous to convey a clear doctrine, indeed on some viewers can impress itself as simply meaningless. This is conversion without full acknowledgement of its significance. The character of this conversion is opaque to the viewer. In particular, Paul himself is given no visible interiority. There is no indication that he will rise from underneath the horse a changed man or, even if he does, whether he will understand the nature of the change. Still less is the viewer in possession of such certainties. The process of conversion remains impervious and mysterious. It is certainly not as grand or cataclysmic as the story in Acts recounts. In that way it stands as an obstinate reminder of the danger of reading too quickly into the meaning and structure of religious experience in late sixteenth-century Europe, or the obscure political world of conversion between one doctrinal side and the other.

In approaching the conversion of Donne it would be wise not to assume too easy access into its motivation. Yet to some Donne's motives have appeared an open book. To one, it appears obvious that 'Donne's need for a God who would make him suffer, voiced so stridently in the "Holy Sonnets", can be related to this sensitivity about missed martyrdom, as well as to the feeling of inner coldness which is part of the same dissatisfied complex'.[8] To another, the *Holy Sonnets* speak just as directly of agonized acceptance of Calvinist predestination, a willing immersion in the theology of despair.[9] Somewhere between the two, a third finds less precisely but no less transparently 'an image of a soul working out its salvation in fear and trembling'.[10] These accounts, so different in their conclusions, are identical in their assumption of the legibility of emotion. Yet the difference in the conclusions itself belies such legibility. Depending on the point of view, Donne is either a catholic apostate racked by guilty conscience, or a crypto-catholic cleverly hiding behind expedient protestantism, or a lip-service conformist not caring either way. Or he is an all-round Church of England good egg; even, on the fringes, a typical Jacobean puritan dean holding Arminianism at bay. The following account will approach Donne's religion somewhat differently. By the early seventeenth century religious identities in England are not constructed around fixed points of doctrine. Donne, like any intellectual interested in divinity, has to fashion his religion by means of a bewildering process of interpretation. This is what leads Annabel Patterson, in rejecting the psychological simplicities of the biographical tradition, to comment instead on the 'mass of

---

[8] Carey, *Donne*, p. 49.   [9] Stachniewski, *Persecutory Imagination*, p. 254.
[10] Gardner (ed.), *Divine Poems*, p. xxxi.

contradictions' Donne's conduct evinces, and to demand of commentary a pressure of linguistic response in proportion with the complexities of Donne's own discourse.[11] Indeed, identity in Donne can be thought of as consisting in acts of discourse and of interpretation.

Biographers have hunted in vain for definitive signs of Donne's conversion.[12] Walton made it the subject of his *Life*, indeed made the life of Donne a continuous conversion. Evelyn Simpson preferred to view Donne's religious journey as 'a number of spiritual crises': a catholic upbringing followed by 'a period of doubt', a youth full of loose living regulated by the order of marriage, the desire for worldly fulfilment finally transcended by emergence into holy orders.[13] 'Perhaps', she observes, 'the word "conversion" is not the appropriate term for any of these crises.'[14] However, Simpson continues to place faith in enigmatic autobiographical passages littered throughout Donne's works, such as the remark late in his life (in a Sermon of April 1627) that '*I date my life from my Ministery*; for *I received mercy*, as I received the ministery, as the *Apostle* speaks.'[15] Yet Donne is not here reminiscing but quoting from I Timothy, 1: 12. Donne's life acquires meaning only as it duplicates Paul's.

Conversion is always a narrative of doubling and of repetition. It is never original, but conforms to a pattern. Verification lies in such conformity, for which the Damascus experience, the conversion of conversions, provides the prototype. Herein lies a paradox, for Damascus is as much anti-type as archetype. Every conversion is modelled on Paul's but none can stand the comparison. Calvin refused to apply the story of Paul to his own life, and (controversially) doubted its applicability to Luther— who, he said, 'did not see everything at once'.[16] Of himself, he was content to tell an obscure and reticent story, which refers to a *subita conversio* in his youth but records this as part of a yearlong process.[17] The word *subita* is glossed elsewhere by Calvin as meaning 'unexpected' (*inconsiderata*) rather than more simply 'sudden' (*repentina*).[18] Somewhat to the chagrin of his followers, Calvin found his own life concurred with what he felt to

[11]　Patterson, 'All Donne', p. 42.　　　　[12]　Gosse, *Life and Letters*, ii. 102–3.

[13]　Simpson, *Study of the Prose Works*, pp. 31–3.　　　[14]　*Sermons*, vii. 36.

[15]　Ibid., 403.

[16]　*Traité des Scandales* (1550), cited in Bouwsma, *Calvin*, p. 11.

[17]　The account written with the hindsight of thirty years in the Preface to the *Commentary on the Psalms* (1557) has been subjected to endless exegesis, notably in recent years by P. Sprenger, *Das Rätsel um die Bekehrung Calvins* (Neukirchen, 1960); A. Ganocszy, *Le jeune Calvin* (Wiesbaden, 1966); more briefly in Parker, *Calvin*, pp. 22–3 and 162–5; and Bouwsma, *Calvin*, pp. 10–11.

[18]　*Commentaria in De Clementia*, ed. by Battles and Hugo, pp. 55–6; cited in a detailed exegesis of the Psalms paragraph by Parker, *Calvin*, p. 163.

be general experience: 'We are converted little by little to God, and by stages.'[19]

The road to Damascus forms a negative identity used to justify an experience lying comfortably outside the extraordinary. As an example to the faithful it is contradictory. On the one hand there is desire for emulation, in the need for a religious experience as obvious, as unequivocal, as falling off a horse. But applied to the self, the example enforces a sensation of lack. It possesses an unexpectedness not to be expected again. The conversion of St Paul is the conversion which occurs to no other sinner, which rebukes every other sinner. Yet it offers a glimmer of transcendence almost realizable in that once, if only once, it was realized.

As Dean of St Paul's, Donne preached frequently on the Feast of the Conversion, the patronal feast of the cathedral's year. On one such occasion, in January 1625, he chose to explicate the text of Acts, in typically contradictory terms.[20] The Pauline experience is cited for its sheer untypicality: 'It is not safe concluding out of single Instances', Donne says (vi. 208). Paul is a prodigy, and his sensational transformation a one-off. It is 'a true Transubstantiation' (209), a monstrous metamorphosis; struggling for suitable metaphors, Donne paraphrases from Chrysostom with goggle-eyed extravagance:

Agnus ex Lupo, that here is another manner of Lycanthropy, then when a man is made a Wolfe; for here a Wolfe is made a Lambe, *Ex lupo Agnus*. *Ex vepribus racemus*, sayes that Father, A bramble is made a vine; *Ex zizaniis frumentum*, Cockle and tares become wheat; *Ex pirata gubernator*, A Pirat becomes a safe Pilot; *Ex novissimo primus*, The lees are come to swim out on the top, and the last is growne first (vi. 209–10)

These fantastic conceits—seemingly so typical of Donne but patristic in origin—conjure up the bizarre metaphysics of this most orthodox of conversions. They reveal the submerged, impossible metaphor in the concept of conversion, of an alteration in chemical state, an alchemy of person.

The editors of the sermons infer a personal investment for Donne in the narrative, suggesting 'he felt a special sympathy with St Paul, as he certainly did with St Augustine, because of his own earlier unregenerate years and his own struggles against the desires of the flesh'.[21] This misunderstands the careful way in which Donne balks at such simplistic 'sympathy'. It also ignores the more oblique relationship between apostolic and personal

---

[19] Commentary on Jeremiah 31: 18, cited in Bouwsma, *Calvin*, p. 11.
[20] *Sermons*, vi. no. 10, Sunday after the conversion of St Paul, 30 January 1624/5: Acts 9: 4.
[21] *Sermons*, i. 140.

conversion buried in a recondite corner of Donne's sermon. Saul, after all, was converted not from 'desires of the flesh' but from persecuting the faithful. It is this part of Saul's story that Donne finds most capable of general comparison:

> Many bloody Executioners were converted to Christ, even in the act of that bloody Execution; Then when they took a delight in tearing out the bowels of Christians, they were received into the bowels of Christ Jesus, and became Christians. Men that rode to Market, and saw an Execution upon the way; Men that opened a window to take ayre, and saw an execution in the street; The Ecclesiasticall Story abounds with examples of occasionall Convertits, and upon strange occasions; but yet the Church celebrates no Conversion, but this.   (vi. 209)

It is not difficult to identify in this paragraph the gist of a comparison with Donne's own bloody times. The reference is specific: it applies neither to the crucifixions of early Christians (including Paul himself) nor to the burnings of English protestants under Henry VIII and Mary Tudor. To an Elizabethan or Jacobean ear the disembowelment of Christians could mean only the execution of catholic priests for treason in the persecutions following Elizabeth's excommunication in 1570.

A popular literature of martyrdom grew up around these excruciating executions which included numerous records of witnesses who 'saw an execution in the street'. One remarkable case of such 'occasionall Convertits' was the young Henry Walpole, 'Cambridge wit, minor poet, satirist, flaneur'.[22] Walpole converted to catholicism when, a spectator at the scaffold of the Jesuit priest Edmund Campion, he was spattered by the martyr's blood. He in turn joined the Jesuit order, became a priest, and, after torture, was executed in 1595. Walpole contributed a poem to the hagiographical classic, *A True Reporte of the Death and Martyrdome of M.Campion Jesuite and Preiste at Tiborne the First of December 1581.*[23] The significance of Donne's reference to these 'strange occasions' is less clearly hagiographical. More immediate to Donne than the illustrious martyrdom of Father Campion was the obscure case of William Harrington, who, on 18 February 1594, was 'drawne from Newgate to Tiburne, and there hanged, cut downe aliue, strugled with the hangman, but was bowelled and quartered'.[24] Harrington was arrested in the Lincoln's Inn cham-

---

[22] Waugh, *Edmund Campion*, p. 198.

[23] ARCR 4. The author is now believed to have been Thomas Alfield. See Southern, *Recusant Prose*, pp. 376–9 and White, *Saints and Martyrs*, pp. 217–18; Walpole's poem is entitled 'The Complaynt of a Catholike for the death of M Edmund Campion', F4^v–G2^r; see also White, *Saints and Martyrs*, pp. 221–2.

[24] Stow, *Chronicle*, p. 439.

bers of Donne's younger brother Henry. Harrington denied being a priest but was betrayed by Henry's testimony when he broke down under cross-examination.[25] Henry himself, facing trial for harbouring a priest (itself a capital offence), died of plague a few days after being moved to Newgate from the Clink.

What possessed the elder Donne to remind his auditors of those bloody executioners who from 'delight in tearing out the bowels of Christians . . . were received into the bowels of Christ Jesus, and became Christians'? He himself was conspicuously not among the 'occasionall Convertits'. Far from honouring the blood of martyrs, he had betrayed them, libelling them as *Pseudo-Martyrs* in the work which led to his own preferment and ordination. The comparison with the glorious turncoat Saul suggests not sympathy of conversion but his own stubborn unconvertedness. In the Preface to *Pseudo-Martyr* itself, Donne had written with a strange, self-conscious exposure of his complicity in the controversy of conversion:

I have been ever kept awake, in a meditation of Martyrdome, by being derived from such a stock and race, as, I beleeve, no family, (which is not of farre larger extent, and greater branches,) hath endured and suffered more in their persons and fortunes, for obeying the Teachers of Romane Doctrine, then it hath done.[26]

Yet for all its apparent openness, this autobiographical reference, like the one in the later sermon, is oppressed by irony. Donne's narrative of conversion deliberately contrasts different theories of the 'truth' of personal narratives. He overturns the conventional trope of individual suffering. Every catholic witness of the true faith prefaced its account with the personal credentials of the author, preferably accrued over generations. Among Donne's family saints was the English martyr of martyrs, Sir Thomas More. Donne wears this badge on his sleeve (using the master vocabulary, 'endured and suffered') but it is a badge of betrayal. His family's suffering gives him the proper authority merely to debunk the very meaning of the 'Martyrdome'.

By contrast, catholics claimed for their martyrs an authenticity beyond reproach. In the new lives of the English saints, persecution was proof of truth. The sufferings, particularly the heroic deaths, of missionary priests were compared to the early Christians of Nero's reign. This propaganda began with *De persecutione Anglicana* of 1581 by Robert Persons, the head

---

[25] Morris, 'Martyrdom of Harrington', prints all documentation surrounding the deaths of both Harrington and Donne.

[26] *Pseudo-Martyr*, p. 8.

of the English mission.[27] Persons's work of controversy was followed by a literature of consolation and complaint, of which the principal work is Southwell's *Epistle of Comfort* of 1588. Here the wounds of martyrs are precisely 'badges of tryumph'.[28] Reassuring his readers that the 'theatre of cruelty' in which they were embroiled was worthwhile, Southwell exhorted patience in the face of torment.[29] The apostolic mission of the new martyrs is proved by citations from the classic source from antiquity, Tertullian's *Ad Martyres*. Martyrdom is declared 'the noblest acte of Fortitude' (138[r]), an immediate sign of divine grace.

The gruesome charity of Southwell's writing turns even the blood of martyrs into flowers of virtue. There seems no limit to his capacity to transcend suffering through metaphor: in one place the quartering of the martyr is transformed into the crushing of coriander (149[v]), in another, 'blood by their woundes gushing out' is made into 'sweete & acceptable . . . balme' (154[r]). Grace renders brutal death as graceful, brutality is almost gratefully endured. And yet, Southwell carefully argues, violence is not itself the condition of grace: *causa, non poena, martyrem facit*, he quotes from Augustine.[30] Indeed, by an equally immediate sign, Southwell claims that the suffering of heretics only reinforces their disgrace: 'the vyolence that proueth, purifyeth, and clenseth the good; damnethe, wasteth, and spoyleth the badd' (184[v]). In a return on his own tropes of metaphorical redemption, he concludes with logic but with a certain interruption of charity:

And so what torturing so euer the wicked or heretickes suffer, it shall auayle them to nothinge but to theyre payne. For if all were Martyres, that dye for theyre relygion, then many heresyes both contrary emong themselues, and repugnant to the euident doctrine of Christ, sholde be truethes, which is impossible.   (183[r])

What was 'impossible' to Southwell seemed quite possible to Donne. He struggles to find a *causa* to justify Southwell's confidence. Foxe had presented the torturing of these same 'heretics' as the work of the Antichrist. The antithesis between the two views was an invitation to dubiety. *Pseudo-Martyr* shows a crisis of faith in the witness of martyrdom. For Donne, it

---

[27] List of works in Milward, *Controversies of the Elizabethan Age*, pp. 65–73.

[28] *An Epistle of Comfort*, 193[v].

[29] The phrase 'theatre of cruelties' is the title of a book of engravings depicting protestant violence (*Theatrum crudelitatum*) by Richard Verstegan, first produced in 1587. Vibrant illustrations of the atrocities of the English 'Calvinists' against catholics (including Campion) are given on pp. 70–86.

[30] *Contra Cresconium grammaticum*, Bk. III. 47, 51 (CSEL, 52, 459). Southwell also refers to the many discussions of martyrdom in *De civitate Dei*; see *Epistle*, 185[v].

was not obvious how to distinguish Thomas More from Tyndale, or Campion from Cranmer, as men 'that dye for theyre relygion'. In this sense, *Pseudo-Martyr* is a work in equal parts of bad faith and benevolent scepticism. It exposes heroic death to a corrupt and corrosive irony, yet it does so by means of a passionate appeal to life.

This involves some violence to Donne's conscience:

Since, as we say of Agues, that no man dies by an Ague, nor without an Ague; So at Executions for Treasons, we may justly say, No man dies for the Romane Religion, nor without it.   (p. 27)

This affront to the patrimony of his ancestors is justified by a complex argument. Martyrdom was an action without words, but in *Pseudo-Martyr* is made to seem uninterpretable. Distinguishing the deaths of the genuine from the heretical requires a knowledge of the 'secret and inward instinct and moving of the Holy Ghost', and such inwardness by definition has no outward signs of authenticity: 'although (I say) this instinct lie not in proofe, nor can be made evident' (p. 35).

Campion on the scaffold is said to have quoted St Paul, *Spectaculum facti sumus Deo, Angelis et hominibus*, 'We are made a spectacle, or a sight unto God, unto his Angels, and unto men'.[31] Yet this ancient motto of martyrs (used from Origen onwards) applied ambiguously to Campion himself. The account of Campion's trial and execution was controversial, and the *spectaculum* of his dismembered body was exposed to viciously different interpretations. The *True Reporte . . . Observid and written by a Catholicke preist, which was present thereat*, which quotes these final words, appeared as a reply to what was already a substantial bibliography on the other side of the story. This began with George Eliot's *A very true Report of the apprehension and taking of that Arche Papist Edmond Campion the Pope his right hand, with three other lewd Iesuite priests*, followed quickly by Anthony Munday's *A Discoverie of Edmund Campion, and his Confederates, their most horrible and traiterous practises, against her Majesties most royall person, and the realme*. Both were in print within two months of Campion's execution.[32]

The smell of treachery lingers round this grisly discourse. Eliot had betrayed Campion to the authorities in the buttery of a catholic safe house in Berkshire, and was himself an ex-recusant turned informer. Munday, an eminently versatile poet, actor, and playwright, had spent time as a

[31] Alfield, *True Reporte*, B4ᵛ–C1ʳ; see White, *Saints and Martyrs*, p. 220.
[32] Milward, *Controversies of the Elizabethan Age*, pp. 61–4.

seminary student at the English College in Rome. Motive here, however corruptible, is also inscrutable. It was quickly said that Munday had been a spy all along, but it is impossible to tell either way. In any event, he vindicated his action as that of a loyal patriot, on the grounds that Campion was a convicted traitor. Whether as turncoat or convert, Munday was no Saul, but then he lived in a different time.

If Donne's record of faith seems less discreditable than Munday's, it is not exactly credulous either. Perhaps he longed for a conversion so pure it eluded politics, but if so it eluded him. The subtle manœuverings of his loyalties, whatever the assertions of biographers, are lost to us as they probably were to him. In 1591 he was a recusant, seemingly; in 1594 his brother died, almost a martyr; in 1597 he found employment as secretary to Sir Thomas Egerton, Lord Keeper of the Seal. To do so he must at least nominally have accepted a requirement to conform, an action condemned by the Pope and by the English Mission. Southwell had died at the scaffold two years earlier to protect such an expression of conscience. Donne found it hard to kick against the pricks. But then Egerton himself had once been a recusant; only later, swapping sides, he had acted as counsel for the prosecution at Campion's trial.

Donne described his religious vicissitudes in the Preface to *Pseudo-Martyr*:

I had a longer worke to doe then many other men; for I was first to blot out certaine impressions of the Romane religion, and to wrastle both against the examples and against the reasons, by which some hold was taken   (p. 13)

Written perhaps fifteen years later, it has been said 'time has distanced Donne's apostasy'.[33] If anything, time has rendered this account a closed book, even in its acknowledged frankness. The blank phrase 'to blot out certaine impressions' says nothing about either 'apostasy' or 'conversion'. To confess 'openly' of such matter was hardly wise; in the same passage, Donne remarks that 'in a jealous, and obnoxious state, a Decipherer can pick out Plots, and Treason, in any familiar letter which is intercepted' (p. 10), never mind in a publication addressed to the king. He writes of the misinterpretation to which his state of soul was subject, aware of how this statement of conscience may yet also be misinterpreted:

And although I apprehended well enough, that this irresolution not onely retarded my fortune, but also bred some scandall, and endangered my spirituall reputation,

---

[33] Carey, *Donne*, p. 29.

by laying me open to many mis-interpretations; yet all these respects did not transport me to any violent and sudden determination, till I had, to the measure of my poore wit and judgement, survayed and digested the whole body of Divinity, controverted betweene ours and the Romane Church.   (p. 13)

This provisional autobiography, carefully unimprovisatory, is heavy with the implications of its own reading: 'irresolution', 'scandall', 'reputation', 'many misinterpretations', are still causes for caution. His etiolated clauses resist 'any violent and sudden determination' by the reader of whatever slow conjecture instigated his own spiritual metamorphosis. It is anything but an invitation to sympathetic identification with the 'truth'.

Far from sudden epiphany, Donne's lycanthropy is a work of controversy, involving (here for once Donne implies no irony) a survey of 'the whole body of Divinity'. Searching for evidence of Donne's conversion to Anglicanism, Walton seized on this dense paragraph and attempted to translate it into a spiritual classic, imbuing it with as much dramatic energy as he could muster. His paraphrase shows Donne throwing down the law and other studies 'to rectifie all scruples' of religion. But scruples and qualifications surround Donne's report of conversion. Despite his best intentions, Walton was embarrassed by the lack of emergency in Donne's account: 'The Cause was weighty: and wilful delays had been inexcusable both towards God and his own Conscience: he therefore proceeded in this search with all moderate haste'.[34] As evidence of this not immoderate haste, Walton narrates that Donne undertook a systematic examination of the complete works of Cardinal Bellarmine, conveniently available in three massive tomes.[35] The climax of Donne's Damascus, Walton tells us with barely controlled excitement, was an interview with the Dean of Gloucester (whose name Walton cannot remember) at which Donne presented him with 'all the Cardinals works marked with many weighty observations under his own hand'. Although Walton appears to have seen these heavily annotated volumes, they have not survived.[36] However, it is doubtful they could reveal the blinding flash of Donne's conversion any more lucidly than Donne does himself.

---

[34] Walton, *Lives*, p. 26.
[35] Bald, p. 69, assumes that Walton's reference must be to the *Disputationes de controversiis Christianae Fidei, adversus huius temporis haereticos* (Ingolstadt, 1586–93); there are numerous citations from this work in Donne's *Sermons*, e.g. vii. 190–1.
[36] Keynes, *Bibliography of Donne*, p. 262.

11 CAMPION'S BRAG AND CAMPION'S BLOODY REASONS

Donne had his reasons for converting, and he also had his Reasons. When he recalled in *Pseudo-Martyr* his labour 'to wrastle both against the examples and against the reasons' of the Roman religion, his wording was explicit. Campion had published *Ten Reasons* (*Rationes Decem*) in 1581 from Persons's secret press in Oxfordshire to persuade his countrymen of the truth of the old faith. The sensational story of how this little book was smuggled surreptitiously into the church of St Mary in Oxford and placed on the benches for the perusal of the assembled university at its June Commencement was a catholic favourite.[37] Even among protestants the term 'Reasons' was a byword for the art of religious persuasion. Donne's conversion was controversial through and through.

Although Walton understood this lexical reference, it has been lost on modern scholarship.[38] The presiding assumption is that theology is an activity separate from the personal and psychological sphere of religious experience. Theology is conceived as a language subsequent, and supplementary, to the spiritual life which it (merely) 'describes'. This mistakes the way that spiritual life is invested in theological language. Any experience, any psychology, is inseparable from the language in which it operates and by which it is identified. To ascribe to language a secondary role of description is to accord to experience an instinctual status appropriate only to a life without such capacity for description. An experience that is rationalized is thick with linguistic description.

The saturation of piety with theology was understood with peculiar self-consciousness in the later sixteenth century. The primacy of theology in Calvinism has of course been widely recognized, although it has not always been connected with its practice of conversion. However, this primacy has been held to be a sign of Calvinism's peculiarity, not of its typicality. Yet if Marian catholicism is marked by a return to the fabric and fixtures of pre-Reformation devotion, Elizabethan recusancy, as we have seen, was intensely doctrinal. When William Allen created his underground movement to maintain the faith, he saw the need for arguments as well as priests.[39]

Beginning in 1570, the literary genre of 'motives' and 'reasons' reached

---

[37] ARCR 135.1. Waugh's version is typically colourful, pp. 136–7.

[38] Walton, *Lives*, p. 26, paraphrasing this passage, describes Donne's reading of Bellarmine as 'the examination of his Reasons'. Bellarmine's work was well known to Donne (see above) but Campion better fits the English context of the memoir.

[39] Milward, *Controversies of the Elizabethan Age*, pp. 39–46.

its height in 'Campion's Brag'. This tiny masterpiece of apology addressed itself to the privy council with an equipoise of humility and challenge, aggression and charity. Posed as an open letter and quickly made public, it set out a 'playne confession' of Campion's purposes and intentions.[40] It was a manifesto for martyrdom: point by point, Campion avowed causes that gave the council reasons enough to quarter him. Alongside personal readiness to 'deliuer my body into durance' is a simultaneous witness of theology. The Brag demanded 'iii sortes of indifferent and quiet audiences' for a trial of doctrine: before the council itself, 'before the Doctors, Maisters, and chosen men of both Vniversities', and before 'the force of the lawe spirituall, and temperall'. In this process he undertook 'to vowe the fayth of our Catholike church, by proofes inuincible, scriptures, councells, fathers, hystories, naturall & morall reasons'.[41] Thus a letter which began as an individual testament had become a political disputation.

But 'proofes inuincible' were not incontrovertible. Indeed, the Brag was only ever printed as part of a volume of confutation—in fact two, one by the furious puritan William Charke and one more temperate by Meredith Hanmer.[42] This monstrous hydra of counter-textuality (which also included Persons and the loquacious William Fulke) is an epitome of the age. After Campion elaborated the Brag in his *Rationes Decem* official reaction was concerted: under the instruction of the Bishop of London, the Regius Professors of Divinity at both universities (Whitaker at Cambridge and Laurence Humphrey at Oxford) wrote Latin replies. The usual ratchet ensued: Whitaker's reply was answered in a *Confutatio* by the Scottish Jesuit John Dury, and the *Confutatio* in a further *Defensio* by Whitaker. This controversy rumbled on following Campion's death; meanwhile, in his last days, he was granted a disputation with protestant divines, which took place in the Tower in intervals from torture. Reports of these euphemistically named 'private conferences' were published to bolster the protestant case; Fulke naturally was involved—earning his epitaph (in Dennington church in Suffolk) the 'Rhemisks terror'—along with the deans of St Paul's and of Windsor. Further 'conferences' of condemned seminary priests with Fulke and others such as John Reynolds also reached the press.

In these last, strange, and fatal interviews, as in the *Reasons* and their

---

[40] Text from Meredith Hanmer's confutation, *The great bragge and challenge of M.Champion a Iesuite*, B1^r.

[41] *The great bragge*, F2^v.

[42] Charke, *An answere to a seditious pamphlet* (1580) [*STC* 5005]; for the controversy, see Milward, *Controversies of the Elizabethan Age*, pp. 54–6.

replies, the terminal and interminable subject is controversial theology: the interpretation of scripture, the ministry of the church, the function of priesthood, the sacrifice of the mass, merit, works, and faith.[43] The proof of faith, tested on the rack and at the scaffold, consisted not only in the *Spectaculum* of martyrdom but in the elucidation of minute verbal detail. Campion claimed 'such assurance in my [quarrel], and my evidence so [impregnable]', that:

> none of the protestantes, nor all the protestantes liuing, nor anye secte of our aduersaryes, how so euer they [face] men downe in their Pulpits and ouerrule them in their kingdome of Grammarians and vnlearned eares, can maintayn their doctrine in disputation.[44]

But Campion, too, had to fight for his place in the 'kingdome of Grammarians'.

If we are to believe Walton's admittedly vague chronology, Donne began research into 'the Body of Divinity, as it was then controverted betwixt the *Reformed* and the *Roman Church*' in 1591. But *Pseudo-Martyr*, on which Walton built his anecdotal history, was published only in 1610. A more immediate pretext for the reference there to Donne's conversion by 'examples and reasons' is the 1606 printing of a comprehensive edition of the Campion controversies. Published as *An Answere to the Ten Reasons of Edmund Campian the Iesuit, in confidence whereof he offered disputation to the Ministers of the Church of England, in the controversie of faith*, this was a translation of Whitaker's work by the puritan preacher Richard Stock. It also included the first English version of Campion's *Reasons* and of Dury's *Defence of those Reasons*. Versions of the *Reasons* existed in French, German, Flemish, and Polish by this date, but Campion Englished was a dangerous concept.[45] By one of those ironies in which the history of controversy abounds, purportedly seditious material was disseminated in the interest of suppressing sedition.

Treason was in the air: Stock's imprint came in the wake of the Powder Plot and the new Oath of Allegiance. The parliament of 1606, postponed from 5 November 1605, passed an 'Act for the better discovery and repressing of Popish Recusants'. The Act required all Catholics to abjure as 'impious and heretical' the 'damnable doctrine' that an excommunicated

---

[43] This list is taken from the title pages of the conferences of Reynolds with the priest John Hart, and Fulke and others with Campion; Milward, *Controversies of the Elizabethan Age*, nos. 218 and 220.

[44] *The great bragge*, F4ʳ, with Southern's emendations noted in parentheses.

[45] Milward, *Controversies of the Elizabethan Age*, p. 57; a catholic translation of Campion (*Campian Englished*) finally appeared in 1632 (ARCR 116).

monarch might lawfully be murdered by his own subjects. Since this doc-trine was confirmed as orthodox by Pope Paul V, and pious by Cardinal Bellarmine, the oath became the subject of a controversy throughout Europe outstanding even in this period in obduracy and obloquy.[46] The king himself was the openly secret author of *Triplici nodo, triplex cuneus, or An Apologie for the Oath of Allegiance* in 1607, and when this was refuted by Bellarmine, published a second edition in 1609 with the royal name on the title-page. Quick to the royal side came Bishop Andrewes of Chichester and the Dean of Salisbury, John Gordon, who exposed Bellarmine's theol-ogy to extended scrutiny in a series of works which made tortuous play with Bellarmine's pseudonym Matteo Torti: *Tortura Torti* (1609), *Antitor-tobellarminus* (1610), and *Anti-Bellarmino-tortor, sive Tortus Retortus* (1612). Alongside these Latin diversions a smaller English squib evolved, largely surrounding the output of the veteran polemicist Persons, in which Donne's *Pseudo-Martyr* played a cameo role.

Persons had already entered into a vigorous quarrel with Thomas Morton on the question of religious faith and political loyalty, a question given explosive topicality when Guy Fawkes intervened in its mid course. The ensuing treason trials prompted Morton to make a brilliant confla-tion between the political theory of resistance and the catholic doctrine of 'equivocation', a method long practised by recusant priests to avoid self-incrimination while preserving their conscience. Persons's replies (culmi-nating in the last work of his lifetime, *A Quiet and Sober Reckoning*) were masterpieces of equivocation, employing an irony later admired by Jonathan Swift.[47]

By 1607, when Morton became Dean of Gloucester, Donne appears to have been on good terms. It is conjectured that Morton may have employed him in the voluminous research required for his many contro-versies; less speculatively, that Donne sometimes read Morton's work in manuscript before publication.[48] Walton went the whole hog and invented an epistolary dialogue in which Morton unsuccessfully urged Donne to 'wave your Court-hopes, and enter into holy Orders' (p. 33). Walton as ever is eager to create a smooth narrative of religious introspection. The significance of Donne's relationship with Morton, and his intimate knowledge of the controversies that surrounded Morton, lies instead in

---

[46] Milward, *Controversies of the Jacobean Age*, pp. 89–119, lists over a hundred works in fifteen years occasioned by, though not always directly concerned with, the argument about the oath.

[47] *The Tatler*, no. 230, *Prose Writings*, ii. 177.

[48] Gosse, *Life and Letters*, i. 149; Bald, *John Donne*, pp. 210–12.

the deep complicity of Donne's reading and writing in the main lines of anti-catholic suppression in the aftermath of the Powder Plot.

In a world where to betray a thought might betray friends or faith altogether, the capacity of language to conceal as much as reveal became a prized asset. Indeed the beauty of language lay in the impossibility of discriminating between concealment and revelation. What was the difference between conviction and conviction? In the controversies over oaths, Morton and his opponents took to impersonating each other's voices: a seminary priest, ironically now identifiable only by his pseudonym, wrote *The Protestants Apologie for the Roman Church*, to which Morton replied with *A Catholike Appeale for Protestants*. There followed *Protestants Demonstrations*, and *The English Protestants Recantation*, both by anonymous catholics. In exasperation at such impersonations, *The Fal of Babel* complained in 1608 that 'a view of their writings, and bookes being taken, it cannot be discerned by any man living, what they would say, or how be understoode'.

On the question of the oath, Donne assured Sir Henry Goodyer in a private letter, 'I think truly there is a perplexity (as farre as I see yet) and both sides may be in justice, and innocence'.[49] Perhaps a year later Donne could see further, since *Pseudo-Martyr*, while complex, is not at all perplexed as to where justice lay in the matter of the oath: 'if it be taken in the sharpest sense, the Oath may nevertheless be taken without prejudice'.[50] In a public book as opposed to a private letter it could hardly be otherwise. Bald vigorously defends Donne from the imputation of duplicity, arguing that Donne changed his mind, but his mind was not what mattered. Donne was not free to say what he liked. *Pseudo-Martyr*'s apparently careless diversions into autobiography are carefully constructed. Donne, it was generally suspected, had been in the 1590s a rigid non-swearer; a decade later, he was now a converted swearer. Proof of his conversion was thus vital to his purpose. Reticence in such a case was impossible: it was too close to the expedient silence which, like any loyal catholic, Donne had shown in failing to proceed to public examinations at university, so omitting to swear to the Thirty-Nine Articles. What better way was there of establishing his credentials than openly betraying his former secret faith? How better to vindicate his new loyalty, than publish a treatise on the ultimate proof-test of fealty, the Oath of Allegiance?

It is possible to feel some distaste in Donne excoriating the time-serving William Barlow that he should 'write for religion, without it' and then

[49] *Letters*, p. 161.   [50] *Pseudo-Martyr*, p. 268.

make the slur in *Pseudo-Martyr* that 'at Executions for Treasons, we may justly say, No man dies for the Romane Religion, nor without it'. Or that he should take George Gervase to task for casting 'snares and tortures' on the swearers of the oath, whereas Gervase had been tortured and executed for refusing it.[51] Yet the self-consciousness of such betrayals is part of his act of sincerity in converting. Outspokenness is a trade-off for former silence; vulgarity for equivocation. Neither faithfulness nor infidelity can necessarily be taken completely at face value. To ascribe to Donne a cynical motive is as perilous as to ascribe a pious one, a false conversion as a true one. What was true conversion, and what were merely 'sophistications, and illusions, and forgeries'?[52]

In 1606, the year of the oath, one man's conversion was another's subversion. When protestantism stood accused of *Calvino-Turcismus* Matthew Sutcliffe replied by reflex, redubbing catholicism *Turco-Papismus*. Beyond name-calling lay a subjective world of interiority. Conversion was enveloped in a theology of conversion. Each was invested in a language so implicated that words and phrases twisted themselves in self-negation. Campion's forthright challenge to 'justifie the . . . faith' and thereby reconvert the privy council, the universities, and even the queen in person, was inextricably linked with the little matter of confuting Luther's doctrine of justification by faith. Not for the first time in the sixteenth century, the quibbling verb 'justifie' doubled back on itself in meaning. Campion founded his *Reasons* on a specific refutation of Luther's arguments concerning faith, incurring the automatic reaction of the Calvinist arch-Turk Whitaker in a loyal justification of 'the doctrine of iustification, which *Luther* learned from *S.Paul*'.[53] Reading this work in Stock's English, with its simultaneous translation of Campion's anti-Luther, Whitaker's anti-Campion, Dury's anti-Whitaker, and Whitaker's anti-Dury, is a bewildering exercise. Arguments pile up on top of each other, and the careless reader is liable to forget which is which, especially since each author cites the same citations.

Campion's Reasons for rejecting Luther formed a familiar catalogue. Luther's bondage of the will amounted to the axiom that 'God is the author and cause of sinne, willing, prompting, making, commaunding, and working it' (p. 184). The protestant God was made to command the impossible (p. 230). In granting certainty of grace to the elect, God permits the elect to commit wantonness and commits the rest to despair. Whitaker's

---

[51] Ibid., 157 and n.   [52] Letter to Goodyer, p. 160.
[53] Stock (tr.), *Answere to the Ten Reasons*, p. 32.

reply is equally run of the mill, returning to gobbets of scripture worn down by dispute since the diatribes between Erasmus and Luther: the hardening of Pharaoh's heart (p. 197); Christ's use of moral exhortations (p. 230).[54] The dispute is interesting not so much for its arguments as its methodology, in evidence especially in the Ninth Reason concerning sophisms.

Campion accused the protestants of four cardinal sins of language: *sciamachia*, 'fighting with shadow'; *logomachia*, 'a contention about words'; *homonymia*, 'a mistaking of the sense of words'; and *circulatio*, 'a going about the bush' (p. 272). Unwittingly, Campion laid bare the grounds of this theology in language, and took away the solid base of his own theory. Whitaker's critique of Campion was based on the same apprehension:

for all these are very vnlearnedly concluded; either *by mistaking words of double signification*; or by *wresting phrases figuratively spoken*: or *without any consequent*; or *from ignorance of the Elenche*; or (to conclude) altogether trifling   (p. 272)

Words vie with words, and dwindle into '*equiuocation*' (p. 279) and 'ambiguous signification' (p. 281). In one extraordinary passage, Whitaker allows the gospel to indulge in irony. God's commands show not that 'therefore those things may be performed of us' (as Campion, following Erasmus, had asserted), but are spoken 'ironically', for otherwise 'men may be conuerted vnto the Lord, by their owne meere will and disposition'. Dury responded with disbelief, for once forbearing denunciation and gaving Whitaker a second chance to take back his astounding suggestion: '*Do you think that God calleth men to repentance ironically?*' Whitaker was not abashed:

but when men will not seek God, being called thereto by his bountie; no maruaile though hee withdraw from them and (as it were) laugh at their madnes: of which ironies there be many examples in Scriptures.   (p. 269)

If, in a moment of madness, Whitaker was prepared to make Jesus an ironist, he is unprepared to apply the irony back to his own writing. Whitaker and Campion accuse each other of sophistries, but cannot acknowledge their own complicity in language. In the process, they create a dangerous world, in which lines of allegiance are drawn with deadly clarity. Donne's writing shows no such zealous neutrality. He sees instead 'miscitings, and mis-interpretations' on each side. Even Cardinal Cajetan,

---

[54] The debate between Luther and Erasmus continued to be cited throughout the century. In 1582, Beza appended '*Aliquot loci*' from *De servo arbitrio* to *De praedestinationis doctrina*; the passages concerning the hardening of pharaoh's heart and the grammar of verbs are quoted pp. 157–71. This appendix was reprinted in *Tractationes theologicae*, iii.

an orthodox among the orthodox, he remarks in *Pseudo-Martyr*, was accused by the papal curia of both heretical radicalism and temporizing caution (*Hebraizando* and *Erasmizando*)—as if he were both Luther and Erasmus. Donne's own path among the 'Barbarismes and Solaecismes' of language is weary and wary. To the Jesuits of his youth, the imputation of treason was a necessary risk, a martyr's wager. In resisting such heroism, Donne risked the opposite imputation of betrayal and opportunity. In this his 'conversion' was perhaps more symptomatic of his time than the lonely courage of the martyrs. Yet it should not be confused with simple ambition, still less with agnosticism. He may not have been an English Augustine in the manner of his conversion, as Walton enthusiastically claimed, but in the engagement of his religion in the dark matter of language he might still justly be called Augustinian.[55]

III THE NOISE OF THE *HOLY SONNETS*

The dating of the *Holy Sonnets* has undergone the same vicissitudes as the timing of Donne's conversion: the two have moved hand in hand.[56] For centuries, Walton's supposition that the divine poems belong to the period of Donne's ministry went unchallenged. The poetry, as surely as its author, was converted from profane to sacred. Present scholarship disputes a rigid distinction between Jack Donne and Dr Donne, and ascribes most of the *Holy Sonnets* to 1609–10, the same uneasy year as the composition of *Pseudo-Martyr*. The coincidence of chronology has not invited much comparison, however. The two kinds of writing seem diametrically opposed: public and controverted as against private and introverted. *Pseudo-Martyr*, the first work published by Donne with his name on the title-page, was dedicated to the king in direct appeal for patronage. By contrast, three of the *Holy Sonnets* exist in only one manuscript. Others which survive in more, still provoke the question of to whom such unreasonable poems might reasonably be addressed; sometimes their only satisfactory audience is God or Donne himself:

> Oh my blacke Soule! now thou art summoned
> By sicknesse, deaths herald, and champion;
> Thou'art like a pilgrim, which abroad hath done
> Treason, and durst not turne to whence hee's fled,

---

[55] 'Now the *English Church* had gain'd a second St *Austine*', Walton, *Lives*, pp. 47–8.
[56] Strier, ' "Holy Sonnets", 1608–10', summarizes the positions, pointing out the theological confusions of many commentators (361).

> Or like a thiefe, which till deaths doome be read,
> Wisheth himselfe delivered from prison;
> But damn'd and hal'd to execution,
> Wisheth that still he might be'imprisoned;
> Yet grace, if thou repent, thou canst not lacke;
> But who shall give thee that grace to beginne?
> Oh make thy selfe with holy mourning blacke,
> And red with blushing, as thou art with sinne;
> Or wash thee in Christs blood, which hath this might
> That being red, it dyes red soules to white.
>
> (IV)[57]

Addressed to itself ('Oh my blacke Soule!'), the poem has no interlocutor. In the sestet, it gestures outwards only to turn back in on itself, in peculiarly self-directed interrogations ('But who shall give thee...?') and imperatives ('Oh make thy selfe ... Or wash thee'). The poem's privacy seemingly allows no interruption.

However, this is no bottom-drawer poem. It survives in fifteen manuscript copies.[58] The original owners of these manuscripts are mostly unknown, but one was a miscellany compiled for the Cavendish family, probably for Sir William, the first Duke of Newcastle.[59] This miscellany contains a large number of poems by Jonson as well as ninety-eight by Donne. The presence of divine alongside profane poems, as in the Newcastle MS, was commonplace. One large collection of Donne's works (the Dobell MS) contains manuscript copies of three sermons, two 'characters', and the *Paradoxes and Problems*, as well as 119 poems (including 'Oh my blacke Soule!'). Even a manuscript containing none of Donne's sacred pieces, such as the first Dalhousie, includes religious pieces by other writers. Not all these pieces are poems: odd though it may seem to a modern eye, a trial testimony by the Archbishop of Canterbury, George Abbott, and a Latin prayer coexist with such pious ditties as 'The Flea' and 'Elegy, Going to Bed'.[60]

Arthur Marotti has suggested reasons for placing both *Pseudo-Martyr* and the *Holy Sonnets* within the network of Jacobean patronage.[61] Addressing *Pseudo-Martyr* to James I follows a trend in the dedication of

---

[57] Text from Gardner (ed.), *Divine Poems*; for ease of reference, Grierson's numbering is given.

[58] Beal, *Index of English Literary Manuscripts*, vol. i part 1 DnJ 2472–2486.

[59] BL Harley MS 4955 (usually referred to as H49); Beal, vol. i part 1, p. 250.

[60] Sullivan (ed.), *Dalhousie Manuscripts*, pp. 15–20, 106, 61.

[61] Marotti, *Coterie Poet*, pp. 180–1, and for a general survey of the religious works, pp. 245–68.

religious and controversial works to the monarch. Theology was a furrowed route to favour, as shown by the personal interest taken by the king in controversies such as the Oath of Allegiance. It was natural for Donne to seek favour among aristocratic patrons, women as well as men, by turning from the erotic to the divine. The short sonnet cycle *La Corona* was sent to Magdalen Herbert (George's mother) with a letter of recommendation and a dedicatory sonnet. Richard Sackville, third Earl of Dorset, was sent a similar dedicatory sonnet to accompany six so-called 'Holy Sonnets', now believed to be six poems on last things—including 'Oh my blacke Soule!'—later published in 1633 among the nineteen poems under that title.[62] Far from being inappropriate to the function of compliment, Marotti argues, the rhetoric of the *Holy Sonnets* enabled familiarity with his patrons. Later, Donne circulated copies of his sermons for the same reasons among the same sorts of patrons, including Magdalen, now Lady Danvers, and Dorset's wife, Lady Anne Clifford, of whom Donne remarked 'that she knew well how to discourse of all things, from Predestination, to Slea-silk'.[63] He was well rewarded, receiving from Dorset the rich and prestigious living of St Dunstan-in-the-West in 1624.[64] Dorset, significantly, was also the dedicatee of the 1620 collected edition of Southwell's works, which contained prose works such as *Marie Magdalens Funerall Teares* as well as the poems.[65]

'Oh my blacke Soule!' is purportedly a meditation on sickness as a prelude to divine judgement. The metaphor of redemption is the standard scriptural stamp used in hagiographical portraits of martyrdom, Christ's blood which 'dyes red soules to white'. The poem also makes more 'public' profession of theology:

> Yet grace, if thou repent, thou canst not lacke;
> But who shall give thee that grace to beginne?

Such a statement might seem to have no need for secrecy, but this sentence covers its traces with syntactic quibbles. The main clause disappears in

---

[62] This argument was first proposed by Gardner, Introduction to *Divine Poems*, pp. xlviii–ix.

[63] Bald, *John Donne*, p. 324.

[64] Ibid., 455; on the value of this living, see ibid., 425–6.

[65] This volume, which also included *A Short Rule of Good Life* and *The Triumphs of Death* (originally written in 1591 in commemoration of Sackville's mother) was published by William Barrett, the priest involved in the Cambridge controversy of 1595; the printer was Richard Field, who printed Shakespeare's *Venus and Adonis* and *Lucrece*. See McDonald and Brown, (eds.) Southwell, *Poems*, p. lxxv, and Janelle, *Southwell*, p. 316.

front of the reader's eyes. A statement of absolute generality is subjected to a succession of qualifying clauses that wither it away.

The two lines are like a reverse syllogism, but provide no hard and fast logic. Several interpretations of grace are considered, keeping the reader as well as the sinner in limbo. The main clause suggests 'thou canst not lacke [grace]', as if to imply unconditional universal salvation; the qualifying clause 'if thou repent' implies a conditional soteriology of penitence. It is as if we are witnessing the offer of universal salvation being withdrawn in front of our eyes, attenuated into insignificance. The reader, expecting theological explanation of the sinner's chances, struggles to extract a conclusive theological meaning. Instead, the conclusion is a rhetorical question, the superfluous dangling clause, 'But who shall give thee that grace to beginne?' Beyond questions, there are only commands, voiced into a vacuum from the self to the self, urging what cannot in any event be urged—an autoptic 'blushing' or a self-sanctifying sacrament:

> Oh make thy selfe with holy mourning blacke,
> And red with blushing, as thou art with sinne;
> Or wash thee in Christs blood, which hath this might
> That being red, it dyes red soules to white.

What impresses itself on the reader is not so much an unsatisfying theology as an elusive one, suppressed as soon as voiced. It is as contingent as the eschatological status of the sinner. Theology converts itself in endless modulations. And yet theology is an absolutely necessary adjunct to the personal narrative of the sinner: there is nothing he can say about himself without bringing theology in. Modern accounts of devotional poetry somehow regard theology as supplementary to the more immediate matter of experience. Even Marotti, concerned to show that the apparently 'personal' concerns of religion are also social, regards theology as a subterfuge for politics. But these matters are intimately connected. A metahistory of theology encloses that most cataclysmic of all interior religious narratives—the conversion of St Paul. Indeed, without theology, the psychological history is meaningless.

Calvin, as ever, is the sixteenth-century commentator most aware of these concerns:

in this story we have, so to speak, a universal type of that grace which the Lord puts out every day in calling of us . . . Accordingly, when we are converted to God it happens against our nature and by the marvelous and secret power of God.[66]

---

[66] *Opera Calvini*, xlviii. 202 (Acts 9: 5); *Calvin's Commentaries*, p. 259.

The merest analysis of Luke's stark narrative of a man falling to the ground invests it with meaning: Calvin proposes that Paul 'is called back to salvation against the intention of his own mind' (9: 3). This is a conversion with no initiative from the sinner, which calls him out of sin without his calling for it. Triumphantly, Calvin makes this a prototype for protestant grace, the sheer gift of God manifesting his 'secret power'. Commentary merges into controversy with seamless ease:

The Papists certainly also ascribe the credit for our conversion to the grace of God, but only partly, because they think that we co-operate   (9: 5).

Calvin assures his readers conversion instead confirms predestination in its absolute and singular authority.

Donne's sermons on the conversion of St Paul are marked on the contrary by a theological reticence, almost by a refusal to comment. The need for reticence is explained in a Lent sermon preached at Whitehall soon after his ordination. This made direct reference to the conversion of St Paul, using it as a blueprint for grace. This occasioned some remarkable comment on the controversies of theology: 'Whether this grace, which God presents so, be resistible or no, whether man be not perverse enough to resist this grace, why should any perverse or ungracious man dispute?'[67] Donne thunders against these 'new terms in divinity', such as '*Resistibility* and *Irresistibility* of grace', which have become 'every Artificers wearing now', but which never appeared in the writings of the church Fathers, 'a language that pure antiquity spake not'. The sermon urges restraint in the discussion of grace. 'It should not be disputed of in Schools, much less serv'd in every popular pulpit to curious ears; least of all made table-talke, and houshold-discourse' (i. 255). Yet Donne cannot resist the temptation to offer his own determination of this indeterminable point. Having declared the subject out of bounds in the pulpit, his exposition continues by asserting that 'Christ promises to come to the door, and to knock at the door, and to enter if any man open; but he does not say he will break open the door: it was not his pleasure to express such an earnestness, such an Irresistibility in his grace, so' (i. 255–6). This is not a disciplined refusal to speculate, but an open denial of 'Irresistibility'. Although he goes on to reclaim his orthodoxy by confirming 'his ends shall not be prevented; his ways shall not be precluded', he has already said enough to damn himself in Calvinist eyes.

A sermon on the feast of the conversion in January 1625 is more careful.

---

[67] *Sermons*, i. 255 (Luke, 23: 40, 20 February 1617).

It had to be, since in 1622 James had published Directions to Preachers which were quite explicit on the point. The king's letter to Archbishop Abbott in August recollected that 'abuses and extravagancies' of the pulpit had been properly repressed by act of council throughout history, and fulminated against modern preachers who 'by reading of late writers and ungrounded divines, do broach many times unprofitable, unsound, seditious, and dangerous doctrines'.[68] The directions which followed were breathtaking in their compass:

> That no preacher of what title or denomination soever, under the degree of bishop or dean at the least, do from henceforth presume to preach in any popular auditory the deep points of predestination, election, reprobation, or the universality, efficacy, resistibility or irresistibility of God's grace, but leave these themes to be handled by learned men, and that moderately and modestly.[69]

Such a mandate to stifle controversial discourse by Calvinist preachers on their favourite topics was inevitably controversial. Abbott was put in a deeply embarrassing position. Fuller reports that 'some counted it a cruel act, which cut off half the preaching in England'—an ironic glance at the ban in the directions on preaching in the afternoons, an obvious time for summer sedition. The Venetian ambassador wrily commented to the Doge that 'the idea of bridling the tongues of preachers in matters pertaining to their faith is like damming torrents, which only rage the more furiously'.[70] The king none the less worked to stem the torrent further. Donne, who as Dean of St Paul's was one of the few excepted from the ban, was ordered to preach in public at Paul's Cross in its favour.[71]

It was an odd brief, a sermon preaching the proscription of sermons. As text, Donne chose part of the Song of Deborah (Judges 5: 20), 'They fought from heaven; the stars in their courses fought against Sisera'. John Chamberlain, in a letter to that staunch supporter of the government, Sir Dudley Carleton, commented drily that it was 'somwhat a straunge text for such a busines', although he does not suggest what might have been a more appropriate scriptural citation for suppressing scripture.[72] Possibly Donne felt he had been granted a poisoned chalice; he later wrote to Goodyer that 'the Directions which his Majesty gave for preachers, had scandalized

---

[68] Summarized by Abbott in his letter to the bishops of August 12; Wilkins, *Concilia*, iv. 465.

[69] Fuller, *Church History*, v. 556.

[70] 'Il voler anco raffrenar le lingua a predicanti ministri nelle cose stimate attinenti alla lor religione reisce come trattener torrenti che impedisti maggiormente infuriano', (ambassador A. Valdaresso, 9 September 1622), *CSPV*, 17 (1621–3), 411; see also 445.

[71] MacLure, *Register of Sermons*, pp. 121–2.

[72] *Letters of Chamberlain*, ii. 451; *CSPD*, James I, 1619–23, p. 449.

many', continuing that he hoped that he had given 'comfortable assurance of his Majesties constancy in Religion'.[73] Even the zealously uncontroversial Bishop of Lincoln, John Williams, had mixed feelings, considering the directions a necessary restraint on those who 'would be meddling with controversies they scarcely understand' but also potentially '*limiting of the Spirit of God*'.[74] The reception of Donne's sermon was ambiguous. Chamberlain, usually the most garrulous reporter, is non-plussed: 'how he made yt hold together I know not, but he gave no great satisfaction, or as some say spake as yf himself were not so well satisfied' (ii. 451). Yet Donne, 'satisfied' or not, worked hard to have his justification published, the first of his sermons to be printed. He sent it to a number of patrons for comment and approval; Sir James Hay, now the Earl of Carlisle, showed it to the king, who (Carlisle wrote to Donne) gave 'his own word, That it was a piece of such perfection, as could admit neither addition nor diminution'. Whether this gnomic sentence is really the unmitigated satisfaction some of Donne's biographers have assumed may be questioned.[75] In any event, the king consented to publication, although on Carlisle's advice it was dedicated to the Duke of Buckingham rather than to James himself.

Perhaps James did not understand the sermon. Although it is one of Donne's most important public utterances, it mystified his editors and has often eluded commentary.[76] Gosse thought James to be identified with the Sisera of the text in Judges, a wild mistake since Sisera was the violent enemy of the Israelites and was assassinated in marvellous style by a Hebrew woman armed only with a tent-peg: Donne retells the story in his sermon. No less strangely, Bald asserts there is 'no mention at all of the list of forbidden topics' of theology in Donne's sermon. One-third of the sermon deals with these forbidden topics, but so circumspectly Bald may be forgiven for having missed them. The sermon is hedged round with caveats and *mea culpas*. Despite this, unmentionable topics turned out to be more or less unavoidable because the directions are so indiscreetly indiscrete in their censorship. Attempting to avoid any subject whatsoever

---

[73] *Letters*, pp. 231–2.

[74] Hacket, *Scrinia reserata*, p. 90. Those who consider Donne's own career as ruthlessly time-serving might consider the parallel career of Williams, who was employed by Sir Thomas Egerton at the same time as Donne, and who rose with astonishing speed to be Lord Keeper of the Seal and eventually Archbishop of York. The reference to Williams in the sermon is at iv. 201.

[75] Shami's analysis ('Donne and the Pulpit Crisis') of the full circumstances surrounding this sermon has overturned the biographical consensus of Bald and Carey.

[76] See, however, the suggestive analysis in Patterson, *Censorship and Interpretation*, pp. 98–100.

in his elaborate circumlocutions, Donne stumbles on forbidden fruit. He gingerly trespasses the territory of God's grace, suggesting that those 'who expressed their faith in *Workes*' shall have 'a place in the *Booke of life*; indelibly in the Booke of life'. Having expressed himself so indelicately, Donne hesitates, attempting to pre-empt the inference that he has committed any serious indiscretion: 'and doe not thinke, that they have done all, or done enough, if they have done something some one time'.[77] Heaven forbid that he might be thought to have said that works work sufficiently to be efficacious of, or even sufficient for, grace.

The sermon is marked by an overpowering will to its own oppression. And yet it bears the scars of self-censorship even as it cuts out its own tongue. Donne excoriates erratic preaching, which, 'be the intention never so sincere, will presage, and prognosticate, and predivine sinister and mischievous effects from it' (197). Caught in the throat of the words 'presage, and prognosticate, and predivine' is the shibboleth 'predestinate', invoked as it is extinguished. In the desperate effort to shy from all controversy, Donne falls inexorably into it. To promote the peace of the Church of England, he recounts one of the least peaceable episodes in its short history, the ineffable Lambeth Articles of 1595. Even here, Donne's censorship is so exact he omits their name, putting Bald and other commentators off the scent (iv. 200). The details of this half-secret, half-open war of words were lost on most of his audience, too, but his references are specific enough to be obvious to anyone in the higher clergy. Donne makes glancing reference to the coalition of the heads of Cambridge houses, to the deliberations of Whitgift (not named), to the scrupulous determination of the Articles, to Whitaker's sermon *Ad Clerum*, and to the intervention of Queen Elizabeth.

Donne means the Lambeth Articles to tell an exemplary moral tale of government suppression, but their invocation is two-edged. The Lambeth Articles had enjoyed a posthumous history quite as peculiar as their original inception. At the Hampton Court Conference called to clarify the religious polity of the new reign in January 1604, a puritan group, which included Chaderton, one of the heads of house involved in 1595, attempted to resurrect the Lambeth Articles as official doctrine. John Reynolds, who led the puritan representatives, described them as 'nine assertions orthodoxical', and suggested that they be inserted after the Thirty-Nine Articles as a clarification of Articles 16 and 17. It seemed an opportune moment: the new king's religious views were uncertain, but he took a personal interest

[77] *Sermons*, iv. 186–7.

in theology in some contrast to his predecessor. Whitgift, his archbishop, who was old and ill, appeared unlikely to intervene with his habitual iron hand, and indeed survived the conference by only a month. However, the campaign for the Articles was to have no easy run: Overall and Andrewes, who had taken a carefully ambiguous stance in relation to the Articles in 1595, were also present at the conference, perhaps at the instigation of Sir Fulke Greville.[78] In more direct opposition stood the Bishop of London, Richard Bancroft, soon to replace Whitgift as archbishop.

The history of the conference has itself become shrouded in controversy. Historians have argued in different places that it represents either the high water mark of English Calvinism, or the sign of its ultimate defeat, or else the beginnings of English Arminianism. The documentary evidence is hardly immaculate. The main source is *The summe and substance of the conference*, by William Barlow, then Dean of Chester, but Barlow wrote with a strong bias towards the episcopal argument. Several manuscript memoranda survive which have been used recently to rebut Barlow, but these are no more impartial. The idea of an impartial account in such an area is probably bogus, as also is the assumption of clear divisions of party to which labels can easily be attached.

Donne despised Barlow, but owned a copy of *The summe and substance* which he heavily annotated.[79] Barlow's account should be read as a dramatic narrative not a record of fact, and reverberates with sudden irruptions of point and counterpoint, conducted over strange exchanges of volatile speech acts. Reynolds (in Barlow's narrative) begins from the imprudent premiss that the Thirty-Nine Articles in 'some things were defective', and continues in still more dangerous fashion that Article 16 might on a quick reading 'seem contrary to the doctrine' of Article 17. The insertion of the Lambeth Articles, he moves, would resolve these 'places obscure'.[80] At this point in Barlow's drama the Bishop of London cannot contain himself. Spluttering an old Latin papal curse, *schismatici contra episcopos non sunt audiendi*, and mocking the schismatics' outlandish style of dress as 'Turkey gowns', he wonders aloud whether clemency towards such open questioning of established doctrine can be allowed. The late queen, he recalls with approval, was not notably generous in such cases (p. 179).

---

[78] Tyacke, *Anti-Calvinists*, p. 22.

[79] Donne's copy survives in the Cambridge UL; Keynes, *Bibliography*, p. 264 [L17]. Donne's satirical spoof book-list *The Courtier's Library* contains the item 'An Encomium on Dr Shaw, chaplain to Richard III, by Dr Barlow' (no. 31). Shaw preached a sermon implying that the Princes in the Tower were illegitimate.

[80] Barlow, *Summe and substance*, in Cardwell (ed.), *History of Conferences*, p. 178.

The reaction of the king in this narrative is fascinatingly ambiguous. He is put out by the interruption of the intemperate bishop, but asks him to make a specific case. The bishop complains of those who 'neglecting holinesse of life' have 'presumed too much of persisting of grace, laying all their religion on predestination'. With savage ridicule, he reduces the predestinatory logic to a grammatical tautology, a meaningless condition, 'If I shall be saved, I shall be saved', reminiscent of Faustus's desperate wager, 'what will be, shall be' (p. 180). But his own case turns on a similarly brittle logical methodology (pp. 180–1).

The king replies with a balance bordering on weightlessness, worrying on one side that 'God's omnipotency might be called in question, by impeaching the doctrine of his eternal predestination'; on the other that 'a desperate presumption might be arreared, by inferring the necessary certainty of standing and persisting in grace' (p. 181). This is as near to saying nothing as is possible. On the politics of the Lambeth Articles, however, his ignorance is more sphinx-like in its cunning. He affects not to know of them, and asks to be reminded of their content and circumstances. On receiving information, he demurs from the motion to include them with the Thirty-Nine. The very explicitness and comprehensiveness of the Lambeth propositions is the problem: the king declares his dislike of their logical elaborateness, their complex clauses, and inverted conditionals, 'thinking it unfit to thrust into the book every position negative'. To allow for every scruple the Articles of Religion would have to be 'as big as the Bible'; indeed, the king opines, 'were the articles so many and sound', they could never satisfy every problem in advance, for 'who can prevent the contrary opinions of men til they be heard?' (p. 185)

It is debatable whether these are the king's actual words. In any event the Lambeth Articles were not officially adopted in 1604 as they had not been in 1595. On 5 March 1604 there was a proclamation inhibiting further discussion.[81] Such a position should not be taken as anti-Calvinist, however; the government was equally careful in not condemning the Articles in one jot. From the beginning of the Elizabethan polity to the beginning of King Charles's reign, the aim of government pronouncements on predestination seems consistent: to keep open debate to a minimum. Donne's 1622 sermon explicitly endorsed such a policy and defended an 'Inhibition' on preachers who persisted in 'medling with any of those poynts' (*Sermons*, iv. 200). But in reinforcing the boundary he comes dangerously close to overstepping it himself. He implies disapproval of the Lambeth Articles, and

---

[81] *SRP*, i. 74–7.

makes other sly insinuations of a partisan approach. Recommending catechism to replace afternoon preaching, he remarks: 'And if wee should tell some men, That *Calvins Institutions* were a *Catechisme*, would they not love Catechising the better for that name?' (iv. 203). A gibe at Calvin's *Institutes* is a dangerous game, however oblique. Donne quickly restores his position by rhapsodizing the Thirty-Nine Articles as the supreme 'Superedification' of doctrine, 'high inough, and deepe inough' for any man, but he is careful not to expound them any further, recognizing that 'they imbrace *Controversies* too, in poynts that are necessarie' (iv. 205–6). Reynolds, after all, had found controversies in the interstices between different Articles.

Donne's sermon on the feast of the conversion of St Paul just over two years later operates under the constraints of the directions. It hesitates to make too clear a statement of divine grace but longs for a sensational sentence, for a grace as pure as Saul's. The sermon concludes with a long peroration of the voice of God, which breaks with sudden violence into the life of Saul, changing everything in its wake. The voice which calls Saul out of the blue is the voice which at the creation announced itself unequivocally: '*Dixit, & facta sunt*, God spoke, and all things were made'.[82] In its clarity of intention and meaning, the divine speech act reveals no slippage between word and meaning or between word and world. It is the ultimate illocutionary act ('God spoke, and all things were made'), utterance without *différance*.

But the self-fulfilling panache of God's sentence is denied to mortal speech acts. In fact, in the translation between divine locutor and human auditor, grace itself becomes unrecognizable. The declaratory perfection of the creator's fiat is located in the fact that God was his own audience as well as his own subject. The human audience has a habit of mishearing grace, of mistaking providence for mere happening. So it is with the Pauline conversion, Donne says:

we heare no voyce, we doe not discern that this noyse, or this sound comes from any certain person; we do not feele them to be mercies, nor to be judgements uttered from God, but naturall accidents, casuall occurrencies, emergent contingencies, which as an Atheist might think, would fall out though there were no God (vi. 217).

The unitary 'voyce' of the grace of conversion is dispersed into random 'noyse', indistinguishable and uninterpretable.

---

[82] *Sermons*, vi. 216; it is a quotation from Psalm 33: 9.

Thus it is that the voice of Donne's own essays in poetic grace appear instead as mere 'noyse'. The peremptory imperatives that abound in the *Holy Sonnets* seem aimed at nobody out of nowhere. It is this unperformability which gives this poetry its sense of religious futility, of wild gesture. The sinner senses a need for grace and makes hopeless cries for transformation; but can only be transformed by a grace which should already have intervened preveniently.

This is the true exemplariness of Saul, in revealing the perplexity of the involuntariness of grace. As Caravaggio's painting demonstrates with virtuoso mundanity, the involuntary has all the appearance of everyday accident. Indeed, in being detached from causality, the incident on the road is made strangely inconsequential. This most supernatural of voices which appears out of nowhere sounds like mere 'noyse', and this most providential of actions as the most ordinary of 'casuall occurrencies'. In fact it is this casualness (from the root *casu*, by accident) which renders the moment as archetypally one of grace.

Archetypally but also ambiguously, because to the atheist it is just as natural to read this narrative of sublime clumsiness as simple contingency, Caravaggio's 'accident in a blacksmith's shop'. By definition, this experience, this blinding flash, is without physical evidence. Conversion to grace is irremediably prone to ambiguity. By what signs can it be known? Indeed, when does it take place, even if believed in? The person in grace is always already in grace, even before grace comes. And yet it is not clear (if at all) how the sinner is marked by the change. Is Paul suddenly sinless? Or does he sin less and less, gradually? And if another sinner, not quite so graced as Paul, sins not at all for a while but then slides back, is this still a sign of grace, or proof that grace never came after all? If, on the other hand, Saul cannot resist, it seems doubtful if the grace is really his. Grace reveals in this way the deep paradox of the gift: it can only be given if it is received.

IV DONNE'S DANGEROUS QUESTION

Grace may or may not be irresistible, but the language of grace, the language of the theology used to inscribe it—in some sense no doubt language itself—is full of resistances. Donne longed for a language free of resistances, but his own poetry and prose abound in them, and offer vexed commentary on them. This becomes apparent when diction and metaphor is put aside for a while in order to reveal in relief the linguistic structure of Donne's religious poems. The grammar of these poems projects a bewildering confusion of theological accents, which refuse to conform to a rigid doctrinal pattern. Like the road to Damascus, this way is obscured by the 'noyse' of grace, demanding interpretation but not delivering it. The 'noyse' of the *Holy Sonnets* insists itself on the reader's attention but fails to provide a coherent 'voyce':

> Spit in my face yee Jewes, and pierce my side,
> Buffet, and scoffe, scourge, and crucifie mee
>
> (XI, 1–2)

Six imperative verbs pile on each other with diminishing returns. The commands are not only self-lacerating but self-involuted: they refer to no addressee. The imperative mode finds no interlocutor but is reflected onto the subject in redoubled rebuke.

This solipsistic trope is also present in the most notoriously noisy of Donne's poems:

> Batter my heart, three-person'd God; for, you
> As yet but knocke, breathe, shine, and seeke to mend;
> That I may rise, and stand, o'erthrow mee, 'and bend
> Your force, to breake, blowe, burn and make me new.
>
> (XIV, 1–4)

The poem is both admired and deprecated for the aggressively sexualized blasphemy of its ending, appealing for the rape of grace. It is equally blasphemous in its strident commands, bullying God to take the dominating role in the partnership with self-consciously masochistic bravado:

> Divorce mee, 'untie, or breake that knot againe,
> Take mee to you, imprison mee, for I
> Except you'enthrall mee, never shall be free,
> Nor ever chast, except you ravish mee.
>
> (XIV, 11–14)

And yet it is hard to perceive the poem as being within God's hearing: these are shouts in the dark, with a strangely directionless and unmotivated energy of articulation. The violence is over-determined, as if in compensation for the marked absence of the violent intervention of grace.

Indeed the raucous perversity of the poem's sexuality is in some contrast with its zealously orthodox theology. This begins with the fussily correct appellation, 'three-person'd God', and is apparent in the economy of grace projected throughout the poem: the soul, fallen through original sin, is 'like an usurpt towne, to'another due' (l. 5). No amount of good works ('Labour to' admit you') can possibly be fruitful, and 'Reason', the gift of creation, 'is captiv'd' by the corruption of the Fall. One region remains free from the enemy's thrall, the freedom of love, expressed with a sonneteer's lilt:

> Yet dearely'I love you, and would be lov'd faine
> (l. 9)

But love, too, is not offered unconditionally by the soul unless and until it is initiated by grace; the poem awaits this transcendence, unable to make any effort of its own in advance of grace. The five imperative verbs of the final quatrain ('Divorce mee, 'untie, or breake . . . / Take mee to you, imprison mee'), therefore occupy a peculiar place in the theology of the poem. They demand an action which cannot be prevented, but which cannot be provoked either. The soul is in a state of inertia. In that sense the energy of the imperative verbs which the soul urges upon itself is made redundant. The proliferation of different commands only emphasizes the failure of every one in its turn, as does the wavering conjunction 'or' (l. 11), implying the equal superfluity of each. As a result, the poem ends in suspense, committed to submission but not yet permitted to submit. The soul is still waiting for release, and remains poised in unsatisfied and interminable passivity:

> for I
> Except you'enthrall mee, never shall be free,
> Nor ever chast, except you ravish mee.

Futile imperatives lurch into the strange negative conditionals of its ending, 'Except . . . never . . . nor . . . except'. After the bravado of the opening command, the poem eventually gives up the ghost, admitting defeat in the contorted logic of a final double negative ('not . . . if not').

Screaming for conversion, the sonnets point to their sullen unconvertedness. 'As due by many titles' lists in order in its octave eight entitlements, by which his self belongs to God. At the opening of the sestet, however, the catalogue is interrupted by two sharply posed questions cutting across the grain of the preceding syntax:

> Why doth the devill then usurpe in mee?
> Why doth he steale, nay ravish that's thy right?
> (II, 9–10)

The rest of the poem is forced to unravel the implied consequences of these questions, not so much in contradiction of the octave as in determined ignorance of it. It is a different poem, abandoning co-ordinate syntax in favour of muddled subordination, one clause tacked on to the last in improvised reply without any respect for the line unit:

> Except thou rise and for thine owne worke fight,
> Oh I shall soone despaire, when I doe see
> That thou lovs't mankind well, yet wilt not chuse me,
> And Satan hates mee, yet is loth to lose mee.
>
> (II, 11–14)

With each breath he undoes the force of the last. The characteristic 'except' introduces a condition attached oddly to God, only to give way to an exclamation ('Oh I shall soone despaire') itself grammatically subordinate to a further series of qualification upon qualification upon qualification ('when . . . yet . . . And . . . yet'). Everything is made to hang by the most tenuous thread to the final frighteningly loose afterthought, 'And Satan hates mee'. The tenuous grammar is matched by the tenuous rhymes, which allows a feminine to match a masculine ending, producing a theologically dying fall, a loss of faith, and a graceless cadence.[83]

All the more contorted in its grammatical logic is 'If poysonous miner-alls'. This poem begins with four if-clauses which are left dangling, only for their completion to be effected not by a consequence but by two aggressive questions, the interrogative 'why?' repeated within five words:

> If poysonous mineralls, and if that tree,
> Whose fruit threw death on else immortall us,
> If lecherous goats, if serpents envious
> Cannot be damn'd; Alas; why should I bee?
> Why should intent or reason, borne in mee,
> Make sinnes, else equall, in mee, more heinous?
>
> (IX, 1–6)

A further 'why?' follows before the end of the octave. This quizzical and querulous poem torments itself with questions and conditions, testing the reader's wit and nerves with its theological twists. Wishing itself in a state of inorganic oblivion in preference to the imputation of sin and mortality, the poem centres on the paradox of the fatal consequences of 'intent or reason'. As if in answer, the very contortions of 'intent or reason' in evidence in the poem's wracked speech acts seem to prove his point. Who would wish for wakefulness in a consciousness like this? The state of sin is bodied forth in fallen syntax.

---

[83] The rhymes have been extensively commented; see the summary in Gardner, p. 66.

It is as if language cannot bear grace. Propositional assertion is incapable of completion, constantly giving way to hypothesis or interrogation. There is not a single indicative clause in the whole poem. After the divine inquisition of the octave the sestet turns inward in self-introspective reproach, continuing the grammatical mode of interrogation before abandoning semantics altogether in exclamation:

> But who am I, that dare dispute with thee?
> O God, Oh!
>
> (IX, 9–10)

Is this an exhalation, a groan, or an expletive? If the last, against whom is it directed? Perhaps he is swearing at himself or, then again, perhaps at God himself. The latter possibility is reinforced by the way that the poem now changes grammatical tack again, to place new demands on God to 'make a heavenly Lethean flood' of the sinner's tears. Yet still the longed-for oblivion will not come. The subject wills his own unconsciousness but cannot enforce his will. An exterior action is required which the poem cannot itself enact, and after the failure of its own imperatives it drifts into a final conditional clause:

> That thou remember them, some claime as debt,
> I thinke it mercy, if thou wilt forget.
>
> (IX, 13–14)

This brilliantly equivocal sentence sums up the uncertain syntax of the poem. Beginning with its relative clause, the rest of the sentence struggles to catch up; looking out for a main clause, seeming to find it ('I thinke it mercy'), and then revealing a further subordination to the ultimate anti-climax of an inconclusive 'if'. For anyone who knows Donne's secular poetry (as his first readers obviously did) it is the antithesis of the 'masculine persuasive force' considered his trade-mark. There is something virtuoso about this anti-climactic, anti-deictic verse. The grammatical subject commits suicide in front of us, erasing himself into subordination.

There is a constant tension in the *Holy Sonnets* between the eschatological doctrine which dominates the dictional surface of the poems and the prevaricating and protesting syntax which purports to justify that doctrine but eminently fails to do so. It is this tension which has enabled critical response to divide between those who see the poems as vauntingly orthodox and those who see them as irrepressibly sceptical. It would be more accurate to say that they are both orthodox and dubious, and never more dubious than when orthodox. The syntax embodies a reflex of dissidence against the demands of assertion. The most obvious form of dissent is in the relentless commands which erupt in every poem. These commands portend a sense of doctrine against the grain and perhaps against the will, of obedience only achievable by coercion. Such a grace seems not predestined so much as prescribed. But lack of stress can be as undermining as an over-stress. The little word 'or' acts as a constant source of linguistic dubiety. When the last quatrain of 'Oh my blacke Soule!' enjoins the sinner 'Oh make thy selfe with holy mourning blacke' with overwhelming urgency, the action of penitence is suddenly interrupted by an alternative source of transcendence, 'Or wash thee in Christs blood'. The force of 'Or' here is unclear: could it mean a double condition, both of which are necessary for grace (penitence and sacrament); or is it a fail-safe device, so that if one fails the other can be tried? The hesitation seems antipathetic to grace, as if God might be changing his mind or having it both ways.

The endless questions have a more complex action. The semantics of questions is an area much misunderstood. It is often assumed that a question must have an addressee, in much the same way that it is assumed that an imperative must have an addressee; indeed sometimes the question is held to be a kind of demand, an instruction to the addressee to answer the question. But this is simplistic, resulting from an emphasis on the circumstances of conversation which ignores the illocutionary force of the question as a grammatical entity.[84] Lyons's application of speech act theory to interrogation is quick to notice that 'we can pose questions which we not merely expect to remain unanswered, but which we know, or believe, to be unanswerable' (ii. 755). Questions answer to innumerable motives of qualification or scepticism.

A Sermon preached on New Year's Day in 1625 offers extended analysis. The Feast of the Circumcision occasioned a disquisition on obedience to God's commands in general, and a long digression on the problems of questioning those commands. This leads Donne into a deeply considered citation from Luther on the question of questions:

Periculosa & pestilens quaestio, Quare; saies *Luther* also, It is a Dangerous and Infectious *Monosillable, How* or *Why*: If I will aske a *reason*, why God commands such a thing.[85]

[84] Lyons, *Semantics*, ii. 753–5.
[85] *Sermons*, vi. 187–8. The wording from Luther's *In primum librum Mose enarrationes* is a slight misquotation: *Pernitiosa igitur et pestilens cogitatio est de Quare*, WA 42.670.26.

Donne, like Luther before him, is impressed by Abraham's amazing capacity to obey God, no questions asked, even when asked to circumcise himself at the age of 99 years. Unquestioning obedience is a necessary antidote to the alternative, the impossible, unfathomable 'why?', a monosyllable which is 'Dangerous' because 'I have nothing to answer me, but mine owne *reason*' and which is 'infectious' because it has no barriers and no limits. Once we have asked 'why?', where will it all end?

So if that *infectious inquisition*, that *Quare* (*Why* should God command this or this particular?) be entred into me, all my *Humilitie* is presently infected, and I shall looke for a reason, why God made a world, or why he made a world no sooner then 6000. yeares agoe, and why he saves *some*, and why *but* some, and I shall examine God upon all the *Interrogatories* that I can frame (vi. 188)

Once initiated, the interrogation envelops the whole of the Creed, the Pater Noster, and the Ten Commandments. It is, he says (quoting Luther once more), '*Otiosa & exitialis vocula, Quare*, It is an Execrable and Damnable Monosillable, *Why*', which calls into question God's 'goodnesse', 'power', and 'wisdome'.[86]

To call these things into question is to question whether God is God, since God by definition is all-good, all-powerful, and all-wise. The wise course therefore is to eschew such enquiries altogether. If the question is the wrong question, it is better left unasked. Sometimes a little knowledge is a dangerous thing: 'There is as much strength in, and safe relying upon some ignorances, as some knowledges' (vi. 189). Asking too many questions led Eve and Adam to the Fall. Luther's meditation on questions compares Abraham's faithful silences favourably with Adam's need to know—why God had created him, why the one fruit was forbidden, why he would die if he ate it.[87] Abraham had the sense or grace not to ask why, even when he had good reason to, on the frequent occasions when God had asked him to do something patently unreasonable. Continuing the theme, Luther extended the ban on questions. Whenever *de praedestinatione volumus Philosopheri* ('we want to philosophize about predestination', WA 42.670.28) it is time for us to stop asking why. Donne paraphrases in his sermon: 'It was the Devill that opened our eies in Paradise, it is our parte to shut them so farre, as not to gaze upon Gods secret purposes' (*Sermons* vi. 189).

Donne's citation from Luther has been taken as a conservative and com-

---

[86] WA 42.671.37.
[87] In his gloss on Genesis 3: 1, Luther argued that the Hebrew grammar of Satan's question was equivalent to the Latin *Quare?* (WA 42.164.37).

forting gesture, abandoning human reason in the face of divine mystery.[88] It was certainly a convenient passage to find in Luther in the light of the 1622 directions, which forbade useless enquiries into the operations of divine grace. Indeed, while Luther specifically mentions *praedestinatio* as the most contagious of all 'infectious inquisitions', Donne goes so far as to erase the very word from his prohibition. Like any wise preacher in late Jacobean England, he omitted to mention the word entirely. The directions made such extremes of delicacy expedient, but the probability that it is none the less the real object of Donne's urgent proscription is shown by the little euphemism 'Gods secret purposes', a Calvinist code for eternal providence. And lurking in the midst of Donne's discourse is a question so devilish that hardly any Jacobean divine was prepared to own up to it, why God 'saves *some*, and why *but* some'?

Rather like God mentioning the tree to Adam in the first place, this puts the serpent back in paradise even in the act of forbidding him entrance. Donne puts the very question into the heads of his audience that he claims he wants them not to ask. Having let the cat out of the bag, Donne appends a list of all the best, or worst, questions in the Bible in order to prove his point that such questions should never be put. Among these posers from Old and New Testaments he includes the murmuring of the Children in the Desert, '*Wherefore have you brought us hither to die here?*', and the cry of Job, '*Why did I not die in birth?*' These questions, so like the questions of the *Holy Sonnets*, carry with them the volatile speech acts of the sonnets, providing a theological counterweight to the official purpose of censorship. No doubt it would have been better not to ask them, but here they are asked, and in the asking Donne frankly admits his own inability to answer them. They remain unanswered, apparently unanswerable, and the act of forbidding them only adds to their inadmissable, incalculable power.

Donne's disquisition on dangerous monosyllables, like Luther's before him, is a more powerful essay on human and divine rationality and irrationality than his more comfortably sceptical modern critics allow. To 'aske a *reason*, why God commands such a thing' may be dangerous, but to ban the question is equally dangerous, because it risks making God appear openly irrational. It also undermines his argument, which must itself appear irrational. How can the rejection of rationality appear as anything other than irrational? As a result, every proposition Donne utters begins to appear paradoxical. He behaves as if the statement 'I have nothing to

---

[88] Carey, *Donne*, p. 242.

answer me, but mine owne *reason*' is a manifest falsity. On the other hand, he approves as self-evident Augustine's curious observation that 'He that seekes a reason of the will of God, seekes for something greater then God'. From Augustine also he takes what appears to be his trump card, '*Why* God commands any thing, God himselfe knowes' (vi. 189).

Donne's English translation transforms Augustine's ordinary Latin saying (*Dominus cur iusserit, viderit*) into a desperate paradox poised sensationally between axiom and blasphemy. The demotic bluntness of 'God himselfe knowes' is a marvellous bluff, daring his audience to smile while retaining the outward appearance of saintly orthodoxy. It is a sentence which acknowledges the high risks which it takes with doctrine. Luther in this respect is an appropriate source for him to quote, because Luther was the master of this style of high theological irony. In the final section of *De servo arbitrio* it became his typical manner:

As you can see, God so orders this corporeal world in its external affairs that if you respect and follow the judgement of human reason, you are bound to say either that there is no God or that God is unjust. (WA 18.784.36; Rupp and Watson, p. 330)

This sentence is so laconic as to be frightening. The bleakness of the conclusion (*aut nullum esse Deum, aut iniquum esse Deum*), uttered with an even-handedness which is all the more brutal for not admitting to any terror or surprise, bewilders the reader into forgetting for a moment the force of the premiss ('if you follow human reason'). The conclusion affects the reader with a shattering logic of uncompromising clarity: this is an either/or between human reason and divine goodness.

It is hard to think of a more shocking sentence in sixteenth-century theology. One aspect of the shock is that it is so close to scriptural orthodoxy. Paul's epigrammatic description of the gospel of Christ as being Ἰουδαίοις μὲν σκάνδαλον ἔθνεσιν δὲ μωρίαν ('unto the Jews a stumbling-block, and unto the Greeks foolishness', 1 Corinthians 1: 23) is as well worn as any cliché in the Bible, so much so that its real implications are rarely considered. Like most statements praising folly, it has been turned back into homely common sense or domesticated mystic wisdom. Erasmus laboured wittily to restore the original chutzpah of Paul's saying in *Encomium Moriae*, but found Luther's version of folly a stumbling-block of intransigent proportions. It is not hard to see why. Luther's aphorism is a scandal, a piece of open atheism. Luther knew as much: as a supporting citation, he used one of the classic atheist mottoes, from Ovid's *Amores: sollicitor nullos esse putare deos.*[89]

It is possible to see the history of sixteenth- and early seventeenth-century theology as a collective act of recoil in the face of Luther's terrifying sentence. Catholic theology, most publicly in the canons of Trent, attempted by turns to ignore and to refute it. The canons painstakingly reasserted the rationality of a belief in a good God. Many protestant theologians reacted with a form of intellectual amnesia, repeating Luther's soteriology but masking over its implications. Perhaps only Calvin understood the sentence properly, and even he laboured mostly to paper it over with overwhelming system. Within the *Institutio* he confessed at one point that the tongues of theologians must become silent in the face of the eternal decree: *Decretum quidem horribile, fateor,* or, in the more personal terms of the French version, 'je confesse que ce décret nous doit épouvanter'.[90] McNeill writes appropriately that Calvin here is 'awestruck but unrelenting in his declaration that God is the author of reprobation'.[91] Later Calvinists, on the other hand, responded to Luther's horrifying suggestion as if there was nothing too horrific about it. Beza cited Luther's claim for the irrationality of divine justice as only reasonable.[92]

Luther's scandalous flirtation with atheism is the more shocking because it comes from the century's most radical fideist, and because it is followed by a powerful reaffirmation of faith in the existence and righteousness of God. *De servo arbitrio* poises on the abyss of atheism and then plunges in as a wild gesture of faith. Only by risking unbelief so recklessly, Luther avers, can faith itself be rescued. In this way, Luther imitates Paul's flirtation with blasphemy in Romans, 'What shall we say then? Is there unrighteousness with God? God forbid' (9:14). Of all the 'infectious inquisitions' in the Bible, this is the most hazardous of all. It is a question which screams for an answer, and yet hopes that there is no case to be answered or that the question might somehow be rhetorical. In either case, it is not at all clear that it is given an answer. What kind of an answer is μὴ γένοιτο? Is Paul making an emphatic denial, is he protesting too much, or is he just shutting himself up? The speech acts of this dynamic passage in Paul refuse any facile explanation, at some level resist any interpretation whatever.

The *Holy Sonnets* are not unlike such Pauline and Lutheran statements in their volatile and inexplicable syntax. They struggle to say the unsayable, and to unsay the sayable. They are caught between 'infectious

---

[89] *Amores*, iii, ix (viii), 36, ed. by Kenney, p. 96. [90] *Institutio*, 3, 23, 7.
[91] *Institutes*, p. 955 n. [92] *De praedestinatione*, pp. 179–82.

inquisition' and what elsewhere Donne calls 'inordinate expostulation', in the gap between τί οὖν ἐροῦμεν; and μὴ γένοιτο.[93] At other times, they offer more than their share of theological assertion and affirmation. These shifts of temper are not always convincing, but they are not meant either to be convinced or convincing. We should not be too easily persuaded by their scepticism any more than we should by their credence. The *Holy Sonnets* try out faith and faithlessness by turns. What makes them continually rewarding is not the ultimate triumph of either but the uneasy tension between the two, the way that the one depends on the other. Just as Paul risked the unrighteousness of God to explain God's righteousness, and just as Luther risked atheism to mark out faith, so the *Holy Sonnets* are by turns clumsy, ugly, brutal, and momentarily redeemed.

V SHALL BE, THAT IS, MAY BE

Jacobus Arminius, later infamous Professor of Theology at Leiden, early in his career dubbed the ninth chapter of Romans *difficillimaeque explicationis*, the most difficult text in the whole of scripture, a place shrouded in *densissimus . . . tenebris* ('the thickest shade').[94] Of all these treacherous *loci*, Arminius shuddered most at that *periculosa quaestio*, the ineffable inference *numquid iniquitas apud Deum?* (9:14, Vulgate). To illuminate the darkness, he found respite in a gnomic Latin verb, *Absit*, the Vulgate version of Paul's impenetrable exhalation, μὴ γένοιτο. For Arminius, *Absit* is a straightforward negation, an interpretation which he justifies by means of some conveniently obfuscatory modal logic:

Primo negat consequentiam: deinde reddit rationem negationis. Negat consequentiam quam dicit: *Absit*. Hoc est: nullo modo hoc in cogitationem nobis venire debet, ullam in Deo esse iniustitiam, qui in se iustus, imò ipsa iustitia existens, nihil agit, ac ne agere quidem potest, nisi quod cum istâ suâ naturâ congruit solidissimè. (p. 277)

[First he denies the consequence: then he renders a reason for that denial. He denies the consequence when he says, 'God forbid'. That is, it ought by no means to enter our thoughts that there is any injustice in God, who, just in himself, nay, existing as Justice itself, does nothing, and indeed can do nothing, except what is most thoroughly in agreement with that nature of his.][95]

---

[93] *Sermons*, ii. 51–2.
[94] *Analysis Cap.IX. ad Romanos*, written in Amsterdam in 1593 but published only posthumously as an appendix to *Examen modestum libelli*, p. 261.
[95] *Works*, iii. 499.

Aristotelian logic muffles the paradox by making the *periculosa quaestio* redundantly rhetorical. God is *in se iustus*, indeed *ipsa iustitia existens*, and so, partaking of the category *iustitia*, cannot admit its opposite *iniustitia*. In this sense, there is no need for the reply, *Absit*, because the question is already a contradiction in terms. Yet Arminius's careful demonstration contains an implicit acknowledgement of its own vulnerability. If the consequential logic is self-evident, why is there any need so strenuously to deny the counter-argument, such that God's injustice must be erased from our minds (*nullo modo hoc in cogitationem nobis venire debet*)? Arminius allows that the impersonal verb *Absit* is no simple negation, for by protesting so much it reveals a desperate need to protest. It is as if Arminius confronts the unrighteousness of God and then turns his face away in horror.

This former pupil of Beza dedicated the latter years of his life to a reformation of Beza's doctrine of predestination which threw Dutch Calvinism into political turmoil.[96] Arminius himself seems to have been surprised by the acrimony, regarding himself as a true apostle of Calvin involved in a revised exposition of scripture's hardest places. Outside the arcane reaches of the divine will, indeed, his theology appears sometimes to be indistinguishable from his fiercest Calvinist opponents, although this did not stop them from taking opposition on other points for granted.[97] Controversy, as always, created differences as well as revealed them. Arminius, on the other hand, writes as if guided by the insuperable purpose of reason, in defence of a God whose object by definition is always good.[98] In this he followed the Spanish Jesuits (particularly Luis de Molina) in describing God's permissive will as a 'middle act between willing and not willing'.[99] In the unflinching exercise of logic and an inalienable sense of the rightness of his argument Arminius's work finds its clarity and its unrelenting tension.

His elaborate examination of the necessity of sin takes place in an answer to a treatise on predestination by the eminent English Calvinist Perkins. In its original form, however exemplary in its topics of controversy, the quarrel between Perkins and Arminius remained a private affair. Perkins died before Arminius finished his reply, and it remained

---

[96] Beza and Arminius are compared in White, *Predestination, Policy and Polemic*, ch. 2.

[97] Kendall, *Calvin and English Calvinism*, p. 142. Arminius approved for instance the practical syllogism; Kendall, p. 148.

[98] 'Examination of Gomarus', *Works*, iii. 588.

[99] *Examen modestum*, p. 21; compare Molina, *Divine Foreknowledge*, disputation 52, p. 168. On Arminius and Molina, see Dekker, *Rijker dan Midas*, ch. 4.

unpublished in Arminius's lifetime. In the years between the death of Perkins in 1602 and the eventual imprint of the *Examen modestum libelli, quem D.Guliemus Perkinsius . . . edidit . . . de praedestinationis modo & ordine* in 1612, however, the political context for debate on predestination was transformed. Even the title took on new significance. If Arminius intended his examination as a modest enquiry to a fellow-theologian and fellow-Calvinist whose writings he admired, the *Examen modestum* of 1612 appeared as an ironic challenge, a modest proposal or else great brag directed at the heart of dogmatic puritanism. Perkins by now was a canonical doctor, the English Moses, and predestination was his sacred tablet.[100] Calvin, Beza, Perkins constituted the 'trinity of the orthodox'.[101] Arminius's little book, and Arminius's name, acquired a posthumous significance of outlandish proportions when translated across the North Sea.

Sir Henry Wotton, ambassador to Venice and a close friend of Donne, is reported by Walton to have spent nearly a year in Leiden, finding Arminius 'a man of most rare Learning, . . . a most strict life, and of a most meek spirit'.[102] With ambassadorial care, he is even-handed between theological adversaries. He declares differences from Arminius 'in some points', but wishes Perkins had lived to consider Arminius's reply himself, since 'he was also of most meek *spirit*, and of great and sanctified *Learning*' (p. 133). Most of all Wotton wishes the controversy had remained as Arminius desired, in loving privacy, and regrets the contumacious consequence of its publication. Would that all could refrain from 'tampering with, and thereby perplexing the *Controversie*'.

Wotton's words speak volumes about the public state of theology in Jacobean England. Within a year of Arminius's death, the Dutch *Remonstrance* of 1610 threw northern European Calvinism into spasm with its Five Articles on grace declaring that Christ died for all, that grace is not irresistible, and that perseverance in faith is an open question. The controversy was exacerbated in England when Arminius's successor at Leiden, Conrad Vorstius, was accused of Socinianism. James I declared Vorstius 'a wretched Heretique, or rather Atheist' and intervened to have him removed from his professorial chair. In the same year, 1612, the last two Englishmen ever to be burned for heresy were charged with the anti-trinitarian taboo.

---

[100] Perkins's funeral sermon by James Montagu used the text of Joshua 1: 2, 'Moses my servant is dead'.
[101] Hill, *Puritanism and Revolution*, p. 213.   [102] Walton, *Life of Wotton*, p. 132.

Wotton, in a manner which mirrors official policy, urged peaceful discretion on the topic of predestination, but the problem was that Perkins and his followers had been so extravagantly explicit, and Arminius in his turn so scandalously lucid in opposition. Perkins and Arminius in their different ways are marked by a determination to be indiscreet, to say the ultimate word on the ultimate question. The careful obscurities of the religious settlement were left behind in the urge to define and to discriminate. The need for theology to explain the arcane intentions of God threatened to escape the shackles imposed by government on doctrinal wrangles. Predestinarian speculation emerged in open warfare to be silenced eventually only by an international conference of divines, the Synod of Dort of 1618–19. Here James instructed the British delegation to desist from 'innovation in doctrine' and to endeavour 'that certain positions be moderately laid down, which may tend to the mitigation of heat on both sides'.[103]

The Acts of the Synod were commonly conceived to represent a victory for the anti-Arminian view, and English Calvinism celebrated accordingly. However, any hope that theology could be tamed by a Synod quickly subsided. The Directions for Preachers in 1622 show the application of censorship on the opposite camp, as James reacted nervously to puritan suspicions regarding the marriage negotiations with Spain. The volatile response of the king to predestinarian dispute has led to variable guesses as to his own predilections, but James was probably more concerned, as Tudor monarchs had been, to keep open debate to a minimum. His instructions to the Dort delegates follow the old formula, forbidding ministers to 'deliver in the pulpit to the people those things which are the highest points of the schools, and not fit for vulgar capacity, but disputable on both sides'.[104]

In the final year of the king's reign, controversy broke out again over a book published, oddly enough, by one of the royal chaplains, Richard Montagu. Montagu's *A Gagg for the new Gospell? No: a New Gagg for an Old Goose* (1624) was written in reply to a piece of catholic propaganda. Yet it aroused a storm of puritan protest, rejecting Montagu's defence of English protestantism as Arminian and even quasi-papistical.[105] Among his denouncers was Samuel Ward, who had attended Perkins on his deathbed and later served as one of the four British delegates at Dort. Montagu was terrified, scurrying to the dying king and any remotely sympathetic bishop

---

[103] Fuller, *Church History*, v. 462–3.   [104] Ibid., 462.
[105] Montagu is discussed in detail by Tyacke, *Anti-Calvinists*, ch. 6.

for support, and dedicating his defence (the *Appello Caesarem* of 1625) to the new king, Charles.

Montagu's *Gagg* is an epitome of a hundred years' disputation over what he calls (with some distaste) 'points of inextricable obscurity almost, of the concordance in working of Grace, and Predestination with Free-Will'.[106] Shedding little light of his own, Montagu stumbles over the hard places of doctrine, setting himself up for his own fall. After rehearsing various positions on free will, he turns to the old problem of the commandments of God. Here he encounters the by now familiar cruces of biblical interpretation, and becomes entrapped in the nexus of English modal auxiliaries used to translate them. However, Montagu's argument cannot be aligned simply with Arminius, despite the complaints of his detractors. He shares interpretations with Perkins as well as Perkins's adversary. Bizarrely, as he twists this way and that, he follows first Erasmus and then Luther on the semantics of exhortations.

He examines the very text taken by Erasmus in his *Diatribe* to be the first proof-text of free will, Ecclesiasticus 15: 15, 'If thou wilt observe the commandments, and keep acceptable fidelity for ever, they shall preserve thee'. Adding other like texts, familiar Erasmian examples from Old and New Testaments, he comments: 'All which, and others of that Nature, proue this, *Gods Commandements* must be kept'. Having hesitated on the edge of Erasmus's interpretation, he plumps instead for Luther's: 'Nor doth our Sauiour here promise any ability to doe it: or specifie any performance of it: but exhorteth them rather to shew their loue vnto him, by striuing to doe what hee gaue them in charge' (p. 128). Montagu asserts that 'will' does not equal 'shall', and that 'must' may not imply 'can', before concluding that 'may' does not always include 'would' or even 'could'. He tartly denies the consequence that 'Some men haue done it, therfore euery man, or any man, may doe it' (p. 129).

These conclusions would not look out of place in Perkins. But when he came to consider the case of commandments in relation to man in a state of faith, he asserted contingency:

> Besides, if Faith cannot be lost, the *Dogge* cannot be said, *to returne vnto his owne vomit*: nor doth the *Swine to wallowing in the myre*. If righteousnesse had cannot be lost, why doe we pray continually against that, *Lead vs not into temptation*? (p. 164)

Montagu's modalities shift according to context, showing signs of strain

---

[106] *Gagg for the new Gospell?*, p. 110.

and confusion. Perhaps it is no wonder he complains 'what great Towers of *Babel*' (p. 154) have built up over the foundational words of scripture. But it was all one to his opponents. By taking up such an antagonistic position on falling faith, he was branded an Arminian altogether. In *Appello Caesarem* Montagu complained that 'I disavow the name and title of ARMINIAN' and 'the time is yet to come that I ever read word in ARMINIUS'.[107] He quoted Perkins in favour of his own arguments (p. 87). But he also fuelled controversy himself with vituperations against the 'novellizing PURITANS' and 'their desperate doctrine of predestination' (p. 60). Montagu's became a new rallying point for divisive opinion on both fronts, and another theological conference was called at York House in 1626 to resolve his case.[108] Greville's protégé Preston represented the puritan argument.

Donne gave a copy of *A Gagg* to Izaak Walton in 1625.[109] It has been surmised that Donne was sympathetic to the book.[110] However, his direct involvement in the enormous public furore provoked by Montagu's case is typically oblique. He was on the bench of the High Commission which investigated William Prynne's anti-Arminian campaign in 1627 in the wake of the *Gagg*, and signed the summons against Prynne.[111] Prynne inveighed against the 'pur-blinde, squint eyed, ide-all Arminian Nouellists', much to the annoyance of Bishop Laud.[112] But Laud also examined one of Donne's sermons in the same year for signs of affiliation with Archbishop Abbott, who had refused to license *Appello Caesarem*. Donne was mortified that his sermon should have made any theological point worth investigation, and Laud graciously passed on the king's forgiveness for 'certain slips'.[113]

The speed of Laud's enquiry, and of Donne's self-defence, is a warning against any hasty ascription of party to Donne's theology. Open factionalism was a luxury available only to the highest or the most foolhardy. Perhaps it is for this reason that Donne has been confidently termed an 'orthodox Anglican divine of the school of Andrewes and Laud', whereas equally confidently it has been asserted that 'his theology is characteristic of the "High Church Calvinism" of men like Downame, Bridges, Carleton,

---

[107] *Appello Caesarem*, pp. 10–11.
[108] White, *Predestination, Policy and Polemic*, p. 224. Montagu attended the second session, and was challenged by Preston; Tyacke, *Anti-Calvinists*, pp. 177–80.
[109] Keynes, *Bibliography*, no. L216, p. 279. The copy contains marginalia by Walton.
[110] Bald, *John Donne*, p. 482.   [111] Ibid., 419.
[112] *Old Antithesis to New Arminianisme*, A3ʳ. The book examined by the High Commission in 1627 was *The Perpetuitie of a Regenerate Mans Estate*.
[113] Laud's Diary, Wednesday, 4 April 1627; quoted in Bald, *John Donne*, p. 494.

Hall and Montague (James, not Richard)?.[114] Donne was careful not to be so casually open in his sympathies. Andrewes, more secure in his eminence, considered Arminius to be as dangerous in his explicitness as Whitaker in the opposite camp a generation earlier.

Arminius accused Perkins of *aequivocatio . . . seu amphibologia in verbis*, but more properly it could be said that for both *aequivocatio* is the enemy. They each search for a univocal interpretation, for a definition to unite all believers. If Perkins makes God's decree his first and only law, Arminius dismisses it as a legal fiction that makes God's creation futile. And yet *amphibologia* dogs them at every step. The babel of modal grammar defeats their desperate attempts to control it. In a marginal note in his section on exhortations, Arminius appeals for support to Augustine's *Ad Simplicianum de diversis quaestionibus*. It is an odd source of comfort. It is doubtful whether Simplician himself derived much reassurance from being shown by one of the cleverest minds in history that the most difficult questions in Christian doctrine were more difficult than he could possibly have imagined. Augustine's dazzling exegesis of Romans 9: 10–29 places caveat upon caveat in the elucidation of predestination. The excruciating argumentative violence of Paul's scrupulous syntax is revealed here in its full complexity, and is replicated in Augustine's turn upon turn on himself. Why does God favour one man and not another: Jacob and not Esau? Augustine displaces every possible justification ever located in the person of Jacob, paragraph by paragraph. Not by works, nor by foreknowledge of works, neither by faith, nor by foreknowledge of faith, nor even by willing assent, nor even by foreknowledge of will or assent, can Jacob's election be found. For not only the work, and not only the faith, but even the good will to believe and to do good, is given by God. It is not that God only has mercy if we consent, but rather that if God has mercy, he grants the will to consent also.

Perkins and Arminius in turn tried to rid the Pauline epistles of ambiguity, to obliterate the impossible, irrational question of God's injustice by an absolute negation. Augustine, by contrast, celebrates *aequivocatio*. His grace abounds in ambiguity. Indeed, it seems as if grace is revealed only through ambiguity. For grace comes without motivation and seemingly without cause. It is the gift without debt, the recompense which comes in advance. Grace is an occurrence outside of any man's power, unaccountable and unforeseeable. The supreme example, quoted at the finale to Augustine's first book to Simplician, is the conversion of Saul. The will of

---

[114] Simpson, *Study of the Prose Works*, p. 75; Shuger, *Habits of Thought*, pp. 164–5.

Saul 'was thrown prostrate by one word from on high, and a vision came to him whereby his mind and will were turned from their fierceness and set on the right way towards faith' (I, ii, 22; CC, 44, 55).

In a Whitehall sermon of April 1626, Donne preached the text of Matthew 9: 13, 'I am not come to call the righteous, but sinners to repentance'. It describes the conversion of the sinner who does not come to meet Christ of his own volition, but is met by Christ in gratuitous and spontaneous love:

> for no man had either disposition in himself, or faculty in himself, neither will nor power to rise and meet him, nor so much as to wish that Christ would call him, till he did call him. (vii. 144)

Grace therefore comes completely without warning. No predisposition or presentiment anticipates it, but it comes like the cry of the drowning man in a storm at sea, *Lord, Lord.*

Conversio defies the ordinary usages of language to express it, for it is a moment without preparation, even without syntax. Donne's sermons show a constant effort to suggest the incapacity of ordinary grammar to express the unfathomable grammar of grace: 'There is then forgiveness for *sin*, for *all sin* . . . but it is *In futuro remittetur, It shall be forgiven*. It is not *Remittebatur*, It was forgiven' (v. 84).[115] Grace works by prolepsis:

> It is not, in such a sense, *Remittebatur*, It was forgiven; nor it is not *Remittitur*, that even then, when the sin is committed, it is forgiven . . . It is but *Remittetur*, Any sin *shall be*, that is, may be *forgiven*, if the meanes required by God, and ordained by him, be entertained. (v. 84)

In this verbal declination, from 'was forgiven' to 'is forgiven' to '*shall be . . . forgiven*', Donne describes the impossible moment of grace. Already written in the book of life, and eternally predestinated by God, it none the less lies in wait in an unforeseeable future. With a beautiful modal hesitation, Donne suspends his grammar still further to qualify '*shall be, that is, may be*'. Grace is always one step further off.

Anything else would be to 'change Gods Grammer', to introduce 'a dangerous solecisme':

> for it is not They were forgiven before they were committed, nor they are forgiven in the committing, but They shall be, by using the meanes ordained by God, they may be; and so *They shall be forgiven unto men*, saies the Text (v. 85).

---

[115] The text for this Whitsun sermon is Matthew 12: 31. The date is uncertain; Potter and Simpson suggest 1623.

Grace is an enigma, a grammar unto itself. It reaches back to the original decree before time itself, and forward beyond time to the last judgement. This involves Donne in further fantastical exercises of tense, as in the commemorative sermon for George Herbert's mother, Lady Danvers, preached at Chelsea in July 1627:

He saies, *he will*, and he *doe's it*. For it is not, *Ecce veniam*, but *Ecce venio, Behold I do come upon thee as a Thiefe*; There, the *future*, which might imply a *dilatorinesse*, is reduc't to an infallible *present*; It is so sure, that he *will* doe it, that he is said, to *have* done it already (viii. 68).

'Gods grammer' plays havoc with human tenses, for 'God is a future God'; his very name disturbs the rules of language, demands the invention of a new language.

In something like a linguistic joke, Donne notes that 'as God himself is eternall and cannot bee considered in the distinction of times' so the language in which God delivered his written word, Hebrew, has 'the least consideration of Time of any other language':

Evermore in expressing the mercies of God to man, it is an indifferent thing to the holy Ghost whether he speak in the present, or the future, or in the time that is past: what mercies soever he hath given us, he will give us over againe; And whatsoever he hath done, and will doe, hee is always ready to doe at the present. (ix. 335)

The temporal uncertainties of Hebrew, which gave endless trouble to commentators, translators, and theologians, are turned for a moment into a trope of God's illimitability. But Donne also attempts to render this uncertainty within English, using those casual, faithful signifiers, the modal auxiliaries. The modal verbs are the true heroes of Donne's great final divine poem, 'A Hymne to God the Father':

> Wilt thou forgive that sinne where I begunne,
>   Which is my sin, though it were done before?
> Wilt thou forgive those sinnes through which I runne,
>   And doe them still: though still I doe deplore?
> When thou hast done, thou hast not done,
>   For, I have more.
>
> Wilt thou forgive that sinne by which I'have wonne
>   Others to sinne? and, made my sinne their doore?
> Wilt thou forgive that sinne which I did shunne
>   A yeare, or two: but wallow'd in, a score?
> When thou hast done, thou hast not done,
>   For, I have more.

> I have a sinne of feare, that when I'have spunne
> My last thred, I shall perish on the shore;
> Sweare by thy selfe, that at my death thy Sunne
> Shall shine as it shines now, and heretofore;
> And, having done that, Thou hast done,
> I have no more.

The whole poem is a play on the impossibility of tense. The 'sinne where I begunne', the original sin of Adam, inhabits the present Donne's past and future. It belongs properly not to the present, nor even to Donne's own past, but to a distant origin in another lifetime ('it were done before'); and yet it is inscribed into his every new action (it 'is my sin').

At the same time, the verbs of the poem apply to no particular time, but consignify a continuous present, in which I 'doe them still'. This contains an indeterminable future as well as an unquantifiable past. Rather like the Hebrew aspect of uncompleted action, his 'sinnes' are tied to no tense system at all. Even by doing them he has not done with them. This play with verbal time gives point to the magnificent pun at the poem's centre:

> When thou hast done, thou hast not done,
> For, I have more.

The double take of the poet's name is made the more powerful by the rigorous grammatical logic in which the poem's theology is encased. The gruff demotic tone of the everyday idiom, 'thou hast done', is made to articulate simultaneously an eschatalogical statement and a certain grim predestinarian humour. By dislocating the referentiality of tense, the contradictory sentence, 'thou hast done, thou hast not done' is made into a summary of the sinful condition: *semper iustus et iniustus*.

Like so many of the religious poems of the period, the last stanza reverses the poetic tropes of the foregoing stanzas in a reversion of theology from sin to grace. The wonderful economy of this poem is to do this throughout by means of the same simple auxiliaries. First there is the sudden interposition of an immediate future in the movement from 'I have a sinne of feare' to 'I shall perish on the shore'. For the first occasion in the poem, the threat of real time looms over the sinner, in the shape of what appears to be a natural tense sequence: from 'have' to 'shall'. The continuous present gives way to a measurable future, the identifiable point in time of the poet's death. The poem descends into the hell of desperation, both 'sinne of feare' and 'feare of sinne'. But at this point the poem twists its verbal logic all over again:

> Sweare by thy selfe, that at my death thy Sunne
> Shall shine as it shines now, and heretofore;

The imperative verb, 'Sweare', is a modal shock. It brings the addressee, God, into closer view, and with the same blasphemous vehemence as is so characteristic of the 'Holy Sonnets'. The urgency is expressed by the opposed pronouns 'my death thy Sunne'. But the poet is not making a threat, he is looking for a promise. The imperative verb does not cajole but yearns for release.

This is expressed by the new auxiliary verb 'Shall'. The poem has already moved from the simple interrogative 'Wilt thou' of the first two stanzas to the stronger modal force of 'I shall perish'. Now it moves from the epistemic to the deontic. 'I shall perish' implies a logic of the future, an epistemological statement. The promise which he attempts to extract from God, 'Sweare . . . thy Sunne / Shall shine', enforces an obligation. It has no knowledge of its eschatalogical future, but pleads for a gift of redemption. This readies the poem for its final motion out of the realm of 'now, and heretofore' into the realm of grace:

> And, having done that, Thou hast done,
> I have no more.

The laconic and comic gravity of the poem is maintained to the last. The modal auxiliaries are taken through one last change, in the shift from imperfect to perfect, from 'having done that' to 'Thou hast done'. In a line of supreme simplicity, Donne makes the four monosyllables, 'I have no more', a miniature indication of grace.

In his last surviving sermon preached on the feast of his patronal saint, in 1628, Donne made one final essay in the strange lycanthropy of conversion. His text comes from Acts 28: 6, 'They changed their minds, and said, That he was a God':

They changed, sayes our Text; not their mindes; there is no evidence, no appearance, that they exercised any, that they had any; but they changed their passions. Nay, they have not so much honour, as that afforded them, in the Originall; for it is not *They changed*, but *They were changed*, passively; Men subject to the transportation of passion, doe nothing of themselves, but are meerely passive   (viii. 327)

The controversial phrase, 'meerely passive', a point of contention between catholics and protestants for a hundred years, is here used uncontroversially as a synecdoche for the transformation of grace. It expresses a grammatical, not a psychological, statement. The Greek verb μεταβαλόμενοι is passive in form. Conversion comes as a gift, from God knows where. The fragile grammar of the Greek verb used by Luke keeps faith with this uncertainty, the ambiguity of grace. 'Poore intricated soule! Riddling, perplexed, labyrinthicall soule!', Donne laments. The soul is given no assurance, Donne admits, to the perplexity of providence.

Caravaggio's Paul lies slumped on the ground. To supply evidence for transcendent transformation is something the painting cannot provide, only 'blind faith'. It is only in such a way that we can finally read the strange religion of Donne. After a century of Reformation, religious identities on all sides were complex and controversial. Later history has looked too hard for clear signs of doctrine, believing that in a world that cares so much about religious difference, the differences must be clear cut. Donne's conversions show a religion that is slower and more painful in making its mind up, which is hardly able to declare itself to itself, let alone others. The language of religion is now too dense, too marked by previous conflict, to allow easy redemption. In this way, Donne's writing shows the paradox of religion and literary culture in the wake of Reformation. For a time, a religion founded on writing appeared to offer a unifying power, a religion apparently without limits. Instead, the new literature of religion identified new differences, new contradictions, and new limits. A God that seemed to be immanent in language was just as much occluded in language. Yet this hardly stops Donne from looking for this God of limits, indeed the desire for divine intellection appears insatiable, almost to be an end in itself. With his promise of 'Gods Grammer', a grammar constantly prone to solecism, Donne gives only the faintest glimpse of a grammar of grace. In this theology full of resistance he offers the small hope, or smaller consolation, that 'S.Paul, and he that speaks in S.Paul, is too good a Grammarian, too great a Critique, for thee to dispute against' (viii. 333). 'The God of heaven rectifie in us our naturall Logique', Donne asks. Any truth beyond this, lies beyond language.

Epilogue

—The whole entirely depends, added my father, in a low voice, upon the *auxiliary verbs*, Mr Yorick.

Had Yorick trod upon Virgil's snake, he could not have looked more surprised.

 Laurence Sterne, *The Life and Opinions of Tristram Shandy Gentleman*

10 Revolutionary English

At the beginning of *Paradise Lost*, in one of the most familiar phrases in English literature, Milton invokes the aid of the heavenly muse to 'justifie the wayes of God to men'.[1] Both in the audacity of its intellectual ambition and in its invitation to controversy the phrase could be said to sum up a hundred and fifty years of Reformation writing. Perhaps the poem could in that sense fittingly be called the final chapter of the English Reformation. In this phrase the Reformation comes full circle. What begins with the promise of justification for men ends with a promise of justification for God.

As well as brazen or even boastful, the word 'justify' is strangely vulnerable or even fallible. It seems to make God's grace scarcely accessible to God in the face of the world he has created. For this reason, perhaps unknowingly, Alexander Pope emended the word 'justify' to the more consolatory if graceless 'vindicate the ways of God to man'.[2] It is easier in the end to put the blame on man. It is also easy to see how Milton might feel God needed vindication against his assembled pandemonium of enemies amidst the restoration of the monarchy after 1660. However, a God who needs justifying is one who seems on the face of things less than perfectly justified, possibly not altogether justifiable. At the very least his reasoning needs explaining; at worst, in William Empson's words, God is on trial for his behaviour.[3] Either way, Milton sets himself the task of bringing the best possible or least indefensible defence against Paul's scandalous charge, 'Is there then unrighteousness with God?'

The word 'justify' had undergone extraordinary travails by the time Milton came to use it. An early editor identified quickly the Pauline reference in Milton's line, and its source in the Psalms, 'That thou mightest be justified in thy sayings', so problematic in Reformation exegesis from the time of Luther on.[4] Contemporary readers were well aware of the hermeneutic knot: Richard Montagu in 1624 commented astutely on the possibilities of misinterpretation attendant on the juxtaposition of the two registers of 'Christian learning' and the secular legal courts.[5] Montagu

---

[1] All quotations are from the 2nd edn. of 1674.   [2] *An Essay on Man* (1733), i. 16.
[3] *Milton's God*, p. 94.   [4] *Paradise Lost*, ed. by Thomas Newton, i. 11.
[5] *A Gagg for the new Gospell?*, p. 140.

finds the word prone to inevitable and unfortunate ambiguity and contro-versy. He identifies a 'three-fold extent' in the word, adding three glosses pregnant with possibility for Milton's later usage: 'to *make iust* and right-eous'; 'to *make more iust* and righteous'; and, finally, 'to *declare* and pro-nounce iust and righteous'. To say any of these of God is strange indeed: is not God just already? How could he become more just who is justice itself? What would it mean to declare God to be just as if he is not so in fact?

I THE NECESSARY FALL

> Thus Satan talking to his neerest Mate
> With Head up-lift above the wave, and Eyes
> That sparkling blaz'd, his other Parts besides
> Prone on the Flood, extended long and large
> Lay floating many a rood, in bulk as huge
> As whom the Fables name of monstrous size,
> *Titanian*, or *Earth-born*, that warr'd on *Jove*,
> *Briareos* or *Typhon*, whom the Den
> By ancient *Tarsus* held, or that Sea-beast
> *Leviathan*, which God of all his works
> Created hugest that swim th' Ocean stream:
> Him haply slumbring on the *Norway* foam
> The Pilot of some small night-founder'd Skiff,
> Deeming some Island, oft, as Sea-men tell,
> With fixed Anchor in his skaly rind
> Moors by his side under the Lee, while Night
> Invests the Sea, and wished Morn delayes:
> So stretcht out huge in length the Arch-fiend lay
> Chain'd on the burning Lake, nor ever thence
> Had ris'n or heav'd his head, but that the will
> And high permission of all-ruling Heaven
> Left him at large to his own dark designs,
> That with reiterated crimes he might
> Heap on himself damnation, while he sought
> Evil to others, and enrag'd might see
> How all his malice serv'd but to bring forth
> Infinite goodness, grace and mercy shewn
> On Man by him seduc't, but on himself
> Treble confusion, wrath and vengeance pour'd.
>   (I, 192–220)

The sentence which passes judgement on Satan is the longest in the poem. It consists of perhaps twenty-two different clauses, although the reader might be forgiven for losing count. It is a Leviathan of a sentence, meandering in deviations and digressions. No wonder the pilot of the ill-starred skiff gets lost, misconstruing as we do. The punctuation, which typically for Milton is very light, gives clear navigation at only two points.[6] It is a sentence in which it is as easy to miss the plot as it is difficult to find the subject. For what is the subject: is it Satan, or the sea-beast, is it the hapless pilot, or the will of heaven? As the sentence unfolds, the grammar dilates and divagates. At the same time, the object of the reader's attention is similarly difficult to grasp. It is only as an afterthought that the real problem emerges; the dreadful suspense inspired by the monstrous sea-beast is a ruse, hiding a more frightful nexus within: the theology of divine providence.

Even so, while the theology comes upon the sentence as if by accident, it appears to arrive with seemingly irresistible force, like the final breaker in the wake of the whale. Its place in the logic of the poem is therefore somewhere between contingency and necessity. In this way, the extraordinarily etiolated syntax of the sentence, which even for a great master of subordination is something of a lifetime's masterpiece, is altogether to the point. Most masterly of all is the way the whole sentence turns out to be a gigantic, monstrous counterfactual:

> nor ever thence
> Had ris'n or heav'd his head, but that the will
> And high permission of all-ruling Heaven
> Left him at large to his own dark designs,

a counterfactual which none the less has diverse causes and diverse effects. The sentence builds up to a shattering climax, in which the final clauses have an overwhelming brute force:

> Infinite goodness, grace and mercy shewn
> On Man by him seduc't, but on himself
> Treble confusion, wrath and vengeance pour'd.

But the ambiguity of syntax is still present to the last, and leaves awful unanswered questions. Is the ultimate indictment a result or a purpose? Is it an irrevocable command of God or an irredeemable choice of Satan?

It hardly needs emphasizing that this is the crux of the poem and also of Reformation theology.[7] And yet as the grammar of the sentence delays,

---

[6] In order to clarify the syntax and certify the theology, 19th-century editors commonly divided the passage into three sentences, and used semi-colons liberally.

[7] An account as brief as this can do no justice to the great library of commentary that the question of Milton's theodicy has invoked. Reference may be made especially to the survey of arguments in Danielson, *Milton's Good God*, with its attendant bibliography.

shifts, and wavers, so does the reader's interpretation of this powerful crux, caught in uncertainty as to who is doing the damning, who the saving. Does Satan will his own destruction, or is it 'pour'd' on him by God? In one version, Satan is a free agent who determines evil in the full knowledge of the consequences, thus deserving all and every punishment. In the other version, his evil actions are ordained for the greater good, part of a plan which is beyond him and outside his control.

The issue as ever is whether this question is available either to grammatical or to theological determination. It is the saving grace of Christian theology that it tries so hard to assert both contradictions at once. In a similar way, Milton's syntax makes no clear choice, indeed never states the choice in such crude terms. Every clause in this most elusive of sentences seems to be an elaborate means of avoiding foreclosing the argument. Eschatology and syntax unravel themselves one clause at a time, searching for and simultaneously recoiling from any final closure. Most irresolute of all is the terminally indecisive relative pronoun 'that', which promises and fails on its own promise to deliver the identity of the efficient cause, 'nor ever thence . . . but that'. Caught in this indecision is the unassuming auxiliary verb, 'might':

> That with reiterated crimes he might
> Heap on himself damnation,

a 'might' which hovers between permission and coaction, what he might do if he chose, and what he might do if made to. It is a classical site of the ambiguity between deontic and epistemic modality. Grammarians might argue as to whether the clause is therefore a result or an intention, but we are given no easy answer: for the indeterminacy is itself dependent on a double subordinate clause, 'but that . . . That . . . he might'. With sinuous duplicity, the sentence refuses to choose between its ambiguous paths, and takes the reader down both in turn. And yet the questions raised by this indecision could not be more fraught and more insistent. How did Satan come to be where he is? Who put him there? Did Satan fall or was he pushed?

II MILTON'S ENGLISH

It is perhaps the predetermined doom of literary criticism to make Milton's mind up for him, to decide once and for all whether he is a would-be determinist or a be-damned Freewiller. Empson claims 'we are specifically told that God's actions towards Satan were intended to lead him into greater evil', assisting his case by silently emending 'permission' to 'fore-knowledge' in line 213.[8] R. L. Brett, in reply, accused Empson of making an elementary grammatical slip: 'the word *might* implies a permissive freedom for Satan given by God, who as the passage proceeds to make clear, will bring ultimate good from Satan's evil action.'[9] Empson could not let the matter rest, adding a caustic rejoinder in his next edition: 'I doubt this; surely "he castrated him that he might be chaste" is good seventeenth-century grammar and not permissive'.[10] Like Luther's flea to Erasmus's elephant, Empson insisted on having the last word. Yet it is uncharacteristic of him to conclude so brusquely 'But anyway the problems of free will are larger than English grammar' (p. 368). It would be more proper to say that the two problems are coincident, and that the ambiguity of the one is inseparable from the complexity of the other.

English grammatical theory in the seventeenth century was only beginning to acquire the terminology to conceptualize the problem, never mind resolve it. The first use of the term 'auxiliaries' to describe 'might' and its humdrum companions appears to be John Wallis's *Grammatica linguae Anglicanae* of 1653.[11] The borrowing of the term from the Latin word for the secondary army of non-Roman non-legionary troops is not inappropriate for a member of Cromwell's vernacular New Model Army.[12] Wallis had an impeccable puritan heritage and received his intellectual training at Emmanuel College, Cambridge. He deciphered codes for the Parliamentarians before being rewarded by becoming Savilian Professor of Geometry at Oxford in 1649.[13] His puritan rationalism is typical of many of the founder members of the Royal Society. He controverted with Thomas Hobbes; in his arithmetical work, he anticipated Isaac Newton's differential calculus. It is also compatible with an interest in theology: he wrote works on infant baptism, the sabbath, the trinity, and the Athanasian creed. To mark his affinity with Milton, he also wrote a long poem on the life of David.[14] Wallis's vernacular enthusiasm, unlike Milton's, was no bar to continuing favour under the Restoration, and his

---

[8] *Milton's God*, p. 42.   [9] Review of *Milton's God*, in *Critical Quarterly*, 3 (1961), 287.

[10] Letter to *Critical Quarterly*, 3 (1961), 368; see also appendix to *Milton's God*, p. 278.

[11] *Verba auxiliaria*, Wallis, *Grammatica*, chs. 9–10; this predates the first ref. in *OED*, but of course Wallis writes in Latin.

[12] The term auxiliary was familiar among republican writers from its use in Machiavelli's *Il Principe*. In the civil wars of the 1640s, 'auxiliaries' were irregular troops, such as urban militias, distinguished from the standing armies.

[13] Webster, *Great Instauration*, pp. 40–1.

[14] *History of David's Troubles*. Wallis was in holy orders and became Doctor of Divinity; Webster, *Great Instauration*, p. 159.

grammar went through eleven editions by 1765. Yet in its practical scientific empiricism his grammar is emphatically a work of the Commonwealth, developing a new theory of English speech-sounds at the same time as its author was devising a method for deaf-mutes to speak.

The linguistic enfranchisement of the English modal auxiliaries, those foot-soldiers of the vernacular republic, is part of a revolutionary approach to the formal properties of English verbs. Leaving aside the auxiliaries, he notes, English has only two tenses—present and imperfect past (*Praesens et Praeteritum Imperfectum*). This observation, standard in modern English grammars although not in modern English thinking (which often clings obstinately to classical categories) is startling in its historical context. Even Ben Jonson, who pared English verbal forms down to 'three only *Tymes*', retained the imperative as a vestigial future tense.[15] Wallis simplified the analysis of inflections still further, while at the same time attempting to do justice to the extraordinary grammatical life of auxiliaries. He identified nine major modal verbs, which with the auxiliary use of the primary verbs *be*, *have*, and *do*, and the numerous phrasal forms, may be used singly or in combinations of up to four at a time in an apparently endless variety of permutations. Wallis responded with a connoisseur's pleasure to the delicate poetry of these forms which gives life to the plainest English sentence.[16] He attempted to classify their capacity to embody both philosophical refinement (in the delineation of time or speaker-perspective) and minute social register. Wallis seems to be the first author to note that *shall* is merely declarative in the first person, whereas in the second and third it promises or threatens, while with *will* the roles are reversed.[17]

The auxiliaries play an important part in Wallis's redrawing of the boundaries between Latin and the vernacular. There is, he declares, an *immanis discrepentia* in structure and usage between English and the classical languages. His forerunners in grammar, however accomplished, have always fallen into error by attempting to regulate English according to antique practice. The only way forward is a *nova methodus* founded on vernacular principles. In place of the latinate fictions of case, gender, mood, and tense which have been forced willy-nilly on a language 'altogether alien to them', he proposes to follow the lines of common syntax.[18]

---

[15] *Workes*, ii. 61. Jonson notes briefly some of the peculiar syntax of auxiliaries (without recognizing them as a category), ii. 78.

[16] He divides them into two groups, *integra* (*have* and *be*) and *mutila* (all the others are called 'defective' because they are used in a limited number of ways).

[17] *Grammatica* (1653), pp. 94–5.   [18] Praefatio, A7ᵛ.

The most striking features of this, he observes in startling fashion, are that in the syntax of nouns almost nothing is done by declensions and almost everything by means of prepositions, and in the syntax of verbs almost nothing by conjugations and almost everything by means of the auxiliaries.

Wallis's Preface makes a declaration of linguistic independence with a significantly political resonance (*veram nativae suae linguae rationem*). In addition to this incipient nationalism, there is a further strain of linguistic politics. The fluid syntax of the English prepositions and auxiliaries is a triumph of liberty against the servile yoke of terminist regulation. English, in Wallis's terms, is the least rule-bound of languages and therefore the most flexible and the freest. It is the perfect language for the rationalist as it is the least dependent on irrational custom. In a remarkable turn on the humanist apology for the inferiority of the vulgar tongue, which held sway throughout the Tudor and Stuart grammatical programmes, Wharton's *A New English-Grammar* of 1655 went a step further, declaring English to be the superior of Latin precisely because 'it needeth little or no Grammar at all'.

III LANGUAGE AND ERROR

In grammatical theory Milton himself was a conservative. He devised textbooks for his nephews and other pupils on both grammar and logic, which in his penurious post-Restoration old age he published. By this time they were anachronisms, although even at the time of writing they were out of date. Milton was one of the last proponents of classical Ramism, a vestige from his days at Christ's College, Cambridge, the college of Chaderton and Perkins. In his analysis of language Milton sounds at times like the last of the Elizabethans, and it is symptomatic that he begins the preface to his *Ars Logicae* with a citation in praise of Ramus from Sir Philip Sidney.[19]

On the question of mood, the *Accedence Commenc't Grammar* harks back even further to the Henrician models of Lily, describing moods as 'Signs'.[20] Milton shows some awareness of modern trends in reducing the number of moods to four, but he still treats the auxiliaries according to Latin usage, describing them as the means by which 'The Potential or Subjunctive is Englisht' (viii. 98). Although he knows more recent sources

---

[19] *Prose Works of Milton*, viii. 208.
[20] Ibid., 98. Lily's book had an exceptionally long life, forming the basis of most English grammars up to the nineteenth century.

such as John Danes's *Light to Lilie* of 1637, he does not show Danes's interest in applying formal criteria to meaning.

It is in practice rather than in theory that Milton's grammar becomes radical. Here his usage shows such variation as to justify Danes's apt aphorism that there are 'as many moods as there are affections of the mind'.[21] In particular, his use of the modal auxiliaries in *Paradise Lost* anticipates the extraordinary philosophical survey of the semantics of the auxiliaries in a follower of Wallis, Christopher Cooper, whose *Grammatica linguae Anglicanae* of 1685 was the last vernacular grammar to be printed in Latin. Cooper attributed a different modal signification to each of eight different auxiliaries. This account of mood is a miniature essay in theology, whereby *can* is said to denote 'absolute causal ability' whereas *could* and *might* denote 'conditional ability'; *may* expresses 'absolute liberty', *will* 'absolute inclination', and *shall* 'absolute necessity'.

It is not always clear that Milton's God speaks English as his native language. As he looks down on Heaven and Hell he shares for a moment with the Son his own peculiar vision of past, present, and future, contemplating with a suitably Olympian air Satan's bleakest prospects:

> And now
> Through all restraint broke loose he wings his way
> Not farr off Heav'n, in the Precincts of light,
> Directly towards the new created World,
> And Man there plac't, with purpose to assay
> If him by force he can destroy, or worse,
> By some false guile pervert;
>
> (III, 86–92)

As God unfolds his narrative of Satan's progress, we are made to wonder whether he understands the rule (so recently identified by Wallis) about the difference between the first and third person usages of *shall* and *will*:

> and shall pervert
> For man will hark'n to his glozing lyes,
> And easily transgress the sole Command,
> Sole pledge of his obedience: So will fall,
> Hee and his faithless Progenie
>
> (III, 92–6)

The words *shall* and *will*, as a glance at the dictionary will show, are among the most disarmingly complex in the language. What could God mean by

---

[21] *Light to Lilie*, p. ix.

these awkward auxiliaries? Does he know enough about English idiom to realize the difference when he uses first one then the other? Modern linguistics, as was seen in Chapter 5, distinguishes between an epistemic usage, which in this case would imply a statement of knowledge in the form of a prediction about the future, and a deontic, which should express instead God's desires, intentions, instructions. By Wallis's analysis the third person *shall* must be deontic but the third person *will* epistemic, in which case God would be in two minds. In the sixteenth century, however, the case was not so clear cut: the examination of Tyndale's usage in Chapter 5 showed that *shall* could be either epistemic or deontic in all persons, according to context.[22] It may be that Wallis is too hard and fast, as are some modern grammarians who make too little allowance for the considerable regional and dialectal variation in auxiliary practice. It may even be wrong to think that language always makes hard distinctions: might not the language itself sometimes be in confusion or even in error? Why should it be easy for me to discriminate between what I think will happen and what I want to happen? Even if the language knew for me, would I know the difference?

In the case of Milton's God, the rules of language are stretched even further, perhaps to breaking-point. He seems to be saying to the Son that he can predict Satan's (and man's) future unequivocally but that he has not predetermined it. God only knows, God only foreknows what is going to happen. Yet it seems nothing can be said so simply. By repeating the point, and by changing the verb ('and shall pervert | For man will hark'n') he appears to protest too much, and to will the future into happening. Ordinarily this might not matter, except that God's wishes have a habit of coming true. God can make a command when the person is not present, and can make something happen just by commanding it. The deontic possibilities present in 'shall pervert' exert all the greater pressure here, hope, desire, or promise carrying a surplus menace of threat or eternal punishment.

This is one of God's most important pronouncements in the poem, asserting the centrality of the doctrine of free will in the history of the Fall of man. It is also a central statement in Milton's promise of justifying God. God's justice is upheld because he is not the cause of man's sin, which man freely chose. None the less it reads uncomfortably. Not the least of the

---

[22] Barber, *Early Modern English*, pp. 259–60, is unclear on this issue, noting merely that 'will . . . could also signal wish or desire' and '*shall* . . . could be used all through our period to signal obligation or necessity'. An acute account of the grammar of these verbs is given in Palmer, *Modality and the English Modals*, pp. 137–8.

problems is that it comes from God's own lips. This is not Milton justifying God but God justifying God:

> whose fault?
> Whose but his own? ingrate, he had of mee
> All he could have; I made him just and right,
> Sufficient to have stood, though free to fall.
> (III, 96–9)

Self-justification ('he had of mee | All he could have') mixed liberally with blame-throwing ('whose fault? | Whose but his own?') never sounds pleasant from someone in supreme power. However, it is also not clear that, just by wishing it, he can make his knowledge of the future so pristinely epistemic, so clean of deontic imputation. The problems are exacerbated in a passage which has become one of the most controversial in the whole poem:

> This my long sufferance and my day of grace
> They who neglect and scorn, shall never taste;
> But hard be hard'nd, blind be blinded more,
> That they may stumble on, and deeper fall.
> (III, 198–201)

Like the hardening of Pharaoh's heart, this is the hardest of hard sayings. What makes it so unresisting is the blank certainty of its modalities. It is difficult to see 'shall' and 'may' and the imperative 'be' as benign, impartial predictions here. God's foreknowledge and God's predestination merge in the obligatory syntax of his modal auxiliaries.

In *Paradise Lost*, it has been famously observed, language falls.[23] The observation has been copiously illustrated in the subtle gradations of Milton's lapsarian vocabulary. The reader participates in the fall by paranomasia, word by word. Sometimes it seems to be being suggested that Milton has some divine power over this process, charming the words into obedience with his lexicographical mastery. How Milton could acquire such special access is not explained. To find such a place he would have to escape outside language, somewhere God only knows. *Paradise Lost* is not such a place. If language has fallen it has fallen already, as Milton and his best commentators know only too well. The only place to observe the fall of language is within a language which is also fallen. The world of words in *Paradise Lost* is one of constant fallibility and gullibility, for author and reader alike. Not even God is immune from this error.

---

[23] Ricks, *Milton's Grand Style*, p. 109; see also Fish, *Surprised by Sin*, p. 103.

In the devious and errant paths of Milton's syntax language reveals its inevitable ambivalence. In this, as much as in Milton's dogmatic assurances, *Paradise Lost* is an archetypal Reformation artefact. The poet's labour to retain control and mastery over this language is like the work of a great theological exegete over the recalcitrant meanings of the Bible. Milton the grammarian manifests contrary moods, marshalling his sentences into predetermined order or allowing them to wander at will. By 1654, the Preface to Hobbes's treatise *Of libertie and Necessity* was complaining that 'the controversies betwixt *Rome* and the *Reformation*, are long since beaten out of the pit'. This querulous note was made in response to the way that scriptural exegetes 'involve their consciences in the bryars of a thousand needless scruples [and] spin out volumes out of half sentences, nay, out of points and accents'.[24] It was a world that was now disappearing. *Paradise Lost* is an elegy not only to the lost paradise of Eden, and the abandoned hopes of Commonwealth, but also to the energies and creativity of the long Reformation. It is also the crowning laurel in the contribution of the Reformation to the English language and its literature.

[24] *Of libertie and Necessity*, Dedicatory epistle, A3ʳ. The epistle is dated 20 August 1646, and was probably written by John Davies of Kidwelly, the book's publisher.

Bibliography

PRIMARY SOURCES

Actes made in session of this present parlyament (London: Thomas Barthelet, 1543).

Alexander of Villedieu, *Das Doctrinale des Alexander de Villa-Dei*, ed. D. Reichling, *Monumenta Germaniae Paedagogica*, 12 (Berlin: A. Hofmann, 1893).

Alfield, Thomas, *A True Reporte of the Death and Martyrdome of M. Campion Jesuite and Preiste, and M. Sherwin, and M. Bryan Preistes, at Tiborne the First of December 1581* (London: 'Rowlande', 1582).

Andrewes, Lancelot, *XCVI Sermons* (London: George Miller, 1629).

Aquinas, Thomas, *Summa contra gentiles*, Book III, 2 vols. (Notre Dame, 1975).

—— *Summa Theologiae*, Blackfriars edn., 60 vols. (London: Eyre & Spottiswoode, 1964–75).

Aretino, Pietro, *I Sette Salmi de la Penitentia di David* (Venice: Francesco Marcolini, 1536).

Aristotle, *Categoriae et liber de interpretatione*, ed. L. Minio-Paluello, rev. edn. (Oxford: Clarendon, 1956).

—— *Ethica Nicomachea*, ed. I. Bywater, repr. edn. (Oxford: Clarendon, 1975).

—— *Metaphysica*, ed. W. Jaeger (Oxford: Clarendon, 1957).

Arminius, Jacobus, *Examen modestum libelli, quem D. Guliemus Perkinsius . . . edidit . . . de praedestinationis modo & ordine* (Leiden: G. Basson, 1612).

—— *The Works of James Arminius*, tr. James and William Nichols, 3 vols. (London: Longman, 1825–75).

Arnoldi, Bartholomäus, *Figure Donati: Aureum opusculum artis grammatices* (Strasburg: J. Grüninger, 1505).

Articuli Lambethani (London: G.D[ugard], 1651).

Ascham, Roger, *The Whole Works*, 3 vols., ed. J. A. Giles (London: J. Russell Smith, 1865).

—— *English Works*, ed. W. A. Wright (Cambridge: Cambridge University Press, 1904).

Augustine, *Confessiones*, ed. L. Verheijen, CC, 27 (Turnhout: Brepols, 1981).

—— *Contra Cresconium grammaticum at Donatistam*, ed. M. Petschenig, CSEL, 52 (Leipzig: G. Freytag, 1909).

—— *Contra epistulam Manichaei quam uocant fundamenti*, ed. J. Zycha, CSEL, 25 (Leipzig: G. Freytag, 1891).

—— *De civitate Dei*, ed. B. Dombart and A. Kalb, 2 vols., CC, 47–8 (Turnhout: Brepols, 1955).

——*De correptione et gratia*, ed. G. Folliet, CSEL, 92 (Vienna: Österreichischen Akademie der Wissenschaften, 2000).

——*De diversis quaestionibus ad Simplicianum*, ed. A. Mutzenbecher, CC, 44 (Turnhout: Brepols, 1970).

——*De doctrina christiana*, ed. J. Martin, CC, 32 (Turnhout: Brepols, 1962).

——*De dono perseverantiae*, ed. J.-P. Migne, rev. edn., PL, 45 (Paris: Garnier, 1865).

——*De natura et gratia*, ed. C. Urba and J. Zycha, CSEL, 60 (Leipzig: G. Freytag, 1913).

——*De peccatorum meritis et remissione*, ed. C. Urba and J. Zycha, CSEL, 60 (Leipzig: G. Freytag, 1913).

——*De spiritu et litera*, ed. C. Urba and J. Zycha, CSEL, 60 (Leipzig: G. Freytag, 1913).

——*Enarrationes in Psalmos*, ed. D. E. Dekkers and J. Fraipont, 3 vols., CC, 38–40 (Turnhout: Brepols, 1956).

——*Epistulae*, ed. A. Goldbacher, 5 vols., CSEL, 34, 44, and 57–8 (Leipzig: G. Freytag, 1895–1923).

——*Earlier Writings*, tr. J. H. S. Burleigh (Philadelphia: Westminster, 1953).

——*Anti-Pelagian Writings*, tr. P. Holmes and R. Wallis, repr. edn. *NPNF*, 5 (Grand Rapids: Eerdmans, 1978).

——*Expositions on the Psalms*, tr. C. Crowe, repr. edn. *NPNF*, 8 (Grand Rapids: Eerdmans, 1989).

Bacon, Francis, *The Two Bookes of the Proficience and Advancement of Learning*, London 1605, facs. edn., English Experience, 218 (Amsterdam, 1970).

Barlow, William, *The Summe and Substance of the Conference in his Maiesties Privy-Chamber, at Hampton Court. Ianuary 14, 1603* (London: J. Windet, 1604).

Barnes, Robert, *A Supplicatyon made by Robert Barnes doctoure in diuinite vnto the most excellent and redoubted prince kinge henrye the eyght* (Antwerp: Simon Cock, 1531).

——*The supplication of doctour Barnes vnto the moost gracyous kynge Henrye the eyght with the declaration of his articles condemned for heresy by the byshops* (London: H. Syngleton, 1550?).

Baro, Peter, *Summa trium de praedestinatione sententiarum* (Harderwick, 1613).

Bencius, Franciscus, *Orationes & Carmina, cum disputatione de stylo et scriptione*, 2nd edn. (Ingolstadt: D. Sartorius, 1595).

Beza, Theodore, *Tractationes theologicae*, 3 vols. (Geneva: Eustace Vignon, 1576–82).

——*De praedestinationis doctrina et vero vsv tractatio absolutissima* (Geneva: Eustace Vignon, 1582).

Biblia cum glosa ordinaria et expositione lyre literali et morali, 6 vols. (Basle: Johann Froben, 1506–8).

——*Biblia sacra iuxta vulgatam versionem*, ed. Robert Weber, 2 vols. (Stuttgart: Württembergische Bibelanstalt, 1969).

Beza, Theodore, *Biblia. the bible, that is, the holy scripture . . . translated out of Douche and Latyn in to Englishe*, tr. Miles Coverdale ([Cologne?: E. Cervicornus?, 1535]).

—— *The bible and holy Scriptures conteyned in the olde and newe Testament translated according to the Ebrue and Greke, and conferred With the best translations in diuers languages* (Geneva: R. Hall, 1560).

—— *The Holie Bible* (London: R. Jugge, 1568) [The Bishops' Bible].

Biel, Gabriel, *Collectorium circa quattuor libros Sententiarum*, ed. Wilfrid Werbeck and Udo Hofmann, 6 vols. (Tübingen: J. C. B. Mohr, 1973–92).

Bradford, John, *Two notable Sermons, Made by that worthy Martyr of Christ Maister Iohn Bradford* (London: Iohn Awdeley and Iohn Wyght, 1574).

—— *The Writings*, ed. A. Townsend, 2 vols., Parker Society (Cambridge: Cambridge University Press, 1848–53).

Bradwardine, Thomas, *De causa Dei contra Pelagium libri tres* (London: I. Billius, 1618).

Brassicanus, Johannes, *Grammatice institutiones* (Strasbourg: Matthias Schürer, 1512).

Bucer, Martin, *Epistola D. Pauli ad Ephesios. In eandem commentarius* (Zurich: C. Froschover, 1527).

—— *Metaphrases et enarrationes perpetuae epistolarum D. Pauli Apostoli* (Strasbourg: W. Rihel, 1536).

—— *Scripta Anglicana fere omnia* (Basle: Petrus Perna, 1577).

Bullinger, Heinrich, *In omnes apostolicas epistolas, divi videlicet Pauli xiiii, et vii canonicas commentarii* (Basle: C. Froschover, 1539).

Bullokar, William, *Pamphlet for Grammar 1586*, ed. J. R. Turner, *The Works of William Bullokar*, 2 vols. (Ilkley: Scolar Press, 1980), vol. ii.

Calvin, Jean, *Christianae religionis institutio* (Basle: C. Froschover, 1536).

—— *Institutio Christianae religionis* (Strasbourg: W. Rihel, 1539).

—— *Institution de la religion chrestienne: en laquelle est comprinse une somme de pieté, et quasi tout ce qui est necessaire a cognoistre en la doctrine de salut* (Geneva: Michel Du Bois, 1541).

—— *In omnes Pauli apostoli epistolas, atque etiam in epistolam ad Hebraeos commentarii* (Geneva: Jean Crespin, 1554).

—— *Harmonia ex tribus Euangelistis composita, Matthaeo, Marco & Luca* (Geneva: Robert Estienne, 1555).

—— *Commentaires sur les cinq livres de Moyse* (Geneva: François Estienne, 1564).

—— *Sermons vpon the Fifth Booke of Moses called Deuteronomie*, tr. Arthur Golding (London: H. Middleton, 1583).

—— *Opera Calvini quae supersunt omnia*, ed. W. Baum, E. Cunitz, and E. Reuss, 59 vols., CR (Braunschweig: C. A. Schwetschke, 1863–1900).

—— *Opera selecta*, ed. P. Barth and W. Niesel, 2nd edn., 5 vols. (Munich: C. Kaiser, 1957–9).

—— *Institution de la religion chrestienne*, ed. Jean-Daniel Benoît, 5 vols. (Paris: Vrin, 1957–63).

——*Institutes of the Christian Religion*, ed. J. T. McNeil, tr. F. L. Battles, 2 vols. (Philadelphia: Westminster Press, 1960).

——*Iohannis Calvini Commentarius in epistolam Pauli ad Romanos*, ed. T. H. L. Parker, Studies in the History of Christian Thought, 22 (Leiden: E. J. Brill, 1981).

——*Des scandales*, ed. O. Fatio, Textes littéraires français (Geneva: Droz, 1984).

Campensis, Ioannes, *Enchiridion Psalmorum* (Lyon: Sebastian Gryphius, 1533).

Campion, Edmund, *Campian Englished* (Rouen: J. Cousturier, 1632).

Cardwell, E. (ed.), *A History of Conferences and other proceedings connected with the revision of the Book of Common Prayer* (Oxford: Oxford University Press, 1840).

Carleton, Dudley, *Letters during his Embassy in Holland* (London, 1775).

——*Dudley Carleton to John Chamberlain, 1603–1624: Jacobean Letters*, ed. Maurice Lee (New Brunswick: Rutgers University Press, 1972).

Chaderton, Laurence, *An excellent and godly sermon, most needefull for this time, wherein we liue in all securitie and sinne* (London: Christopher Barker, 1580).

Chamberlain, John, *The Letters*, ed. N. E. McClure, 2 vols. (Philadelphia: American Philosophical Society, 1939).

Clajus, Johannes, *Grammatica Germanicae Linguae ex bibliis Lutheri Germanicis at aliis eius libris collecta* (Leipzig: J. Rhamba, 1578).

Cooper, Christopher, *Grammatica linguae Anglicanae* (London: J. Richardson, 1685).

Coverdale, Miles, *Certain most godly, fruitful, and comfortable letters of such true Saintes and holy Martyrs of God* (London: Iohn Day, 1564).

Danes, John, *A Light to Lilie* (London: R. Young, 1637).

Denzinger, Heinrich (ed.), *Enchiridion Symbolorum definitionum et declarationum de rebus fidei et morum*, 32nd edn. (Freiburg im Briesgau: Herder, 1963).

Donatus, *Ars grammatica*, ed. Heinrich Keil, *Grammatici Latini*, 8 vols., repr. edn. (Hildesheim: G. Olms, 1961), iv. 353–402.

Donne, John, *Deuotions vpon Emergent Occasions* (London: Thomas Jones, 1624).

——*Letters to Severall Persons of Honour* (London: J. Flesher, 1651).

——*Poetical Works*, ed. H. J. C. Grierson, 2 vols. (Oxford: Oxford University Press, 1912).

——*Essays in Divinity*, ed. E. M. Simpson (Oxford: Clarendon Press, 1952).

——*The Sermons*, ed. E. M. Simpson and G. R. Potter, 10 vols. (Berkeley: University of California Press, 1953–62).

——*Ignatius his Conclave*, ed. T. S. Healy (Oxford: Clarendon Press, 1969).

——*The Divine Poems*, ed. Helen Gardner, 2nd edn. (Oxford: Clarendon Press, 1978).

——*Pseudo-Martyr*, ed. A. Raspa (Montreal: McGill-Queen's University Press, 1993).

Dürer, Albrecht, *Diary of his Journey to the Netherlands 1520–1521* (London: Lund Humphries, 1971).

Eberhard of Béthune, *Graecismus*, ed. J. Wrobel, Corpus grammaticorum medii aevi, 1 (Breslau: G. Koebner, 1887).

Ellis, J., *A Defence of the Thirty Nine Articles . . . to which are added the Lambeth Articles* (London: R. Bonwicke, 1710).

Erasmus, *Moriae Encomium Erasmi Roterodami declamatio* (Strasbourg: M. Schürer, 1511).

——*Adagiorum chiliades tres* (Basle: Johan Froben, 1513).

——*De duplici copia rerum ac verborum commentarii duo. De ratione studii & instituendi pueros commentarii totidem* (Paris: O. Senant, 1515?).

——*Nouum instrumentum omne, diligenter ab* ERASMO ROTERODAMO *recognitum & emendatum*, 2 vols. (Basle: Johan Froben, 1516).

——*Antibarbarorum liber unus* (Basle: J. Froben, 1520).

——*Nouum testamentum omne tertio ab Erasmo recognitum*, 3rd edn., 2 vols. (Basle: Johan Froben, 1522).

——*De libero arbitrio ΔIA TPIBH siue collatio* (Basle: Johan Froben, 1524).

——*Opera Omnia*, ed. J. Leclerc, 10 vols. (Leiden: Pieter van der Aa, 1703–6).

——*Opus Epistolarum*, ed. P. S. Allen, 12 vols. (Oxford: Clarendon Press, 1906–58).

——*Christian Humanism and the Reformation: Selected Writings*, ed. and tr. John C. Olin (New York: Harper & Row, 1965).

——*Opera Omnia*, 9 vols. in parts (Amsterdam: North-Holland, 1969–).

——*Collected Works of Erasmus*, 72 vols. (Toronto: University of Toronto Press, 1974–).

——*Annotations on the New Testament: The Gospels*, ed. Anne Reeve (London: Duckworth, 1986).

——*Annotations on the New Testament: Acts, Romans, I and II Corinthians*, ed. Anne Reeve and M. A. Screech, Studies in the History of Christian Thought, 42 (Leiden: E. J. Brill, 1990).

——*Les préfaces au Novum Testamentum*, ed. Y. Delègue and J.-P. Gillet, Histoire et société, 20 (Geneva: Labor et Fides, 1990).

Fenner, Dudley, *The Artes of Logike and Rethorike, plainlie set foorth in the English tongue, easie to be learned and practised* (Middelburg: R. Schilders, 1584).

Fisher, John, *The treatise concernynge the fruytfull saynges of Dauyd the kynge & prophete in the seuen penytencyall psalmes* (London: Wynkyn de Worde, 1508).

——*The sermon of John the bysshop of Rochester made agayn ye pernicious doctryn of Martin Luther* (London: Wynkyn de Worde, 1521).

——*Assertionis Lutheranae Confutatio* (Antwerp: M. Hillenius, 1523).

——*The English Works*, ed. J. Mayor, (London: EETS, 1876).

Foxe, John, *Actes and Monuments of these latter and perrilous dayes* (London: Iohn Day, 1563).

——*The first [second] volume of the Ecclesiasticall history contaynyng the Actes and Monumentes*, 2 vols. (London: Iohn Daye, 1570).

——(ed.), *The Whole Workes of W. Tyndall, Iohn Frith, and Doct. Barnes, those worthy Martyrs, and principall teachers of this Churche of England* (London: John Daye, 1573).

Fraunce, Abraham, *The Arcadian Rhetorike* (London, 1588).

—— *The Lawiers Logike* (London: W. How, 1588).

Fuller, Thomas, *The History of the Worthies of England* (London: J. G. W. L. and W. G., 1662).

—— *The Church History of Britain from the Birth of Jesus Christ until the Year 1648*, ed. J. S. Brewer, 6 vols. (Oxford: Oxford University Press, 1845).

Gil, Alexander, *Logonomia Anglica* (London: J. Beale, 1619).

Greaves, Paul, *Grammatica Anglicana, praecipue quatenus a Latina differt, ad vnicam P. Rami methodum concinnata* (Cambridge: John Legatt, 1594).

The Greek New Testament, ed. K. Aland, M. Black, C. M. Martini, B. M. Metzger, and A. Wikgren, 3rd edn. (London: United Bible Societies, 1975).

Greville, Fulke, *The Tragedy of Mustapha* (London: J. Windet, 1609).

—— *Certaine learned and elegant workes of Fulke, Lord Brooke, written in his youth and familiar exercise with Sir Philip Sidney* (London: E. Purslowe, 1633).

—— *Life of Sir Philip Sidney*, ed. Nowell Smith (London, 1907).

—— *Poems and Dramas*, ed. Geoffrey Bullough, 2 vols. (Edinburgh, 1939).

—— *The Remains: being poems of monarchy and religion*, ed. G. A. Wilkes (Oxford: Clarendon, 1965).

—— *Selected Poems*, ed. Thom Gunn (London: Faber, 1968).

Hacket, John, *Scrinia reserata* (London: E. Jones, 1693).

Hanmer, Meredith, *The great bragge and challenge of M. Champion a Iesuite* (London: Thomas Marsh, 1581).

Harding, Thomas, *An Answere to Maister Iuelles Chalenge* (Louvain: John Bogard, 1564).

Hegius, Alexander, 'Invectiva in modos significandi', ed. J. Ijsewijn, *Forum for Modern Language Studies*, 7 (1971), 299–318.

Herbert, George, *The Works*, ed. F. E. Hutchinson (Oxford: Clarendon Press, 1941).

Hobbes, Thomas, *Of libertie and Necessity. A Treatise, Wherein all Controversie concerning Predestination, Election, Free-Will, Grace, Merits, Reprobation, &c is fully decided and declared* (London: John Davies, 1654).

Hooker, Richard, *Certayne Divine Tractates and other Godly Sermons* (London: Henrie Fetherstone, 1618).

—— *Works*, ed. John Keble, 3 vols., 7th edn., (Oxford: Clarendon Press, 1888).

—— *Works*, ed. W. Speed Hill, 5 vols., Folger Library Edition (Cambridge, Mass: Belknap Press, 1972–90).

Hume, Alexander, *Grammatica noua in vsum iuuentutis Scoticae* (Edinburgh: T. Finlason, 1612).

—— *Of the Orthographie and Congruitie of the Britan Tongue: A Treates, noe shorter then necessarie, for the Schooles*, ed. H. B. Wheatley, (London: EETS, 1865).

Hutten, Ulrich von, *Schriften*, ed. Eduard Böcking, 5 vols. (Leipzig: Teubner, 1859–61).

John of Garland, *Compendium Grammatice*, ed. Thomas Haye (Cologne: Böhlau, 1995).

John of Salisbury, *Metalogicon*, tr. D. McGarry (Berkeley: University of California Press, 1955).

—— *Metalogicon*, ed. J. B. Hall, CC, 98 (Turnhout: Brepols, 1991).

Jonson, Ben, *The Workes*, 2 vols. (London: Richard Bishop, 1640).

Kähler, Ernst, *Karlstadt und Augustinus: Der Kommentar des Andreas Bodenstein von Karlstadt zu Augustins De Spiritu et Litera*, Hallische Monographien, 19 (Halle: Niemayer, 1952).

Lee, Edward, *Annotationes E. Leei in annotationes Noui Testamenti D. Erasmi* (Basle: J. Froben, 1520).

Lever, Ralph, *The Arte of Reason, rightly termed, Witcraft* (London: H. Bynneman, 1573).

Lily, William, *A Shorte Introduction of Grammar, generally to be vsed in the Kynges Maiesties dominions*, English Linguistics 1500–1800, 262 (Menston: Scolar Press, 1970).

—— and John, Colet, *Ioannes Coleti aeditio una cum . . . G. Lilij grammatices rudimentis [1527]*, ed. R. C. Alston, English Linguistics 1500–1800, 298 (Menston: Scolar Press, 1971).

Linacre, Thomas, *De emendata structura latini sermonis libri sex [1524]*, English Linguistics 1500–1800, 83 (Menston: Scolar Press, 1968).

—— *Progymnasmata grammatices vulgaria* (London: J. Rastell, 1512).

Lombard, Peter, *Sententiae in IV libris distinctae*, 2 vols., Collegii S. Bonaventurae ad Claras Aquas, 3rd edn. (Rome: Grottaferrata, 1971–81).

Lords' Journals [*Journal of the House of Lords*, 235 vols. (Westminster, 1509–)].

Luther, Martin, *Amore et studio elucidande veritatis: hec subscripta disputabuntur Wittenberge* (Nuremberg: H. Höltzel?, 1517).

—— *Disputatio pro declaratione virtutis indulgentiarum* (Basle: Adam Petri, 1517).

—— *Eynn Sermon von dem Ablasz vnnd gnade* (Wittenberg: J. Grunenberg, 1518).

—— *Resolutiones disputationum de indulgentiarum virtute* (Wittenberg: J. Grunenberg, 1518).

—— *An den Christlichen Adel deutscher Nation* (Wittenberg: M. Lotter, 1520).

—— *De servo arbitrio ad D. Erasmum* (Wittenberg: Hans Lufft, 1525).

—— *Opera Omnia*, 7 vols. (Wittenberg: Hans Lufft et al., 1545–72).

—— *D. Martin Luthers Werke: kritische Gesamtausgabe*, 68 vols. (Weimar: Hermann Böhlau, 1883–1999).

—— *D. Martin Luthers Werke: die Deutsche Bibel*, 12 vols. (Weimar: Hermann Böhlau, 1906–61).

—— *D. Martin Luthers Werke: Tischreden*, 6 vols. (Weimar: Hermann Böhlau, 1912–21).

—— *D. Martin Luthers Werke: Briefwechsel*, 18 vols. (Weimar: Hermann Böhlau, 1930–85).

—— *Luther's Works*, ed. J. Pelikan and H. T. Lehmann, 56 vols. (Philadelphia: Fortress, 1955–86).

—— *Lectures on Romans*, ed. W. Pauck (Philadelphia: Westminster Press, 1961).

Manutius, Aldus, *Rudimenta grammatices Latinae linguae* (Venice: Aldus Manutius, 1501).

Marlowe, Christopher, *The Works*, ed. C. F. Tucker Brooke (Oxford: Clarendon Press, 1910).

Marot, Clément and Theodore Beza, *Pseaumes Octantetrois de Dauid, mis en rime Françoise* (Geneva: Thomas Courteau, 1565).

Martin, Gregory, *The New Testament of Jesus Christ, 1582*, facs. edn. (Ilkley: Scolar Press, 1975) [The Rhemes New Testament].

Marx, Karl, 'Contribution to the Critique of Hegel's Philosophy of Right', *Early Writings*, ed. T. B. Bottomore (London: C. A. Watts, 1963), pp. 43–59.

Meier, John (ed.), *Ältere Deutsche Grammatiken in Neudrucken*, 4 vols. (Strasbourg: K. Trübner, 1894–7).

Melanchthon, Philipp, *De rhetorica libri tres* (Wittenberg: J. Grunenberg, 1519).

—— *Loci communes rerum theologicarum* (Basle: A. Petri, 1521).

—— *Elementa Latinae grammatices* (Cologne: E. Cervicor, 1526).

—— *Dialectices libri quattuor* (Lyon: M. Trechsel, 1534).

—— *The Justification of Man by Faith Only* (London: W. Powell, 1548).

—— *Historia de vita et actis Lutheri* (Erfurt: G. Sthurmerus, 1548).

—— *Opera quae supersunt omnia*, ed. C. G. Bretschneider, 28 vols. (Halle: C. A. Schwetschke, 1834–59).

—— *Melanchthons Werke*, ed. Robert Stupperich, 7 vols. (Gütersloh: G. Mohn, 1931–75).

Milton, John, *Paradise Lost. A Poem in Twelve Books*, 2nd edn. (London: S. Simmons, 1674).

—— *Paradise Lost*, ed. Thomas Newton, 7th edn., 2 vols. (London: J. Beecroft etc., 1770).

—— *Complete Prose Works*, 8 vols. (New Haven: Yale University Press, 1953–82).

Molina, Luis de, *On Divine Foreknowledge*, tr. Alfred J. Freddoso (Ithaca: Cornell University Press, 1988).

Montagu, Richard, *A Gagg for the new Gospell? No: a New Gagg for an Old Goose* (London: Thomas Snodham, 1624).

—— *Appello Caesarem. A Iust appeale from two most vniust informers* (London: Matthew Lownes, 1625).

Montaigne, Michel de, *Essais de Michel de Montaigne. Cinquiesme edition, augmentée d'un troisiesme liure: et de six cens additions aux deux premiers* (Paris: Abel l'Angelier, 1588).

—— *Essais*, ed. M. le Jars de Gournay, 2 vols. (Paris: Abel l'Angelier, 1595).

—— *Essayes*, tr. John Florio, 6 vols. (London: Gibbings, 1906).

—— *Les Essais de Michel de Montaigne*, ed. P. Villey, rev. V.-L. Saulnier (Paris: Presses Universitaires de France, 1965).

—— *Essays*, tr. M. A. Screech (Harmondsworth: Penguin, 1991).

Monumenta Germaniae Paedagogica, ed. Karl Kehrbach, 12 vols. (Berlin: A. Hofmann, 1886–93).

Monumenta Paedagogica Societatis Iesu, vols. ii and iii, ed. L. Lukacs, Monumenta Historica Societatis Iesu, 107 (Rome, 1974).

More, Thomas, *Correspondence*, ed. Elizabeth Rogers (Princeton: Princeton University Press, 1947).

—— *The Complete Works*, ed. Louis L. Martz, Richard S. Sylvester, and Clarence H. Miller, 15 vols. (New Haven: Yale University Press, 1963–97).

Myconius, Friedrich, *Historia reformationis* (Leipzig: George Weidman, 1718).

Nashe, Thomas, *Works*, ed. R. B. McKerrow, 5 vols. (Oxford: Blackwell, 1958).

Ockham, William of, *Summa logicae*, ed. Philotheus Boehner, *Opera philosophica et theologica* (St Bonaventure, NY.: St Bonaventure University, 1974).

Ovid, *Amores, Ars Amatoria, Remedia Amoris*, ed. E. J. Kenney, 2nd edn., Oxford Classical Texts (Oxford: Clarendon Press, 1994).

Pagninus, Sanctes, *Biblia* (Leiden: A. du Ry, 1528).

Pauck, Wilhelm (ed.), *Melanchthon and Bucer* (Philadelphia: Westminster Press, 1969).

Peacham, Henry, *The Garden of Eloquence* (London: H. Jackson, 1593).

Perkins, William, *Prophetica, siue de sacra et vnica ratione concionandi* (Cambridge: J. Legate, 1592).

—— *A Golden Chaine; or, The Description of Theologie, containing the order of the Causes of Saluation and Damnation*, tr. Robert Hill (Cambridge: J. Legate, 1597).

—— *The Workes of that famous and worthie minister of Christ, in the vniuersitie of Cambridge, M. William Perkins*, 3 vols. (Cambridge: John Legatt, 1608–9).

Perotti, Niccolò, *Rudimenta grammatices* (Rome: A. Pannartz, 1473).

Persons, *De persecutione Anglicana, epistola* (Bononiae, apud Io. Baptistam Algazarium [Rouen: G. Flinton, at Persons's press], 1581).

Peter Helias, *Summa super Priscianum*, ed. Leo Reilly, 2 vols. (Toronto: Pontifical Institute of Mediaeval Studies, 1993).

Pontanus, Jacobus, *Poeticarum institutionum libri III*, 2nd edn. (Ingolstadt: A. Sartorius, 1597).

Pope, Alexander, *An Essay on Man*, ed. Maynard Mack, Twickenham Edition of the Works of Alexander Pope, 3/1 (London: Methuen, 1950).

Priscian, *Institutiones grammaticarum libri XVIII*, ed. Martin Hertz, *Grammatici Latini*, ed. Heinrich Keil, 8 vols., repr. edn. (Hildesheim: G. Olms, 1961), vols. ii–iii.

Prynne, William, *The Church of England's Old Antithesis to New Arminianisme* (London: A. Mathewes, 1629).

Puttenham, George, *The Arte of English Poesie*, ed. G. D. Willcock and A. Walker, repr. edn. (Cambridge: Cambridge University Press, 1970).

Rabelais, François, *Le Tiers Livre*, ed. M. A. Screech, Textes littéraires français (Geneva: Droz, 1964).

—— *The Histories of Gargantua and Pantagruel*, tr. J. M. Cohen, repr. edn. (Harmondsworth: Penguin, 1987).

Ramus, Peter, *Dialectique* (Paris: A. Wechel, 1555).

—— *Grammatica* (Paris: A. Wechel, 1572).

—— *The Logike of the moste excellent philosopher P. Ramus Martyr, Newly translated . . . Per M. Roll Makylmenaeum Scotum* (London: Thomas Vautrollier, 1574).

—— *Commentariorum de religione christiana, libri quatuor* (Frankfurt: A. Wechel, 1576).

—— *Scholae in liberales artes* (Basle: E. Episcopius, 1578).

—— *The Latine Grammar of P. Ramus* (London: R. Waldegrave, 1585).

Ratio studiorum et institutiones scholasticae Societatis Iesu, ed. G. M. Pachtler, *Monumenta Germaniae Paedagogica*, 2 (Berlin: A. Hofmann, 1887).

Reuchlin, Johan, *De rudimentis Hebraicis* (Pforzheim: T. Amshelm, 1506).

—— *Septem psalmi poenitentiales hebraici cum grammatica tralacione latina* (Tübingen: Thomas Amshelm, 1512).

—— *In Septem psalmos poenitentiales hebraicos interpretatio de uerbo ad uerbum, et super eisdem commentarioli sui* (Wittenberg: Joseph Clug, 1529).

Rupp, Gordon, and Philip Watson, (eds.), *Luther and Erasmus: Free Will and Salvation* (Philadelphia: Westminster Press, 1969).

Scaliger, Julius Caesar, *De causis linguae Latinae libri tredecim* (Lyon: Sebastian Gryphius, 1540).

—— *Poetices libri septem* (Lyon: Antonius Vincentius, 1561).

Schroeder, H. J., *The Canons and Decrees of the Council of Trent* (New York, 1941).

Shakespeare, William, *The First Folio*, ed. Charlton Hinman, facs. edn. (New York: Norton, 1968).

Sidney, Philip, *The countesse of Pembrokes Arcadia* (London: J. Windet, 1590).

—— *Prose Works*, ed. Albert Feuillerat, 4 vols. (Cambridge: Cambridge University Press, 1912–26).

—— *Poems*, ed. William Ringler (Oxford: Clarendon Press, 1962).

—— *An Apology for Poetry*, ed. Geoffrey Shepherd (Manchester: Manchester University Press, 1973).

Sidney, Mary and Philip, *The Psalms*, ed. J. C. A. Rathmell (New York: New York University Press, 1963).

Smith, G. G. (ed.), *Elizabethan Critical Essays*, 2 vols., repr. edn. (Oxford: Clarendon Press, 1950).

Some, Robert, *Three Questions Godly, Plainly, and Briefly Handled* (Cambridge: J. Legat, 1596).

Southwell, Robert, *An Epistle of Comfort, to the Reverend Priestes, & to the Honorable, Worshipful, & other of the Laye sort restrayned in Durance for the Catholicke Fayth* (Paris [London: Arundel House?, 1587/8?]).

—— *Saint Peters Complaint, With Other Poemes* (London: John Wolfe, 1595).

—— *Saint Peters Complaynt. With other Poems* (London: Gabriel Cawood, 1595).

—— *Maeoniae; or, Certaine excellent Poems and spirituall Hymnes: Omitted in the last Impression of Peters Complaint* (London: John Busbie, 1595).

—— *Saint Peters Complaint. With other Poems* (Edinburgh: R. Waldegrave, 1599).

Southwell, Robert, *S. Peters Complaint and Saint Mary Magdalens Funerall Teares. With sundry other selected, and deuout Poems* (St Omer: English College, 1616).

—— *St Peters Complaint, Mary Magdalens Teares, with other workes of the author R.S.* (London: William Barrett, 1620).

—— *An Humble Supplication to her Maiestie* [1600] ed. R. C. Bald (Cambridge: Cambridge University Press, 1953).

—— *The Poems of Robert Southwell, S.J.*, ed. James McDonald and Nancy Pollard Brown (Oxford: Clarendon Press, 1967).

—— *Two Letters and Short Rules of a Good Life*, edited by Nancy Pollard Brown (Charlottesville: University of Virginia Press, 1973).

—— *Spiritual Exercises and Devotions*, tr. P. E. Hallett, 2nd edn. (London, 1974).

Stapleton, Thomas, *Vniuersa iustificationis doctrina hodie controuersa* (Paris: M. Sonnium, 1582).

—— *Authoritatis ecclesiasticae circa S. Scripturarum approbationem . . . defensio* (Antwerp: J. Keerberg, 1592).

—— *Opera quae extant omnia*, 4 vols. (Paris: R. Fouet etc., 1620).

Steward, Richard, *Three Sermons, to which is added a fourth Sermon . . . by . . . Samuel Harsnett* (London: Gabriel Bedel and Thomas Heath, 1656).

Stock, Richard, *An Answere to the Ten Reasons* (London: Felix Kyngston, 1606).

Stow, John, *A Summarie of the Chronicles of England* (London: R. Bradocke, 1598).

Sullivan, Ernest (ed.), *The First and Second Dalhousie Manuscripts: Poems and Prose by John Donne and Others*, facs. edn., (Columbia: University of Missouri Press, 1988).

Swift, Jonathan, *Prose Writings*, ed. Herbert Davis, 16 vols. (Oxford: Blackwell, 1939–74).

Tansillo, Luigi, *Le Lagrime di S. Piero* (Venice: Francesco Rampazetto, 1560).

—— *Le Lagrime di San Pietro del signor Luigi Tansillo; con le Lagrime della Maddalena del Signor Erasmo da Valvasone* (Venice: Simon Cornetti, 1592).

Temple, William, *Temple's Analysis of Sidney*, ed. John Webster (Binghampton: SUNY Press, 1984).

Tertullian, *Ad martyres*, ed. J.-P. Migne, PL 1 (Paris: Garnier, 1844).

Thomas of Erfurt, *Grammatica speculativa*, ed. G. L. Bursill-Hall (London: Classics of Linguistics, 1972).

[Tottel's Miscellany] *Songes and sonettes, written by the right honorable Lorde Henry Howard late Earle of Surrey, and other* (London: Richard Tottel, 1557).

Trutfetter, Jodokus, *Breviarium dialecticum* (Erfurt: Wolfgang Schenk, 1500).

—— *Summule totius logice* (Erfurt: L. Schenk, 1501).

Tudor Royal Proclamations, ed. P. Hughes and J. Larkin, 3 vols. (New Haven: Yale University Press, 1964–9).

Tyndale, William, *A compendious introduccion, prologe or preface vn to the pistle off Paul to the Romayns* ([Worms: P. Schoeffer, 1526]).

—— *That fayth the mother of all good workes iustifieth vs* [*The parable of the wicked mammon*] ([Antwerp: M. de Keyser, 1528]).

—— *The obedience of a Christen man and how Christen rulers ought to governe* ([Antwerp: M. de Keyser, 1528]).

—— *The fyrst boke of Moses called Genesis* [*The seconde–thirde–fourth–fifth boke*] ([Antwerp: M. de Keyser, 1530]).

—— *The prophete Jonas, with an introduccion before teachinge to vnderstonde him* ([Antwerp: M. de Keyser, 1531]).

—— *The newe testament* (Antwerp: M. Emperowr [M. de Keyser], 1534).

——*Doctrinal Treatises and Introductions to Different Portions of the Holy Scriptures by William Tyndale*, ed. Henry Walter, Parker Society (Cambridge: Cambridge University Press, 1848).

—— *The Newe Testamente dylygently corrected and compared with the Greke*, facs. edn. by N. Hardy Willis, Royal Society of Literature (Cambridge: Cambridge University Press, 1939).

—— *An Answere vnto Sir Thomas Mores Dialoge*, ed. Anne M. O'Donnell and Jared Wicks, *Independent Works of William Tyndale*, vol. iii (Washington: Catholic University of America Press, 2000).

Valla, Lorenzo, *Opera omnia*, facs. edn. Eugenio Garin, 2 vols. (Turin: Bottega d'Erasmo, 1962).

——*De linguae latinae elegantia*, ed. Santiago López Moreda, 2 vols. (Cáceres: Universidad de Extremadura, 1999).

Valvasone, Erasmo da, see Tansillo, Luigi.

Verstegan, Richard, *Theatrum Crudelitatum Haereticorum Nostri Temporis* (Antwerp: Adrian Hubert, 1588).

Vives, Juan Luis, *De disciplinis libri XX* (Antwerp: M. Hillen van Hoochstraten, 1531).

—— *Opera in duos distincta tomos* (Basle: Nicolas l'Evesque, 1555).

—— *In Pseudodialecticos*, ed. Charles Fantazzi (Leiden: Brill, 1979).

Wallis, John, *Grammatica linguae Anglicanae* (Oxford: Leonard Lichfield, 1653).

—— *The History of David's Troubles; or, Human Frailty Delineated. A Sacred Poem* (Oxford: Leonard Lichfield, 1741).

—— *Grammar of the English Language*, ed. J. A. Kemp (London: Longman, 1972).

Walton, Izaak, *The Lives of John Donne, Sir Henry Wotton, Richard Hooker, George Herbert and Robert Sanderson*, repr. edn. (Oxford: Oxford University Press, 1973).

Whitaker, William, *Ad rationes decem Edmundi Campiani iesuitae . . . responsio* (London: Thomas Vautrollier, 1581).

——*Disputatio de sacra scriptura, contra R. Bellarminum & T. Stapletonum* (Cambridge: T. Thomas, 1588).

——*Praelectiones doctissimi viri Guilielmi Whitakeri . . . in quibus tractatur controuersia de ecclesia. His accesit Doct. Whitakeri ultima concio ad clerum* (Cambridge: J. Legat, 1599).

——*Tractatus . . . de peccato originali . . . adversus . . . Thomas Stapletoni* (Cambridge: J. Legat, 1600).

Wilkins, David, *Concilia magnae Brittaniae et Hiberniae*, 4 vols. (London: R. Gosling, 1737).

Wilson, Thomas, *The rule of Reason, conteinyng the Arte of Logique* (London: Richard Grafton, 1551).

—— *The Arte of Rhetorique, for the use of all soche as are studious of Eloquence* (London: John Kingston, 1560).

Wimpfeling, Jacob, *Isidoneus Germanicus* (Strasbourg: J. Grüninger, 1497?).

Wyatt, Thomas, *Certayne psalmes chosen out of the psalter of Dauid commonly called thee .vii. penytntiall psalmes, drawen into englyshe meter by Sir Thomas Wyat* (London: Thomas Raynold and John Harrington, 1549).

—— *Life and Letters*, ed. Kenneth Muir (Liverpool: Liverpool University Press, 1963).

—— *Collected Poems*, ed. Kenneth Muir and Patricia Thomson (Liverpool: Liverpool University Press, 1969).

Yepes, Diego de, *Historia particular de la persecucion de Inglaterra* (Madrid: Luis Sanchez, 1599).

Zwingli, Huldrych, *Sämtliche Werke*, ed. E. Egli, G. Finsler, and W. Köhler, Corpus Reformatorum, 14 vols. (Berlin: C. A. Schwetschke, Leipzig: Heinsius Nachfolger, and Zurich: Berichthaus, 1905–59).

SECONDARY SOURCES

Ackroyd, P. R., C. F. Evans, G. W. H. Lampe, and S. L. Greenslade (eds.), *The Cambridge History of the Bible*, 3 vols. (Cambridge: Cambridge University Press, 1963–70).

Adams, H. M., *Catalogue of Books Printed on the Continent of Europe, 1501–1600 in Cambridge Libraries*, 2 vols. (Cambridge: Cambridge University Press, 1967).

Allison, Anthony and D. M. Rogers, *The Contemporary Printed Literature of the English Counter-Reformation between 1558 and 1640*, 2 vols. (Aldershot: Scolar Press, 1989–94).

Alston, R. C., *A Bibliography of the English Language from the Invention of Printing to the Year 1800*, 11 vols. (Ilkley: Scolar Press, 1974–7).

Arber, Edward, *A Transcript of the Registers of the Company of Stationers of London, 1554–1640*, 5 vols. (London: private press, 1875–94).

Aston, Margaret, *Lollards and Reformers: Images and Literacy in Late Medieval Religion* (London: Hambledon Press, 1984).

—— *England's Iconoclasts, I: Laws Against Images* (Oxford: Clarendon Press, 1988).

—— *Faith and Fire: Popular and Unpopular Religion 1350–1600* (London: Hambledon Press, 1993).

Augustijn, Cornelis, 'Hyperaspistes I: La doctrine d'Érasme et de Luther sur la «Claritas Scripturae»', *Colloquia Erasmiana Turonensia*, 2 vols. (Paris: Vrin, 1972), ii. 737–48.

—— *Erasmus: His Life, Works and Influence* (Toronto: University of Toronto Press, 1991).

—— *Erasmus: der Humanist als Theologe und Kirchenreformer*, Studies in Medieval and Reformation Thought, 59 (Leiden: E. J. Brill, 1996).

Austin, J. L., *Philosophical Papers*, 3rd edn. (Oxford: Oxford University Press, 1979).

—— *How to Do Things with Words* (Oxford: Clarendon Press, 1962).

Bagchi, David, *Luther's Earliest Opponents: Catholic Controversialists 1518–1525* (Minneapolis: Fortress Press, 1991).

Bainton, Roland H., *Erasmus of Christendom* (London: Collins, 1970).

Bald, R. C., *John Donne: A Life* (Oxford: Clarendon Press, 1970).

Barber, Charles, *Early Modern English* (London: André Deutsch, 1976).

Barnes, Jonathan, *Aristotle* (Oxford: Oxford University Press, 1982).

Barnett, Mary Jane, 'Erasmus and the Hermeneutics of Linguistic Praxis', *Renaissance Quarterly*, 49 (1996), 542–72.

Bataillon, Marcel, *Érasme et l'Espagne*, rev. edn., 3 vols. (Geneva: Librairie Droz, 1991).

Beal, Peter, *Index of English Literary Manuscripts*, vol. i 1450–1625, 2 parts (London: Mansell, 1980).

Bentley, Jerry H., *Humanists and Holy Writ: New Testament Scholarship in the Renaissance* (Princeton: Princeton University Press, 1983).

Benveniste, Emile, *Le Vocabulaire des institutions indo-européennes*, 2 vols. (Paris: Minuit, 1969).

Benzing, Josef, *Lutherbibliographie: Verzeichnis der gedruckten Schriften Martin Luthers bis zu dessen Tod* (Baden-Baden: Heitz, 1966).

Biersack, Manfred, 'La conoscenza delle fonti protestanti di Bellarmino nelle *Lectiones lovanienses*, in prospettiva della doctrina circa la predestinazione e la grazia', *Roberto Bellarmino*, ed. Gustavo Galeota (Capua: Archidiocesi di Capua, 1990), pp. 159–87.

Biller, Peter and Anne Hudson, (eds.), *Heresy and Literacy, 1100–1530* (Cambridge: Cambridge University Press, 1994).

Bizer, Ernest, *Fides ex Auditu*, 3rd edn. (Neukirchen: Neukirchener Verlag, 1966).

Bonhoeffer, Dietrich, *Ethics* (London: SCM, 1955).

Bornkamm, *Luther in Mid-Career, 1521–1530* (London: Darton, Longman, & Todd, 1983).

Bossy, John, *The English Catholic Community 1570–1850* (London: Darton, Longman & Todd, 1975).

—— *Giordano Bruno and the Embassy Affair* (New Haven: Yale University Press, 1991).

Bouwsma, William J., *Calvin: A Sixteenth Century Portrait* (New York: Oxford University Press, 1988).

Bray, John S., *Theodore Beza's Doctrine of Predestination* (Nieuwkoop: de Graaf, 1975).

Brecht, Martin, *Martin Luther: His Road to Reformation 1483–1521* (Philadelphia: Fortress Press, 1985).

Brecht, Martin, and Eberhard Zwink (eds.), *Eine glossierte Vulgata aus dem Umkreis Martin Luthers*, Vestigia Bibliae, 21 (Bern: Peter Lang, 1999).

Breen, Quirinus, *Calvin: A Study in French Humanism* (Grand Rapids: Eerdmans, 1931).

—— 'John Calvin and the Rhetorical Tradition', *Church History*, 26 (1957), 3–21.

Breward, Ian, *The Works of William Perkins* (Abingdon: Duffield, 1970).

Brigden, Susan, *London and the Reformation* (Oxford: Clarendon Press, 1989).

Brodrick, James, *Robert Bellarmine: Saint and Scholar*, rev. edn. (London: Burns & Oates, 1961).

Brown, Nancy Pollard, 'The Structure of "Saint Peter's Complaint"', *Modern Language Review*, 61 (1966), 3–11.

Burke, Peter, *The Art of Conversation* (Cambridge: Polity Press, 1993).

Bursill-Hall, G. L. *A Census of Medieval Latin Grammatical Manuscripts* (Stuttgart: Frommann-Holzboog, 1981).

Bush, Sargent, and Carl Rasmussen, *The Library of Emmanuel College, Cambridge, 1584–1637* (Cambridge: Cambridge University Press, 1986).

Butler, Ernest, *Syntax of the Moods and Tenses in New Testament Greek*, 3rd edn. (Edinburgh: T. & T. Clark, 1898).

Carey, John, *Donne: Life, Mind and Art* (London: Faber & Faber, 1981).

Carruthers, Mary, *The Book of Memory: A Study of Memory in Medieval Culture* (Cambridge: Cambridge University Press, 1990).

Cavallo, Guglielmo, and Roger Chartier (eds.), *A History of Reading in the West*, tr. Lydia G. Cochrane (Cambridge: Polity Press, 1999).

Cave, Terence, *The Cornucopian Text: Problems of Writing in the French Renaissance* (Oxford: Clarendon Press, 1979).

Chantraine, G., *Érasme et Luther: libre et serf arbitre* (Paris: Lethielleux, 1981).

Chomarat, Jacques, 'Les Annotations de Valla, celles d'Érasme et la grammaire', *Histoire de l'exégèse au XVIe siècle*, ed. O. Fatio and P. Fraenkel (Geneva: Droz, 1978), pp. 202–28.

—— *Grammaire et rhétorique chez Érasme*, 2 vols. (Paris: Société de l'édition 'Les belles lettres', 1981).

Chrisman, Miriam, *Lay Culture, Learned Culture: Books and Social Change in Strasbourg 1480–1599* (New Haven: Yale University Press, 1982).

—— *Bibliography of Strasbourg Imprints, 1480–1599* (New Haven: Yale University Press, 1982).

Clarke, Elizabeth, *Theory and Theology in George Herbert's Poetry* (Oxford: Clarendon Press, 1997).

Clebsch, William A., *England's Earliest Protestants 1520–1535* (New Haven: Yale University Press, 1964).

Clegg, Cyndia Susan, *Press Censorship in Elizabethan England* (Cambridge: Cambridge University Press, 1997).

Collinson, Patrick, *The Elizabethan Puritan Movement* (London: Jonathan Cape, 1967).

—— 'Concerning the name Puritan, a comment', *Journal of Ecclesiastical History*, 31 (1980), 463–88.

—— *Godly People: Essays on English Protestantism and Puritanism* (London: Hambledon Press, 1983).

—— *English Puritanism* (London: Historical Association, 1983).

—— *The Birthpangs of Protestant England: Religious and Cultural Change in the Sixteenth and Seventeenth Centuries* (London: Macmillan, 1988).

Connell, Dorothy, *Sir Philip Sidney: The Maker's Mind* (Oxford: Clarendon Press, 1977).

Cooper, C. H. and T. Cooper, *Athenae Cantabrigienses*, 3 vols. (Cambridge, 1858–1913).

Courtenay, William J., *Schools and Scholars in Fourteenth-Century England* (Princeton: Princeton University Press, 1987).

Cressy, David, *Literacy and the Social Order: Reading and Writing in Tudor and Stuart England* (Cambridge: Cambridge University Press, 1980).

Cummings, Brian, 'Justifying God in Tyndale's English', *Reformation*, 2 (1997), 143–71.

—— 'Literally Speaking; or, The Literal Sense from Augustine to Lacan', *The Literal*, ed. Andrew Benjamin, *Paragraph*, 21 (1998), 200–26.

—— 'Reformed Literature and Literature Reformed', *The Cambridge History of Medieval English Literature*, ed. David Wallace (Cambridge: Cambridge University Press, 1999), pp. 821–51.

Daniell, David, *William Tyndale: A Biography* (New Haven: Yale University Press, 1994).

Danielson, Dennis, *Milton's Good God: A Study in Literary Theodicy* (Cambridge: Cambridge University Press, 1982).

Davidson, Donald, *Essays on Actions and Events*, repr. edn. (Oxford: Clarendon Press, 1985).

Davies, Philip R., 'Potter, Prophet and People: Jeremiah 18 as Parable', *Hebrew Annual Review*, 11 (1987), 23–33.

Davis, John F., *Heresy and Reformation in the South-East of England, 1520–1559* (London: Royal Historical Society, 1983).

Davis, Natalie Zemon, *Society and Culture in Early Modern France* (Stanford: Stanford University Press, 1975).

—— *The Gift in Sixteenth-Century France* (Oxford: Oxford University Press, 2000).

Dekker, Evert, *Rijker dan Midas: vrijheid, genade en predestinatie in de theologie van Jacobus Arminius* (Zoetermeer: Boekencentrum, 1993).

De Molen, Richard L., *Essays on the Work of Erasmus* (New Haven: Yale University Press, 1978).

Denifle, Heinrich, *Luther und Luthertum in der ersten Entwicklung*, 2 vols. (Mainz: Franz Kirchheim, 1904–9).

Derrida, Jacques, *De la grammatologie* (Paris: Minuit, 1967).

Derrida, Jacques, *Marges de la philosophie* (Paris: Minuit, 1972).

—— *Given Time: I. Counterfeit Money*, tr. Peggy Kamuf (Chicago: University of Chicago Press, 1992).

Devlin, Christopher, *The Life of Robert Southwell* (London: Longman, 1956).

Dickens, A. G., *The English Reformation*, rev. edn. (London: Collins, 1967).

—— *The German Nation and Martin Luther* (London: Arnold, 1974).

Duffy, Eamon, *The Stripping of the Altars: Traditional Religion in England, 1400–1580* (New Haven: Yale University Press, 1992).

Dummett, Michael, *Frege: Philosophy of Language*, 2nd edn. (London: Duckworth, 1981).

Duncan-Jones, Katherine, *Sir Philip Sidney: Courtier Poet* (New Haven: Yale University Press, 1991).

Durston, Christopher and Jacqueline Eales (eds.), *The Culture of English Puritanism, 1560–1700* (London: Macmillan, 1996).

Ebeling, Gerhard, *Luther: An Introduction to his Thought* (London: Collins, 1970).

—— *Introduction to a Theological Theory of Language* (London: Collins, 1973).

—— *Lutherstudien*, 3 vols. (Tübingen: J. C. B. Mohr, 1971–89).

Eisenstein, Elizabeth L., *The Printing Press as an Agent of Change*, 2 vols. (Cambridge: Cambridge University Press, 1979).

Elton, Geoffrey, *Policy and Police: The Enforcement of the Reformation in the Age of Thomas Cromwell* (Cambridge: Cambridge University Press, 1972).

Empson, William, *Milton's God*, rev. edn. (Cambridge: Cambridge University Press, 1981).

Enselging, R., *Der Bürger als Leser: Lesergeschichte in Deutschland 1500–1800* (Stuttgart: Metzler, 1974).

Erichson, Alfred, *Bibliographia Calviniana: catalogus chronologicus operum Calvini* (Nieuwkoop: B. de Graaf, 1960).

Erikson, Erik H., *Young Man Luther: A Study in Psychoanalysis and History* (New York: Norton, 1958).

Evans, G. R., *The Language and Logic of the Bible*, 2 vols. (Cambridge: Cambridge University Press, 1984–5).

Fenlon, Dermot, *Heresy and Obedience in Tridentine Italy: Cardinal Pole and the Counter Reformation* (Cambridge: Cambridge University Press, 1972).

Ferguson, Margaret W., *Trials of Desire: Renaissance Defenses of Poetry* (New Haven: Yale University Press, 1983).

Fish, Stanley E., *Surprised by Sin: The Reader in Paradise Lost* (Berkeley: University of California Press, 1967).

Foestermann, C. E., *Liber Decanorum Facultatis Theologicae Academiae Vitebergensis* (Leipzig: C. Tauchnitz, 1838).

Foucault, Michel, *Les mots et les choses: une archéologie des sciences humaines* (Paris: Gallimard, 1966).

—— *The History of Sexuality: An Introduction*, Eng. tr. (Harmondsworth: Penguin, 1979).

—— *The Order of Things*, Eng. tr., repr.edn. (London: Tavistock/Routledge, 1989).
—— *The Archaeology of Knowledge*, Eng. tr., repr. edn. (London: Routledge, 1997).
Fox, Alistair, *Thomas More: History and Providence* (Oxford: Blackwell, 1982).
—— *Politics and Literature in the Reigns of Henry VII and Henry VIII* (Oxford: Blackwell, 1989).
Froelich, Karlfried, 'The Printed Gloss', *Biblia Latina cum glossa ordinaria*, facs. edn., 4 vols. (Turnhout: Brepols, 1992), i., pp. xii–xxvi.
Ganoczy, Alexandre, *The Young Calvin*, tr. David Foxgrover and Wade Provo (Edinburgh: T. & T. Clark, 1987).
—— and Scheld, Stefan, *Die Hermeneutik Calvins: geistesgeschichtliche Voraussetzungen und Grundzüge* (Wiesbaden: Franz Steiner, 1983).
Gaskin, Richard, *The Sea Battle and the Master Argument: Aristotle and Diodorus Cronus on the Metaphysics of the Future* (Berlin: de Gruyter, 1995).
Geisendorf, Paul-F., *Théodore de Bèze* (Geneva: Labor et Fides, 1949).
Gilmont, Jean-François, *Jean Calvin et le livre imprimé* (Geneva: Droz, 1997).
—— (ed.), *The Reformation and the Book*, tr. K. Maag (Aldershot: Ashgate, 1998).
Gilson, Etienne, *Introduction à l'étude de Saint Augustin*, 2nd edn. (Paris: Vrin, 1943).
Girardin, Benoît, *Rhétorique et théologique: Calvin, le Commentaire de l'Épître aux Romains*, Théologie historique, 54 (Paris: Beauchesne, 1979).
Goodwin, Gordon, *A Catalogue of the Harsnett Library at Colchester* (London: Richard Amer, 1888).
Gosse, Edmund, *The Life and Letters of John Donne*, 2 vols. (London: Heinemann, 1899).
Grafton, Anthony, *Commerce with the Classics: Ancient Books and Renaissance Readers* (Ann Arbor: University of Michigan Press, 1997).
—— and Jardine, Lisa, *From Humanism to the Humanities* (London: Duckworth, 1986).
Gravier, M., *Luther et l'opinion publique* (Paris: Aubier, 1942).
Green, Ian, *The Christian's ABC: Catechisms and Catechizing in England c.1530–1740* (Oxford: Clarendon Press, 1996).
Greenblatt, Stephen, *Renaissance Self-Fashioning: From More to Shakespeare* (Chicago: Chicago University Press, 1980).
—— *Shakespearean Negotiations: The Circulation of Social Energy in Renaissance England* (Oxford: Clarendon Press, 1988).
Grice, H. P., 'Logic and conversation', *Studies in the Way of Words* (Cambridge, Mass.: Harvard University Press, 1989), pp. 22–40.
Grossmann, Maria, *Humanism in Wittenberg, 1485–1517*, Bibliotheca Humanistica & Reformatorica, 11 (Nieuwkoop: de Graaf, 1975).
Haigh, Christopher, *English Reformations: Religion, Politics and Society under the Tudors* (Oxford: Clarendon Press, 1993).
Hall, Basil, 'Calvin against the Calvinists', *John Calvin*, ed. G. E. Duffield, Courtenay Studies in Reformation Theology, 1 (Abingdon: Duffield, 1966), pp. 19–37.

Hall, Basil, 'The Early Rise and Gradual Decline of Lutheranism in England', *Reform and Reformation: England and the Continent*, ed. Derek Baker, *Studies in Church History* (Oxford, 1979), pp. 103–31.

——'Martin Bucer in England', *Martin Bucer: Reforming Church and Community*, ed. D. F. Wright (Cambridge: Cambridge University Press, 1994), pp. 144–60.

Haller, William, *The Rise of Puritanism* (New York: Columbia University Press, 1938).

Hamel, Adolf, *Der junge Luther und Augustin*, 2 vols. (Gütersloh: G. Mohn, 1934–5).

Hamilton, A. C., *Sir Philip Sidney: A Study of his Life and Works* (Cambridge: Cambridge University Press, 1977).

Hammond, Gerald, 'William Tyndale's Pentateuch: Its Relation to Luther's German Bible and the Hebrew Original', *Renaissance Quarterly*, 33 (1980), 351–85.

Handford, Stanley, *The Latin Subjunctive: Its Usage and Development from Plautus to Tacitus* (London: Methuen, 1947).

Hannay, Margaret, *Philip's Phoenix: Mary Sidney, Countess of Pembroke* (Oxford: Oxford University Press, 1990).

Hare, R. M., *Freedom and Reason* (Oxford: Clarendon Press, 1963).

Heath, Terrence, 'Logical Grammar, Grammatical Logic, and Humanism in Three German Universities', *Studies in the Renaissance*, 18 (1971), 9–64.

Hibbard, Howard, *Caravaggio* (London: Thames & Hudson, 1983).

Higman, Francis M., *Piety and the People: Religious Printing in France, 1511–1551* (Ipswich: Scolar Press, 1996).

Hill, Christopher, *Puritanism and Revolution*, repr. edn. (Harmondsworth: Penguin, 1986).

Hill, Geoffrey, *The Lords of Limit: Essays on Literature and Ideas* (London: André Deutsch, 1984).

Hillerbrand, H. J., *The Reformation in its Own Words* (London: SCM, 1964).

Hirsch, Emanuel, 'Initium Theologiae Lutheri', *Festgabe für Julius Kaftan zu seinem 70. Geburtstage* (Tübingen: J. C. B. Mohr, 1920), pp. 150–69.

Holborn, Louise, 'Printing and the Growth of a Protestant Movement in Germany from 1517–1524', *Church History*, 11 (1942), 1–15.

Holl, Karl, *Gesammelte Aufsätze zur Kirchengeschichte*, 6th edn., 3 vols. (Tübingen: J. C. B. Mohr, 1932).

Honselmann, Klemens, *Urfassung und Drucke der Ablaßthesen Martin Luthers und ihre Veröffentlichung* (Paderborn: F. Schöningh, 1966).

Howell, W. S., *Logic and Rhetoric in England, 1500–1700* (New York: Russell & Russell, 1956).

Hudson, Anne, 'Wyclif and the English Language', *Wyclif in his Times*, ed. Anthony Kenny (Oxford: Clarendon Press, 1986), pp. 85–103.

Huizinga, Johan, *Erasmus and the Age of the Reformation*, repr. edn. (Princeton: Princeton University Press, 1990).

Hunt, R. W., *The History of Grammar in the Middle Ages: Collected Papers*, ed. G. L. Bursill-Hall, Studies in the History of Linguistics, 5 (Amsterdam: Benjamins, 1980).

Irvine, Martin, *The Making of Textual Culture: 'Grammatica' and Literary Theory, 350–1100* (Cambridge: Cambridge University Press, 1994).

Iserloh, Erwin, *Luthers Thesenanschlag: Tatsache oder Legende?* (Wiesbaden: Franz Steiner, 1962).

Janelle, Pierre, *Robert Southwell the Writer: A Study in Religious Inspiration* (London: Sheed & Ward, 1935).

Jardine, Lisa, 'The Place of Dialectic Teaching in Sixteenth-century Cambridge', *Studies in the Renaissance*, 21 (1974), 31–62.

——'Lorenzo Valla and the Intellectual Origins of Humanist Dialectic', *Journal of the History of Philosophy*, 15 (1977), 143–64.

——*Erasmus, Man of Letters* (Princeton: Princeton University Press, 1993).

——*Worldly Goods: A New History of the Renaissance* (London: Macmillan, 1996).

——and Anthony Grafton, ' "Studied for Action": How Gabriel Harvey read his Livy', *Past & Present*, 129 (1990), 30–78.

Jedin, Hubert, *A History of the Council of Trent*, 2 vols. (London: Nelson, 1957–61).

Jespersen, Otto, *The Philosophy of Grammar* (London: Allen and Unwin, 1924).

Jones, Richard Foster, *The Triumph of the English Language* (Stanford: Stanford University Press, 1953).

Junghans, Helmar, *Der junge Luther und die Humanisten* (Göttingen: Vandenhoek & Ruprecht, 1985).

Kendall, R. T., *Calvin and English Calvinism to 1649* (Oxford: Oxford University Press, 1979).

——'The Puritan Modification of Calvin's Theology', *John Calvin: His Influence in the Modern World*, ed. W. S. Reid (Grand Rapids: Zondervan, 1982).

Keynes, Geoffrey, *A Bibliography of Dr John Donne*, 4th edn. (Oxford: Clarendon Press, 1973).

King, John N., *English Reformation Literature: The Tudor Origins of the Protestant Tradition* (Princeton: Princeton University Press, 1982).

Kinney, Daniel, 'More's Letter to Dorp: Remapping the Trivium', *Renaissance Quarterly*, 34 (1981), 179–210.

Kleineidam, Erich, *Universitas Studii Erffordensis: Überblick über die Geschichte der Üniversität Erfurt*, 4 vols. (Leipzig: St Benno, 1969–81).

Knappen, M. M., *Tudor Puritanism* (Chicago: University of Chicago Press, 1939).

Kohls, Ernst-Wilhelm, 'La position théologique d'Érasme et la tradition dans le "De libero arbitrio" ', *Colloquium Erasmianum* (Mons: Centre Universitaire de l'État, 1968), pp. 69–88.

Kretzmann, Norman, Anthony Kenny, and Jan Pinborg (eds.), *The Cambridge History of Later Medieval Philosophy* (Cambridge: Cambridge University Press, 1982).

Küng, Hans, *Justification*, 2nd edn. (London: Burns & Oates, 1981).

Lake, Peter, *Moderate Puritans and the Elizabethan Church* (Cambridge: Cambridge University Press, 1982).

—— 'Puritan Identities', *Journal of Ecclesiastical History*, 35 (1984), 112–23.

—— 'Calvinism and the English Church 1570–1635', *Past and Present*, 114 (1987), 32–76.

—— *Anglicans and Puritans? Presbyterianism and English Conformist Thought from Whitgift to Hooker* (London: Unwin Hyman, 1988).

—— 'Religious Identities in Shakespeare's England', *A Companion to Shakespeare*, ed. D. S. Kastan (Oxford: Blackwell, 1999), pp. 57–84.

Leclercq, Jean, *The Love of Learning and the Desire for God: A Study of Monastic Culture*, 2nd edn. (London: SPCK, 1978).

Leedham-Green, E. S., *Books in Cambridge Inventories*, 2 vols. (Cambridge: Cambridge University Press, 1986).

Le Huray, Peter, *Music and the Reformation in England 1549–1660*, repr. edn. (Cambridge: Cambridge University Press, 1978).

Lehmberg, Stanford E., *The Later Parliaments of Henry VIII 1536–1547* (Cambridge: Cambridge University Press, 1977).

Lewalski, Barbara Kiefer, *Protestant Poetics and the Seventeenth-Century Religious Lyric* (Princeton: Princeton University Press, 1979).

Lloyd Jones, G., *The Discovery of Hebrew in Tudor England* (Manchester: Manchester University Press, 1983).

Lohse, Bernhard (ed.), *Der Durchbruch der reformatorischen Erkenntnis bei Luther* (Darmstadt: Wissenschaftliche Buchhandlung, 1968).

—— (ed.), *Der Durchbruch: Neuere Untersuchungen* (Stuttgart: F. Steiner, 1988).

—— *Martin Luther's Theology: Its Historical and Systematic Development* (Edinburgh: T. & T. Clark, 1999).

Lubac, Henri de, *Exégèse médiévale: les quatre sens de l'écriture*, 4 vols. (Paris: Aubier, 1959–64).

Lyons, John, *Semantics*, 2 vols. (Cambridge: Cambridge University Press, 1977).

McConica, J. K., 'Erasmus and the Grammar of Consent', *Scrinium Erasmianum*, ed. J. Coppens, 2 vols. (Leiden: E. J. Brill, 1969), ii. 77–99.

Macculloch, Diarmaid, *Thomas Cranmer: A Life* (New Haven: Yale University Press, 1996).

McEachern, Claire and Debora Shuger, *Religion and Culture in Renaissance England* (Cambridge: Cambridge University Press, 1997).

McGrath, Alister E., *Luther's Theology of the Cross: Martin Luther's Theological Breakthrough* (Oxford: Blackwell, 1985).

—— *Iustitia Dei: A History of the Christian Doctrine of Justification*, 2 vols. (Cambridge: Cambridge University Press, 1986).

Maclean, H., 'Greville's "Poetic"', *Studies in Philology*, 61 (1964), 170–91.

Maclure, Millar, *The Paul's Cross Sermons 1534–1642* (Toronto: University of Toronto Press, 1958).

——*Register of Sermons Preached at Paul's Cross 1534–1642*, rev. edn. (Ottawa: Dovehouse Press, 1989).

McNair, P., 'Ochino on Sedition: An Italian Dialogue of the Sixteenth Century', *Italian Studies*, 15 (1960), 36–49.

McSorley, H. J., *Luther: Right or Wrong? An Ecumenical-Theological Study of the Bondage of the Will* (New York: Newman, 1969).

Mansi, Giovanni Domenico (ed.), *Sacrorum Conciliorum nova et amplissima collectio*, repr. edn., 54 vols. (Graz: Akademische Druck, 1960–1).

Marenbon, John, *Early Medieval Philosophy (480–1150): An Introduction* (London: Routledge, 1983).

——*Later Medieval Philosophy (1150–1350): An Introduction* (London: Routledge, 1987).

——*The Philosophy of Peter Abelard* (Cambridge: Cambridge University Press, 1997).

Margolin, Jean-Claude, 'Érasme et le silence', *Érasme: Le prix des mots et de l'homme* (London: Variorum, 1986), pp. 163–78.

Marius, Richard, *Martin Luther: The Christian between God and Death* (Cambridge, Mass.: Harvard University Press, 1999).

Marotti, Arthur F., *John Donne, Coterie Poet* (Madison: University of Wisconsin Press, 1986).

——*Manuscript, Print and the English Renaissance Lyric* (Ithaca: Cornell University Press, 1995).

Marranzini, Alfredo, 'Il problema della giustificazione nell'evoluzione del pensiero di Seripando', *Girolamo Seripando e la chiesa del suo tempo* (Rome: Storia e letteratura, 1997), pp. 227–69.

Marrou, H. I., *Saint Augustin et la fin de la culture antique* (Paris: Bocard, 1938).

——*A History of Education in Antiquity* (New York: Sheed and Ward, 1956).

Martz, Louis, *The Poetry of Meditation*, rev. edn. (New Haven: Yale University Press, 1962).

Mason, H. A., *Humanism and Poetry in the Early Tudor Period* (London: Routledge & Kegan Paul, 1959).

Matheson, Peter, *Cardinal Contarini at Regensburg* (Oxford: Clarendon Press, 1972).

Mauss, Marcel, *The Gift: The Form and Reason for Exchange in Archaic Societies*, tr. W. D. Halls (New York: Norton, 1990).

Menchi, Silvana Seidel, *Erasmus als Ketzer: Reformation und Inquisition im Italien des 16. Jahrhunderts*, Studies in Medieval and Reformation Thought, 49 (Leiden: E. J. Brill, 1993).

Metzger, Bruce M., *The Text of the New Testament: Its Transmission, Corruption and Restoration*, 3rd edn. (New York: Oxford University Press, 1992).

Michael, Ian, *English Grammatical Categories and the Tradition to 1800* (Cambridge: Cambridge University Press, 1970).

Miller, Perry, *The New England Mind: The Seventeenth Century*, repr. edn. (Cambridge, Mass.: Harvard University Press, 1954).

Milton, Anthony, *Catholic and Reformed: The Roman and Protestant Churches in English Protestant Thought 1600–1640* (Cambridge: Cambridge University Press, 1995).

Milward, Peter, *Religious Controversies of the Elizabethan Age: A Survey of Printed Sources* (London: Scolar Press, 1977).

—— *Religious Controversies of the Jacobean Age: A Survey of Printed Sources* (London: Scolar Press, 1978).

Minnis, Alastair, *Medieval Theory of Authorship* (London: Scolar Press, 1984).

Morgan, John, *Godly Learning: Puritan Attitudes Towards Reason, Learning, and Education, 1560–1640* (Cambridge: Cambridge University Press, 1986).

Morris, John, 'The Martyrdom of William Harrington', *The Month*, 20 (1874), 411–23.

Muller, R. A., *Christ and the Decree: Christology and Predestination in Reformed Theology from Calvin to Perkins* (Grand Rapids, 1988).

Nellen, H. J. M., and E. Rabbie (eds.), *Hugo Grotius Theologian*, Studies in the History of Christian Thought, 55 (Leiden: E. J. Brill, 1994).

Nelson, W., 'The Teaching of English in Tudor Grammar Schools', *Studies in Philology*, 49(1952), 119–43.

Nijhoff, W., and M. E. Kronenberg, *Nederlandsche Bibliographie van 1500 tot 1540*, 3 vols. (The Hague: M. Nijhoff, 1923–40).

Norbrook, David, *Poetry and Politics in the English Renaissance* (London: RKP, 1984).

Nussbaum, Martha C., *The Fragility of Goodness* (Cambridge: Cambridge University Press, 1986).

Nuttall, A. D., *Overheard by God: Fiction and Prayer in Herbert, Milton, Dante and St John* (London: Methuen, 1980).

Nygren, Anders, *Agape and Eros*, tr. Philip Watson (London: SPCK, 1953).

Oberman, Heiko A., 'Some Notes on the Theology of Nominalism, with Attention to its Relation to the Renaissance', *Harvard Theological Review*, 53 (1960), 47–76.

—— *The Harvest of Medieval Theology: Gabriel Biel and Late Medieval Nominalism* (Cambridge, Mass.: Harvard University Press, 1963).

—— ' "Iustitia Christi" and "Iustitia Dei": Luther and the Scholastic Doctrines of Justification', *Harvard Theological Review*, 59 (1966), 1–26.

—— *The Dawn of the Reformation: Essays in Late Medieval and Early Reformation Thought* (Edinburgh: T. & T. Clark, 1986).

—— *Luther: Man between God and the Devil* (New Haven and London: Yale University Press, 1989).

O'Connell, M. R., *Thomas Stapleton and the Counter Reformation* (New Haven: Yale University Press, 1964).

Olin, John C., *Six Essays on Erasmus and a Translation of Erasmus's Letter to Carondelet, 1523* (New York: Fordham University Press, 1979).

O'Malley, J. W., 'Erasmus and Luther, Continuity and Discontinuity as Key to their Conflict', *Sixteenth-Century Journal*, 5 (1974), 47–65.

Ong, W. J., *Ramus, Method and the Decay of Dialogue* (Cambridge, Mass.: Harvard University Press, 1957).

——*Ramus and Talon Inventory* (Cambridge, Mass.: Harvard University Press, 1958).

Overfield, James H., *Humanism and Scholasticism in Late Medieval Germany* (Princeton: Princeton University Press, 1984).

Padley, G. A., *Grammatical Theory in Western Europe 1500–1700: The Latin Tradition* (Cambridge: Cambridge University Press, 1976).

——*Grammatical Theory in Western Europe 1500–1700: Trends in Vernacular Grammar I* (Cambridge: Cambridge University Press, 1985).

——*Grammatical Theory in Western Europe 1500–1700: Trends in Vernacular Grammar II* (Cambridge: Cambridge University Press, 1988).

Paetow, Louis John, *The Arts Course at Medieval Universities* (Champaign: University of Illinois, 1910).

Pagels, Elaine, *Adam, Eve and the Serpent* (New York: Random House, 1988).

Palmer, F. R., *Mood and Modality* (Cambridge: Cambridge University Press, 1986).

——*Modality and the English Modals*, 2nd edn. (London: Longman, 1990).

Parker, T. H. L., *Calvin's New Testament Commentaries* (London: SCM, 1971).

——*John Calvin: a Biography* (London: Dent, 1975).

——*Commentaries on Romans, 1532–1542* (Edinburgh: T. & T. Clark, 1986).

Patterson, Annabel, *Censorship and Interpretation: The Conditions of Writing and Reading in Early Modern England* (Madison: University of Wisconsin Press, 1984).

——'All Donne', *Soliciting Interpretation: Literary Theory and Seventeenth-Century English Poetry*, ed. E. Harvey and K. E. Maus (Chicago: University of Chicago Press, 1990), pp. 37–67.

Payne, John B., 'Toward the Hermeneutics of Erasmus', *Scrinium Erasmianum*, ed. J. Coppens, 2 vols. (Leiden: E. J. Brill, 1969), ii. 13–49.

——'The significance of Lutheranizing changes in Erasmus's interpretations of Paul's Letters', *Histoire de l'exégèse au XVIe siècle*, ed. O. Fatio and P. Fraenkel (Geneva: Librairie Droz, 1978), pp. 312–30.

Penny, D. Andrew, *Freewill or Predestination: The Battle over Saving Grace in Mid-Tudor England* (Woodbridge: Royal Historical Society, 1990).

Peter, Rodolphe, and Jean-François Gilmont, *Bibliotheca Calviniana: Les oeuvres de Jean Calvin publiées au XVIe siècle*, 3 vols. (Geneva: Droz, 1991–2000).

Phillips, Margaret Mann, *Erasmus and the Northern Renaissance*, rev. edn. (Bury St Edmunds: Boydell, 1981).

Pigden, Charles R., 'Ought-Implies-Can: Erasmus, Luther and R. M. Hare', *Sophia*, 29 (1990), 2–30.

Porter, Harry, *Reformation and Reaction in Tudor Cambridge* (Cambridge: Cambridge University Press, 1958).

Prescott, Anne Lake, 'King David as a "Right Poet": Sidney and the Psalmist', *English Literary Renaissance*, 19 (1989), 131–51.

Questier, Michael C., *Conversion, Politics and Religion in England, 1580–1625* (Cambridge: Cambridge University Press, 1996).

Rabil, Albert, *Erasmus and the New Testament: the Mind of a Christian Humanist* (San Antonio: Trinity University Press, 1972).

Raeder, Siegfried, *Das Hebräische bei Luther untersucht bis zum Ende der ersten Psalmenvorlesung* (Tübingen: J. C. B. Mohr, 1961).

——*Grammatica Theologica: Studien zu Luthers Operationes in Psalmos* (Tübingen: J. C. B. Mohr, 1977).

Rashdall, Hastings, *The Universities of Europe in the Middle Ages*, rev. edn. by F. M. Powicke and A. B. Emden, 3 vols., (Oxford: Oxford University Press, 1936).

Rebholz, Ronald, *The Life of Fulke Greville, First Lord Brooke* (Oxford: Clarendon Press, 1971).

Rees, Joan, *Fulke Greville, Lord Brooke, 1554–1628 : A critical biography* (London: RKP, 1971).

Rex, Richard, *The Theology of John Fisher* (Cambridge: Cambridge University Press, 1991).

Ricks, Christopher, *Milton's Grand Style* (Oxford: Clarendon Press, 1963).

Rummel, Erika, *Erasmus's Annotations on the New Testament* (Toronto: University of Toronto Press, 1986).

——*Erasmus and his Catholic Critics*, Bibliotheca Humanistica & Reformatorica, 45, 2 vols. (Nieuwkoop: de Graaf, 1989).

——*The Humanist–Scholastic Debate in the Renaissance and Reformation* (Cambridge, Mass.: Harvard University Press, 1995).

——*The Confessionalization of Humanism in Reformation Germany* (Oxford: Oxford University Press, 2000).

Rupp, E. Gordon, *Studies in the Making of the English Protestant Tradition* (Cambridge: Cambridge University Press, 1947).

——*Luther's Progress to the Diet of Worms 1521* (London: SCM, 1951).

——*The Righteousness of God: Luther Studies* (London: Hodder & Stoughton, 1953).

——*Patterns of Reformation* (London: SPCK, 1969).

Saussure, Ferdinand de, *Course in General Linguistics*, tr. Roy Harris (London: Duckworth, 1983).

Schmidt-Lauber, Gabriele, *Luthers Vorlesung über den Römerbrief 1515/16* (Cologne: Böhlau, 1994).

Schmitt, Charles B. and Quentin Skinner (eds.), *The Cambridge History of Renaissance Philosophy* (Cambridge: Cambridge University Press, 1988).

Schwiebert, Ernest G., 'The Theses and Wittenberg', *Luther for an Ecumenical Age*, ed. Carl S. Meyer (St Louis: Concordia Press, 1967).

Screech, M. A., *Ecstasy and the Praise of Folly* (London: Duckworth, 1980).

Scribner, R. W., *For the Sake of Simple Folk: Popular Propaganda for the German Reformation*, rev. edn. (Oxford: Clarendon Press, 1994).

Shami, Jeanne, 'John Donne and the Pulpit Crisis of 1622', *John Donne Journal*, 14 (1995), 1–58.

Shell, Alison, *Catholicism, Controversy and the English Literary Imagination, 1558–1660* (Cambridge: Cambridge University Press, 1999).

Short-Title Catalogue of Books Printed in the German-Speaking Countries and German Books Printed in Other Countries from 1455 to 1600 now in the British Museum (London: British Museum, 1962).

Shuger, Debora Kuller, *Habits of Thought in the English Renaissance: Religion, Politics and the Dominant Culture* (Berkeley and Los Angeles: University of California Press, 1990).

—— *The Renaissance Bible* (Berkeley: University of California Press, 1998).

Sider, Ronald J., *Andreas Bodenstein von Karlstadt: The Development of his Thought 1517–1525* (Leiden: Brill, 1974).

Simon, Joan, *Education and Society in Tudor England* (Cambridge: Cambridge University Press, 1966).

Simpson, E. M., *A Study of the Prose Works of John Donne*, 2nd edn. (Oxford: Clarendon Press, 1948).

Sinfield, Alan, *Faultlines: Cultural Materialism and the Politics of Dissident Reading* (Berkeley: University of California Press, 1992).

Smalley, Beryl, *The Study of the Bible in the Middle Ages*, 2nd edn. (Notre Dame: University of Notre Dame Press, 1964).

Smits, Luchesius, *Saint Augustin dans l'oeuvre de Jean Calvin*, 2 vols. (Assen: van Gorcum, 1957–8).

Southern, A. C., *Elizabethan Recusant Prose 1559–1582* (London: Sands, 1950).

Spingarn, J. E., *A History of Literary Criticism in the Renaissance*, repr. edn. (New York: New York University Press, 1950).

Spitz, Lewis W., *Luther and German Humanism* (Aldershot: Variorum, 1996).

Stachniewski, John, *The Persecutory Imagination: English Puritanism and the Literature of Religious Despair* (Oxford: Clarendon Press, 1991).

Steinmetz, David, *Misericordia Dei: The Theology of Johannes von Staupitz in its Medieval Setting*, Studies in Medieval and Reformation Thought, 4 (Leiden: E. J. Brill, 1968).

Stern, Virginia F., *Gabriel Harvey: His Life, Marginalia and Library* (Oxford: Clarendon Press, 1979).

Stock, Brian, *The Implications of Literacy: Written Language and Models of Interpretation in the Eleventh and Twelfth Centuries* (Princeton: Princeton University Press, 1983).

—— *Augustine the Reader* (Cambridge, Mass.: Harvard University Press, 1996).

Strier, Richard, *Love Known: Theology and Experience in George Herbert's Poetry* (Chicago: University of Chicago Press, 1983).

Strier, Richard, 'John Donne Awry and Squint: The "Holy Sonnets", 1608–10', *Modern Philology*, 86 (1989), 357–84.

Strype, John, *Life and Acts of Whitgift*, 3 vols. (Oxford, 1822).

Surtz, E., *The Works and Days of John Fisher* (Cambridge, Mass.: Harvard University Press, 1967).

Taylor, Charles, *Sources of the Self: The Making of Modern Identity* (Cambridge: Cambridge University Press, 1989).

Tentler, T. N., *Sin and Confession on the Eve of the Reformation* (Princeton: Princeton University Press, 1977).

Thornton, Dora, *The Scholar in his Study: Ownership and Experience in Renaissance Italy* (New Haven: Yale University Press, 1997).

Thurot, Charles, *Notices et extraits de divers manuscrits latins pour servir à l'histoire des doctrines grammaticales au moyen âge* (Paris, 1869).

Tracy, James D., *Erasmus of the Low Countries* (Berkeley: University of California Press, 1996).

Trinkaus, Charles, *In Our Image and Likeness: Humanity and Divinity in Italian Renaissance Thought*, 2 vols. (London: Constable, 1970).

Trueman, Carl R., *Luther's Legacy: Salvation and English Reformers, 1525–1556* (Oxford: Clarendon Press, 1994).

Tyacke, Nicholas, *Anti-Calvinists: The Rise of English Arminianism c. 1590–1640* (Oxford: Clarendon Press, 1987).

Veith, Gene, *Reformation Spirituality* (London: Associated University Press, 1985).

Verzeichnis der im deutschen Sprachbereich erschienenen Drucke des XVI. Jahrhunderts, 24 vols. (Stuttgart: Anton Hiersemann, 1983–97).

Vignaux, Paul, *Luther, commentateur des Sentences* (Paris: Vrin, 1935).

Vincent, Gilbert, *Exigence éthique et interprétation dans l'œuvre de Calvin* (Geneva: Labor et fides, 1984).

Vogelsang, Erich, *Die Anfänge Luthers Christologie nach der ersten Psalmenvorlesung* (Berlin and Leipzig: de Gruyter, 1929).

Wallace, Dewey D., 'The Anglican Appeal to Lutheran Sources', *Historical Magazine of the Protestant Episcopal Church*, 52 (1983), 355–67.

Waller, Gary, 'Fulke Greville's Struggle with Calvinism', *Studia Neophilologica*, 44 (1972), 295–314.

—— '"This matching of contraries": Calvinism and Courtly Philosophy in the Sidney Psalms', *English Studies*, 55 (1974), 22–31.

Walsham, Alexandra, *Church Papists: Catholicism, Conformity and Confessional Polemic in Early Modern England* (London: RHS/Boydell Press, 1993).

—— *Providence in Early Modern England* (Oxford: Oxford University Press, 1999).

Waswo, Richard, *Language and Meaning in the Renaissance* (Princeton: Princeton University Press, 1987).

Watson, Foster, *The English Grammar Schools to 1660: Their Curriculum and Practice* (Cambridge: Cambridge University Press, 1908).

Waugh, Evelyn, *Edmund Campion*, 3rd edn. (Oxford: Oxford University Press, 1961).

Webster, Charles, *The Great Instauration: Science, Medicine, and Reform 1626–1660* (London: Duckworth, 1975).

Weiner, Andrew D., *Sir Philip Sidney and the Poetics of Protestantism* (Minneapolis: University of Minnesota Press, 1978).

Weingreen, J., *A Practical Grammar for Classical Hebrew*, 2nd edn. (Oxford: Oxford University Press, 1959).

Weis, R., *Humanism in England in the Fifteenth Century* (Oxford: Blackwell, 1941).

Welsby, Paul A., *Lancelot Andrewes 1555–1626* (London: SPCK, 1958).

Wendel, François, *Calvin: The Origins and Development of his Religious Thought* (London: Collins, 1963).

White, H. C., *Tudor Books of Saints and Martyrs* (Madison: University of Wisconsin Press, 1963).

White, Peter, *Predestination, Policy and Polemic: Conflict and Consensus in the English Church from the Reformation to the Civil War* (Cambridge: Cambridge University Press, 1992).

Wilkes, G. A., 'The Sequence of the Writings of Fulke Greville', *Studies in Philology*, 56 (1959), 489–503.

Williams, Bernard, *Moral Luck* (Cambridge: Cambridge University Press, 1981).

Worden, Blair, *The Sound of Virtue: Philip Sidney's Arcadia and Elizabethan Politics* (New Haven: Yale University Press, 1996).

Woudhuysen, H. R., 'Enigmatic Relations', *Times Literary Supplement*, 19 August 1986, p. 895.

——*Sir Philip Sidney and the Circulation of Manuscripts, 1558–1640* (Oxford: Clarendon Press, 1996).

Zlotowitz, Meir, *Bereishis/Genesis: A New Translation with a Commentary Anthologized from Talmudic, Midrashic and Rabbinic Sources* (New York: Mesorah Publications, 1977).

Index